INTERNATIONAL MONETARY FUND

International
Financial Statistics

COUNTRY NOTES

2007

INTERNATIONAL FINANCIAL STATISTICS

Vol. LX, 2007
Prepared by the IMF Statistics Department
Robert W. Edwards, Director

For information related to this publication, please:
  fax the Statistics Department at (202) 623–6460,
  or write Statistics Department
      International Monetary Fund
      Washington, D.C. 20431
  or e-mail your query to **StatisticsQuery@imf.org**
For copyright inquiries, please fax the Editorial Division at (202) 623–6579.
For purchases only, please contact Publication Services (see information below).

International Financial Statistics (IFS) is a standard source of statistics on all aspects of international and domestic finance. *IFS* publishes, for most countries of the world, current data on exchange rates, international liquidity, international banking, money and banking, interest rates, prices, production, international transactions (including balance of payments and international investment position), government finance, and national accounts. Information is presented in tables for specific countries and in tables for area and world aggregates. *IFS* is published monthly and annually.

Address orders to:
International Monetary Fund
Attention: Publication Services
Washington, D.C. 20431
U.S.A.
Telephone: (202) 623–7430
Telefax: (202) 623–7201
E-mail: publications@imf.org
Internet: *http://www.imf.org*

ISSN 0250-7463
ISBN 978-1-58906-655-7

POSTMASTER: Send address changes to International Financial Statistics, Publication Services, 700 19th St., N.W., Washington, D.C. 20431. Postage for periodicals paid at Washington, D.C. USPS 049–610

Recycled paper

CONTENTS

"Country" in this publication does not always refer to a territorial entity that is a state as understood by international law and practice; the term also covers the euro area and some nonsovereign territorial entities, for which statistical data are provided internationally on a separate basis.

SELECTION OF STATISTICAL PUBLICATIONS

International Financial Statistics (IFS)
Acknowledged as a standard source of statistics on all aspects of international and domestic finance, *IFS* publishes, for most countries of the world, current data on exchange rates, international liquidity, international banking, money and banking, interest rates, prices, production, international transactions (including balance of payments and international investment position), government finance, and national accounts. Information is presented in tables for specific countries and in tables for area and world aggregates. *IFS* is published monthly and annually. *Price:* Subscription price is US$695 a year (US$445 to university faculty and students) for twelve monthly issues and the yearbook. Single copy price is US$89 for a monthly issue and US$145 for a yearbook issue.

Balance of Payments Statistics Yearbook (BOPSY)
Issued in three parts, this annual publication contains balance of payments and international investment position data. Part 1 provides detailed tables on balance of payments statistics for approximately 170 countries and international investment position data for 105 countries. Part 2 presents tables of regional and world totals of major balance of payments components. Part 3 contains descriptions of methodologies, compilation practices, and data sources used by reporting countries *Price:* US$129.

Direction of Trade Statistics (DOTS)
Quarterly issues of this publication provide, for 156 countries, tables with current data (or estimates) on the value of imports from and exports to their most important trading partners. In addition, similar summary tables for the world, industrial countries, and developing countries are included. The yearbook provides, for the most recent seven years, detailed trade data by country for approximately 186 countries, the world, and major areas. *Price:* Subscription price is US$209 a year (US$179 to university faculty and students) for the quarterly issues and the yearbook. Price for a quarterly issue only is US$34, the yearbook only is US$92, and a guide only is US$12.50.

Government Finance Statistics Yearbook (GFSY)
This annual publication provides detailed data on transactions in revenue, expense, net acquisition of assets and liabilities, other economic flows, and balances of assets and liabilities of general government and its subsectors. The data are compiled according to the framework of the 2001 *Government Finance Statistics Manual*, which provides for several summary measures of government fiscal performance. Price: US$94.

CD-ROM Subscriptions
International Financial Statistics (IFS), Balance of Payments Statistics (BOPS), Direction of Trade Statistics (DOTS)), and Government Finance Statistics (GFS) are available on CD-ROM by annual subscription. The CD-ROMs incorporate a Windows-based browser facility, as well as a flat file of the database in scientific notation. *Price of each subscription:* US$520 a year for single-user PC license (US$295 for university faculty and students). Network and redistribution licenses are negotiated on a case-by-case basis. Please contact Publication Services for information.

Subscription Packages
Combined Subscription Package
The combined subscription package includes all issues of *IFS, DOTS, BOPSY, GFSY,* and *Staff Papers,* the Fund's economic journal. *Combined subscription price:* US$1,195 a year (US$889 for university faculty and students). Airspeed delivery available at additional cost; please inquire.

Combined Statistical Yearbook Subscription
This subscription comprises *BOPSY, GFSY, IFSY,* and *DOTSY* at a combined rate of US$415. Because of different publication dates of the four yearbooks, it may take up to one year to service an order. Airspeed delivery available at additional cost; please inquire.

IFS on the Internet
The Statistics Department of the Fund is pleased to make available to subscribers the *International Financial Statistics (IFS)* database through an easy-to-use online service. The *IFS* database contains time series data beginning in 1948. The browser software provides a familiar and easy-to-use Windows interface for browsing the database, selecting series of interest, displaying the selected series in a spreadsheet format, and saving the selected series for transfer to other software systems, such as Microsoft Excel®. Single user license price for the *IFS Online Service* is $575, and $345 for academic users. Dependent on certain criteria, a range of scaled discounts is available. For full details of qualification for these discounts and online payment, please visit http://www.imfstatistics.org or email us directly at publications@imf.org.

Address orders to
Publication Services, IMF, Washington, DC 20431, USA
Telephone: (202) 623-7430   Telefax: (202) 623-7201   E-mail: publications@imf.org
Internet: http://www.imf.org

Note: Prices include the cost of delivery by surface mail. Enhanced delivery is available for an additional charge.

INTRODUCTION

The Fund's principal statistical publication, *International Financial Statistics (IFS)*, has been published monthly since January 1948. Beginning in 1961, the monthly was supplemented by a yearbook, and in 1991 and 2000, respectively, *IFS* was introduced on CD-ROM and the Internet. *IFS* contains country tables for most Fund members, as well as for Aruba, the Central African Economic and Monetary Community (CEMAC), the euro area, the Eastern Caribbean Currency Union (ECCU), the Netherland's Antilles, the West African Economic Monetary Union (WAEMU) and some nonsovereign territorial entities for which statistics are provided internationally on a separate basis. Also, selected series are drawn from the country tables and published in area and world tables.

International Financial Statistics, Country Notes presents, in two sections, brief information on the data published in *IFS*. The first section provides a description of the compilation techniques underlying selected area and world tables. The second identifies for each country the standard sources of the statistics and provides some explanatory material on each country's data, including any breaks in the series. Prior to the May 2003 issue of *IFS*, this information appeared within the individual world and country pages and often overflowed to the rear portion of the publication. As part of the redesign of *IFS*, the notes from the monthly and yearbook editions have been combined into this separate volume.

Although the topics addressed by the notes provided for each country may differ, they typically cover the following:

- Date of Fund Membership
- Standard Sources identified by the country (e.g., the Bank of Albania's *Monthly Statistical Report*)
- Exchange Rates
- International Liquidity
- Money and Banking
- Interest Rates
- Prices, Production and Labor
- International Transactions
- Government Finance
- National Accounts

Country Notes is designed to be a companion volume to each version of *IFS*: the monthly print edition, the yearbook, the CD-ROM, and the Internet. It will normally appear as an annual volume and will be shipped with the print edition of the *International Financial Statistics Yearbook* during August each year. Because one main volume of *Country Notes* will be produced each year, any supplementary notes will be provided on a cumulative basis at the rear of the monthly print edition of *IFS* until the next volume of *Country Notes* is published.

In addition, the complete set of updated country notes are accessible from the *IFS Online Service* Internet site at www.imfstatistics.org and appear on the CD-ROM edition of *IFS*. A print edition of the *Country Notes* volume may be ordered separately by subscribers of the CD-ROM or the Internet editions of *IFS*.

WORLD NOTES

Real Effective Exchange Rate Indices

The indicators of real effective exchange rates based on *relative unit labor costs (line 65um)* and *relative normalized unit labor costs (line reu)* in manufacturing represent the product of the index of the ratio of the relevant indicator (in national currency) for the country listed to a weighted geometric average of the corresponding indicators for 20 other industrial countries (again in national currency, and including in addition to the other 16 countries listed on this table, Australia, New Zealand, Greece, and Portugal) and the index of the nominal effective exchange rate, which is calculated by weighting the exchange rates for the countries listed in the same manner as the other indicators. This index for the nominal effective exchange rate is presented as *line neu* in the country pages of the 17 countries in the table and Greece. The reference base is 2000=100.

Several of the measures of real effective exchange rates are subject to frequent and sometimes substantial revision. To an important extent, these revisions stem from the procedures used to estimate several of the indicators. Thus, the national data underlying the two labor cost series and the value-added deflator series are calculated by benchmarking the best available monthly or quarterly series on reasonably comprehensive and comparable, but periodically revised, annual data from the national accounts. While such benchmarking makes these series particularly susceptible to revision, it also permits the calculation of up-to-date quarterly series which, on an annual basis, are also reasonably comprehensive and comparable.

The total trade weights used to construct the nominal effective exchange rates and the associated real effective exchange rates for the five indices are designed to make them particularly relevant with respect to movements in costs and prices affecting exports and imports of manufactured goods. The weights, which are built up from aggregate trade flows for manufactured goods (SITC 5–8) averaged over the period 1999–2001, take into account the relative importance of a country's trading partners in its direct bilateral relations with them, in both the home and foreign markets; of the competitive relations with third countries in particular markets; and of the differences among countries in the importance of foreign trade to the manufacturing sector.

Estimates shown for the Euro Area for relative unit labor costs and relative normalized unit labor costs are generated using a subset of the trade weights described in the paragraph above, where the weights for the Euro Area relate to the trade of the Euro Area as a whole with its partners in the system. A synthetic euro has been constructed for the period before the introduction of the euro using trade weights drawn from the same weighting scheme, Euro Area member exchange rates, and the official lock-in rates, which were used to determine the initial value of the euro. This method (national currency series times lock-in rates times Euro Area member trade weights specific to this system) has also been used to estimate the Euro Area unit labor cost and normalized unit labor cost series denominated in euros.

The nature and scope of the various national indicators entering into the indices are briefly described below. While mention is made of specific deficiencies in some of the selected measures of costs and prices, the emphasis is on what they purport to measure. Because these measures of costs and prices contain a considerable amount of staff estimation, they are not published in *IFS*.

Unit labor costs are defined as compensation of employees per unit of real output (or value added) in the manufacturing sector. Account is taken of employer-paid social insurance premia and other employment taxes, as well as wages and salaries. For the most recent quarters, however, indices typically refer more narrowly to wages or wages and salaries per unit of total output of manufactured goods (rather than that of value added in the manufacturing sector).

Normalized unit labor costs in manufacturing are calculated by dividing an index of actual hourly compensation per worker by the normalized index of output per man-hour in local currency. The data printed are the product of this variable after weighting (to obtain the relative measure) and the nominal effective exchange rate (**neu**). The purpose of normalizing output per man-hour is to remove distortions arising from cyclical movements which occur largely because changes in hours worked do not correspond closely to changes in the effective inputs of labor. The Hodrick-Prescott filter, which smooths a time series by removing short-run fluctuations while retaining changes of larger amplitude, is the method used to normalize output per man-hour. The monthly series are estimated by extrapolating the quarterly local currency series for the period needed, interpolating these estimates from quarterly into monthly series and reweighting the interpolated monthly series to obtain the monthly relative series. **Where the monthly data are extrapolated, data for the corresponding quarters are not shown.** Monthly nominal effective exchange rates are computed using monthly exchange rates and the same weights as are used for quarterly nominal effective exchange rates, and real effective rates are calculated using the nominal effective rates and interpolated relative monthly normalized unit labor costs. The extrapolation and interpolation of the quarterly series is acceptable because the quarterly series have been smoothed and the trend of these series is retained in the extrapolation. The interpolated monthly trend series is used to adjust the more current nominal effective exchange rate. The annual series (for both relative, and relative normalized, unit labor costs) may not correspond with the average of the quarterly series because only the annual series include Switzerland.

An indicator of real effective exchange rates based on relative consumer prices is also shown *(line rec)* to afford comparison with a wider group of partner—or competitor—countries. The weighting scheme is based on disaggregated trade data for manufactured goods and primary products covering the three-year period 1999–01 and is derived according to the same methodology as that followed for other countries discussed in the Introduction (section 1). The consumer price index that is used as a cost indicator is that shown on the country pages *(line 64)*. However, it should be borne in mind that, especially for the industrial countries, consumer price indices are, in a number of respects, conceptually inferior to the other measures of domestic costs and prices discussed above for the purpose of compiling indices of real effective exchange rates, owing to the inclusion of various factors which may differ across countries, for example, net taxes on production.

Estimates shown for the Euro Area for relative consumer prices are generated using a subset of the trade weights described in the above, where the weights for the Euro Area relate to the trade of the Euro Area as a whole with its partners in the system. A synthetic euro has been constructed for the period before the introduction of the euro using trade weights drawn from the same weighting scheme, Euro Area member exchange rates, and the official lock-in rates, which were used to determine the initial value of the euro. The Euro Area consumer price series from January 1995 onward is the Harmonized Index of Consumer Prices, provided by the ECB, and prior to this period, it is the trade-weighted average of the individual member countries' consumer price indices. Trade weights used in the construction are specific to this system and are the same as those used in the construction of the synthetic euro.

As indicated in the Introduction, movements in these indices need to be interpreted with considerable caution. While every effort is made to use national data that are as internationally comparable as possible, the degree to which it is practicable to assure comparability is limited by the character of the available data. For this reason, the table provides a wide array of available indicators.

Industrial Production

The aggregate Industrial Production Index for the industrial countries as a group is calculated by the Statistics Department from industrial and manufacturing production indices that are published in the country pages. The index covers industrial activities in mining, quarrying, manufacturing, and electricity, gas, and water. The coverage of each country's production index is detailed in the footnotes of the country pages. No attempt has been made to standardize the coverage of industrial country series before aggregation.

Non-seasonally adjusted industrial production (lines 66) or manufacturing production (lines 66ey) indices are presented for 22 industrial countries. The aggregate index thus includes non-seasonally adjusted production data.

The aggregate index is calculated using a weighted geometric mean of country indices. The individual country production series are weighted by the 2000 value added in industry, as derived from individual countries' national accounts and expressed in U.S. dollars. Different weighting bases—1963, 1970, 1975, 1980, 1984–86, 1990, 1995, and 2000—have been used, and the index series are chain-linked by the technique of ratio splicing at the overlap years and are shifted to the reference base 2000=100.

The weights used in the calculation are identical in concept for all countries and cover, where possible, mining, quarrying, manufacturing, and electricity, gas, and water.

Although industrial production data for some countries are not available for more recent periods, the aggregate index will be calculated for any period for which data for more than 60 percent of the area index aggregate have been reported.

Commodity Prices

Indices of market prices for primary commodities are prepared by the Commodities Unit, IMF Research Department. They are compiled as period averages in terms of U.S. dollars and expressed using a 2000=100 weights reference period in accordance with all indices published in IFS. The All Non-Fuel Commodities indices include 62 market price series (marked by an * in the Commodity Price table) which represent 45 primary commodities. They do not include fuel (petroleum, natural gas, and coal) and precious metals (gold and silver). The commodity price index for the World is calculated by weighting commodity price indices with the average export earnings of the commodities selected during the years 1995 through 1997 in 175 countries.

† For the periods prior to 1982 the World index and its components (food, beverages, agricultural raw materials, metals except fertilizers) were calculated by backward recursion of percent changes based on the previously used indices. (00176axd)

The commodities covered and the weights used are as follows:

1. *Food Commodities*—21.7 percent: bananas—0.6 percent, cereals (maize, rice, and wheat)—6.1 percent, meat (beef, lamb, swine meat, and poultry)—3.6 percent, vegetable oils and protein meals (coconut oil, fishmeal, groundnuts, olive oil, palm oil, soybeans, soybean meal, soybean oil, and sunflower oil)—5.2 percent, seafood (fish and shrimp)—3.8 percent, oranges—0.5 percent, and sugar—1.9 percent. (00176exd)

2. *Beverages*—3.1 percent: cocoa beans—0.7 percent, coffee—2.0 percent, and tea—0.4 percent. (00176dwd)

3. *Agricultural Raw Materials*—11.3 percent: cotton—1.1 percent, hides—3.0 percent, rubber—1.1 percent, timber—5.0 percent, and wool (fine and coarse)—1.1 percent. (00176bxd)

4. *Metals*—16.1 percent: aluminum—6.1 percent, copper—5.1 percent, iron ore—1.8 percent, lead—0.3 percent, nickel—1.2 percent, tin—0.3 percent, uranium—0.7 percent, and zinc—0.9 percent. (00176ayd)

5. *Energy*—47.8 percent: coal—3.4 percent, natural gas—4.5 percent, and petroleum—39.9 percent. (00176end)

The World Bank Price Index for Primary Commodities for the Low- and Middle-Income Countries (LMICs) is compiled by the Commodity Policy and Analysis Unit of the World Bank's International Economics Department. The weights for the index are based on the average export earnings during the period 1987–89 of countries classified by the World Bank as being Low- and Middle- Income Countries, expressed in U. S. dollars, on a 1990=100 base. The LMICs index is comprised of 34 price series covering 32 commodities.

Aluminum: London Metal Exchange*, standard grade, spot price, minimum purity 99.5 percent, c.i.f. U.K. ports (*Wall Street Journal,* New York, and *Metals Week,* New York).[3] Prior to 1979, U.K. producer price, minimum purity 99 percent (*Metal Bulletin,* London). (15676drz)

Bananas: Latin America*: Central America and Ecuador, first class quality tropical pack, Chiquita, Dole and Del Monte, U.S. importer's price f.o.b. U.S. ports (Sopisco News, Guayaquil).[1] (24876u.z)

Barley: Canada*: Canadian No. 1 Western Barley, spot price (Winnipeg Commodity Exchange). (15676baz)

Beef: Australia/NZ (U.S. Ports)*: frozen boneless, 85 percent visible lean cow meat, U.S. import price, f.o.b. U.S. port of entry (*The Yellow Sheet,* The National Provisioner Daily Market and News Service, Chicago, Illinois).[3] Prior to December 1975, 90 percent visible. (19376kbz)

United States: Utility grade, all weights in New York, Chicago and San Francisco, mid-month. (11176k.z)

Argentina (frozen) unit value. (21374kaz)

Brazil (unit value). (22374m.z)

Butter: New Zealand (London). (19676flz)

New Zealand (unit value). (19674flz)

Coal: Australia*: Thermal coal. 12000 btu/pound, less than 1% sulfur, 14% ash, f.o.b. piers, Newcastle/Port Kembla (World Bank). (19376coz)

Australia (unit value). (19374vrz)

South Africa: Steam, f.o.b. Richards Bay, for period up to 2001, 11,500 btu/lb, less than 1% sulfur, 16% ash for 1990–2001; beginning 2002, 11,200 btu/lb. (19976coz)

Cocoa Beans: New York and London*: International Cocoa Organization daily price. Average of the daily prices of the nearest three active future trading months on the New York Cocoa Exchange at noon and the London Terminal market at closing time. c.i.f. U.S. and European ports (*The Financial Times,* London).[3] (65276r.zM44)
Brazil (unit value). (22374r.z)

Coconut Oil: Philippines/Indonesia (New York)*: Philippines (*DataStream*). (56676aiz)

Coffee: Other milds*: Arithmetic average of El Salvador Central Standard, Guatemala prime washed, Mexico prime washed, prompt shipment, ex-dock, New York.[3] (38676ebz)
Brazil (New York): Unwashed arabica, Santos No. 4, ex-dock, New York.[3] (22376ebz).
Brazil (unit value). (22374e.z)
Uganda (New York)*: Robusta: New York cash price. Côte d'Ivoire Grade II, and Uganda Standard. Prompt shipment, ex-dock, New York. Prior to July 1982, arithmetic average of Angolan Ambriz and 2AA and Ugandan Native Standard (*Patton's Complete Coffee Coverage,* New York).[3] (79976ecz)

Copper: United Kingdom*: London Metal Exchange, grade A cathodes, spot price, c.i.f. European ports (*Wall Street Journal,* New York, and *Metal Bulletin,* London).3 Prior to July 1986, higher grade, wire bars or cathodes. (11276c.z)

Copra: Philippines: Phil/Indo, c.i.f. Northwest European ports (*Oil World,* Hamburg).[1] (56676agz)

Cotton: Liverpool Index*: Midd. 13/32 inches, Liverpool Index 'A', average of the cheapest fourteen of ten styles; c.i.f. Liverpool (*Cotton Outlook,* Liverpool from January 1968 to May 1981 strict middling, SM 11/16 inches; prior to 1968, Mexican SM 11/16 .[1] (11176f.zM40)

DAP (diammonium phosphate): US Gulf: Standard size, bulk spot, f.o.b. (11176arzM17)

Fish: Norway*: Fresh Norwegian Salmon, farm bred, export price (NorStat). (14276fiz)

Fish Meal: Peru Fish meal/pellets 65% protein, CIF (*DataStream*). Prior to 1964, FAO estimate, Peruvian. (29376z.z)
Iceland (unit value). (17674zaz)

Gasoline: Regular unleaded. Petroleum Product Assessments (Reuter's News Services). (11176rgz)

Gold: United Kingdom: 99.5 percent fine. London, afternoon fixing.[3] (11276krz)

Groundnuts: Any origin*: U.S. Runner, 40–50 percent shelled basis, c.i.f. Rotterdam. (69476bhz)

Groundnut Oil: Any Origin: c.i.f. Rotterdam (*Oil World,* Hamburg).[1]

Hides: United States*: Wholesale dealer's price, packer's heavy native steers, over 53 lbs. (formerly over 58 lbs.), Chicago, f.o.b. shipping point (*Wall Street Journal,* New York).[3] Prior to November 1985, U.S. Bureau of Labor Statistics, Washington, D.C. (11176p.z)

Iron Ore: Brazil*: Carajas fines, 67.55 percent FE (iron) content, contract price to Europe, f.o.b. Ponta da Madeira (Companhia Vale de Rio Doce, Rio de Janeiro, Brazil).[1] (22376gaz)

Jute: Raw Bangladesh BWD, f.o.b. Chittagong/Chalna (World Bank, Washington, D.C. Beginning 1977, UNCTAD source.)[2] (51376x.z)

Lamb: New Zealand (London)*: PL, frozen, wholesale price at Smithfield Market, London (National Business Review, Auckland, New Zealand). (19676pfz)

Lead: United Kingdom*: London Metal Exchange, 99.97 percent pure, spot, c.i.f. European ports (*Wall Street Journal,* New York, and *Metals Week,* New York).[3] (11276v.z)
United States: Common grade domestic pigs in New York. (00176v.z)

Linseed Oil: Any origin, ex-tank Rotterdam (*Oil World,* Hamburg). (11176niz)

Maize: United States (U.S. Gulf Ports)*: U.S. No. 2 yellow, prompt shipment, f.o.b. Gulf of Mexico ports (USDA *Grain and Feed Market News,* Washington, D.C.).[3] (11176j.zM17)

Natural Gas: Russian Federation: Russian border price in Germany (World Gas Intelligence, New York). (92276ngz)
Indonesia: Indonesian Liquid Natural Gas in Japan (World Gas Intelligence, New York). (53676ngz)
United States: Natural Gas Spot Price, Henry Hub, Lousiana. (11176ngz)

Newsprint: Finland (unit value). (17274ulz)

Nickel: United Kingdom*: London Metal Exchange, melting grade, spot, c.i.f. North European ports (*Wall Street Journal,* New York, and *Metals Week,* New York). Prior to 1980, INCO price, c.i.f. Far East and American ports (*Metal Bulletin,* London).[3] (15676ptz)

Olive Oil: United Kingdom*: ex-tanker prices, extra virgin olive oil, 1%>ffa (free fatty acid) (DataStream). (11276liz)

Oranges: French import price*: miscellaneous oranges, (FRuiTROP). (13276raz)

Palm Kernel Oil: Malaysia: c.i.f. Rotterdam (*World Oil,* Hamburg). (54876dfz)

Palm Oil: Palm Oil Futures (first contract forward) 4–5 percent FFA (*Bursa Malaysian Derivatives Berhad*).1 Prior to 1974, UNCTAD.[2] (54876dgz)
Malaysia (unit value). (54874dgz)

Pepper: Malaysia: Black, average U.S. wholesale price, bagged, carlots, f.o.b. New York. Average of daily quotations.(54876dlz)
Singapore: White Sarawak 100%, closing quotations (Market News Service, I.T.C., Geneva). (57676dlz)

Petroleum: Average Crude Price: U.K. Brent (light), Dubai (medium), and West Texas Intermediate, equally weighted. † Prior to 1983, Alaska North Slope (heavy) was used in the composition of this line instead of West Texas Intermediate. Annual data through 1994 for this earlier version are available in the 1995 *IFS* yearbook, with quarterly and monthly data available in the monthly issues through the January 1996 issue. (00176aaz)
Dubai: Medium, Fateh 32° API, spot, f.o.b. Dubai (*Petroleum Market Intelligence,* New York, *International Crude Oil and Product Prices,* Beirut, and *Bloomberg Business News*). † Prior to 1984, Middle East Light 34° API, spot (*Petroleum Intelligence Weekly,* New York). † Prior to 1974, Saudi Arabian Light 34° API, posted price, ex Ras Tanura (*Platt's Oil Price Handbook and Almanac,* New York). (46676aaz)
United Kingdom: Light, Brent Blend 38° API, spot, f.o.b. U.K. ports (*Petroleum Market Intelligence,* New York, *Platt's Oilgram Price Report,* New York, and *Bloomberg Business News*). † Prior to 1984, North African Light 37/44° API (*Petroleum Intelligence Weekly,* New York). † Prior to 1974, Libyan Brega 40° API, posted price, ex Marsa El Brega (*Platt's Oil Price Handbook and Almanac,* New York). † Prior to 1961, Qatar Um Said 39° API posted price, f.o.b. (*Platt's Oil Price Handbook and Almanac,* New York). (11276aaz)
United States: West Texas Intermediate 40° API, spot, f.o.b. Midland Texas (New York Mercantile Exchange, New York). In 1983–84 (Platt's Oilgram Price Report, New York).[3] (11176aazM17)

Phosphate Rock: Morocco (Casablanca): 70 percent BPL, contract, f.a.s. (*British Sulphur Monthly Newsletter*). Prior to 1981, 72 percent BPL, f.a.s.[1] (68676awz)

Potash: Canada: Muriate of potash, f.o.b., Vancouver. Average of daily quotations. (15676qrz)

Plywood: Philippines: Lauan, 3-ply, extra, 91 cm x 182 cm x 4 mm, wholesale price, spot, Tokyo. (56676wxz)

Pulp: Sweden (North Sea Ports): Softwood, sulphate bleached, air-dry weight, c.i.f. (14476slzz)

Rice: Thailand*: White milled 5 percent broken, nominal price quotes, f.o.b. Bangkok (USDA *Rice Market News,* Little Rock, Arkansas).[1] (57876n.zM81)

Thailand (unit value). (57874n.z)

Rubber: Malaysia*: No. 1 R.S.S., prompt shipment, f.o.b. Malaysian/Singapore ports (*The Financial Times,* London).[3] (548761.z)

Malaysia (unit value). (54874l.z)

Thailand (unit value). (57874l.z)

Shrimp: United States*: Mexican, west coast, white, No. 1 shell-on, headless, 26 to 30 count per pound, wholesale price at New York (World Bank). (11176blz)

Silver: United States: 99.9 percent grade refined, Handy and Harman, New York. Average of daily quotations. (11176y.z)

Sisal: East African, ungraded, c.i.f. European ports (UNCTAD).[2] (63976mlz)

Sorghum: United States: No. 2 yellow, prompt shipment, f.o.b. Gulf of Mexico ports (*USDA Grain and Feed Market News,* Washington, D.C.) (11176trz)

Soybeans: Soybean futures contract (first contract forward) No. 2 yellow and par*: (*Chicago Board of Trade*). (11176jfz)

Brazil (unit value). (22374s.z)

Soybean Meal: Soybean Meal Futures (first contract forward) Minimum 48 percent protein (*Chicago Board of Trade*). (11176jjz)

Soybean Oil: Soybean Oil Futures (first contract forward) exchange approved grades (*Chicago Board of Trade*). Prior to April 1973, Dutch crude oil, ex-mill. (11176jiz)

Sugar: EU Import Price*: Unpacked sugar, c.i.f. European ports. Negotiated export price for sugar from ACP countries to EU under the Sugar Protocol (Lomé Convention). (EU office, Washington, D.C.).[3] (11276i.z)

Free Market*: CSCE contract No. 11, nearest future position (Coffee, Sugar and Cocoa Exchange, New York Board of Trade). (00176iaz)

U.S. Import Price*: CSCE contract No. 14, nearest future position (Coffee, Sugar and Cocoa Exchange, New York Board of Trade). (11176iazM02)

Brazil (unit value). (22374i.z)

Philippines (unit value): Centrifugal. (55674i.z)

Sunflower Oil: Sunflower Oil, US export price from Gulf of Mexico (*DataStream*). (11276soz)

Superphosphate: United States (U.S. Gulf Ports): Triple-super-phosphate, bulk, spot, f.o.b. Gulf of Mexico Ports (*Fertilizer Week,* CRU International Ltd., London).[3] (11176asz)

Swine Meat: United States (Iowa)*: 51–52% (.8–.99 inches of back fat at measuring point) lean Hogs, USDA average base cost price of back fat measured at the tenth rib (USDA). (11176smz)

Tea: Average Auction (London)*: Mombasa auction price for best PF1, Kenyan Tea. Replaces London auction price beginning July 1998.[3] (11276s.z)

Sri Lanka (unit value). (52474s.z)

Timber: Hardwood Logs*: Malaysia, meranti, Sarawak best quality, sale price charged by importers, Japan (World Bank, Washington, D.C.). From January 1988 to February 1993, average of Sabah and Sarawak in Tokyo weighted by their respective import volumes in Japan. From February 1993 to present, Sarawak only.[2] (54876vxz)

Hardwood Sawnwood*: Malaysian sawnwood, dark red meranti, select and better quality, standard density, c.i.f. U.K. Port (Tropical Timbers, Surrey, England).[2] (54876rmz)

Softwood Logs*: Average value of Douglas-fir, Western hemlock and other softwoods exported from Washington, Oregon, Northern California and Alaska (Pacific Northwest Research Station, USDA Forest Service, Portland, OR).[2] (11176vxz)

Softwood Sawnwood*: Average value of Douglas-fir, Western hemlock and other softwoods exported from Canada.[2] (11176rmz)

Tin: Any Origin (London)*: London Metal Exchange, standard grade, spot, c.i.f. European ports (*Wall Street Journal,* New York). From December 1985 to June 1989, Malaysian Straits, minimum 99.85 percent purity, Kuala Lumpur Tin Market settlement price. Prior to November 1985, London Metal Exchange (*Wall Street Journal,* New York and *Metals Week,* New York).[3] (11276q.z)

Bolivia (unit value). (21874q.z)

Malaysia (unit value): Primary tin. (54874q.z)

Thailand (unit value): Tin metal. (57874q.z)

Tobacco: U.S. Import Unit Value of general unmanufactured tobacco. (USDA, Foreign Agricultural Service). (11176m.z)

Uranium: Restricted*: Metal Bulletin Nuexco Exchange Uranium (U308 restricted) price. (00176umz)

Urea: Ukraine: Bulk, spot, for 1985–91 (June) f.o.b. Eastern Europe; 1991 (July)—2000 (May 17) f.o.b. Black Sea (primarily Yuzhnyy), from May 18, 2000 onwards f.o.b. Yuzhnyy, Ukraine. (92676urz).

Wheat: Australia (unit value). (19374d.z)

United States*: No. 1, hard red winter, ordinary protein, prompt shipment, f.o.b. Gulf of Mexico ports (USDA *Grain and Feed Market News,* Washington, D.C.)[3] (11176d.z)

Argentina (unit value). (21374d.z)

Wool: Australia-New Zealand 48's*: Coarse wool, 23 micron (AWEX, Australian Wool Exchange) Sydney, Australia. (11276hdz)

Australia–New Zealand 64's*: Fine wool, 19 micron (AWEX, Australian Wool Exchange) Sydney, Australia. (11276hez)

Australia (unit value): Greasy wool. (19374haz)

Zinc: United Kingdom*: London Metal Exchange, high grade cash, c.i.f. U.K. ports, 98 percent pure, spot (*Wall Street Journal,* New York, and *Metals Week,* New York).[3] Prior to January 1987, standard grade. (11276t.z)

Bolivia (unit value). (21874t.z)

---

[1] Average of weekly quotations.
[2] Monthly quotations.
[3] Average of daily quotations.

COUNTRY NOTES

Albania   914

Date of Fund Membership:
October 15, 1991

Standard Sources:
B: Bank of Albania, *Monthly Statistical Report, Balance of Payments Quarterly Statistical Bulletin*
S: Institute of Statistics

Exchange Rates:

Market Rate (End of Period and Period Average):
† Beginning in July 1992, a floating exchange rate system (independent float) was introduced. The exchange rate for the lek is the weighted average midpoint rate of six commercial banks and four foreign exchange bureaus that cover most of the foreign exchange transactions.

Monetary Authorities:
Comprises the Bank of Albania (central bank) only.
Foreign Assets (line 11): Beginning in September 1995, includes U.S. government bonds purchased by the central bank as collateral for the par bonds it issued to foreign creditors as part of a restructuring of Albania's foreign debt. These U.S. government bonds, held by the Bank of England as the collateral agent, are not included in foreign exchange reserves (*line 1d.d*). Both the U.S. government bonds and the par bonds are recorded in the accounts of the central bank at their maturity values.
Claims on Central Government (line 12a): In March 1995, certain suspense liability accounts have been netted against claims on central government.
Other Liabilities to Banks (line 14n): Comprise liabilities arising from the reverse repurchase operation of the central bank.
Other Items (Net) (line 17r): Since March 1995, certain suspense liability accounts previously classified as other items have been netted against claims on government. In October 1995, the contra-entry in other assets of foreign liabilities that were forgiven under a debt restructuring agreement was extinguished. † Beginning in December 2001, data are based on an improved classification and sectorization of the accounts. † Beginning in December 2002, data are based on a new reporting system which provides an improved classification and sectorization of the accounts.

Banking Institutions:
Comprises commercial banks. *Other Claims on Monetary Authorities (line 20n)* comprise repurchase agreements of banks with the central bank. † Beginning in February 2001, *Other Claims on Monetary Authorities (line 20n), Claims on Central Government (line 22a),* and *Credit from Monetary Authorities (line 26g)* are based on improved classification of repurchase agreements of banks with the central bank. † Beginning in December 2001, data are based on an improved classification and sectorization of the accounts. † Beginning in December 2002, data are based on a new reporting system which provides an improved classification and sectorization of the accounts.

Banking Survey:
† See note to section 20.

Money (National Definitions):
M1 comprises currency outside depository corporations and national-currency-denominated demand deposits and sight deposits of residents other than central government.
M2 equals M1 *plus* national-currency-denominated term deposits of residents other than central government.
M3 equals M2 *plus* foreign-currency-denominated deposits of residents other than central government.

Interest Rates:

Bank Rate (End of Period):
The Bank of Albania's main policy rate. Starting in March 2001, the data refer to the rate on weekly repurchase agreements. † Prior to March 2001, the data refer to the basic rate at which the Bank of Albania lends to commercial banks.

Treasury Bill Rate:
Weighted average rate of accepted bids on three-month treasury bills during the last auction of the month.

Deposit Rate:
† In June 1993, the central bank set a band around a guideline rate with the lower end of the band enforced as the minimum deposit rate. Data beginning in June 1993 refer to the guideline rate. † Beginning in October 1995, data refer to the weighted average rate on new 12-month deposits of the three commercial banks with the highest level of outstanding deposits.

Lending Rate:
† From July 1992 to June 1995, the central bank announced guideline rates to assist banks in setting their lending rates. Data from July 1992 to June 1995 refer to the guideline rate for loans of 12-month maturity. † Beginning in July 1995, the central bank ceased announcing the guideline rates, and the banks are left on their own to determine their lending rates. Data beginning in July 1995 refer to the maximum interest rate charged by a state-owned commercial bank on loans with 12-month maturity. † Data beginning in October 1995 refer to the weighted average rate on new 12-month loans of the three commercial banks with the highest level of outstanding loans.

Prices:

Producer Prices:
Source S. Weight Reference Period: 1998; Geographical Coverage: covers all industrial activities; Number of Items in the Basket: about 250 goods produced by a sample of 460 enterprises; Basis for Calculation: compiled in accordance with the NACE, Rev. 1 and the classification of products by activities (CPA).

Consumer Prices:
Source S. Weights Reference Period: December 2001; Geographical Coverage: covers price changes of goods and services consumed by households in 11 cities; Number of Items in the Basket: 267 items; Basis for Calculation: 2000 Household Budget Survey by INSTAT.

Wages:
Source S. Average wages cover only the public sector and are measured on a gross basis include payments for overtime.

International Transactions:
Source S.

Government Finance:

Annual data are as reported for the *Government Finance Statistics Yearbook (GFSY)* and cover general government. The fiscal year ends December 31.

National Accounts:

Source S. As indicated by the country, data are compiled according to the recommendations of the *1993 SNA*.

Algeria 612

Date of Fund Membership:

September 26, 1963

Standard Source:

S: Department of Statistics, *Bulletin of General Statistics*

Exchange Rates:

Official Rate: (End of Period and Period Average):
Central bank midpoint rate. The official rate is based on a fixed relationship between the dinar and a composite of currencies.

International Liquidity:

Gold (National Valuation) (line 1and) is equal to *Gold (Million Fine Troy Ounces) (line 1ad)*, valued at SDR 35 per fine troy ounce and converted into U.S. dollars at the dollar/SDR rate **sa** on the country page for the United States. Source E: OECD

Monetary Authorities:

Comprises the Central Bank of Algeria only. † Beginning in 1992, data reflect the introduction of a new reporting system. † Beginning in December 2001, data are based on a new reporting system which provides improved classification and sectorization of the accounts.

Banking Institutions:

Comprises state-owned commercial banks (except Caisse Nationale d'Épargne et de Prévoyance) and private-sector-owned commercial banks. † Beginning in 1992, data reflect improved classification including the separate identification of *Claims on Nonfinancial Public Enterprises (line 22c)*, which were previously included with *Claims on Private sector (line 22d)*. † Beginning in December 2001, includes the Caisse Nationale d'Épargne et de Prévoyance and a mutual bank (banking department of the Caisse Nationale de Mutualité Agricole). Data are based on a new reporting system which provides improved classification and sectorization of the accounts.

Banking Survey:

† See notes on monetary authorities and banking institutions.

Nonbank Financial Institutions:

Comprises finance companies ("établissements financiers" in accordance with the Algerian Law on Money and Credit).

Money (National Definitions):

M1 (*means of payment*) comprises banknotes and coins held by the public; demand deposits of nonbank financial institutions, local governments, nonfinancial corporations, and households with banking institutions; demand deposits of households and public nonfinancial quasi-corporations with the postal administration (Centres des Chèques Postaux); and demand deposits of households and social security funds with the Treasury.

M2 comprises M1; time, savings, and foreign currency deposits of nonbank financial institutions, social security funds, nonfinancial corporations, and households with banking institutions; and blocked import deposits of nonfinancial corporations with commercial banks. † Beginning in January 2007 includes deposits of insurance corporations, finance companies, and households with the central bank and excludes blocked import deposits of nonfinancial corporations with commercial banks.

Interest Rates:

Discount Rate (End of Period):
Rate charged by the Bank of Algeria on loans to banks and finance companies through a call for tender system.

Money Market Rate:
Weighted average rate on transactions in the interbank market on the last working day of the period.

Treasury Bill Rate:
Weighted average rate at issuance for treasury bills with maturity of 26 weeks sold at the last auction of the period.

Deposit Rate:
Average rate offered by commercial banks on 12-month term deposits to nonfinancial corporations and households.

Lending Rate:
Average rate charged by commercial banks on short term rediscountable loans granted to nonfinancial corporations for general purpose.

Prices, Production, Labor:

Producer Prices:
Source S. Weights Reference Period: 1989; Coverage: 157 public and private companies; Number of Items in Basket: 300.

Consumer Prices:
Source S. Weights Reference Period: 1989; Geographic Coverage: Algiers; Number of Items in Basket: 260; Basis for Calculation: National Survey on Household Consumption conducted in 1988.

Industrial Production:
Source S. Weights Reference Period: 1989.

Crude Petroleum Production:
Calculated from production quantities reported in the *Oil Market Intelligence*.

International Transactions:

Exports:
Annual data on the volume of petroleum exports are obtained by weighting volumes for crude and refined petroleum by their relative 1995 export values. Monthly data on volume of crude petroleum exports are based on production quantities shown in the *Petroleum Intelligence Weekly*.

Imports, c.i.f.:
Source S data.

Government Finance:

Annual data are as reported for the *Government Finance Statistics Yearbook (GFSY)* and cover budgetary central government. The fiscal year ends December 31.

National Accounts:

Source S.

Angola 614

Date of Fund Membership:

September 19, 1989

Standard Sources:

B: National Bank of Angola, *Economics and Statistics Bulletin*
S: National Institute of Statistics, *Statistical Bulletin*

Exchange Rates:

On September 22, 1990, the new kwanza (NKZ) replaced the kwanza at par. Beginning in July 1995, a monetary reform took place, and the readjusted kwanza (KZR), equal to 1,000 new kwanzas, was introduced. On November 12, 1999, the kwanza, equal to 1,000,000 readjusted kwanzas, was introduced.

Market Rate (End of Period and Period Average):
Through June 1996, the market rate was determined by the National Bank of Angola (central bank) and applied to sales of foreign exchange to commercial banks on the basis of allocations that were administratively set at fixing sessions held from time to time. Beginning on July 1, 1996, the market rate was administratively fixed to the U.S. dollar. Beginning in June 1998, the market rate is determined weekly in accordance with a crawling peg scheme. On May 1999, a free market exchange rate system was introduced. The rate is determined as the weighted average of the rates quoted by banking institutions and exchange bureaus.

International Liquidity:

Foreign Exchange (line ld.d) is the U.S. dollar value of the central bank's deposits in foreign banks and holdings of foreign currency.

Monetary Authorities:

Comprises the National Bank of Angola (NBA) only. Data for 1995 and 1996 are partially estimated. Estimates are based on available balance sheet data of the NBA with adjustments to reconcile these data with information from foreign correspondent banks and operational data of the NBA. Counterpart entries to these adjustments are included in *Other Items (Net) (line 17r)*. *Other Items (Net)* also reflect weaknesses in accounting data, which have been addressed beginning in the third quarter of 1997. † Beginning in December 1999, data are based on a new plan of accounts.

Banking Institutions:

Comprises the Banco Português do Atlântico, Banco Totta & Açores, Banco de Comércio e Indústria, Banco de Fomento e Exterior, Banco Africano de Investimentos, Banco de Poupança e Crédito, Banco Comercial Angolano, and Caixa de Crédito Agro Pecuário e Pescas, which was liquidated in May 2001. † See note

on monetary authorities. Beginning in December 2001, includes Banco Sol. Beginning in January 2002, includes Banco Espírito Santo-Angola. Beginning in October 2003, includes Banco Regional do Keve.

Banking Survey:

† See note on monetary authorities.

Money (National Definitions):

Reserve Money comprises currency in circulation, banks' required and excess reserve deposits, and local government and private sector deposits at the BNA.

M1 comprises currency outside of depository corporations and transferable deposits in national and foreign currency of local governments, nonfinanicial public enterprises, and the private sector with depository corporations. Currency outside of depository corporations refers to the notes and coins issued by the BNA less the amount held by the BNA and commercial banks.

M2 comprises *M1* and time and other deposits in national and foreign currency of nonfinanical public enterprises and the private sector.

M3 comprises *M2* and BNA bonds, certificates of deposit, and repurchase agreements in national and foreign currency held with the depository corporations by nonfinanical public enterprises and the private sector.

Interest Rates:

Discount Rate (End of Period):
Rate charged by the National Bank of Angola on loans to commercial banks.

Deposit Rate:
Minimum rate set by the National Bank of Angola on commercial banks' time deposits in national currency with maturities of 91 to 180 days. † Beginning in May 1999, rate offered by commercial banks on 91- to 180-day time deposits in national currency. † Beginning in January 2000, average rate offered by commercial banks on time deposits of up to 90 days in national currency. † Beginning in December 2000, weighted average rate offered by commercial banks on time deposits of up to 90 days in national currency. The rate is weighted by deposit amounts.

Lending Rate:
Maximum rate set by the National Bank of Angola on commercial banks' loans in national currency with maturities of 180 days. † Beginning in May 1999, rate charged by commercial banks on 180-day loans in national currency. † Beginning in January 2000, average rate charged by commercial banks on loans of up to 180 days in national currency. † Beginning in December 2000, weighted average rate charged by commercial banks on loans of up to 180 days in national currency. The rate is weighted by loan amounts.

Prices:

Consumer Prices:
Source S. Weights Reference Period: December 2001; Geographical Coverage: province of Luanda; Number of Items in Basket: 224; Basis for Calculation: weights are based on the results obtained from a survey conducted from February 2000 to February 2001.

International Transactions:

Source B trade data in U.S. dollars.

National Accounts:

Source B.

Anguilla 312

Standard Sources:

A: Eastern Caribbean Central Bank, *Annual Report and Statement of Accounts*
B: Eastern Caribbean Central Bank, *Economic and Financial Review*
C: Eastern Caribbean Central Bank, *National Accounts Statistics*
N: Eastern Caribbean Central Bank, *Commercial Banking Statistics*
S: Central Statistical Office

Exchange Rates:

Official Rate: (End of Period and Period Average):
The official rate is pegged to the U.S. dollar.

Monetary Authorities:

The accounts are compiled from data contained in the balance sheet of the Eastern Caribbean Central Bank (ECCB). The monetary authorities' accounts for Anguilla represent country attributable data for ECCB claims on and liabilities to the government of Anguilla and its resident deposit money banks, and estimates of Anguilla's notional share of the ECCB's foreign assets and liabilities and currency in circulation within the region. † Beginning in December 2001, data are based on a new reporting system which provides improved classification and sectorization of the accounts.

Banking Institutions:

Comprises commercial banks. † Beginning in December 2001, data are based on a new reporting system which provides improved classification and sectorization of the accounts.

Banking Survey:

† See notes on monetary authorities and banking institutions.

Money (National Definitions):

M1 comprises notes and coins held by the public and demand deposits in national currency of the private sector in commercial banks.
M2 comprises *M1* plus time, savings, and foreign currency deposits of the private sector in commercial banks.

Interest Rates:

Discount Rate (End of Period):
Rate charged by the ECCB on loans of last resort to commercial banks.

Money Market Rate:
Fixed rate on loans between commercial banks. The rate includes the commission charged by the ECCB as agent. † Beginning in October 2001, weighted average rate on loans between commercial banks. The rate is weighted by loan amounts.

Savings Rate:
Maximum rate offered by commercial banks on savings deposits in national currency. † Beginning in June 2003, weighted average rate offered by commercial banks on savings deposits in national currency. The rate is weighted by deposit amounts.

Savings Rate (Foreign Currency):
Weighted average rate offered by commercial banks on savings deposits in foreign currency. The rate is weighted by deposit amounts.

Deposit Rate:
Maximum rate offered by commercial banks on three-month deposits. † Beginning in March 1991, weighted average rate offered by commercial banks on deposits in national currency. The rate is weighted by deposit amounts.

Deposit Rate (Foreign Currency):
Weighted average rate offered by commercial banks on deposits in foreign currency. The rate is weighted by deposit amounts.

Lending Rate:
Maximum rate charged by commercial banks on prime loans. † Beginning in March 1991, weighted average rate charged by commercial banks on loans in national currency. The rate is weighted by loan amounts.

Lending Rate (Foreign Currency):
Weighted average rate charged by commercial banks on loans in foreign currency. The rate is weighted by loan amounts.

Prices, Toursim, Labor:

Consumer Prices:
Source S.

International Transactions:

Exports and Imports:
Source S.

National Accounts:

Source C.

Antigua And Barbuda 311

Date of Fund Membership:
February 25, 1982

Standard Sources:

A: Eastern Caribbean Central Bank, *Annual Report and Statement of Accounts*
B: Eastern Caribbean Central Bank, *Economic and Financial Review*
C: Eastern Caribbean Central Bank, *National Accounts Statistics*
N: Eastern Caribbean Central Bank, *Commercial Banking Statistics*

Exchange Rates:

Official Rate: (End of Period and Period Average):
Rates are based on a fixed relationship to the U.S. dollar.
The weighting scheme used to calculate indices of nominal and real effective exchange rates (*lines* **nec** and **rec**) is based on data for tourism receipts and on data for aggregate bilateral non-oil trade flow for 1980–82.

Monetary Authorities:

The accounts are compiled from data contained in the balance sheet of the Eastern Caribbean Central Bank (ECCB). The monetary authorities' accounts for Antigua and Barbuda represent country attributable data for ECCB claims on and liabilities to the government of Antigua and Barbuda and its resident deposit money banks, and estimates of Antigua and Barbuda's notional share of the ECCB's foreign assets and liabilities and currency in circulation within the region. † Beginning in December 2001, data are based on a new reporting system which provides improved classification and sectorization of the accounts.

Banking Institutions:

Comprises commercial banks. † Beginning in December 2001, data are based on a new reporting system which provides improved classification and sectorization of the accounts.

Banking Survey:

† See notes on monetary authorities and banking institutions.

Money (National Definitions):

M1 comprises notes and coins held by the public and demand deposits in national currency of the private sector in commercial banks.
M2 comprises M1 plus time, savings, and foreign currency deposits of the private sector in commercial banks.

Interest Rates:

Discount Rate (End of Period):
Rate charged by the ECCB on loans of last resort to commercial banks.

Money Market Rate:
Fixed rate on loans between commercial banks. The rate includes the commission charged by the ECCB as agent. † Beginning in October 2001, weighted average rate on loans between commercial banks. The rate is weighted by loan amounts.

Treasury Bill Rate:
Rate on three-month treasury bills.

Savings Rate:
Maximum rate offered by commercial banks on savings deposits in national currency. † Beginning in June 2003, weighted average rate offered by commercial banks on savings deposits in national currency. The rate is weighted by deposit amounts.

Savings Rate (Foreign Currency):
Weighted average rate offered by commercial banks on savings deposits in foreign currency. The rate is weighted by deposit amounts.

Deposit Rate:
Maximum rate offered by deposit money banks on three-month time deposits. † Beginning in March 1991, weighted average rate offered by commercial banks on deposits in national currency. The rate is weighted by deposit amounts.

Deposit Rate (Foreign Currency):
Weighted average rate offered by commercial banks on deposits in foreign currency. The rate is weighted by deposit amounts.

Lending Rate:
Maximum rate charged by commercial banks on prime loans. † Beginning in March 1991, weighted average rate charged by commercial banks on loans in national currency. The rate is weighted by loan amounts.

Lending Rate (Foreign Currency):
Weighted average rate charged by commercial banks on loans in foreign currency. The rate is weighted by loan amounts.

International Transactions:

Data for exports and imports are from source B.

National Accounts:

Source C. As indicated by the country, data have been revised following the implementation of the *1993 SNA*.

Argentina 213

Date of Fund Membership:

September 20, 1956

Standard Sources:

B: Central Bank of the Republic, *Statistical Bulletin*
S: National Institute of Statistics and Census, *Quarterly Statistical Bulletin, Monthly Statistics*

Exchange Rates:

From January 1, 1970, the peso ley ($ ley) was established as the monetary unit replacing the peso moneda nacional at the exchange rate of one peso ley for 100 peso moneda nacional (m$n). On June 1, 1983, the peso argentino ($a), equal to 10,000 peso ley was introduced. On June 14, 1985, the austral (A), equal to 1,000 peso argentino was introduced. On January 1, 1992 the peso, equal to 10,000 australes, was introduced. The *Official Rate (End of Period* and *Period Average)* was pegged to the U.S. dollar through 2001. By the end of 2001, and amidst a partial freeze on bank deposits and the introduction of exchange and capital controls, Argentina abandoned the Convertibility System and devalued the peso through Law 25.561: "Public Emergency and Reform of the Exchange Regime." By means of this law a new exchange regime was established, based on an Official Exchange Market with a fixed rate of 1.40 pesos per U.S. dollar for trade and financial transactions, and a Free Exchange Market for all other transactions. A unified floating exchange rate regime was introduced on February 11, 2002, with the exchange rate determined by market conditions.

International Liquidity:

As of April 1, 1991, international reserve assets back the monetary liabilities of the Central Bank of the Republic of Argentina. *Gold (National Valuation) (line 1and)* is the U.S. dollar value of official holdings of gold as reported in the country's standard sources. *Foreign Exchange (line 1d.d):* The decline in foreign exchange holdings of the Central Bank in August 1995 was partly due to a decrease in reserve requirements at the Central Bank that could be met by a corresponding increase in the banks' deposits abroad in certain foreign banks. *Line 3..d* mainly comprises payments agreements balances and export bills held by the Central Bank of Argentina.
Argentina's national definition of international reserves includes the central bank's holdings of gold, SDRs, reserve position in the

Fund, foreign exchange, net assets of the ALADI agreement (multilateral payment system), and domestic government securities payable in foreign exchange.

Monetary Authorities:

Comprises the Central Bank of the Republic of Argentina (CBRA) only. Accounts classified as central government include also positions with nonfinancial public enterprises.

The definition of foreign assets of the monetary authorities in *IFS* differs from the definition of foreign assets in the *Bulletin* in that the latter excludes the foreign exchange received by the CBRA under swaps from domestic financial entities' current account balances in foreign currencies. † Beginning in January 1990, data may not be comparable with data for earlier periods because of a change in the valuation system and adjustments to the accounts of the CBRA. † Beginning in January 1994, data are based on more detailed sectorization of the accounts.

Deposit Money Banks:

Comprises national, provincial, and municipal banks, Caja Nacional de Ahorro y Seguro (savings bank), and private commercial banks including branches of foreign banks. Holdings of public securities and accrued income on loans, which are classified as *Claims on Central Government (line 22a),* include also positions with state and local governments and nonfinancial public enterprises. *Claims on Official Entities (line 22bx)* comprise mainly claims on nonfinancial public enterprises. Positions in financial derivatives are included in unclassified assets and liabilities which are shown in other items net. † Beginning in January 1990, data are based on an improved reporting system. † See note on monetary authorities.

Monetary Survey:

Money (line 34) excludes deposits of other banking institutions. † See notes on monetary authorities and deposit money banks.

Other Banking Institutions:

Comprises investment finance companies, credit cooperatives, and savings and loan associations for housing. † See notes on monetary authorities and deposit money banks.

Banking Survey:

† See notes on monetary authorities and deposit money banks.

Money (National Definitions):

Base Money comprises currency in circulation, reserve deposits, and correspondent accounts of banking institutions in national currency with the CBRA. Currency in circulation refers to notes and coins issued by the CBRA less the amount held by the CBRA. *M1* comprises currency in circulation outside the banking system and transferable deposits in national and foreign currency. Currency in circulation outside the banking system refers to notes and coins issued by the CBRA less the amount held by banking institutions, including the CBRA. Transferable deposits refer to current account deposits of state and local governments, public nonfinancial corporations, private sector, and residents abroad with banking institutions.

M2 comprises M1 and savings deposits in national and foreign currency of state and local governments, public nonfinancial corporations, private sector, and residents abroad with banking institutions.

M3 comprises M2, fixed deposits, and other deposits in national and foreign currency of state and local governments, public nonfinancial corporations, private sector, and residents abroad with banking institutions.

M3 Total comprises M3 and transferable, savings, time, and other deposits of nonresidents (in national and foreign currency).

Interest Rates:

Money Market Rate:
Average rate on loans denominated in national currency of up to 15 days between domestic financial institutions. The rate is weighted by daily loan amounts.

Money Market Rate (Foreign Currency):
Average rate on loans denominated in U.S. dollars of up to 15 days between domestic financial institutions. The rate is weighted by daily loan amounts.

Deposit Rate:
Average rate offered on 30- to 59-day time deposits in national currency. The rate is weighted by deposit amounts.

Deposit Rate (Foreign Currency):
Average rate offered on 30- to 59-day time deposits in U.S. dollars. The rate is weighted by deposit amounts.

Lending Rate:
Arithmetic average rate at which a selected group of banks is willing to lend to most creditworthy business customers on 30-day loans denominated in national currency.

Lending Rate (Foreign Currency):
Arithmetic average rate at which a selected group of banks is willing to lend to most creditworthy business customers on 30-day loans denominated in U.S. dollars.

Prices, Production, Labor:

Share Prices:
Composite stock price index (MERVAL) of the Buenos Aires Stock Exchange, weights reference period: June 30, 1986. The index covers shares based on their trading volume and is weighted by market capitalization. The component companies and their weights are updated on a quarterly basis according to their participation in the market during the last six months.

Producer Prices:
Source S. Weights Reference Period: 1993; Coverage: agriculture, fisheries, minerals, manufacturers, and electric energy; Number of Items in Basket: 2800 prices are monitored every month; Basis for Calculation: weights are based on the gross production value for the primary sector, the results of the National Economic Census of 1994 for the manufacturing sector, and the foreign trade data for exports and imports.

Consumer Prices:
Source S. Weights Reference Period: 1999; Geographical Coverage: whole national territory; Number of Items in Basket: 182; Basis for Calculation: weights are derived from the Survey of Household Expenditure and Revenue conducted between February 1996 and January 1997.

Wages: Monthly Earnings (Manufacturing):
Source S index, weights reference period: 2001. Data cover wages, including overtime pay and holiday pay, of production workers in manufacturing firms employing 10 or more people.

Manufacturing Production, Seasonally Adjusted:
Source S, weights reference period: 1993. Calculated by main economic activities in accordance with ISIC Rev. 3. Data are based on surveys of 83 leading enterprises, supplemented by information from trade associations and administrative information on 100 products.

Crude Petroleum Production:
Index based on data (in thousands of cubic meters) directly supplied by the Central Bank.

International Transactions:

Value of Exports and Imports:
Trade data are from source S, with the exception of imports f.o.b. which are supplied by the Central Bank.
Trade indices are from source S, weights reference period: 1993. Aggregate volume data are Laspeyres, and unit value indices are Paasche indices.

Government Finance:

Monthly, quarterly, and annual data cover the consolidated central government and are derived from *Public Sector Accounts—Public Sector on a Cash Basis—Savings, Investment, and Financing,* a monthly publication of the Ministry of Economy, Public Works, and Services. Revenue and expenditure data are adjusted to exclude taxes collected by the central government and shared with provincial governments, and expenditure data include transfers to nonfinancial public enterprises. The fiscal year ends December 31.

National Accounts:

Source B. As indicated by the country, data have been revised following the implementation of the *1993 SNA.* Statistical Discrepancy included in "Changes in Inventories."

Armenia   911

Date of Fund Membership:
May 28, 1992

Standard Sources:
B: Central Bank of Armenia
S: Ministry of Statistics of Republic of Armenia

Exchange Rates:
The ruble was the legal tender in Armenia until November 21, 1993. The dram, equal to 200 rubles, was introduced on November 22, 1993.

Official Rate: (End of Period and Period Average):
The official rate is determined by the Central Bank of Armenia (CBA) and is set on a daily basis as a weighted average of the previous day's interbank and foreign exchange auction rates.

International Liquidity:
Prior to January 1996, *Foreign Exchange (line 1d.d)* includes convertible and nonconvertible currencies.

Monetary Authorities:
Comprises the Central Bank of Armenia (CBA) only. † Beginning in December 2001, data are based on a new reporting system which provides improved classification and sectorization of the accounts.

Banking Institutions:
Comprises commercial banks. † Beginning in December 2001, data are based on a new reporting system which provides improved classification and sectorization of the accounts.

Banking Survey:
† See notes on monetary authorities and banking institutions .

Money (National Definitions):
Reserve Money comprises notes and coins issued by the CBA, required reserve and other deposits of banking institutions with the CBA, and deposits of the private sector in national and foreign currency with the CBA.
M1 comprises currency in circulation and transferable deposits. Currency in circulation refers to notes and coins issued by the CBA less the amount held by banking institutions. Transferable deposits refer to current account deposits in national currency of other financial corporations, public nonfinancial corporations, and the private sector with the CBA and banking institutions.
M2 comprises M1 and term deposits in national currency of other financial corporations, public nonfinancial corporations, and the private sector with the CBA and banking institutions.
M2X comprises M2 and foreign currency deposits of other financial corporations, public nonfinancial corporations, and the private sector with the CBA and banking institutions.

Interest Rates:
All interest rate data are from source B.

Discount Rate (End of Period):
Corresponds to the credit auction rate, which is the basic rate at which the CBA lends to commercial banks.

Refinancing Rate (End of Period):
Basic rate at which the CBA lends to the central government. † Beginning in December 1999, repo rate at which the CBA conducts repurchase agreements with resident banks.

Money Market Rate:
Loan-amount-weighted average rate of interbank loans and deposits.

Treasury Bill Rate:
Weighted average yield on 91-day treasury bills. † Beginning in May 1996, weighted average yield on three- to six-month (including 182-day) treasury bills. † Beginning in March 2001, weighted average yield on nine- to twelve-month treasury bills.

Deposit Rate:
Weighted average rate offered by commercial banks on new deposits in domestic currency with maturities of 15 days to less than a year. The rate is weighted by deposit amounts.

Lending Rate:
Weighted average rate charged by commercial banks on new loans in domestic currency with maturities of 15 days to less than a year. The rate is weighted by loan amounts.

Government Bond Yield:
Weighted average yield on medium-term coupon bonds with partial repayment sold in the primary market. Several types of bonds with maturities ranging between one to five years are included.

Prices, Production, Labor:

Source S.

Industrial Production:

Monthly data do not include data of small and medium enterprises, which are included in quarterly data. Annual data are revised by final reports.

Producer Prices:

Data are compiled on the basis of registered prices of 286 representative goods from 111 enterprises.

Wages:

Average monthly nominal wages, including benefits in kind per worker, are compiled on the basis of monthly reports provided by 9,000 economic entities.

Consumer Prices:

Source S. Weights Reference Period: previous year; Geographical Coverage: Yerevan and nine large population centers in the Republic; Number of Items in Basket: 400; Basis for Calculation: the weights are calculated on the basis of annual data from sample surveys of households.

International Transactions:

Source S. *Exports* and *Imports* are based on customs records that include coverage of citizens' (shuttle) trade.

Government Finance:

Cash data cover the operations of the consolidated central government. The fiscal year ends December 31.

National Accounts:

Source S. *Gross Domestic Product, Production Approach (line 99b)* is compiled from the production approach using data on gross output and intermediate consumption from production surveys. Because official GDP is calculated using the production approach, the statistical discrepancy (*line 99bs*) represents the difference between GDP from the production approach (*line 99b*) and the sum of the expenditure components shown. Concepts, definitions, and methodology are in accordance with the *1993 SNA*, as indicated by the country. Estimates include hidden activities but exclude illegal activities. *GDP Volume Measures:* Beginning in 1994, data at previous year prices are used to construct *line 99bvp*.

Aruba   314

Standard Sources:

B: Centrale Bank van Aruba, *Quarterly Bulletin*
S: Central Bureau of Statistics

Exchange Rates:

Official Rate: (End of Period and Period Average):
The official rate is pegged to the U.S. dollar.

International Liquidity:

Gold (National Valuation) (line 1and) is obtained by converting the value in national currency terms, as reported in the country's standard source, using the prevailing exchange rate, as given in *line* **ae**. Title to the gold held in various forms by the Central

Bank of the Netherlands Antilles as of December 31, 1985 was formally transferred to the Gold Fund of the Netherlands Antilles and Aruba by means of a deed of transfer dated December 19, 1986. The Gold Fund then distributed gold to the Bank van de Nederlandse Antillen and the Centrale Bank van Aruba based on the Mutual Regulation. During 1998, the distribution of gold was finalized. *Lines 7a.d* and *7b.d* are derived from the accounts of the commercial banks and exclude the nonresident assets and liabilities of offshore banks operating in Aruba.

Monetary Authorities:

Comprises the Central Bank of Aruba, which was established on January 1, 1986, when Aruba obtained a separate status within the Kingdom of the Netherlands. Prior to that date, Aruba formed part of the Netherlands Antilles. *Central Government Deposits (line 16d)* includes development funds received from the Netherlands Government and held temporarily pending expenditures on current development projects in Aruba.

Deposit Money Banks:

Data refer to the four commercial banks licensed to carry out operations with residents and nonresidents. The two offshore banks established in Aruba transact exclusively with nonresidents and are themselves classified as such in national sources. *Claims on Private Sector (line 22d)* includes claims on nonfinancial public enterprises.

Interest Rates:

Discount Rate:

The rate at which the central bank makes collateralized loans to commercial banks. Data are end-of-period.

Deposit Rate:

Beginning in September 1998, data refer to the weighted-average rate on new deposits. Prior to September 1998, data are end-of period and refer to deposit money banks' offered rates on six-month deposits above Af. 10,000.

Lending Rate:

Beginning in September 1998, data refer to the weighted average rate on new loans. Prior to September 1998, data are end-of-period and refer to deposit money banks' current account lending rate.

Prices and Tourism:

Consumer Prices:

Source S. Data are compiled on a September 2000 weights reference period and cover all income groups. The weights were derived from a 1998 household income and expenditure survey consisting of 498 households. By the end of 2006, the CBS will adjust the weights for products and services again based on the Income and Expenditure Survey held during the period April—May 2006, which consists of 796 households.

International Transactions:

Source S. Data through December 1999 exclude imports into and exports from the Free Zone. Mineral fuels trade is also excluded.

National Accounts:

Source S. As indicated by the country, the National Accounts of Aruba follows the guidelines, concepts, definitions, classifications, and accounting rules of the *System of National Accounts 1993 (1993 SNA)*.

Australia   193

Date of Fund Membership:
August 5, 1947

Standard Sources:
A: Reserve Bank, *Report and Financial Statements*
B: Reserve Bank, *Statistical Bulletin*
C: Commonwealth Cash Flow Statements
D: Department of the Treasury
S: Australian Bureau of Statistics, *Monthly Review of Business Statistics, Digest of Current Economic Statistics, Life Insurance Bulletin*

Exchange Rates:
Market Rate (End of Period and Period Average):
Central bank midpoint rate.

International Liquidity:
Gold (National Valuation) (line 1and) is obtained by converting the value in national currency terms, as reported in the country's standard sources, using the prevailing exchange rate, as given in *line* **dg** or *line* **ag**. This line follows national valuation procedures, which revalue gold monthly on the basis of the average U.S. dollar price of gold prevailing in the London market during the month.

Monetary Authorities:
Consolidates the Reserve Bank of Australia (RBA) and monetary functions undertaken by the Treasury. The contra-entry to Treasury IMF accounts and coin issues is included in *line 12a*. Data relate to the note issue and central banking departments of the RBA. † Beginning in June 1989, data are based on an improved sectorization of the accounts.

Banking Institutions:
Comprises trading and savings banks. Data for deposits with savings banks are interpolated weekly averages based on end-of-month figures; other data for savings banks are end of period. *Claims on State and Local Governments (line 22b)* comprise securities issued by local and semigovernmental authorities. *Demand Deposits (line 24)* comprise interest-bearing and non-interest-bearing current deposits of the private sector. † Before December 1971, data relate to net foreign assets. † Beginning in November 1984, foreign assets and liabilities are compiled under a new, more comprehensive statistical collection. † Beginning in June 1989, the coverage of accounts has been expanded to include domestic assets and liabilities denominated in foreign currencies as well as foreign assets and foreign liabilities denominated in Australian dollars. Beginning in July 2000, data are for the last business day of the month. † Beginning in March 2002, data are based on a new reporting system, which provides an improved classification and sectorization of the accounts. Data on public sector securities are reported net of short positions, which may result in negative values of *Claims on Central Government (line 22a)*

and *Claims on State and Local Governments (line 22b)*. *Demand deposits (line 24)* include accounts with checking facility of the private sector, nonfinancial public enterprises, and state, territory, and local governments.

Banking Survey:
† See notes on monetary authorities and banking institutions .

Money (National Definitions):
Money Base comprises holdings of notes and coins by the private sector, deposits of banks with the RBA, and other RBA liabilities to the private nonbank sector.
M1 comprises notes and coins held by the public and demand deposits of the private nonbank sector in banks.
M3 comprises M1 and all other deposits and certificates of deposits of the private non-authorized deposit-taking institutions sector in authorized deposit-taking institutions. Beginning in April 2002, excludes certificates of deposits denominated in foreign currency.
Broad money comprises M3 and non-deposit borrowings from the private sector by all financial intermediaries, excluding holdings of currency and deposits in banks by registered financial corporations and cash management trusts. Beginning in April 2002, excludes certificates of deposits denominated in foreign currency.

Interest Rates:
Discount Rate:
Rediscount rate offered by the RBA to holders of treasury notes. Rates shown are average for period.

Money Market Rate:
Weighted average short-term rate of outstanding loans. † Beginning in January 1995, rate paid on unsecured overnight loans of cash as calculated by the Australian Financial Markets Association and published on Reuters page at 11 a.m. † Beginning in January 1999, weighted average rate of the interest rates at which banks have borrowed and lent exchange settlement funds during the day. The rate is weighted by loan amounts.

Treasury Bill Rate:
Weighted average yield on thirteen-week treasury notes allotted at last tender of month. †Beginning in January 1995, estimated closing yield in the secondary market on thirteen-week treasury notes.

Deposit Rate:
Investment rate offered by savings banks. † Beginning in December 1981, average rate offered by major banks on three-month fixed deposits of 10,000 Australian dollars.

Lending Rate:
Maximum rate charged by banks on overdrafts of less than 100,000 Australian dollars. † Beginning in January 1977, rate charged by banks on loans to small and large businesses.

Government Bond Yield:
Short-Term: Yield on two-year Treasury bonds. † Beginning in June 1981, assessed secondary market yield on two-year non-rebate bonds. † Beginning in June 1992, assessed secondary market yield on three-year non-rebate bonds. Yield is calculated before brokerage and on the last business day of the month. *Long-Term:* Yield on 15-year Treasury bonds † Beginning in July 1969,

assessed secondary market yield on ten-year non-rebate bonds. Yield is calculated before brokerage and on the last business day of the month.

Prices, Production, Labor:

Share Prices:
End-of-month share price index covering shares quoted in the Australian Stock Exchange (ASX), base December 31, 1979. Through March 2000, data refer to the All Ordinaries Index. Beginning in April 2000, index refers to the S&P/ASX 200.

Prices: Manufacturing Output:
Source S index of articles produced by manufacturing industry, weights reference period: 1996–97. The index includes prices of articles produced by domestic manufacturers for sale or transfer to other domestic sectors or for export or for use as capital equipment.

Consumer Prices:
Source S. Weights Reference Period: 1998–99; Geographical Coverage: Eight capital cities; Number of Items in Basket: Goods and services actually acquired by the reference population in the weighting base period; Basis for Calculation: Weights are based on Household Expenditure Survey and are updated at approximately five-yearly intervals.

Wages:
Average weekly earnings, ordinary time (excludes overtime) for full-time adult males for the pay period ending on or before the middle of the quarter.

Industrial Production, Seasonally Adjusted:
Source S. Weights Reference Period: Current financial year (July 1–June 30); Sectoral Coverage: mining, manufacturing and electricity, gas and water industrial sectors; Basis for Calculation: from 1985–86 the elemental volume indexes are aggregated together to form annually reweighted chain Laspeyres indexes which are referenced to the current price values of the latest but one complete financial year.

Manufacturing Employment, Seasonally Adjusted:
Source S data for the middle month of the quarter on civilians employed in manufacturing establishments. For coverage see the explanatory notes to "The Labor Force, Australia," published by the Australian Bureau of Statistics.

International Transactions:

All trade value and volume data are from source S. Beginning July 1985, nonmerchandise trade is excluded from total trade value. Nonmerchandise trade includes such items as coin being legal tender and goods for temporary exhibition.

Exports:
Data refer to total exports, f.o.b.

Imports, c.i.f.:
Prior to June 1976, data are based on imports, f.o.b., adjusted by the f.o.b./c.i.f. factor supplied by the Australian Bureau of Statistics. Since July 1976, the Australian Bureau of Statistics has supplied imports, c.i.f. data. † Beginning October 1985, import statistics exclude posted articles with a value of less than $1,000 inclusive (previously $250) and will not be strictly comparable with data for previous periods.

Volume of Exports:
Laspeyres index of exports of merchandise annually chained. Volume indices for individual commodities are based on data in physical quantities.

Volume of Imports:
Laspeyres index of imports of merchandise annually chained.

Export Prices:
Source S Laspeyres export prices index (including re-exports), weights reference period: annually reweighted and chained.

Wheat:
Source S Australian Wheat Board price.

Coal/Greasy Wool (Unit Value):
Data are calculated by *IFS* from reported value and volume data.

Import Prices:
Source B Laspeyres import price index, f.o.b., weights reference period: annually reweighted and chained.

Government Finance:

Prior to May 2003, monthly cash data are derived from sources C and D. Source C is used for revenue, expenditure, and financing, whereas source D is used for debt. Monthly data cover the operations of the budgetary central government (Commonwealth Public Account) and include the budget appropriations to central government agencies with individual budgets. However, excluded are own revenues of central government agencies with individual budgets and the expenditures from those revenues. Total debt, *line 63* for budgetary central government includes government securities on issue. From July 1995, debt data include Income Equalization Deposits and exclude Treasury Bond holdings by the Loan Consolidation and Investment Reserve Trust Fund. † Owing to changes associated with the introduction of accrual accounting cash data provided from September quarter 1999 are not comparable with earlier data. From 1999 onward, data for the month of June are derived as a residual. From July 2003, quarterly accrual data are reported by source S.

Annual data from 2003, are as reported in the *Government Finance Statistics Yearbook* and cover the budgetary central government cash data. The fiscal year ends June 30.

National Accounts:

† As indicated by the country, data have been revised from midquarter 1959 onwards following the implementation of improved compilation methods and the *1993 SNA*. Lines *99a.c* and *99b.c* include a statistical discrepancy. GDP chain-linked volume measures are calculated based on the prices and weights of the previous year, using Laspeyres formula in general.

Austria   122

Data are denominated in schillings prior to January 1999 and in euros from January 1999 onward. An irrevocably fixed factor for converting schillings to euros was established at 13.7603 schillings per euro. Beginning in January 1999, with the implementation of Stage Three of the European Economic and Monetary Union (EMU), a euro area-wide definition of residency was introduced: All positions with residents of other euro area (EA) countries, including the European Central Bank (ECB), are classified as domestic positions, and foreign assets and foreign liabilities include only positions with non-euro area residents. In 2002, the schilling was retired from circulation and replaced by euro banknotes and coins. Descriptions of the changes in the methodology and presentation of Austria's accounts following the introduction of the euro are shown in the introduction to *IFS* and the notes on the euro area page.

Date of Fund Membership:
August 27, 1948

Standard Sources:
A: National Bank, *Annual Report*
B: National Bank, *Mitteilungen*
S: Statistical Office, *Statistische Nachrichten*
V: Eurostat

Exchange Rates:
Official Rate: (End of Period and Period Average):
Prior to January 1999, the official rate referred to the midpoint rate in the Vienna market. In January 1999, the schilling became a participating currency within the Eurosystem, and the euro market rate became applicable to all transactions. In 2002, the schilling was retired from circulation and replaced by euro banknotes and coins. For additional information, refer to the section on exchange rates in the introduction to *IFS* and the footnotes on the euro area page.

International Liquidity:
Beginning in January 1999, *Total Reserves minus Gold (line 1l.d)* is defined in accordance with the Eurosystem's statistical definition of international reserves. The international reserves of Austria per the Eurosystem statistical definition at the start of the monetary union (January 1, 1999) in billions of U.S. dollars were as follows: *Total Reserves minus Gold,* $17,257; *Foreign Exchange,* $15,676; *SDRs,* $149; *Reserve Position in the Fund,* $1,433; *Other Reserve Assets,* $0; *Gold,* $3,972; *Gold (million fine troy ounces),* 13.820 ounces. *Foreign Exchange (line 1d.d):* Between January 1995 and December 1998, gold and foreign exchange holdings excluded deposits at the European Monetary Institute (EMI), and the holdings of European currency units (ECUs) issued against these deposits were included in *line 1d.d. Gold (Eurosystem Valuation) (line 1and):* Prior to January 1999, the value of gold was obtained by converting the value in national currency, as reported in the country's standard sources, using the schilling/dollar conversion rates utilized for balance sheet purposes. These conversion rates differed from the prevailing exchange rates reported in *IFS.* Beginning in December 1979, gold in national sources was valued at 60,000 schillings per kilogram. From January 1999 onward, gold is valued at market prices at the end of each quarter. Memorandum data are provided on *Non-Euro Claims on Euro Area Residents* and *Euro Claims on Non-Euro Area Residents,* which represent positions as of the last Friday in each month. For additional information, refer to the section on international liquidity in the introduction to *IFS* and the footnotes on the euro area page.

Monetary Authorities:
Comprises the National Bank of Austria, which beginning in January 1999 is part of the Eurosystem, and coin issue of the Austrian Mint, which is a subsidiary of the National Bank of Austria. Beginning in 2002, *Currency Issued (line 14a)* includes euro banknotes and coins and, until December 2002, any unretired schillings. The recorded value of euro banknotes is based on a monthly allocation of total euro banknotes in circulation based on the National Bank of Austria's paid up share of the ECB's capital; it does not correspond to either the actual amount of euro banknotes placed in circulation by the National Bank of Austria which is shown in memo line *Currency Put into Circulation (line 14m)*, nor the actual circulation of banknotes within the domestic territory. See section *Euro banknotes and coins* in the introduction to *IFS.* † In December 1995, the institutional coverage of the data on the government sector was revised in accordance with the *1995 ESA.* Prior to January 1999, the contra-entries to Treasury-IMF accounts, treasury loans to banks, and coin issue were included in *Claims on General Government (line 12a).* From January 1999 onward, the contra-entries are included in *Other Items (Net) (line 17r).* *Foreign Assets (line 11)* and *Foreign Liabilities (line 16c):* Prior to January 1999, securities holdings were valued at market value at year end; beginning in January 1999, securities holdings are recorded at market value each month. Beginning in 2002, *Claims on Banking Institutions (line 12e.u)* and *Liabilities to Banking Institutions (line 14c.u)* include "Intra-Eurosystem claims/liabilities related to banknote issue," which is a single net value representing the difference between the value of euro banknotes allocated to the National Bank of Austria according to the accounting scheme of the Eurosystem for issuing euro banknotes, and the value of euro banknotes put into circulation by the National Bank of Austria. See section *Euro banknotes and coins* in the introduction to *IFS.* Prior to January 1999, securities repurchase agreements between the National Bank of Austria and banking institutions, which were used for open-market operations, were recorded as transactions in the underlying security. Beginning in January 1999, these are recorded as collateralized loan instruments. Prior to January 1999, *Claims on Banking Institutions (line 12e)* included post-World War II European Recovery Program loans that are administered by banks but were made to other resident sectors. *Bonds and Money Market Instruments (line 16n.u)* include subordinated debt in the form of securities, other bonds, and money market paper. *Other Items (Net) (line 17r)* : Includes capital accounts, including reserve positions, provisions of the National Bank of Austria's pension fund, and holding gains/losses from revaluation of foreign exchange holdings. Beginning in January 1999, includes liabilities to the National Bank of Austria for post-World War II European Recovery Program loans that are administered by banks but were made to other resident sectors. For a description of the accounts, refer to the section on monetary authorities in the introduction to *IFS.* Beginning with the data for end-November 2000, Monetary Authorities' *Foreign Assets (line 11), Foreign Liabilities (line 16c), Claims on Banking Institutions (line 12e.u),* and *Liabilities to Banking Institutions (line 14c.u)* are affected by a change from gross to net presentation of positions relating to the TARGET (Trans-European Automated Real-Time Gross

Settlement Express Transfer) euro clearing system. (See *Recording of TARGET system positions* under *European Economic and Monetary Union (EMU)* in the introduction to *IFS*.) Memo line *Net Claims on Eurosystem (line 12e.s)* equals gross claims on, less gross liabilities to, the ECB and other members of the Eurosystem. Comprises euro-denominated claims equivalent to the transfer of foreign currency reserves to the ECB, Intra-Eurosystem claims/liabilities related to banknote issue, net claims or liabilities within the TARGET clearing system, and other positions.

Banking Institutions:

† Beginning in 1974, banks' external accounts are based on the foreign exchange record, which provides an improved resident/nonresident distinction. † Beginning in 1984, data are based on improved classification. † Beginning in 1995, data on claims on government were revised to reflect the institutional classification of the government sector in the *European System of Accounts 1995 (1995 ESA)*. Prior to January 1999, comprised joint stock, private, savings, and mortgage banks, agricultural credit associations, industrial credit corporations, post office savings bank, miscellaneous other credit institutions, and branches of Austrian banks resident outside Austria. Data were derived from supervisory reports that differed in accounting, valuation, and residency criteria from data compiled under the Eurosystem's regulatory standards. Beginning in January 1999, consists of all resident units classified as other monetary financial institutions (other MFIs), in accordance with *1995 ESA* standards, including money market funds. Numerous units classified within the banking sector prior to January 1999 are excluded thereafter, because they do not have the characteristics of MFIs. Monthly statistical reports are not required for several hundred small MFIs, but data are estimated to represent the entire MFI universe. *Claims on Monetary Authorities (line 20)* and *Credit from Monetary Authorities (line 26g)*: Prior to January 1999, *lines 20 and 26g* recorded securities repurchase agreements between the National Bank of Austria and MFIs used in open-market operations as transactions in the underlying security. Beginning in January 1999, these are recorded as collateralized loan instruments. *Other Deposits (line 25)* includes subordinated instruments other than those classified as securities. *Money Market Fund Shares (line 26m.u)* include shares/units issued by money market funds. *Bonds and Money Market Instruments (line 26n.u)* include subordinated debt in the form of securities, other bonds, and money market paper. *Other Items (Net) (line 27r)*: Beginning in January 1999, includes accruals of liabilities to third parties and holdings of shares issued by other MFIs. For a description of the accounts, refer to the section on banking institutions in the introduction to *IFS*.

For a description of the methodology and accounts, refer to the section Banking Survey (National Residency) in the introduction to *IFS*.

Banking Survey (National Residency):

For a description of the methodology and accounts, refer to the section Banking Survey (National Residency) in the introduction to *IFS*.

Banking Survey (Euro Area-wide Residency):

For a description of the methodology and accounts, refer to the section Banking Survey (Euro Area-wide Residency) in the introduction to *IFS*.

Money (National Definitions):

Prior to January 1999, *Central Bank Money (line 19ma)* consisted of bank notes and coins (excluding gold and silver coins) in circulation plus balances of resident banks, government, and other liabilities to residents at the National Bank of Austria. *Extended Monetary Base (line 19mb)* consisted of National Bank of Austria money holdings of banks and nonbanks; banks' holdings were adjusted for changes in reserve requirements and changes in the composition of deposits with banks. *Money M1 (line 39m)* consisted of currency outside banks (excluding gold and silver coins) plus demand deposits (including demand deposits of nonbanks with the National Bank of Austria) with resident banks excluding banks' cash holdings and interbank deposits. Beginning in January 1999, national monetary aggregates series are discontinued. Euro Area aggregates are presented on the euro area page.

Interest Rates:

Discount Rate (End of Period) (line 60):
Prior to January 1999, Source B. Referred to the rate at which the National Bank of Austria discounted eligible paper. The National Bank of Austria also lent against government and other eligible securities at the lombard rate, which was usually above the discount rate. Beginning in January 1999, central bank policy rates are discontinued. See Eurosystem policy rate series on the euro area page.

Money Market Rate (line 60b):
Rates refer to one-day interbank loans among banks in Vienna. Monthly data are unweighted averages of daily mean rates.

Deposit Rate (line 60l):
Deposits up to one year at monetary financial institutions. † Prior to December 1997, data refer to rates on savings deposits without agreed maturity (due at call).

Deposit Rate (lines 60lhs, 60lhn, 60lcs, and 60lcn):
See notes in the Introduction to *IFS*.

Lending Rate (line 60p):
Loans to enterprises up to one year.

Lending Rate (lines 60phs, 60pns, 60phm, 60phn, 60pcs, and 60pcn):
See notes in the Introduction to *IFS*.

Government Bond Yield (line 61):
Data refer to all government bonds issued and not yet redeemed and are weighted with the share of each bond in the total value of government bonds in circulation. The data include bonds benefitting from tax privileges under the tax reduction scheme. For additional information, refer to the section on interest rates in the introduction to *IFS* and the footnotes on the euro area page.

Prices, Production, Labor:

Share Prices:
Data are from source B index, referring to average quotations of 41 shares on the Vienna Stock Exchange, base December 31, 1967. † Prior to January 1986, data refer to end-of-period quotations; thereafter, to monthly averages of daily quotations.

Wholesale Prices:

Data refer to source B index of general wholesale prices, base 2005. The source of the data is a monthly survey among 220 wholesale establishments. The weights for the 61 groups, reflecting the ÖCPA (the Austrian version of the Classification of Products by Activities in the European Union) are based on the results of the structural business statistics of 2003 for wholesale trade.

Consumer Prices:

Source S. Weights Reference Period: 2004/2005; Geographical Coverage: All Austria; Number of Items in Basket: 760; Basis for Calculation: Weights are derived from a family budget survey, which is carried out every five years, in combination with national accounts data on national household consumption within the economic territory.

Wages: Monthly Earnings (line 65):

Data are from source S, covering manufacturing and mining and excluding sawmills.

Wages (line 65a):

Source S, covering all employed persons within the Austrian Economy. Index based on agreed minimum wages for employees over 18 years of age.

Industrial Production:

Source S. Weights Reference Period: 2000; Sectoral Coverage: starting in 1996, mining and quarrying, manufacturing, electricity, gas and steam, and construction; Basis for Calculation: weights are based on gross value added to factor costs derived from structural statistics and applied to quantity relatives or, in some cases, to deflated value relatives.

Employment:

Data are from source B, based on social security statistics covering total employment at the end of each month.

International Transactions:

Value data on total *Exports* and *Imports* are from source B.

Government Finance:

Prior to 1999, annual cash data on federal government are as reported for the *Government Finance Statistics Yearbook (GFSY)* and cover consolidated central government operations, including social security and extrabudgetary operations. However, data on central government outstanding debt relate to the budgetary central government only. Quarterly data differ from source B in which budgetary and extrabudgetary accounts are reported separately, whereas they are consolidated in *IFS*. From 1999, accrual data on general government are derived from source V. The fiscal year ends December 31.

National Accounts:

Line 93i includes a statistical discrepancy. As indicated by the country, from 1976 onward data have been revised following the implementation of the *ESA 95*. From 1999, euro data are sourced from the Eurostat database. Data are published at current and chained 2000 euro. Eurostat introduced chain-linked GDP volume measures to both annual and quarterly data with the release of the third quarter 2005 on November 30, 2005. Chain linked GDP volume measures are expressed in the prices of the previous year and re-referenced to 2000.

Azerbaijan, Rep. of   912

Date of Fund Membership:
September 18, 1992

Standard Sources:
B: National Bank of Azerbaijan
S: State Committee on Statistics

Exchange Rates:

The manat, which was first introduced on August 15, 1992 and circulated alongside the Russian ruble at a fixed rate of 10 rubles per manat, became the sole legal tender in Azerbaijan on January 1, 1994. On January 1, 2006, the new manat, equivalent to 5,000 of the old manat was introduced.

Official Rate: (End of Period and Period Average):

Multiple exchange rates were in existence from 1992 through February 1995. The official exchange rate was pegged to the ruble at the rate of 10 rubles per manat until end-November 1993, when the National Bank of Azerbaijan (NBA) fixed the exchange rate for the manat against the U.S. dollar at a rate of US$1=118 manats. The fixed exchange rate against the U.S. dollar was maintained until March 25, 1994, when the NBA reverted to a ruble peg for the manat at a rate of 10 rubles per manat. On March 25, 1994, with the re-pegging of the manat to the ruble, the official exchange rate moved from 118 manats to 174 manats per U.S. dollar. On May 24, 1994, the NBA began quoting the official manats per U.S. dollar exchange rate on the basis of a weighted average of exchange rates quoted by commercial banks. Starting in March 1995, the exchange rate was unified and the official exchange rate is determined by the NBA at the rate established by the Baku Interbank Currency Exchange (BICEX), the Organized Interbank Foreign Exchange Market (OIFEM), the Common Interbank Foreign Exchange Market (CIFEM), and the commercial banks.

International Liquidity:

Data for *Foreign Exchange (line .1d.d)* comprise the NBA's convertible currency cash and other liquid claims on nonresidents denominated in convertible currencies and in post–1993 Russian rubles.

Monetary Authorities:

Comprises the National Bank of Azerbaijan (NBA) only. Through December 2001, *Claims on Central Government* include the contra-entry of the obligations with the Fund assumed by the NBA as the depository institution for Azerbaijan's relations with the Fund. † Beginning in January 1998, data reflect the introduction of a new plan of accounts. † Beginning in December 2001, data are based on a new reporting system which provides an improved classification and sectorization of the accounts.

Banking Institutions:

Comprises commercial banks. † Beginning in March 2000, data reflect the introduction of a new plan of accounts. † Beginning in December 2001, data are based on a new reporting system which provides an improved classification and sectorization of the accounts.

Banking Survey:

† See notes on monetary authorities and banking institutions .

Money (National Definitions):

Reserve Money comprises notes and coins issued by the NBA, deposits of other depository corporations with the NBA, and deposits of other financial corporations, public nonfinancial corporations, and private sector with the NBA.

M1 comprises currency in circulation and transferable deposits. Currency in circulation refers to notes and coins issued by the NBA less the amount held by other depository corporations. Transferable deposits refer to current account deposits in national currency of other financial corporations, public nonfinancial corporations, and private sector with the NBA and other depository corporations.

M2 comprises M1; savings and time deposits in national currency of other financial corporations, public nonfinancial corporations, and private sector with the NBA and other depository corporations; securities other than shares in national currency issued by other depository corporations held by other financial corporations, public nonfinancial corporations, and private sector; and guarantee deposits and payables on financial leasing, brokerage operations, and factoring operations in national currency.

M3 comprises M2; foreign currency deposits of other financial corporations, public nonfinancial corporations, and private sector with the NBA and other depository corporations; securities other than shares in foreign currency issued by other depository corporations held by other financial corporations, public nonfinancial corporations, and private sector; and guarantee deposits and payables on financial leasing, brokerage operations, and factoring operations in foreign currency.

Interest Rates:

All interest rate data are from source B.

Refinancing Rate (End of Period):
Basic six-month rate at which the NBA lends to commercial banks.

Treasury Bill Rate:
Weighted average rate on three-month treasury bills sold at auction.

Deposit Rate:
Weighted average rate offered by commercial banks on 12-month deposits in national currency. The rate is weighted by deposit amounts.

Deposit Rate (Foreign Currency):
Weighted average rate offered by commercial banks on 12-month deposits in foreign currency. The rate is weighted by deposit amounts.

Lending Rate:
Weighted average rate charged by commercial banks on 12-month loans in national currency. The rate is weighted by loan amounts.

Lending Rate (Foreign Currency):
Weighted average rate charged by commercial banks on 12-month loans in foreign currency. The rate is weighted by loan amounts.

Prices:

Consumer Prices:
Source S. Percent changes derived from annually chained Laspeyres index which includes 268 items, uses weight from the Household Budget Survey representative for all socio-economic groups and geographic areas.

International Transactions:

Source S. Data exclude military goods, precious metals, and goods procured in foreign ports.

Government Finance:

Through 1999, annual data are as reported for the *Government Finance Statistics Yearbook* and cover the consolidated central government. The fiscal year ends December 31.

National Accounts:

Source S.

Bahamas, The   313

Date of Fund Membership:
August 21, 1973

Standard Sources:
B: Central Bank, *Quarterly Statistical Digest, Quarterly Economic Review*
S: Department of Statistics, *Quarterly Statistical Summary, Statistical Abstract 1978*

Exchange Rates:

The official exchange rate is pegged to the U.S. dollar and applies to most transactions. An investment currency rate, which is also pegged to the U.S. dollar, applies to certain capital transactions between residents and nonresidents and to direct investments outside The Bahamas.

Principal Rate relates to the official rate.

Secondary Rate relates to the investment currency rate.

The weighting scheme used to calculate indices of nominal and real effective exchange rates (*lines* **nec** and **rec**) is based on data for tourism receipts as well as on data for merchandise trade.

International Liquidity:

† Prior to January 1977, data for *line 1d.d* include small foreign exchange holdings by the government, which were transferred to the Central Bank of The Bahamas as of this date. *Lines 7a.d* and *7b.d* relate to the foreign accounts of commercial banks. There are numerous other financial institutions in The Bahamas, primarily branches of foreign banks, that engage exclusively in foreign operations. Their assets and liabilities with the monetary system are regarded as part of the foreign sector in sections 10, 20, and 30. Hence, *lines 7a.d* and *7b.d* include accounts of commercial banks with offshore banks. Data are not available on the accounts of all such Bahamian-based intermediaries.

Monetary Authorities:

Comprises the Central Bank of The Bahamas only.

Deposit Money Banks:

Comprises commercial banks and the authorized dealers that are permitted to undertake domestic business and are licensed to deal in gold and all foreign currencies.

Other Banking Institutions:

Comprises licensed banks and trust companies that are permitted to undertake domestic business, other than commercial banks (reported in section 20). These data exclude the accounts of numerous financial intermediaries transacting primarily, and in most cases exclusively, with nonresidents for which complete data are not available (see note in the international liquidity section).

Money (National Definitions):

Base Money comprises currency in circulation, banker's correspondent and other accounts with the Central Bank of The Bahamas (CBB), and transferable deposits of nonbank depository corporations CBB in national currency. Currency in circulation refers to notes and coins issued by the CBB.

M1 comprises currency in circulation and transferable deposits. Currency in circulation refers to notes and coins issued by the CBB less the amount held by banking institutions. Transferable deposits refer to current account deposits in national currency of nonbank financial institutions, public nonfinancial corporations, private sector, and the national insurance fund with the CBB and banking institutions.

M2 comprises M1 and fixed and savings deposits in national currency of nonbank financial institutions, public nonfinancial corporations, and private sector with banking institutions.

M3 comprises M2 and foreign currency deposits of nonbank financial institutions, public nonfinancial corporations, and private sector with banking institutions.

Interest Rates:

All interest rate data are from source B.

Bank Rate (End of Period):
Rate at which the Central Bank of The Bahamas makes loans and advances to the commercial banks.

Treasury Bill Rate:
Average discount rate for three-month bills denominated in Bahamian dollars.

Savings Rate:
Average of rates quoted by commercial banks for savings deposits.

Deposit Rate:
Average of rates quoted by commercial banks for three-month time deposits.

Lending Rate:
Prime rate, which is the rate that commercial banks charge their most creditworthy business customers on short-term loans.

Prices, Production, Labor:

Consumer Prices:
Source S. Weights Reference Period: July–August 1994; Geographical Coverage: Covers the two major islands of New Providence and Grand Bahama; Number of Items in Basket: 253

items for which prices are collected from some 60 or more housing units and 417 retail establishments; Basis for Calculation: Weights were derived from the July/August 1994 Household Budgetary Survey.

Tourist Arrivals:
Source B.

International Transactions:

All trade data are from source B. Trade data since 1988 are those compiled by the Central Bank of the Bahamas and published in source B. These data differ significantly from *DOTS* which are compiled by the Department of Statistics and published in source S. Beginning in 1990, trade statistics exclude certain oil and chemical products.

Government Finance:

Data are derived from source B. Source B data originate from monthly Treasury Statistical Summary Printouts and annual Treasury Accounts. † Data beginning in 1988 cover the budgetary central government and no longer cover operations of the National Insurance Board, which is a social security fund. The discrepancies between the annual data and the sum of the monthly and quarterly data result from the annual data revisions, which could not be allocated by months and quarters. † From 1993 onward, fiscal years begin on July 1, rather than on January 1. † Prior to July 2004, to the extent possible, existing subannual *IFS* data were converted to the main aggregates that are presented in the *GFSM 2001* Statement of Sources and Uses of Cash (see the Introduction of the monthly *IFS* publication for details). The fiscal year ends June 30.

National Accounts:

Source S. As indicated by the country, beginning in 1989, data have been revised following the implementation of improved compilation methods and the *1993 SNA. Gross Saving (line 99s)* is derived from the gross national disposable income account. A statistical discrepancy exists with gross savings derived from gross capital formation.

Bahrain, Kingdom of   419

Date of Fund Membership:
September 7, 1972

Standard Sources:

A: Central Bank of Bahrain, *Annual Report*
B: Central Bank of Bahrain, *Quarterly Statistical Bulletin*
M: Ministry of Finance and National Economy (MOFNE), *National Accounts*
S: Central Statistics Organization, *Statistical Abstract*

Exchange Rates:

Official Rate: (End of Period and Period Average):
Central bank midpoint rate. The official rate shows limited flexibility against the U.S. dollar. Since 1980 the Bahraini Dinar has been fixed to the SDR at a rate of BD 0.47619 per SDR. As of

December 25, 2001 the Bahraini Dinar was formally pegged to the U.S. Dollar at a rate of $2.659 per BD.

International Liquidity:

Gold (National Valuation) (line 1and) is obtained by converting the value in national currency terms, as reported in the country's standard sources, using the prevailing exchange rate, as given in *line* **ag** or *line* **wg**.

Offshore banking units (OBUs), which began operations in 1976, deal freely with nonresidents but are permitted to undertake only limited domestic operations, essentially with the monetary system and the government. OBUs are treated as residents of Bahrain. † Prior to 1991, data for *lines 7a.d* and *7b.d* include positions with offshore banking units, which were classified as nonresident institutions. Data are as given in source B.

Monetary Authorities:

Consolidates the Central Bank of Bahrain, which effective September 7, 2006 is the successor to the Bahrain Monetary Agency with monetary functions undertaken by the MOFNE. The contra-entry to MOFNE IMF accounts and government foreign assets is included in *line 16d.* † See note on deposit money banks.

Deposit Money Banks:

† Beginning in 1991, data are compiled from a new set of statistical returns, and the institutional coverage is extended to include all kinds of resident banks, that is, full commercial banks (FCUs), offshore banking units (OBUs), and investment banks (IBs). Deposit money banks' claims on and liabilities to nonresidents therefore exclude positions with OBUs (previously treated as nonresidents), and their claims on and liabilities to resident banks include positions with OBUs. *Reserves (line 20)* includes vault cash and balances held with the Central Bank of Bahrain.

Monetary Survey:

† See note on deposit money banks.

Other Banking Institutions:

Comprises offshore banking units and investment banks.

Interest Rates:

Data are from source B.

Money Market Rate:

Rate offered on six-month interbank deposits.

Treasury Bill Rate:

Average interest rate (discount basis) per annum on allotted treasury bills with 91 days to maturity. Monthly averages are simple averages of weekly averages. For periods during which no auctions of treasury bills were held, no data are published.

Deposit Rate:

† Through May 1998, data refer to the weighted average of interest rates on time deposits with maturities of at least three months and under six months. Beginning June 1998, data refer to time deposits between BD10,000–50,000 with maturities of three to twelve months.

Lending Rate:

From September 1, 1988 to July 31, 1994, data refer to the maximum recommended rate on consumer loans with maturities of at least twelve months and under fifteen months. Beginning August 1, 1994, data refer to the weighted average of interest rates on consumer loans with maturities of at least twelve months and under fifteen months. Beginning June 1998, data refer to the weighted average rate on all personal loans extended in the last month of the quarter. The interest-rate survey is conducted quarterly with deposit money banks.

Prices, Production, Labor:

Consumer Prices:

Source S. Weights Reference Period: 1994–1995; Geographical Coverage: whole national territory; Basis for Calculation: 1995 household survey.

Petroleum Production:

Source: Ministry of Oil and Industry data.

International Transactions:

Exports and Imports, c.i.f.:

All data are from source B. If uncurrent, total value data are obtained as the sum of petroleum and other trade (excluding gold). The latter series are supplied by the Central Bank of Bahrain and are not published.

Government Finance:

Annual data are as reported for the *Government Finance Statistics Yearbook (GFSY)* and cover budgetary central government. The fiscal year ends December 31.

National Accounts:

Source M.

Bangladesh 513

Date of Fund Membership:

August 17, 1972

Standard Sources:

A: Bangladesh Bank, *Annual Report*
B: Bangladesh Bank, *Bulletin*
S: Bangladesh Bureau of Statistics, *Monthly Statistical Bulletin, Economic Indicators of Bangladesh*

Exchange Rates:

Official Rate: (End of Period and Period Average):
As of January 1, 1992, the official exchange rate and the secondary exchange market rate were unified.

International Liquidity:

Gold (National Valuation) (line 1and) is obtained by converting the value in national currency terms, as reported in the country's standard sources, using the prevailing exchange rate, as given in line **ae** or **we.** Data on gold in national sources revalue gold monthly at 75 percent of the average London market prices for the preceding month.

Monetary Authorities:

Consists of the Bangladesh Bank only. † Beginning in June 1982 and in June 1987 data are based on an improved classification and sectorization of the accounts. † Beginning in December

2001, data are based on a new reporting system which provides improved classification and sectorization of the accounts.

Banking Institutions:

Comprises scheduled banks and agricultural and industrial development banks. † Beginning in June 1982 and in June 1987 data are based on an improved classification and sectorization of the accounts. † Beginning in December 2001, comprises commercial banks, National Savings Scheme, and nonbank depository corporations (Grameen Bank, private finance and leasing companies, land mortgage cooperative banks, cooperative banks, and cooperative societies). Data are based on a new reporting system which provides improved classification and sectorization of the accounts.

Banking Survey:

† See notes on monetary authorities and banking institutions.

Money (National Definitions):

Reserve Money comprises currency in circulation, banker's correspondent and other accounts with the Bangladesh Bank (BB), and transferable deposits of nonbank depository corporations and private sector with the BB in national currency. Currency in circulation refers to notes and coins issued by the BB and the Ministry of Finance.

M1 comprises currency in circulation and transferable deposits. Currency in circulation refers to notes and coins issued by the BB and the Ministry of Finance less the amount held by commercial banks. Transferable deposits refer to current account deposits in national currency of nonbank depository corporations, nonbank financial institutions, state and local governments, public nonfinancial corporations, and private sector with the BB and commercial banks.

M2 comprises M1 and time and savings deposits in national currency and foreign currency deposits of nonbank depository corporations, nonbank financial institutions, state and local governments, public nonfinancial corporations, and private sector with commercial banks.

M3 comprises currency in circulation, transferable, time, and savings deposits in national and foreign currency of nonbank financial institutions, state and local governments, public nonfinancial corporations, and private sector with the BB, commercial banks, nonbank depository corporations and the national savings scheme. Currency in circulation refers to notes and coins issued by the BB and the Ministry of Finance less the amount held by commercial banks and nonbank depository corporations.

Interest Rates:

Discount Rate (End of Period):
Discount rate offered by the Bangladesh Bank on loans to commercial banks.

Deposit Rate:
Average rate offered by commercial banks on three- to six-month fixed or term deposits.

Lending Rate:
Maximum rate charged by commercial banks on loans and advances for agricultural production, including forestry and fishing.

Prices, Production, Labor:

Share Prices:
Composite stock price index of the Dhaka Stock Exchange Limited, base 1994–95.

Consumer Prices:
Source B. Weights Reference Period: 1995–96; Geographical Coverage: national index; Number of Items in Basket: covers items relating to eight commodity groups; Basis for Calculation: weights are determined based on the Household Expenditure Survey of 1995–96.

Industrial Production:
Source S quantum index of industrial production, all industries, weights reference period 1988–89. The index covers manufacturing, mining, and electricity.

International Transactions:

Trade data are from source B. Value of *Exports* refers to total exports receipts which include cash, barter, and special trade. *Imports, c & f* data include cost and freight, but exclude insurance.

International Investment Position:
The data on Other Investment, General Government are compiled on a fiscal year ending June 30.

Government Finance:

Annual data are as reported for the *Government Finance Statistics Yearbook (GFSY)* and cover budgetary central government. The fiscal year ends June 30.

National Accounts:

Source B. As indicated by the country, data from 1990 onwards are according to the *1993 SNA.*

Barbados   316

Date of Fund Membership:
December 29, 1970

Standard Sources:
A: Central Bank, *Annual Statistical Digest*
B: Central Bank, *Economic and Financial Statistics*
S: Statistical Service, *Statistics of Monthly Overseas Trade, Monthly Digest of Statistics*

Exchange Rates:

Official Rate: (End of Period and Period Average):
The official rate is pegged to the U.S. dollar.

International Liquidity:

† Beginning in 1972, *line 1dbd* includes sinking funds held against domestic government debt.

Monetary Authorities:

Comprises the Central Bank of Barbados only. *Line 12f* includes loans to Barbados Development Bank.

Deposit Money Banks:

Comprises eight foreign commercial banks operating in Barbados. *Line 22f* includes loans to Barbados Development Bank.

† Prior to June 1969, deposits of nonresidents are included in *Demand Deposits* and *Time, Savings, and Foreign Currency Deposits* rather than in *Foreign Liabilities*.

Monetary Survey:
† See note to deposit money banks.

Other Banking Institutions:
Comprises trust companies with operations in Barbados.

Banking Survey:
† See note to deposit money banks.

Interest Rates:
All interest rate data are from source B.

Bank Rate (End of Period):
Central Bank of Barbados' general rediscount rate.

Treasury Bill Rate:
Average tender rate for three-month treasury bills.

Savings Rate:
Rate offered by commercial banks on savings deposits.

Deposit Rate:
Weighted average rate offered by commercial banks on time and savings deposits. The rate is weighted by deposit amounts.

Lending Rate:
Prime lending rate charged by commercial banks. Data represent the maximum of the range of rates quoted by commercial banks.

Prices, Production, Labor:

Consumer Prices:
Source B. Base Period: July 2001; Geographical Coverage: Whole national territory; Number of Items in Basket: 340; Basis for Calculation: Weights are derived from the household budget survey of 1998–1999.

Industrial Production:
Source B index covers mining and quarrying, electricity and gas, manufacturing industries, base 1994, as compiled by the Statistical Service.

International Transactions:

Exports and Imports:
All trade data are from source B. Total exports include domestic exports and re-exports.

Government Finance:
Data are derived from source B and cover budgetary central government. The statistical discrepancy results from net errors and omissions in the recording of financing transactions. The fiscal year ends March 31.

National Accounts:
Source A data as reported by the national authorities. Data for *line 96f* include increases or decreases in stocks.

Belarus   913

Date of Fund Membership:
July 10, 1993

Standard Sources:
B: National Bank of Belarus
N: Ministry of Finance
S: Ministry of Statistics and Analysis of Belarus

Exchange Rates:

Official Rate: (End of Period and Period Average):
The official rate is the rate used by the National Bank of Belarus (NBB) and, since December 1993, has been determined in auctions organized by the Interbank Currency Exchange.
On August 20, 1994, the rubel (Rbl) replaced the Belarussian ruble as the unit of account at the rate of ten Belarussian rubles per rubel. On January 1, 2000, the national currency was redenominated. The new rubel is equal to 1,000 old rubels.

International Liquidity:
Data for *Total Reserves minus Gold (line 11.d)* comprise the country's holdings of SDRs, reserve position in the Fund, and convertible foreign exchange.

Monetary Authorities:
Comprises the National Bank of Belarus (NBB) only. † Beginning in December 2001, data are based on an improved classification and sectorization of the accounts. † Beginning in December 2004, data are based on a new reporting system which provides an improved classification and sectorization of the accounts.

Banking Institutions:
Comprises commercial banks. † Beginning in January 1996, data are based on an improved reporting system which provides an improved classification and sectorization of the accounts. † Beginning in December 2001, data are based on an improved classification and sectorization of the accounts. † Beginning in December 2004, data are based on a new reporting system which provides an improved classification and sectorization of the accounts.

Banking Survey:
† See notes on monetary authorities and banking institutions.

Money (National Definitions):
Base Money comprises currency in circulation, required reserves deposits of banks in the National Bank of the Republic of Belarus (NBB), bankers' correspondent and other accounts at the NBB, banks' investment in NBB securities, and transferable and time deposits of nonfinancial public enterprises, non-profit organizations, and the private sector at the NBB. Currency in circulation refers to notes and coins issued by the NBB less the amount held in offices of the NBB.
M1 comprises currency in circulation and transferable deposits. Currency in circulation refers to notes and coins issued by the NBB less the amount held in offices of the NBB and commercial banks. Transferable deposits refer to the current account deposits and other demand accounts including accrued interest in national currency of other financial institutions, nonfinancial public enterprises, and private sector with the NBB and commercial banks.
M2 comprises M1 and time deposits. Time deposits include time and savings deposits, deposits in escrow, and accrued interest in national currency of other financial institutions, nonfinancial public enterprises, and private sector with the NBB and commercial banks.

$M2^*$ comprises M2 and securities other than shares issued by commercial banks in national currency held by other financial institutions, nonfinancial public enterprises, and private sector. $M3$ comprises $M2^*$ plus transferable and time deposits in foreign currency and deposits in precious metals of other financial institutions, nonfinancial public enterprises, and private sector with the NBB and commercial banks and securities other than shares issued by commercial banks in foreign currency held by other financial institutions, nonfinancial public enterprises, and private sector.

Interest Rates:

All interest rate data are from source B.

Refinancing Rate (End of Period):
Actual average rate at which the NBB lends to commercial banks. Includes concessionary rates charged on directed loans. † Beginning in January 2000, the practice of directed lending to commercial banks at concessionary rates was discontinued, and the data refer to the announced rate at which the NBB lends to commercial banks.

Deposit Rate:
Weighted average rate offered by commercial banks on deposits in domestic currency. Rate is weighted by deposit amounts.

Lending Rate:
Weighted average rate charged by commercial banks on loans in domestic currency. Rate is weighted by loan amounts.

Prices and Labor:

Producer Prices:
Source S. Weights Reference Period: 1999; Sectoral Coverage: covers all industry and is broken down into 14 main industrial branches; Number of Items in the Basket: covering more than 4,500 representative goods reported by 1,401 enterprises; Basis for Calculation: are compiled in accordance with the guidelines of the *System of National Accounts 1993 (SNA 1993)*.

Consumer Prices:
Source S. Weights Reference Period: 1999; Geographical Coverage: the entire Republic of Belarus; Number of Items in the Basket: 408 goods and services, covering 45,000 prices and tariffs; Basis for Calculation: based on data on families' expenditures for purchases of goods and services obtained from the Annual Household Survey and are compiled and processed in accordance with the guidelines of the *System of National Accounts 1993 (SNA 1993)*.

Wages:
Source S. Average wages and salaries of employees, including in-kind payments, in all branches of economy.

International Transactions:

Source S. Data consist from merchandise trade data compiled by the State Customs Committee (SCC) of the Republic of Belarus on the basis of customs declarations and export/import of goods not recorded by the SCC.

Government Finance:

Monthly data are derived from source N and cover the central budget sector excluding social security. Annual data are as reported for the *Government Finance Statistics Yearbook (GFSY)* and cover consolidated central government. † Prior to 2003, to the ex-tent possible, existing subannual *IFS* data were converted to the main aggregates that are presented in the *GFSM 2001* Statement of Sources and Uses of Cash (see the Introduction of the monthly *IFS* publication for details). The fiscal year ends December 31.

National Accounts:

Source S. As indicated by the country, data are compiled according to the recommendations of the *1993 SNA*. The base year for constant price estimates is changed every five years and GDP volume 2000 is computed and presented in 2000 prices and 1995 prices, making it possible to link the series and obtain a longer-term series in uniform prices. On January 1, 2000, the denomination of the Belarussian rubel took place (1000 times decrease in the face value of money unit).

Belgium   124

Data refer to Belgium except where noted. Data are denominated in Belgian francs prior to January 1999 and in euros from January 1999 onward. An irrevocably fixed factor for converting Belgian francs to euros was established at 40.3399 Belgian francs per euro. Beginning in January 1999, with the implementation of Stage Three of the European Economic and Monetary Union (EMU), a euro area-wide definition of residency was introduced: All positions with residents of other euro area (EA) countries, including the European Central Bank (ECB), are classified as domestic positions, and foreign assets and foreign liabilities include only positions with non-euro area residents. In 2002, the franc was retired from circulation and replaced by euro banknotes and coins. Descriptions of the changes in the methodology and presentation of Belgium's accounts following the introduction of the euro are shown in the introduction to *IFS* and in the notes on the euro area page.

Date of Fund Membership:

December 27, 1945

Standard Sources:

A: National Bank, *Annual Report*
B: National Bank, *Statistical Bulletin*
S: National Institute of Statistics, *Bulletin of Statistics*
V: Eurostat

Exchange Rates:

Market Rate (End of Period and Period Average):
Prior to March 5, 1990, there was a dual exchange rate system, in which the primary rate, maintained within the cooperative exchange arrangement under the European Monetary System (EMS), was applicable to most current transactions, and the secondary, or free market rate, was applicable to most capital transactions. Between March 5, 1990 and December 31, 1998, the market rate maintained within the EMS was applicable to all transactions. Prior to January 1999, the market rate was the midpoint rate in the official market in Brussels. In January 1999, the Belgian franc became a participating currency within the Eurosystem, and the euro market rate became applicable to all transactions. In 2002, the franc was retired from circulation and replaced by euro banknotes and coins. For additional information, refer to the section on exchange rates in the introduction to *IFS* and on the euro area page.

International Liquidity:

Beginning in January 1999, *Total Reserves minus Gold (line 1l.d)* is defined in accordance with the Eurosystem's statistical definition of international reserves. The international reserves of Belgium per the Eurosystem statistical definition at the start of the monetary union (January 1, 1999) in billions of U.S. dollars were as follows: *Total Reserves minus Gold,* $12,670; *Foreign Exchange,* $10,166; *SDRs,* $609; *Reserve Position in the Fund,* $1,895; *Other Reserve Assets,* $0; *Gold,* $2,738; *Gold (million fine troy ounces),* 9.525 ounces. From December 1998 through May 1999, holdings of monetary gold include an amount of gold on loan to Luxembourg. *Foreign Exchange (line 1d.d):* Beginning in March 1979, gold and foreign exchange holdings excluded deposits at the European Monetary Cooperation Fund (EMCF), and the holdings of European currency units (ECUs) issued against these deposits were included in *line ld.d. Gold (Eurosystem Valuation) (line 1and):* Prior to January 1990, only 20 percent of official gold was valued at market prices. From January 1990 onward, all official gold has been valued at market prices. Memorandum data are provided on *Non-Euro Claims on Euro Area Residents* and *Euro Claims on Non-Euro Area Residents,* which represent positions as of the last Friday in each month. For additional information, refer to the section on international liquidity in the introduction to *IFS* and on the euro area page.

Monetary Authorities:

Comprises the National Bank of Belgium, which beginning in January 1999 is part of the Eurosystem, and coin issue of the Treasury. Beginning in 2002, *Currency Issued (line 14a)* includes euro banknotes and coins and, until December 2002, any unretired francs. The recorded value of euro banknotes is based on a monthly allocation of total euro banknotes in circulation based on the National Bank of Belgium's paid up share of the ECB's capital; it does not correspond to either the actual amount of euro banknotes placed in circulation by the National Bank of Belgium which is shown in memo line *Currency Put into Circulation (line 14m),* nor the actual circulation of banknotes within the domestic territory. See section *Euro banknotes and coins* in the introduction to *IFS.* Prior to January 1999, the contra-entry to coin issue was included in *Claims on General Government (line 12a).* From January 1999 onward, the contra-entry for government coin issue is included in *Other Items (Net) (line 17r).* † Beginning in 1980, foreign currencies participating in the exchange rate mechanism of the EMS were valued at their midpoint rates, while gold and other foreign currencies were valued at historical prices. † During 1991–98, gold was revalued annually at market prices, and other assets and liabilities denominated in foreign currencies were valued at market exchange rates. *Bonds and Money Market Instruments (line 16n.u)* include subordinated debt in the form of securities, other bonds, and money market paper. For a description of the accounts, refer to the section on monetary authorities in the introduction to *IFS.* Beginning with the data for end-November 2000, Monetary Authorities' *Foreign Assets (line 11), Foreign Liabilities (line 16c), Claims on Banking Institutions (line 12e.u),* and *Liabilities to Banking Institutions (line 14c.u)* are affected by a change from gross to net presentation of positions relating to the TARGET (Trans-European Automated Real-Time Gross Settle-

ment Express Transfer) euro clearing system. (See *Recording of TARGET system positions* under *European Economic and Monetary Union (EMU)* in the introduction to *IFS.*) Beginning in 2002, *Claims on Banking Institutions (line 12e.u)* and *Liabilities to Banking Institutions (line 14c.u)* include "Intra-Eurosystem claims/liabilities related to banknote issue," which is a single net value representing the difference between the value of euro banknotes allocated to the National Bank of Belgium according to the accounting scheme of the Eurosystem for issuing euro banknotes, and the value of euro banknotes put into circulation by the National Bank of Belgium. See section *Euro banknotes and coins* in the introduction to *IFS.* Memo line *Net Claims on Eurosystem (line 12e.s)* equals gross claims on, less gross liabilities to, the ECB and other members of the Eurosystem. Comprises euro-denominated claims equivalent to the transfer of foreign currency reserves to the ECB, Intra-Eurosystem claims/liabilities related to banknote issue, net claims or liabilities within the TARGET clearing system, and other positions.

Banking Institutions:

† Prior to 1992, data include the Rediscount and Guarantee Institute. Certain breaks in the series may occur in 1992 owing to the radical reform of the reporting procedure of the credit institutions that was introduced at that time. First, the contents of the report forms were revised, and second, all types of institutions had to report according to the same scheme. Formerly, there were distinct report forms for deposit banks, savings banks, and public credit institutions. From 1992 until January 1999, comprised only the commercial banks. From January 1999 onward, data cover the money market funds. *Claims on Monetary Authorities (line 20)* and *Credit from Monetary Authorities (line 26g):* Monetary Authorities refers to the National Bank of Belgium and coin issue of the Treasury. *Money Market Fund Shares (line 26m.u)* include shares/units issued by money market funds. *Bonds and Money Market Instruments (line 26n.u)* include subordinated debt in the form of securities, other bonds, and money market paper. For a description of the accounts, refer to the section on banking institutions in the introduction to *IFS.*

Banking Survey (National Residency):

For a description of the methodology and accounts, refer to the section Banking Survey (National Residency) in the introduction to *IFS.*

Banking Survey (Euro Area-wide Residency):

For a description of the methodology and accounts, refer to the section Banking Survey (Euro Area-wide Residency) in the introduction to *IFS.*

Money (National Definitions):

Beginning in January 1999, national monetary aggregates series are discontinued. Euro area aggregates are presented on the euro area page.

Interest Rates:

Discount Rate (End of Period) (line 60):
Before January 1999, Source B. Official rate applied by the National Bank of Belgium to rediscounts of commercial paper and bank acceptances presented by financial intermediaries. The

discount rate was abolished on December 15, 1998. From January 1999 onward, see Eurosystem policy rate series on the euro area page.

Money Market Rate (line 60b):
† Before 1991, the call money rate. From 1991 until January 1999, represented the averages of borrowing and lending rates for three-month interbank transactions. From January 1999 onward, represents the three-month EURIBOR rate, which is an interbank deposit bid rate. See euro area page.

Deposit Rate (line 60l):
† Before 1993, the indicative rates published by banks. Thereafter the rate on three-month time deposits, weighted by volume of deposits in a monthly survey of banks.

Deposit Rate (lines 60lhs, 60lhn, 60lcs, and 60lcn):
See notes in the Introduction to *IFS*.

Lending Rate (line 60p):
Published rate for liquidity credit from the four major banks; banks can charge a higher or lower rate to certain customers.

Lending Rate (lines 60phs, 60pns, 60phm, 60phn, 60pcs, and 60pcn):
See notes in the Introduction to *IFS*.

Government Bond Yield (line 61):
Represents yield on ten-year government bonds. For additional information, refer to the section on interest rates in the introduction to *IFS* and on the euro area page.

Prices, Production, Labor:

All data on prices are from source B.

Industrial Share Prices:
Data refer to 10th-of-month quotations for all industrial shares on the Brussels and Antwerp exchanges, base 1970.

Home and Import Goods:
Data include agricultural and industrial products, weights reference period: 2000.

Industrial Production Prices:
Data refer to the domestic goods of the industrial products component of the general wholesale price index, weights reference period: 2000.

Consumer Prices:
Source B. Weights Reference Period: January 2004–December 2004; Geographical Coverage: Whole national territory; Number of Items in Basket: 507; Basis for Calculation: The Household Budget Survey was organized by the National Statistical Institute, covering the period January 2004–December 2004.

Wages:
Source B, weights reference period: Q3 1980. The index covers male members over 21 years old in industry.

Industrial Production:
Data are sourced from the OECD database, weights reference period: annually re-weighted and chained. The indices exclude construction.

International Transactions:

BLEU trade data refer to the Belgium-Luxembourg Economic Union and exclude transactions between the two countries. Beginning in 1997, trade data are for Belgium only, which includes trade between Belgium and Luxembourg. (For 1997, certain goods transiting from non-EU members to EU members through the Belgium-Luxembourg Economic Union are recorded as imports and exports of the BLEU.) BLEU trade data and Belgium trade data are not comparable, owing to differences in compilation methods. The Laspeyres volume and Paasche unit value indices of trade, weights reference period: 1993, are from the *Monthly Bulletin of Foreign Trade*. The annual, but not the quarterly or monthly, indices of *Volume of Exports* are adjusted for changes in coverage.

Import Prices:
† Source B Index, weights reference period: 1980 refers to the import component of the Industrial products group of the general wholesale price index of Belgium (country code 124).

Government Finance:

Data on general government are derived from source V. Monthly cash data are provided by the Ministry of Finance. Transactions and debt data cover budgetary operations of the central government Treasury but exclude operations of social security funds and other central government agencies with individual budgets. Lending minus repayments receipts are included in revenue, and payments are included in expenditure. † Beginning in 1999, monthly, quarterly, and annual data cover only budgetary operations and are not comparable to data from previous years. † Beginning in 1970, annual data on central government are as reported for the *Government Finance Statistics Yearbook (GFSY)* and cover consolidated central government. † From 1996 onwards, annual data are compiled on the basis of European Standard Accounting rules and are not comparable with data for previous years. The fiscal year ends December 31.

National Accounts:

Source B. As indicated by the country, from 1985 onwards data have been revised following the implementation of the *ESA 95*. Beginning in 1999, euro data are sourced from the Eurostat database. Eurostat introduced chain-linked GDP volume measures to both annual and quarterly data. Chain-linked GDP volume measures are expressed in the prices of the previous year and re-referenced to 1995.

Belize 339

Date of Fund Membership:
March 16, 1982

Standard Sources:
A: Central Bank of Belize, *Annual Report*
B: Central Bank of Belize, *Statistical Digest*
S: Central Statistical Office, *External Trade Bulletin*

Exchange Rates:

Official Rate: (End of Period and Period Average):
Rates are based on a fixed relationship to the U.S. dollar.

Monetary Authorities:

Comprises the Central Bank of Belize (CBB) only. † Beginning in December 2001, data are based on an improved classification and sectorization of the accounts. † Beginning in January 2006, data are based on a new reporting system which provides an improved classification and sectorization of the accounts.

Banking Institutions:

Comprises commercial banks. † Beginning in December 2001, data are based on an improved classification and sectorization of the accounts. † Beginning in January 2006, data are based on a new reporting system which provides an improved classification and sectorization of the accounts.

Banking Survey:

† See notes on monetary authorities and banking institutions.

Nonbank Financial Institutions:

Comprises the Development Finance Corporation. *Foreign Liabilities (line 46c)* largely relate to borrowings from the Caribbean Development Bank.

Money (National Definitions):

M1 comprises currency in circulation outside the banking system and transferable deposits. Transferable deposits include the demand and checkable savings deposits of local governments, nonfinancial public corporations, other financial corporations, and the private sector in national and foreign currency and demand deposits of nonresidents in national currency with commercial banks.

M2 comprises M1, time and savings deposits of local governments, nonfinancial public corporations, other financial corporations, and the private sector in national and foreign currency, time deposits of nonresidents in national and foreign currency, and savings deposits of nonresidents in national currency with commercial banks.

Interest Rates:

All interest rate data are from source B.

Discount Rate (End of Period):
Rate at which the CBB makes advances to commercial banks against government securities.

Treasury Bill Rate:
Discount rate on treasury bills.

Savings Rate:
Rate offered by commercial banks on savings deposits.

Deposit Rate:
Weighted average of deposit rates at commercial banks. Rate is weighted by deposit amounts.

Lending Rate:
Weighted average of lending rates of commercial banks. Rate is weighted by loan amounts.

Prices:

Consumer Prices:
Source B, Weights Reference Period: 1990; Geographical Coverage: national index; Number of Items in the Basket: 107 items, together with rents, are included in the index. Second quarter figures for 1980, 1983, and 1984 are interpolated. Data are compiled on a quarterly basis; Basis for Calculation: index was de-rived from a national household expenditure survey conducted from June 1990 through March 1991.

International Transactions:

Source S data.

Government Finance:

Annual data cover budgetary accounts only. The fiscal year ends March 31.

National Accounts:

Line 99b includes a statistical discrepancy.

Benin   638

Date of Fund Membership:
July 10, 1963

Standard Sources:

B: Banque Centrale des Etats de l'Afrique de l'Ouest (Central Bank of West African States), *Notes d'information et Statistiques (Informative Notes and Statistics)*
N: Institut National de la Statistique et de l'Analyse Economique Benin is a member of the West African Economic and Monetary Union, together with Burkina Faso, Côte d'Ivoire, Guinea-Bissau, Mali, Niger, Senegal, and Togo. The Union, which was established in 1962, has a common central bank, the Central Bank of West African States (BCEAO), with headquarters in Dakar, and national branches in the member states. Mali and Guinea-Bissau joined the Union on June 1, 1984 and May 2, 1997, respectively.

Exchange Rates:

Official Rate: (End of Period and Period Average):
Prior to January 1999, the official rate was pegged to the French franc. On January 12, 1994, the CFA franc was devalued to CFAF 100 per French franc from CFAF 50 at which it had been fixed since 1948. From January 1, 1999, the CFAF is pegged to the euro at a rate of CFA franc 655.957 per euro.

International Liquidity:

Gold is revalued on a quarterly basis at the rate communicated by the BCEAO, which corresponds to the lowest average fixing in the London market.

Monetary Authorities:

Comprises the national branch of the BCEAO only. The amount of currency outside banks is estimated by subtracting from the amount of CFA franc notes issued by Benin the estimated amounts of Benin's currency in the cash held by the banks of all member countries of the Union.

Deposit Money Banks:

Comprises commercial banks and the Development Bank, and includes certain banking operations of the Treasury and the Post Office. The Treasury accepts customs duty bills (reported separately in *line 22d.i*). Through its many branches, the Postal Checking System acts as the main depository for the private sector in the interior of Benin. *Claims on the Private Sector (line 22d)* include doubtful and litigious debts. † Beginning in 1979, *Central Government Deposits (line 26d)* include the deposits of the public establishments of an administrative or social nature (EPAS) and exclude those of the savings bank; *Demand and Time Deposits (lines 24 and 25)* include deposits of the savings bank and exclude deposits of EPAS; and *Claims on Private Sector (line 22d)* exclude claims on other financial institutions.

Monetary Survey:

The data reported agree with source B aggregates, as given in the table on the position of the monetary institutions, except for *line 31n,* for which source B treats long-term foreign liabilities and SDR allocations as a foreign liability, whereas *IFS* reports the former separately and includes the latter in *line 37r.* Moreover, valuation differences exist as a result of the *IFS* calculations of reserve position in the Fund and the SDR holdings, both components of *line 11,* based on Fund record. † Beginning in 1979, *Claims on Other Financial Institutions (line 32f)* includes claims of deposit money banks on other financial institutions; see deposit money bank notes for explanation of other break symbols.

Other Banking Institutions:

Liquid Liabilities (line 55l): † See notes on deposit money banks and monetary survey.

Interest Rates:

Bank Rate (End of Period):
Rate on repurchase agreements between the BCEAO and the banks. † Prior to October 1, 1993 data refer to basic discount rate offered by the BCEAO.

Money Market Rate:
Rate paid on overnight interbank advances.

Deposit Rate:
Rate offered by banks on time deposits of CFAF 500,000–2,000,000 for under six months.

Prices:

Consumer Prices:
Source N. Weights Reference Period: 1996; Geographical Coverage: Metropolitan area of Cotonou; Number of Items in Basket: 345; Basis for Calculation: The weights come from a household expenditure survey in 1996 (EDM96) in Cotonou.

International Transactions:

All trade data are from source B. Ships' stores, bunkers, and imports of gold are included. Data on trade crossing land frontiers may be understated.

Government Finance:

Annual data are as reported for the *Government Finance Statistics Yearbook (GFSY)* and cover budgetary central government. The fiscal year ends December 31.

National Accounts:

Source N.

Bhutan   514

Date of Fund Membership:
September 28, 1981

Standard Sources:

B: Royal Monetary Authority of Bhutan, *Selected Economic Indicators*
S: Central Statistical Office, *Statistical Yearbook of Bhutan*

Exchange Rates:

Official Rate: (End of Period and Period Average):
Official midpoint rate. Since Bhutan's currency was introduced in 1974, the ngultrum has been pegged at par to the Indian rupee, which also circulates freely within Bhutan.

International Liquidity:

Foreign Exchange (line 1d.d) consists of all foreign assets of the Royal Monetary Authority of Bhutan and the convertible currency and Indian rupee-denominated foreign assets of other depository corporations.

Monetary Authorities:

Comprises the Royal Monetary Authority of Bhutan, which was established in 1983. † Data are based on a standardized report form for central bank, which accords with the concepts and definitions of the IMF's *Monetary and Financial Statistics Manual (MFSM),* 2000. Departures from the *MFSM* methodology are explained below. Securities other than shares and shares and other equity are recorded at acquisition cost rather than at market price or fair value. Accrued interest is included in *Other Items (Net)* rather than in the outstanding amounts of the financial assets and liabilities.

Deposit Money Banks:

Comprises commercial banks. Beginning in January 1994, foreign liabilities of one of the commercial banks were assumed by the Royal Monetary Authority of Bhutan. † Data are based on a standardized report form for other depository corporations, which accords with the concepts and definitions of the *Monetary and Financial Statistics Manual (MFSM).* Departures from the *MFSM* methodology are explained below. Securities other than shares and shares and other equity are recorded at acquisition cost rather than at market price or fair value. Accrued interest is included in *Other Items (Net)* rather than in the outstanding amounts of the financial assets and liabilities.

Monetary Survey:

† The sectorization and classification of accounts have been revised beginning in June 1993, following the introduction of a more detailed reporting of accounts. See notes on central bank and other depository corporations.

Money (National Definitions):

M1 comprises currency outside banks and demand deposits. *Currency outside banks* is equal to the amount of domestic currency notes and coins issued by the RMA *less* domestic currency note and coin holdings of the RMA and commercial banks. Demand deposits consist of current accounts and savings deposits.

Savings deposits are interest-bearing deposits that can be withdrawn on demand without penalty.

$M2$ is equal to $M1$ plus Quasi-money. *Quasi-money* comprises time and foreign-currency deposits that other financial corporations, public nonfinancial corporations, and private sector hold at the RMA and commercial banks.

Interest Rates:

Bank Rate (End of Period):
Rate determined by the Monetary Operation Committee of RMA on RMA bills of 91-day maturity that are sold to the commercial banks.

Deposit Rate:
Rate offered by commercial banks on three- to six-month deposits.

Lending Rate:
Rate charged on loans for general trade by the financial institutions operating in Bhutan.

Prices, Production, and Tourism:

Consumer Prices:
Source S index for all Bhutan, weights reference period: 2003. The indices prior to Q3 2003 represent half-yearly averages. The quarterly index and the half-yearly index cannot be directly compared because of a different periodicity and a considerable break in continuity (the expenditure basket has been completely changed).

Electricity Production:
The large increase in 1986–87 is due to the beginning of production of the Chukha hydroelectric facility. From July 1988 onwards, the data refer to Chukha production only.

Tourist Arrivals:
The data refer to tourists on package tours paid for in convertible currencies. Tourists from India are not included.

International Transactions:

All value data for merchandise trade are customs data, as adjusted by the Department of Trade and Industry to include, inter alia, exports of electricity and imports of aircraft.

Government Finance:

Annual data are as reported for the *Government Finance Statistics Yearbook (GFSY)* and cover budgetary central government. † Through 1986, fiscal year begins April 1; from 1988 onward, fiscal year ends June 30. Data for 1988 fiscal year cover 15 months. † From 1989 onward, data on grants include grants received in kind. Also, data on expenditure include the value of grants in kind.

National Accounts:

Source S.

Bolivia   218

Date of Fund Membership:

December 27, 1945

Standard Source:

B: Banco Central de Bolivia, *Boletín Estadístico (Statistical Bulletin)*

Exchange Rates:

On January 1, 1987 the boliviano, equal to 1,000,000 pesos, was introduced.

Market Rate (End of Period and *Period Average)* is determined through auction held by the Central Bank.

For the purpose of calculating the real effective exchange rate index (*line* **rec**), no attempt has been made to seasonally adjust the data for consumer prices (*line 64*).

International Liquidity:

Gold (National Valuation) (line 1and) is the U.S. dollar value of official holdings of gold as reported in the country's standard sources.

Monetary Authorities:

Comprises the Central Bank of Bolivia (CBB) only. † Beginning in December 1987, data reflect the introduction of improved sectorization and classification of domestic and foreign accounts.† Beginning in December 1996, data are based on an improved sectorization of the accounts. † Beginning in December 2001, data are based on a new reporting system which provides an improved classification and sectorization of the accounts.

Banking Institutions:

Comprises commercial banks, State Bank, and specialized banks. † Beginning in December 1987, data reflect the introduction of improved sectorization and classification of domestic and foreign accounts. † Beginning in December 1996, comprises commercial banks, State Bank, specialized banks, savings and loans associations, savings and credit cooperatives, and financial funds. † Beginning in December 2001, data are based on a new reporting system which provides an improved classification and sectorization of the accounts.

Banking Survey:

† See notes on monetary authorities and banking institutions.

Banking Survey:

† See note on monetary authorities.

Money (National Definitions):

Base Money comprises notes and coins issued and bankers' reserves. Bankers' reserves include the demand deposits, legal reserve requirements, funds for external payments, other funds, securities and liabilities as result of swaps in national currency, foreign currency, and national currency with value maintenance of commercial banks and other banking institutions in the CBB.

$M1$ comprises notes and coins in circulation outside the banking system and demand deposits in national currency of the private sector in commercial banks and other banking institutions. Demand deposits include demand and sight deposits, inactive current accounts, and certified checks.

$M'1$ comprises notes and coins in circulation outside the banking system and demand deposits in national currency, foreign currency, and national currency with value maintenance of the private sector in commercial banks and other banking institutions.

$M2$ comprises $M1$ and savings deposit in national currency of the private sector in commercial banks and other banking institutions.

$M'2$ comprises $M'1$ and savings deposit in national currency, foreign currency, and national currency with value maintenance of the private sector in commercial banks and other banking institutions.

M3 comprises M2 plus time deposits and other deposits in national currency of the private sector in commercial banks and other banking institutions. Other deposits include other demand deposits and other deposits subject and not subject to legal reserve requirements.

M'3 comprises M'2 plus time deposits and other deposits in national currency, foreign currency, and national currency with value maintenance of the private sector in commercial banks and other banking institutions.

M4 comprises M3 plus CBB certificates of deposit and treasury bills in national currency held by the private sector.

M'4 comprises M'3 plus CBB certificates of deposit and treasury bills in national currency, foreign currency, and national currency with value maintenance held by the private sector.

Interest Rates:

All interest rate data are from source B.

Discount Rate (End of Period):
Rate charged by the CBB on loans to financial institutions collateralized by public (Treasury or CBB) securities in national currency.

Discount Rate (Foreign Currency) (End of Period):
Rate charged by the CBB on loans to financial institutions collateralized by public (Treasury or CBB) securities in foreign currency.

Money Market Rate:
Weighted average rate on loans between financial institutions in national currency. The rate is weighted by daily loan amounts and the maturity of the loan.

Money Market Rate (Foreign Currency):
Weighted average rate on loans between financial institutions in foreign currency. The rate is weighted by daily loan amounts and the maturity of the loan.

Treasury Bill Rate:
Rate on 91-day treasury bills denominated in national currency auctioned by the CBB.

Treasury Bill Rate (Foreign Currency):
Rate on 91-day treasury bills denominated in foreign currency auctioned by the CBB.

Savings Rate:
Average rate offered by commercial banks on savings deposits in national currency.

Savings Rate (Foreign Currency):
Average rate offered by commercial banks on savings deposits in foreign currency.

Deposit Rate:
Average rate, including surcharges and commissions, offered by commercial banks on time deposits in national currency † Beginning in January 1987, weighted average rate, including surcharges and commissions, offered by commercial banks on time deposits in national currency. The rate is weighted by deposit amounts.

Deposit Rate (Foreign Currency):
Weighted average rate, including surcharges and commissions, offered by commercial banks on time deposits in foreign currency. The rate is weighted by deposit amounts.

Lending Rate:
Average rate, including surcharges and commissions, charged by commercial banks on loans in national currency. † Beginning in January 1987, weighted average rate, including surcharges and commissions, charged by commercial banks on loans in national currency. The rate is weighted by loan amounts.

Lending Rate (Foreign Currency):
Weighted average rate, including surcharges and commissions, charged by commercial banks on loans in foreign currency. The rate is weighted by loan amounts.

Prices and Production:

Consumer Prices:
Source S. Weights Reference Period: 1991; Geographical Coverage: the four largest cities in the country: La Paz, Santa Cruz, Cochabamba, and El Alto; Number of Items in the Basket: 332 items; Basis for Calculation: 1990 Household Budget Survey (EPF). Based on the data, the baskets for each city and at the national level were prepared and their respective structures and weights determined.

Crude Petroleum Production:
Source B data (in thousand cubic meters).

International Transactions:

Value of Exports and Imports:
All data are from source B. Exports of *Tin* refer to tin concentrates and tin metallic. Total export values are adjusted downward for smelting of minerals abroad. Commodity export values include smelting costs.

Volume of Exports:
IFS average of tin, natural gas, zinc, antimony, silver, and wolfram with a 1995 value of exports as weights. *Export Volume* indices for individual commodities are based on source B data in physical quantities.

Unit Value of Exports:
IFS average of tin, natural gas, zinc, antimony, silver, and wolfram with a 1995 value of exports as weights. *Export Unit Value* indices for individual commodities are calculated for *IFS* from reported value and volume data.

Government Finance:

Monthly, quarterly, and annual data are as reported by source B and are derived from data provided by the Fiscal Programming Unit of the National Secretariat of Finance. Data cover the consolidated general government comprising the budgetary central government, decentralized agencies including the social security institutions, and regional and local governments. Revenue data include grants and repayments of loans extended by the government. Expenditure data include lending by the government. The fiscal year ends December 31.

National Accounts:

Source S. As indicated by the country, data are compiled according to the recommendations of the *1968 SNA* and the *1993 SNA*.

Bosnia & Herzegovina   963

Date of Fund Membership:
December 20, 1995

Standard Source:

B: Central Bank of Bosnia and Herzegovina, *Quarterly Bulletin*

Exchange Rates:

Official Rate: (End of Period and Period Average):
The official rate is pegged to the euro. Prior to January 1999, the official rate was pegged to the deutsche mark at a 1:1 rate.

Monetary Authorities:

Comprises the Central Bank of Bosnia and Herzegovina (CBBH) and monetary authority functions undertaken by the central government. The CBBH was established in August 1997 under a currency board arrangement. The Central Bank Law prohibits CBBH from extending loans and credits to government and other domestic entities and from incurring foreign liabilities. *Foreign Liabilities (line 16c)* represents obligations of the central government with the Fund. Central Government (*line 16d: Central Government Deposits*) refers to the country-wide government under the Council of Ministers.

Deposit Money Banks:

Comprises all commercial banks in Bosnia and Herzegovina. Data include the National Bank of Republika Srpska for the period August 1997–December 1998, the National Bank of Bosnia and Herzegovina for the period August 1997–December 2000, and Payment Bureaus' giro accounts in foreign currencies for the period August 1997–December 1999. State Government (*line 22ab: Claims on State Government*) refers to entity governments of the Federation and Republika Srpska. Local government (*line 22b: Claims on Local Government*) refers to cantonal and municipality government units. Central government (*line 26d: Central Government Deposits*) refers to the country-wide government under the Council of Ministers. Other resident sectors (*line 22d: Claims on Other Resident Sectors*) include other financial corporations, nonfinancial public and private enterprises, households, and nonprofit institutions serving households.

Monetary Survey:

Consolidates the accounts of monetary authorities and deposit money banks.

Interest Rates:

Source B.

Deposit Rate (End of Period):
Prior to January 2002, data refer to average of end-of-period minimum and maximum rates offered by commercial banks on time and savings deposits of households. † Beginning in January 2002, data refer to weighted average rate offered by commercial banks on time and savings deposits of households in convertible marka. The rate is weighted by the amount of new deposits accepted during the reference period.

Lending Rate (End of Period):
Prior to January 2002, data refer to average of end-of-period minimum and maximum rates charged by commercial banks on short-term loans to nonfinancial private enterprises. † Beginning in January 2002, data refer to weighted average rate charged by commercial banks on short-term loans to nonfinancial private

enterprises and cooperatives. The rate is weighted by the amount of new loans extended during the reference period.

International Transactions:

Exports and imports data are sourced from the *Annual Report* of the Central Bank of Bosnia and Herzegovina. Data are compiled by the Customs Administration of the Federation of Bosnia and Herzegovina and the Customs Administration of Republika Srpska.

National Accounts:

Source is the *Annual Report* of the Central Bank of Bosnia and Herzegovina. Gross domestic product data are compiled by the Entities Institutes of Statistics.

Botswana   616

Date of Fund Membership:
July 24, 1968

Standard Sources:

A: Bank of Botswana, A*nnual Report*
C: Department of Customs and Excise, *External Trade Statistics*
S: Central Statistics Office, *Statistical Bulletin*

Exchange Rates:

Official Rate: (End of Period and Period Average):
The official rate is pegged to a basket of currencies.

Monetary Authorities:

Comprises the Bank of Botswana only. † Beginning in December 2001, data are based on a new reporting system which provides improved classification and sectorization of the account.

Banking Institutions:

Comprises commercial banks. † Beginning in December 2001, includes the Botswana Savings Bank and Botswana Building Society. Data are based on a new reporting system which provides improved classification and sectorization of the accounts.

Banking Survey:

† See notes on monetary authorities and banking institutions.

Money (National Definitions):

M1 comprises currency in circulation and transferable deposits less commercial banks holdings of checks and other cash items in the process of collection. Currency in circulation refers to notes and coins issued by the Bank of Botswana (BOB) less the amount held by banks. Transferable deposits refer to the current account deposits in national currency of other financial corporations, state and local governments, public nonfinancial corporations, and private sector with the BOB and banks.
M2 comprises M1 and other deposits. Other deposits include time and savings deposits in national and foreign currency of other financial corporations, state and local governments, public nonfinancial corporations, and private sector with banks.
M3 comprises M2 and Bank of Botswana Certificates (BoBCs)

issued in national currency held by other financial corporations and private sector.

Interest Rates:

Bank Rate (End of Period):
The Bank of Botswana's lending rate.

Savings Rate:
Average rate offered by commercial banks on savings deposits in national currency.

Deposit Rate:
Rate offered by commercial banks on 88-day fixed deposits in national currency. Quarterly and annual data are averages of end-of-period monthly data.

Deposit Rate (Foreign Currency):
Rate offered by commercial banks on 88-day fixed deposits in U.S. dollars. Quarterly and annual data are averages of end-of-period monthly data.

Lending Rate:
Commercial banks' prime lending rate. Quarterly and annual data are averages of end-of-period monthly data.

Government Bond Yield:
Yield on 12-year government bonds.

Prices, Production, Labor:

Share Prices:
Share price index is based on a domestic company index as determined by the Botswana Stock Exchange, base 1989.

Consumer Prices:
Source S. Weights Reference Period: 2002–03; Geographical Coverage: national index; Number of Items in Basket: 384; Basis for Calculation: weights are determined based on the Household Expenditure Survey of 2002–03.

Mining Production:
Source C index, weights reference period 1976.

International Transactions:

All value data on trade are derived from source C. *Imports, c.i.f.* and *Imports, f.o.b.* include duty and are therefore not comparable to corresponding balance of payments data.

Government Finance:

† Beginning in 1986, data is reported from the records of the Ministry of Finance and Development and are reported by source A. The data cover the operations of budgetary central government. † Beginning in 2000, annual data is derived from monthly and quarterly data. Annual data between 1986–1999 were reported separately from monthly and quarterly data. Prior to 1986 data are as reported from the *Government Finance Statistics Yearbook (GFSY)* and cover budgetary central government. The fiscal year ends March 31.

National Accounts:

Source S. Data are compiled by industrial origin and expenditure categories. Official GDP data at constant prices have 1993–94 as the weights reference period. *Line 99b* includes a statistical discrepancy.

Brazil   223

Date of Fund Membership:
January 14, 1946

Standard Sources:

B: Central Bank, *Bulletin*
N: Ministry of Industry, Commerce and Tourism, Secretariat of Foreign Commerce (SECEX)
S: Brazilian Institute of Statistics and Geography (IBGE)

Exchange Rates:

Beginning on November 1, 1942, a cruziero (Cr$) was worth a thousand réis. On February 13, 1967 the new cruzeiro (NCr$) was instituted as a transitory monetary unit equivalent to 1,000 cruzeiros. Effective May 15, 1970 the cruziero (Cr$) was re-established at par with the new cruzeiro. On February 28, 1986, the cruzado (Cz$), equal to 1,000 cruzeiros, was introduced. On January15, 1989 the new cruzado (NCz$), equal to 1,000 old cruzados, was introduced. On March 16, 1990 the cruzeiro (Cr$) replaced the new cruzado at an exchange rate of one new cruzado for one cruzeiro. On August 1, 1993 the cruzeiro real (Cr$), equal to 1,000 cruzeiros, was introduced. On July 1, 1994 the real (R$), equal to 2,750 cruzeiros reais, was introduced.

Principal Rate (End of Period and Period Average):
From March 1990 through September 1994, the official rate floated independently with respect to the U.S. dollar. From October 1994 through January 17, 1999, the official rate was determined by a managed float. Since January 18, 1999, the official rate floats independently with respect to the U.S. dollar.

International Liquidity:

Foreign Exchange (line 1d.d) includes domestic government securities payable in foreign currency. *Gold (National Valuation) (line 1and)* is valued on the basis of the daily average closing quotations in London during the preceding two months. *Other Liquid Foreign Assets (line 1e.d)* comprises the value of liquid export bills. The Brazilian definition of liquid international reserves comprises the sum of *Total Reserves minus Gold (line 1l.d), Gold (National Valuation) (line 1and),* and *Other Liquid Foreign Assets (line 1e.d).* † Prior to January 1986, data for *Total Reserves minus Gold (line 1l.d)* and *Foreign Exchange (line 1d.d)* include foreign exchange held by the Central Bank of Brazil (CBB) and Bank of Brazil. Beginning in 1986, data include the foreign exchange held by the CBB only.

Monetary Authorities:

Consolidates the accounts of the Central Bank of Brazil (CBB) and Bank of Brazil. † Beginning in December 1971 and in December 1978, data are based on improved sectorization of the accounts. † Beginning in January 1986, comprises the Central Bank of Brazil only. † Beginning in June 1988, data are based on an improved classification and sectorization of the accounts. Beginning in December 1998, data on repurchase agreements, previously included in other items (net), have been classified in the assets according to the economic sector to which credit was granted and in the liabilities according to the economic sector from which credit was received. † Beginning in December 2001, data are based on an improved classification and sectorization of the accounts.

Banking Institutions:

Comprises commercial banks and investment banks. † Beginning in December 1971 and in December 1978, data are based on improved sectorization of the accounts. Beginning in December 1978, includes the National Bank of Cooperative Credit. † Beginning in January 1986, includes the Bank of Brazil. † Beginning in June 1988, includes multiple banks, Federal Savings Bank, state savings bank, National Bank for Economic and Social Development, state development banks, finance and investment companies, and housing credit companies. Data reflect the introduction of a new accounting system, which provides an improved sectorization of the accounts. Beginning in December 1996, includes mortgage companies. Beginning in December 1998, includes financial investment funds. Data on repurchase agreements, previously included in other items (net), have been classified in the assets according to the economic sector to which credit was granted and in the liabilities according to the economic sector from which credit was received. † Beginning in December 2001, data are based on an improved classification and sectorization of the accounts.

Banking Survey:

† See notes on monetary authorities and banking institutions .

Nonbank Financial Institutions:

Comprises leasing companies, stock brokerage houses, and distributor companies. Beginning in December 1998, includes fostering agencies. Data on repurchase agreements, previously included in other items (net), have been classified in the assets according to the economic sector to which credit was granted and in the liabilities according to the economic sector from which credit was received. † Beginning in December 2001, data are based on an improved classification and sectorization of the accounts.

Money (National Definitions):

Base Money (BM) comprises notes and coins issued and required and excess reserves on sight deposits with financial institutions. Sight deposits include demand deposits, advance notice deposits, third party float, collection of taxes, cashier's checks, and realized guarantees.

BA comprises base money plus required cash reserves on savings and time deposits and mutual fund shares, and federal securities valued by their yield curve outside the Central Bank of Brazil (CBB), except the *Letras do Banco Central-Série Especial* (LBC-E) used for the swap of state securities.

B2 comprises BA plus state and local securities outside the CBB, at face value, and LBC-E.

M1 comprises currency held by the public, and demand deposits. Demand deposits include deposits of the private sector; of the federal, state, and municipal governments; of the federal, state, and municipal enterprises; and of the financial institutions that are not subject to reserve requirements. M1 also includes domestic currency deposits of nonresidents, travelers' checks issued and not cashed, certified checks with a fixed payment date, payroll checks, and customers' credit balances on loan and financing accounts.

M2 comprises M1 plus interest-bearing deposits, savings deposits, and securities issued by depository corporations.

M2A comprises M1 plus short-term shares in FIF, including FAF prior to 1995, short-term FRF, and nonmarket funds *(Fundos Extramercado)* administered by the Bank of Brazil for investment by state enterprises.

M3 comprises M2 plus shares in mutual investment funds and repurchase agreements registered in the Special Settlement and Custody System (SELIC).

M3A comprises M2A plus shares in 30-day FIF, including FRF prior to 1995, foreign-capital fixed-income funds, and savings deposits.

M4 comprises M3 plus federal, state, and municipal liquid securities held by the public.

M4A comprises M3A plus shares in 60- and 90-day FIF, private securities (which include bank certificates of deposit, bills of exchange, housing and mortgage bills, and automatic investment deposits, but exclude those held by financial institutions and mutual funds), and federal, state, and municipal securities (excluding those held by financial institutions and FIF).

Interest Rates:

Discount Rate (End of Period):
Bank rate (TBAN) charged by the CBB on noncollaterilized loans to financial institutions. † Beginning in March 2000, TBAN was abolished, and the CBB established new rules for lending to financial institutions, taking into account the maturity of the operation and the collateral used by the borrowing institutions. The CBB decided to use the SELIC rate (see note on money market rate) plus two points as the discount rate. In April 2002, the CBB introduced a new payments system and changed the method for calculating the discount rate based on repurchase agreements using government securities. Beginning in April 2002, corresponds to SELIC plus one point. Beginning in July 2002, corresponds to SELIC plus six points.

Money Market Rate:
Average rate on loans between commercial banks. † Beginning in January 1980, the SELIC overnight rate is a weighted average rate on loans between financial institutions involving firm sales of or repurchase agreements based on federal securities in the Special Settlement and Custody System (SELIC). The rate is weighted by loan amounts.

Treasury Bill Rate:
Effective yield on *Letras do Tesouro Nacional* (LTN) of 31 days or longer, calculated from the discount. The yield is that of the last issue of the month, is calculated on a daily basis, and applies only to business days.

Treasury Bill Rate (Foreign Currency):
Effective yield on *Notas do Tesouro Nacional—Emissão D* (NTN-Series D) of three months or longer issued with exchange rate guarantee. The yield includes the purchase discount or premium and the coupon rate of six percent per year, compounded twice a year for notes for longer than six months and paid at maturity for shorter terms. The yield is that of the last issue of the month and does not include the exchange rate change.

Savings Rate:
Rate paid by the Brazilian savings and loan system (SBPE) on 30-day savings deposits.

Deposit Rate:

Average rate offered by banks on 60-day time deposits. † Beginning in January 1989, average rate offered by banks on certificates of deposit of 30 days or longer.

Lending Rate:

Weighted average of the rates charged by banks on loans with fixed interest rates and with own funds to individuals and corporations. The rate is weighted by loan amounts.

Prices, Production, Labor:

Share Prices:

Average index of daily share prices in the São Paulo Securities Exchange (BOVESPA), weights reference period: January 2, 1968.

Wholesale Prices:

Source S. Weights Reference Period: August 1994; Coverage: the index is structured to measure the rate of change of prices of a sample of merchandise at the wholesale level in business to business transactions in the following productive areas of the country: Alagoas, Amazonas, Bahia, Ceara, Espírito Santo, Goiás, Maranhão, Mato Grosso do Sul, Minas Gerais, Pará, Paraíba, Panará, Pernambuco, Piauí, Rio de Janeiro, Rio Grande do Norte, Rio Grande do Sul, Rondônia, Santa Catarina, Sergipe, São Paulo e Tocantis; Number of Items in Basket: 462 commodities/products; Basis for Calculation: weights are revised monthly due to relative changes in the components of the index.

Consumer Prices:

Source S. Weights Reference Period: June 1994; Geographical Coverage: whole national territory; Number of Items in Basket: 512; Basis for Calculation: weights are derived from a Household Expenditure Survey conducted between October 1995 and September 1996.

Industrial Production, Seasonally Adjusted:

Source S. Weights Reference Period: 2002; Sectoral Coverage: mining sector and processing industry; Basis for Calculation: the weighting system is fixed and follows the structure of the "Industrial Value Added of 1985" based on the Industrial Census of 1985.

International Transactions:

All trade value and volume data are from source N.

Volume of Exports and Imports:

Data on total volume are based on quantities in metric tons. *Unit Value of Exports* and *Imports* indices are calculated from value and volume indices.

Export Volume indices for coffee are based on source B data in metric tons. *Export Unit Value* indices for coffee are calculated for *IFS* from reported value and volume data. The coffee wholesale price index is the Brazil (New York) index shown in the commodity prices world table.

Government Finance:

Monthly and quarterly data are derived from source B. The data cover the operations of the National Treasury including the collection and transfer of earmarked revenues for social expenditure purposes. Revenue data include repayments of loans, and expenditure data include lending operations. The fiscal year ends December 31.

National Accounts:

Data are from source B. *Line 93i* data are included in *line 96f* when they are not separately shown. † As indicated by the country, data have been revised following the implementation of the *1993 SNA*.

Brunei Darussalam   516

Date of Fund Membership:

October 10, 1995

Standard Sources:

B: Brunei Currency and Monetary Board (BCMB)
F: Ministry of Finance
S: Department of Economic Planning and Development

Exchange Rates:

Official Rate: (End of Period and Period Average):

Refers to Singapore's midpoint interbank rate at noon. The Brunei dollar is legal tender in Brunei Darussalam and the Singapore dollar is a customary tender. Under the Currency Interchangeability Agreement of 1967, Brunei Darussalam and Singapore accept each other's currency at par without charge.

International Liquidity:

Foreign Exchange (line 1d.d) comprises the BCMB's foreign currency holdings, liquid correspondent accounts with nonresidents banks, and holdings of foreign securities and shares.

Monetary Authorities:

Comprises the BCMB only. The BCMB is the depository agency for the IMF's holdings of Brunei currency, while the Ministry of Finance is the fiscal agent for conducting financial transactions with the IMF. The contra-entry to the Ministry of Finance IMF accounts is included in *Central Government Deposits (line 16d)*.

Banking Institutions:

Comprises commercial banks, finance companies, and a trust fund.

Money (National Definitions):

M0 comprises currency in circulation.
Money comprises currency outside the banking system and demand deposits of nonfinancial public corporations, other financial corporations, and private sector at commercial banks in national currency.
Quasi Money comprises savings and time deposits of nonfinancial public corporations, other financial corporations, and private sector at commercial banks, finance companies, and trust fund in national currency.
Broad Money comprises money and quasi money.

Interest Rates:

Deposit Rate:

Average rate offered by commercial banks on three-month time deposits in national currency.

Lending Rate:

Minimum rate, fixed by the Brunei Association of Banks, charged by commercial banks on loans to preferred customers in national currency. † Beginning on May 16, 2005, the minimum rate is market determined.

Prices:

Consumer Prices:
Source S. Base Year: 2002; Geographical Coverage: all income groups and all districts of the country; Number of Items in Basket: 557 items, of which 247 food items, 310 non-food items; Basis for Weights Calculation: the basket of goods and services and the weights are derived from the Household Income and Expenditure Survey, conducted during October 1997–September 1998.

International Transactions:

Source S. Based on customs data.

National Accounts:

Source S. As indicated by the country, data follow the implementation of the *1968 SNA*.

Bulgaria   918

Date of Fund Membership:

September 25, 1990

Standard Sources:

B: Bulgarian National Bank, *Monthly Bulletin, Semiannual Report, Annual Report*
N: *Report on Execution of the State Budget*
S: National Statistical Institute, *Report on Current Economic Business* (monthly bulletin), *Statistical Yearbook*

Exchange Rates:

On July 5, 1999 the lev was re-denominated: the post-July 5, 1999 lev is equal to 1,000 of the pre-July 5, 1999 leva. All data are expressed in terms of the post-July 5, 1999 lev.

Official Rate: (End of Period and Period Average):
Beginning July 1, 1997, the official rate is pegged to the deutsche mark at one Bulgarian lev (LEV) per 1 deutsche mark. When the euro became the legal tender in the Federal Republic of Germany, the official exchange rate of the lev to the euro was determined by the conversion rate of the deutsche mark to the euro. Thus established exchange rate is published by the Bulgarian National Bank in the State Gazette, and it is LEV 1 per euro 0.5113 (euro 1 per LEV 1.95583). Prior to July 1997, data refer to market rate, calculated as the volume weighted average of the previous day's interbank rates.

International Liquidity:

Gold (National Valuation) (line 1and) is the U.S. dollar value of official holdings of gold which, beginning in February 2005, are valued at market prices. †For the period July 1997 to January 2005, gold was valued at either 500 Bulgarian leva per fine troy ounce or at the end-of-period London gold market price, whichever is lower. † Prior to July 1997, gold was valued at US$300 per fine troy ounce.

Monetary Authorities:

Comprises the Bulgarian National Bank. With reference to June 1995 onward, data are based on a new accounting system and are compiled in accordance with the European Central Bank's framework for monetary statistics using the national residency approach. † Prior to June 1995, deposits of the national Social Security Fund are included in *Central Government Deposits (line 16d)*; beginning in June 1995, transferable and other deposits of the national Social Security Fund are included, respectively, in *Reserve Money (line 14)* and in *Other Deposits (line 15)*. Prior to June 1997, *Foreign Liabilities (line 16c)* includes some foreign liabilities incurred by the central government.

Banking Institutions:

Beginning in February 2007, comprises credit institutions (licensed commercial banks) and money market funds, which represent all resident units classified as other monetary financial institutions (other MFIs) in accordance with the *1995 ESA*. Prior to February 2007, comprises only licensed commercial banks in Bulgaria (beginning in December 1997, non-operating banks were excluded). With reference to June 1995 onward, data are based on a new accounting system and are compiled in accordance with the European Central Bank's framework for monetary statistics using the national residency approach. † Prior to June 1995, deposits of the national Social Security Fund are included in *Central Government Deposits (line 26d)*. Beginning in June 1995, transferable and other deposits of the national Social Security Fund are included, respectively, in *Demand Deposits (line 24)* and in *Other Deposits (line 25)*.

Monetary Survey:

See notes on monetary authorities and deposit money banks.

Money (National Definitions):

M1 comprises currency outside MFIs and overnight deposits of non-central government non-MFI resident sectors with resident MFIs.
M2 is equal to M1 plus deposits with agreed maturity up to two years and deposits redeemable at notice with terms up to three months of non-central government non-MFI resident sectors with resident MFIs.
M3 is equal to M2 plus marketable instruments (which comprise repurchase agreements contracted by MFIs with non-government non-MFI resident sectors, shares/units of money market funds, and debt securities issued by resident MFIs with maturity of up to two years).

Interest Rates:

Source B.

Bank Rate (End of Period):
Data refer to Basic Interest Rate (BIR). BIR is the official reference rate announced by the Bulgarian National Bank (BNB) and published in the State Gazette. † Since February 1, 2005, BIR is equal to the arithmetic average of the values of the LEONIA reference rates for the business days of the previous calendar month (the LEONIA - (Lev OverNight Index Average) reference rate is a weighted average of rates on all overnight unsecured lending transactions in the interbank market in Bulgaria by a representative panel of banks). The BIR is in effect from the first to the last

day of the calendar month to which it refers. † During period July 1, 1997 (the date of establishment of the currency board) to January 31, 2005, BIR was set equal to the annual yield on the three-month government securities based on the outcome of the primary auction. This rate was in effect from the day of the auction and was recalculated based on the results of the subsequent auction. † Prior to January 1997, BIR was one of BNB's main policy instruments and was determined by its Board of Directors based on the annual yield on short-term (7 to 28-day) government securities.

Money Market Rate:
Beginning in December 2004, the LEONIA reference rate. † Prior to December 2004, weighted average rate on deposits transacted in the interbank market.

Treasury Bill Yield:
Beginning in January 2006, weighted average yield to maturity on treasury bills with terms up to one year traded in secondary market. † Prior to January 2006, weighted average yield on newly issued treasury bills with terms up to one year sold at primary auctions.

Deposit Rate:
Beginning in February 2000, weighted average rate offered by credit institutions on new one-month deposits in leva to the household sector. † Prior to February 2000, weighted average rate offered by credit institutions on time deposits in leva to the non-financial corporations and the household sectors.

Lending Rate:
Weighted average rate charged by credit institutions on new loans (including overdrafts) in leva to the non-financial corporations and the household sectors with terms up to one year.

Government Bond Yield:
Beginning in January 2006, weighted average yield to maturity on treasury bonds with term over one year traded in secondary market. † Prior to January 2006, weighted average yield of the newly issued government bonds with terms over one year sold at primary auctions.

Prices:

Producer Prices:
Source S. Weights Reference Period: 2000; Sectoral Coverage: covers mining, manufacturing, and electricity, water, and gas supply; Number of Items in the Basket: the sampling method compilation involves a three-stage sampling process: first of PRODCOM groups, second of reporting units, and then of specific products (transactions); Basis for Calculation: monthly surveys of industrial products sold on domestic market and non-domestic market.

Consumer Prices:
Source S. Weights Reference Period: 1995; Geographical Coverage: the whole country; Number of Items in the Basket: 531 goods and services divided into 12 major consumption groups; Basis for Calculation: the commodity basket is re-weighted each year based on the annual Household Budget Survey (HBS) data.

International Transactions:

Source B. Based on customs data.

Government Finance:

Cash data cover operations of consolidated central government, comprising budgetary, extrabudgetary, and social security funds. † Beginning in 1994, quarterly and annual data are reported by the Bulgarian National Bank and are taken from source N and unpublished reports on the operations of the consolidated central government. Beginning in 1996, annual and quarterly data are obtained by aggregating monthly data. Beginning in January 2002, general government data are presented in the *GFSM 2001* Statement of Sources and Uses of Cash. The fiscal year ends December 31.

National Accounts:

Source S. As indicated by the country, data are compiled according to the recommendations of the *1995 ESA* and the *1968 SNA*.

Burkina Faso   748

Date of Fund Membership:
May 2, 1963

Standard Source:
B: Banque Centrale des Etats de l'Afrique de l'Ouest (Central Bank of West African States), *Notes d'information et Statistiques (Informative Notes and Statistics)*
Burkina Faso is a member of the West African Economic and Monetary Union, together with Benin, Côte d'Ivoire, Guinea-Bissau, Mali, Niger, Senegal, and Togo. The Union, which was established in 1962, has a common central bank, the Central Bank of West African States (BCEAO), with headquarters in Dakar, and national branches in the member states. Mali and Guinea-Bissau joined the Union on June 1, 1984 and May 2, 1997, respectively.

Exchange Rates:

Official Rate: (End of Period and Period Average):
Prior to January 1999, the official rate was pegged to the French franc. On January 12, 1994, the CFA franc was devalued to CFAF 100 per French franc from CFAF 50 at which it had been fixed since 1948. From January 1, 1999, the CFAF is pegged to the euro at a rate of CFA franc 655.957 per euro.

International Liquidity:

Gold is revalued on a quarterly basis at the rate communicated by the BCEAO, which corresponds to the lowest average fixing in the London market.

Monetary Authorities:

Comprises the national branch of the BCEAO only. The amount of currency outside banks is estimated by subtracting from the amount of CFA franc notes issued by Burkina Faso the estimated amounts of Burkina Faso's currency in the cash held by the banks of all member countries of the Union.

Deposit Money Banks:

Comprises commercial banks and specialized development banks, and includes certain banking operations of the Treasury and the Post Office. The Treasury accepts customs duty bills (reported separately in *line 22d.i*). Through its many branches, the Postal Checking System acts as the main depository for the private sector in the interior of Burkina Faso. *Claims on the Private Sector (line 22d)* include doubtful and litigious debts. † Beginning in 1979, *Central Government Deposits (line 26d)* include the deposits of the public establishments of an administrative or social nature (EPAS) and exclude those of the savings bank; *Demand and Time Deposits (lines 24 and 25)* include deposits of the savings bank and exclude deposits of EPAS; and *Claims on Private Sector (line 22d)* exclude claims on other financial institutions.

Monetary Survey:

The data reported agree with source B aggregates, as given in the table on the position of the monetary institutions, except for *line 31n*, for which source B treats long-term foreign liabilities and SDR allocations as a foreign liability, whereas *IFS* reports the former separately and includes the latter in *line 37r*. Moreover, valuation differences exist as a result of the *IFS* calculations of reserve position in the Fund and the SDR holdings, both components of *line 11*, based on Fund record. † Beginning in 1979, *Claims on Other Financial Institutions (line 32f)* includes claims of deposit money banks on other financial institutions; see deposit money bank notes for explanation of other break symbols.

Other Banking Institutions:

Liquid Liabilities (line 55l): † See notes on deposit money banks and monetary survey.

Interest Rates:

Bank Rate (End of Period):
Rate on repurchase agreements between the BCEAO and the banks. † Prior to October 1, 1993 data refer to basic discount rate offered by the BCEAO.

Money Market Rate:
Rate paid on overnight interbank advances.

Deposit Rate:
Rate offered by banks on time deposits of CFAF 500,000–2,000,000 for under six months.

Prices and Labor:

Consumer Prices:
Source B. Weights Reference Period: 1996; Geographical Coverage: City of Ouagadougou; Number of Items in Basket: 320; Basis for Calculation: The weights are derived from a household expenditure survey conducted in the city of Ouagadougou in 1996.

International Transactions:

All trade data are from source B. Trade indices are compiled on weights reference period 1986.

Government Finance:

Data are derived from information provided by source B and cover budgetary central government and capital expenditure financed by foreign grants. The fiscal year ends December 31.

National Accounts:

Source B.

Burundi 618

Date of Fund Membership:
September 28, 1963

Standard Source:
B: Central Bank, *Monthly Bulletin*

Exchange Rates:

Official Rate: (End of Period and Period Average):
The official rate is pegged to an undisclosed basket of currencies and is adjusted from time to time.

International Liquidity:

Gold (National Valuation) (line 1and) is obtained by converting the value in national currency terms, as reported in the country's standard sources, using the prevailing exchange rate, as given in **line ae** or **we**. This line follows national valuation procedures which revalue gold semiannually beginning December 1977 at the average price of the opening and closing quotations on the London market of the last day of each period.

Monetary Authorities:

Comprises Bank of the Republic of Burundi only. The profit resulting from the revaluation of gold (see note on international liquidity) is placed in a reserve set for the purpose. *Nonfinancial Public Enterprise Deposits (line 14e)* includes deposits of other financial institutions. *Restricted Deposits (line 16b)* comprises required stabilization funds and import deposits.

Deposit Money Banks:

† Beginning in 1980, data are based on an improved sectorization of the accounts. † Beginning in 1991, data reflect changes in the coverage of the other monetary institutions. Beginning in November 1998, the data reflect the liquidation of CAMOFI, one other monetary institution. Since then, this subsector comprises only the CCP (sight and saving deposits with the postal administration).

Monetary Survey:

† See notes on monetary authorities and deposit money banks.

Other Banking Institutions:

Comprises Banque Nationale pour le Développement Économique (BNDE) and Société Burundaise de Financement (SBF). † Beginning in January 1997, includes the Fonds de Promotion de l'Habitat Urbain (FPHU). Beginning in January 2000, includes one leasing finance company. Savings and credit cooperatives are not included.

Interest Rates:

Discount Rate (End of Period):
The discount rate is applicable for the refinancing of short-term commercial claims held by banks.

Lending Rate:
Rate on short-term cash advances (two years or less).

Prices:

Consumer Prices:
Source B. Weights Reference Period: January 1991; Geographical

Coverage: Bujumbura; Basis for Calculation: the weights are derived from a household budget survey conducted in 1979.

International Transactions:
All trade data are from source B. *Value of Exports* and *Imports* are based on customs data.

Government Finance:
Data are derived from source B and cover central government operations. They comprise receipts and outlays from the ordinary and extraordinary budget as well as Treasury receipts and outlays from extrabudgetary accounts. Data on government operations do not cover operations of the National Social Security Institute or of other central government agencies with own budgets. † Beginning in 1992, data are presented in a new format and are not directly comparable with data for earlier periods. Debt data cover outstanding debt of the nonfinancial public sector comprising direct government debt, onlent government debt, and debt guaranteed by the government. The fiscal year ends December 31.

National Accounts:
Source B.

Cambodia   522

Date of Fund Membership:
December 31, 1969

Standard Source:
B: National Bank of Cambodia
S: National Institute of Statistics

Exchange Rates:
Official Rate: (End of Period and Period Average):
Official buying rate of the National Bank of Cambodia (NBC).

International Liquidity:
† Prior to 1994, *Foreign Exchange (line 1d.d)* excludes portion of official reserves that was held by the Foreign Trade Bank. Beginning in 1994, official foreign reserves were centralized at the National Bank of Cambodia.

Monetary Authorities:
Comprises the accounts of the NBC, which undertakes all monetary authority functions. Beginning in July 2004, covers the accounts of the NBC's head office and all NBC provincial branches. Prior to that date, the NBC's provincial branches were classified as deposit money banks.

Deposit Money Banks:
Comprises the state-owned banks, privately owned commercial banks, branches of foreign banks, and the NBC's provincial branches. Beginning in July 2004, the NBC's provincial branches are excluded from the accounts of deposit money banks and included in the accounts of monetary authorities.

Interest Rates:
Deposit Rate:
Simple average of rates on domestic-currency savings deposits reported by the 10 banks with the largest deposit holdings.

Lending Rate:
Simple average of rates on foreign currency loans to private enterprises reported by the 10 banks with the largest deposit holdings.

Prices and Labor:
Consumer Prices:
Source S. Weight Reference Period: July–December 2000; Geographical Coverage: Phnom Penh and five provincial cities; Number of Items in Basket: 225 (227 for Phnom Penh); Basis for Calculation: weights are based on the 1999 Cambodian socio-economic survey.

International Transactions:
All trade data are from source B.

Government Finance:
Monthly cash data are as provided by the Ministry of Finance. These data cover the operations of the National Budget at the central and regional level, as well as expenditure financed by foreign grants and loans. Receipts from privatization are classified as domestic financing. Annual data are obtained by aggregating monthly data. Beginning in January 2006, general government data are presented in the *GFSM 2001* Statement of Government Operations. The fiscal year ends December 31.

National Accounts:
Source S.

Cameroon   622

Date of Fund Membership:
July 10, 1963

Standard Source:
B: Banque des Etats d'Afrique Centrale (BEAC) (Bank of the Central African States), *Etudes et Statistiques (Studies and Statistics)*

Exchange Rates:
Official Rate: (End of Period and Period Average):
Prior to January 1999, the official rate was pegged to the French franc. On January 12, 1994, the CFA franc was devalued to CFAF 100 per French franc from CFAF 50 at which it had been fixed since 1948. From January 1, 1999, the CFAF is pegged to the euro at a rate of CFA franc 655.957 per euro.

International Liquidity:
Gold (National Valuation) (line 1and) is obtained by converting the value in national currency, as reported in the country's standard sources, using the prevailing exchange rate, as given in *line* **ae**. Prior to January 1999, the national currency/dollar conversion rates utilized for balance sheet purposes are used. These conversion rates differ from the prevailing exchange rates reported in *IFS*. This line follows the national valuation procedure which corresponds to that of the Bank of France (*cf* the international liquidity note on the *IFS* page for France).

Monetary Authorities:
Comprises the national branch of the Bank of the Central African States only. Claims on central government include assumption of certain nonperforming bank loans.

Deposit Money Banks:

Comprises active commercial banks. Claims and deposits of nonactive banks or banks in the process of liquidation are excluded. The counterpart of government assumption of certain nonperforming bank loans is reclassified to capital accounts.

Interest Rates:

Discount Rate (End of Period):

Basic rediscount rate offered by the BEAC. † Beginning July 1994, rate charged by the BEAC to financial institutions on refinancing operations.

Deposit Rate:

Minimum rate offered by deposit money banks on savings accounts.

Lending Rate:

Maximum rate charged by deposit money banks on all loans, excluding charges and fees.

Prices and Production:

Industrial Production:

Source S. Laspeyres-type index. The industrial production index (IPI) covers the manufacturing industry as well as the production and distribution of water, electricity, gas, and oil refining. It measures changes in the volume of production of a basket of 242 goods representative of the 18 manufacturing branches covered. Data are collected through on-site visits to 170 enterprises in Cameroon. The IPI product weights in the index are based on the gross value added calculated on the basis of the 1995/96 Annual Survey of Industry (EAI).

Consumer Prices:

Source B. Weights reference period: 1983/1984; Coverage: weighted average of the price indices of five major cities; Number of Items in Basket: 266; Basis for Calculation: fixed-weight Laspeyres index, 1983–1984 Budget Consumption Survey.

International Transactions:

All trade data are from source B. Data on total exports may not include all crude oil exports.

Government Finance:

Annual data are as reported for the *Government Finance Statistics Yearbook (GFSY)* and cover budgetary central government. Annual data refer to a fiscal year different from calendar year. The fiscal year ends June 30.

National Accounts:

Line 99b includes a statistical discrepancy. The framework of the national accounts for data corresponding to the new weights reference period 1989/90 is patterned on the *1993 SNA*.

Canada   156

Date of Fund Membership:

December 27, 1945

Standard Sources:

B: Bank of Canada, *Review*
S: Statistics Canada

Exchange Rates:

Market Rate (End of Period and Period Average):

The exchange rate floats independently. Midpoint rate quoted by the Bank of Canada at noon in the Montreal-Toronto interbank exchange market.

International Liquidity:

Lines 7a.d and *7b.d* comprise Canadian dollar and foreign currency accounts of nonresidents booked in Canada.

Monetary Authorities:

Comprises the Bank of Canada only. † Beginning in December 2001, data are based on a new reporting system which provides improved classification and sectorization of the accounts.

Banking Institutions:

Comprises chartered banks and Quebec savings banks. Beginning in March 1967, includes trust and mortgage loan companies, local credit unions, and *caisses populaires*. † Beginning in December 1981, all wholly- and majority-owned subsidiaries of the chartered banks (including mortgage loan subsidiaries and foreign banking subsidiaries) are consolidated in accordance with Canadian banking law. Unconsolidated data are not available on a monthly basis. In addition, data for *lines 24 and 25,* which were previously calculated from monthly averages of Wednesday figures in the absence of an adequate classification of month ends, are now calculated mostly from month-end figures. Adjustments have been made to exclude foreign currency transactions booked outside Canada from the *IFS* presentation. Beginning September 1987, excludes the Quebec savings banks. † Beginning in December 2001, includes life insurance company annuities, government owned savings institutions, money market mutual funds, and non-money market mutual funds and excludes *caisses populaires*. Data are based on a new reporting system which provides improved classification and sectorization of the accounts.

Banking Survey:

† See notes on monetary authorities and banking institutions.

Nonbank Financial Institutions:

Comprises sales finance and consumer loan companies. Beginning in June 1977, includes insurance companies and segregated funds. † Beginning in March 1999, comprises insurance companies, segregated funds, and other nondepository credit intermediaries, which are establishments, both public (government sponsored enterprises) and private, primarily engaged in extending credit or lending funds raised by credit- market borrowing (e.g., by issuing commercial paper and other debt instruments) and by borrowing from other financial intermediaries. † Beginning in December 2001, includes investment funds. Data are based on a new reporting system which provides improved classification and sectorization of the accounts.

Financial Survey:

† See notes on monetary authorities, banking institutions, and nonbank financial institutions.

Money (National Definitions):

M1 comprises currency outside banks, chartered bank demand deposits, and adjustments to M1.

Gross M1 comprises currency outside banks, personal checking accounts and current accounts excluding Government of Canada deposits, and adjustments to M1 (continuity adjustments as well as adjustments for demand deposits of chartered banks). Adjustments are made to reconstruct past data and make them consistent with how the current data are structured. Changes in the financial industry can result in new data that are inconsistent with the former presentation causing significant discontinuities in the series and making the data useless for econometric work. The Bank of Canada adjusts its monetary aggregates each time one of the following events takes place: the acquisition of a trust company by a bank, the acquisition of an entity in a sector that was not previously included in the monetary aggregates (i.e., an investment dealer), the formation of a bank from a trust company or companies, and the acquisition of a bank by a trust company. Monetary aggregates are also adjusted to exclude interbank deposits. Continuity adjustments have been made to eliminate discontinuities resulting from the 1980 Bank Act revision and the introduction of a new reporting system for the banks. In addition, float denotes funds in transition between the time a check is deposited or a payment is sent and the time the payment is settled. Net denotes monetary aggregates that do not include float.

M1+ Gross comprises currency outside banks, personal and non-personal chequable deposits held at chartered banks , all chequable deposits at trust and mortgage loan companies, credit unions and caisses populaires (excluding deposits of these institutions) and continuity adjustments.

M1++ Gross comprises M1+ Gross , non-chequable notice deposits held at chartered banks, all non-chequable deposits at trust and mortgage loan companies, credit unions and caisses populaires less interbank non-chequable notice deposits and continuity adjustments.

M2 Net comprises M1, non-personal notice deposits and personal savings deposits with chartered banks, and adjustments (continuity adjustments as well as notice deposits of other chartered banks).

M2 Gross comprises currency outside banks, personal deposits and non-personal demand and notice deposits held at chartered banks and continuity adjustments.

M2+ Net comprises M2 Net, trust and mortgage loan companies total deposits, credit unions and caisses populaires total deposits, life insurance company individual annuities, personal deposits at government owned savings institutions, money market mutual funds, and adjustments (adjustments as well as credit union and caisses populaires share capital, less the sum of Receiver General deposits at trust and mortgage loan companies, trust and mortgage loan company holdings of currency and demand and notice deposits with other deposit-taking institutions, and credit union and caisses populaires holdings of currency and demand and notice deposits with other deposit-taking institutions (other than provincial centrals and federations).

M2+ Gross comprises M2 Gross, deposits of non-banks (trust and mortgage loan companies, government savings institutions, deposits and shares at credit unions and caisses populaires, life insurance company individual annuities and money market mutual funds) and continuity adjustments.

M2++ Net comprises M2+ Net, Canada Savings Bonds, cumulative contribution to non-money market mutual funds other than Canadian-dollar money market mutual funds (already part of M2+ Net).

M2++Gross comprises M2+Gross, Canada Savings Bonds and other retail instruments , cumulative net contributions to mutual funds other than Canadian dollar money market mutual funds (which are already included in M2+ Gross) and continuity adjustments.

M3 Net comprises M2 Net, non-personal term deposits and foreign currency deposits of residents with chartered banks, and adjustment (continuity adjustments as well as term deposits of other chartered banks).

M3 Gross comprises M2 Gross, non-personal term and foreign currency deposits of residents with chartered banks, and continuity adjustments.

Interest Rates:

All interest rate data are from source B.

Bank Rate (End of Period):
Rate at which the Bank of Canada is prepared to respond to requests of chartered banks for temporary advances and enter into purchase and resale agreements with money market dealers. Rate is set at¼ of 1 percent above the latest average rate on three-month treasury bills established at the preceding weekly tender.

Money Market Rate:
Rate refers to the overnight money market financing rate. Monthly figures are the average for the seven days ending the last Wednesday of the month.

Corporate Paper Rate:
Rate of 90-day prime corporate paper. Quarterly and annual data are averages of data for the last Wednesday in each month.

Treasury Bill Rate:
Weighted average of the yields on successful bids for three-month bills. Monthly data relate to the tender rates of the last Wednesday of the month.

Savings Rate:
Rate offered by chartered banks on non-chequeable savings deposits in national currency.

Deposit Rate:
Rate offered by chartered banks on 90-day commercial certificates of deposit in national currency. † Beginning in January 1974, rate offered by chartered banks on 90-day deposits in national currency.

Lending Rate:
Rate that chartered banks charge on large business loans to their most creditworthy customers; when there are differences among banks, the most typical rate is taken. Monthly figures are for the last Wednesday of the month.

Government Bond Yield:
Average yield to maturity. *Medium-term* series refers to issues with original maturity of 3–5 years. *Long-term* series refers to issues with original maturity of 10 years and over.

Prices, Production, Labor:

Industrial Share Prices:
Source B data on closing quotations at the end of the month on the Toronto Stock Exchange for a composite of 300 shares, base 1975.

Prices: Industry Selling:
Source S data on aggregate industry selling prices (gross weighted), weights reference period 1997, covering about 90 percent of the value of manufacturing output in 1997.

Consumer Prices:
Source S. Geographical Coverage: All provinces, Whitehorse and Yellowknife; Number of Items in Basket: 182 item categories; Basis for Calculation: Weights are based on Family Expenditure Survey and are updated at approximately four-yearly intervals.

Wages: Hourly Earnings:
Source S data in dollars per hour, covering manufacturing firms employing 20 or more persons. Data refer to the last pay period of the month including overtime, vacation pay, cost of living, allowances, etc.

Industrial Production, Seasonally Adjusted:
Source S. Weights Reference Period: 1997; Sectoral Coverage: entire economy of Canada; Basis for Calculation: GDP in constant 1997 prices based on the production approach for all industries using the 1997 North American Industrial Classification.

Gold Production:
Data are from *Statistics Canada* and are expressed in kilograms.

Manufacturing Employment:
Source B data covering manufacturing firms employing 20 or more persons. Data relate to the last pay period of the month.

International Transactions:

Exports:
Source B data on merchandise exports multiplied by a factor for inland freight adjustment, derived from the *Balance of Payments Statistics Yearbook.* Beginning January 1990, the inland freight adjustment is not made to these data, because the valuation basis for exports was revised to include these expenses.

Imports, f.o.b.:
Source B data on merchandise imports.
The general trade indices are source S data. The *Unit Value* indices are constant weighted and are calculated as a Laspeyres index, weights reference period 1997. The *Volume* indices are source S Laspeyres indices, seasonally adjusted, weights reference period: 1997.

Government Finance:

Monthly and quarterly data are derived from the 'Statement of Financial Operations' of the Public Works and Government Services Agency and cover budgetary and nonbudgetary transactions. † Data classification changes may have been introduced between 1987 and 1988, as a result of revisions applied from 1988 through 1995. † Beginning in 1996, annual data are as reported for the *Government Finance Statistics Yearbook (GFSY)* and cover consolidated central government. The fiscal year ends March 31.

National Accounts:

Data are derived from source B. *Lines 99a.c* and *99b.c* include a statistical discrepancy. As indicated by the country, from 1995 onwards data have been revised following the implementation of the *1993 SNA.* GDP chain linked volume measures are calculated based on prices and weights of the previous year, using Laspeyres formula in general.

Cape Verde   624

Date of Fund Membership:
November 20, 1978

Standard Source:
B: Bank of Cape Verde, *Annual Balance Sheets*

Exchange Rates:

Official Rate: (End of Period and Period Average):
On March 30, 1998, the Cape Verde escudo began to be pegged to the Portuguese escudo. From January 1, 1999, the official rate is pegged to the euro at a rate of CVEsc 110.27 per euro.

International Liquidity:

Data on foreign exchange *(line 1d.d)* are derived from data denominated in national currency from components of monetary authorities' foreign assets *(line 11),* using the end-of-period market rate *(line ae)* for conversion to U.S. dollars.

Monetary Authorities:

Comprises the Bank of Cape Verde (BCV). † Beginning in September 1993, data are based on an improved sectorization of the accounts. † Beginning in December 1995, data are based on an improved sectorization of the accounts. † Beginning in December 2001, data are based on a new reporting system which provides improved classification and sectorization of the accounts.

Banking Institutions:

Comprises the Caixa Econômica of Cape Verde. † Beginning September 1993, includes the Banco Comercial do Atlântico. Data are based on an improved sectorization of the accounts. † Beginning in December 1995, data are based on an improved sectorization of the accounts. Beginning in February 1996, includes the Totta and Azores Bank. † Beginning in December 2001, comprises commercial banks and the Caixa Econômica of Cape Verde. Data are based on a new reporting system which provides improved classification and sectorization of the accounts.

Banking Survey:

† See notes on monetary authorities and banking institutions .

Money (National Definitions):

Base Money comprises currency in circulation and commercial banks' deposits with BCV in national and foreign currency. Currency in circulation refers to notes and coins issued by the BCV less the amount held in the vaults of the BCV.
M1 comprises currency in circulation and demand deposits in national currency of other financial corporations, state and local governments, nonfinancial public corporations, and the private sector with the BCV and commercial banks.
M2 comprises *M1,* time, savings, and foreign currency deposits, cashiers' cheques and money orders, repurchase agreements, and legally restricted deposits of other financial corporations, state and local governments, nonfinancial public corporations,

and private sector with the BCV and commercial banks. Deposits of the private sector include the deposits of nonresident emigrant workers.

Interest Rates:

Rediscount Rate (End of Period):
Rate at which the BCV lends to commercial banks in national currency.

Treasury Bill Rate:
Average yield on 182-day treasury bills denominated in national currency.

Deposit Rate:
Maximum rate offered by commercial banks on 90-day time deposits. † Beginning in January 1995, maximum rate offered by commercial banks on 61- to 90-day time deposits. † Beginning in May 2006, weighted average rate offered by commercial banks on deposits of 31 to 90 days in national currency.

Lending Rate:
Maximum rate charged by commercial banks on 90-day loans. † Beginning in May 2006, weighted average rate offered by commercial banks on 90- to 181-day loans in national currency.

Prices:

Consumer Prices:
Source B. Weights Reference Period: 1989; Geographical Coverage: covering three consumption points which representing rural areas (cities of Praia, Mindelo and Assomada); Number of Items in the Basket: contains approximately 220 items for Praia, 205 for Mindelo, and 183 for Assomada; Basis for Calculation: was obtained from data gathered in the 1988/89 First Household Expenditure and Income Survey (*IDRF*), conducted between July 1988 and June 1989, which covered six islands of the archipelago, representing some 95 percent of the resident population.

International Transactions:

Source B.

National Accounts:

Source B. As indicated by the country, data are compiled according to the recommendations of the *1968 SNA*.

CEMAC   758

The treaty establishing the Central African Economic and Monetary Community (Communauté économique et Monétaire de l'Afrique Centrale (CEMAC)) was signed in March 1994 and entered into force on August 1999, after its ratification by the six member states: Cameroon, the Central African Republic, Chad, the Republic of Congo, Equatorial Guinea, and Gabon. The treaty was built on the achievements of the monetary cooperation arrangement in effect under the common central bank since 1959 and on those of the Customs and Economic Union of Central Africa (Union Douanière et économique de l'Afrique Centrale (UDEAC)) established in 1966.

The main objective of the treaty is to provide macroeconomic stability and credibility required to sustain the fixed exchange rate for the common currency. To achieve this objective, the member countries share a common regional central bank established in 1972, the Bank of Central African States (Banque des

états de l'Afrique Centrale (BEAC)), which has issued the common currency, the CFA franc (CFA stands for "Coopération Financière en Afrique Centrale"), since 1972. Equatorial Guinea, which is not a founding member, joined the BEAC in 1985. Prior to 1972, the countries shared the Central Bank of Equatorial African States and of Cameroon (Banque Centrale des états de l'Afrique équatoriale et du Cameroun (BCEAEC)), which issued the common currency, the CFA franc (CFA stood for "Communauté Financière Africaine). The CEMAC Treaty integrates the Central African Monetary Union (Union Monétaire en Afrique Centrale (UMAC)) Covenant and the Central African Economic Union (Union Économique en Afrique Centrale (UEAC)) Covenant. The BEAC and the regional banking commission (Commission Bancaire en Afrique Centrale (COBAC)), a banking supervision agency established in 1990, are the UMAC's principal bodies.

Compared to the data published in the individual *IFS* pages for the CEMAC member countries, the consolidated data published for the CEMAC as a whole embody two major methodological differences: (1) where relevant, a CEMAC-wide residency criterion is applied instead of a national residency criterion; (2) BEAC headquarters' transactions are included in the data presented in the sections "International Liquidity" and "Monetary Authorities." BEAC headquarters' transactions are not allocated to the member countries' national data.

Date of Fund Membership:

Cameroon, the Central African Republic, Chad, the Republic of Congo, and Gabon on July 10, 1963; Equatorial Guinea on December 22, 1969.

Standard Source:

B: Banque des Etats d'Afrique Centrale (BEAC) (Bank of the Central African States), *Etudes et Statistiques (Studies and Statistics)*

Exchange Rates:

Official Rate: (End of Period and Period Average):
Prior to January 1999, the official rate was pegged to the French franc. On January 12, 1994, the CFA franc (CFAF) was devalued to CFAF 100 per French franc from CFAF 50 at which it had been fixed since 1948. From January 1, 1999 onward, the CFAF is pegged to the euro at the rate of CFAF 655.957 per euro.

Fund Position:

Data are the aggregation of positions of CEMAC countries. *SDRs (line 1b.d)* includes SDR holdings by BEAC headquarters.

International Liquidity:

Data include holdings by BEAC headquarters and BEAC member country national directorates. *Gold (National Valuation) (line 1and)* is obtained by converting the value in national currency, as reported by the BEAC, using the prevailing exchange rate, as given in *line ae.* Prior to January 1999, the national currency/dollar conversion rates utilized for balance sheet purposes were used. These conversion rates differ from the prevailing exchange rate reported in *IFS.* The national valuation procedure for gold corresponds to that of the Bank of France (see note on International Liquidity on the *IFS* page for France).

Monetary Authorities:

Data, compiled from the BEAC balance sheet, cover headquarters and national directorates.

Deposit Money Banks:

This section consolidates national data by application of a CEMAC-wide residency criterion. For more details on national data, see country notes.

Interest Rates:

Discount Rate (End of Period):
Basic rediscount rate offered by the BEAC. † Beginning July 1994, rate charged by the BEAC to financial institutions on refinancing operations.

Deposit Rate:
Minimum rate offered by deposit money banks on savings accounts.

Lending Rate:
Maximum rate charged by deposit money banks on all loans, excluding charges and fees.

Central African Republic   626

Date of Fund Membership:
July 10, 1963

Standard Sources:

A: Ministry for Economy, Finance, Planification, and International Cooperation, *Les comptes de la Nation* (National Accounts)
B: Banque des Etats d'Afrique Centrale (BEAC) (Bank of the Central African States), *Etudes et Statistiques (Studies and Statistics)*

Exchange Rates:

Official Rate: (End of Period and Period Average):
Prior to January 1999, the official rate was pegged to the French franc. On January 12, 1994, the CFA franc was devalued to CFAF 100 per French franc from CFAF 50 at which it had been fixed since 1948. From January 1, 1999, the CFAF is pegged to the euro at a rate of CFA franc 655.957 per euro.
For the purpose of calculating the real effective exchange rate index (*line* **rec**), the wholesale price index is used (*line 63*).

International Liquidity:

Gold (National Valuation) (line 1and) is obtained by converting the value in national currency, as reported in the country's standard sources, using the prevailing exchange rate, as given in *line* **ae**. Prior to January 1999, the national currency/dollar conversion rates utilized for balance sheet purposes are used. These conversion rates differ from the prevailing exchange rates reported in *IFS*. This line follows the national valuation procedure which corresponds to that of the Bank of France (*cf* the international liquidity note on the *IFS* page for France).

Monetary Authorities:

Comprises the national branch of the Bank of the Central African States only. Claims on central government include assumption of certain nonperforming bank loans.

Deposit Money Banks:

Comprises active commercial banks. Claims and deposits of non-active banks or banks in the process of liquidation are excluded.

The counterpart of government assumption of certain nonperforming bank loans is reclassified to capital accounts.

Interest Rates:

Discount Rate (End of Period):
Basic rediscount rate offered by the BEAC. † Beginning July 1994, rate charged by the BEAC to financial institutions on refinancing operations.

Deposit Rate:
Minimum rate offered by deposit money banks on savings accounts.

Lending Rate:
Maximum rate charged by deposit money banks on all loans, excluding charges and fees.

Prices and Labor:
All data on prices are from source B.

Wholesale Prices:
Data refer to the wholesale price index in Bangui, weights reference period: 1981. The weights are derived from import and production data for 1982. The index includes 63 items and covers foodstuffs, fuel, electricity, and industrial materials and products.

Consumer Prices:
Data refer to the consumer price index for African households in Bangui, weights reference period: 1975, covering 160 items. The index is based on a household survey conducted among 5,000 households throughout the country.

International Transactions:
Source A.

National Accounts:
Source A. The national accounts are compiled primarily with reference to the *1993 SNA*.

Chad   628

Date of Fund Membership:
July 10, 1963

Standard Source:

B: Banque des Etats d'Afrique Centrale (BEAC) (Bank of the Central African States), *Etudes et Statistiques (Studies and Statistics)*

Exchange Rates:

Official Rate: (End of Period and Period Average):
Prior to January 1999, the official rate was pegged to the French franc. On January 12, 1994, the CFA franc was devalued to CFAF 100 per French franc from CFAF 50 at which it had been fixed since 1948. From January 1, 1999, the CFAF is pegged to the euro at a rate of CFA franc 655.957 per euro.

International Liquidity:

Gold (National Valuation) (line 1and) is obtained by converting the value in national currency, as reported in the country's standard sources, using the prevailing exchange rate, as given in *line* **ae**. Prior to January 1999, the national currency/dollar conversion rates utilized for balance sheet purposes are used. These conversion rates differ from the prevailing exchange rates reported in *IFS*. This line follows the national valuation procedure which corresponds to that of the Bank of France (*cf* the international liquidity note on the *IFS* page for France).

Monetary Authorities:

Comprises the national branch of the Bank of the Central African States only. Claims on central government include assumption of certain nonperforming bank loans.

Deposit Money Banks:

Comprises active commercial banks. Claims and deposits of non-active banks or banks in the process of liquidation are excluded. The counterpart of government assumption of certain nonperforming bank loans is reclassified to capital accounts.

Interest Rates:

Discount Rate (End of Period):

Basic rediscount rate offered by the BEAC. † Beginning July 1994, rate charged by the BEAC to financial institutions on refinancing operations.

Deposit Rate:

Minimum rate offered by deposit money banks on savings accounts.

Lending Rate:

Maximum rate charged by deposit money banks on all loans, excluding charges and fees.

Prices and Labor:

Consumer Prices:

Source B index, weights reference period: 1972 for African households in N'Djamena. The index covers 155 items. The weights were derived from the budget/consumption survey conducted over 12 months in 1972 in N'Djamena.

International Transactions:

Beginning with 1982, trade data are obtained from the *Balance of Payments Statistics*.

Government Finance:

† Prior to 1986, data cover budgetary central government only. Beginning in 1986, data are as reported for *the Government Finance Statistics Yearbook* by the Bank of the Central African States and cover budgetary central government and the Autonomous Amortization Fund accounts. † Beginning in 1991, data are as reported by the Banque des Etats de l'Afrique Centrale. The fiscal year ends December 31.

National Accounts:

Data are from source B. The national accounts framework for data corresponding to the new base year 1995 is patterned on the *1993 SNA*.

Chile   228

Date of Fund Membership:

December 31, 1945

Standard Sources:

A: Central Bank, *Annual Report*
B: Central Bank, *Biweekly Economic and Financial Report, Monthly Bulletin*

Exchange Rates:

Market Rate (End of Period and Period Average):

Weighted average of the midpoint rates between the buying and selling rates of U.S. dollars by banks and foreign exchange houses that are part of the official exchange market. Since 1985, the exchange regime was based on a system of floating bands. In January 1997, the exchange rate band was broadened to 12.5 percent on either side of the reference rate (basket of currencies of the country's three major trading partners readjusted for domestic inflation discounted by relevant external inflation). In June 1998, the fluctuation margin was reduced from 25 percent to 5.5 percent. In September 1998, the margins of the band were broadened to 7 percent and a band broadening factor 0.013575 percent was introduced. In December 1998, it was broadened to 16 percent and the daily broadening factor retained. On September 2, 1999, the fluctuation band was indefinitely suspended and the peso was allowed to float freely.

International Liquidity:

Gold (National Valuation) (line 1and) is the U.S. dollar value of official holdings of gold as reported in the country's standard sources. This line follows national valuation procedures which revalue gold quarterly on the basis of the average morning quotations in London during the preceding three months, less a discount of 10 percent.

Monetary Authorities:

Comprises the Central Bank of Chile (CBC) only. † Beginning in January 1976, data are based on an improved classification and sectorization of the accounts. † Beginning in December 1997, data are based on a new reporting system, which provides an improved classification and sectorization of the accounts. †Beginning in December 2001, data are based on a new reporting system which provides improved classification and sectorization of the accounts.

Banking Institutions:

Comprises commercial banks, the government-owned Banco del Estado, finance companies, mutual funds and credit unions. † Beginning in January 1976, data are based on an improved classification and sectorization of the accounts. Beginning in January 1979, includes finance companies. † Beginning in December 1997, includes mutual funds. Data are based on a new reporting system which provides an improved sectorization of the accounts. † Beginning in December 2001, includes credit unions. Data are based on a new reporting system which provides improved classification and sectorization of the accounts.

Banking Survey:

† See notes on monetary authorities and banking institutions.

Nonbank Financial Institutions:

Comprises eight pension funds. † Beginning in December 2001, data are based on a new reporting system which provides improved classification and sectorization of the accounts.

Money (National Definitions):

Base Money comprises notes and coins in circulation and deposits of the banking system at the Central Bank of Chile.

M1 comprises notes and coins in circulation outside the banking system, checks issued by the central bank, demand deposits of the private sector in national currency (net of checks to be cleared), other sight deposits of the private sector in national currency, and savings deposits of the private sector in national currency with a maturity of less than 30 days in banking institutions.

M1A comprises M1 plus other sight deposits in commercial banks and finance companies.

M2A comprises M1A plus time deposits of the private sector in commercial banks and finance companies.

M3 comprises M2, foreign currency deposits of the private sector in banking institutions, central bank bills, treasury promissory notes, and letters of credit held by the private sector in banking institutions, mutual funds' shares of the private sector with a maturity longer than one year, and voluntary savings quotas of pension funds, less investment of mutual funds and pension funds in instruments included in M3.

M4 comprises M3 plus central bank bills held by the private sector in commercial banks and finance companies.

M5 comprises M4 plus treasury promissory notes held by the private sector in commercial banks and finance companies.

M6 comprises M5 plus letters of credit held by the private sector in commercial banks and finance companies.

M7 comprises M6 plus foreign currency deposits of the private sector in commercial banks and finance companies.

Interest Rates:

All interest rate data are from source B.

Discount Rate (End of Period):
Rediscount rate charged by the CBC on liquidity loans to banks.

Money Market Rate:
Weighted average overnight rate on loans between financial institutions in national currency.

Savings Rate:
Weighted average rate offered by financial institutions on savings deposits with unconditional withdrawal in national currency. The rate is weighted by deposit amounts.

Deposit Rate:
Weighted average rate offered by banks on 30- to 89-day deposits in national currency.† Beginning in January 1985, weighted average rate offered by financial institutions on 30- to 89-day deposits in national currency. The rate is weighted by deposit amounts. The rate is converted to percent per annum by compounding monthly rates of interest.

Deposit Rate (Foreign Currency):
Weighted average rate offered by financial institutions on 30- to 89-day deposits in foreign currency. The rate is weighted by deposit amounts.

Lending Rate:
Weighted average rate charged by banks on 30- to 89-day loans in national currency. † Beginning in January 1985, weighted average rate charged by financial institutions on 30- to 89-day loans in national currency. The rate is weighted by loan amounts. The rate is converted to an annual percentage by compounding monthly rates of interest.

Lending Rate (Foreign Currency):
Weighted average rate charged by financial institutions on 30- to 89-day loans in foreign currency. The rate is weighted by loan amounts.

Prices, Production, Labor:

Industrial Share Prices:
Index of industrial share prices, base December 1974. † Beginning in January 1978, index of industrial share prices, base December 29, 1978. † Beginning in June 1980, index of industrial share prices, base December 30, 1980, refers to the average of daily quotations.

Wholesale Prices:
Source B. Data are disseminated on the "Indice de Precios al por Mayor" (wholesale price index), a Laspeyres index (weights reference period June 1992), covering the agriculture and livestock, mining, fishing, and manufacturing production sectors. The weights used for the index were established on the basis of the internal absorption or destination side of the 1986 input output matrix.

Consumer Prices:
Source S. Weights Reference Period: December 1998; Geographical Coverage: The Great Santiago Area; Number of Items in Basket: 368; Basis for Calculation: The relevant weights were established on the basis of a survey of family budgets carried out in Greater Santiago from August 1996 to July 1997.

Wages:
Hourly earnings, weights reference period January 2006.

Employment:
Data are derived from the results of the new National Employment Survey, based on the Population and Households Census of 1992.

Manufacturing Production:
Source S. Weights Reference Period: 2000; Sectoral Coverage: entire manufacturing industry; Basis for Calculation: the sample is based on the importance of products and establishments, as determined by gross production value and value added.

Mining Production:
Source S. Weight Reference Period: 1990. The index is based on surveys of Chile's mining establishments, excluding limestone.

International Transactions:

Source B value data on trade, which are derived from customs returns, have been updated with central bank exchange record data for current periods. Value data on *Exports* and *Imports, c.i.f.* are from source B.

Import Prices:
Source B index on wholesale import prices, weights reference period June 1992, compiled by INE.

Government Finance:

Quarterly data are provided by the Ministry of Finance and cover the operations of the consolidated central government. From 1999 through 2004, annual data are as reported for the

Government Finance Statistics Yearbook (GFSY) and cover consolidated central government. † Beginning in 2005, quarterly data are as reported in the GFSM 2001 analytical framework and cover consolidated central government. The fiscal year ends December 31.

National Accounts:

Source B. As indicated by the country, the national accounts are compiled according to the recommendations of the 1993 SNA.

China, P.R.: Mainland 924

The data refer to the People's Republic of China, excluding the Hong Kong Special Administrative Region (HKSAR) and the Macao Special Administrative Region (MSAR). Data on transactions and assets and liabilities vis-à-vis HKSAR and MSAR are treated as international transactions and external positions respectively.

Date of Fund Membership:

December 27, 1945

Standard Sources:

A: State Statistical Bureau, Statistical Yearbook of China
B: People's Bank of China, Zhongguo Jinrong (Chinese Finance)
C: General Administration of Customs, China's Customs Statistics (Quarterly)
D: Ministry of Finance
S: National Bureau of Statistics, Communiques, Monthly Bulletin of Statistics–China

Exchange Rates:

† Beginning January 1, 1994, the People's Bank of China quotes the midpoint rate against the U.S. dollar based on the previous day's prevailing rate in the interbank foreign exchange market. Banks which are licensed to conduct foreign exchange business will quote their transaction rates within the floating margins set by the People's Bank of China. Prior to this date, the official exchange rate of renminbi was adjusted according to movements in the value of a basket of internationally traded currencies.

International Liquidity:

Foreign Exchange (line 1d.d): † Beginning in 1984, data include foreign government securities. † Prior to 1992, Foreign Exchange includes foreign exchange holdings of the Bank of China. Starting in that year, line 1d.d comprises foreign exchange holdings of the People's Bank of China only.
Banking Institutions: Liabilities (line 7b.d) includes specialized banks' borrowings from overseas affiliates, deposits of foreign banks, bonds issued abroad, and loans from foreign governments.

Monetary Authorities:

Comprises the accounts of the People's Bank of China. † Data classification from 1993 onwards has been revised. Claims on Central Government (line 12a) and Central Government Deposits (line 16d) relate to the units of the central government included in the budget. † Prior to 1997, Central Government Deposits (line 16d) also includes some deposits of provincial and local government units. † For the period 1993 to 1996, data on foreign assets are net figures. † Beginning in January 2002, Claims on Other Banking Institutions (line 12f) exclude nonbank financial institutions. Reserve Money (line 14) does not include deposits of the non-central government units.

Banking Institutions:

The data cover the Bank of China, the Agriculture Bank of China, the People's Construction Bank of China, the Industrial and Commercial Bank of China, and the Rural Credit Cooperatives. Beginning in January 2002, other sectors (line 22d: Claims on Other Sectors) exclude nonbank financial institutions. Beginning in January 2004, Postal Savings Bureaus (PSBs) are classified as other depository corporations due to changes in regulations governing PSBs' financial activities. PSBs are not subject to reserve requirements but to a required amount of deposits at the People's Bank of China.

Banking Survey:

Consolidates the accounts of the People's Bank of China and the Banking Institutions. † Data prior to 1985 exclude rural credit cooperatives and the People's Construction Bank of China. Money (line 34) does not include deposits of the non-central government units.

Interest Rates:

Bank Rate (End of Period):
Rate charged by the People's Bank of China on 20-day loans to financial institutions.

Deposit Rate (End of Period):
Interest rates on institutional and individual deposits of one-year maturity.

Lending Rate (End of Period):
† Prior to 1989, rate on working capital loans to state industrial enterprises. Thereafter, rate on working capital loans of one-year maturity.

Prices, Production, Labor:

Producer Prices:
Source S. The series provides changes from the corresponding period of the previous year and is the ex-factory prices of industrial products.

Consumer Prices:
Source S. The series provides changes from the corresponding period of the previous year and covers urban and rural residents.

Industrial Production:
Source S. The series provides changes from the corresponding period of the previous year and is the growth rate of the value added of industry.

International Transactions:

Sources C and S. Trade data are based on customs records. Prior to 1980, the data are provided by the Ministry of Foreign Trade and exclude exports of complete plants in the form of foreign aid. Beginning 1980, data are provided by the General Administration of Customs and are more comprehensive.

Government Finance:

Prior to 1990, data are from source A and represent a consolidation of the central government, provinces, counties, and municipal governments. Revenue includes repayments of loans extended and foreign borrowing, and Expenditure include lending. Beginning in 1990, annual data are from source D. The data cover the budgetary central government. The deficit/surplus does not equal financing due to unavailability of complete financing data on a monthly basis. The fiscal year ends December 31.

National Accounts:

Source A. Constant price estimates are based on index numbers and use data with several base years chained together.

China, P.R.: Hong Kong   532

The data refer to the Hong Kong Special Administrative Region (HKSAR). Data on transactions and assets and liabilities vis-à-vis The Mainland of China are treated as international transactions and external positions respectively.

Standard Sources:

B: Hong Kong Monetary Authority, *Monthly Statistical Bulletin*
S: Census and Statistics Department, Hong Kong, *Hong Kong Monthly Digest of Statistics, Hong Kong Annual Digest of Statistics, Quarterly Report of Gross Domestic Product Estimates, Estimates of Gross Domestic Product 1961–1996*

Exchange Rates:

Market Rate (End of Period and Period Average):
The closing midpoint (average of selling and buying rates) telegraphic transfer rates provided by the Hang Seng Bank Limited.

International Liquidity:

Foreign Exchange (line 1d.d): † Beginning in July 1997, the data include the foreign exchange reserves of the HKSAR Government's Land Fund. † Beginning in November 1998, assets of the Land Fund are placed with the Exchange Fund.

Monetary Authorities:

Comprises the Hong Kong Monetary Authority. † Beginning in January 1999, *Reserve Money (line 14)* also includes Exchange Fund bills and notes. *Currency Outside Banks (line 14a):* Currency issuance corresponds to the amount of noninterest-bearing certificates of indebtedness (CI) that the Hong Kong Monetary Authority issues to three commercial banks as backing for the Hong Kong banknotes that these commercial banks issue. The CIs are issued at a rate of HK$7.8 per U.S. dollar under the exchange rate system established in October 1983 whereby the Hong Kong dollar was officially linked to the U.S. dollar. In the accounts of the banking institutions, banknote liabilities are exactly offset by the CI holdings of the three banks that issue the banknotes. Beginning in November 1998, assets of the HKSAR Government's Land Fund are placed with the Exchange Fund. The Land Fund's foreign exchange assets are included in *Foreign Assets (line 11)*, and its other assets are included in *Other Items (Net) (line 17r)*. The contra-entry to the Land Fund's total assets is included in *Government Deposits (line 16d)*.

Banking Institutions:

Comprises all authorized banking institutions, covering licensed banks, restricted licence banks, and deposit-taking companies.

Foreign Assets (line 21) and *Foreign Liabilities (line 26c):* Data are based on information collected in a separate monthly survey of banking institutions. Because these data are not fully reconcilable with banking institutions' balance sheet accounts in respect of what may be inferred as foreign assets and liabilities, corresponding adjustments are made to the data in order to derive estimates of domestic assets and liabilities within the balance sheet framework.

Interest Rates:

All interest rate data are from source B.

Discount Rate (End of Period):
Exchange Fund's overnight liquidity adjustment facility offer rate.

Money Market Rate:
Midpoint (average of offer and bid rates) overnight closing rates in the interbank money market quoted by the Standard Chartered Bank.

Treasury Bill Rate:
Annualized yields on Exchange Fund bills of 91-day maturity.

Deposit Rate (Period Average):
Rate on average one-month time deposits of ten major banks. Prior to January 1995, data refer to the maximum rates paid by licensed banks under the interest rate rules of the Hong Kong Association of Banks.

Lending Rate:
Rate quoted by the Hongkong and Shanghai Banking Corporation Limited.

Prices, Production, Labor:

Share Prices:
Source B, base July 31, 1964. † Beginning in 1996, monthly data refer to simple averages of daily values of closing Hang Seng indices. Quarterly and annual data are simple averages of the monthly data. Prior to 1996, data refer to simple averages of daily values of closing Hang Seng indices over the reference period. The constituent stocks of the Hang Seng index are 33 stocks representative of the market. The aggregate market value of these stocks accounts for 75 percent of the total market capitalization on the Stock Exchange of Hong Kong Limited.

Producer Prices:
Source S, weights reference period: annually re-weighted and chained; Laspeyres index which measures the changes in producer prices of manufactured goods. The index covers the more important products identified from the Annual Survey of Industrial Production, and the data are obtained from the Quarterly Survey of Industrial Production. The survey sample covers about 1700 establishments.

Consumer Prices:
Source S. Weights reference period: 2004–2005; Geographical Coverage: The whole HKSAR territory; Number of Items in Basket: 984; Basis for Calculation: The weights are derived from the expenditure patterns of households collected from the Household Expenditure Survey, and the indices are re-based and the weights revised every five years.

Wages: Average Earnings (Manufacturing):
Source S index, weights reference period: first quarter 1999. Payroll per person. Payroll covers wages and salaries, bonuses

and gratuities, commissions, and cash payments in other forms paid directly to employees for normal work time and overtime.

Wage Rates (Manufacturing):
Source S index, weights reference period: September 1992. Data are based on the Labor Earnings Survey and refer to nominal wage indices for September of each year. Data cover a similar range of remuneration as the payroll per person index but only for normal work time.

Manufacturing Production:
Source S. Weights reference period: weights are annually re-weighted; Sectoral Coverage: all manufacturing industries; Basis for Calculation: sales data are used as weights for aggregating production indices at product level into indices at industry level.

International Transactions:

All trade data are from source S. Trade statistics refer to movements of merchandise between the HKSAR and its trading partners, by land, air, ocean, and to a limited extent, post. Imports are c.i.f. values, whereas exports are f.o.b. values. Value index, unit value index, and quantum index. Weights reference period: 2000.

National Accounts:

As indicated by the authorities, concepts and definitions are in accordance with the *1993 SNA*.

China, P.R.: Macao   546

The data refer to the Macao Special Administrative Region (MSAR). Data on transactions and assets and liabilities vis-à-vis the Mainland of China are treated as international transactions and external positions, respectively.

Standard Sources:

B: Monetary Authority of Macao, *Monthly Bulletin of Monetary Statistics*
S: Statistics and Census Service of Macao, *Monthy Bulletin of Statistics, Yearbook of Statistics, Employment Survey, Manpower Needs and Wages Survey, Revised Estimates of Gross Domestic Product 1982–89, External Trade Statistics*
F: Revenue Bureau of Macao, *Monthly Bulletin of Public Finance*

Exchange Rates:

Market Rate (End of Period and Period Average):
The midpoint rate of the average buying and selling rates quoted by Reuters and fixed at 9:00 a.m. each day.

International Liquidity:

Foreign Exchange (line 1d.d) includes the claims on banks abroad, financial investments abroad, and other foreign exchange reserves of the Monetary Authority of Macao (AMCM) but does not include the foreign assets of the Reserve Fund, which are considered not to be readily available for use by the AMCM for balance of payments purposes.

Monetary Authorities:

Comprises the Monetary Authority of Macao. *Foreign Assets (line 11)* includes the foreign assets of the Reserve Fund (formerly the Land Fund created in 1987). The Reserve Fund is owned by the MSAR government, but management of the Fund was entrusted to the AMCM in April 2000. *Currency Outside Banks (line 14a):* Currency issuance reflects the amount of non-interest bearing certificates of indebtedness (CIs) that the AMCM issues to two note-issuing commercial banks as backing for the pataca (P) notes that these commercial banks issue. The CIs are issued at a rate of P 1.03 per Hong Kong dollar under the exchange rate mechanism whereby the pataca is officially linked to the the Hong Kong dollar.

Banking Institutions:

Comprises all authorized banking institutions and the postal savings bank. † From January 1998 onward, all banking institutions in Macao SAR fully apply the residency criterion in classifying their deposits and credit provided to customers. Prior to January 1998, two banks did not fully apply the residency criterion. Also prior to June 2001, claims on nonfinancial public enterprises were included in *Claims on Other Sectors (line 22d)*.

Money (National Definitions):

M1 comprises currency in circulation, banking institutions, and demand deposits of resident non-central government sectors with banking institutions.
M2 comprises M1 plus the savings, notice, time, and certificates of deposits of resident non-central government sectors with banking institutions.

Interest Rates:

All interest rate data are from source B.

Interbank Rate:
The end-of-period one-month MAIBOR, the Macao Interbank Offered Rates.

Deposit Rate:
Weighted average rate quoted by three major banks on three-month deposits; the weights are the shares of each bank in the volume of deposits.

Lending Rate:
Weighted average rate quoted by three major banks on loans; the weights are the shares of each bank in the volume of loans.

Prices and Labor:

Consumer Prices:
Source S. Weights Reference Period: July 2004-June 2005; Geographical Coverage: whole national territory; Number of Items in Basket: 661; Basis for Calculation: weights are derived from the 2002–2003 Household Budget Survey.

International Transactions:

All trade data are from source S. The trade statistics are based on information given by the importers and exporters in the trade licenses and declarations.

Government Finance:

Annual data are as reported for the *Government Finance Statistics Yearbook (GFSY)* and cover Macao SAR consolidated general government. † Beginning in 2003, quarterly data are as reported in the *GFSM 2001* analytical framework and cover consolidated general government. The fiscal year ends December 31.

National Accounts:
Source S.

Colombia 233

Date of Fund Membership:
December 27, 1945

Standard Sources:
B: Bank of the Republic, *Monthly Review*
S: National Department of Statistics, *Monthly Bulletin*

Exchange Rates:
The exchange rate was operated as a managed float within an intervention band. On September 25, 1999 the crawling band was abandoned and the peso was allowed to float independently.

International Liquidity:
Monetary Authorities: Other Assets (line 3..d) comprises contributions to nonmonetary international organizations and net bilateral payments agreements assets.
Data for *lines .3..d, .4..d, .7a.d, .7b.d,* and *.7f.d* are converted from pesos to U.S. dollars at a booking rate different from exchange rate **ae.**

Monetary Authorities:
Comprises the Bank of the Republic (BR) only. † Beginning in January 1978, the financial funds (for the financing of agriculture, industry, housing, etc.) are considered as part of the Bank of the Republic in the treatment of the accounts of these funds with commercial and specialized banks. † Beginning in January 1989, data reflect the introduction of a new system of accounts, which provides an improved sectorization of the accounts. † Beginning in December 2001, data are based on a new reporting system which provides improved classification and sectorization of the accounts.

Banking Institutions:
Comprises commercial banks and savings and housing corporations (CAVS). † Beginning in December 1974, includes finance corporations and Financiera Energética Nacional (FEN). † Beginning in January 1978, data exclude the accounts of the Agricultural Bank (Caja de Crédito Agrario, Industrial y Minero). See note on monetary authorities regarding the treatment of financial funds. † Beginning in December 1990, includes the Agricultural Bank, Social Savings Bank, commercial financing companies, and financial cooperatives. Data reflect the introduction of a new system of accounts, which provides an improved sectorization of the accounts. Beginning in December 1991, includes the Banco de Comercio Exterior (BANCOLDEX), and Financiera de Desarrollo Territorial (FINDETER). Beginning in December 1994, includes the Central Mortgage Bank. † Beginning in December 2001, includes a specialized cooperative (COOPCENTRAL). Data are based on a new reporting system, which provides improved classification and sectorization of the accounts. Beginning in March 2002, excludes CAVS.

Monetary Survey:
† See notes on monetary authorities and deposit money banks.

Nonbank Financial Institutions:
Comprises Instituto de Fomento Industrial (IFI) and the Fondo para el Financiamiento del Sector Agropecuario (FINAGRO). Beginning in October 1993, includes the Fondo Nacional de Desarrollo (FONADE). Beginning in November 1998, includes the Fondo de Garantías de Instituciones Financieras (FOGAFIN). Beginning in January 2002, includes the Instituto Colombiano de Crédito Educativo y Estudios Técnicos en el Exterior (ICETEX). Beginning in December 2004, includes Fondo Nacional del Ahorro (FNA), Fondo de Garantías de Entidades Cooperativas, and the Fondo Nacional de Garantías (FNG) Beginning in January 2005, excludes Instituto de Fomento Industrial (IFI).

Banking Survey:
† See notes on monetary authorities and banking institutions.

Money (National Definitions):
Reserve Money comprises notes and coins issued and deposits of financial intermediaries and special entities in the BR. The deposits of special entities correspond to deposits of FEN, BANCOLDEX, FINAGRO, FINDETER, FOGAFIN, and BR employees.
M1 comprises notes and coins in circulation outside the banking system and demand deposits. Demand deposits include deposits of the private sector, of central, state, and municipal governments, of decentralized agencies, and of nonfinancial public enterprises.
M2 comprises M1 plus savings deposits and certificates of time deposits of the central, state, and municipal governments, decentralized agencies, public nonfinancial corporations, and private sector with banking institutions.
M3 comprises M2 plus fiduciary deposits, other sight deposits of the central, state, and municipal governments, decentralized agencies, public nonfinancial corporations, and private sector with other depository corporations, mortgage certificates issued by the Central Mortgage Bank held by the public, and bonds in circulation issued by banking institutions. Other sight deposits include guaranteed and tax deposits, cashier's, certified, and traveler's checks, and canceled accounts.

Interest Rates:
All interest rate data are from source B.
Discount Rate (End of Period):
Rate charged by the BR on loans to commercial banks. † Beginning in September 1986, corresponds to DTF (see note for deposit rate) plus two points. Beginning in October 1990, corresponds to DTF plus eight points. Beginning in June 1992, corresponds to DTF plus seven points. Beginning in December 1999, corresponds to DTF plus five points. Beginning in September 2001, corresponds to the Lombard rate plus one point. The Lombard rate is the maximum rate charged by the BR to provide liquidity to financial institutions.
Money Market Rate:
Weighted average rate on loans between financial institutions. The rate is weighted by loan amounts.

Deposit Rate:

Fixed-term deposits (DTF): Weighted average rate paid by banking institutions on 90-day certificates of deposit. The rate is weighted by deposit amounts.

Lending Rate:

Weighted average rate charged by banking institutions on loans. The rate is weighted by loan amounts. † Beginning in May 1999, weighted average rate charged by banking institutions on commercial, ordinary, and short-term (tesorería) and long-term preferential loans. The rate is weighted by loan amounts and, owing to the revolving nature of the short-term preferential loans, their weight was established as one fifth of the daily disbursement.

Prices, Production, Labor:

Source S.

Share Prices:

Index of prices on the Bogotá Stock Exchange, base, March 15, 1976. † Beginning in January 1991, index of prices on the Bogotá Stock Exchange, base January 2, 1991. † Beginning in July 2001, general share price index on the Colombia Stock Exchange, base July 3, 2001.

Producer Prices:

Source B index, fixed-weight Laspeyres index (June 1999=100). The PPI covers 76 percent of domestically produced goods and 24 percent of imports. The index is based on the prices of 730 goods traded in the wholesale market, and classified by origin; 460 goods are locally produced and 270 are imported. The PPI is calculated on the basis of 6,900 quotes for the various articles it comprises. Prices are obtained every month from a survey of a sample of 2,200 reporting entities. It covers 18 cities in which the Banco de la República has branches. Basic information for calculating the weights was obtained from the national accounts reported by Departamento Administrativo Nacional de Estadísticas (DANE) for 1994, and from the Annual Manufacturing Survey and the Foreign Trade Yearbooks. The Index weights are fixed, and at the beginning of 1999 have been revised on the basis of the 1994 national accounts compiled by DANE.

Consumer Prices:

Source S index, weights reference period December 1998. The index covers prices of a basket of 176 items (so-called basic expenditure) purchased by individual households located in the urban areas, which include the country's 13 largest cities, namely, Bogotá, Medellín, Cali, Barranquilla, Bucaramanga, Manizales, Pasto, Pereira, Cartagena, Neiva, Montería, Cúcuta, and Villavicencio (the data exclude the population of rural areas). The weights were last revised in 1998, with data from the 1994–95 Income and Expenditure Survey.

Manufacturing Production:

Source S. Weights Reference Period: 1990; Sectoral Coverage: the manufacturing sector; Basis for Calculation: the index measures output and sales values and is presented in nominal and real terms.

Crude Petroleum Production:

Source B data (in thousands of barrels). Data for January 1996 onwards are based on production quantities as reported in the *Oil Market Intelligence*.

Employment:

Prior to 2001, the National Household Survey covered the seven principal cities of the country. From 2001 onward, the survey includes the 12 main cities.

International Transactions:

Total *Exports* and *Imports* in U.S. dollars are from source S. Current data on *Exports* and *Imports f. o. b.* are transmitted by the Bank of the Republic and are based on preliminary registration figures of the Colombian External Trade Institute (INCOMEX). *Coffee* exports in U.S. dollars are from source B (table 5.2.2), as compiled by the National Federation of Colombian Coffeegrowers.

Volume of Exports for *Coffee* are based on source B (table 5.2.2) data in physical quantities.

Export and Import Prices:

Data refer to source B indices of wholesale/producer prices of export goods and of import goods, respectively. The coffee export price index refers to the source B New York price quotation, as reported by the National Federation of Colombian Coffeegrowers.

Government Finance:

Data are derived from source B. Data cover budgetary central government and exclude the transactions of the decentralized agencies and the social security institutes. Revenue data include the repayments of loans granted to entities that do not form part of the nonfinancial public sector, and financing data include privatization receipts. The fiscal year ends December 31.

National Accounts:

Beginning in 1970, data are compiled by the National Department of Statistics (DANE). As indicated by the country, beginning in 1994, data are compiled according to the *1993 SNA*.

Comoros   632

Date of Fund Membership:
September 21, 1976

Standard Source:
A: Banque Centrale des Comores, *Rapport Annuel (Annual Report)*

Exchange Rates:

Official Rate: (End of Period and Period Average):
Prior to January 1999, the official rate was pegged to the French franc. On January 12, 1994, the Comorian franc was devalued to CF 75 per French franc from CF 50 at which it had been fixed since 1948. From January 1, 1999, the CFAF is pegged to the euro at a rate of CFA franc 491.9677 per euro.

International Liquidity:

Data expressed in U.S. dollars on *Foreign Exchange (line 1d.d)* and *Gold (line 1and)* are derived from data denominated in national currency from components of the monetary authorities' *Foreign Assets (line 11)*, using the end-of-period market rate (*line* **ae**).

Monetary Authorities:

Data cover the Central Bank's accounts and certain accounts of the Treasury related to its monetary authority functions. † Beginning in 1998, data are based on an improved reporting and classification of accounts.

Deposit Money Banks:

Comprises the Banque pour l'industrie et le commerce-Comores. † Beginning in 1998, data are based on an improved reporting and classification of accounts.

Monetary Survey:

† Beginning in 1998, data are based on an improved reporting and classification of accounts.

Other Banking Institutions:

Data cover the Banque de Developpement des Comores and the Caisse Nationale d'Epargne. † Beginning in 1998, data are based on an improved reporting and classification of accounts.

Banking Survey:

† Beginning in 1998, data are based on an improved reporting and classification of accounts.

Interest Rates:

Discount Rate (End of Period):
Rediscount rate charged by the Banque Centrale des Comores (BCC) and set at the Euro Overnight Index Average + 1.5 percent.

Deposit Rate:
Rate offered on saving passbooks.

Lending Rate:
Commercial bank lending rates are regulated by the BCC in the form of a minimum and a maximum rate. Data provided is a simple average of the minimum and maximum rates.

International Transactions:

All trade data are from source A. Based on customs records.

Government Finance:

Annual data are as reported for the *Government Finance Statistics Yearbook (GFSY)* and cover the central government. The fiscal year ends December 31.

Congo, Democratic Republic of   636

Date of Fund Membership:
September 28, 1963

Standard Sources:

A: Central Bank of Congo, *Annual Report*
B: Central Bank of Congo, *Quarterly Bulletin*
S: National Office of Research and Development, *Quarterly Bulletin of General Statistics*

Exchange Rates:

On July 1, 1998 the Congo franc, equal to 100,000 new zaïres, was introduced. On October 22, 1993 the new zaïre, equal to three million old zaïres, was introduced.

Official Rate: (End of Period and Period Average):
The market rate is freely determined in the interbank foreign exchange market. Beginning in December 2003, data refer to the official exchange rate as set by the Central Bank of Congo.

International Liquidity:

Line 1and is equal to *line 1ad,* converted into U.S. dollars at the dollar price of gold used by national sources, as reported to *IFS.*

Monetary Authorities:

Comprises the Bank of Zaïre and the monetary authority functions of the Treasury. Prepayments for exchange are required to be made at commercial banks for the full c.i.f. value of imports when the banks open letters of credit abroad on behalf of importers. Import deposits are required to be made at commercial banks for 40 percent of the c.i.f. value of goods when applications for import licenses are presented. Both forms of import prepayments absorb liquidity. Prepayments for exchange at the Bank of Zaïre include outstanding external payment arrears.

Deposit Money Banks:

Consolidates the following banks: Banque Commerciale Zaïroise, Union Zaïroise de Banques, Banque du Peuple, Barclays Bank-Zaïre, Banque de Paris et des Pays-Bas, Banque Internationale pour l'Afrique au Zaïre, Banque de Kinshasa, First National City Bank-Zaïre, Banque Grindlay International au Zaïre, and Banque de Credit Agricole.

Monetary Survey:

In the monetary survey (see Introduction for the standard method of calculation), *line 34* includes *Post Office Checking Deposits (line 24..i)* with the contra-entry in *line 32an.*

Interest Rates:

Discount Rate (End of Period):
Data are as reported to *IFS.*

Deposit Rate:
Simple average rate offered by commercial banks on time deposits of one to three months.

Lending Rate:
Simple average rate charged by commercial banks on short-term loans.

Prices:

All data are from source B.

Consumer Prices:
The index, weights reference period August 1995, covers all income groups in Kinshasa.

International Transactions:

Trade data are on a payments basis. As of January 1984, all trade data are reported in SDRs and converted into U.S. dollars by *IFS* using the average exchange rate.

Balance of Payments:
Data refer to the first half rather than to the second quarter of the year.

Government Finance:

Annual data are as reported for the *Government Finance Statistics Yearbook (GFSY)* and cover budgetary central government. The fiscal year ends December 31.

National Accounts:

Source B. *Line 99e* includes a statistical discrepancy.

Congo, Republic of   634

Date of Fund Membership:
July 10, 1963

Standard Source:
B: Banque des Etats d'Afrique Centrale (BEAC) (Bank of the Central African States), *Etudes et Statistiques (Studies and Statistics)*

Exchange Rates:
Official Rate: (End of Period and Period Average):
Prior to January 1999, the official rate was pegged to the French franc. On January 12, 1994, the CFA franc was devalued to CFAF 100 per French franc from CFAF 50 at which it had been fixed since 1948. From January 1, 1999, the CFAF is pegged to the euro at a rate of CFA franc 655.957 per euro.

International Liquidity:
Gold (National Valuation) (line 1and) is obtained by converting the value in national currency, as reported in the country's standard sources, using the prevailing exchange rate, as given in *line* **ae**. Prior to January 1999, the national currency/dollar conversion rates utilized for balance sheet purposes are used. These conversion rates differ from the prevailing exchange rates reported in *IFS*. This line follows the national valuation procedure which corresponds to that of the Bank of France (*cf* the international liquidity note on the *IFS* page for France).

Monetary Authorities:
Comprises the national branch of the Bank of the Central African States only. Claims on central government include assumption of certain nonperforming bank loans.

Deposit Money Banks:
Comprises active commercial banks. Claims and deposits of nonactive banks or banks in the process of liquidation are excluded. The counterpart of government assumption of certain nonperforming bank loans is reclassified to capital accounts.

Interest Rates:
Discount Rate (End of Period):
Basic rediscount rate offered by the BEAC. † Beginning July 1994, rate charged by the BEAC to financial institutions on refinancing operations.

Deposit Rate:
Minimum rate offered by deposit money banks on savings accounts.

Lending Rate:
Maximum rate charged by deposit money banks on all loans, excluding charges and fees.

Prices and Production:
All data on prices are from source B.

Consumer Prices:
Data refer to the consumer price index for African families in Brazzaville (weights reference period: December 1977) and the second largest city of Pointe Noire (weights reference period: December 1997 for Brazzaville and 1989 for Pointe-Noir).

Crude Petroleum Production:
Data refer to the volume of production in thousand metric tons.

International Transactions:
All trade data are from source B.

Value of Exports and Imports:
Bunkers and ship's stores are included. Data exclude imports from other countries of the Union douanière et économique de l'Afrique centrale (UDEAC) (Central African Customs Union). *Imports* are adjusted to include diamond imports as derived from diamond exports minus 10 percent for diamond handling. *Imports, f.o.b.* are calculated from *Imports, c.i.f.* by applying a freight and insurance factor estimated for *IFS*.

Government Finance:
Annual data are as reported for the *Government Finance Statistics Yearbook* and cover the consolidated central government. The fiscal year ends December 31.

National Accounts:
Source B.

Costa Rica   238

Date of Fund Membership:
January 8, 1946

Standard Source:
B: Central Bank, *Statistical Bulletin, National Accounts of Costa Rica*

Exchange Rates:
Market Rate (End of Period and Period Average):
A system of managed floating is in effect. For the purpose of calculating the real effective exchange rate index (*line* **rec**), the wholesale price index is used (*line 63*).

International Liquidity:
Gold (National Valuation) (line 1and) is obtained by converting the value in national currency terms, as reported in the country's standard sources, using the prevailing exchange rate, as given in *line* **de**, *line* **ae**, or *line* **we**. This line follows national valuation procedures, which revalue gold monthly at the price of gold in London on the last day of each month.

Monetary Authorities:
Comprises the Central Bank of Costa Rica (CBCR) only. † Beginning in December 1997, data are based on an improved sectorization of the accounts.

Deposit Money Banks:
Comprises commercial banks and a mortgage bank. Beginning in December 1999, includes finance companies, savings and credit cooperatives, and savings and loans associations.

Monetary Survey:
† See note on monetary authorities.

Other Banking Institutions:
Comprises a mortgage bank, the cooperative development, mortgage, and rural credit departments of the National Bank of Costa

Rica, and the mortgage departments of two other commercial banks. Beginning in September 1995, these institutions were classified as deposit money banks.

Money (National Definitions):

Base Money comprises currency in circulation and reserve deposits and correspondent accounts of commercial banks in national currency with the CBCR. Currency in circulation refers to notes and coins issued by the CBCR.

M1 comprises currency in circulation and transferable deposits. Currency in circulation refers to notes and coins issued by the CBCR less the amount held by commercial banks. Transferable deposits refer to current account deposits in national currency of nonbank financial institutions, state and local governments, public nonfinancial corporations, and private sector with commercial banks.

M2 comprises M1 and quasi-money in national currency. Quasi-money refers to fixed, savings, and overdue deposits; certificates of deposit; certified checks; and deposits in litigation of nonbank financial institutions, state and local governments, public nonfinancial corporations, and private sector with commercial banks; and securities other than shares issued by commercial banks and the CBCR held by nonbank financial institutions, state and local governments, public nonfinancial corporations, and private sector.

M3 comprises M2 and quasi-money in foreign currency. Quasi-money refers to demand, fixed, savings, and overdue deposits; certificates of deposit; certified checks; and deposits in litigation of state and local governments, public nonfinancial corporations, and private sector with commercial banks and the CBCR; and securities other than shares issued by commercial banks and the CBCR held by nonbank financial institutions, state and local governments, public nonfinancial corporations, and private sector.

Interest Rates:

Discount Rate (End of Period):
Rediscount rate offered by the Central Bank of Costa Rica to state-owned commercial banks.

Deposit Rate:
Rate offered by state-owned commercial banks on one-month time deposits. Data refer to a simple arithmetic average of the rates reported by each of the four state-owned commercial banks.

Lending Rate:
Rate charged by state-owned commercial banks on loans to the agricultural sector. Data refer to a simple arithmetic average of the rates reported by each of the four state-owned commercial banks.

Prices and Labor:

Producer Prices:
Source B, modified Laspeyres index, reference period December 1999=100. Weights were derived from a 1997 industrial survey. Index covers manufacturing industry with production for domestic market.

Consumer Prices:
Source B. Weights Reference Period: November 1987-November 1988; Geographical Coverage: the first four sub-regions of the central region of Costa Rica; Number of Items in Basket: 264; Basis for Calculation: the weights are derived from the National Household Income and Expenditure Survey.

International Transactions:

Exports and Imports:
Source B data, compiled by the Directorate General of Statistics and Census in U.S. dollars.

Balance of Payments:
The entries shown in the columns for the second and fourth quarters correspond to data for the first half and the second half of each year, respectively.

Government Finance:

Monthly, quarterly, and annual data are as reported by source B and are derived from the cash flow of the Directorate of the National Treasury in the Ministry of Finance. Data cover operations of the central administration (budgetary accounts and special Treasury accounts). The central administration does not receive grants in cash and does not engage in lending minus repayments operations. Data do not cover operations of the Costa Rican Social Security Fund or of any other central government units with individual budgets. Domestic and foreign debt data have the same coverage as the cash flow data of the Directorate of the National Treasury and are derived from the *Balance de la Hacienda Pública* of the Directorate of National Accounting in the Ministry of Finance. † From 1987 onwards, monthly and quarterly data were revised to have the same presentation as the Treasury cash flow. † Beginning in 2003, annual data are as reported for the *Government Finance Statistics Yearbook (GFSY)* and cover budgetary central government. † Beginning in January 2006, data are as reported in the *GFSM 2001* analytical framework and cover budgetary central government. The fiscal year ends December 31.

National Accounts:

Source B. Beginning in 1991, data are compiled according to the *1993 SNA*, as indicated by the country.

Côte d'Ivoire   662

Date of Fund Membership:
March 11, 1963

Standard Source:

B: Banque Centrale des Etats de l'Afrique de l'Ouest (Central Bank of West African States), *Notes d'information et Statistiques (Informative Notes and Statistics)*

Côte d'Ivoire is a member of the West African Economic and Monetary Union, together with Benin, Burkina Faso, Guinea-Bissau, Mali, Niger, Senegal, and Togo. The Union, which was established in 1962, has a common central bank, the Central Bank of West African States (BCEAO), with headquarters in Dakar, and national branches in the member states. Mali and Guinea-Bissau joined the Union on June 1, 1984 and May 2, 1997, respectively.

Exchange Rates:

Official Rate: (End of Period and Period Average):
Prior to January 1999, the official rate was pegged to the French franc. On January 12, 1994, the CFA franc was devalued to CFAF 100 per French franc from CFAF 50 at which it had been fixed since 1948. From January 1, 1999, the CFAF is pegged to the euro at a rate of CFA franc 655.957 per euro.

International Liquidity:

Gold is revalued on a quarterly basis at the rate communicated by the BCEAO, which corresponds to the lowest average fixing in the London market.

Monetary Authorities:

Comprises the national branch of the BCEAO only. The amount of currency outside banks is estimated by subtracting from the amount of CFA franc notes issued by Côte d'Ivoire the estimated amounts of Côte d'Ivoire's currency in the cash held by the banks of all member countries of the Union.

Deposit Money Banks:

Comprises commercial banks and specialized development banks, and includes certain banking operations of the Treasury and the Post Office. The Treasury accepts customs duty bills (reported separately in *line 22d.i*). Through its many branches, the Postal Checking System acts as the main depository for the private sector in the interior of Côte d'Ivoire. *Claims on the Private Sector (line 22d)* include doubtful and litigious debts. † Beginning in 1979, *Central Government Deposits (line 26d)* include the deposits of the public establishments of an administrative or social nature (EPAS) and exclude those of the savings bank; *Demand and Time Deposits (lines 24 and 25)* include deposits of the savings bank and exclude deposits of EPAS; and *Claims on Private Sector (line 22d)* exclude claims on other financial institutions.

Monetary Survey:

The data reported agree with source B aggregates, as given in the table on the position of the monetary institutions, except for *line 31n,* for which source B treats long-term foreign liabilities and SDR allocations as a foreign liability, whereas *IFS* reports the former separately and includes the latter in *line 37r.* Moreover, valuation differences exist as a result of the *IFS* calculations of reserve position in the Fund and the SDR holdings, both components of *line 11,* based on Fund record. † Beginning in 1979, *Claims on Other Financial Institutions (line 32f)* includes claims of deposit money banks on other financial institutions; see deposit money bank notes for explanation of other break symbols.

Other Banking Institutions:

Liquid Liabilities (line 55l): † See notes on deposit money banks and monetary survey.

Interest Rates:

Bank Rate (End of Period):
Rate on repurchase agreements between the BCEAO and the banks. † Prior to October 1, 1993 data refer to basic discount rate offered by the BCEAO.

Money Market Rate:
Rate paid on overnight interbank advances.

Deposit Rate:
Rate offered by banks on time deposits of CFAF 500,000–2,000,000 for under six months.

Prices, Production, Labor:

Consumer Prices:
Source B. Weights Reference Period: 1996; Geographical Coverage: Abidjan area; Number of Items in Basket: 392; Basis for Calculation: The weights come from a household budget survey conducted in Abidjan in 1996.

Industrial Production:
Source B, Laspeyres type index, weights reference 1984 Q4–1985 Q3. The index covers mining, manufacturing, and energy; sectors are weighted by their share of total value added at factor cost of 1985.

International Transactions:

All data are from source B.

Government Finance:

Annual data are as reported for the *Government Finance Statistics Yearbook* and cover the budgetary central government. The fiscal year ends December 31.

National Accounts:

Source B.

Croatia   960

Date of Fund Membership:

December 14, 1992

Standard Sources:

B: Croatian National Bank, *Bulletin* (monthly)
S: Statistics Office of the Republic of Croatia, *Monthly Bulletin*

Exchange Rates:

Market Rate (End of Period and Period Average):
The midpoint rate announced by the Croatian National Bank based on the results of the interbank foreign exchange auctions. From December 23, 1991 to May 30, 1994, the Croatian dinar was the official currency of Croatia. On May 30, 1994 the kuna, equal to 1000 dinars, was introduced.

Monetary Authorities:

Comprises the Croatian National Bank.
Claims on Central Government (line 12a) comprise claims on central government budgetary units and central government funds; they also include claims arising from the assumption by the government of certain liabilities of the central bank of the Former Socialist Federal Republic of Yugoslavia to the Croatian National Bank.
Central Government Deposits (line 16d) comprise deposits of the central government budgetary units and central government funds.
Claims on Other Financial Institutions (line 12g) and *Liabilities to Other Financial Institutions (line 16j)* include positions with th housing savings banks, investment funds, and savings and loan cooperatives.

† Beginning in December 2001, data are based on an improved sectoral and instrument classification of accounts.

Banking Institutions:

Comprises banks licensed by CNB in accordance with the *Banking Act* and banks in liquidation proceedings; beginning in July 1999, the coverage includes savings banks. *Claims on Other Financial Institutions (line 22g)* and *Liabilities to Other Financial Institutions (line 26j)* include positions with the housing savings banks, the investment funds, and the savings and loan cooperatives. *Claims on Central Government (line 22a)* comprise claims on central government budgetary units and central government funds; they also include claims arising from the assumption by the government of certain liabilities of the central bank of the Former Socialist Federal Republic of Yugoslavia to Croatian banks. *Central Government Deposits (line 26d)* comprise deposits of the central government budgetary units and central government funds. † Beginning in December 2001, data are based on an improved sectoral and instrument classification of accounts.

Banking Survey:

See notes on monetary authorities and banking institutions.

Money (National Definitions):

Reserve Money comprises currency in circulation, licensed banks' deposits at the CNB, and deposits of housing savings banks, savings and loan cooperatives, investment funds, and other resident non-central government sectors. Currency in circulation refers to currency and coins issued by CNB.

M1 comprises currency outside licensed banks, and transferable deposits in national currency of housing savings banks, investment funds, savings and loan cooperatives and other resident non-central government sectors at the central bank and licensed banks.

M4 (broad money) comprises *M1*, savings, time, and foreign currency deposits of housing savings banks, investment funds, savings and loan cooperatives and other resident non-central government sectors, and bonds and money market instruments in national and foreign currency issued by licensed banks and held by other resident non-central government sectors.

Interest Rates:

Discount Rate (End of Period):
Basic rate at which the Croatian National Bank lends to the commercial banks.

Money Market Rate:
Short-term rate determined on the Zagreb Money Market.

Deposit Rate:
Average rate offered by commercial banks on deposits weighted by volume of new deposits received during the last reporting month.

Lending Rate:
Average rate charged by commercial banks on credits weighted by volume of new credits granted during the last reporting month. † Beginning in January 2002, rates on interbank loans and loans to the central government which carry lower interest rates, are ex-

cluded. Thus, the average rate has increased reflecting mainly rates on balances' overdrafts for households and enterprises.

Prices, Production, Labor:

Share Prices:
CROBEX share price index of Zagreb Stock Exchange (base July 1, 1997=100).

Wholesale Prices:
Source S. Based on a basket of industrial products, base 1995 = 100.

Consumer Prices:
Source S. Weights Reference Period: 2001; Geographical Coverage: Whole territory of the Republic of Croatia; Number of Items in Basket: 540; Basis for Calculation: Weights are based on the 2001 Household Budget Survey and are updated at approximately five-yearly intervals.

Industrial Production:
Source S. Weights Reference Period: 1995; Sectoral Coverage: mining and quarrying, manufacturing and electricity, gas and water supply sectors; Basis for Calculation: weights are calculated as the value added for units of production.

Wages and Employment:
Source S. Data are based on a regular monthly sample of 70 percent of all employees, including the self-employed. Annual data represent averages of the monthly data. Prior to 1996, data did not include private farmers and employed persons at the Ministry of Internal Affairs and Ministry of Defense. Since 1996, these areas and estimates of employees in small businesses (up to 10 employed persons) have been included.

International Transactions:

Source S data on *Exports and Imports, c.i.f.* are provisional customs statistics pending improvements in the management of customs declarations. Beginning in 1992, the data include foreign trade with countries of the Former Socialist Federal Republic of Yugoslavia.

Government Finance:

Monthly and quarterly data are as reported by the Ministry of Finance and cover budgetary central government. Annual data are obtained by aggregating of quarterly data. † Prior to January 2004, to the extent possible, existing subannual IFS data were converted to the main aggregates that are presented in the *GFSM 2001* Statement of Sources and Uses of Cash (see the Introduction of the monthly *IFS* publication for details). Beginning in January 2004, monthly data are as reported in the *GFSM 2001* analytical framework and cover budgetary central government. The fiscal year ends December 31.

National Accounts:

As indicated by the country, data are in accordance with the *ESA 95*. Beginning in 1995, data are sourced from the Eurostat database. Eurostat introduced chain-linked GDP volume measures to both annual and quarterly data. Chain-linked GDP volume measures are expressed in the prices of the previous year and re-referenced to 1995.

Cyprus 423

Date of Fund Membership:
December 21, 1961

Standard Sources:
A: Central Bank, *Annual Report*
B: Central Bank, *Bulletin*
S: Statistics and Research Department, *Monthly Economic Indicators, Cyprus Imports and Exports Statistics*

Exchange Rates:
Official Rate: (End of Period and Period Average):
Central bank midpoint rate. The exchange rate is adjusted daily.

International Liquidity:
Line 1d.d includes Treasury foreign exchange.
Gold (National Valuation) (line 1and) is obtained by converting the value in national currency terms, as reported in the country's standard sources, using the prevailing exchange rate, as given in *line* **dg** or *line* **ag**.

Monetary Authorities:
Consolidates Central Bank of Cyprus and monetary authority functions undertaken by the central government. The contra-entry to Treasury IMF accounts and government foreign assets is included in *line 16d*. † Beginning in 1988, data reflect improved classification in the report forms.

Deposit Money Banks:
† Beginning in 1988, data reflect improved classification in the report forms.
Prior to January 2002, comprises commercial banks and the Co-operative Central Bank which channel the excess liquidity of village cooperative societies to other societies. They also carry on normal commercial banking functions with the community at large. In the former capacity they facilitate the flow of loan-able funds within the agricultural sector, including its light service industries. In the second function they serve as brokers for the flow of liquidity between the agricultural sector and the rest of the community, including the placement of government loans. The deposit money bank accounts specifically exclude other financial institutions which do not accept transferable demand deposits. † Beginning in January 2002, data also include specialized credit institutions, which are classified under deposit money banks in accordance with the framework of the European Central Bank.

Monetary Survey:
† Beginning in 1988, data reflect improved classification in the report forms.

Other Banking Institutions:
† Prior to 1988, only specialized credit institutions were included. From 1988 to December 2001, comprises specialized credit institutions, co-operative credit institutions, and international banking units. † Beginning in January 2002, data exclude specialized credit institutions, which are reclassified under deposit money banks in accordance with the framework of the European Central Bank.

Interest Rates:
All interest rate data are from source B.
Discount Rate (End of Period):
Prior to 1996, data refer to the rate charged by the Central Bank of Cyprus for the discount of treasury bills. † Beginning in January 1996, data refer to marginal lending rate charged by the Central Bank of Cyprus for its overnight facility with collateral.
Money Market Rate:
Average rate for overnight deposits in the interbank market.
Treasury Bill Rate:
Data refer to weighted average rate on 13-week treasury bills sold at auctions during the month.
Deposit Rate:
Prior to March 1997, data refer to the deposit rate ceiling set by the Central Bank of Cyprus for time (fixed or notice) deposits of one year in the amount of over CYP 5,000. † For the period of March 1997 to December 2000, data refer to the deposit rate ceiling set by the Central Bank of Cyprus for all types of time (fixed or notice) deposits. † Beginning in January 2001, data refer to the average of the representative nominal interest rates on one-year fixed deposits as reported by the three largest banks.
Lending Rate:
Prior to December 2000, data refer to the lending rate ceiling set by the Central Bank of Cyprus. † For the period of January-November 2001, data refer to the simple average of minimum nominal interest rates on loans to enterprises as reported by the three largest banks. † Beginning in December 2001, data refer to the simple average of the representative nominal interest rates on loans to enterprises as reported by the three largest banks.
Government Bond Yield:
Data refer to weighted average yield on ten-year development stocks sold at auctions during the month.

Prices, Production, Labor:
Wholesale Prices:
Source B index, weights reference period: 1990. The index includes 374 reporting agents in Nicosia, Limassol, and Larnaca. Prices, covering 1,346 items, are collected for 284 commodities with sales valued at more than £ 100,000.
Consumer Prices:
Source B retail price index, weights reference period: 2005.
Industrial Production:
Source B indices, weights reference period: 2000.
Mining Production:
Source B indices, weights reference period: 2000.

International Transactions:
Exports and Imports, c.i.f.:
All data are from source B. Monthly figures do not necessarily agree with annual figures, as valuation adjustments are made only at the end of each year. Total exports include re-exports. Import data refer to civil imports. Non-civil imports have accounted

for less than 1 percent of total imports in recent years. *Imports, f.o.b.* are calculated from *Imports, c.i.f.* by applying a freight and insurance factor derived from the *Balance of Payments Statistics.*

Balance of Payments:

The entries shown in the columns for the second and fourth quarters correspond to data for the first half and the second half of each year, respectively.

Government Finance:

Monthly, quarterly, and annual data are derived from source S and cover consolidated central government. The fiscal year ends December 31.

National Accounts:

Beginning in 1995, data are sourced from the Eurostat database. Chain linked GDP volume measures are expressed in the prices of the previous year and re-referenced to 2000.

Czech Republic   935

Date of Fund Membership:

January 1, 1993

Standard Sources:

B: Czech National Bank, *Monetary Statistics* (monthly)
S: Czech Statistical Office, *Monthly Statistics of the Czech Republic*

Exchange Rates:

Official Rate: (End of Period and Period Average):
Czech National Bank midpoint rate.

International Liquidity:

Gold (National Valuation) (line 1and) is valued at the price of 60.61 koruny per gram.

Monetary Authorities:

Comprises the Czech National Bank. Central government comprises budgetary and extrabudgetary units. † Beginning in January 1997 data are based on an improved classification of accounts due to availability of more detailed information. † Beginning in January 2002, data are compiled in accordance with the European Central Bank's framework for monetary statistics using a national residency approach. Prior to January 2002, *Reserve Money (line 14)* includes positions that are subsequently shown as *Other Liabilities to Banking Institutions (line 14n).*

Banking Institutions:

Beginning in January 2004, comprises all resident units classified as other monetary financial institutions (other MFIs) in accordance with *1995 ESA* standards, including the money market funds. Prior to January 2004, comprises only financial institutions with bank licenses, namely the commercial banks, savings banks, and building societies. General government comprises budgetary and extrabudgetary units of central government, local governments, and the National Property Fund. † Beginning in January 1997, data are based on an improved classification of accounts due to availability of more detailed information. † Begin-

ning in January 2002, data are compiled in accordance with the European Central Bank's framework for monetary statistics using a national residency approach. Prior to January 2002, data on *line 22a* refer to Claims on General Government, and data on *line 26d* refer to General Government Deposits; also, prior to January 2002, *Reserves (line 20)* include positions that are subsequently shown separately as *Other Claims on Monetary Authorities (line 20n).*

Banking Survey:

See notes on banking institutions. † Beginning in January 1997, data are based on an improved classification of accounts due to availability of more detailed information. † Beginning in January 2002, data are compiled in accordance with the European Central Bank's framework for monetary statistics using a national residency approach. Prior to January 2002, data on *line 32an* refer to Claims on General Government (net).

Money (National Definitions):

M1 comprises currency outside depository corporations and overnight deposits. Currency outside depository corporations is equal to currency in circulation less currency and coin holdings of other depository corporations.
M2 equals M1 plus deposits with agreed maturity up to 2 years and deposits redeemable at notice up to 3 months.
M3 equals M2 plus repurchase agreements contracted with other (non-MFI) resident sectors, money market fund shares/units, and debt securities issued with maturity up to 2 years.

Interest Rates:

Bank Rate (End of Period):
Rate on a 14-day repurchase agreement between the Czech National Bank and the commercial banks.

Money Market Rate:
Rate on the three-month interbank deposits.

Treasury Bill Rate:
Average rate weighted by volume, on the three-month Treasury bills sold at auctions.

Deposit Rate:
Beginning in January 2001, average rate, weighted by stocks, offered by commercial banks on the outstanding koruny-denominated deposits of non-financial sectors. † Prior to January 2001, average rate offered by commercial banks on all deposits weighted by stocks.

Lending Rate:
Beginning in January 2001, average rate, weighted by stocks, charged by commercial banks on the outstanding koruny-denominated credits to non-financial sectors. † Prior to January 2001, average rate charged by commercial banks on all outstanding credits weighted by stocks.

Government Bond Yield:
Yield to maturity on a five-year government bond.

Prices, Production, Labor:

Data are from source S.

Producer Prices:
Source S. Laspeyres index, weights reference period: 1999, covers three main industrial activities: mining and quarrying;

manufacturing; and production and distribution of electricity, heat, and water. The index covers 5700 items. The weights are calculated from the structure of sales of the industrial enterprises on the domestic market.

Consumer Prices:

Source S. Weights Reference Period: 1999; Geographical Coverage: whole national territory; Number of Items in Basket: 790; Basis for Calculation: the weights are based on household expenditure as measured by family budget statistics.

Wages:

Data refer to average monthly wages in Koruny, including agricultural cooperatives, source S. Data based on 20 or more employees in enterprises (except banking and insurance companies) and all state employees (except armed forces).

Industrial Production:

Source S. Weights Reference Period: 2000; Sectoral Coverage: mining and quarrying, manufacturing and electricity, gas and water supply sectors; Basis for Calculation: weights are calculated as the shares of value added created in the whole industry.

Industrial Employment:

Data on average number of workers employed in enterprises of 25 or more employees, reported in thousands. † Beginning 1995, the data cover enterprises of 100 or more employees. Starting in 1997, data cover enterprises of 20 or more employees. Since January 2007(Eurostat methodology) besides employees, the indicator of industrial employment has covered persons working out of employment, too, i.e. persons working base on contract of services and other employed but not just employees. It is an amount adapted to full time. It also induces figures of average monthly wages and productivity of labor. A year-on-year comparability is guaranteed.

International Transactions:

Source S. † From 1995 onward, the value of goods for processing is included in total trade values on a gross basis.

Government Finance:

Monthly, quarterly, and annual data are as supplied by the Ministry of Finance and cover budgetary central government. Extra-budgetary accounts (including those of the National Property Fund) are excluded. The fiscal year ends December 31.

National Accounts:

Source S. Concepts and definitions are in accordance with the *ESA 95*, as indicated by the country. Eurostat introduced chain-linked GDP volume measures to both annual and quarterly data with the release of the third quarter 2005 on November 30, 2005. Chain linked GDP volume measures are expressed in the prices of the previous year and re-referenced to 1995.

Denmark   128

Date of Fund Membership:

March 30, 1946

Standard Sources:

A: National Bank, *Reports and Accounts*
B: National Bank, *Monetary Review*
S: Statistical Office, *Statistiske Efterretninger* (Statistical Bulletin), *Statistisk Manedsoversigt, Economic Trends* (Quarterly Supplement)

Exchange Rates:

Market Rate (End of Period and Period Average):
Midpoint rate in the Copenhagen market fixed at 11:50 a.m. by the Danmarks National Bank each business day in a meeting attended by authorized foreign exchange dealers.

International Liquidity:

Gold (National Valuation) (line 1and) is valued according to the gold fixing price in London on the last banking day of each month. † prior to June 2005, *Gold (National Valuation)* was obtained by converting the value in national currency terms, as reported in the country's standard sources, using the prevailing exchange rate, as given in *line* **ae** or **we.** Prior to 2005, valuation of gold holdings took place only at the end of each calendar year.
Foreign Exchange (line 1d.d) is based on market value. † Prior to June 2005, these data were adjusted to market value only at year end.
Monetary Authorities: Other Liabilities (line 4..d) is based on market value. † Prior to June 2005, these data were adjusted to market value only at year end.

Monetary Authorities:

Comprises Denmark's National bank only. *Line 11* includes ECUs issued against the deposit with the EMI of U.S. dollars and gold; gold is valued at market-related prices (see Introduction). Beginning January 1985, *Claims on Central Government (line 12a)* and *Government Deposits (line 16d)* declined considerably because certain claims on the government began to be netted out in *line 16d.* From December 1987 through May 1991, the accounts of the monetary authorities include the accounts of the postal giro system. Beginning with the data for end-November 2000, data on Monetary Authorities' *Foreign Assets (line 11)* and *Foreign Liabilities (line 16c)* are affected by a change from gross to net presentation of positions relating to the TARGET (Trans-European Automated Real-Time Gross Settlement Express Transfer) euro clearing system. (See *Recording of TARGET system positions* under *European Economic and Monetary Union (EMU)* in the introduction to *IFS.*) † Beginning in July 2000, data are compiled in line with standards prescribed by ECB regulations using a national residency approach. From July 2000 onward, *Claims on Banking Institutions (line 12e)* include claims on other banking institutions; *Money Market Instruments (line 16n)* are separately identified from *Reserve Money (line 14)*; and *Time Deposits (line 15)* and *Capital Accounts (line 17a)* are separately identified from *Other Items (line 17r).* Prior to July 2000, *Currency Outside Banking Institutions (line 14a)* relates to currency outside deposit money banks, a subset of banking institutions.

Banking Institutions:

Comprises commercial banks and other monetary institutions. Other monetary institutions include the major savings bank and accounts of the postal checking system. Excluded accounts of small savings banks, which are only available annually, are minor.

† Beginning December 1987, the accounts of the deposit money banks exclude the accounts of their nonresident branches.

† Through December 1990, deposit money banks' claims on other banking institutions and local governments are included in *Claims on Private Sector (line 22d)*. The accounts of the deposit money banks were completely restructured from January 1991. † From June 1991, the accounts of the deposit money banks include the postal giro system. † Beginning in July 2000, data are compiled in line with standards prescribed by ECB regulations using a national residency approach. Prior to July 2000, banking institutions comprise the consolidated accounts of deposit money banks and thereafter comprise the consolidated accounts of deposit money banks and other banking institutions. Prior to July 2000, money market instruments issued by the monetary authority are included in *Reserves (line 20)* and thereafter are included as part of *Other Claims on Monetary Authorities (line 20c)*. Beginning in July 2000, *Claims on Other General Government (line 22b)*, *Money Market Instruments (line 26m)*, *Bonds (line 26n)*, and *Central Government Deposits (line 26d)* are separately identified.

Banking Survey:

IFS line 34 and *line 34* plus *line 35* differ from the source B measures on M1 and M2, as given in the money supply table, in that *IFS* nets uncleared checks. † Beginning in July 2000, data are compiled in line with standards prescribed by ECB regulations using a national residency approach. See notes on monetary authorities and banking institutions above for additional details.

Money (National Definitions):

M1 comprises currency outside depository corporations and demand deposits.

M2 equals M1 *plus* time deposits with original maturity less than two years and deposits at notice with original maturity less than three months.

M3 equals M2 *plus* repurchase agreements, money-market securities and shares, and bonds issued with an original maturity less than two years.

Interest Rates:

Discount Rate (End of Period):
Source B.

Money Market Rate:
Arithmetic average of offered interbank rates. † Prior to January 1993, weighted average of three-month interbank rates.

Deposit Rate:
Calculated from interest accrued on krone-denominated deposit accounts (excluding deposits under capital pension schemes) divided by average deposit balance in the quarter. † Prior to 2002, banks' deposit rates were based on information collected by the Danish Financial Supervisory Authority. Since then, Denmark's Nationalbank has been responsible for collecting these data and a number of methodological changes were introduced. These include a reduction in the number of reporters from 98 to 23 banks, and a refocusing of the data on banks' domestic deposit taking operations. † Prior to second quarter of 1993, calculated from interest accrued on both krone- and foreign currency-denominated deposit accounts (including deposits under capital pension schemes) divided by average deposit balance in the quarter.

† Prior to 1990, weighted average of rates on time deposits for one to less than twelve months.

Lending Rate:
Calculated from interest accrued on krone-denominated loan accounts divided by average loan balance in the quarter. † Prior to 2002, banks' lending rates were based on information collected by the Danish Financial Supervisory Authority. Since then, Denmark's Nationalbank has been responsible for collecting these data and a number of methodological changes were introduced. These include a reduction in the number of reporters from 98 to 23 banks, and a refocusing of the data on banks' domestic lending operations. † Prior to second quarter of 1993, calculated from interest accrued on both krone- and foreign currency-denominated loan accounts divided by average loan balance (including nonperforming loans from 1991) in the quarter. † Prior to 1990, weighted average rates on overdrafts.

Government Bond Yield:
Yield on five-year government bonds.

Mortgage Bond Yield:
Yield on 20-year mortgage credit bonds.

Prices, Production, Labor:

Share Prices, Industrial and Shipping:
Data are from source S and are represented by a Laspeyres-type index, base January 1, 1983. The index refers to end-of-month quotations and covers a sample of shares on the Copenhagen exchange.

Prices, Home and Import Goods:
Data refer to source S index, weights reference period: 1998. *Home Goods* is a component of the above index.

Consumer Prices:
Source S. Weights Reference Period: 1999; Geographical Coverage: whole country; Basis for Calculation: the weights are based on a Household Budget Survey combined with the weights of the consumer groups in the national accounts.

Wages: Hourly Earnings:
Data are in kroner from source S and represent mainly male workers in manufacturing industries, including construction, employing 20 or more persons. † Prior to 1988, enterprises employing six or more persons were sampled. Annual data are calculated independently and are not an average of quarterly data.

Industrial Production:
Data are sourced from the OECD database, weights reference period: 2000. Data are derived from a sample of all major enterprises with at least 200 employees and selected smaller enterprises; some 1350 enterprises out of 5700 are sampled. Enterprises in electricity, gas, and water as well as in the ship building sector are excluded.

Agricultural Production:
The series is from source S, weights reference period: 1985.

International Transactions:

Value of Exports and Imports:
Source S. Trade data before 1988 does not include ships etc. Trade data are all published in the *Monthly Bulletin of External Trade*.

Trade indices:
These are Fisher indices from source S, weights reference period: 1995.

Import Prices:
The index is from source S, weights reference period: 1998. The series is a component of the *Home and Import Goods* producer price index.

Government Finance:
From 1990 to 1999, annual data are as reported for the *Government Finance Statistics Yearbook (GFSY)* and cover consolidated central government. From 1999, accrual data on general government are derived from source V. The fiscal year ends December 31.

National Accounts:
Source S. † Beginning in 1988, data have been revised significantly following the implementation of the *1993 SNA*, as indicated by the country. Beginning in 1990, data are sourced from the Eurostat database. Eurostat introduced chain-linked GDP volume measures to both annual and quarterly data with the release of the third quarter 2005 on November 30, 2005. Chain-linked GDP volume measures are expressed in the prices of the previous year and re-referenced to 1995.

Djibouti   611

Date of Fund Membership:
December 29, 1978

Standard Source:
S: Direction Nationale de la Statistique (National Department of Statistics), *Annuaire des Statistiques du commerce exterieur de Djibouti (External Trade of Djibouti Statistics Yearbook)*

Exchange Rates:
Official Rate: (End of Period and Period Average):
The official rate is pegged to the U.S. dollar. Cross rates are based on a fixed relationship to the U.S. dollar.

International Liquidity:
Data expressed in U.S. dollars for *Foreign Exchange (line 1d.d)* are derived from data denominated in national currency for components of the monetary authorities' *Foreign Assets (line 11),* using the end-of-period market rate *(line* **ae**).

Monetary Authorities:
Data cover the National Bank's accounts and certain accounts of the Treasury related to its monetary authority functions.

Deposit Money Banks:
Data cover the Banque Indo-Suez Mer-Rouge, Banque pour le Commerce et l'Industrie, and Commercial Bank of Ethiopia. Prior to 1998, coverage also includes Banque de Credit et du Commerce, Commercial and Savings Bank of Somalia, and Banque de Djibouti et du Moyen Orient which were operating at that time.

Other Banking Institutions:
Data cover the Caisse de Developpement de Djibouti.

Interest Rates:
Deposit Rate:
Simple average of minimum and maximum rates offered by commercial banks on time deposits of at least 1,000,000 Djibouti Francs with maturity of one month and more.

Lending Rate:
Simple average of minimum and maximum rates charged by commercial banks on overdrafts of under 10,000,000 Djibouti Francs.

International Transactions:
All trade data are from source S. Trade indices: Data are compiled on weights reference period: 1990.

Dominica   321

Date of Fund Membership:
December 12, 1978

Standard Sources:
A: Eastern Caribbean Central Bank, *Annual Report and Statement of Accounts*
B: Eastern Caribbean Central Bank, *Economic and Financial Review*
C: Eastern Caribbean Central Bank, *National Accounts Statistics*
N: Eastern Caribbean Central Bank, *Commercial Banking Statistics*
S: Ministry of Finance, Trade and Industry, Statistical Division

Exchange Rates:
Official Rate: (End of Period and Period Average):
The official rate is pegged to the U.S. dollar. Rates are based on a fixed relationship to the U.S. dollar.

Monetary Authorities:
The accounts are compiled from data contained in the balance sheet of the Eastern Caribbean Central Bank (ECCB). The monetary authorities' accounts for Dominica represent country attributable data for ECCB claims on and liabilities to the government of Dominica and its resident deposit money banks, and estimates of Dominica's notional share of the ECCB's foreign assets and liabilities and currency in circulation within the region. † Beginning in December 2001, data are based on a new reporting system which provides improved classification and sectorization of the accounts.

Banking Institutions:
Comprises commercial banks. † Beginning in December 2001, data are based on a new reporting system which provides improved classification and sectorization of the accounts.

Banking Survey:
† See notes on monetary authorities and banking institutions.

Money (National Definitions):
M1 comprises notes and coins held by the public and demand deposits in national currency of the private sector in commercial banks.

M2 comprises M1 plus time, savings, and foreign currency deposits of the private sector in commercial banks.

Interest Rates:

Discount Rate (End of Period):
Rate charged by the ECCB on loans of last resort to commercial banks.

Money Market Rate:
Fixed rate on loans between commercial banks. The rate includes the commission charged by the ECCB as agent. † Beginning in October 2001, weighted average rate on loans between commercial banks. The rate is weighted by loan amounts.

Treasury Bill Rate:
Rate on three-month treasury bills.

Savings Rate:
Maximum rate offered by commercial banks on savings deposits in national currency. † Beginning in June 2003, weighted average rate offered by commercial banks on savings deposits in national currency. The rate is weighted by deposit amounts.

Savings Rate (Foreign Currency):
Weighted average rate offered by commercial banks on savings dposits in foreign currency. The rate is weighted by deposit amounts.

Deposit Rate:
Maximum rate offered by deposit money banks on three-month time deposits. † Beginning in March 1991, weighted average rate offered by commercial banks on deposits in national currency. The rate is weighted by deposit amounts.

Deposit Rate (Foreign Currency):
Weighted average rate offered by commercial banks on deposits in foreign currency. The rate is weighted by deposit amounts.

Lending Rate:
Maximum rate charged by commercial banks on prime loans. † Beginning in March 1991, weighted average rate charged by commercial banks on loans in national currency. The rate is weighted by loan amounts.

Lending Rate (Foreign Currency):
Weighted average rate charged by commercial banks on loans in foreign currency. The rate is weighted by loan amounts.

Prices:

Consumer Prices:
Source S. Weights Reference Period: January 2001; Geographical Coverage: whole national territory; Number of Items in Basket: 394; Basis for Calculation: weights are derived from the 1997–1998 Household Expenditure Survey.

International Transactions:

All trade data are from source S.

National Accounts:

Source C. As indicated by the country, data have been revised following the implementation of the *1993 SNA*.

Dominican Republic   243

Date of Fund Membership:
December 28, 1945

Standard Source:
B: Central Bank, *Monthly Bulletin*

Exchange Rates:

Until September 4, 2000, the exchange rate system was based on an independent float of the peso. On September 5, 2000, the exchange rate was devalued 2 percent under a managed floating regime; since then, and through November 19, 2001, the central bank was setting once a week, the official exchange rate equal to the previous week's average of the commercial bank rate. Effective November 20, 2001, the buying exchange rate is the weighted average buying rate on the private market on the business day immediately prior to the operation date. Effective March 13, 2002, the selling exchange rate is the weighted average selling rate on the private foreign exchange market on the business day immediately preceding the operation. The abovementioned private market includes commercial banks and foreign exchange dealers. Effective exchange rate indices (*lines* **nec** and **rec**) are calculated as trade-weighted rate indices for U.S. dollars per peso, based on trade at the official, free market, and other exchange rates adjusted for the effects of surcharges on foreign exchange used for international trade.

International Liquidity:

Gold (National Valuation) (line 1and) is obtained by converting the value in national currency terms, as reported in the country's standard sources, using the prevailing exchange rate, as given in *line* **ae** or **we**. This line follows national valuation procedures which revalued gold monthly beginning June 1978 through January 1981 on the basis of the average minimum gold price in the Zurich and London markets during the month and thereafter on the basis of the daily average price in the London market.

Monetary Authorities:
Comprises the Central Bank of the Dominican Republic only.

Deposit Money Banks:
Comprises commercial banks.

Other Banking Institutions:
Comprises development banks, mortgage banks, specialized banks, and savings and loan associations.

Interest Rates:

Money Market Rate:
Simple average of rates at which commercial banks borrow funds in the interbank market.

Savings Rate:
Average rate offered by commercial banks on savings deposits in national currency.

Savings Rate (Foreign Currency):
Average rate offered by commercial banks on savings deposits in U.S. dollars.

Deposit Rate:

Weighted average rate offered by commercial banks on time deposits. The rate is weighted by deposit amounts. Prior to 1996, rate is calculated as a simple average.

Deposit Rate (Foreign Currency):

Average rate offered by commercial banks on time deposits in U.S. dollars.

Lending Rate:

Weighted average rate charged by commercial banks on non-preferential loans. The rate is weighted by loan amounts. Prior to 1996, rate is calculated as a simple average.

Lending Rate (Foreign Currency):

Average rate charged by commercial banks on non-preferential loans in U.S. dollars.

Prices and Labor:

Consumer Prices:

Source B national consumer price index, weights reference period January 1999. Prior to 1978, data refer only to consumer prices in Santo Domingo.

International Transactions:

Exports and Imports, f.o.b.:

All trade data are from source B. Export and import values exclude trade in the processing zone.

Volume of Exports:

IFS average of sugar, ferronickel, coffee, and cocoa beans with a 1995 value of exports as weights.

Unit Value of Exports:

IFS average of sugar, ferronickel, coffee, and cocoa beans with a 1995 value of exports as weights.

Government Finance:

Monthly, quarterly, and annual data are derived from tables prepared by source B and cover budgetary central government. Data do not cover operations of the social security funds or of other central government agencies with own budgets. Data differ from national presentations in that some transactions are reclassified according to Government Finance Statistics methodology. The fiscal year ends December 31.

National Accounts:

Data are from source B. As indicated by the country, data are compiled according to the recommendations of the *1993 SNA*.

ECCU 309

The Eastern Caribbean Currency Union (ECCU) was formed when the Eastern Caribbean Central Bank (ECCB) was created. The governments participating in the East Caribbean Currency Authority (ECCA) signed the Eastern Caribbean Central Bank Agreement Act 1983 on July 5, 1983 to establish the ECCB. In accordance with the Agreement, the ECCB was formally established on October 1, 1983, on which date the ECCA was deemed to have ceased to exist. Effective from this date, all the assets and liabilities of the ECCA, together with all its rights and obliga-

tions that are not inconsistent with the provisions of this Agreement, were transferred to the ECCB.

The ECCB is the monetary authority for the governments of Anguilla, Antigua and Barbuda, Dominica, Grenada, Montserrat, St. Kitts and Nevis, St. Lucia, and St. Vincent and the Grenadines. The ECCB is governed by two acts: the Eastern Caribbean Central Bank Agreement of 1983 which establishes and defines the powers and operations of the ECCB and the Uniform Banking Act of 1993 which defines the operations of financial institutions within the ECCU area including their relations with the ECCB. The Monetary Council, the governing body of the ECCB, comprises the Finance Minister of each of the eight members. The core purposes of the ECCB are to regulate the availability of money and credit, promote and maintain monetary stability, promote credit and exchange conditions and a sound financial structure conducive to the balanced growth and development of the territories of the participating governments, and actively promote the economic development of the territories of the participating governments.

The ECCB issues and manages a common currency for the area, the Eastern Caribbean dollar, with a fixed exchange rate pegged at EC$2.70 to US$1.00 since July 1976. The ECCB has the sole right to issue notes and coins for its member countries. The ECCB serves as a banker to its participating governments as well as to the commercial banks operating in the area. Governments maintain accounts with the ECCB through which transactions are conducted. Commercial banks maintain accounts with the ECCB to satisfy legal reserve requirements, to facilitate interbank transactions, and as a means of holding excess funds. The ECCB may grant advances to commercial banks to meet short-term liquidity needs.

The consolidated data published for the ECCU has one major methodological difference compared to the data published in *IFS* for the individual countries. The ECCU-wide residency criterion is applied instead of the national residency criterion.

Date of Fund Membership:

Antigua and Barbuda (February 25, 1982), Dominica (December 12, 1978), Grenada (August 27, 1975), Saint Kitts and Nevis (August 15, 1984), Saint Lucia (November 15, 1979), and Saint Vincent and the Grenadines (December 28, 1979). Anguilla and Montserrat are not members of the IMF.

Standard Sources:

A: Eastern Caribbean Central Bank, *Annual Report and Statement of Accounts*
B: Eastern Caribbean Central Bank, *Economic and Financial Review (Quarterly)*; Eastern Caribbean Central Bank, *Financial Statistics Yearbook*
C: Eastern Caribbean Central Bank, *National Accounts Statistics*
N: Eastern Caribbean Central Bank, *Commercial Banking Statistics*

Exchange Rates:

Official Rate: (End of Period and Period Average):
The official rate is pegged to the U.S. dollar.

Monetary Authorities:

Comprises the Eastern Caribbean Central Bank (ECCB) only.
† Beginning in December 2001, data are based on a new reporting

system which provides improved classification and sectorization of the accounts.

Banking Institutions:

Comprises commercial banks. This section consolidates national data by application of an ECCU-wide residency criterion. † Beginning in December 2001, data are based on a new reporting system which provides improved classification and sectorization of the accounts.

Banking Survey:

† See notes on monetary authorities and banking institutions.

Money (National Definitions):

M1 comprises notes and coins held by the public and demand deposits in national currency of the private sector in commercial banks.

M2 comprises *M1* plus time, savings, and foreign currency deposits of the private sector in commercial banks.

Interest Rates:

Discount Rate (End of Period):
Rate charged by the ECCB on loans of last resort to commercial banks.

Money Market Rate:
Fixed rate on loans between commercial banks. The rate includes the commission charged by the ECCB as agent. † Beginning in October 2001, weighted average rate on loans between commercial banks. The rate is weighted by loan amounts.

Savings Rate:
Maximum rate offered by commercial banks on savings deposits in national currency. † Beginning in June 2003, weighted average rate offered by commercial banks on savings deposits in national currency. The rate is weighted by deposit amounts.

Savings Rate (Foreign Currency):
Weighted average rate offered by commercial banks on savings deposits in foreign currency. The rate is weighted by deposit amounts.

Deposit Rate:
Maximum rate offered by commercial banks on three-month deposits. † Beginning in October 2003, weighted average rate offered by commercial banks on deposits in national currency. The rate is weighted by deposit amounts.

Deposit Rate (Foreign Currency):
Weighted average rate offered by commercial banks on deposits in foreign currency. The rate is weighted by deposit amounts.

Lending Rate:
Maximum rate charged by commercial banks on prime loans. † Beginning in March 1991, weighted average rate charged by commercial banks on loans in national currency. The rate is weighted by loan amounts.

Lending Rate (Foreign Currency):
Weighted average rate charged by commercial banks on loans in foreign currency. The rate is weighted by loan amounts.

National Accounts:

Source C.

Ecuador   248

Date of Fund Membership:

December 28, 1945

Standard Sources:

A: Central Bank, *Annual Report*
B: Central Bank, *Bulletin*

Exchange Rates:

Principal Rate (End of Period and Period Average):
Through December 1999, the principal rate refers to the market-determined rate. On January 7, 2000, the Ecuadorian government passed a decree dollarizing the economy. On March 13, 2000, the Ecuadorian congress approved a new exchange system, whereby the U.S. dollar is adopted as the main legal tender in Ecuador for all purposes, including means of payment, store of value, and unit of account. On March 20, the Central Bank of Ecuador started to exchange the existing local currency (sucres) for U.S. dollars at the fixed exchange rate of 25,000 sucres per U.S. dollar. Beginning on April 30, 2000, all transactions are denominated in U.S. dollars.

International Liquidity:

Gold (National Valuation) (line 1and) is obtained by converting the value in national currency terms, as reported in the country's standard sources, using the prevailing exchange rate, as given in *line* **ae** or **we.**

Monetary Authorities:

Comprises the Central Bank of Ecuador (CBE) only. † Beginning in January 1990 and in January 1998, data are based on improved sectorization and classification of the accounts. † Beginning in December 1999, data reflect the introduction of the U.S. dollar as the main legal tender. † Beginning in December 2001, data are based on improved sectorization and classification of the accounts. † Beginning in July 2002, data are based on a new reporting system which provides improved classification and sectorization of the accounts.

Banking Institutions:

Comprises private banks (both open and in the process of liquidation), private finance companies, National Financial Corporation, Housing Bank of Ecuador, savings and loans associations, and financial cooperatives. † Beginning in January 1990, includes the National Development Bank. Data are based on improved sectorization and classification of the accounts. Beginning in January 1998, excludes the National Finance Corporation. Data are based on improved sectorization and classification of the accounts. † Beginning in December 1999, data reflect the introduction of the U.S. dollar as the main legal tender. † Beginning in December 2001, data are based on improved sectorization and classification of the accounts. † Beginning in July 2002, excludes Filanbanco (private bank) due to the lack of reporting. Data are based on a new reporting system which provides improved classification and sectorization of the accounts. Beginning in January 2004, excludes the Housing Bank of Ecuador.

Banking Survey:

† See notes on monetary authorities and banking institutions .

Nonbank Financial Institutions:

Comprises the National Finance Corporation and credit card companies. † Beginning in December 1999, data reflect the introduction of the U.S. dollar as the main legal tender. † Beginning in December 2001, data are based on improved sectorization and classification of the accounts. Beginning in March 2002, excludes credit card companies. † Beginning in July 2002, data are based on a new reporting system which provides improved classification and sectorization of the accounts. Beginning in January 2004, includes the Housing Bank of Ecuador.

Interest Rates:

All interest rate data are from source B.

Discount Rate (End of Period):

Legal rate charged by the CBE to discount eligible commercial paper offered by commercial banks in national currency. † Beginning in March 2000, legal rate charged by the CBE to discount eligible commercial paper offered by commercial banks in U.S. dollars.

Savings Rate:

Weighted average rate offered by private banks on savings deposits in national currency. † Beginning in January 1999, weighted average rate offered by private banks on savings deposits in U.S. dollars.

Deposit Rate:

Weighted average rate offered by private banks on 30- to 83-day time deposits in national currency. † Beginning in January 1999, weighted average rate offered by private banks on 30- to 83-day time deposits in U.S. dollars.

Lending Rate:

Weighted average rate charged by private banks on 92- to 172-day loans in national currency. † Beginning in January 1999, weighted average rate charged by private banks on 92- to 172-day loans in U.S. dollars.

Prices and Production:

Producer Prices:

Source B. Weight Reference Period: 1995; Coverage: main production centers; Number of Items in the Basket: covers a total of 1,576 items (462 agricultural and livestock goods, 140 fishing goods, and 974 mining and manufacturing goods) and approximately the same number of establishments; Basis for Calculation: measured for agricultural and livestock goods are in farm and ex-factory for the manufacturing and mining goods and port for the fishing goods.

Consumer Prices:

Source B. Weights Reference Period: 2004; Geographical Coverage: covering eight cities with a population of more than 20,000; Number of Items in the Basket: 299 items; Basis for Calculation: Survey of Incomes and Expenses of Urban Homes, conducted during the period from February 2003 to January 2004.

Crude Petroleum Production:

Source B data in thousands of barrels.

International Transactions:

Source B.

Government Finance:

† Beginning in 1973, annual data are identical to data reported in the *Government Finance Statistics Yeabook* and cover budgetary central government. † Beginning in 1986, annual data are derived from monthly data. Monthly, quarterly, and annual data are derived from source B and cover budgetary central government. The fiscal year ends December 31.

National Accounts:

Data are from source B. Prior to the first quarter of 1999 and annual of 1993, data in national currency has been converted using the average exchange rate (*line* **rf**). For subsequent periods, the data are reported in U.S. dollars. As indicated by the country, data are compiled according to the recommendations of the *1993 SNA*.

Egypt   469

Date of Fund Membership:

December 27, 1945

Standard Sources:

B: Central Bank, *Economic Review*
S: Central Agency for Public Mobilization and Statistics, *Monthly Bulletin of Foreign Trade*

Exchange Rates:

Market Rate (End of Period and Period Average):

† Beginning in October 1991, data refer to the rate quoted by the Central Bank of Egypt based on Egypt's foreign exchange market conditions.

Beginning in October 1991, a unified exchange rate replaced the multiple exchange rate system. Since then, the Egyptian Pound is traded freely in a single exchange market with the authorities intervening to maintain the rate in a tight band against U.S. dollars.

Egypt's exchange rate regimes prior to October 1991 are as follows: Until May 11, 1987, the *central bank pool,* which continues to exist, handled (1) on the receipts side, exports of petroleum, cotton, and rice; Suez Canal dues and Sumed pipeline royalties; and (2) on the payments side, imports of certain essential foodstuffs (including wheat, wheat flour, edible oils, tea, and sugar); insecticide and fertilizers; and specified public sector capital transactions. It covered all public sector external debt service payments except for service payments on suppliers' credits related to public sector capital goods imports. The *commercial bank pool,* which was formally closed in March 1988, received proceeds of workers' remittances, tourism, and exports not going through the central bank pool, while providing foreign exchange for public sector payments not covered by the central bank pool. In addition, transactions involving residents' holdings of foreign exchange deposits in free accounts with domestic banks were effected outside the banking system, and there also existed an unofficial market in Port Said (a free trade zone) and illegal street markets. The outside-banks markets shared common sources of supply with the commercial bank pool (workers' remittances and tourism) and satisfied demand by the private sector for exchange for both visible and invisible transactions.

A *new bank foreign exchange market* (the new bank market), in which all authorized commercial banks and two travel agencies were permitted to operate, began operations on May 11, 1987. In opening the market, the authorities set the initial exchange rate to reflect the rates in the outside-banks markets; subsequently, the daily rate for the market has been determined de jure by a committee of representatives from eight participating banks on the basis of market supply, demand, and other factors as evolved by the committee. On the supply side, the new bank markets' resources are drawn mainly from workers' remittances, tourist expenditures, the purchase of foreign bank notes, and specified public and private sector export earnings. On the uses side, the new market is permitted to provide foreign exchange for specified public sector visible and invisible transactions, private sector imports, and certain private sector invisible payments primarily related to imports. Authorized banks are permitted to sell for private sector debt servicing up to 10 percent of their foreign exchange receipts, provided that the debtors' own foreign exchange accounts have been drawn down.

Over 1987/88–1988/89, transactions through the central bank pool accounted for approximately two thirds and one fourth of merchandise exports and imports, respectively, and 40 percent of invisible transactions. Although the buying rate in the central bank pool was changed on August 15, 1989 from LE 0.7=US$1 to LE 1.1=US$1, the Central Bank established three subaccounts to shield most transactions in the pool from the rate change, and most transactions continue to be carried out effectively at the rate of LE 0.7 = US$1.

Principal Rate relates to the central bank fixed official rate through December 1978, the unified exchange rate from January 1979 through July 1981, and the central bank pool rate thereafter.

Secondary Rate relates to the parallel market exchange rate through December 1978, the official incentive buying rate established by the authorities that applies to exchange transactions by authorized banks from August 1981 through December 1984, the premium rate quoted at authorized banks from January 1985 through June 1986, the authorized commercial bank (flexible) rate from July 1986 through March 1988, and the new bank free market rate thereafter. The banks free market rate was established in May 1987 and gradually absorbed most transactions from the authorized banks rate until the latter was abolished in March 1988.

Tertiary Rate relates to transactions effected outside banks and can only be considered as indicative of the exchange rates at which such transactions take place.

Since February 27, 1991, foreign exchange transactions were carried out through two markets, the primary market and the free market. Effective October 8, 1991, the primary market was eliminated, and all foreign exchange transactions are effected through the free market.

International Liquidity:

Gold (*National Valuation*) (*line 1and*) is the U.S. dollar value of official holdings of gold, which is valued at the daily average of gold fixing in London during the preceding three months, less a discount of 25 percent or at 75 percent of its final fixing on the last working day in June, whichever is less.

Lines 7a.d and *7b.d* are the U.S. dollar equivalents of *lines 21* and *26c,* respectively. They therefore exclude the accounts of banks operating exclusively with the foreign sector (see note on deposit money banks).

Monetary Authorities:

Consolidates the Central Bank of Egypt and monetary authority functions undertaken by the central government. The contra-entry to Treasury IMF accounts and coin issues is included in *line 12a.* Beginning January 2004, comprises Central Bank of Egypt (CBE) only. *Claims on Nonfinancial Public Enterprises (line 12c)* is equal to the sum of claims on public economic authorities and claims on public sector companies. *Claims on Deposit Money Banks (line 12e)* include claims on business and investment banks. *Central Government Deposits (line 16d)* excludes deposits of public enterprises, which are included in *Reserve Money (line 14).* † Beginning in 1980, data are based on improved classification and sectorization. † Beginning in December 2001, data are based on an improved classification and sectorization of accounts. † Beginning in January 2004, data are based on a new reporting system which provides an improved classification and sectorization of the accounts.

Banking Institutions:

Comprises commercial banks, business and investment banks (except the Arab International Bank, for which no data are available), and the Arab African International Bank since December 1982. *Claims on Nonfinancial Public Enterprises (line 22c)* is equal to the sum of claims on public economic authorities and claims on public sector companies. Public economic authorities' deposits are included in *Demand Deposits (line 24), Time, Savings, and Foreign Currency Deposits (line 25)* and *Restricted Deposits (line 26b). Restricted Deposits (line 26b)* is equal to the sum of all domestic, earmarked, import deposits except those of the central government. *Demand Deposits (line 24)* and *Time, Savings, and Foreign Currency Deposits (line 25)* include deposits in foreign currency which have been revalued, using the booking rates currently employed by the banks for all assets and liabilities denominated in foreign currencies, in accordance with instructions given by the Central Bank of Egypt. Foreign currency items in the process of collection are included in *Other Items (Net) (line 27r).* † Beginning in 1980, data are based on improved classification and sectorization. † Beginning in December 2001, data are based on an improved classification and sectorization of accounts. Beginning in January 2004, data are based on new reporting system which provides an improved classification and sectorization of the accounts.

Banking Survey:

† See notes on monetary authorities and banking institutions.

Other Banking Institutions:

Comprises the specialized banks and the Post Office Savings Bank. The specialized banks include the Arab Land Bank, Credit Foncier Egyptien, Industrial Development Bank, Principal Bank for Development and Agricultural Credit, the Post Office Savings Bank, and a free-zone bank (Manufacturers Hanover Trust). Manufacturers Hanover Trust is not presently included in the reporting system.

Apart from the institutions described above, the remaining Egyptian financial institutions of significant size are the four public sector insurance companies, for which data are not included in *IFS*. † Beginning in 1980, data are based on improved classification and sectorization.

Interest Rates:

Discount Rate (End of Period):
Source B. The rate at which the Central Bank discounts eligible commercial paper to commercial banks. Operations with the agricultural and cooperative credit organizations are carried at different rates according to the purpose of the loan and the type of guarantee. Direct credit and loans against securities granted to certain public institutions are subject to various rates close to the discount rate. The Bank sets up quantitative limits of discounting to banking institutions. There is no schedule of penalties, and normally loans do not exceed the authorized limits. Discount operations are a privilege granted to banks at the discretion of the Central Bank. The volume of discounts is large.

Treasury Bill Rate:
Weighted average based on the last auction of the month.

Deposit Rate:
Upper margin offered on fixed term deposits for less than one year.

Lending Rate:
Upper margin on commercial bank loans to the general public; the rates on agricultural and export credits are generally lower.

Prices and Labor:

Industrial Share Price (End of Period):
Weighted average based on daily closing quotations, covering whole industrial sector. Base 1992.

Wholesale Prices:
Source B index, weights reference period: 1986–1987, covering domestically produced agricultural and industrial goods and imported goods.

Consumer Prices:
Source B index, weights reference period: 1999–2000, covering the total urban population. The weights are based on a household expenditure survey.

International Transactions:

Exports and Imports, c.i.f.:
Source S data. Exports cover domestic exports. Import data refer to goods cleared through customs and differ from balance of payments data, which are based on exchange control statistics, i.e., on actual payments for imports. The large differences are due to differences in both coverage and valuation, especially with regard to goods released from customs under the temporary admissions system. Both sets of statistics also substantially underestimate the value of petroleum imports. Data on Suez Canal dues are received directly from the Central Bank of Egypt.

Government Finance:

Annual data are as reported for the *Government Finance Statistics Yearbook (GFSY)* and cover budgetary central government. The fiscal year ends June 30.

National Accounts:

Source B. † Compilation procedures were revised in 1970. Data for 1970 to 1979 relate to calendar year. Beginning in 1980, data relate to a fiscal year ending June 30. *Line 99b* includes a statistical discrepancy.

El Salvador 253

Date of Fund Membership:
March 14, 1946

Standard Sources:
B: Central Bank, *Monthly Review*
N: Central Bank, Superintendency of Banks and Other Financial Institutions, *Statistics*

Exchange Rates:

Market Rate (End of Period):
On June 1, 1990 the exchange system was unified. The exchange rate is determined by commercial banks and exchange houses authorized to operate in the foreign exchange market. Since January 1993, the central bank has intervened in the market to maintain the value of the colón at C 8.755 per U.S. dollar. Beginning in January 2001, because of the introduction of the 'Integration Law-*La Ley de Integración Monetaria*,' that makes the U.S. dollar legal tender, the exchange rate has been fixed to colón 8.75 per U.S. dollar.

International Liquidity:
Line 1and is equal to *line 1ad*, converted into U.S. dollars at the dollar price of gold used by national sources, as reported to *IFS*.

Monetary Authorities:
Comprises the Central Reserve Bank of El Salvador only. † Beginning in December 2000 and December 2001, data are based on a new reporting system, which provides an improved classification and sectorization of the accounts.

Banking Institutions:
† Beginning in January 1982, data are based on an improved classification and sectorization of the accounts. † Beginning in December 2000 and December 2001, data are based on a new reporting system, which provides an improved classification and sectorization of the accounts.

Banking Survey:
† See notes on monetary authorities and banking institutions.

Nonbank Financial Institutions:
Comprises the Multisector Investment Bank. † Beginning in December 2001, data are based on a new reporting system which provides an improved classification and sectorization of the accounts.

Money (National Definitions):
Base Money comprises currency in circulation, liquidity reserves, and other deposits of banking institutions with the Central

Reserve Bank of El Salvador (CRBES) in national currency. Currency in circulation refers to national notes and coins issued by the CRBES. Liquidity reserves refers to deposits, monetary stabilization bonds, and certificates of deposit that can be used as substitutes for required reserves issued by the CRBES in national currency held by banking institutions.

M1 comprises currency in circulation and transferable deposits. Currency in circulation refers to national notes and coins issued by the CRBES less the amount held by banking institutions. Transferable deposits refers to sight deposits, certified checks, and cashier's checks in national currency of the private sector with banking institutions.

M2 comprises M1 and time and savings deposits in national currency of the private sector with banking institutions.

M3 comprises M2, foreign currency deposits of the private sector with banking institutions, securities other than shares issued in national currency issued by banking institutions held by the private sector, and other deposits of the private sector in national currency with the CRBES not included in M1.

Interest Rates:

Money Market Rate:
Average of rates on 1- to 7-day loans between commercial banks.

Deposit Rate:
Rate offered by commercial banks and finance companies on 180-day time deposits in national currency.

Deposit Rate (Foreign Currency):
Rate offered by commercial banks and finance companies on 180-day time deposits in foreign currency.

Lending Rate:
Rate charged by commercial banks on loans of one year or less in national currency.

Lending Rate (Foreign Currency):
Rate charged by commercial banks on loans of one year or less in foreign currency.

Prices and Labor:

Consumer Prices:
Source B. Weights Reference Period: April 1991–March 1992; Geographical Coverage: San Salvador metropolitan area and the three largest departmental capitals in the country; Number of Items in Basket: 241; Basis for Calculation: The weights are derived from the urban household income and expenditure survey conducted in the period April 1991–March 1992.

Wholesale Prices:
Source B index, weights reference period: January 1978. The index covers 176 articles and relates to goods both produced and consumed in the country, as well as exports and imports. Coffee is included.

Producer Prices:
Source B index, weights reference period: 1992. Its geographic coverage includes the San Salvador and Santa Ana metropolitan areas. The index covers 139 producer goods. The index weights are based on the 1992 Economic Censuses developed by the General Bureau for Statistics and Censuses.

International Transactions:

Trade values are source B data, as compiled by the General Directorate of Statistics and Census.

Government Finance:

† Beginning in January 1994, monthly, quarterly, and annual data are derived from the *Quarterly Review* of the Central Reserve Bank of El Salvador and cover budgetary central government. Until 1993, the data covered the central government's budgetary operations recorded in the General Account of the Treasury, the Development Loan Fund, and the IDB Revolving Loan Fund. Debt data cover central government and official entities. The fiscal year ends December 31.

National Accounts:

Source B. Prior to 1978, *lines 99a* and *99b* include a statistical discrepancy. As indicated by the country, the national accounts are compiled according to the recommendation of the *1968 SNA*.

Equatorial Guinea   642

Date of Fund Membership:

December 22, 1969

Standard Source:

B: Banque des Etats d'Afrique Centrale (BEAC) (Bank of the Central African States), *Etudes et Statistiques (Studies and Statistics)*

Exchange Rates:

Official Rate: (End of Period and Period Average):
Prior to January 1999, the official rate was pegged to the French franc. On January 12, 1994, the CFA franc was devalued to CFAF 100 per French franc from CFAF 50 at which it had been fixed since 1948. From January 1, 1999, the CFAF is pegged to the euro at a rate of CFA franc 655.957 per euro.

Monetary Authorities:

Comprises the national branch of the Bank of the Central African States only. Claims on central government include assumption of certain nonperforming bank loans.

Deposit Money Banks:

Data cover the Banco de Credito y Desarrollo, the Banco Exterior de Guinea Ecuatorial, and the Banque Internationale de l'Afrique Occidentale (BIAO-Guinea Ecuatorial). The counterpart of government assumption of certain nonperforming bank loans is reclassified to capital accounts.

Interest Rates:

Discount Rate (End of Period):
Basic rediscount rate offered by the BEAC. † Beginning July 1994, rate charged by the BEAC to financial institutions on refinancing operations.

Deposit Rate:
Minimum rate offered by deposit money banks on savings accounts.

Lending Rate:
Maximum rate charged by deposit money banks on all loans, excluding charges and fees.

Eritrea   643

Date of Fund Membership:
July 6, 1994

Standard Source:
B: Bank of Eritrea

Exchange Rates:
Official Rate: (End of Period and Period Average):
Central bank midpoint rate. Until October 1997, the Ethiopian birr was the legal tender. In November 1997, the Eritrean nakfa was introduced, at par with the birr.

International Liquidity:
Gold (National Valuation) (line 1and) is obtained by converting for current periods the value in national currency as recorded by the Bank of Eritrea, using the prevailing exchange rate, as given in *line* **ae**. The Bank of Eritrea adjusts the value of its gold holdings once a year at end-December, to bring it close to a valuation based on the London exchange quotation, using the official exchange rate. Thereafter, the valuation in nakfa remains constant during the year, except for changes in stock.

Monetary Authorities:
Comprises the Bank of Eritrea only. † Beginning in December 2001, data are based on a new reporting system which provides an improved classification and sectorization of the accounts.

Banking Institutions:
Comprises the Commercial Bank of Eritrea and the Housing and Commerce Bank of Eritrea. † Beginning in December 2001, data are based on a new reporting system which provides an improved classification and sectorization of the accounts.

Banking Survey:
† See notes on monetary authorities and banking institutions.

Money (National Definitions):
Monetary Base comprises currency in circulation, deposits of banking institutions in national and foreign currency at the Bank of Eritrea, and deposits of local governments, public nonfinancial corporations, and the private sector in national currency at the Bank of Eritrea.
M1 comprises currency in circulation outside banking institutions and demand deposits in national currency, other than those of the central government, held at the Bank of Eritrea and banking institutions.
M2 comprises M1 plus savings and fixed deposits in national currency, other than those of the central government, at banking institutions.

Estonia   939

Date of Fund Membership:
May 26, 1992

Standard Sources:
B: Bank of Estonia, *Banking Monthly Review*
S: Statistical Office of Estonia, *Estonian Statistics*

Exchange Rates:
Official Rate: (End of Period and Period Average):
The kroon was introduced in June 1992 and was pegged to the Deutsche mark. Effective January 1, 1999, the official rate is pegged to the euro.

Monetary Authorities:
Comprises the Bank of Estonia only. *Claims on Private Sector* refers to loans to the Bank of Estonia's employees and claims arising from the assumption by the Bank of Estonia of loans made by commercial banks to private enterprises. The Bank of Estonia does not lend to private enterprises. There are no claims on local government, because the Bank of Estonia is prohibited from granting credits to local budgets, directly or indirectly. † Beginning in September 1993, data are based on an improved classification and sectorization of the accounts.

Banking Institutions:
Comprises six commercial banks and two authorized savings and lending associations. In 1992 there were 41 banking institutions. In 1995, 1996, 1997, and 1998 there were 18, 15, 12, and six banks, respectively, in addition to the two authorized savings and lending associations.

Banking Survey:
† See note on monetary authorities.

Interest Rates:
All interest rate data are from source B.
Money Market Rate:
Weighted average rate on overnight loans between banks in national currency. The rate is weighted by daily loan amounts. † Beginning in January 2000, three-month Tallinn Interbank Offered Rate (TALIBOR).

Deposit Rate:
Weighted average rate offered by banks on time and savings deposits in national currency to individuals and nonbank financial institutions. The rate is weighted by deposit amounts.

Lending Rate:
Weighted average rate charged by banks on short-term loans in national currency to individuals and nonbank financial institutions. The rate is weighted by loan amounts.

Prices and Labor:
Data are from source S.
Share Prices:
Tallinn Stock Exchange (TALSE) index, base June 3, 1996. The index covers common shares traded in the TALSE and is weighted by market capitalization. The monthly index is calculated from the average of the daily closing quotations.

Producer Prices:

From 2002, the producer price index (PPI) data are calculated on the basis of an annually chain-linked Laspeyres index. Until 2002, a fixed base index was calculated. The index covers the Estonian manufacturing, mining, and energy industries. The index measures the developments in producer prices of products sold both in the domestic market and for export. The data are based on monthly surveys. Approximately 700 prices are reported by about 200 enterprises over the entire country. The price concept used for the index is the price received by the producer, excluding VAT and excise duties.

Consumer Prices:

Source S. Geographical Coverage: Whole territory of Estonia; Number of Items in Basket: All goods and services bought by the reference population for the purpose of final consumption; Basis for Calculation: Weights are based on Family Expenditure Survey and are updated at approximately one-yearly intervals.

Monthly Earnings:

The published average gross wages and salaries have been converted into full-time units (part-time employees converted into full-time units) that allow comparing different average wages regardless of the length of working time. The average gross wages include payments for actual worked time and remuneration for time not worked. The average gross wages and salaries exclude payments to employees with contract of agreement. Since 1999, sick benefits to employees from social security funds are not included in the average gross wages as, according to changes made in the law, the employer no longer calculates and pays out sick benefits.

International Transactions:

Data for *Exports* and *Imports, c.i.f.* are from source S. The general trade system of recording trade transactions is used.

Balance of Payments:

Data are from source B.

Government Finance:

Annual data are as reported for the *Government Finance Statistics Yearbook (GFSY)* and cover budgetary central government. The fiscal year ends December 31.

National Accounts:

Beginning in 1993, data are sourced from the Eurostat database. Data from source S. Data are based on the *ESA 95* rules and concepts. The official figure of GDP is derived by the output approach. The expenditure approach is balanced with the output side estimates via the introduction of the "statistical discrepancy." The estimates of GDP include both formal and informal part of the economy.

Ethiopia   644

Date of Fund Membership:

December 27, 1945

Standard Source:

B: National Bank, *Quarterly Bulletin*

Exchange Rates:

Official Rate: (End of Period and Period Average):

Until May 1993, the birr was pegged to the U.S. dollar. During May 1993–July 25, 1995, the exchange rate system in Ethiopia consisted of two exchange rates: the official and auction exchange rates. On July 25, 1995, these exchange rates were unified, with the official exchange rate set as the marginal rate resulting from auctions. Effective October 25, 2001, the exchange rate is determined by the interbank foreign exchange market.

International Liquidity:

Gold (National Valuation) (line 1and) is obtained by converting the value in national currency terms, as reported in the country's standard sources, using the prevailing exchange rate, as given in *line* **ae** or **we**.

Monetary Authorities:

Comprises the National Bank of Ethiopia (NBE) only.

Deposit Money Banks:

Comprises the Commercial Bank of Ethiopia, Construction and Business Bank Awash International Bank S.C., Dashen Bank S.C., Bank of Abyssinia S.C., Wegagen Bank S.C., United Bank S.C., and Nib International Bank S.C. † Prior to December 1979, loans and advances of the commercial banks were included in *Claims on Private Sector (line 22d)*. Beginning in December 1979, these loans and advances are separated into *line 22d* and *Claims on Other Financial Institutions (line 22f)*. † Beginning in September 1983, data are based on an improved sectorization and classification of the accounts and exclude the Djibouti branch of the Commercial Bank of Ethiopia.

Monetary Survey:

† See note on deposit money banks.

Other Banking Institutions:

Comprises the Development Bank of Ethiopia only.

Banking Survey:

† See note on deposit money banks.

Money (National Definitions):

Base Money comprises notes and coins issued, deposits of commercial banks and Development Bank of Ethiopia, statutory deposits of insurance companies, and deposits of regional governments with the National Bank of Ethiopia (NBE).

M1 comprises currency in circulation outside the banking system and demand deposits. Demand deposits include statutory deposits of insurance companies and deposits of regional governments with the NBE; and demand deposits of the private sector, regional governments, nonfinancial public enterprises, nonfinancial cooperatives, and nonbank financial agencies and nontransferable nonresident deposits in national currency with commercial banks.

M2 comprises M1 plus fixed and savings deposits of the private sector, regional governments, nonfinancial public enterprises, nonfinancial cooperatives, and nonbank financial agencies with commercial banks in national and foreign currency.

Interest Rates:

Discount Rate:
Rate charged by the NBE on loans to commercial banks.

Treasury Bill Rate:
Average rate of yields on 28-, 91-, and 182-day treasury bills issued at face value. † Beginning in July 2003, weighted average yield on 91-day treasury bills.

Savings Rate:
Minimum rate offered by commercial banks on savings deposits.

Deposit Rate:
Weighted average rate offered by commercial banks on time deposits of less than one year. The rate is weighted by deposit amounts.

Lending Rate:
Rate charged by the Commercial Bank of Ethiopia on loans for exports. † Beginning in July 2003, minimum rate charged by commercial banks on loans to various sectors of the economy.

Government Bond Yield:
Rate paid by the NBE on its holdings of government bonds. † Beginning in November 2003, simple average yield on government bonds.

Prices and Labor:

Consumer Prices:
Source B. Weights Reference Period: December 2000; Geographical Coverage: Whole national territory; Number of Items in Basket: From 85 to 175; Basis for Calculation: The weights are derived from the results of the Household Income, Consumption and Expenditure Survey (HICES) conducted in 1999/2000.

International Transactions:

Value of Exports and *Imports* are customs data. Data on imports are unadjusted for the undervaluation of crude petroleum imports.

Government Finance:

Data are as reported in the *Government Finance Statistics Yearbook* and cover budgetary central government. The fiscal year ends July 7.

National Accounts:

† Beginning 1992, data excludes Eritrea. † Beginning 1992, *line 96f* includes a statistical discrepancy.

Euro Area   163

The original participating members of Stage Three of the EMU are Austria, Belgium, Finland, France, Germany, Ireland, Italy, Luxembourg, Netherlands, Portugal, and Spain. Greece joined in January 2001, and Slovenia in January 2007. The euro area is an official descriptor for the monetary union and is defined by its actual membership as of a specified date. Thus, the accession of Greece and Slovenia created breaks in series.

The European Economic Community, established in 1958, formed the basis for European integration and creation of the EMU through a three-stage process. On July 1, 1990, the European Community entered Stage One of monetary union, which led to freedom of capital movements, increased cooperation among central banks, free usability of the European currency unit (ECU), and improvement of economic convergence among member states of the European Union (EU). The Maastricht Treaty, signed in February 1992, provided the legal basis for Stage Two, which began with the establishment of the European Monetary Institute (EMI). During Stage Two, the member states achieved greater economic convergence, enhanced coordination of monetary policies, and prohibited monetary financing of governments by central banks. The European Central Bank (ECB), successor to the EMI, was established on June 1, 1998, as part of Stage Two. Stage Three began on January 1, 1999 when the euro—the euro area currency unit—was introduced, the conversion rates for national currencies were irrevocably fixed, the new exchange rate mechanism (ERM II) became effective for two of the four EU countries that did not join the initial EMU, and the Eurosystem (the ECB and the national central banks of the countries that adopted the euro) began conducting a single monetary policy for the euro area. In 2002, euro banknotes issued by the Eurosystem and euro coins issued by the national authorities replaced the national currencies of the euro area countries. A description of the methodology and presentation of accounts for the euro area is presented in the introduction to *IFS*. † Following the participation of Greece in the Eurosystem, a break occurs in all series beginning with January 2001. Similar breaks in series resulted from accession of Slovenia into the Eurosystem in January 2007.

Standard Sources:

B: European Central Bank, *Monthly Bulletin*
V: Eurostat

Exchange Rates:

Market Rate (End of Period and Period Average):
The euro was created on January 1, 1999 as the legal currency of the euro area countries, with an initial value established by setting one euro equal to one European currency unit (ECU), which was the accounting unit of the European Union. During 1999–2001, national denominations coexisted with the euro as physical circulating currencies and for denomination of financial instruments and transactions. The national currencies have irrevocable fixed conversion factors against the euro, based on the configuration of exchange rates when the euro was created. The irrevocably fixed, six significant digit conversion factors of national currencies per euro are as follows: Austrian schilling 13.7603, Belgian franc 40.3399, Finnish markka 5.94573, French franc 6.55957, German mark 1.95583, Greek drachmas 340.750, Irish pound .787564, Italian lira 1,936.27, Luxembourg franc 40.3399, Netherlands guilder 2.20371, Portuguese escudo 200.482, Slovenian tolar 239.640, and Spanish peseta 166.386. In 2002, euro banknotes issued by the Eurosystem and euro coins issued by national authorities replaced the national currencies of the euro area countries. Only euro exchange rates are presented. For further information see the section on exchange rates in the introduction to *IFS*.

International Liquidity:

Total Reserves Minus Gold (Eurosystem Definition) (line 1l.d): Beginning in January 1999, the statistical definition of the international reserves for the Eurosystem (the ECB and euro area national central banks) is based on the Eurosystem's statistical definition of international reserves, adopted by the ECB's Statistics Committee in December 1998. Reserves are defined on a euro area-wide residency basis to include only positions with non-euro area residents. Claims denominated in euros are excluded from reserves. The international reserves of the euro area per the Eurosystem statistical definition at the start of the monetary union (January 1, 1999) in billions of U.S. dollars were as follows: *Total Reserves minus Gold,* $269,140; *Foreign Exchange,* $235,103; *SDRs,* $6,982; *Reserve Position in the Fund,* $26,238; *Other Reserve Assets,* $820; *Gold,* $116,094; *Gold (million fine troy ounces),* 403.778 ounces. *Gold (Eurosystem Valuation) (line 1and)* from January 1999 onward is revalued at market rates and prices at the end of each quarter. Memorandum data are provided on *Non-Euro Claims on Euro Area Residents* and *Euro Claims on Non-Euro Area Residents,* which represent positions as of the last Friday in each month. For additional information, see the section on international liquidity in the introduction to *IFS.*

Monetary Authorities: (Eurosystem):

Covers the aggregated accounts of the Eurosystem. Includes coin issue of governments, with the contra-entries recorded in *Other Items (Net) (line 17r).* The classifications of economic sectors and financial instruments used in the accounts are based on the Eurosystem's regulatory standards for monetary statistics. *Claims on, and Liabilities to, the Euro Area Banking Sector (lines 12e.u and 14c.u)* include claims on, and liabilities to, the ECB, national central banks, and banking institutions (other MFIs) in the euro area. In contrast, Eurosystem members' Intra-Eurosystem claims/liabilities related to banknote issue are recorded as part of *Other Items (Net) (line 17r),* where they effectively net to zero, and not as part of lines *12e.u* and *14c.u. Bonds and Money Market Instruments (line 16n.u)* include subordinated debt in the form of securities, other bonds, and money market paper. Beginning with the data for end-November 2000, Monetary Authorities' *Foreign Assets (line 11), Foreign Liabilities (line 16c), Claims on Banking Institutions (line 12e.u),* and *Liabilities to Banking Institutions (line 14c.u)* are affected by a change from gross to net presentation of positions relating to the TARGET (Trans-European Automated Real-Time Gross Settlement Express Transfer) euro clearing system. (See *Recording of TARGET system positions* under *European Economic and Monetary Union (EMU)* in the introduction to *IFS.*) For additional information and description of the accounts, see the section on monetary authorities in the introduction to *IFS.*

Banking Institutions: (Other Monetary Financial Institutions):

Consists of the aggregated accounts of all units in the euro area classified as other monetary financial institutions (other MFIs), defined in accordance with 1995 *ESA* standards. *Claims on, and Liabilities to, the Euro Area Banking Sector (lines 20..u and 26g.u)* include claims on, and liabilities to, the ECB, national central banks, and banking institutions (other MFIs) in the euro area. *Money Market Fund Shares (line 26m.u)* include shares/units issued by money market funds. *Bonds and Money Market Instruments (line 26n.u)* include subordinated debt in the form of securities, other bonds, and money market paper. For additional information and description of the accounts, see the section on banking institutions in the introduction to *IFS.*

Banking Survey (Euro Area-wide Residency):

Consolidated accounts of the banking sector of the euro area, comprising the Eurosystem and banking institutions (other MFIs). Euro-area residency is based on the membership in the Eurosystem as any specific date. Euro area membership increased in January 2001 when Greece joined and in January 2007 when Slovenia joined. For additional information and description of the accounts, see the section Banking Survey (Euro Area-wide Residency) in the introduction to *IFS.*

Money (Eurosystem Definition):

Euro area monetary aggregates comprise monetary liabilities of MFIs (the Eurosystem and banking institutions) and central government monetary liabilities to non-MFI euro area residents. Monetary liabilities of governments consist primarily of postal system savings accounts and Treasury Department deposit facilities in some euro area countries. Beginning in 2002, includes euro banknotes and coins and unretired national currency banknotes and coins.

M1 (line 59mau) comprises currency in circulation and overnight deposits.

M1 Growth Rate (line 59max). The M1 growth rates are calculated by the European Central Bank (ECB) on the basis of adjusted flows rather than a simple comparison of end-of-period levels. The flows for the current period are calculated by adjusting the difference between the stock at the end of the period and the stock at the end of the previous period for effects that do not arise from transactions, such as reclassifications, foreign exchange revaluations, and other revaluations. Flows data used to compile the euro area M1 Growth Rate are adjusted to eliminate the net effect on stocks of the enlargement of the Euro area due to Greece's membership in January 2001 and Slovenia's membership in January 2007. Further details on methodology are available on the ECB website.

M2 (line 59mbu) comprises M1 plus deposits with agreed maturity up to two years and deposits redeemable at notice up to three months.

M3 (line 59mcu) comprises *M2* plus repurchase agreements, money market fund shares and money market paper, and debt securities up to two years.

Nonmonetary Liabilities of MFIs (line 59mfu) comprises the other liabilities of MFIs—deposits with agreed maturity over two years, deposits redeemable at notice over three months, debt securities over two years, and capital and reserves.

Interest Rates:

Consists of three policy rates used by the Eurosystem and five market weights calculated as weighted averages of rates prevailing in euro area countries. Source B.

Eurosystem Marginal Lending Facility Rate (line 60) is the rate at a Eurosystem standing facility at which eligible counterparties can obtain overnight credit against eligible assets. The terms and conditions of the facility are identical throughout the euro area.

Eurosystem Refinancing Rate (line 60r) is the rate for the Eurosystem's main open-market refinancing operations in the form of regular liquidity-providing reverse transactions with a weekly frequency and two-week maturity.

Eurosystem Deposit Facility Rate (line 60x) is the rate at a Eurosystem standing facility at which eligible counterparties can make overnight deposits with national central banks.

Interbank Rate (Overnight) (line 60a) and *Interbank Rate (Three-Month Maturity) (line 60b)* are interbank deposit bid rates.

Deposit Rate (line 60l) is a weighted average euro area retail bank deposit rate for deposits with an agreed maturity up to one year, using instrument specific weights drawn from monthly MFI balance sheet statistics.

Deposit Rate (lines 60lhs, 60lhn, 60lcs, 60lcn, and 60lcr):
See notes in the Introduction to *IFS*.

Lending Rate (line 60p) is a weighted average euro area retail bank lending rate for loans to enterprises up to one year, using instrument specific weights drawn from monthly MFI balance sheet statistics.

Lending Rate (lines 60phs, 60pns, 60phm, 60phn, 60pcs, and 60pcn):
See notes in the Introduction to *IFS*.

Government Bond Yield (line 61) is a euro area yield for 10-year government bonds calculated on the basis of harmonized national government bond yields weighted by GDP. For additional information, refer to the section on interest rates in the introduction to *IFS*.

Prices, Production, Labor:

Producer Prices:
Source V index, weights reference period: 2000, an aggrega-tion for the euro area of the industrial price indices of the 11 member countries, using 2000 industry sales weights excluding construction.

Harmonized CPI:
Source V index, the Harmonized Index of Consumer Prices (HICP), referring to a basket consisting of commodity groups common to all member states of the European Union with expenditure weights annually updated, excluding the imputed consumption cost of owner-occupied housing and certain other items.

Wages/Labor Costs:
Source V index. Average labor costs in the whole economy. Data for 1997 and earlier can be obtained from Eurostat.

Industrial Production:
Source V index, weights reference period: 2000, seasonally adjusted. An aggregation for the euro area of the industrial production indices of the 11 member countries, using 2000 industry value-added weights excluding construction.

Employment, Unemployment and Unemployment Rate:
Source V. Seasonally adjusted compiled following the recommendations of the International Labor Office.

International Transactions:

Merchandise Exports and Imports:
Source V. Excludes intra-euro area trade. Refers to customs sources for trade with nonmember countries of the European Union and survey sources for trade with those EU countries that are not members of the EMU. Data for 1997 and earlier can be obtained from Eurostat.

Volume and Unit Value data:
Source V, weights reference period: 2000.

Balance of Payments:
Statistics for 1998 for the euro area, compiled by the European Central Bank (ECB), provide only a summary presentation of the key aggregates. Statistics are compiled by aggregating gross cross-border transactions of euro area residents vis-à-vis non-euro area residents as reported by the 11 participating countries. Transactions between residents of the participating member states are not included. The methodological concepts follow international standards i.e., the IMF *Balance of Payments Manual*, fifth edition; in addition, further harmonization proposals in special fields have been developed and agreed within the European System of Central Banks (ESCB), in consultation with the European Commission (Eurostat).

As euro area reserve assets flows for 1998 are aggregates of national data, they include transactions in instruments issued by other residents of the euro area; they do not correspond to the 1999 Eurosystem's definition of reserve assets.

Government Finance:

Data are derived from source V. For a description of the definitions, refer to section 8 in the introduction. The fiscal year ends December 31.

National Accounts:

Source V. As indicated by Eurostat, series are based on the *ESA 95*. *Line 99b.r* is based on Eurostat data at 1995 prices. Data for 1997 and earlier can be obtained from Eurostat. Eurostat introduced chain-linked GDP volume measures to both annual and quarterly data with the release of the third quarter 2005 on November 30, 2005. Chain linked GDP volume measures are expressed in the prices of the previous year and re-referenced to 1995.

Fiji   819

Date of Fund Membership:
May 28, 1971

Standard Sources:
B: Reserve Bank of Fiji, *Quarterly Review*
S: Bureau of Statistics, Current Economic Statistics

Exchange Rates:

Official Rate: (End of Period and Period Average):
Central bank midpoint rate. The official rate has a fixed relationship with a weighted basket of currencies.

The weighting scheme used to calculate indices of nominal and real effective exchange rates (*lines* **nec** and **rec**) is based on data for tourism receipts as well as on data for merchandise trade.

International Liquidity:

Line 1d.d includes treasury foreign exchange holdings.
Gold (National Valuation) (line 1and) is obtained by converting the value in national currency terms, as reported in the country's standard sources, using the prevailing exchange rate, as given in *line* **ae** or **we**.

Monetary Authorities:

Comprises the Reserve Bank of Fiji (RBF) only. Data refer to the Currency Board through August 1973, to the Central Monetary Authority until November 1983, and to the RBF thereafter.

Deposit Money Banks:

Comprises commercial banks.

Monetary Survey:

† See note on monetary authorities.

Nonbank Financial Institutions:

Comprises life insurance companies.

Money (National Definitions):

M1 comprises currency in circulation outside the banking system, demand deposits, and local bills payable. Demand deposits include transferable deposits of local governments, statutory bodies, and the private sector less checks in the process of clearance in national currency with commercial banks.

M2 comprises M1 plus savings and time deposits of the local governments, statutory bodies, and the private sector with commercial banks in national and foreign currency.

Interest Rates:

All interest rate data are from source B.

Bank Rate (End of Period):
Minimum rate charged by the RBF on short-term loans to commercial banks and public enterprises.

Money Market Rate:
Weighted average of interbank money market overnight rates.

Treasury Bill Rate:
Bond equivalent yield on treasury bills allotted to banks and nonmonetary financial institutions.

Deposit Rate:
Rate offered by deposit money banks on one- to three-month time deposits of less than F$250,000; these rates are regulated by the RBF.

Lending Rate:
Rate charged by commercial banks on loans.

Government Bond Yield:
Weighted average yield on five-year government bonds.

Prices, Production, Labor:

Source S.

Consumer Prices:
Source S. Weights Reference Period: 1993; Geographical Coverage: covers price changes of goods and services consumed by all households in the seven urban areas of the Fiji islands (Suva, Lami, Nausori, Lautoka, Nadi, Ba, and Labasa); Number of Items in the Basket: 331 elementary groups of goods or services; Basis for Calculation: urban households extracted from the Household Income and Expenditure Survey of 1990–1991.

Wage Rates:
Source S. Covers all employees. The data are derived from annual employment survey.

Industrial Production:
Source S. Weight Reference Period: 1995; Coverage: covers the production of mining and quarrying, manufacturing, and electricity and water industries.

Tourist Arrivals:
Source S. Index calculated from total number of visitor arrivals by sea and air. Data exclude residents and persons in transit.

Industrial Employment:
Data are derived from annual sample surveys of nonagricultural establishments.

International Transactions:

Source B. Export data include re-exports.

Government Finance:

Data are provided by the Ministry of Finance. External debt data are from the Commonwealth Secretariat Debt Recording Management System, and domestic debt data are from the Reserve Bank of Fiji. The fiscal year ends December 31.

National Accounts:

Source S. As indicated by the country, data are compiled according to the recommendations of the *1968 SNA. Line 99b* includes a statistical discrepancy.

Finland   172

Data are denominated in markkaa prior to January 1999 and in euros from January 1999 onward. The markka's irrevocable fixed conversion factor to the euro is 5.94573 markkaa per euro. Beginning in January 1999, with the implementation of Stage Three of the European Economic and Monetary Union (EMU), an alternative euro area-wide definition of residency was introduced: All positions with residents of other euro area (EA) countries, including the European Central Bank (ECB), are classified as domestic positions, and foreign assets and foreign liabilities include only positions with non-euro area residents. In 2002, the markka was retired from circulation and replaced by euro banknotes and coins. Descriptions of the changes in the methodology and presentation of Finland's accounts following the introduction of the euro are shown in the introduction to *IFS* and in the footnotes on the euro area page.

Date of Fund Membership:

January 14, 1958

Standard Sources:

B: Bank of Finland, *Financial Markets—Statistical Review*
N: Ministry of Finance, *Economic Survey*
S: Statistics Finland, *Bulletin of Statistics*
V: Eurostat

Exchange Rates:

Official Rate: (End of Period and Period Average):
Prior to January 1999, the market rate referred to the markka's central bank midpoint rate. In January 1999, the markka became a participating currency within the Eurosystem, and the euro

market rate became applicable to all transactions. In 2002, the markka was retired from circulation and replaced by euro banknotes and coins. For additional information, refer to the section on exchange rates in the introduction to *IFS* and the footnotes on the euro area page.

International Liquidity:

Beginning in January 1999, *Total Reserves minus Gold (line 1l.d)* is defined in accordance with the Eurosystem's statistical definition of international reserves. The international reserves of Finland per the Eurosystem statistical definition at the start of the monetary union (January 1, 1999) in billions of U.S. dollars were as follows: *Total Reserves minus Gold,* $9,196; *Foreign Exchange,* $8,025; *SDRs,* $344; *Reserve Position in the Fund,* $826; *Other Reserve Assets,* $0; *Gold,* $575; *Gold (million fine troy ounces),* 2.002 ounces. *Foreign Exchange (line 1d.d)*: Beginning in January 1995, gold and foreign exchange holdings excluded deposits at the European Monetary Institute (EMI), and the holdings of European currency units (ECUs) issued against these deposits are included in *line 1d.d. Gold (Eurosystem Valuation) (line 1and)* is obtained by converting the value in national currency terms as reported in the country's standard sources, using the prevailing exchange rate, as given in *line* **de**, *line* **ae**, or *line* **we**. In December 1979 gold was revalued at the average daily quotations in London during November 1979 less a discount of 25 percent. From January 1999 onward, gold is revalued at market prices at the end of each quarter. Memorandum data are provided on *Non-Euro Claims on Euro Area Residents* and *Euro Claims on Non-Euro Area Residents,* which represent positions as of the last Friday in each month. For additional information, refer to the section on international liquidity in the introduction to *IFS* and on the euro area page.

Monetary Authorities:

Comprises the Bank of Finland, which is part of the Eurosystem beginning in January 1999. Beginning in 2002, *Currency Issued (line 14a)* includes euro banknotes and coins and, until December 2002, any unretired markkas. The recorded value of euro banknotes is based on a monthly allocation of total euro banknotes in circulation based on the Bank of Finland's paid up share of the ECB's capital; it does not correspond to either the actual amount of euro banknotes placed in circulation by the Bank of Finland which is shown in memo line *Currency Put into Circulation (line 14m)*, nor the actual circulation of banknotes within the domestic territory. See section *Euro banknotes and coins* in the introduction to *IFS*. *Bonds and Money Market Instruments (line 16n.u)* include subordinated debt in the form of securities, other bonds, and money market paper. Beginning in 2002, *Claims on Banking Institutions (line 12e.u)* and *Liabilities to Banking Institutions (line 14c.u)* include "Intra-Eurosystem claims/liabilities related to banknote issue," which is a single net value representing the difference between the value of euro banknotes allocated to the Bank of Finland according to the accounting scheme of the Eurosystem for issuing euro banknotes, and the value of euro banknotes put into circulation by the Bank of Finland. See section *Euro banknotes and coins* in the introduction to *IFS*. For a description of the accounts, refer to the section on monetary authorities in the introduction to *IFS*. Beginning with the data for end-November 2000, Monetary Authorities' *Foreign Assets (line 11)*, *Foreign Liabilities (line 16c)*, *Claims on Banking Institutions (line 12e.u)*, and *Liabilities to Banking Institutions (line 14c.u)* are affected by a change from gross to net presentation of positions relating to the TARGET (Trans-European Automated Real-Time Gross Settlement Express Transfer) euro clearing system. (See *Recording of TARGET system positions* under *European Economic and Monetary Union (EMU)* in the introduction to *IFS*.) Memo line *Net Claims on Eurosystem (line 12e.s)* equals gross claims on, less gross liabilities to, the ECB and other members of the Eurosystem. Comprises euro-denominated claims equivalent to the transfer of foreign currency reserves to the ECB, Intra-Eurosystem claims/liabilities related to banknote issue, net claims or liabilities within the TARGET clearing system, and other positions.

Banking Institutions:

Prior to January 1999, comprised commercial banks, cooperative banks, savings banks, and branches of foreign credit institutions engaged in deposit-taking activities in Finland. Balance sheet data of deposit money banks include data of Finnish banks' foreign branches through the end of 1996. † Beginning in January 1991, data are based on improved sectorization. *Claims on Monetary Authorities (line 20)* and *Credit from Monetary Authorities (line 26g)* refer to the Bank of Finland. *Money Market Fund Shares (line 26m.u)* include shares/units issued by money market funds. *Bonds and Money Market Instruments (line 26n.u)* include subordinated debt in the form of securities, other bonds, and money market paper. For a description of the accounts, refer to the section on banking institutions in the introduction to *IFS*.

Banking Survey (National Residency):

For a description of the accounts and the methodology, refer to the section Banking Survey (National Residency) in the introduction to *IFS*.

Banking Survey (Euro Area-wide Residency):

For a description of the accounts and the methodology, refer to the section Banking Survey (Euro Area-wide Residency) in the introduction to *IFS*.

Interest Rates:

Discount Rate (End of Period) (line 60):
Source B. Prior to January 1999, the discount rate provided the basis for determining the interest rates charged by commercial banks. Over time, it had minor significance and was used mostly as a reference rate for loans and deposits. Beginning in January 1999, central bank policy rates are discontinued. See Eurosystem policy rate series on the euro area page.

Money Market Rate (line 60b):
Source B. Rate refers to the three-month Helibor rate and, beginning in January 1999, refers to the three-month EURIBOR rate. Monthly data are the average of daily rates for the month.

Deposit Rate (line 60l):
Source B. Rate is a stock-weighted average of deposit rates of total deposits with banking institutions at end-of-month.

Deposit Rate (lines 60lhs, 60lhn, 60lcs, and 60lcn):
See notes in the Introduction to *IFS*.

Lending Rate (line 60p):
Data are from source B. Represents mean value of the end-of-month lending rate weighted by market value of stocks.

Lending Rate (lines 60phs, 60pns, 60phm, 60phn, 60pcs, and 60pcn):
See notes in the Introduction to *IFS*.

Government Bond Yield (line 61):
Data are period averages of quotations for a fixed rate serial bond with an average remaining maturity of 10 years. For additional information, refer to the section on interest rates in the introduction to *IFS* and on the euro area page.

Prices, Production, Labor:

Industrial Share Prices:
Source S index, base 1990, refer to the average of daily buying quotations.

Prices: Domestic Supply:
Source B basic price index of domestic supply, weights reference period 2000. About 1100 enterprises are surveyed in an effort to include in each NACE industrial class all large size enterprises (producers, exporters, or importers). The weights were derived from industrial statistics, foreign trade statistics, and national accounts. The weighting system is revised every five years. The index is rebased every five years.

Producer Manufacturing:
Source B producer price index for manufactured products, base 2000.

Consumer Prices:
Source S. Weights Reference Period: 2005; Geographical Coverage: The whole country; Number of Items in Basket: 500; Basis for Calculation: The index uses weights derived from the 2005 National Accounts and is rebased every five years.

Wages: Hourly Earnings:
Source B index of salary and wage earnings in mining, quarrying, and electricity, weights reference period 2000. From January 1985 this index covers manufacturing only.

Industrial Production:
Source S. Weights Reference Period: 2000; Sectoral Coverage: industrial sector; Basis for Calculation: the variable weight chain index in which the weights are changed yearly both within the industry and between industries is used.

Industrial Employment:
Index constructed from source S data on employment in mining, manufacturing, electricity, gas, and water.

International Transactions:

Exports and Imports:
Total exports and imports, c.i.f. are from source B; newsprint export value is from source S data. *Imports, f.o.b.* are calculated from *Imports, c.i.f.* by applying a freight and insurance factor estimated for *IFS*.

Volume of Exports:
Source B Paasche index of volume of exports, weights reference period 1980. Newsprint export volume is from source S.

Volume of Imports:
Source B Paasche index of volume of imports, weights reference period 1980.

Unit Value of Exports:
Source B Laspeyres index of unit value of exports, weights reference period 1980.

Newsprint:
Source S value of exports of newsprint divided by quantity of newsprint exports.

Unit Value of Imports:
Source B Laspeyres index of unit value of imports, weights reference period 1980.

Export Prices:
Source B, f.o.b. price index of exported goods, weights reference period 2000.

Import Prices:
Source B basic price index of domestic supply of imported goods, weights reference period 2000.

Government Finance:

From 1999 onward annual, quarterly, and monthly cash data on central government are as reported by the Bank of Finland. Debt data on central government do not include the outstanding debt of the social security funds and selected extrabudgetary funds. Data on general government are derived from source V. The fiscal year ends December 31.

National Accounts:

Source N. *Line 93i* includes a statistical discrepancy. As indicated by the country, from 1988 onwards data have been revised following the implementation of the *ESA 95*. Beginning in 1999, euro data are sourced from the Eurostat database. Eurostat introduced chain-linked GDP volume measures to both annual and quarterly data with the release of the third quarter 2005 on November 30, 2005. Chain linked GDP volume measures are expressed in the prices of the previous year and re-referenced to 2000.

France   132

Data are denominated in French francs prior to January 1999 and in euros from January 1999 onward. An irrevocably fixed factor for converting French francs to euros was established at 6.55957 French francs per euro. Beginning in January 1999, with the implementation of Stage Three of the European Economic and Monetary Union (EMU), a euro area-wide definition of residency was introduced: All positions with residents of other euro area (EA) countries, including the European Central Bank (ECB), are classified as domestic positions, and foreign assets and foreign liabilities include only positions with non-euro area residents. In 2002, the franc was retired from circulation and replaced by euro banknotes and coins. Descriptions of the changes in the methodology and presentation of France's accounts following the introduction of the euro are shown in the introduction to *IFS* and in the footnotes on the euro area page.

Date of Fund Membership:

December 27, 1945

Standard Sources:

B: 1. Bank of France, *Statistiques monétaires définitives, Statistiques monétaires provisoires, Quarterly Bulletin*
2. National Council of Credit, *Annual Report*
E: OECD
N: Ministry of Economics, Finance and Budget, *Les Notes Bleues, Statistics and Financial Studies* (Quarterly), *Statistics and Financial Studies* (Annual)
S: National Institute of Statistics and Economic Research (INEE), *Monthly Statistics Bulletin, Informations Rapides*
V: Eurostat

Exchange Rates:

Market Rate (End of Period and Period Average):
In January 1999, the French franc became a participating currency within the Eurosystem, and the euro market rate became applicable to all transactions. In 2002, the franc was retired from circulation and replaced by euro banknotes and coins. For additional information, refer to the section on exchange rates in the introduction to *IFS* and on the euro area page.

International Liquidity:

Beginning in January 1999, *Total Reserves minus Gold (line 1l.d)* is defined in accordance with the Eurosystem's statistical definition of international reserves. The international reserves of France per the Eurosystem statistical definition at the start of the monetary union (January 1, 1999) in billions of U.S. dollars were as follows: *Total Reserves minus Gold,* $39,422; *Foreign Exchange,* $33,862; *SDRs,* $1,107; *Reserve Position in the Fund,* $4,453; *Other Reserve Assets,* $0; *Gold,* $29,425; *Gold (million fine troy ounces),* 102.370 ounces. *Foreign Exchange (line 1d.d)*: Between March 1979 and December 1998, gold and foreign exchange holdings excluded deposits at the European Monetary Cooperation Fund (EMCF), and the holdings of European currency units (ECUs) issued against these deposits were included in *line 1.d.d. Gold (Eurosystem Valuation) (line 1and)*: For January–May 1975, gold was valued at the average dollar price quoted on the London market on January 7 and converted into French francs at the dollar rate in Paris. During June 1975 to December 1998, the gold was the average over the three preceding months of the dollar price of gold in London converted to French francs at the franc/dollar rate in Paris. From January 1999 onward, gold is valued at market prices at the end of each quarter. Memorandum data are provided on *Non-Euro Claims on Euro Area Residents* and *Euro Claims on Non-Euro Area Residents,* which represent positions as of the last Friday in each month. For additional information, refer to the section on international liquidity in the introduction to *IFS* and on the euro area page.

Monetary Authorities:

Consolidates the Bank of France, which beginning in January 1999 is part of the Eurosystem, and coin issue of the Treasury. *Foreign Assets (line 11)* uses Fund records for SDR holdings and reserve position in the Fund (converted at end-of-month exchange rates), which may differ slightly from the Bank of France records. † Beginning in 1975, gold holdings in *line 11* are revalued at market price: the contra-entry of valuation difference is included in *line 17r.* † Beginning in 1979, the ECU counterpart of the U.S. dollar and gold deposits with the EMCF is included in *line 11*; the contr-entry is recorded in *line 17a,* and the difference in valuation of gold between the Bank of France method and that of the EMCF is included in *line 17r.* † Between January 1996 and December 1998, gold, receivables from the EMI, and ECUs payable to the EMI (subsequently, the ECB) were treated as off-balance-sheet items in accordance with the revised accounting system of the Bank of France. Prior to January 1999, *Claims on General Government (line 12a)* included the contra-entry of the central government coin issue (see *line 14a*). From January 1999 onward, the contra-entry is in *Other Items (Net) (line 17r).* *Currency in Circulation (line 14a)* is derived by adding the central government coin issue to the central bank currency issue minus currency held by banks and cash advances to overseas (outre-mer) French territories (IEDOM & IEOM). Beginning in 2002, *Currency Issued (line 14a)* includes euro banknotes and coins and, until December 2002, any unretired francs. The recorded value of euro banknotes is based on a monthly allocation of total euro banknotes in circulation based on the Bank of France's paid up share of the ECB's capital; it does not correspond to either the actual amount of euro banknotes placed in circulation by the Bank of France which is shown in memo line *Currency Put into Circulation (line 14m),* nor the actual circulation of banknotes within the domestic territory. See section *Euro banknotes and coins* in the introduction to *IFS. Bonds and Money Market Instruments (line 16n.u)* include subordinated debt in the form of securities, other bonds, and money market paper. *Capital Accounts (line 17a)* includes gold revaluation and the counterpart to SDR allocations. For a description of the accounts, refer to the section on monetary authorities in the introduction to *IFS.* Beginning with the data for end-November 2000, Monetary Authorities' *Foreign Assets (line 11), Foreign Liabilities (line 16c), Claims on Banking Institutions (line 12e.u),* and *Liabilities to Banking Institutions (line 14c.u)* are affected by a change from gross to net presentation of positions relating to the TARGET (Trans-European Automated Real-Time Gross Settlement Express Transfer) euro clearing system. (See *Recording of TARGET system positions* under *European Economic and Monetary Union (EMU)* in the introduction to *IFS.*) Beginning in 2002, *Claims on Banking Institutions (line 12e.u)* and *Liabilities to Banking Institutions (line 14c.u)* include "Intra-Eurosystem claims/liabilities related to banknote issue," which is a single net value representing the difference between the value of euro banknotes allocated to the Bank of France according to the accounting scheme of the Eurosystem for issuing euro banknotes, and the value of euro banknotes put into circulation by the Bank of France. See section *Euro banknotes and coins* in the introduction to *IFS.* Memo line *Net Claims on Eurosystem (line 12e.s)* equals gross claims on, less gross liabilities to, the ECB and other members of the Eurosystem. Comprises euro-denominated claims equivalent to the transfer of foreign currency reserves to the ECB, Intra-Eurosystem claims/liabilities related to banknote issue, net claims or liabilities within the TARGET clearing system, and other positions.

Banking Institutions:

† Beginning in 1977, data reflect institutional changes and an extension in coverage to include "finance companies" specializing

in granting credits to households and private companies. † Beginning in 1978, data reflect other institutional changes in the banking sector, including the development of new financial assets. Prior to January 1999, consolidated the accounts of the commercial banks, the specialized banks as defined in source B3 (*Caisse des dépôts et consignations, Caisses d'épargne, Sociétés financières et Maisons de titre, Institutions financières spécialisées et assimilées*), and the private sector deposits with the Postal System and Treasury of Metropolitan France and Monaco. *IFS* data differed in some aspects from source B3 data. *Demand Deposits (line 24)* excluded deposits in foreign currency. *Other Deposits (line 25)* included demand deposits in foreign currency, investments *(placements)* on demand and term, and contractual savings *(épargne contractuelle)*. From January 1999 onward, consolidates the accounts of all resident units classified as other monetary financial institutions (other MFIs), as defined by the 1995 *ESA* standards. Accounts of the Caisse Nationale des Télécommunications and the Caisse Nationale des Autoroutes—affiliates of the *Institutions financières spécialisées et assimilées*—and private sector deposits with the Postal System and Treasury are not included, but the money market funds are included. *Money Market Fund Shares (line 26m.u)* include shares/units issued by money market funds. *Bonds and Money Market Instruments (line 26n.u)* include subordinated debt in the form of securities, other bonds, and money market instruments, including certificates of deposit and other negotiable paper. For a description of the accounts, refer to the section on banking institutions in the introduction to *IFS*.

Banking Survey (National Residency):

Prior to January 1999, consolidated the monetary authorities, banking institutions, and private sector deposits with the Postal System and Treasury. *Foreign Assets (Net) (line 31n)* differed from foreign assets (net) published in source B3 (tables 1.1.4.1 and 1.1.4.2), because *line 16c* excluded gold revaluation and SDR allocations (see Monetary Authorities). From January 1999 onward, consolidates the monetary authorities and banking institutions. For a description of the methodology and the accounts, refer to the section Banking Survey (National Residency) in the introduction to *IFS*.

Banking Survey (Euro Area-wide Residency):

For a description of the methodology and accounts, refer to the section Banking Survey (Euro Area-wide Residency) in the introduction to *IFS*.

Money (National Definitions):

Prior to January 1999, M1 was the same as Currency in Circulation (line 34a.n) plus Demand Deposits (line 34b.n). M2 consisted of Currency in Circulation (line 34a.n) plus Demand Deposits (line 34b.n) plus Passbook Savings. M3 consisted of Currency in Circulation (line 34an) plus Demand Deposits (line 34b.n) plus Other Deposits (line 35..n), Contractual Savings Excepted, plus Money Market Instruments (line 36m). M4 consisted of Currency in Circulation (line 34a.n) plus Demand Deposits (line 34b.n) plus Other Deposits (line 35..n), Contractual Savings Excepted, plus Money Market Instruments (line 36m) plus Treasury Money Market Instruments and Enterprises Commercial Paper. In January 1999, national monetary aggregates series were discontinued. Euro area aggregates are presented on the euro area page.

Interest Rates:

Rate on Repurchase Agreements (line 60a):
Prior to January 1999, referred to the interest rate for official repurchase agreements with the Bank of France. The rate typically served as the lower bound for short-term market rates. In January 1999, central bank policy rates were discontinued. Refer to Eurosystem policy rate series on the euro area page.

Money Market Rate (line 60b):
Prior to January 1999, represents the monthly average of rates for overnight loans against private bills, based on opening quotations. From January 1999 onward, represents the three-month EURIBOR rate, which is an interbank deposit bid rate. See euro area page.

Deposit Rate (line 60l):
Rate on tax-exempt "A" passbook deposits at savings bank.

Deposit Rate (lines 60lhs, 60lhn, 60lcs, 60lcn, and 60lcr):
See notes in the Introduction to *IFS*.

Lending Rate (line 60p):
Rate on short-term bank loans.

Lending Rate (lines 60phs, 60pns, 60phm, 60phn, 60pcs, and 60pcn):
See notes in the Introduction to *IFS*.

Government Bond Yield (line 61):
Average yield to maturity on public sector bonds with original maturities of more than five years. Monthly yields are based on weighted averages of weekly data. For additional information, refer to the section on interest rates in the introduction to *IFS* and on the euro area page.

Prices, Production, Labor:

All price series are from source S.

Share Prices:
Base December 1987. The index covers the common shares of the 40 enterprises having the largest capitalization. Price data refer to averages of end-of-week quotations for each month. † Prior to 1987, the index was calculated from the sample of 180 shares on the Paris exchange.

Prices: Producer Prices:
Beginning in 1999, in addition to the Prices of intermediate industrial goods (*line 63a*, weights reference period: 2000) and the imported raw materials index (*line 63b*, weights reference period: 2000), France publishes a Producer Price Index covering all sectors of the industry. The PPI (weights reference period: 2000) is a Laspeyres index collected on a sample of 4400 industrial producers. The actual weights refer to 2000 sales.

Consumer Prices:
Source S. Weights Reference Period: annually re-weighted; Geographical Coverage: all cities of mainland France and of the overseas departments (Guadeloupe, Martinique, Guyana, Réunion) with a population greater than 2,000; Number of Items in Basket: 305; Basis for Calculation: Weights for these groupings are derived from national accounts final consumption data of the antepenultimate year.

Labor Costs:

Include wages and other labor costs established by law or contracts, weights reference period: October 1997. The index covers manufacturing of mechanical and electrical machinery and equipment.

Industrial Production:

Source S. Weights Reference Period: 2000; Sectoral Coverage: manufacturing, mining, construction and energy; Basis for Calculation: the weighting system is renewed every five years. Data are sourced from the OECD database.

Industrial Employment:

Source S index. The series covers all salaried personnel in manufacturing and mining.

International Transactions:

Exports and *Imports, f.o.b.:* Source B data. *Imports c.i.f.:* Data are from the *Statistics of Foreign Trade* of Customs. Beginning in 1997, reported exports and imports data include trade of French Guiana, Guadeloupe, Martinique, and Reunion. The f.o.b./c.i.f. factor is established at the beginning of each year by the Customs director of forecasting.

Volume data: Source E, weights reference period: 1995 fixed weight indices. *Unit Value* data: Source S, weights reference period: 1995, current weights indices. The indices exclude electricity, military and railway equipment, electronics, analyzing and controlling instruments, shipbuilding and aeronautics, and machine tools. From January 1994 onwards, the methodology was changed to broaden the geographical coverage and improve the validation procedures and the representativeness of the products selected. From January 2005 onward, the indices take into account the enlargement of the European Union.

Government Finance:

Monthly and quarterly cash data are derived from source S and cover Treasury accounts only. Monthly, quarterly, and annual debt data on central government are derived from source B. Data on general government are derived from source V. The fiscal year ends December 31.

National Accounts:

Source B. As indicated by the country, from 1997 onwards data have been revised following the implementation of the *ESA 95*. Beginning in 1999, euro data are sourced from the Eurostat database. Eurostat introduced chain-linked GDP volume measures to annual data with the release of the third quarter 2005 on November 30, 2005. Chain linked GDP volume measures are expressed in the prices of the previous year and re-referenced to 1995.

Gabon   646

Date of Fund Membership:

September 30, 1963

Standard Source:

B: Banque des Etats d'Afrique Centrale (BEAC) (Bank of the Central African States), *Etudes et Statistiques (Studies and Statistics)*

Exchange Rates:

Official Rate: (End of Period and Period Average):

Prior to January 1999, the official rate was pegged to the French franc. On January 12, 1994, the CFA franc was devalued to CFAF 100 per French franc from CFAF 50 at which it had been fixed since 1948. From January 1, 1999, the CFAF is pegged to the euro at a rate of CFA franc 655.957 per euro.

International Liquidity:

Gold (National Valuation) (line 1and) is obtained by converting the value in national currency, as reported in the country's standard sources, using the prevailing exchange rate, as given in *line* **ae**. Prior to January 1999, the national currency/dollar conversion rates utilized for balance sheet purposes are used. These conversion rates differ from the prevailing exchange rates reported in *IFS*. This line follows the national valuation procedure which corresponds to that of the Bank of France (*cf* the international liquidity note on the *IFS* page for France).

Monetary Authorities:

Comprises the national branch of the Bank of the Central African States only. Claims on central government include assumption of certain nonperforming bank loans.

Deposit Money Banks:

Comprises active commercial banks. Claims and deposits of nonactive banks or banks in the process of liquidation are excluded. The counterpart of government assumption of certain nonperforming bank loans is reclassified to capital accounts.

Interest Rates:

Discount Rate (End of Period):

Basic rediscount rate offered by the BEAC. † Beginning July 1994, rate charged by the BEAC to financial institutions on refinancing operations.

Deposit Rate:

Minimum rate offered by deposit money banks on savings accounts.

Lending Rate:

Maximum rate charged by deposit money banks on all loans, excluding charges and fees.

Prices and Production:

All data on prices are from source B.

Consumer Prices:

Source B. Weights reference period: 1975; Coverage: 9942 African families in Libreville; Number of Items in Basket: 125; Basis for Calculation: fixed-weight Laspeyres index, 1975 Family Expenditure Survey.

Crude Petroleum Production:

Calculated from production quantities reported in the *Oil Market Intelligence.*

International Transactions:

All trade data are from source B.

Value of Exports and Imports:

Data exclude transactions to and from other countries of the Union douanière et économique de l'Afrique centrale (UDEAC)

(Central African Customs Union). If uncurrent, export data are derived by adding the value of oil exports and the value of other exports. Current monthly entries on other exports are estimated by carrying forward latest available entries. *Imports, c.i.f., from DOTS:* Data are based on reported data and estimates from *Direction of Trade Statistics (DOTS).*

National Accounts:

Source B. As indicated by the country, data are compiled according to the *1968 SNA.*

Gambia, The   648

Date of Fund Membership:

September 21, 1967

Standard Sources:

B: Central Bank of The Gambia, *Quarterly Bulletin*
S: Central Statistics Division, *Summary of External Trade*

Exchange Rates:

Market Rate (End of Period and Period Average):
Cross rates are based on a fixed relationship to the pound sterling.

International Liquidity:

Data for *line 1d.d* include small foreign exchange holdings by the government.

Monetary Authorities:

Consolidates Central Bank of The Gambia (CBG) and monetary authority functions undertaken by the central government. The contra-entry to Treasury IMF accounts and government holdings of foreign exchange is included in *line 16d.* † Beginning in December 1978, data are based on an improved sectorization of the domestic accounts. † Beginning in January 1984, domestic currency deposits made by the government in lieu of external debt service payments (i.e., special accounts) are included in *line 16b,* with a contra-entry in *line 16c.* Deposit money bank deposits with the central bank, arising from the receipt from their customers of domestic currency payments on account of external debt service (i.e., commercial arrears), are treated similarly. In addition, *line 16b* includes the contra-entry of The Gambia Produce Marketing Board export proceeds, as access to that account is limited.

Deposit Money Banks:

Comprises the following commercial banks: The Gambia Commercial and Development Bank, Banque Internationale pour le Commerce et L'Industrie du Senegal, and Standard Bank Gambia. † Beginning in December 1978, data are based on an improved sectorization of the domestic accounts. † Beginning in January 1984, a contra-entry to domestic currency payments received from customers to meet external debt service obligations, commercial arrears, is shown in *line 26b.*

Monetary Survey:

† See notes on monetary authorities and deposit money banks.

Money (National Definitions):

Reserve Money comprises currency in circulation and commercial banks' deposits at the CBG. Currency in circulation refers to notes and coins issued by the CBG.
Narrow Money comprises currency outside the banking system, demand deposits of nonfinancial public corporations at the CBG in national currency, and demand deposits of nonfinancial public corporations and private sector at commercial banks in national currency.
Quasi Money comprises time and savings deposits of nonfinancial public corporations and private sector at commercial banks in national and foreign currency.
Broad Money comprises narrow money and quasi money.

Other Banking Institutions:

Comprises post office savings deposits.

Interest Rates:

Discount Rate (End of Period):
Rate at which the Central Bank of The Gambia discounts commercial paper for banks.

Savings Rate:
Maximum rate offered by commercial banks on three- to six-month savings deposits.

Deposit Rate:
Maximum rate offered by commercial banks on three-month time deposits in national currency.

Lending Rate:
Maximum rate charged by commercial banks on industrial loans in national currency.

Prices:

All data on prices are from source B.

Consumer Prices:
Source B. Weights Reference Period: 1974; Geographical Coverage: low income households in the greater Banjul area; Number of Items in the Basket: 135 items; Basis for Calculation: survey of the consumption of low income households conducted in 1968/69 by the Central Statistics Department (CSD).

International Transactions:

Export data include re-exports.

Government Finance:

Annual data are as reported in the *Government Finance Statistics Yearbook (GFSY)* and cover budgetary central government. The fiscal year ends June 30.

National Accounts:

Source B. As indicated by the country, concepts and definitions are broadly in accordance with the *1968 SNA.*

Georgia   915

Date of Fund Membership:

May 5, 1992

Standard Sources:

B: National Bank of Georgia (NBG)
F: Ministry of Finance
S: State Department for Statistics

Exchange Rates:

The lari was introduced and made the sole legal tender in October 1995.

Official Rate: (End of Period and Period Average):
Since April 1993, the official rate has been set by the NBG on the basis of the rate determined by the periodic auctions conducted by the Tbilisi Interbank Currency Exchange (TICEX). This exchange was established by the NBG and a group of commercial banks.

International Liquidity:

Gold (National Valuation) (line 1and) is equal to *Gold (Million Fine Troy Ounces) (line 1ad)* valued at the London fixing rate, discounted by ten percent, for the end of period. *Foreign Exchange (line 1d.d)* comprises the NBG's cash holdings, liquid correspondent accounts with nonresident banks, and foreign government securities.

Monetary Authorities:

Comprises the National Bank of Georgia (NBG) only. † Beginning in January 2001, data reflect the introduction of a new plan of accounts, which provides an improved sectorization and classification of the accounts. † Beginning in December 2001, data are based on a new reporting system which provides improved classification and sectorization of the accounts.

Banking Institutions:

Comprises commercial banks. † Beginning in December 2001, data are based on a new reporting system which provides improved classification and sectorization of the accounts.

Banking Survey:

See notes on monetary authorities and banking institutions.

Money (National Definitions):

Reserve Money comprises notes and coins issued by the National Bank of Georgia (NBG) excluding cash in the vault of the NBG, required reserves of credit institutions with the NBG, and correspondent and other accounts of credit institutions (including banks with licences withdrawn).
M2 comprises currency outside banks and deposits in national currency with commercial banks, excluding deposits of the banking and government sectors.
M3 comprises M2 plus deposits in foreign currency, excluding deposits of the banking and government sectors.

Interest Rates:

All interest rate data are from source B.

Money Market Rate:
Weighted average rate on loans determined in the interbank credit auction market. The rate is weighted by the loan amounts.

Treasury Bill Rate:
Weighted average rate on treasury bills. The rate is weighted by issuance amounts.

Deposit Rate:
Weighted average rate offered by commercial banks on three-month deposits in national currency. The rate is weighted by the deposit amounts.

Deposit Rate (Foreign Currency):
Weighted average rate offered by commercial banks on three-month deposits in foreign currency. The rate is weighted by the deposit amounts.

Lending Rate:
Weighted average rate charged by commercial banks on three-month loans in national currency. The rate is weighted by the loan amounts.

Lending Rate (Foreign Currency):
Weighted average rate charged by commercial banks on three-month loans in foreign currency. The rate is weighted by the loan amounts.

Prices:

Producer Prices:
Source S. Weights Reference Period: December 2000; Coverage: measures ex-factory gate prices, excluding indirect taxes and the cost of freight and packaging; Number of Items in the Basket: 400 price quotations reported by 200 enterprises; Basis for Calculation: the weights are revised annually based on production values for the previous year.

Consumer Prices:
Source S. Weights Reference Period: December 1997; Geographical Coverage: five largest cities, which represent the major regions of Georgia; Number of Items in the Basket: 296 items; Basis for Calculation: the weights are revised every two years on the basis of a household budget survey of approximately 3,500 households.

International Transactions:

Source S.
Exports and *Imports (c.i.f.)* are compiled from the monthly customs statistics. Adjustments to the customs data are made to account for humanitarian aid (since 1998 data on humanitarian aid are included in the customs data) and the exports and imports of electricity and gas. Informal trade is excluded from the data coverage.

Government Finance:

† Prior to 2006, annual data are as reported for the *Government Finance Statistics Yearbook (GFSY)* and cover general government. Data are as reported by source F. Beginning in January 2006, monthly data are as reported in the *GFSM 2001* analytical framework and cover the general government. The fiscal year ends December 31. @bhead:National Accounts:
Source S. Data are as reported by the State Department for Statistics of Georgia.

Germany   134

With the coming into effect on July 1, 1990 of the treaty on German Economic, Monetary, and Social Union (GEMSU) between the former Federal Republic of Germany (FRG) and the former

German Democratic Republic (GDR), the deutsche mark became the sole currency of the GEMSU area, and customs borders between the two states were abolished. On October 3, 1990, the former GDR became part of the FRG under international law. The membership of the FRG in the Fund, under the designation Germany, remains unchanged. The presentation of exchange rates and Fund accounts shown for Germany in *IFS* is unaffected by the unification of the former FRG and the former GDR.

Data on international liquidity, money and banking, and international transactions cover the former FRG and the former GDR beginning with end-June (second quarter) 1990 for stock data and July 1990 for flow data. Data on prices, production, labor market, and national accounts cover the former FRG and the former GDR from 1991 onward. Data on industrial employment and wages refer only to the former FRG.

Data are denominated in deutsche marks prior to January 1999 and in euros from January 1999 onward. An irrevocably fixed factor for converting deutsche marks to euros was established at 1.95583 deutsche marks per euro. In 2002, the deutsche mark was retired from circulation and replaced by euro banknotes and coins. Beginning in January 1999, with the implementation of Stage Three of the European Economic and Monetary Union (EMU), a euro area-wide definition of residency was introduced: All positions with residents of other euro area (EA) countries, including the European Central Bank (ECB), are classified as domestic positions, and foreign assets and foreign liabilities include only positions with non-euro area residents. Descriptions of the changes in the methodology and presentation of Germany's accounts following the introduction of the euro are shown in the introduction to *IFS* and in the notes on the euro area page.

Date of Fund Membership:
August 14, 1952

Standard Sources:
B: Deutsche Bundesbank, *Monthly Report, Supplement to the Monthly Reports*
C: Deutsche Bundesbank, *Monthly Report*
S: Federal Statistical Office, *Aussenhandel, Reihe 1, Wirtschaft und Statistik*
N: Deutsche Bundesbank, *Saisonbereinigte Wirtschaftszahlen*
V: Eurostat

Exchange Rates:
Market Rate (End of Period and Period Average):
Prior to January 1999, the market rate was the midpoint rate determined during official sessions of the Frankfurt foreign exchange market. In January 1999, the deutsche mark became a participating currency within the Eurosystem, and the euro market rate became applicable to all transactions. In 2002, the deutsche mark was retired from circulation and replaced by euro banknotes and coins. For additional information, refer to the section on exchange rates in the introduction to *IFS* and the notes on the euro area page.

International Liquidity:
Beginning in January 1999, *Total Reserves minus Gold (line 1l.d)* is defined in accordance with the Eurosystem's statistical definition

of international reserves. The international reserves of Germany per the Eurosystem statistical definition at the start of the monetary union (January 1, 1999) in billions of U.S. dollars were as follows: *Total Reserves minus Gold,* $75,408; *Foreign Exchange,* $65,536; *SDRs,* $2,609; *Reserve Position in the Fund,* $7,263; *Other Reserve Assets,* $0; *Gold,* $34,200; *Gold (million fine troy ounces),* 118.925 ounces. *Foreign Exchange (line 1d.d):* Between March 1979 and December 1998, gold and foreign exchange holdings excluded deposits at the European Monetary Cooperation Fund (EMCF), and the holdings of European currency units (ECUs) issued against these deposits were included in *line 1d.d. Gold (Eurosystem Valuation) (line 1and):* Prior to January 1999, gold was valued using the prevailing exchange rate given in *line ae* to convert the value in national currency terms, as reported in the country's standard sources. From January 1999 onward, gold is revalued at market prices at the end of each quarter. Memorandum data are provided on *Non-Euro Claims on Euro Area Residents* and *Euro Claims on Non-Euro Area Residents,* which represent positions as of the last Friday in each month. For additional information, refer to the section on international liquidity in the introduction to *IFS* and the notes on the euro area page.

Monetary Authorities:
Comprises the Deutsche Bundesbank, which beginning in January 1999 is part of the Eurosystem, and coin issue of the Treasury. Prior to January 1999, the contra-entry to Treasury coin issue was included in *Claims on General Government (line 12a).* From January 1999 onward, the contra-entry is included in *Other Items (Net) (line 17r).* Beginning in 2002, *Currency Issued(line 14a)* includes euro banknotes and coins and, until December 2002, any unretired deutsche marks. The recorded value of euro banknotes is based on a monthly allocation of total euro banknotes in circulation based on the Deutsche Bundesbank's paid up share of the ECB's capital; it does not correspond to either the actual amount of euro banknotes placed in circulation by the Deutsche Bundesbank which is shown in memo line *Currency Put into Circulation (line 14m),* nor the actual circulation of banknotes within the domestic territory. See section *Euro banknotes and coins* in the introduction to *IFS.* Beginning in 2002, *Claims on Banking Institutions (line 12e.u)* and *Liabilities to Banking Institutions (line 14c.u)* include "Intra-Eurosystem claim/liability related to banknote issue," which is a single net value representing the difference between the value of euro banknotes allocated to the Deutsche Bundesbank according to the accounting scheme of the Eurosystem for issuing euro banknotes, and the value of euro banknotes put into circulation by the Deutsche Bundesbank. See section *Euro banknotes and coins* in the introduction to *IFS.* Prior to January 1999, *Liabilities to Banking Institutions (line 14c)* differed from central bank money in that *IFS* included, and source B excluded, banking institutions' excess reserves at the Deutsche Bundesbank and required reserves against foreign liabilities. Beginning in March 1978, the banking institutions' holdings of domestic notes and coins were excluded from central bank money by source B. For a description of the accounts, refer to the section on monetary authorities in the introduction to *IFS.* Beginning with the data for end-November 2000, Monetary Authorities' *Foreign Assets (line 11), Foreign Liabilities (line 16c), Claims on Banking Institutions (line 12e.u),* and *Liabilities to Banking*

Institutions (line 14c.u) are affected by a change from gross to net presentation of positions relating to the TARGET (Trans-European Automated Real-Time Gross Settlement Express Transfer) euro clearing system. (See *Recording of TARGET system positions* under *European Economic and Monetary Union (EMU)* in the introduction to *IFS*.) Memo line *Net Claims on Eurosystem (line 12e.s)* equals gross claims on, less gross liabilities to, the ECB and other members of the Eurosystem. Comprises euro-denominated claims equivalent to the transfer of foreign currency reserves to the ECB, Intra-Eurosystem claims/liabilities related to banknote issue, net claims or liabilities within the TARGET clearing system, and other positions.

Banking Institutions:

† Beginning in 1985, coverage of financial institutions was broadened to include all cooperative banks.Prior to January 1999, comprised the consolidated accounts of commercial banks, specialized banks, savings banks, commercial and agricultural credit cooperatives, private and public mortgage banks, the postal banking system, and private and public building societies. *Foreign Assets (line 21)* differed from source B data in that *IFS* excluded, and source B included, participation in nonresident banks. *Money Market Fund Shares (line 26m.u)* include shares/units issued by money market funds. *Bonds and Money Market Instruments (line 26n.u)* include subordinated debt in the form of securities, other bonds, and money market paper. Prior to January 1999, *Bonds and Money Market Instruments (line 26n)* included long-term nonmarketable obligations and *Capital Accounts (line 27a)* included general provisions. Beginning in January 1999, consists of all resident units classified as other monetary financial institutions (other MFIs), in accordance with *1995 ESA* standards, including money market funds. Beginning in January 1999, *Other Deposits (line 25)* includes long-term nonmarketable obligations previously classified as bonds, and *Other Items (Net) (line 27r)* includes provisions previously included in capital accounts. For a description of the accounts, refer to the section on banking institutions in the introduction to *IFS*.

Banking Survey (National Residency):

For a description of the methodology and accounts, refer to the section Banking Survey (National Residency) in the introduction to *IFS*.

Banking Survey (Euro Area-wide Residency):

For a description of the methodology and accounts, refer to the section Banking Survey (Euro Area-wide Residency) in the introduction to *IFS*.

Money (National Definitions):

Prior to January 1999, seasonally adjusted series were based on national methodology for adjusting the data: *Central Bank Money (line 19m.c)* was defined as currency in circulation plus required reserves against domestic liabilities.
M1 (line 39mac) comprised currency outside banks plus domestic nonbanks' sight deposits including government deposits other than with Bundesbank.
M2 (line 39mbc) comprised M1 plus domestic nonbanks' time deposits and funds borrowed for less than four years.
M3 (line 39mcc) comprised M2 plus domestic nonbanks' savings deposits at 3-months' notice.

Extended Money M3 (line 39mdc) comprised M3 plus domestic nonbanks' deposits with domestic banks' foreign branches and foreign subsidiaries and bearer bonds of under two-year maturity. From August 1994, included domestic and foreign money market funds shares in the hands of domestic nonbanks. Beginning in January 1999, national monetary aggregates series were discontinued. Euro area aggregates are presented on the euro area page.

Interest Rates:

Discount Rate (End of Period) (line 60):
Prior to January 1999, Source B. In January 1999, central bank policy rates were discontinued. See Eurosystem policy rate series on the euro area page.

Money Market Rate (line 60b):
Period averages of ten daily average quotations for overnight credit. Data in source B were the weekly high and low quotations.

Treasury Bill Rate (line 60c):
Rate on 12-month Federal debt register claims.

Deposit Rate (line 60l):
Rate on three-month deposits in denominations of less than one million marks.

Deposit Rate (lines 60lhs, 60lhn, 60lcs, and 60lcn):
See notes in the Introduction to *IFS*.

Lending Rate (line 60p):
Rate on current-account credit in denominations of less than one million marks.

Lending Rate (lines 60phs, 60pns, 60phm, 60phn, 60pcs, and 60pcn):
See notes in the Introduction to *IFS*.

Government Bond Yield (line 61):
Bonds issued by the Federal government, the railways, the postal system, the Länder governments, municipalities, specific purpose public associations, and other public associations established under special legislation. Average yields on all bonds with remaining maturity of more than three years, weighted by amount of individual bonds in circulation.

For additional information, refer to the section on interest rates in the introduction to *IFS* and the notes on the euro area page.

Prices, Production, Labor:

Share Prices:
Source B index, base December 30, 1987, refers to the CDAX share price index (previously called all-share price index FWBX) of the Deutsche Börse A.G. It shows average price movements of all ordinary and preference shares officially listed on the Frankfurt stock exchange of companies with headquarters in Germany.

Producer Prices:
Source S. Laspeyres index, weights reference period: 2000, which measures the trend of prices for goods produced by the mining, manufacturing industry, and power and water supply sectors, which are sold to domestic consumers. The weights were calculated on the basis of turnover.

Consumer Prices:
Sources S. Weights Reference Period: 2000; Geographical Coverage: all regions of the Federal Republic of Germany; Number of Items in Basket: 750; Basis for Calculation: the weights are based

on surveys of household expenditures on goods and services, and are revised every five years.

Industrial Production:
Data are sourced from the OECD database, weights reference period: 2000. The indices exclude construction.

International Transactions:

Exports and Imports, c.i.f.:
Source B data.
Trade indices are from source S, weights reference period: 1995.

Export and Import Prices:
Source B indices, weights reference period: 2000.

Government Finance:

Monthly and quarterly cash data are derived from source C. Transactions and debt data cover the budgetary federal government but exclude operations of the Federal Equalization Office and social insurance institutions. † Data cover government operations within the territory of the united Germany. † Data for social security funds and the European Recovery Program are on a cash basis only beginning in 1974 and 1975, respectively. † Beginning in 1990, central government extrabudgetary operations include operations of the German Unity Fund. † From 1992 onward, annual data refer to government operations within the territory of unified Germany; through 1991 annual data cover government operations within the territory of the former Federal Republic of Germany. † From 1995 onward, the debts of the Treuhandanstalt, classified as a nonfinancial corporation, have been assumed by the Redemption Fund for the Inherited Liabilities, a central government body. The fiscal year ends December 31.

National Accounts:

Source N. From 1991 onwards, concepts and definitions are in accordance with the *ESA 95*, as indicated by the country, and GDP *(line 99b.c)* is calculated as the sum of the components. Beginning in 1999, euro data are sourced from the Eurostat database. Eurostat introduced chain-linked GDP volume measures to both annual and quarterly data with the release of the third quarter 2005 on November 30, 2005. Chain-linked GDP volume measures are expressed in the prices of the previous year and re-referenced to 1995.

Population:

† Beginning in 1991, data cover unified Germany.

Ghana   652

Date of Fund Membership:

September 20, 1957

Standard Sources:

A: Bank of Ghana, *Annual Report*
B: Bank of Ghana, *Quarterly Economic Bulletin*
S: Central Bureau of Statistics, *Quarterly Digest of Statistics*

Exchange Rates:

Market Rate (End of Period and Period Average):
The exchange rate of the cedi is determined in the interbank foreign exchange market. In October 1999, the Bank of Ghana adopted a new procedure to calculate the market exchange rate from actual commercial bank transactions instead of from indicative rates.

International Liquidity:

Data for *line 1d.d* include government holdings. *Line 1and* is equal to *line 1ad,* converted into U.S. dollars at the dollar price of gold used by national sources, as reported to *IFS.*

Monetary Authorities:

Consolidates the Bank of Ghana and monetary functions undertaken by the Treasury. † Beginning in December 1991, data reflect the introduction of a new reporting system. † Beginning in December 1998, comprises the Bank of Ghana only. Data are based on a new reporting system, which provides an improved classification and sectorization of the accounts.

Banking Institutions:

Comprises commercial banks. † Beginning in November 1973, the classification of claims on the private sector and claims on the public enterprises is revised. Beginning in January 1992, includes discount houses. † Beginning in December 1998, data are based on a new reporting system, which provides an improved classification and sectorization of the accounts.

Banking Survey:

† See notes on monetary authorities and banking institutions.

Interest Rates:

Discount Rate (End of Period):
Rate at which the Bank of Ghana makes advances against treasury bills. A rate of one percent higher is used in discounts of direct credit to business. There are no quantitative limits on credit to banks at the discount rate. The volume of these operations is relatively small.

Money Market Rate:
Weighted average rate on interbank loans. The rate is weighted by loan amounts.

Treasury Bill Rate:
Rate of discount on 91-day treasury bills.

Savings Rate:
Rate offered by commercial banks on savings deposits.

Deposit Rate:
Rate on offered by commercial banks on three-month time deposits.

Government Bond Yield:
Yield on three-year government bonds.

Prices and Labor:

Consumer Prices:
Source S, weights reference period: 1992. Data refer to the national consumer price index. The weights are computed accord-

ing to the standard consumption basket from the 1992 Ghana Living Standard Survey (GLSS).

International Transactions:

All trade data are from source S.

Value of Exports and Imports:

Imports of military goods, purchase and sale of ships and aircraft, and purchase of fish from foreign fishing vessels are excluded.

Government Finance:

† Beginning in 2001, annual data are as reported for the *Government Finance Statistics Yearbook (GFSY)* and cover budgetary central government. The fiscal year ends December 31.

National Accounts:

Source B.

Greece   174

Data are denominated in drachmas prior to January 2001 and in euros from January 2001, onward. An irrevocably fixed factor for converting drachmas to euros was established at 340.750 drachmas per euro. With Greece's entry into Stage Three of the European Economic and Monetary Union (EMU) in January 2001, a euro area-wide definition of residency is introduced. All positions with residents of other euro area (EA) countries, including the European Central Bank (ECB), are classified as domestic positions, and foreign assets and foreign liabilities include only positions with non-euro residents. In 2002, the drachma was retired from circulation and replaced by euro banknotes and coins. Descriptions of the changes in the methodology and presentation of Greece's accounts following the introduction of the euro are shown in the introduction to *IFS* and in the notes on the euro area page.

Date of Fund Membership:

December 27, 1945

Standard Sources:

B: Bank of Greece, *Monthly Statistical Bulletin*
S: National Statistical Service, *Monthly Statistical Bulletin*

Exchange Rates:

Market Rate (End of Period and Period Average):

Prior to January 2001, the market rate was the central bank midpoint rate. In January 2001, the drachma became a participating currency within the Eurosystem, and the euro market rate became applicable to all transactions. In 2002, the drachma was retired from circulation and replaced by euro banknotes and coins. For additional information, refer to the section on exchange rates in the introduction to *IFS* and the notes on the euro area page.

International Liquidity:

Beginning in January 2001, *Total Reserves minus Gold (line 11.d)* is defined in accordance with the Eurosystem's statistical definition of international reserves and is revalued at market prices at the end of each quarter. † For the period January 1986 to December 2000, data on *Gold (line 1ad)* and *Foreign Exchange (line 1d.d)* exclude the deposits made with the European Monetary Institute (EMI) of gold and gross U.S. dollar holdings: the holdings of European currency units (ECUs) issued by the EMI against these deposits are included in *1d.d.* †Prior to December 1975, data on import documentary credits are excluded from *line 1d.d* at the time of account opening. After this date, such credits are excluded at the time of payment. *Gold (Eurosystem Valuation) (line 1and)* : Prior to December 1985, gold was valued at SDR 35 per fine troy ounce and converted into U.S. dollars at the dollar/SDR rate **sa** on the country page for the United States. † For the period December 1985 to December 2000, gold is revalued each December at 65 percent of the average buying market price of gold during that month. From January 2001 onward, gold is revalued at market prices at the end of each quarter. Memorandum data are provided on *Non-Euro Claims on Euro Area Residents and Euro Claims on Non-Euro Area Residents*, which represent positions as of the last Friday in each month. For additional information, refer to the section on international liquidity in the introduction to *IFS* and the notes on the euro area page.

Monetary Authorities:

Comprises the Bank of Greece, which beginning in January 2001 is part of the Eurosystem, and coin issue of the Treasury. † Beginning in 1987, tbe data reflect improved classification in the report forms. Prior to January 2001, the contra-entry to Treasury coin issue was included in *Claims on General Government (line 12a)*. From January 2001 onward, the contra-entry is included in *Other Items (Net) (line 17r)*. *Bonds and Money Market Instruments (line 16n.u)* include subordinated debt in the form of securities, other bonds, and money market paper. Beginning in 2002, *Currency Issued (line 14a)* includes euro banknotes and coins and, until December 2002, any unretired drachmas. The recorded value of euro banknotes is based on a monthly allocation of total euro banknotes in circulation based on the Bank of Greece's paid up share of the ECB's capital; it does not correspond to either the actual amount of euro banknotes placed in circulation by the Bank of Greece which is shown in memo line *Currency Put into Circulation (line 14m)*, nor the actual circulation of banknotes within the domestic territory. See section *Euro banknotes and coins* in the introduction to *IFS*. Beginning with the data for end-November 2000, data on Monetary Authorities' *Foreign Assets (line 11)* and *Foreign Liabilities (line 16c)* are affected by a change from gross to net presentation of positions relating to the TARGET (Trans-European Automated Real-Time Gross Settlement Express Transfer) euro clearing system. (See *Recording of TARGET system positions* under *European Economic and Monetary Union* in the introduction to *IFS*.) Beginning in 2002, *Claims on Banking Institutions (line 12e.u)* and *Liabilities to Banking Institutions (line 14c.u)* include "Intra-Eurosystem claims/liabilities related to banknote issue," which is a single net value representing the difference between the value of euro banknotes allocated to the Bank of Greece according to the accounting scheme of the Eurosystem for issuing euro banknotes, and the value of euro banknotes put into circulation by the Bank of Greece. See section *Euro banknotes and coins* in the introduction to *IFS*. Memo line *Net Claims on Eurosystem (line 12e.s)* equals gross claims on, less gross liabilities to, the ECB and other members of the Eurosystem. Comprises euro-denominated claims equivalent to the transfer of foreign currency reserves to the ECB, Intra-Eurosystem claims/liabilities related to banknote issue, net claims or liabilities within the TARGET clearing system, and other positions.

Banking Institutions:

† Beginning in 1987, the data reflect improved classification in the report forms. Prior to January 2001, comprised the consolidated accounts of the commercial banks and specialized credit institutions. Beginning in January 2001, consists of all resident units classified as other monetary financial institutions (other MFIs), in accordance with *1995 ESA* standards, including money market funds. *Money Market Fund Shares (line 26m.u)* include shares/units issued by money market funds. *Bonds and Money Market Instruments (line 26n.u)* include subordinated debt in the form of securities, other bonds, and money market paper. For a description of the accounts, refer to the section on banking institutions in the introduction to *IFS*.

Banking Survey (National Residency):

For a description of the methodology and accounts, refer to the section Banking Survey (National Residency) under *European Economic and Monetary Union* in the introduction of *IFS*. Prior to January 2001, the distinction between foreign and domestic claims and liabilities is based on the currency in which the claims and liabilities are denominated rather than on the residence of the debtor or creditor.

Banking Survey (Euro Area-wide Residency):

For a description of the methodology and accounts, refer to the section Banking Survey (Euro Area-wide Residency) in the introduction to *IFS*.

Interest Rates:

All interest rate data are from source B.

Central Bank Rate (End of Period) (line 60):
Refers to the discount rate offered by the Bank of Greece prior to April 1998 and, thereafter, refers to the interest rate applied to deposits of 14-days maturity placed with the Bank of Greece; the Bank of Greece has made regular interventions in the domestic money market by conducting activities (every Wednesday) for accepting deposits with 14-days maturity. Accordingly, the interest rate applied to these deposits provides an indication of the liquidity conditions as well as the monetary stance. In January 2001, the central bank rates were discontinued. See Eurosystem policy rate on the euro area page.

Treasury Bill Rate (line 60c):
Beginning in January 2000, data refer to the monthly average yield on 12-month treasury bills. Prior to that date, data refer to the end-month rate on new issues of 12-month treasury bills.

Deposit Rate (line 60l):
Before December 1987, refers to the maximum rate offered by deposit money banks on three to six month drachma deposits by individuals and enterprises. Beginning in 1988, data refer to deposits with a maturity of 12 months.

Deposit Rate (lines 60lhs, 60lhn, 60lcs, 60lcn, and 60lcr):
See notes in the Introduction to *IFS*.

Lending Rate (line 60p):
Prior to January 1999, refers to short-term loans to enterprises and households and, thereafter, refers to short-term loans to enterprises only. Beginning in June 1987, this rate was liberalized and includes commissions. Before June 1987, maximum rate charged by commercial banks for short-term working capital loans to industry.

Lending Rate (lines 60phs, 60pns, 60phm, 60phn, 60pcs, and 60pcn):
See notes in the Introduction to *IFS*.

Government Bond Yield (line 61):
Refers to the average daily yield on 10-year fixed-rate government bonds.

Prices, Production, Labor:

Producer Prices:
Source B. Weights Reference Period: 2000; Coverage: about 2960 prices from a number of 1200 enterprises across the country; Number of Items in Basket: 424 products for the domestic market and 185 products for the non-domestic market; Basis for Calculation: based on sales to the domestic and non-domestic market in the year 2000. The index is rebased and the weights are revised every five years (PPI replaced WPI that has been compiled from 1962–2004).

Consumer Prices:
Source B. Weights Reference Period: 2005; Geographical Coverage: covers the entire country; Number of Items in Basket: 784 products from 12 product categories; Basis for Calculation: the weights are calculated on the basis of the results of the Household Budget Survey conducted in February 2004–January 2005.

Wages: Monthly Earnings:
Source S. Base Year: 1999Q1=100; Basis for Calculation: average monthly earnings in Euros obtained from the quarterly Labor Force Survey. The index is broken down by primary, secondary, and tertiary sector of economic activity.

Industrial Production:
Source S. Weights Reference Period: 2000; Sectoral Coverage: mining, electricity, gas and manufacturing ; Basis for Calculation: weighting is done according to the value added at factor cost of the weights reference period. Data are sourced from the OECD database.

International Transactions:

Beginning in 1999, trade data are sourced from the Eurostat database.

Government Finance:

Monthly, quarterly and annual cash data are derived from source B and cover budgetary central government. Data differ from the national presentation in that *Revenue* is adjusted to include foreign transfers. *Expenditure* in source B is also adjusted to exclude amortization. However, expenditures include refunds of taxes and restitutions of revenue to third parties. Data on general government are derived from source V. The fiscal year ends December 31.

National Accounts:

Source B. Beginning in 1988, a statistical discrepancy is included in *line 93i* but, prior to 1988, is in *lines 99a* and *99b*. As indicated by the country, beginning in 1995, concepts and definitions are in accordance with the *1995 ESA*. Beginning in 2001, euro data are sourced from the Eurostat database. Eurostat introduced chain-linked GDP volume measures to both annual and quarterly data with the release of the third quarter 2005 on November 30, 2005. Chain linked GDP volume measures are expressed in the prices of the previous year and re-referenced to 1995.

Grenada   328

Date of Fund Membership:
August 27, 1975

Standard Sources:
A: Eastern Caribbean Central Bank, *Annual Report and Statement of Accounts*
B: Eastern Caribbean Central Bank, *Economic and Financial Review*
C: Eastern Caribbean Central Bank, *National Accounts Statistics*
N: Eastern Caribbean Central Bank, *Commercial Banking Statistics*

Exchange Rates:
Official Rate: (End of Period and Period Average):
Rates are based on a fixed relationship to the U.S. dollar.
The weighting scheme used to calculate indices of nominal and real effective exchange rates (*lines* **nec** and **rec**) is based on data for tourism receipts and on data for aggregate bilateral non-oil trade flow for 1980–82.

Monetary Authorities:
The accounts are compiled from data contained in the balance sheet of the Eastern Caribbean Central Bank (ECCB). The monetary authorities' accounts for Grenada represent country attributable data for ECCB claims on and liabilities to the government of Grenada and its resident deposit money banks, and estimates of Grenada's notional share of the ECCB's foreign assets and liabilities and currency in circulation within the region. † For the period 1975 through 1978 *lines 11* and *14* include net local interbank claims of commercial banks as a proxy for banks' deposits with the ECCB. † Beginning in December 2001, data are based on a new reporting system which provides improved classification and sectorization of the accounts.

Banking Institutions:
Comprises commercial banks. † From 1975 through 1978, *lines 20, 21,* and *26c* include net local interbank claims of commercial banks as a proxy for banks' deposits with the ECCB. Beginning in January 1979, the data reflect improved reporting of commercial bank accounts with the ECCB (*line 20*) and with branches in other member countries (*lines 21 and 26c*). † Beginning in December 2001, data are based on a new reporting system which provides improved classification and sectorization of the accounts.

Banking Survey:
† See notes on monetary authorities and banking institutions.

Money (National Definitions):
M1 comprises notes and coins held by the public and demand deposits in national currency of the private sector in commercial banks.

M2 comprises *M1* plus time, savings, and foreign currency deposits of the private sector in commercial banks.

Interest Rates:
Discount Rate (End of Period):
Rate charged by the ECCB on loans of last resort to commercial banks.

Money Market Rate:
Fixed rate on loans between commercial banks. The rate includes the commission charged by the ECCB as agent. † Beginning in October 2001, weighted average rate on loans between commercial banks. The rate is weighted by loan amounts.

Treasury Bill Rate:
Rate on three-month treasury bills. † Beginning in January 2001, rate on one-year treasury bills.

Savings Rate:
Maximum rate offered by commercial banks on savings deposits in national currency. † Beginning in June 2003, weighted average rate offered by commercial banks on savings deposits in national currency. The rate is weighted by deposit amounts.

Savings Rate (Foreign Currency):
Weighted average rate offered by commercial banks on savings deposits in foreign currency. The rate is weighted by deposit amounts.

Deposit Rate:
Maximum rate offered by deposit money banks on three-month time deposits. † Beginning in March 1991, weighted average rate offered by commercial banks on deposits in national currency. The rate is weighted by deposit amounts.

Deposit Rate (Foreign Currency):
Weighted average rate offered by commercial banks on deposits in foreign currency. The rate is weighted by deposit amounts.

Lending Rate:
Maximum rate charged by commercial banks on prime loans. † Beginning in March 1991, weighted average rate charged by commercial banks on loans in national currency. The rate is weighted by loan amounts.

Lending Rate (Foreign Currency):
Weighted average rate charged by commercial banks on loans in foreign currency. The rate is weighted by loan amounts.

Prices:
Consumer Prices:
Source S. Weights reference period: 1998, covers 122 items. The weights are derived from a household expenditure survey.

International Transactions:
All trade value data are reported directly to *IFS* by the Ministry of Trade, Trade and Industry. *Exports* include re-exports.

Government Finance:
Annual data are as reported for the *Government Finance Statistics Yearbook (GFSY)* and cover budgetary central government. The fiscal year ends December 31.

National Accounts:
Data are as reported by national authorities. As indicated by the country, the national accounts are compiled according to the recommendations of the *1993 SNA*.

Guatemala 258

Date of Fund Membership:
December 28, 1945

Standard Sources:
A: Bank of Guatemala, *Annual Report*
B: Bank of Guatemala, *Statistical Bulletin*

Exchange Rates:

Market Rate (End of Period and Period Average):
Central bank midpoint rate. Effective June 1, 1990, the principal rate refers to the average of the buying and selling rates, set on a weekly basis, for official receipts and payments, imports of petroleum, and coffee exports. In addition, there is a market exchange rate determined by commercial banks and exchange houses. Prior to that date, a system of independent floating was in effect. A multiple exchange rate system, introduced on November 16, 1984, was modified on June 4, 1986 and was abolished in 1991.

International Liquidity:
Line 1and is equal to *line 1ad,* converted into U.S. dollars at the dollar price of gold used by national sources, as reported to *IFS.*

Monetary Authorities:
Comprises the Bank of Guatemala only. † Beginning in December 1997, data are based on an improved sectorization of the accounts. † Beginning in December 2001, data are based on a new reporting system which provides improved classification and sectorization of the accounts.

Banking Institutions:
Comprises private commercial banks, the government-owned Crédito Hipotecario Nacional, and finance companies. Beginning in January 1990, includes the Financiera Nacional. † Beginning in December 1997, data are based on an improved sectorization of the accounts. † Beginning in December 2001, data are based on a new reporting system which provides improved classification and sectorization of the accounts. Beginning in December 2003, includes offshore banks. Beginning in December 2005, includes savings and loans associations.

Banking Survey:
† See notes on monetary authorities and banking institutions.

Money (National Definitions):
Base Money comprises notes and coins issued; legal reserve requirements, excess deposits, and obligatory investments of commercial banks; and deposits of finance companies, offshore banks, and savings and loans associations with the BoG.
M1 comprises currency in circulation outside the banking system and transferable deposits of the private sector in national currency with commercial banks. † Beginning December 2001, comprises currency in circulation outside the banking system and transferable deposits in national currency of other financial corporations, state and local governments, public nonfinancial corporations, and private sector with banking institutions.
M2 comprises M1, demand deposits of the private sector in foreign currency and time and savings deposits of the private sector in national and foreign currency with commercial banks, and mortgage bonds held by the public. † Beginning December 2001, comprises M1, time and savings deposits in national currency and deposits in foreign currency of other financial corporations, state and local governments, public nonfinancial corporations, and private sector with the BoG and banking institutions.
M3 comprises M2 plus securities other than shares issued by the BoG and banking institutions in national and foreign currency held by other financial corporations, state and local governments, public nonfinancial corporations, and private sector.

Interest Rates:

Discount Rate (End of Period):
Rate charged by the Bank of Guatemala on eligible paper presented by commercial banks.

Money Market Rate:
Weighted average rate on loans between commercial banks. The rate is weighted by loan amounts.

Savings Rate:
Weighted average rate offered by commercial banks on savings deposits. The rate is weighted by deposit amounts.

Deposit Rate:
Maximum rate offered by commercial banks on time and savings deposits. † Beginning in January 1997, weighted average rate offered by commercial banks on time and savings deposits. The rate is weighted by deposit amounts.

Lending Rate:
Maximum rate charged by commercial banks on loans. † Beginning in January 1997, weighted average rate charged by commercial banks on loans. The rate is weighted by loan amounts.

Prices and Labor:

Consumer Prices:
Source B consumer price index, CPI, weights reference period: March 1998–April 1999. The index is based on a household income and expenditure survey conducted by the National Institute of Statistics (INE) between March 1998 and April 1999 weights reference period. The CPI is computed by the INE.

International Transactions:
All trade data are from source B.

Government Finance:
Monthly, quarterly, and annual data are derived from source B. Data cover the operations of the budgetary central government but exclude receipt and use of own resources by budgetary units. Data do not cover the operations of the Guatemalan Social Security Institute or of other decentralized agencies with individual budgets. Expenditure and lending minus repayments data are adjusted to a cash basis by including the changes in floating debt. Data on foreign financing differ from those published in source B in that bonds held by nonresidents are included in foreign financing, while in source B they are included in domestic financing. † Prior to 1994, revenue data included grants, and expenditure data included lending minus repayments, without adjustment to a cash basis. The fiscal year ends December 31.

National Accounts:

Data are from source B. As indicated by the country, data are compiled according to the recommendations of the *1953 SNA*.

Guinea   656

Date of Fund Membership:

September 28, 1963

Standard Source:

B: Central Bank of the Republic of Guinea, *Cahiers Monétaires Mensuels (Monthly Monetary Bulletin)*

Exchange Rates:

The official exchange rate of the Guinean franc was set and quoted weekly against the U.S. dollar until end-October 1994; since November 1, 1994, the exchange rate of the Guinean franc is determined in the interbank market for foreign exchange.

International Liquidity:

Data expressed in U.S. dollars on *Foreign Exchange (line 1d.d)* and *Gold (line 1and)* are derived from data denominated in national currency from components of the monetary authorities' *Foreign Assets (line 11),* using the end-of-period market rate (*line* **ae**).

Monetary Authorities:

Comprises the Central Bank of the Republic of Guinea and the operations of the government with the Fund. Beginning in December 1996, *Claims on Other Banking Institutions (line 12f)* excludes the Caisse Nationale de Sécurité Sociale (CNSS), which is included under *Claims on Central Government (line 12a).*

Deposit Money Banks:

Comprises commercial banks.

Interest Rates:

Refinancing Rate (End of Period):
Central bank lending rate for preferential refinancing.

Savings Rate:
Minimum rate on passbook savings deposits.

Deposit Rate:
Minimum rate on term deposits of at least three months.

Lending Rate:
Ceiling rate on medium- and long-term bank loans.

Government Finance:

Data are as reported in the *Government Finance Statistics Yearbook* and cover budgetary central government The fiscal year ends December 31.

Guinea-Bissau   654

Date of Fund Membership:

March 24, 1977

Standard Source:

B: Banque Centrale des États de l'Afrique de l'Ouest, *Notes d'information et statistiques (Informative Notes and Statistics)*

Exchange Rates:

Official Rate: (End of Period and Period Average):
Beginning in end-December 1993, the official exchange rate was adjusted daily to keep the spread between the buying rate in the official and free markets at 2 percent. The free market exchange rate is determined by supply and demand conditions. As of May 2, 1997, Guinea-Bissau has adopted as the national currency the CFA franc following its membership in the West African Monetary Union and the BCEAO. The currency conversion between the Guinean peso and the CFA franc was set at the rate of PG 65 per CFA franc, on the basis of the December 31, 1996 market rates. Prior to January 1999, the official rate was pegged to the French franc at the rate of CFAF 100 per French franc. From January 1, 1999, the CFAF is pegged to the euro at a rate of CFA franc 655.957 per euro.

International Liquidity:

Gold is revalued on a quarterly basis at the rate communicated by the BCEAO, which corresponds to the lowest average fixing in the London market.

Monetary Authorities:

Comprises the national branch of the BCEAO only. The amount of currency outside banks is estimated by subtracting, from the amount of CFA franc notes issued by Guinea-Bissau, the estimated amounts of Guinea-Bissau's currency in the cash held by the banks of all member countries of the Union. Beginning in 1997, data reflect Guinea-Bissau's entry into the West African Monetary Union and the compilation of the data on the Central Bank of West African States' (BCEAO's) basis.

Deposit Money Banks:

Comprises commercial banks and development banks and includes certain banking operations of the Treasury and the Post Office. The Treasury accepts customs duty bills (reported separately in *line 22d.i*). Through its many branches, the Postal Checking System acts as the main depository for the private sector in the interior of Guinea-Bissau. † See note on monetary authorities.

Monetary Survey:

The data reported agree with source B aggregates, as given in the table on the position of the monetary institutions, except for *line 31n,* for which source B treats long-term foreign liabilities and SDR allocations as a foreign liability, whereas *IFS* reports the former separately and includes the latter in *line 37r*. Moreover, valuation differences exist as a result of the *IFS* calculations of reserve position in the Fund and the SDR holdings, both components of *line 11,* based on Fund record. † See note on monetary authorities.

Interest Rates:

Bank Rate (End of Period):
Rate on repurchase agreements between the BCEAO and the banks. † Prior to October 1, 1993 data refer to basic discount rate offered by the BCEAO.

Money Market Rate:
Rate paid on overnight interbank advances.

Deposit Rate:
Rate offered by banks on time deposits of CFAF 500,000–2,000,000 for under six months.

Lending Rate:
Average lending rate charged by banks.

Prices:

Consumer Prices:
Source S. Weights Reference Period: 1996; Geographical Coverage: Bissau metropolitan area; Number of Items in Basket: 51; Basis for Calculation: The weights are derived from the survey of household expenditure in Bissau in 1986.

International Transactions:

All trade value data are from source B.

Balance of Payments:
The figures shown are derived from reports, in terms of U.S. dollars, sent to the IMF by the Central Bank of Guinea-Bissau.

Government Finance:

† Prior to 1987, data are as reported in the *Government Finance Statistics Yeabook (GFSY)* and cover budgetary central government. Beginning in 1987, data are derived from Ministry of Finance sources and cover budgetary central government. The fiscal year ends December 31.

National Accounts:

Source B.

Guyana   336

Date of Fund Membership:

September 26, 1966

Standard Sources:

A: Bank of Guyana, *Annual Report*
B: Bank of Guyana, *Monthly Statistical Bulletin*
S: The Statistical Bureau, Ministry of Economic Development, *Quarterly Statistical Digest, Monthly Account Relating to External Trade*

Exchange Rates:

Market Rate (End of Period and Period Average):
Central bank midpoint rate. From 1984 through February 1991, the Guyana dollar was pegged to a basket of currencies.

Monetary Authorities:

Comprises the Bank of Guyana only. † Beginning in August 1993, data are based on an improved reporting system. † Beginning in December 2001, data are based on a new reporting system which provides an improved classification and sectorization of the accounts.

Banking Institutions:

Comprises commercial banks, new building societies, and trust companies. † Beginning in December 2001, data are based on a new reporting system which provides an improved classification and sectorization of the accounts.

Banking Survey:

† See notes on monetary authorities and banking institutions.

Nonbank Financial Institutions:

Comprises finance companies. † Beginning in December 2001, includes life insurance companies, nonlife insurance companies, and pension funds. Data are based on a new reporting system which provides an improved classification and sectorization of the accounts. Beginning in September 2005, includes asset management companies.

Financial Survey:

† See notes on monetary authorities, banking institutions, and nonbank financial institutions.

Money (National Definitions):

Base Money comprises currency in circulation.
Reserve Money comprises currency issue and deposits of the commercial banks with the Bank of Guyana including the External Payment Deposit Scheme (EPDS). The external payment deposits were local currency deposits made by commercial banks on behalf of importers when restrictions were imposed on foreign exchange transactions. By depositing money in external payment deposits with commercial banks, resident importers could expect to receive foreign currency with which to make their payments. Although this scheme was discontinued after 1990, those depositors that disagreed to take losses arising from the discontinuation still keep the questioned amounts in the accounts pending final settlement.
M1 comprises currency in circulation, demand deposits in national currency of the private sector in commercial banks, and checks outstanding.
M2 comprises *M1* plus time and savings deposits in national currency of the private sector in commercial banks.

Interest Rates:

All interest rate data are from source B.

Treasury Bill Rate:
Average tender rate for three-month treasury bills.

Savings Rate:
Rate offered by commercial banks on small savings deposits in national currency.

Deposit Rate:
Rate offered by commercial banks on three-month time deposits.

Lending Rate:
Prime rate charged by commercial banks on loans to preferred customers.

Prices:

Consumer Prices:
Source S. Weights Reference Period: 1992/3; Geographical Coverage: Georgetown only; Number of Items in Basket: 238; Basis for Calculation: weights were derived from the Household Income and Expenditure Survey (HIES) conducted in 1992/3.

International Transactions:

Exports and Imports:
All trade value data are from source B as compiled by the Statistical Bureau. *Exports* include re-exports.

Volume of Exports:
IFS average of sugar, bauxite, and rice with a 1995 value of exports as weights.

Government Finance:

† Beginning in 1970, data are as reported by the Central Bank of Guyana and cover budgetary central government. † Beginning in 1986, foreign debt includes central government, public guaranteed debt, and Bank of Guyana debt. The fiscal year ends December 31.

National Accounts:

Source B.

Haiti 263

Date of Fund Membership:
September 8, 1953

Standard Source:
B: Bank of the Republic of Haiti, *Quarterly Bulletin of Statistics*

Exchange Rates:

Market Rate (End of Period):
Central bank average rate weighted by the volume of transactions in the banking and informal markets. Since April 1995, the Bank of the Republic of Haiti (BRH) has operated a dollar clearinghouse. Commercial banks quote buying and selling rates for certain other currencies based on the buying and selling rates of the dollar in exchange markets abroad. The market is dominated by commercial banks, with the money changers and other, informal market agents following this market.

Monetary Authorities:

Comprises the Bank of the Republic of Haiti (BRH) only. † Beginning in September 1997, data are based on an improved sectorization of the accounts. † Beginning in December 2001, data are based on an improved classification and sectorization of the accounts. † Beginning in October 2006, data are based on a new reporting system which provides improved classification and sectorization of the accounts.

Banking Institutions:

Comprises commercial banks. † Beginning in September 1997, data are based on an improved sectorization of the accounts. † Beginning in December 2001, data are based on an improved classification and sectorization of the accounts. † Beginning in October 2006, data are based on a new reporting system which provides improved classification and sectorization of the accounts.

Banking Survey:

† See notes on monetary authorities and banking institutions.

Money (National Definitions):

Reserve Money comprises currency in circulation, banker's correspondent and other accounts at the Bank of the Republic of Haiti (BRH), commercial banks' investment in BRH securities, and transferable and time deposits of state and local governments, public nonfinancial corporations, private sector, and other financial corporations at the BRH in national and foreign currency. Currency in circulation refers to notes and coins issued by the BRH less currency in the vaults of the BRH.

M1 comprises currency in circulation and transferable deposits. Currency in circulation refers to notes and coins issued by the BRH less the amount held by commercial banks. Transferable deposits refer to the current account deposits in national currency of the private sector with commercial banks.

M2 comprises M1, savings deposits, time deposits, and securities other than shares issued by commercial banks in national currency held by the private sector. Time deposits refer to both conventional time deposits and bonds and debentures in national currency of the private sector with commercial banks.

M3 comprises M2 plus transferable deposits, savings deposits, and time deposits in foreign currency of the private sector with commercial banks.

Interest Rates:

Central Bank Bond Rate:
Rate on the last monthly issue of 91-day central bank bonds auctioned by the BRH.

Savings Rate:
Average of minimum and maximum rates offered by commercial banks on savings deposits in national currency.

Savings Rate (Foreign Currency):
Average rate offered by commercial banks on savings deposits in foreign currency.

Deposit Rate:
Average of minimum and maximum rates offered by commercial banks on time deposits in national currency.

Deposit Rate (Foreign Currency):
Average rate offered by commercial banks on time deposits in foreign currency.

Lending Rate:
Average of minimum and maximum rates charged by commercial banks on loans in national currency.

Lending Rate (Foreign Currency):
Average rate charged by commercial banks on non-preferential loans in foreign currency.

Prices:

Consumer Prices:
Weights reference period August 2004. Geographical Coverage: 36 towns and rural communities and 9 sectors of the metropolitan region of Port-au-Prince; Number of Items in the Basket: 3,179 basic products, including those represented in the informal sector; Basis for Calculation: weights are based on the results of the 2000 household consumption budget survey and updated in the light of price trends between 2000 and August 2004; in particular, it takes into account the elimination of the subsidy for prices of petroleum products.

International Transactions:

All trade data are supplied directly by the national authorities; they are compiled by the General Customs Office.

Government Finance:

Monthly and annual data are as reported by the Bank of the Republic of Haiti and cover consolidated central government. Annual data refer to a fiscal year different from calendar year. The fiscal year ends September 30.

National Accounts:

Line 99b includes a statistical discrepancy. *Line 96f* includes government consumption expenditures.

Honduras 268

Date of Fund Membership:

December 27, 1945

Standard Source:

B: Central Bank, *Statistical Bulletin*

Exchange Rates:

Market Rate (End of Period and Period Average):

Since July 1994, the exchange rate has been determined through daily auctions by the Central Bank. From February 13, 1992 through June 30, 1992, the principal rate referred to the interbank rate which was the average exchange rate in the exchange house market in the preceding week. In addition, there was a market exchange rate determined by the foreign exchange houses. Prior to that period, the exchange rates had been unified. Effective July 1, 1992, the interbank exchange rate was eliminated, and all foreign exchange transactions are effected through the free market.

International Liquidity:

Gold (National Valuation) (line 1and) is obtained by converting the value in national currency terms, as reported in the country's standard sources, using the prevailing exchange rate, as given in *line* **ae** or **we**.

Monetary Authorities:

Comprises the Central Bank of Honduras (CBH) only. † Beginning in December 1997, data are based on an improved sectorization of the accounts.

Deposit Money Banks:

Comprises commercial banks. † See note on monetary authorities.

Monetary Survey:

† See note on monetary authorities.

Other Banking Institutions:

Comprises development banks, savings and loan associations, and finance companies. † Beginning in December 1997, data are based on an improved sectorization of the accounts.

Banking Survey:

† See notes on monetary authorities, deposit money banks, and other banking institutions.

Money (National Definitions):

Reserve Money (M0) comprises notes and coins issued, deposits of commercial banks and other banking institutions in the CBH in national currency, and securities (monetary absorption certificates) issued by the CBH and used to constitute compulsory investments in addition to the required reserves. Beginning in October 1997, excludes deposits of FONAPROVI in the CBH in national currency.

M1 comprises currency outside the banking system and demand deposits in national currency of the private sector in the CBH, commercial banks, and development banks.

M2 comprises *M1* plus time, savings, and other deposits in national currency of the private sector in commercial banks, development banks, savings and loans associations, and finance companies; other deposits, including deposits for foreign currency purchase in auctions, in national currency of the private sector in the CBH; and securities (monetary absorption certificates) issued by the CBH held by the private sector.

M3 comprises *M2* and time, savings, and other deposits in foreign currency of the private sector in commercial banks, development banks, savings and loans associations, and finance companies.

Interest Rates:

Discount Rate (End of Period):
Rate charged by the CBH on loans to commercial banks.

Savings Rate:
Average rate offered by commercial banks on savings deposits in national currency.

Savings Rate (Foreign Currency):
Average rate offered by commercial banks on savings deposits in foreign currency.

Deposit Rate:
Weighted average rate offered by commercial banks on time deposits in national currency. The rate is weighted by deposit amounts for all maturities.

Deposit Rate (Foreign Currency):
Weighted average rate offered by commercial banks on time deposits in foreign currency. The rate is weighted by deposit amounts for all maturities.

Lending Rate:
Weighted average rate charged by commercial banks on loans in national currency. The rate is weighted by loan amounts for all maturities.

Lending Rate (Foreign Currency):
Weighted average rate charged by commercial banks on loans in foreign currency. The rate is weighted by loan amounts for all maturities.

Government Bond Yield:
Weighted average yield on government bonds. Yields are calculated as volume-weighted yields on government bonds of different maturities traded through weekly public auctions.

Prices and Labor:

Consumer Prices:
Source B Laspeyres index. Weights Reference Period: 1998–1999. Geographical Coverage: whole national territory; Number of Items in Basket: 282; Basis for Calculation: weights are derived

from a Household Expenditure Survey conducted in 1998–1999 on 3746 urban and rural households.

International Transactions:
All trade data are from source B.

Volume of Exports:
IFS average of bananas, coffee, frozen beef, sugar, and wood with a 1995 value of exports as weights.

Export Prices:
IFS average of bananas, coffee, frozen beef, sugar, and wood with a 1995 value of exports as weights.

Government Finance:
Data are derived from source B and cover budgetary central government. The fiscal year ends December 31.

National Accounts:
Source B. Source B. As indicated by the country, the national accounts are compiled according to the recommendation of the *1953 SNA*.

Hungary   944

Date of Fund Membership:
May 6, 1982

Standard Sources:
A: National Bank of Hungary, *Monthly Report*
N: Central Statistical Office, *Statistical Yearbook*
S: Central Statistical Office, *Monthly Statistical Bulletin*

Exchange Rates:
Official Rate: (End of Period and Period Average):
National bank midpoint rate. Beginning October 1991, a unified exchange rate pegged to a composite of currencies was introduced.

International Liquidity:
Foreign Exchange (line 1d.d) comprises holdings of convertible currencies plus swapped gold.

Monetary Authorities:
Comprises the National Bank of Hungary (NBH) only. † Beginning in 1990, *Claims on Central Government (line 12a)* include debt of the central budget, owing to valuation differences previously recorded in *Valuation Changes (line 17rv)*. *Time and Foreign Currency Deposits (line 15)* include foreign currency deposits of banking institutions. †Beginning in January 1999, *Foreign Assets (line 11)* and *Foreign Liabilities (line 16c)* include financial derivatives; beginning in January 2001, these financial derivatives are recorded at market values. *Other Liabilities to Banks (line 14n)* include foreign currency deposits, repurchase agreement deposits, syndicated loans, and noncallable forint deposits of monetary financial institutions (MFIs) other than the NBH.

Banking Institutions:
Aggregates the accounts of resident banks, specialized credit institutions, and co-operative credit institutions classified as "other MFIs," in accordance with the *1995 ESA* standards. *Other Claims on Monetary Authorities (line 20n)* include foreign currency deposits, repurchase agreement deposits, syndicated loans, and noncallable forint deposits of "other MFIs" with the NBH. † Beginning in 1990, *Demand Deposits (line 24)* include sight forint deposits of households, previously shown in *Time, Savings, and Foreign Currency Deposits (line 25)*. Prior to 1990, *Demand Deposits (line 24)* included only current accounts of domestic nonbanks.

Banking Survey:
† See notes on monetary authorities and banking institutions.

Money (National Definitions):
Monetary Base (line 19m) comprises the average of notes and coins plus daily compulsory reserve deposits plus overnight deposits of "other MFIs" with the NBH. The averages of these components are calculated based on daily balances during the reporting month. Prior to April 1998, monetary base consists of the month-end outstanding levels of notes and coins plus the average of daily compulsory reserve deposits and other forint balances of "other MFIs" (excluding overnight deposits) with the NBH. Prior to September 1998, daily averages of compulsory reserves refer only to the last two weeks of the month.
M1 (line 39ma) includes currency outside MFIs and overnight deposits (comprising forint and foreign currency sight deposits) of resident non-MFIs other than central government held with MFIs. Prior to January 1993, M1 comprises currency outside MFIs and forint sight deposits of resident non-MFIs other than central government held with MFIs.
M2 (line 39mb) comprises M1 plus deposits with agreed maturity up to two years of resident non-MFIs other than central government held with MFIs. Prior to January 1993, M2 includes M1 plus time and savings forint deposits and all foreign currency deposits of resident non-MFIs other than central government held with MFIs. Beginning in January 1992, M2 definition was modified; specific instruments issued by "other MFIs" were reclassified as deposits.
M3 (line 39mc) includes M2 plus liabilities arising from repurchase agreements plus debt securities issued by MFIs with original maturity of up to two years plus shares/units issued by money marked funds held with residents other than MFIs and central government. Prior to January 1993, M3 comprises M2 plus securities issued by "other MFIs" (e.g., bonds, CDs, and other debt securities, as defined by the Securities Act).
M4 (line 39md) includes M3 plus government securities (bonds and treasury bills) and domestic NBH bills held by resident non-MFIs.

Interest Rates:
All interest rate data are from source A.

Discount Rate (End of Period):
Basic rate at which NBH offers loans with maturity of more than one year to "other MFI's." As of July 13, 2001, the base rate and rate on two-week deposit facilities at the NBH are identical.

Treasury Bill Rate:
Weighted average yield on 90-day Treasury bills sold at auctions.

Deposit Rate:
Period average rate offered by "other MFIs" on deposits with maturity of up to one year to nonfinancial enterprises, weighted by volume of new deposits received during the last reporting month. † Prior to January 1995, weighted average rate offered by

banks on deposits with maturity of over one month and up to one year. † Prior to January 1990, simple arithmetic rate offered by banks on deposits with maturity of over one month and up to one year.

Lending Rate:
Period average rate charged by "other MFIs" on loans with maturity of less than one year to nonfinancial enterprises, weighted by volume of new credit extended during the last reporting month.

Prices, Production, Labor:

Producer Prices:
Source S. Annuallly revised weights; Coverage: the mining and quarrying, manufacturing, electricity, gas, steam, and water supply sectors; Number of Items in Basket: 7140 selected products; Basis for Calculation: weights are calculated by the value of sales to obtain indices at the 4-digit level of the national classification of activities.

Consumer Prices:
Source S. Annually revised weights; Geographical Coverage: whole national territory; Number of Items in Basket: 900; Basis for Calculation: weights are derived from macrostatistics data after the adjustment of the data with the latest Household Budget Survey.

Industrial Production:
Source S. Weights Reference Period: 2000; Sector Coverage: mining and quarrying, manufacturing, electricity, gas, steam, and water supply sectors; Basis for Calculation: the data are weighted by gross output.

Wages:
Net monthly earnings. Source S. Weights reference period: 1995. The data cover the net monthly earnings of full-time employees of all enterprises in the economy employing more than 10 persons and include the basic wages and salaries, supplements, wages in kind, bonuses, premiums, and payments for time not worked.

International Transactions:

Exports and Imports:
All trade data are from source S. Prior to January 1996, exports and imports data exclude customs free zones. Prior to January 1997, volume of exports and imports exclude customs free zones. *Exports* and *Imports* c.i.f. exclude repairs on goods and operating leasing. Imports f.o.b. only exclude repairs on goods and operating leasing from 1997 onwards. Data on exports and imports include re-exports until June 1989; from July 1989 onward the data exclude re-exports.

Unit values:
Source S, weights reference period: 1995. The series comprise chainlinked versions of indices compiled on a cumulative basis with the corresponding periods of the preceding year as the base.

Balance of Payments:
Services: Credit (line 77ahd) and *Services: Debit (line 77aid):* Beginning in 1982, data are shown on a net basis.
Other Capital, n.i.e. (line 77g.d): Beginning in 1982, includes Net Errors and Omissions (line 77e.d).

Government Finance:
Prior to 2006, cash data are as reported by the Ministry of Finance and cover the consolidated operations of the central government Data on general government are derived from source V. The fiscal year ends December 31.

National Accounts:
As indicated by the country, all data are from source N and are compiled while taking into consideration both the recommendations of the *1993 SNA* as well as the System of Balance of the National Economy (commonly referred to as the Material Product System) and the special institutional features of the Hungarian economic system.

Iceland   176

Date of Fund Membership:
December 27, 1945

Standard Sources:
A: Central Bank, *Annual Report*
B: Central Bank, *Statistical Bulletin*

Exchange Rates:

Official Rate: (End of Period and Period Average):
Central bank midpoint rate. The official rate is determined on the basis of a trade-weighted basket of currencies. Effective March 28, 2001, rates are market determined.

International Liquidity:
Gold (National Valuation) (line 1and) is obtained by converting the value in national currency, as reported in the country's standard sources, using the national currency/dollar conversion rates utilized for balance sheet purposes. These conversion rates differ from the prevailing exchange rates reported in *IFS*. † Beginning in December 1999, gold valuation is based on market prices.

Monetary Authorities:
Comprises Central Bank of Iceland only. † Beginning in December 1999, data are based on revised framework of the central bank balance sheet.

Deposit Money Banks:
Comprises commercial and savings banks. † Data from January 2002 onward reflect changes in the coverage of deposit money banks and in the classification and sectorization of financial instruments.

Monetary Survey:
† See notes to sections 10 and 20.

Interest Rates:

Discount Rate (End of Period):
Central bank's discount rate on overnight loans. † Data prior to March 1998 refer to central bank rates on loans on bills, and prior to 1992, on overdrafts to deposit money banks.

Money Market Rate:
End-of-month yield on the interbank overnight market.

Treasury Bill Rate:

† Before 1992, data refer to yields set by the government in the primary market. Beginning in 1992, data refer to annualized secondary market yield on 90-day treasury bills.

Deposit Rate:

† Before 1988, data refer to interest rate on 3-month deposits. † From 2003 onward, data refer to interest rate on money market accounts.

Housing Bond Rate:

Annualized secondary market real yield on indexed housing bonds of 25-year maturity.

Lending Rate:

Weighted average interest rate on general purpose loans.

Government Bond Yield:

Annualized secondary market real yield on indexed 10-year government bonds.

Prices, Production, Labor:

Consumer Prices:

Source S. Weights Reference Period: March 1997; Geographical Coverage: The entire country; Number of Items in Basket: 4000; Basis for Calculation: the CPI weights cover domestic private consumption based on a continuous household budget survey which covers the entire country and all income groups. The index is rebased every year on the basis of a household budget survey.

Wages:

Source S, weights reference period December 1988. Wage index is calculated and published according to law no. 89/1989. The wage index is based on average for fixed hour earnings each month, calculated and published in the month following calculation.

Total Fish Catch:

Index constructed from source B data in thousand metric tons.

International Transactions:

Exports and Imports, c.i.f.:

Total value data and data on individual commodities are from source B.

Volume of Exports and Imports:

Source B indices of volume of exports and imports, weights reference period 1980. The indices are chain indices computed with preceding year weights.

Unit Value of Exports:

Source B chain index with current year weights of unit values of all merchandise exports, weights reference period 1980.

Unit Value of Imports:

Source B chain unit value index with current year weights of general merchandise imports, base 1980. The volume indices and both unit value indices are interdependent.

Government Finance:

† From 1998 onward, monthly, quarterly and annual data are derived from the records of the State Accounting Office and cover the operations of budgetary central government. Data are as reported by the National Economic Institute. † Beginning in

January 2004, monthly data are reported in the *GFSM 2001* analytical framework The fiscal year ends December 31.

National Accounts:

Source B. As indicated by the country, from 1990 onward figures are according to the *ESA 95*.

India   534

Date of Fund Membership:

December 27, 1945

Standard Sources:

A: Reserve Bank, *Report on Currency and Finance*
B: Reserve Bank, *Bulletin*

Exchange Rates:

Market Rate (End of Period and Period Average):
Effective March 1, 1993, the exchange rate of the rupee is market-determined.

International Liquidity:

Gold (National Valuation) (line 1and) is obtained by converting the value in national currency terms, as reported in the country's standard sources, using the prevailing exchange rate, as given in *line* **ae**.

Monetary Authorities:

Consolidates the Reserve Bank of India and monetary authority functions undertaken by the central government. The contra-entry to Treasury IMF accounts, SDR holdings, and currency issues is included in *line 12a. Foreign Liabilities* are mainly *Use of Fund Credit: Gen. Dept.* (see *line 2e.s*).

Deposit Money Banks:

Comprises commercial and cooperative banks. † Since 1978, a new classification of *Demand and Time Deposits* has reduced *lines 24* and *34* and increased *lines 25* and *35*. Latest monthly data are preliminary.

Interest Rates:

All interest rate data are from source B.

Bank Rate (End of Period):
Standard rate at which the Reserve Bank makes advances to scheduled banks against commercial paper and government securities.

Money Market Rate:
Rate offered in Bombay interbank market. Quarterly and annual data are weighted averages of weekly series.

Lending Rate:
Rate charged on advances from the State Bank of India to the commercial banks. This prime rate regulates all interest rates charged by the commercial banks on various categories of loans.

Government Bond Yield:
† Beginning in 1971, this rate is the average yield on government 5½ percent bonds maturing in the years 1999 and 2000.

Prices, Production, Labor:

All data on prices and production are from source B.

Share Prices:

Data refer to the index of security prices, all India, ordinary shares in all industries, average of weeks ending Saturday, base 1970–71. † Beginning in April 1979, data refer to the monthly average of daily closing figures for the Bombay Stock Exchange Sensitive Index (SENSEX), base 1978–79=100.

Wholesale Prices:

Data refer to Laspeyres index numbers of wholesale prices, base 1993–94 covering 98 primary articles, 318 manufactured products and 19 fuel and power items.

Consumer Prices:

Source B. Weights Reference Period: 1999–2000; Geographical Coverage: 78 industrial cities/towns; Number of Items in Basket: 260; Basis for Calculation: Weights are based on Household Expenditure Survey and are updated at approximately 10-yearly intervals.

Industrial Production:

Source S. Weights Reference Period: 1993–94; Sectoral Coverage: mining, manufacturing, and electricity; Basis for Calculation: the weights for the three sectors (mining, manufacturing, and electricity) are based on gross value added in the base year.

Employment:

Data refer to public sector and establishments of non-agricultural private sector with 10 or more persons employed.

International Transactions:

Value of Exports and Imports:
Source B. Data include indirect transit trade of Nepal, Tibet, Sikkim, and Bhutan and exclude military goods, fissionable materials, bunkers, ships, and aircraft. The general system of recording trade transactions is used.

Unit Value of Exports and Imports:
Data refer to source B Paasche indices, base 1978–79.

Government Finance:

Annual data are as reported for the *Government Finance Statistics Yearbook (GFSY)* and cover budgetary central government. Annual data refer to a fiscal year different from calendar year. The fiscal year ends March 31.

National Accounts:

Lines *99a* and *99b* include a statistical discrepancy. As indicated by the country, from 1987 onwards data have been revised following the implementation of the *1993 SNA.*

Indonesia   536

Date of Fund Membership:

April 15, 1954
Withdrew from membership: August 17, 1965
Readmitted to membership: February 21, 1967

Standard Sources:

A: Bank Indonesia, *Annual Report*
B: Bank Indonesia, *Monthly Bulletin*
S: Central Bureau of Statistics, *Indikator Ekonomi*

Exchange Rates:

Market Rate (End of Period and Period Average):
Central bank midpoint rate.

International Liquidity:

IFS line land follows national valuation procedures, which revalue gold quarterly at 80 percent of the London market quotation on the fifteenth day of the last month of every quarter. *Line land* is equal to *line lad* converted into U.S. dollars at the dollar price of gold used by national sources as reported to *IFS.*

Monetary Authorities:

Comprises the Bank Indonesia only. † Beginning in December 1992, data are based on a new reporting system which provides an improved sectorization of the accounts. † Beginning in December 2001, data are based on an improved classification and sectorization of the accounts. † Beginning in June 2004, data are based on a new reporting system which provides improved classification and sectorization of the accounts.

Banking Institutions:

Comprises commercial banks, which are grouped into state banks, regional government banks, private domestic banks, and foreign and joint venture banks. † Beginning in December 1992, data are based on a new reporting system which provides an improved sectorization of the accounts. † Beginning in December 2001, data are based on an improved classification and sectorization of the accounts. † Beginning in June 2004, includes rural banks. Data are based on a new reporting system which provides improved classification and sectorization of the accounts.

Banking Survey:

† See notes on monetary authorities and banking institutions .

Money (National Definitions):

Base Money comprises currency in circulation, demand deposits of commercial banks at Bank Indonesia (BI) in national currency, demand deposits of the private sector, state and local governments, and nonbank financial institutions at BI in national currency, and some private sector savings deposits at BI in national currency.

M1 comprises currency in circulation outside commercial banks, demand deposits of the private sector, state and local governments, nonfinancial public enterprises, and nonbank financial institutions at BI and commercial banks in national currency, and some private sector savings deposits at BI in national currency.

M2 comprises M1 plus time and savings deposits in national currency and deposits in foreign currency of the private sector, state and local governments, nonfinancial public enterprises, and nonbank financial institutions at BI and commercial banks.

Interest Rates:

All interest rate data are from source B.

Discount Rate (End of Period):
Rate on one-month Bank Indonesia Certificates (SBIs).

Money Market Rate:
Rate on one-day loans between commercial banks.

Deposit Rate:
Average rate offered by commercial banks on six-month time deposits. † Beginning in January 1990, weighted average rate offered by commercial banks on three-month time deposits in national currency. Rate is weighted by deposit amounts.

Deposit Rate (Foreign Currency):
Weighted average rate offered by commercial banks on three-month time deposits in foreign currency. Rate is weighted by deposit amounts.

Lending Rate:
Weighted average rate charged by commercial banks on loans to the private sector for working capital in national currency. Rate is weighted by loan amounts.

Lending Rate (Foreign Currency):
Weighted average rate charged by commercial banks on loans to the private sector for working capital in foreign currency. Rate is weighted by loan amounts.

Prices, Production, Labor:

Share Prices:
Stock price index of the Jakarta Stock Exchange, base August 10, 1982.

Wholesale Prices:
Source S. Data are disseminated on the General Wholesale Price Index (2000=100), a Laspeyres index covering the agricultural, mining and quarrying, industry, import and export sectors. The weights used in the index are based on marketed surplus, including taxes, in the 2000 weights reference period.

Consumer Prices:
Source S. Weights Reference Period: 2002; Geographical Coverage: 45 major urban areas throughout Indonesia; Number of Items in Basket: Between 283 and 397; Basis for Calculation: The weights used in the index are based on the 2002 Cost of Living Survey (CLS).

Industrial Production:
Manufacturing production index (2000=100) measuring changes in real production of large and medium non-oil manufacturing establishments.

Manufacturing Production:
Source S. Weights Reference Period: 1993; Sectoral Coverage: non-oil manufacturing establishments; Basis for Calculation: the production index computation methodology is done using the Discrete Divisia procedure.

International Transactions:

Exports and Imports, c.i.f.:
Data are based on customs statistics.
Trade indices: Source B indices computed according to the Fisher ideal formula with weights reference period 1990.

Government Finance:

† Beginning in 1990, annual data are as reported for the *Government Finance Statistics Yearbook (GFSY)* and cover consolidated central government. The fiscal year ends March 31.

National Accounts:

Source B. Data compiled in accordance with the *1968 SNA*.

Iran, I.R. of   429

Data refer to the Islamic Republic of Iran. Revised annual data in financial sections 10, 20, 30, and 40 relating to Iranian years ending March 20 appeared in the January through March 1972 issues. Beginning with the April 1972 issue, these data refer to December 20.

Date of Fund Membership:
December 29, 1945

Standard Sources:
A: Central Bank, *Annual Report*
B: Central Bank, *Bulletin*
C: Central Bank

Exchange Rates:

Official Rate: (End of Period and Period Average):
The exchange rate system is based on a dual official exchange rate structure; the floating rate and the export rate. The floating rate applies mainly to the imports of essential goods, and the export rate applies to all other transactions. Beginning in March 1993, the exchange rate refers to the official floating rate. Prior to that date, the exchange rate referred to the basic official exchange rate of the Iranian rial, which was pegged to the SDR. † Beginning from March 2002, a unified exchange rate, determined at the inter-bank foreign exchange market, has replaced the dual foreign exchange rate system.

Market Rate:
Data refer to end-of-month average rate determined at the Tehran Stock Exchange.

Weighted Average:
Calculated as a weighted average of the exchange rates that prevailed during the month, where the weights are based on the authorities' estimates of the shares of transactions conducted at various exchange rates.

International Liquidity:

Gold holdings are for months ending the 20th, while *SDR* holdings and the *Reserve Position in the Fund* are as of the end of the month. *Monetary Authorities: Other Assets (line 3..d)* comprise foreign currency subscriptions to other international agencies and net payment agreement balances.

Gold (National Valuation) (line 1and) is equal to *Gold (Million Fine Troy Ounces) (line 1ad)*, valued at SDR 35 per fine troy ounce and converted into U.S. dollars at the dollar/SDR rate **sa** on the country page for the United States. Source E: OECD

Monetary Authorities:
Comprises Bank Markazi Jomhouri Islami Iran only.

Deposit Money Banks:
Comprises commercial banks.

Other Banking Institutions:
Comprises the Agricultural Bank, the Housing Bank, and the Industrial and Mining Bank.

Interest Rates:

Deposit Rate (End of Period):
Data refer to weighted average provisional rate of profits from non-public sectors' deposits with state-owned banks. The rate is weighted by the outstanding amount of the aforementioned deposits at the end of the reference period.

Lending Rate (End of Period):
Data refer to weighted average rate of expected returns on lending facilities extended by state-owned banks to public and non-public sectors. The rate is weighted by the outstanding amount of lending facilities extended to various economic sectors at the end of the reference period.

Prices and Production:

All indices on prices are from Source B.

Share Prices:

Source C, weights reference period: 1990–1991 average. Data cover all companies listed in Tehran Stock Exchange and are produced as a Laspeyres-type index based on average daily prices.

Wholesale Prices:

General index for Iran, includes exports, imports, and home goods, weights reference period: 1997–98.

Wholesale Prices, Home Goods:

Index for domestically produced and consumed goods, with weights reference period: 1997–98.

Consumer Prices:

Source C. Weights Reference Period: 1997–98.

Crude Petroleum Production:

Source B data, updated for current periods using production quantities as reported in the *Oil Market Intelligence.*

International Transactions:

Source C.

Exports:

Data include oil and gas. The volume index for petroleum is obtained by weighting volume indexes for crude petroleum and refined petroleum by their relative values of exports in 1980. Since April 1979, bunker oil has been included in the refined petroleum exports series. Beginning October 1980, data on the value and volume of oil exports and on the value of total exports are rough estimates based on information published in various petroleum industry journals.

Government Finance:

Data are compiled and reported by source A, using unpublished Ministry of Finance data. Data cover the budgetary central government and exclude the operations of the special purpose funds, the Social Insurance Organization, the pension funds, and the procurement and distribution centers. The fiscal year ends March 20.

National Accounts:

Data are as reported by national authorities. *Lines 99a* and *99b* include a statistical discrepancy.

Iraq   433

Date of Fund Membership:

December 27, 1945

Standard Sources:

A: Central Bank, *Annual Report*
B: Central Bank, *Bulletin*

Exchange Rates:

On October 15, 2003, the new national currency known as the "new Iraqi dinar" replaced the existing "old dinar" and the curency used in the North of Iraq, the"swiss dinar." The conversion rates for the new Iraqi dinar were as follows: one "old dinar" for one new Iraqi dinar and one unit of the "swiss" dinar for 150 new Iraqi dinars.

Market Rate (End of Period and Period Average):

Central bank midpoint rate. The exchange arrangement consists of an official rate, a special rate for exports, and a free-market rate. Since May 2004, the Central Bank of Iraq (CBI) has pursued exchange rate stability limiting the fluctuations of the Iraqi dinar to within ±1 percent. The exchange rate of the Iraqi dinar is determined in the foreign exchange market. Auctions are held daily, and eligible bidders may buy and sell foreign exchange at freely determined rates.

International Liquidity:

Gold (National Valuation) (line *1and*) is valued at market rates (London Gold Market).

Production:

Crude Petroleum Production:

Calculated from production quantities reported in the *Oil Market Intelligence.*

International Transactions:

Imports, c.i.f., from DOTS:

Data are based on reported data and estimates from *Direction of Trade Statistics (DOTS).*

Ireland   178

Data are denominated in pounds prior to January 1999 and in euros from January 1999 onward. The pound's irrevocable fixed conversion factor to the euro is 0.787564 pounds per euro. In 2002, the pound was retired from circulation and replaced by euro banknotes and coins. Beginning in January 1999, with the implementation of Stage Three of the European Economic and Monetary Union (EMU), an alternative euro area-wide definition of residency was introduced: All positions with residents of other euro area (EA) countries, including the European Central Bank (ECB), are classified as domestic positions, and foreign assets and foreign liabilities include only positions with non-euro area residents. Descriptions of the changes in the methodology and presentation of Ireland's accounts following the introduction of the euro are shown in the introduction to *IFS* and in the footnotes on the euro area page.

Date of Fund Membership:

August 8, 1957

Standard Sources:

A: Central Bank, *Annual Report*
B: Central Bank, *Quarterly Bulletin*
S: Central Statistics Office, *Statistical Bulletin*
V: Eurostat

Exchange Rates:

Prior to January 1999, the market rate related to the midpoint rate quoted at 2:30 p.m. in the Dublin Market. In January 1999, the pound became a participating currency within the Eurosystem, and the euro market rate became applicable to all transactions. In 2002, the pound was retired from circulation and replaced by euro banknotes and coins. For additional information, refer to the section on exchange rates in the introduction to *IFS* and the footnotes on the euro area page.

International Liquidity:

Beginning in January 1999, *Total Reserves minus Gold (line 1l.d)* is defined in accordance with the Eurosystem's statistical definition of international reserves. The international reserves of Ireland per the Eurosystem statistical definition at the start of the monetary union (January 1, 1999) in billions of U.S. dollars were as follows: *Total Reserves minus Gold,* $7,295; *Foreign Exchange,* $6,677; *SDRs,* $193; *Reserve Position in the Fund,* $426; *Other Reserve Assets,* $0; *Gold,* $130; *Gold (million fine troy ounces),* .451 ounces. *Foreign Exchange (line 1d.d):* Beginning in March 1979, gold and foreign exchange holdings exclude deposits at the European Monetary Cooperation Fund (EMCF), and the holdings of European currency units (ECUs) issued against these deposits are included in *line 1d.d. Gold (Eurosystem Valuation) (line 1and):* During 1994–98, gold was revalued at the midmarket closing price at the valuation date. From January 1999 onward, gold is valued at market prices at the end of each quarter. Memorandum data are provided on *Non-Euro Claims on Euro Area Residents* and *Euro Claims on Non-Euro Area Residents,* which represent positions as of the last Friday in each month. For additional information, refer to the section on international liquidity in the introduction to *IFS* and on the euro area page.

Monetary Authorities:

Comprises the Central Bank of Ireland, which is part of the Eurosystem beginning in January 1999. Beginning in 2002, *Currency Issued (line 14a)* includes euro banknotes and coins and, until December 2002, any unretired pounds. The recorded value of euro banknotes is based on a monthly allocation of total euro banknotes in circulation based on the Central Bank of Ireland's paid up share of the ECB's capital; it does not correspond to either the actual amount of euro banknotes placed in circulation by the Central Bank of Ireland which is shown in memo line *Currency Put into Circulation (line 14m),* nor the actual circulation of banknotes within the domestic territory. See section *Euro banknotes and coins* in the introduction to *IFS. Bonds and Money Market Instruments (line 16n.u)* include subordinated debt in the form of securities, other bonds, and money market paper. For a description of the accounts, refer to the section on monetary authorities in the introduction to *IFS.* Beginning with the data for end-November 2000, Monetary Authorities' *Foreign Assets (line 11), Foreign Liabilities (line 16c), Claims on Banking Institutions (line 12e.u),* and *Liabilities to Banking Institutions (line 14c.u)* are affected by a change from gross to net presentation of positions relating to the TARGET (Trans-European Automated Real-Time Gross Settlement Express Transfer) euro clearing system. (See *Recording of TARGET system positions* under *European Economic and Monetary Union (EMU)* in the introduction to *IFS.*) Beginning in 2002, *Claims on Banking Institutions (line 12e.u)* and *Liabilities to Banking Institutions (line 14c.u)* include "Intra-Eurosystem claims/liabilities related to banknote issue," which is a single net value representing the difference between the value of euro banknotes allocated to the Central Bank of Ireland according to the accounting scheme of the Eurosystem for issuing euro banknotes, and the value of euro banknotes put into circulation by the Central Bank of Ireland. See section *Euro banknotes and coins* in the introduction to *IFS.* Memo line *Net Claims on Eurosystem (line 12e.s)* equals gross claims on, less gross liabilities to, the ECB and other members of the Eurosystem. Comprises euro-denominated claims equivalent to the transfer of foreign currency reserves to the ECB, Intra-Eurosystem claims/liabilities related to banknote issue, net claims or liabilities within the TARGET clearing system, and other positions.

Banking Institutions:

† Beginning in 1982, data reflect the introduction of an improved call report form, which for the first time records data of resident offices on a residency-of-customer basis. From that date, the activities of nonresident offices are, therefore, excluded from the data, and accounts of nonresidents at resident offices are classified under *Foreign Assets (line 21)* and *Foreign Liabilities(line 26c).* Prior to January 1999, consolidated the associated banks, the non-associated banks, building societies, state-sponsored financial institutions, and trustee savings banks. The data were recorded net of provisions for bad and doubtful debts and certain offsets (see source B), and they differed from source B in that *IFS* does not apply a resident/nonresident distinction to capital account items, and *IFS* adjusts certain balance sheet items from an accrual to a cash basis. From January 1999 onward, the data are presented on a euro area-wide residency basis. *Claims on Monetary Authorities (line 20)* and *Credit from Monetary Authorities (line 26g)* refer to the Central Bank of Ireland. *Other Items (Net) (line 27r)* includes a small amount of currency issued by banking institutions. *Money Market Fund Shares (line 26m.u)* include shares/units issued by money market funds. *Bonds and Money Market Instruments (line 26n.u)* include subordinated debt in the form of securities, other bonds, and money market paper. For a description of the accounts, refer to the section on banking institutions in the introduction to *IFS.*

Banking Survey (National Residency):

Beginning in December 1982, *Demand Deposits (line 34b.n)* reflected changes affecting the data of the deposit money banks, including improved sectorization, the exclusion on nonresident accounts, and a change in the method of allocating items in transit. The data differed from the source B measure of M1 as given in the money and other liquid assets table, in that *IFS* includes and source B excludes private sector deposits at the central bank, whereas source B's measure is based on all licensed banks' data and includes interest payable on nongovernment demand deposits. Prior to 2002, *Currency in Circulation (line 34a.n)* includes a small amount of currency issued by banking institutions. For a description of the accounts and the methodology, refer to the section Banking Survey (National Residence) in the introduction to *IFS*

Banking Survey (Euro Area-wide Residency):

For a description of the methodology and accounts, refer to the section Banking Survey (Euro Area-wide Residency) in the introduction to *IFS.*

Nonbank Financial Institutions:

Comprises the accounts of the hire-purchase finance companies, national installment savings, and the post office banks. † Prior to January 1995, consolidated the accounts of building societies, state-sponsored financial institutions, trustees savings banks, hire-purchase finance companies, national installment savings, and the post office savings bank.

Interest Rates:

Discount Rate (End of Period) (line 60):
Short-term facility rate charged by the Bank of Ireland on funds, up to a specified quota, lent to banks experiencing day-to-day liquidity shortages. The discount rate was suspended from

November 23, 1992 to February 5, 1993. † Prior to 1979, data refer to the discount rate. Beginning in January 1999, central bank policy rates are discontinued. See Eurosystem policy rate series on the Euro Area page.

Money Market Rate (line 60b):
Rate on one-month fixed interbank deposits. From May 1994, data refer to closing rates. Prior to this date, average daily rates were used.

Treasury Bill Rate (line 60c):
Yield on 90-day exchequer notes. Prior to February 1992, this rate represented the yield on three-month treasury bills.

Deposit Rate (line 60l):
Rate offered by licenced banks on demand deposits in the range of IR£5,000 to IR£25,000.

Deposit Rate (lines 60lhs and 60lcs):
See notes in the Introduction to *IFS*.

Lending Rate (line 60p):
Lower point of range of rates charged on short-term loans to large commercial customers by the associated banks. Prior to 1991, data refer to the rate charged to AAA customers in the primary, manufacturing, and service sectors.

Lending Rate (lines 60phs, 60pns, 60phm, 60phn, 60pcs, and 60pcn):
See notes in the Introduction to *IFS*.

Government Bond Yield (line 61):
Representative yield on government securities with 15-year maturities. For additional information, refer to the section on interest rates in the introduction to *IFS* and on the euro area page.

Prices, Production, Labor:

Share Prices:
Source B index of share prices, Irish Stock Exchange's equity index of all Official List and USM equities, excluding UK-registered companies, weights reference period: December 1987.

Wholesale Prices:
Source B. Weights Reference Period: 2000; Coverage: the index consists of five series: industrial producer price indices; wholesale price indices for building and construction materials; wholesale price indices for energy products purchased by the manufacturing industry, and General Wholesale Price Index (GWPI); Number of Items in Basket: 7000 commodities; Basis for Calculation: the weights for the producer price index are net sector value weights where sales between the various sectors are excluded. Building and construction materials. Weights for the building and construction materials index are based on the cost of materials used by firms in the building and construction and allied trades industry as returned in a 1998 survey. Weights for capital goods are based on the provisional estimates of the value of fixed capital formation used in the 2001 National Income and Expenditure Accounts. Weights for the energy products index are based on the costs of different types of fuels purchased by industrial establishments as reported in the 2000 Census of Industrial Production. The weights for the GWPI were estimated using the 1990 Input-Output Table with the values updated to 2000.

Wholesale Prices: Output Manufacturing Industry:
Source B index of wholesale prices of output of manufacturing industry, weights reference period: 2000.

Consumer Prices:
Source S. Weights Reference Period: December 2001; Geographical Coverage: whole national territory; Number of Items in

Basket: 613; Basis for Calculation: weights are derived from the 1999–2000 Household Budget Survey.

Wages: Weekly Earnings:
Average weekly earnings by all industrial workers in manufacturing in pounds.

Industrial Production:
Source S. Weights Reference Period: 2000; Sectoral Coverage: manufacturing; mining, quarrying and turf, electricity, gas and water excluding construction; Basis for Calculation: data are reported by all industrial local units with 20 or more persons engaged with details provided on the quantity of production or on the value of production.

Manufacturing Employment:
Source S data, unadjusted, derived from quarterly samples of 1800 establishments with at least three employees, equaling about 90 percent of all employed.

International Transactions:

All value data on trade are from source S.

Volume of Exports:
Data are from source S. Annual indices of volume are Fisher ideal indices derived from an annual unit value index. Monthly indices are derived from monthly value and unit value indices, weights reference period: 1990.

Volume of Imports:
Source S data derived similarly to volume of export indices, base 1990.

Unit Value of Exports:
Data are from source S. Annual unit value indices are Fisher ideal indices. Monthly unit value indices are Laspeyres indices using weights of the previous year. All indices are chained, base 1990.

Unit Value of Imports:
Source S data derived similarly to unit value of export indices, weights reference period: 1990.

Government Finance:

Quarterly and annual cash data on central government are derived from source A Data on general government are derived from source V. The fiscal year ends December 31.

National Accounts:

Source S. As indicated by the country, data are based on the *ESA 95*. Prior to 1990, data are based on the *ESA 79*. GDP chain-linked volume measures are calculated based on the prices and weights of the previous year, using Laspeyres formula in general.

Israel   436

Date of Fund Membership:
July 12, 1954

Standard Sources:
A: Bank of Israel, *Annual Report*
B: Bank of Israel, *Economic Indicators, Banking Statistics*
S: Central Bureau of Statistics of Israel, *Monthly Bulletin of Statistics and Supplements, Foreign Trade Statistics Monthly*

Exchange Rates:

On September 4, 1985 the new sheqel, equal to 1,000 old she-qalim, was introduced.

Market Rate (End of Period and Period Average):
Noon midpoint rate ascertained by the Bank of Israel.

International Liquidity:

† Beginning in January 1997, data for *line 1d.d* include accrued interest on securities. *Gold (National Valuation) (line 1and)* is equal to *Gold (Million Fine Troy Ounces) (line 1ad),* valued at SDR 35 per fine troy ounce and converted into U.S. dollars at the dollar/SDR rate **sa** on the country page for the United States. Source E: OECD Data for *lines 7a.d* and *7b.d* are taken from source B and are slightly different from the corresponding data in *lines 21* and *26c.*

Monetary Authorities:

Comprises Bank of Israel only. Significant amounts shown in *line 17r* are due mainly to the inclusion of redeposits by commercial banks of the full amount of private foreign currency deposits and of time deposits linked to the exchange rate.

Deposit Money Banks:

Comprises the 29 ordinary banking corporations which are fully subject to the liquidity regulations. † As of December 1992, data on *Claims on Other Banking Institutions (line 22f)* are included in *Claims on the Private Sector (line 22d).* Data on claims include accrued interest and are net of provisions for losses. Beginning December 1992, other deposits, which were previously included in *Time and Savings Deposits (line 25),* are included in *Demand Deposits (line 24).* Earmarked government deposits, which were previously included in *Restricted Deposits (line 26b),* are included in *Central Government Deposits (line 26d). Claims on Other Banking Institutions* comprise claims on mortgage banks.

Monetary Survey:

Line 34 is equal to the source B measure of money supply.
Claims on Other Banking Institutions comprise claims on mortgage banks.

Interest Rates:

All rates are converted into annual rates by compounding the simple arithmetic averages of the monthly rates applicable on each day in the month.

Discount Rate:
Average rate on monetary loans offered by tender by the Bank of Israel to commercial banks.

Treasury Bill Rate:
Yield to maturity on short-term treasury bills.

Deposit Rate:
Average rate offered by commercial banks on all short-term deposits up to one year. Prior to September 1988, the rate offered by commercial banks on 14-day fixed deposits of NIS 20,000 was used.

Lending Rate:
Average effective cost of all unindexed credit in Israeli currency, including overdraft credit. Prior to January 1989, the average rate charged by commercial banks on overdrafts.

Prices, Production, Labor:

Share Prices:
Source S index, weights reference period: December 2000, refers to quotations on the 23rd of each month and covers all ordinary shares quoted on the Tel Aviv Exchange.

Wholesale Prices: Industrial Products:
Source S. Weights Reference Period: 2005; Coverage: all products and services sold by establishments in manufacturing, which includes the mining and quarrying industries, excluding the diamond industry; Number of Items in Basket: 1800 types of products and services; Basis for Calculation: weights for the present indices were obtained from the 2004/05 survey of manufacturing.

Consumer Prices:
Source S. Weights Reference Period: 2002; Geographical Coverage: whole national territory; Number of Items in Basket: 1320; Basis for Calculation: weights are derived from the 2002/03 Household Expenditure Surveys.

Wages: Daily Earnings:
Source S. Weights Reference Period: 2004; daily earnings covering total cash remuneration in manufacturing, mining, and quarrying. As of January 1978, the series is based on all employees. Prior to that date, it covered workers only. † The index excludes the diamond sector as of January 1979.

Industrial Production, Seasonally Adjusted:
Source S. Weights Reference Period: 2004; Sectoral Coverage: manufacturing, mining and quarrying, excluding diamonds; Basis for Calculation: the weights used in the index are the gross value added at factor cost obtained from an annual survey of manufacturing. † The index excludes the diamond sector as of January 1979.

Industrial Employment:
Source S. Weights Reference Period: 2004; Coverage: covering all employees engaged in manufacturing, mining, and quarrying. † The index excludes the diamond sector as of January 1979.

International Transactions:

Exports and Imports, c.i.f.:
Source S. *Line 71..d* (imports including military goods) is compiled quarterly.

Export and *Import Volume* indices are from source S; prior to 1980, they are Laspeyres indices obtained by dividing the value indices by the Paasche price indices. Beginning 1980, they are compiled using Fisher's ideal index. † *Export* and *Import Unit Value* indices are source S data; prior to 1976, they are Paasche indices; beginning 1976, they are Laspeyres indices; from 1984 onwards they are compiled using Fisher's ideal index. The weights are revised every two years. For example, for 1981 the weights are calculated on the basis of Israel's trade in 1979. The weights reference period for volume and unit value indices of exports and imports is presently 2000=100. Export volume and unit value indices include ships, aircraft, and diamonds. Import volume and unit value indices exclude ships and aircraft.

Government Finance:

Annual data are as reported for the *Government Finance Statistics Yearbook (GFSY)* and cover consolidated central government. The fiscal year ends December 31.

National Accounts:

Source S. As indicated by the country, from 1995 onward, data are compiled according to the *1993 SNA,* and *line 99b.p* data are annually chained using the prices of the previous year.

Italy 136

Data are denominated in lire prior to January 1999 and in euros from January 1999 onward. An irrevocably fixed factor for converting lire to euros was established at 1,936.27 lire per euro. In 2002, the lira was retired from circulation and replaced by euro banknotes and coins. Beginning in January 1999, with the implementation of Stage Three of the European Economic and Monetary Union (EMU), a euro area-wide definition of residency was introduced: All positions with residents of other euro area (EA) countries, including the European Central Bank (ECB), are classified as domestic positions, and foreign assets and foreign liabilities include only positions with non-euro area residents. Descriptions of the changes in the methodology and presentation of Italy's accounts following the introduction of the euro are shown in the introduction to *IFS* and in the notes on the euro area page.

Date of Fund Membership:
March 27, 1947

Standard Sources:
A: Bank of Italy, *Annual Report*
B: Bank of Italy, *Economic Bulletin, Statistical Bulletin, Statistical Bulletin Supplements*
S: Central Institute of Statistics, *Monthly Bulletin*
V: Eurostat

Exchange Rates:
Market Rate (End of Period and Period Average):
Between September 1992 and December 1998, based on quotations of a sample of banks at 14.15 Central European Time polled by the Bank of Italy. In January 1999, the lira became a participating currency within the Eurosystem, and the euro market rate became applicable to all transactions. In 2002, the lira was retired from circulation and replaced by euro banknotes and coins. For additional information, refer to the section on exchange rates in the introduction to *IFS* and the notes on the euro area page.

International Liquidity:
Beginning in January 1999, *Total Reserves minus Gold (line 1l.d)* is defined in accordance with the Eurosystem's statistical definition of international reserves. The international reserves of Italy per the Eurosystem statistical definition at the start of the monetary union (January 1, 1999) in billions of U.S. dollars were as follows: *Total Reserves minus Gold,* $29,423; *Foreign Exchange,* $24,457; *SDRs,* $111; *Reserve Position in the Fund,* $4,314; *Other Reserve Assets,* $541; *Gold,* $23,991; *Gold (million fine troy ounces),* 83.363 ounces. *Foreign Exchange (line 1d.d)*: Between March 1979 and December 1998, gold and foreign exchange excluded deposits at the European Monetary Cooperation Fund (EMCF), and holdings of European currency units (ECUs) issued against these deposits were included in *line 1d.d. Gold (Eurosystem Valuation) (line 1and)*: Prior to January 1999, gold was valued according to national valuation practices, whereby gold was revalued quarterly on the basis of the average London market price in the preceding six months or the average price of the penultimate working day of the period, whichever was lower. From January 1999 onward, gold is revalued at the market price at the end of each quarter. Memorandum data are provided on *Non-Euro Claims on Euro Area Residents* and *Euro Claims on Non-Euro Area Residents,* which represent positions as of the last Friday in each month. For additional information, refer to the section on international liquidity in the introduction to *IFS* and the notes on the euro area page.

Monetary Authorities:
Comprises the Bank of Italy, which beginning in January 1999 is part of the Eurosystem, and coins issued by the Treasury. At year-end 1998, the Italian Foreign Exchange Office (Ufficio dei Cambi) became a wholly owned subsidiary of the Bank of Italy, which acquired its foreign exchange assets. Beginning in 2002, *Currency Issued (line 14a)* includes euro banknotes and coins and, until December 2002, any unretired lire. The recorded value of euro banknotes is based on a monthly allocation of total euro banknotes in circulation based on the Bank of Italy's paid up share of the ECB's capital; it does not correspond to either the actual amount of euro banknotes placed in circulation by the Bank of Italy which is shown in memo line *Currency Put into Circulation (line 14m)*, nor the actual circulation of banknotes within the domestic territory. See section *Euro banknotes and coins* in the introduction to *IFS*. Beginning in 2002, *Claims on Banking Institutions (line 12e.u)* and *Liabilities to Banking Institutions (line 14c.u)* include "Intra-Eurosystem claims/liabilities related to banknote issue," which is a single net value representing the difference between the value of euro banknotes allocated to the Bank of Italy according to the accounting scheme of the Eurosystem for issuing euro banknotes, and the value of euro banknotes put into circulation by the Bank of Italy. See section *Euro banknotes and coins* in the introduction to *IFS*. Prior to January 1999, treasury bills deposited by the commercial banks and savings banks to fulfill obligatory reserve requirements were eliminated from the balance sheet; *IFS Liabilities to Banking Institutions in Italy (line 14c)* differed from the monetary base data reported in source B, mainly because the latter included deposits of the private sector with the postal system, banks' holdings of government securities which met reserve requirements, and banks' unused margins on credit lines with the Bank of Italy; and *Foreign Liabilities (line 16c)* related to required deposits on all purchases of foreign currency. *Claims on General Government (line 12a)*: Prior to January 1997, holdings of government securities were at book value; beginning in January 1997, holdings are on a market value basis. *Bonds and Money Market Instruments (line 16n.u)* include subordinated debt in the form of securities, other bonds, and money market paper. *Capital Accounts (line 17a)*: Prior to January 1999, included provisions for the pension fund of the Bank of Italy and other special provisions. Beginning in January 1999, includes the equity of the Italian Foreign Exchange Office. For a description of the accounts, refer to the section on monetary authorities in the introduction to *IFS*. Beginning with the data for end-November 2000, Monetary Authorities' *Foreign Assets (line 11)*, *Foreign Liabilities (line 16c)*, *Claims on Banking Institutions (line 12e.u)*, and *Liabilities to Banking Institutions (line 14c.u)* are affected by a change from gross to net presentation of positions relating to the TARGET (Trans-European Automated Real-Time Gross Settlement Express Transfer) euro clearing system. (See *Recording of TARGET system positions* under *European Economic and Monetary Union (EMU)* in the introduction to *IFS*.) Memo line *Net Claims on Eurosystem (line 12e.s)* equals gross claims on, less gross liabilities to, the ECB and other members of the Eurosystem. Comprises euro-denominated claims equivalent to the transfer of foreign currency reserves to the ECB, Intra-Eurosystem claims/liabilities related to banknote issue, net claims or liabilities within the TARGET clearing system, and other positions.

Banking Institutions:

Prior to January 1999, commercial banks only. † Beginning in 1989, data are based on improved classification following the adoption by the Bank of Italy of the sectoral classification and definitions based on the *1995 ESA*. Beginning in January 1999, consists of all resident units classified as other monetary financial institutions (other MFIs), as defined by the *1995 ESA* standards, including money market funds. Positions with residents of San Marino and the Vatican City are treated as nonresident positions. All positions in financial derivatives are off-balance-sheet except for option premiums and margin deposits of customers on futures or other derivatives subject to variation margining. Special public aid loans by the Bank of Italy to banking institutions under the Treasury Decree of September 27, 1974 are normally excluded from the accounts of the banking institutions. Data prior to 1997 covered 92–95 percent of the sector's assets/liabilities. Prior to January 1999, *Claims on Monetary Authorities (line 20)* comprised cash, free reserves, and obligatory reserve deposits in the Bank of Italy. Prior to January 1999, *Foreign Assets (line 21)* and *Foreign Liabilities (line 26c)* were derived from Italian Foreign Exchange Office records, which excluded the accounts of branches of foreign banks. *Money Market Fund Shares (line 26m.u)* include shares/units issued by money market funds. *Bonds and Money Market Instruments (line 26n.u)* include subordinated debt in the form of securities, other bonds, and money market paper. *Other Items (Net) (line 27r)* includes holdings of shares issued by other MFIs. For a description of the accounts, refer to the section on banking institutions in the introduction to *IFS*.

Banking Survey (National Residency):

For a description of the methodology and accounts, refer to the section Banking Survey (National Residency) in the introduction to *IFS*.

Banking Survey (Euro Area-wide Residency):

For a description of the methodology and accounts, refer to the section Banking Survey (Euro Area-wide Residency) in the introduction to *IFS*.

Money (National Definitions):

M1 as calculated by the national authorities and *Money (line 34)* are identical. *M2 (line 39m)* comprises M1 plus bank certificates of deposit with maturity not exceeding 18 months, bank savings deposits, and postal savings deposits. *M2* differs from *Money* and *Quasi-Money (line 34 plus line 35)* in that the latter include residents' foreign currency deposits. Beginning in January 1999, national monetary aggregates series are discontinued. Euro area aggregates are presented on the euro area page.

Interest Rates:

Unless otherwise indicated, interest rate data are from source B.

Discount Rate (End of Period) (line 60):
Prior to January 1999, referred to rate charged by the Bank of Italy for rediscounts on commercial bills; the same rate was also applied to the Bank of Italy's advances and was used as the base for "extraordinary" advances, on which penalties were applied. Beginning in January 1999, central bank policy rates are discontinued. See Eurosystem policy rate series on the euro area page.

Money Market Rate (line 60b):
Three-month interbank rate. Beginning in February 1990, data represent arithmetic averages of daily rates, which are weighted averages of rates based on the volume of transactions for the day. The Bank of Italy compiled the data.

Treasury Bill Rate (line 60c):
Monthly average yield, before tax, on newly issued three-month, six-month, and twelve-month treasury bills, weighted by the respective volumes of the three maturities.

Deposit Rate (line 60l):
Prior to August 1992, data referred to the average paid rate by banks on current accounts and savings accounts. † Beginning in August 1992, data refer to the rate paid by banks on current accounts, savings accounts, and certificates of deposits.

Deposit Rate (lines 60lhs, 60lhn, and 60lcr):
See notes in the Introduction to *IFS*.

Lending Rate (line 60p):
† Beginning in 1990, data refer to the average rate charged by the banking institutions and specialized credit institutions on short-term lira loans.

Lending Rate (lines 60phs, 60pns, 60phm, 60phn, 60pcs, and 60pcn):
See notes in the Introduction to *IFS*.

Government Bond Yield: Long-Term (line 61):
Prior to April 1991, the data are average yields to maturity on bonds with original maturities of 15 to 20 years, issued on behalf of the Treasury by the Consortium of Credit for Public Works. Between April 1991 and December 1998, the data are average yields to maturity on bonds with residual maturities between 9 and 10 years. From January 1999 onward, monthly data are arithmetic averages of daily gross yields to maturity of the fixed-coupon ten-year treasury benchmark bond (last issued bond beginning from the date when it becomes the most traded issue among government securities with residual maturities between nine and ten years), based on prices in the official wholesale market.

Medium-Term (line 61b):
Prior to January 1991, the data are average yields to maturity on treasury bonds with maximum original maturities of nine years. Between January 1991 and December 1998, the data are average yields to maturity on bonds with residual maturity between four and six years. From January 1999 onward, monthly data are arithmetic averages of daily gross yields to maturity of the fixed-coupon five-year treasury benchmark bond (last issued bond beginning from the date when it becomes the most traded issue among government securities with residual maturities between four and five years), based on prices in the official wholesale market. For additional information, refer to the section on international liquidity in the introduction to *IFS* and the notes on the euro area page.

Prices, Production, Labor:

Share Prices:
Source B, base 1975. Data refer to the MIB index calculated by the Milan Stock Exchange and are based on the quoted prices of all stocks traded on that exchange.

Producer Prices:
Source S. Laspeyres index, weights reference period: 2000 measuring variations over time in the prices of goods sold by industrial producers within the domestic market. The index covers 1102 items and its weights are determined on the basis of sales of own-produced manufacturing products for the base period according to the Survey on Economic and Financial Accounts of Enterprises.

Consumer Prices:

Source S. Weights Reference Period: 2000; Geographical Coverage: whole national territory; Number of Items in Basket: 1031; Basis for Calculation: the weights are based on household final consumption expenditure as recorded in the national accounts.

Wages: Contractual:

Source B. Weights reference period: December 2000. Data refer to contractual hourly wages rate in the whole industry.

Industrial Production:

Data are sourced from the OECD database, weights reference period: 2000. The indices cover the whole industry.

Industrial Employment:

Source S data on employees in industry in thousands of persons.

International Transactions:

Trade data are from source S.

Volume indices, weights reference period: 2000. The *Unit* Value data are Fisher indices.

Government Finance:

Monthly, quarterly, and annual cash data on central government are derived from source B Data on general government are derived from source V. The fiscal year ends December 31.

National Accounts:

Source B. Data include the underground economy as part of the reported figures. Data from 1988 onwards are in accordance with the *ESA 95*, as indicated by the country. Beginning in 1999, euro data are sourced from the Eurostat database. Eurostat introduced chain-linked GDP volume measures to both annual and quarterly data with the release of the third quarter 2005 on November 30, 2005. Chain-linked GDP volume measures are expressed in the prices of the previous year and re-referenced to 1995.

Jamaica 343

Date of Fund Membership:

February 21, 1963

Standard Sources:

B: Bank of Jamaica, *Statistical Digest, Monthly Review*
S: Department of Statistics, *Monetary Statistics, National Income and Product*

Exchange Rates:

Market Rate (End of Period and Period Average):

The exchange rate of the Jamaica dollar is determined under the Interbank Foreign Exchange Trading System, which was introduced on September 17, 1990. The interbank foreign exchange market is operated by the commercial banks and the Bank of Jamaica.

International Liquidity:

Data for *line 1d.d* include small foreign exchange holdings by the government. Other official asset holdings reported in *line 3b.d* include the foreign assets held by the Capital Development Fund and the Sugar Industry Authority.

Monetary Authorities:

Comprises the Bank of Jamaica (BOJ) only. † Beginning in December 2001, data are based on a new reporting system which provides improved classification and sectorization of the accounts.

Banking Institutions:

Comprises state and private commercial banks, branches of foreign banks, merchant banks, trust companies, and finance houses. Before December 1973, *Demand Deposits* and *Time and Savings Deposits* include nonresident deposits. Beginning in December 1973, nonresident deposits are included in *Foreign Liabilities*. † Beginning in December 2001, includes building societies. Data are based on a new reporting system which provides improved classification and sectorization of the accounts.

Banking Survey:

† See notes on monetary authorities and banking institutions.

Money (National Definitions):

Base Money comprises currency issued, statutory cash reserves, and current accounts in national currency of commercial banks with the BOJ.

M1 comprises notes and coins in circulation outside commercial banks and demand deposits in national currency of the private sector with commercial banks.

M2 comprises M1 and quasi money. Quasi money comprises time and savings deposits in national currency of the private sector with commercial banks.

Interest Rates:

All interest rate data are from source B.

Bank Rate (End of Period):

Minimum rate at which commercial banks may rediscount eligible paper and treasury bills at the Bank of Jamaica. There are no quantitative limits on credits to commercial banks.

Money Market Rate:

Average rate on overnight interbank transactions in domestic currency.

Treasury Bill Rate:

Average yield of treasury bills issued during the month with maturities closest to 180 days.

Savings Rate:

Minimum rate offered by commercial banks on savings deposits.

Deposit Rate:

Weighted average rate offered by commercial banks on three- to six-month deposits. Rate is weighted by deposit amounts.

Lending Rate:

Weighted average rate charged by commercial banks on all loans, excluding staff loans. Rate is weighted by loan amounts.

Government Bond Yield:

End-of-month yield on government bills of 10 or more years.

Prices:

Industrial Share Prices:

Industrial share price index covering shares quoted in the Jamaican Stock Exchange, base 1969.

Consumer Prices:

Source B. Weights Reference Period: 1988; Geographical Coverage: all Jamaica; Number of Items in Basket: 239 items; Basis for Calculation: Household Expenditure Survey conducted in 1984.

International Transactions:

Source B.

Volume of Exports:
IFS average of alumina, bauxite, and sugar with a 1995 value of exports as weights.

National Accounts:

Source S. As indicated by the country, data are compiled and disseminated according to the recommendations of the *1968 SNA*.

Japan   158

Date of Fund Membership:
August 13, 1952

Standard Sources:
B: Bank of Japan, *Economic Statistics Monthly*
S: Bureau of Statistics, *Monthly Statistics of Japan*

Exchange Rates:

Market Rate (End of Period and Period Average):
Midpoint rate in the interbank foreign exchange market in Tokyo.

International Liquidity:

Gold (National Valuation) (line 1and) is the U.S. dollar value of official holdings of gold as reported in the country's standard sources. Gold is valued at SDR 35 per fine troy ounce and converted into U.S. dollars at the dollar/SDR rate on the *IFS* page *line sa* for the United States.

Data for *lines 7a.d* and *7b.d* include long-term foreign accounts and therefore are not the U.S. dollar equivalents of *lines 21* and *26c*, which comprise only short-term accounts; data are from the Bank for International Settlement's *Annual Report* and *Quarterly Press Release*.

Monetary Authorities:

Comprises the Bank of Japan (BOJ) only. From January 1970 to April 1998, data on *Foreign Assets (line 11)* are provided net of foreign liabilities. † Beginning April 1998, data are based on improved sectorization and classification of the accounts. † Beginning in December 2001, data are based on a new reporting system which provides improved classification and sectorization of the accounts.

Banking Institutions:

Comprises domestically licensed banks, foreign-owned banks in Japan, financial institutions for small business (National Federation of Credit Associations, shinkin banks, Shoko Chukin Bank, Shinkumi Federation Bank, credit unions, Rokinren Bank, labor credit associations), financial institutions for agriculture, forestry, and fishery (Norin Chukin Bank, Credit Federation of Agricultural Cooperatives, agricultural cooperatives, Credit Federation of Fishery Cooperatives, Fisheries Cooperative Association), securities finance institutions, other private financial institutions, government financial institutions, the Trust Fund Bureau, Postal Savings, Postal Annuity and collectively managed trusts. † Beginning April 1998, data are based on improved sectorization and classification of the accounts. † Beginning in December 2001,

data are based on a new reporting system which provides improved classification and sectorization of the accounts.

Banking Survey:

† See notes on monetary authorities and banking institutions.

Nonbank Financial Institutions:

Comprises life and non-life insurance companies and mutual aid insurance companies. Beginning in December 1997, includes pension funds. † Beginning in December 2001, includes securities investment trusts, finance companies, structured-financing special purpose companies and trusts, public financial institutions, financial dealers and brokers, noncollectively managed trusts, and financial auxiliaries. Data are based on a new reporting system which provides improved classification and sectorization of the accounts.

Financial Survey:

† See notes on monetary authorities, banking institutions and nonbank financial institutions.

Money (National Definitions):

M1 comprises notes and coins in circulation outside banking institutions, checks and notes held by banking institutions and demand and savings deposits of the private sector, local governments, public nonfinancial corporations, securities companies, securities finance companies, and Tanshi companies at banking institutions in national currency. The banking institutions surveyed for M1 include the Bank of Japan, domestically licensed banks, Shinkin banks, Norinchukin Bank, and Shoko Chukin Bank. † Beginning in April 1998, the banking institutions surveyed for M1 include foreign banks in Japan, foreign trust banks, and Shinkin Central Bank.

M2 + CDs comprises M1 plus fixed and installment savings deposits, time deposits, and certificates of deposit of the private sector, local governments, public nonfinancial corporations, securities companies, securities finance companies, and Tanshi companies at banking institutions in national and foreign currency and nonresident deposits in national currency. † See note for M1.

M3 + CDs comprises M2 + CDs plus deposits of post offices and other savings and fixed deposits with credit cooperatives, Labor Credit Associations, Agricultural Cooperatives, Fishery Cooperatives, and trust accounts of domestically licensed banks. † Beginning in April 1998, includes savings and fixed deposits of the Shinkumi Federation Bank, National Federation of Labor Credit Associations, Credit Federations of Agricultural Cooperatives, and Credit Federations of Fishery Cooperatives.

Broadly-defined Liquidity comprises M3 plus CDs, pecuniary trusts other than money trusts, investment trusts, bank debentures, commercial paper issued by financial institutions, repurchase agreements and securities lending with cash collateral, government bonds, and foreign bonds.

M1, *M2 plus CDs*, and *M3 plus CDs* are an end-of-month basis while *Broadly-defined Liquidity* is on a month average basis.

Interest Rates:

All interest rate data are from source B.

Discount Rate (End of Period):
Rate at which the Bank of Japan discounts eligible commercial bills and loans secured by government bonds, specially designed securities, and eligible commercial bills. This rate is considered the key indicator of the Bank's discount policy.

Money Market Rate:
From July 1985, lending rate for collateral and overnight loans in the Tokyo Call Money Market. Previously, lending rate for collateral and unconditional loans.

Financing Bill Rate:
Average rate of yield on 13-week Financing Bills.

Deposit Rate:
† Beginning in 1992, average interest rate on unregulated three-month time deposits, ranging in size from three million yen to under ten million yen. Quarterly and annual interest rate data are averages of monthly data.

Certificates of Deposit Rate:
Average interest rate on 90–179 day certificates of deposit issued by domestically licensed banks.

Lending Rate:
† Before 1993, the lending rate excluded overdrafts. Beginning in 1993, weighted arithmetic average of contracted interest rates charged by all banks on both short- and long-term loans, discounts, and overdrafts.

Government Bond Yield:
Prior to December 1998, data refer to arithmetic average yield to maturity of all ordinary government bonds. Beginning in December 1998, data refer to arithmetic average yield on newly issued government bonds with 10-year maturity.

Prices, Production, Labor:
All price data are from source B.

Share Prices:
The index, base January 4, 1968, refers to the average of daily closing prices for all shares listed on the Tokyo exchange.

Wholesale Price Indices:
The index, (Corporate Goods Price Index) weights reference period: 2000, covers 910 domestic products, weighted with 2000 transaction values.

Consumer Prices:
Source B. Weights Reference Period: 2000; Geographical Coverage: The entire country excluding one-person households and those engaged mainly in agriculture, forestry, and fishing; Number of Items in Basket: 598; Basis for Calculation: The weights are based on the 2000 Family Income and Expenditure Survey and are revised once every five years.

Wages: Monthly Earnings:
The series, weights reference period: 2000, refers to the monthly contract cash earnings of regular workers in all industries.

Industrial Production:
Data are sourced from the OECD database, weights reference period: 2000. The indices cover the whole industry.

Manufacturing Employment, Seasonally Adjusted:
The index, weights reference period: 2000, is from source B. It refers to employment of regular workers only and covers all manufacturing establishments with 30 or more regular workers.

International Transactions:
Exports and *Imports, c.i.f.:* Source S data.
Trade indices are from source B, weights reference period: 2000. The unit value indices are Fisher Ideal indices. The volume indices are derived from the value indices divided by the unit value indices.

Export and Import Prices:
The series cover, in principle, all export and import commodities excluding used ships, jewelry, fresh fruits and vegetables, and works of art and are weighted with the value of exports and imports in 2000. The prices are contract prices, f.o.b. for exports and c.i.f. for imports.

Balance of Payments:
Balance of payments data prior to 1985 were converted to the format of the fifth edition of the *Balance of Payments Manual* using a set of conversion keys developed by the Fund.

Government Finance:
Annual data cover budgetary central government. The fiscal year ends March 31.

National Accounts:
Source B. *Exports of Goods and Services (line 90c.c)* includes factor income received from abroad. *Imports of Goods and Services (line 98c.c)* includes factor income payments to abroad, and *lines 90c.c* through *98c.c* add up to *GNP (line 99a.c)*. *Line 98.nc* is not reported to *IFS* and is calculated for *IFS* as the difference between GNP and GDP. As indicated by the country, from 1980 onward data have been revised following the implementation of the *1993 SNA*. GDP chain-linked volume measures are calculated based on the prices and weights of the previous year, using Laspeyres formula in general.

Jordan   439

Date of Fund Membership:
August 29, 1952

Standard Sources:
A: Central Bank, *Annual Report*
B: Central Bank, *Monthly Statistical Bulletin*
S: Department of Statistics, *External Trade Statistics*

Exchange Rates:
Official Rate: (End of Period and Period Average):
Central bank midpoint rate. Prior to 1988, the dinar was officially pegged to the SDR. Since May 1989, the dinar has been pegged to a basket of currencies.

International Liquidity:
Foreign Exchange (line 1d.d):
Prior to December 1993, foreign currency holdings included in *1d.d* are net of foreign currency deposits of licensed banks at the Central Bank of Jordan. Beginning this date, data include these foreign currency deposits. *Gold (National Valuation) (line 1and)* refers to gold valued at US$200 per ounce, in accordance with national valuation procedures.

Monetary Authorities:
Comprises the Central Bank of Jordan (CBJ) only. † Beginning in 1993, *lines 11, 14,* and *16c* reflect foreign currency deposits of licensed banks. Beginning in January 2001, data on the CBJ are on an accruals basis; data prior to January 2001 were on a cash basis.

Deposit Money Banks:
Comprises commercial banks and the Housing Bank. Data include estimates for bank branches in occupied territory. † Begin-

ning in December 1993, *line 26d* includes deposits of the Social Security Corporation, which previously were included in *lines 24* and *25*.

Monetary Survey:

† See notes on monetary authorities and deposit money banks.

Other Banking Institutions:

Comprises the Industrial Development Bank, the Agriculture Credit Corporation, and the Municipal Loan Fund. † Beginning December 1993, comprises Cities and Villages Development Bank, Agricultural Credit Corporation, Industrial Development Bank, the Housing Corporation, and Jordan Co-operative Organization. *Line 45* includes some demand deposits.

Money (National Definitions):

Reserve Money comprises currency in circulation and legal reserve and excess deposits in national currency of commercial banks in national currency with the CBJ. Currency in circulation refers to notes and coins issued by the CBJ.

M1 comprises currency in circulation and transferable deposits. Currency in circulation refers to notes and coins issued by the CBJ less the amount held by commercial banks. Transferable deposits refer to current account deposits in national currency of nonbank financial institutions, state and local governments, public nonfinancial corporations, social security corporation, and private sector with the CBJ and commercial banks.

M2 comprises M1 and quasi-money. Quasi-money refers to time, savings, and foreign currency deposits of nonbank financial institutions, state and local governments, public nonfinancial corporations, social security corporation, and private sector with the CBJ and commercial banks.

Interest Rates:

All interest rate data are from source B.

Discount Rate:
Rate charged by the Central Bank of Jordan on advances to licensed banks.

Money Market Rate:
Weighted average rate on loans between commercial banks. The rate is weighted by loan amounts.

Savings Rate:
Weighted average rate offered by commercial banks on savings deposits in national currency. Rate is weighted by deposit amounts.

Deposit Rate:
Weighted average of interest rates on time deposits in dinars applied by the banks.

Lending Rate:
Weighted average offered by commercial banks on time deposits in national currency. The rate is weighted by deposit amounts.

Prices and Production:

Wholesale Prices:
Source B, Laspeyres index, weights reference period: 1998. Weights from the 1992 Census of Wholesales. The prices are collected from 104 establishments with 142 products in three cities.

Consumer Prices:
Source B. Weights Reference Period: 2002; Geographical Coverage: whole national territory; Number of Items in Basket: 821; Basis for Calculation: weights are derived from the Quin-

quennial Household Income and Expenditure Survey and population estimates.

Industrial Production:
Source B index, weights reference period: 1999, covering selected manufactured commodities. Data refer to the East Bank only.

International Transactions:

All trade data are from source B.
Trade indices: Data are compiled with weights reference period 1994.

Government Finance:

Monthly, quarterly, and annual data are derived from source B (from source A for debt data) and cover budgetary central government. The fiscal year ends December 31.

National Accounts:

Source S. As indicated by the country, beginning in 1992 data are compiled according to the *1993 SNA*.

Kazakhstan   916

Date of Fund Membership:

July 15, 1992

Standard Sources:

B: National Bank of Kazakhstan (NBK), *Monthly Statistical Bulletin*
S: National Statistical Agency, *Monthly Statistical Bulletin*

Exchange Rates:

The tenge was introduced in November 1993.

Official Rate: (End of Period and Period Average):
Prior to August 1995, the official rate was established at periodic interbank auctions. Between August and December 1995, the official rate was set at the beginning of each week by the central bank based on the auction rate for the previous week and taking into account market developments. Beginning in January 1996, the official weekly rate is a weighted average, by volume, of the interbank rates established at daily foreign exchange auctions and in the market outside of the auctions. Monthly data are averages of weekly data.

International Liquidity:

Gold (National Valuation) (line 1and) is equal to *Gold (Million Fine Troy Ounces) (line 1ad)* valued at the London fixing rate for the end of period. Beginning in December 2001, the National Bank of Kazakhstan values foreign currency operations on the basis of the market exchange rate.

Monetary Authorities:

Starting in April 1996, the National Bank of Kazakhstan (NBK) started transferring some of its accounts to the newly created Republican Budget Bank. Up until December 1996, the monetary authorities accounts comprised the National Bank of Kazakhstan and the Republican Budget Bank. Since January 1997, monetary authorities comprise the NBK only. General government comprises central and local government units and their extrabudgetary funds. *Claims on Rest of the Economy (line 12d)* includes claims on nonfinancial public enterprises and on the private sector. † Starting in January 1997, the data for the NBK are compiled on the basis of the new chart of accounts for the NBK and on the basis of the methodology in the forthcoming *Manual on Monetary and Financial Statistics*. Other Deposits (line 15) includes restricted deposits. † Beginning in December 2001, data are based on an improved classification and sectorization of accounts. † Beginning in December 2003, data are based on new reporting system which provides an improved classification and sectorization of the accounts.

Banking Institutions:

Consolidated accounts of the commercial banks. † Prior to December 2001, *Central Government (line 22a)* included central and local government units and their extrabudgetary funds. † Prior to December 2001, *Claims on Rest of the Economy (line 22d)* also included claims on nonfinancial public enterprises and on the private sector. † Beginning in December 1995, data for *Foreign Liabilities (line 26c)* reflect the restructuring of the balance sheet of one of the deposit money banks to exclude obligations for certain outstanding trade credits that were assumed by the government under a government guarantee arrangement. † Starting in January 1997, the data for the commercial banks include data for the Republican Budget Bank and are compiled according to the methodology in the forthcoming *Manual on Monetary and Financial Statistics*. Prior to January 1997, *Demand Deposits (line 24)* includes all deposit liabilities. † Prior to December 2001, *Other Deposits (line 25)* included restricted deposits. † Prior to December 2001, *Central Government Deposits (line 26d)* included central government deposits and liabilities to local government. Starting in October 1997, the data for the commercial banks are compiled on the basis of the new chart of accounts for commercial banks. † Beginning December 2001, data are based on an improved classification and sectorization of accounts. † Beginning in December 2003, data are based on new reporting system which provides an improved classification and sectorization of the accounts.

Banking Survey:

See notes on monetary authorities and banking institutions.

Money (National Definitions):

M1 comprises transferable deposits of individuals and non-bank legal entities in national currency.
M2 comprises *M1* and other deposits in local currency and transferable deposits in foreign currency of individuals and non-bank legal entities.
M3 comprises *M2* and other deposits in foreign currency of individuals and non-bank legal entities.

Interest Rates:

Refinancing Rate (End of Period):
Annualized interest rate until June 1995; thereafter, compound annual rate, which is established as the minimum interest rate for NBK auctions of credit to commercial banks.
Treasury Bill Rate:
Yield based on treasury bill prices established at the last auction of the month.

Prices and Labor:

Producer Prices:
Source S. Weights Reference Period: 1995; Coverage: products from all economic activities, including mining, manufacturing, production, distribution of electric power, gas and water; Num-

ber of Items in Basket: some 230 commodity groups and 450 sub-groups coverage of activities within each main industrial group; Basis for Calculation: The concepts, definitions, and classifications used to compile the PPI are in broad conformity with the guidelines contained in the *1993 SNA* and the *Producer Price Index Manual.*
Consumer Prices:
Source S. Weights Reference Period: December 1995; Geographical Coverage: covers 14 oblasts, 27 districts, the capital at Astana, and three other large cities; Number of Items in Basket: includes 508 quotations of representative goods and services; Basis for Calculation: based on a Household Income Expenditure Survey (HIES, 2002) for the previous year of all resident households, both urban and rural.
Wages:
Information on average monthly wages is derived from monthly reports of large and medium enterprises and quarterly reports of small enterprises engaging in entrepreneurial activity.

International Transactions:

Source S. Exports (line 70..d) and Imports, c.i.f. (line 71..d) exclude informal trade.

Government Finance:

Data are derived from the Ministry of Finance monthly reports on the execution of the state budget. These data cover the general budget, which represents the consolidation of the republican and local budgets. The republican budget covers all the operations of central government entities. The fiscal year ends December 31.

National Accounts:

Source S. As indicated by the country, data are compiled according to the recommendations of the *1993 SNA*.

Kenya   664

Date of Fund Membership:
February 3, 1964

Standard Sources:
B: Central Bank of Kenya, *Economic and Financial Review*
S: Central Bureau of Statistics, *Statistical Digest*

Exchange Rates:

Principal Rate (End of Period and Period Average):
Central bank midpoint rate. With the introduction of a foreign exchange bearer certificate scheme (FEBC) in October 1991, a dual exchange rate system is in effect.

International Liquidity:

Gold (National Valuation) (line 1and) is obtained by converting the value in national currency terms, as reported in the country's standard sources, using the prevailing exchange rate, as given in line **ae** or **we**. Data for *line 1d.d* include small foreign exchange holdings by the government.

Monetary Authorities:

Consolidates the Central Bank of Kenya (CBK) and monetary authority functions undertaken by the central government. The contra-entry to the Treasury IMF accounts and government foreign exchange assets is included in *line 16d.*

Deposit Money Banks:

Comprises commercial banks. Most of the banking business is handled by three banks—two with head offices in London and one with a head office in Nairobi. † Beginning in January 1969, data are based on an improved classification of the accounts.

Monetary Survey:

In the monetary survey (see Introduction for the standard method of calculation), uncleared checks held by the central bank and drawn on commercial banks are netted against demand deposits in arriving at *line 34.* † See note to deposit money banks.

Other Banking Institutions:

Comprises banklike financial institutions, licensed under the banking act, that do not accept transferable deposits.

Money (National Definitions):

Reserve Money comprises currency in circulation and commercial banks' deposits in national and foreign currency with the CBK. Currency in circulation refers to notes and coins issued by the CBK.

M1 comprises currency in circulation and transferable deposits. Currency in circulation refers to notes and coins issued by the CBK less the amount held by commercial banks. Transferable deposits refer to current account deposits in national currency of nonbank financial institutions, state and local governments, public nonfinancial corporations, and private sector with the CBK and commercial banks.

M2 comprises M1 and quasi-money. Quasi-money refers to time and savings deposits of nonbank financial institutions, state and local governments, public nonfinancial corporations, and private sector with commercial banks and other banking institutions excluding the postal savings system.

M3 comprises M2 and foreign currency deposits of nonbank financial institutions, state and local governments, public nonfinancial corporations, and private sector with commercial banks.

Interest Rates:

All interest rate data are from source B.

Discount Rate (End of Period):
Rate of discount on other bills and notes.

Treasury Bill Rate:
Average weekly tender rate for 90-day treasury bills.

Savings Rate:
Weighted average rate offered by commercial banks on savings deposits in national currency. The rate is weighted by deposit amounts.

Savings Rate (Foreign Currency):
Weighted average rate offered by commercial banks on savings deposits in foreign currency. The rate is weighted by deposit amounts.

Deposit Rate:
Upper margin offered on three- to six-month deposits. Beginning in May 1997, weighted average rate offered by commercial banks on three- to six-month deposits. † Beginning in February 2004, weighted average rate offered by commercial banks on three-month deposits in national currency. The rate is weighted by deposit amounts.

Deposit Rate (Foreign Currency):
Weighted average rate offered by commercial banks on three-month deposits in foreign currency. The rate is weighted by deposit amounts.

Lending Rate:
Upper margin on commercial banks' unsecured loans and advances to the general public. † Beginning in February 2004, weighted average rate charged by commercial banks on all loans in national currency. The rate is weighted by loan amounts.

Lending Rate (Foreign Currency):
Weighted average rate charged by commercial banks on all loans in foreign currency. The rate is weighted by loan amounts.

Prices, Production, Labor:

Share Prices:
Geometric mean of prices of all officially listed ordinary and preferred shares on the Nairobi Stock Exchange (NSE), base 1966.

Consumer Prices:
Source B. Weights Reference Period: 1993–1994; Geographical Coverage: whole national territory; Number of Items in Basket: 216; Basis for Calculation: 1993–94 Urban Household Budget Survey, modified Laspeyres index.

Industrial Production:
Source B quantity, index of manufacturing production, base 1976.

International Transactions:

Value data on *Exports* and total *Imports* are from source B.
Trade indices are compiled on weights reference period: 1982; volume indices are reported directly by the Central Bank of Kenya, and unit value indices are from source B.

Government Finance:

Data cover the operations of the budgetary central government (including Appropriations-in-Aid) and are as reported by source B. The data are derived from the monthly budget outturn statement prepared by the Ministry of Finance. Beginning in July 1996, revenue data include privatization proceeds, and the statistical discrepancy is identified separately. † Beginning in January 2001, domestic debt is reported on a gross basis and excludes government deposits and treasury advances to parastatals. The fiscal year ends June 30.

National Accounts:

Source B. From 2000 onward, data have been revised following the implementation of the *1993 SNA.*

Korea   542

Date of Fund Membership:
August 26, 1955

Standard Sources:
A: Bank of Korea, *Economic Statistics Yearbook*
B: Bank of Korea, *Monthly Statistical Bulletin*
S: Economic Planning Board, *Monthly Statistics of Korea*

Exchange Rates:

Market Rate (End of Period and Period Average):
Weighted average of previous day's interbank rates.

International Liquidity:

Line 1d.d refers only to the Bank of Korea's foreign exchange holdings and to the short-term foreign deposits of other domestic banks which are available to the Bank of Korea on demand. Hence, data exclude the bulk of other banks' foreign exchange holdings which are separately reported in *line 7a.d.* Furthermore, *line 7a.d* includes claims of foreign banks' branches on nonresidents.

Gold (National Valuation) (line 1and) is the U.S. dollar value of official holdings of gold as reported in the country's standard sources.

Monetary Authorities:

Consolidates The Bank of Korea and monetary authority functions undertaken by the central government. The contra-entry to Treasury IMF accounts is included in *line 12a.*

Data on *line 16ab* refer to monetary stabilization bonds and accounts which are used by the Bank of Korea as supplementary instruments to control bank liquidity. Under Bank regulation, such bonds and accounts do not form part of reserve requirements and are interest-bearing. Bonds have a maturity of between one and twelve months. Prior to January 1985, *line 16ab* includes small amounts of required bankers' import deposits. Monetary stabilization bonds and accounts held by deposit money banks are reported in *line 20r.* The difference between *lines 16ab* and *20r* represents bonds held by the rest of domestic economy; these are shown in the monetary survey section, *line 36ab.*

Deposit Money Banks:

Consolidates the commercial banks, excluding trust accounts and overseas branches of commercial banks, and the specialized banks. Commercial banks comprise nationwide banks, local banks, and foreign banks. Specialized banks comprise the Industrial Bank of Korea and the credit and banking sectors of the agricultural, fishery, and livestock cooperatives. The agricultural, fishery, and livestock cooperatives are financing, marketing, and raw material purchasing institutions, and their balance sheets reflect their nonfinancial transactions, including their transactions as government agencies for the purchase of commodities. Assets and liabilities relating to such transactions have been omitted from the accounts insofar as it is possible to do so. *Demand Deposits (line 24)* are net of uncleared checks and bills.

Monetary Survey:

In the monetary survey (see Introduction for the standard method of calculation), *line 36ab* is arrived at by netting *line 20r* against the sum of *lines 16ab* and *26ab,* and uncleared checks held by the central bank and drawn on deposit money banks are netted against demand deposits in arriving at *line 34.*

IFS monetary survey aggregates agree with corresponding data in the source B table on the monetary survey except for the following: *Line 31n* differs from the source B measure in that (1) the latter gives gross foreign assets and liabilities of the monetary system, whereas *IFS* follows a net concept, (2) source B includes in foreign assets the subscriptions to international nonmonetary organizations net of their deposits, which in *IFS* are reported in *line 32an,* and (3) source B includes SDR allocations and foreign exchange valuation accounts, which *IFS* reports in *line 37r.*

Line 32an differs from corresponding data in source B because the latter nets government lending funds, which *IFS* reports separately, and because *IFS* includes subscriptions to international nonmonetary organizations net of their deposits, which source B treats as a foreign asset.

The national definition of narrowly defined money (M1 in source B) is identical with *IFS line 34,* and the national definition of broad money (M2 in source B) is equal to the sum of *IFS lines 34* and *35.*

Other Banking Institutions:

Comprises development institutions, trust accounts of commercial banks, and post office savings deposits. Data are derived from source B. *Postal Savings Deposits (line 45..h)* include those of the postal transfer system. *Development Institutions:* Data relate to the Korean Development Bank.

Nonbank Financial Institutions:

Comprises life insurance offices.

Interest Rates:

Data are from source B.

Discount Rate (End of Period):
Rate offered by Bank of Korea on eligible commercial paper presented by commercial banks.

Money Market Rate:
Average daily rate on call money, weighted by the volume of transactions.

Corporate Bond Rate:
Through January 1992, yields on 91-day bills issued by enterprises without collateral. Beginning February 1992, data refer to corporate bond rate.

Deposit Rate:
Beginning in July 1984, maximum guideline rate set by the Bank of Korea on time deposits of one year or more with deposit money banks. † From July 1996, the rate is an average, weighted by the amount of deposits for periods of one year or more but less than two years at nationwide commercial banks.

Lending Rate:
Minimum rate charged to general enterprises by deposit money banks on loans of general funds for up to one year. † From July 1996, the rate is an average, weighted by new loans extended during the period by nationwide commercial banks.

Government Bond Yield:
Arithmetic average of yields, by maturity, on Type 1 National Housing Bonds.

Prices, Production, Labor:

Share Prices:
Based on January 4, 1985=100. Beginning 1983, comprises stock prices weighted by total market values. Prior to 1983, the Dow-Jones Average Index is used.
All data on prices, wages, and employment are from source B.

Producer Prices:
Data are disseminated on the Producer Price Index (PPI), a modified Laspeyres index (2000=100), covering all commodities and selected services traded in the domestic market. The index covers about 4,800 price quotes for 949 items, and about 4,000 firms. Commodity weights are based on shipment values and service weights are based on output values for domestic use.

Consumer Prices:
Source B. Weights Reference Period: 2000; Geographical Coverage: 36 cities; Number of Items in Basket: 516; Basis for Calculation: Weights are based on Family Expenditure Survey and are updated at approximately five-yearly intervals.

Wages:

Data refer to monthly earnings expressed in won, covering wage earners and salaried employees in nonagricultural sectors. The data are taken from a monthly survey of establishments employing ten or more persons and cover persons working for 45 or more days during the past three-month reporting period.

Industrial Production:

Source S. Weights Reference Period: 2000; Sectoral Coverage: mining, manufacturing, electricity and gas industries; Basis for Calculation: the weights of the individual products are based on value added data from the 2000 Mining and Manufacturing Survey.

Manufacturing Employment:

Data refer to persons employed in manufacturing, in thousands.

International Transactions:

Source B data. The data for imports exclude goods financed by U.S. aid programs and by aid relief from private agencies and include goods for processing that do not come into Korean ownership. The data for exports include the value of these processed goods when they are exported.

Volume of Exports and Imports:

Source B indices, weights reference period 1995.

Unit Value of Exports and Imports:

Source B Paasche indices, weights reference period 1995, reported in U.S. dollars and converted to national currency by *IFS*.

Export and Import Prices:

Source B, all commodities contract basis, weights reference period 1990. The export price index includes 216 items, and the import price index includes 147 items. Prior to 1975, the Fisher ideal formula was used, and from 1975 onwards the Laspeyres formula was used.

Government Finance:

Monthly and quarterly data are derived from source B. † Prior to 2001, to the extent possible, existing subannual *IFS* data were converted to the main aggregates that are presented in the *GFSM 2001* Statement of Sources and Uses of Cash (see the Introduction of the monthly *IFS* publication for details). Beginning in 2001, annual data are as reported for the *Government Finance Statistics Yearbook (GFSY)* and cover the consolidated central government. The fiscal year ends December 31.

National Accounts:

Data are from source S and are unadjusted. As indicated by the country, data follow the implementation of the *1993 SNA*.

Kuwait   443

Date of Fund Membership:

September 13, 1962

Standard Sources:

A: Central Bank of Kuwait, *Economic Report*
B: Central Bank of Kuwait, *Quarterly Statistical Bulletin*
S: Central Statistical Office, *Annual Statistical Abstract*

Exchange Rates:

Official Rate: (End of Period and Period Average):

Central bank midpoint rate. The exchange rate is determined on the basis of a fixed but adjustable relationship with a weighted basket of currencies.

International Liquidity:

Gold (National Valuation) (line 1and) is obtained by converting the value in national currency terms, as reported in the country's standard sources, using the prevailing exchange rate, as given in *line* **dg** or *line ag*.

Monetary Authorities:

Comprises the Central Bank of Kuwait only.

Deposit Money Banks:

Beginning in 1981, consolidates commercial banks, specialized banks, and Kuwait Finance House. † Prior to 1981, consolidates commercial banks only.

Monetary Survey:

† See note on deposit money banks.

Other Financial Institutions:

Comprises investment companies.

Interest Rates:

All interest rate data are from source B. With the exception of *Discount Rate (End of Period)*, all interest rate data are period averages.

Discount Rate (End of Period):

Central bank's discount rate on three-month commercial paper.

Money Market Rate:

Average of daily bid and offer quotations for the interbank rate on three-month dinar deposits. The rate is freely determined by the market. The rate on certificates of deposit fluctuates in line with, but is generally slightly lower than, the interbank deposit rate. Rates on time deposits with commercial banks are market determined and also vary with the interbank rate.

Treasury Bill Rate:

Monthly average of maximum acceptable interest rates set by the Central Bank of Kuwait for three-month treasury bills sold at weekly auctions.

Deposit Rate:

Weighted average of interest rates paid by local banks (excluding Kuwait Finance House) on total Kuwaiti dinar deposits of residents and nonresidents.

Lending Rate:

Weighted average of interest rates charged by local banks (excluding Kuwait Finance House) on Kuwaiti dinar credit facilities extended to residents and nonresidents.

Prices, Production, Labor:

Prices:

Source B indices. The wholesale price index, weights reference period 1977–78, measures prices at which wholesalers sell to retailers. The consumer price index, source S, base 1978, comprises all private households including one person households. The weights are derived from a household budget survey conducted in 1977–78.

Crude Petroleum Production:

Source B data updated for current periods using petroleum quantities as reported in the *Oil Market Intelligence.* Data include Kuwaiti share (50 percent) of Neutral Zone oil production.

International Transactions:

Exports and Imports, c.i.f.:
All data are from source B. Data on oil exports exclude gas prior to 1970.

International Investment Position:
Data on IIP assets exclude the external assets held by the general government for which the dissemination is restricted due to legal constraints. However, loans granted by the Kuwaiti Fund for Arab Economic Development (KFAED) and general government trade credits are included.

Government Finance:

Data are derived from source B and cover the operations of the budgetary central government. The fiscal year ends June 30.

National Accounts:

Source B.

Kyrgyz Republic　　917

Date of Fund Membership:
May 8, 1992

Standard Sources:
B: National Bank of the Kyrgyz Republic
F: Ministry of Finance
S: National Statistical Committee

Exchange Rates:
The som was introduced on May 10, 1993 and replaced the Russian ruble at the rate of SOM1=RR200.

Official Rate: (End of Period and Period Average):
All data in this section are from source B. The official rate is determined as the average volume-weighted exchange rate recorded at foreign exchange auctions held by the National Bank of the Kyrgyz Republic. Auctions are held each business Friday (Wednesday and Friday during 1994–96). The end-of-period rate is determined at the last auction of the reference period. The period-average rate is equal to the simple average of the official exchange rates recorded during auctions held during the reference period.

International Liquidity:
Foreign Exchange (line 1d.d) comprises the National Bank of the Kyrgyz Republic's cash, liquid correspondent accounts with non-resident banks, and foreign government securities.

Monetary Authorities:
Comprises the National Bank of the Kyrgyz Republic only. General government comprises central and local governments and their extrabudgetary funds, excluding the state Social Fund.

Banking Institutions:
Consolidated accounts of the commercial banks and the Settlement Savings Corporation. General government comprises central and local governments and their extrabudgetary funds, except the state Social Fund.

Interest Rates:
All interest rate data are from source B.

Lombard Rate (line 60.a):
Rate at which the National Bank of the Kyrgyz Republic extends overnight loans in soms to banks. Calculated on the basis of interest rates on short-term repurchase transactions in the secondary market.

Money Market Rate (line 60b):
Weighted-average rate on interbank loans in soms with maturities of 1 to 90 days. It does not reflect transactions in the interbank repurchase market.

Treasury Bill Rate (line 60c):
Weighted average rate on 3-month treasury bills sold in the primary market.

Deposit Rate (line 60l):
Weighted average rate offered on som time deposits of one- to three-month maturities.

Lending Rate (line 60p):
Weighted average rate on loans in soms for one- to three-month maturities.

Prices:

Producer Prices:
Source S. Weights Reference Period: 2000; Coverage: covering 3 main sectors of industry, 16 subsectors, and 23 groups; Number of Items in the Basket: around 289 price quotes are obtained monthly for 263 selected items; Basis for Calculation: with the production volume of the previous year being used as weights. The weights are updated annually in June on the basis of the annual production survey of enterprises.

Consumer Prices:
Source S. Base Year: 2000; Geographical Coverage: Covers eight main cities and one district (Moskovskiy); Number of Items in Basket: 348 items; Basis for Calculation: based on yearly data from the household budget survey, the weights are updated annually in June. When the weights are updated, a recalculation is performed for previous years by means of a correction factor.

International Transactions:

The data in this section are from sources B and S. *Exports (line 70)* and *Imports, c.i.f. (line 71):* Exports and imports (c.i.f.) are compiled from the monthly customs statistics and from the monthly and quarterly report forms submitted by enterprises. Adjustments to the customs data are made to account for humanitarian aid, 'shuttle' trade, barter trade, and the exports and imports of electricity and gas.

Balance of Payments:
Compiled quarterly in accordance with the fifth edition of the *Balance of Payments Manual, 1993* from the data provided by over 900 enterprises. Other sources of data include the National Bank, the report forms of the commercial banks, the Ministry of Transport and Communications, and other organizations.

Government Finance:

The data in this section are from source F. The monthly and annual data are derived from the reports of the central treasury that cover the cumulative cash transactions of the budgetary central and local governments. The data exclude the transactions of the social fund (earlier the insurance, employment, and pension funds) and other extrabudgetary units. The fiscal year ends December 31.

National Accounts:

Source S. As indicated by the country, the data are compiled in accordance with *1993 SNA* methodology.

Lao People's Dem. Rep   544

Date of Fund Membership:
July 5, 1961

Exchange Rates:
Prior to September 1995, data refer to the midpoint between the buying and selling rates quoted by the Bank of Lao P.D.R. In September 1995, a floating exchange rate policy was adopted, and the commercial banks were allowed to set their rates. Data beginning in September 1995 refer to the simple average of midpoint rates reported by the commercial banks on a daily basis, covering their transactions for the previous day.

Monetary Authorities:
Comprises the Bank of Lao P.D.R., which undertakes all monetary authority functions.

Deposit Money Banks:
Comprises commercial banks, which include state-owned banks, joint venture banks, and branches of foreign banks.

Monetary Survey:
Money (line 34) is the sum of lines 14a and 24 and demand deposits of the nonfinancial public enterprises and private sector with the monetary authorities.

Interest Rates:
Bank Rate (End of Period):
The lending rate of the Bank of Lao P.D.R.

Treasury Bill Rate:
Weighted average auction rate for 6-month treasury bills during the last auction of the month. Beginning in December 1997, weighted average auction rate for treasury bills with 12-month maturity.

Deposit Rate:
Minimum rate fixed by the Bank of Lao P.D.R. on commercial banks' three-month domestic-currency time deposits.

Lending Rate:
Prior to August 1995, data refer to the maximum rate set by the Bank of Lao P.D.R. for commercial banks' nonagricultural loans. The lending rate was liberalized in July 1995; data beginning August 1995 refer to the highest rate quoted by the commercial banks on nonagricultural loans.

Prices:
Consumer Prices:
Source B. Weights Reference Period: December 2005; Geographical Coverage: prices for most of these items are collected on a daily basis in Vientiane; Number of Items in the Basket: 197 items classified in 9 goods components; Basis for Calculation: using weights derived from a household budget survey.

Latvia   941

Date of Fund Membership:
May 19, 1992

Standard Sources:
B: Bank of Latvia, *Monetary Bulletin* (monthly), *Monetary Review* (quarterly), *Annual Report*
S: Central Statistical Bureau of Latvia, *Monthly Bulletin of Latvian Statistics*

Exchange Rates:
Official Rate: (End of Period and Period Average):
Bank of Latvia midpoint rate. Rates quoted by banks and moneychangers closely follow the Bank of Latvia rate. The official rate is pegged to the SDR.

International Liquidity:
Data for *Foreign Exchange (line 1d.d)* comprise the Bank of Latvia's external assets that are readily available to and controlled by the Bank of Latvia for direct financing of payment imbalances, for indirectly regulating the magnitude of such imbalances through intervention in exchange markets to affect the currency exchange rate, and/or for other purposes.
Gold (National Valuation) (line 1and): Gold reserves were valued at 175.50 lats per troy ounce between April 28, 1997 – March 30, 1999. As of March 31, 1999, gold reserves are valued at market price. The periodicity of gold revaluation is daily.

Monetary Authorities:
Comprises the Bank of Latvia only.

Banking Institutions:
Comprises credit institutions (i.e., banks and branches of foreign banks and credit unions). † Prior to December 1994, data for *Claims on Central Government* and *Central Government Deposits* comprise accounts that were maintained on a cumulative flow basis. Thereafter, these data are on a stock basis. Beginning in December 1994, data are based on an improved sectorization and classification of the accounts.

Banking Survey:
† See note on banking institutions.

Interest Rates:
All interest rate data are from source B.
Discount Rate (End of Period):
The Bank of Latvia sets the refinancing rate as a reference rate for the banking system. This rate serves as a general guide for the money market and is not used in monetary operations.

Money Market Rate:
Weighted average rate on overnight loans in national currency transacted in the interbank market. The rate is weighted by loan amounts.

Treasury Bill Rate:
Weighted average auction rate on 91-day treasury bills. † Beginning in January 2000, weighted average auction rate on six-month treasury bills.

Deposit Rate:
Weighted average rate offered by banking institutions on deposits of less than one year in national currency. Rate is weighted by deposit amounts.

Lending Rate:
Weighted average rate charged by banking institutions on loans of less than one year in national currency to enterprises and individuals. Rate is weighted by loan amounts.

Prices, Production, Labor:

Share Prices:

Dow Jones Riga Stock Exchange (RSE) index, base April 2, 1996. The index covers common shares traded in the RSE and is weighted by market capitalization. The index is limited to shares whose market value is greater than one million Latvian lats. However, the component companies are adjusted to ensure that only the largest and most actively traded shares are included. The monthly index is calculated from the average of the daily closing quotations.

Producer Prices:

Source S, annual chain-linked Laspeyres index with a reference base of December of the previous year. In 2002, the index covers 125 out of the 175 classification classes of NACE (Rev. 1). Prices are recorded for over 1400 representative items in almost 350 enterprises, which accounted for 69 percent of sold industrial goods in Latvia in 2000. Since 2001, the weights refer to the value of the volume of production sold of two years prior to the reporting period, and prices of December of the previous year serve as a base for price comparisons.

Consumer Prices:

Source S. Geographical Coverage: 15 regions; Number of Items in Basket: 412; Basis for Calculation: Weights are based on Household Budget Survey and are updated at approximately one-yearly intervals.

Industrial Employment and Wages:

Source S data are based on information obtained from quarterly enterprise surveys. Industrial employment data cover employees in the main job. Wage data comprise wages and salaries to employees in the main job before personal income tax deductions and social security contributions. The latter are payable by employees, while being deducted and transferred to the state budget by the employer. Wage data exclude remuneration in kind.

International Transactions:

Exports and Imports:

Source S data. The special trade system of recording trade transactions is used. Revisions to quarterly data are not apportioned among monthly data. Data include, in addition to those recorded in the customs statistics, estimates of imports of electricity and natural gas each month and quarterly estimates of extraterritorial trade from fishing vessels. Through 1994, the data also include quarterly information on supplies to Russian troops stationed in Latvia and adjustments (based on estimates of consumption) for mineral fuel imports that were not reflected in customs declarations. The volume index for exports is an annual chain-linked Laspeyres index for merchandise trade.

Government Finance:

Monthly, quarterly, and annual cash data are as reported by the Treasury. Data cover the consolidated central government. However, data on grants from some foreign assistance programs are excluded. † Data prior to 1996 cover the budgetary central government only. † From January through March 1996, data cover the budgetary central government and the Social Security Fund. † From 1997 onwards, expenditure on education and health functions was shifted within components of central government and between local government and central government. † Prior to 1998, data reported for *IFS* are not consolidated. The data are consolidated beginning with the data for January 1998. Data on

general government are derived from source V. The fiscal year ends December 31.

National Accounts:

Source S data. As indicated by the country, data are compiled according to the *SNA 93* and the *ESA 95*. Beginning in 1990, data are sourced from the Eurostat database.

Lebanon   446

Date of Fund Membership:

April 14, 1947

Standard Source:

A: Bank of Lebanon, *Annual Report, Quarterly Bulletin*

Exchange Rates:

Market Rate (End of Period and Period Average):
Closing midpoint rate in Beirut.

International Liquidity:

Gold (National Valuation) (line 1and) is obtained by converting the value in national currency terms, as reported in the country's standard sources, using the prevailing exchange rate, as given in *line* **ae** or **we**.

Monetary Authorities:

Consolidates the Bank of Lebanon and monetary authority functions undertaken by the central government. The contra-entry to Treasury IMF accounts is included in *line 12a.*

Deposit Money Banks:

Comprises approximately 70 operating commercial banks.

Interest Rates:

All interest rate data are from source A.

Discount Rate (End of Period):
Rate charged by the Bank of Lebanon to discount advances and paper offered by the commercial banks. Since June 7, 1985, the discount rate has been formally linked to treasury bill rates and commercial bill rates. The discount rate has not been used extensively as an instrument of monetary policy, because discounting by the commercial banks with the Bank of Lebanon occurs very rarely and in relatively small amounts.

Treasury Bill Rate:
Average yield on newly issued three-month treasury bills. † Beginning January 1987, secondary market yield on three-month treasury bills determined by the Central Bank of Lebanon.

Deposit Rate:
Average rate offered by commercial banks on fixed-term deposits.

Lending Rate:
Average rate charged by commercial banks on loans and advances.

International Transactions:

Prior to 1993, exports were taken from Statistical Office data on total exports minus *Government Finance Statistics Yearbook (GFSY)* data on bank notes and coin exports. Imports, c.i.f. were Statistical

Office data on total imports minus *GFSY* data on bank notes and coin imports. Beginning in 1993, the source of the data is the Customs Directorate of the Ministry of Finance. Exports are based on the *official dollar rate,* which is the previous month's average for the U.S. dollar. Imports are calculated using the *customs dollar rate.* From January 1, 1991 though May 15, 1991, the customs dollar rate was equal to 6 Lebanese pounds (LL). From May 16, 1991 through December 31, 1991 the customs dollar rate was equal to 100 LL. From January 1, 1992 through July 15, 1992 it was equal to 200 LL. From July 1992 through July 1995 it was fixed at 800 LL, and since July 15, 1995 the customs dollar rate has been equalized to the official dollar rate. Export values exclude re-export data.

Government Finance:

Prior to 2000, annual data are as reported for the *Government Finance Statistics Yearbook (GFSY)* and cover budgetary central government. † Since 2000, to the extent possible, existing subannual *IFS* data were converted to the main aggregates that are presented in the *GFSM 2001* Statement of Sources and Uses of Cash (see the Introduction of the monthly *IFS* publication for details). The fiscal year ends December 31.

Lesotho   666

Date of Fund Membership:
July 25, 1968

Standard Sources:
A: Central Bank of Lesotho, *Annual Report*
B: Central Bank of Lesotho, *Quarterly Review*
S: Bureau of Statistics, *Statistical Bulletin*

Exchange Rates:
The loti is at par with the South African rand (see notes on South Africa page for description of exchange rates).
The weighting scheme used to calculate indices of nominal and real effective exchange rates (*lines* **nec** and **rec**) is based on data for aggregate bilateral non-oil trade flows for 1988–90.

Monetary Authorities:
Comprises the Central Bank of Lesotho (CBL) only. *Currency Outside Banks (line 14a)* excludes South African rand in circulation, which is legal tender in Lesotho but for which data are not available. † Beginning in December 2001, data are based on a new reporting system which provides improved classification and sectorization of the accounts.

Banking Institutions:
Comprises commercial banks and Lesotho Building Finance Corporation (liquidated in November 1993). † Beginning in December 2001, data are based on a new reporting system which provides improved classification and sectorization of the accounts.

Banking Survey:
† See notes on monetary authorities and banking institutions .

Interest Rates:
Treasury Bill Rate:
Average rate on treasury bills. † Beginning in April 1993, average rate of three issues of 91-day treasury bills. The rate is determined through securities auctions conducted by the CBL.

Savings Rate:
Maximum rate offered by commercial banks on savings deposits.
Deposit Rate:
Rate prevailing at or near the end of the month for 88-day deposits.
Lending Rate:
Rate charged by commercial banks to prime borrowers at or near the end of the month.

Prices:
Consumer Prices:
Source B. Weights Reference Period: April 1997; Geographical Coverage: Maseru, the capital city and six lowland towns. Number of items in basket: 220; Basis for Calculation: the weights used in the index are derived from the Household Budget Survey of 1994/95.

International Transactions:
All trade value data are from source B. *Imports, c.i.f.* include customs duties and are therefore not comparable to corresponding balance of payments data.

Government Finance:
Quarterly data are as reported by the Ministry of Finance and cover the budgetary central government. The fiscal year ends March 31.

National Accounts:
Source S. As indicated by the country, the analytical framework is mainly based on the *1993 SNA.*

Liberia   668

Date of Fund Membership:
March 28, 1962

Standard Sources:
B: Central Bank of Liberia, *Liberia Financial Statistics*
S: Ministry of Planning and Economic Affairs, *Quarterly Statistical Bulletin*

Exchange Rates:
Market Rate (End of Period and Period Average):
Until December 1997, rates are based on a fixed relationship with the U.S. dollar. † Beginning in January 1998, rates are market determined.

International Liquidity:
Small holdings of gold, including commemorative coins, are not shown separately.

Monetary Authorities:
Consolidates the Central Bank of Liberia, which replaced the National Bank of Liberia in October 1999 and monetary authority functions undertaken by the central government. The contra-entry to Treasury IMF accounts is included in *line 12a.* † Beginning in December 1980, data are based on a new reporting system. † Beginning in January 2000, data are based on an improved sectorization and classification of the accounts.

Banking Institutions:

Comprises commercial banks. † See note on monetary authorities.

Banking Survey:

† See note on monetary authorities.

Money (National Definitions):

M1 comprises Liberian dollar notes and coins in circulation outside the banking system and demand deposits of the private sector, nonfinancial public corporations, and nonbank financial institutions at commercial banks in national and foreign currency. *M2* comprises M1 plus time and savings deposits of the private sector, nonfinancial public corporations, and nonbank financial institutions at commercial banks in national and foreign currency.

Interest Rates:

Savings Rate:
Average rate offered by commercial banks on saving deposits.

Deposit Rate:
Average rate offered by commercial banks on time deposits.

Lending Rate:
Average rate offered by commercial banks on overdrafts. † Beginning in January 1998, average rate offered by commercial banks on all loans.

Libya   672

Data refer to the Socialist People's Libyan Arab Jamahiriya.

Date of Fund Membership:

September 17, 1958

Standard Sources:

A: General Directorate for Economic and Social Planning
B: Central Bank of Libya, *Economic Bulletin*
S: Census and Statistics Directorate

Exchange Rates:

Official Rate (End of Period):
Central bank midpoint rate. The official rate is pegged to the SDR.

International Liquidity:

Gold (National Valuation) (line 1and) is obtained by converting the value in national currency terms, as reported in the country's standard sources, using the prevailing exchange rate, as given in *line* **ag** or *line* **wg**.
Foreign nonbank components of *lines 7a.d* and *7b.d* are small and are not reported separately.

Monetary Authorities:

Consolidates the Central Bank of Libya and monetary authority functions undertaken by the central government. The contra-entry to Treasury IMF accounts is included in *line 16d*. † Prior to March 2002, *Claims on Nonfinancial Public Enterprises (line 12c)* include positions arising from contingent operations such as issuance of letters of credit and guarantees; the contra-entries to these positions are in *Foreign Liabilities (line 16c), Time, and Foreign*

Currency Deposits (line 15), and *Other Items (net) (line 17r)*. † Beginning in June 1997, data are based on improved reporting and classification of accounts.

Deposit Money Banks:

Comprises commercial banks including, since December 2000, the regional (ahlia) banks. † From June 1997 to February 2002, *Claims on Nonfinancial Public Enterprises (line 22c)* include positions arising from contingent operations such as issuance of letters of credit and guarantees; the contra-entries to these positions are in *Foreign Liabilities (line 26c)* and *Other Items (net) (line 27r)*. † Prior to January 1999, some central government time deposits are included in *Time and Foreign Currency Deposits (line 25)*.

Monetary Survey:

† See notes on monetary authorities and deposit money banks.

Other Banking Institutions:

Comprise the Development Bank, the Agricultural Bank, and the Savings and Real Estate Investment Bank. † Prior to 1991, data refer to the National Agricultural Bank.

Interest Rates:

All interest rate data are from source B. With the exception of *Discount Rate (End of Period)*, all interest rate data are period averages.

Discount Rate (End of Period):
The rate applies to rediscounts of eligible commercial paper to banks by the Bank of Libya. Ceilings are established by the Bank of Libya for each commercial bank not exceeding 20 percent of its capital and reserves or 10 percent of its deposits, whichever is lower. Borrowing from the Bank is a privilege granted to banks at the discretion of the Central Bank, and the volume of discounts is limited.

Money Market Rate:
Maximum rate on interbank call loans.

Deposit Rate:
Maximum rate on six-month fixed deposits at commercial banks.

Lending Rate:
Maximum rate on secured loans and overdrafts.

Production:

Crude Petroleum Production:
Index constructed from source B data. If uncurrent, the index is calculated from production quantities reported in the *Oil Market Intelligence*.

International Transactions:

All trade data are from source S.

National Accounts:

Source A.

Lithuania   946

Date of Fund Membership:

April 29, 1992

Standard Sources:

B: Bank of Lithuania, *Monthly Bulletin, Quarterly Bulletin*
S: Lithuanian Department of Statistics, *Economic and Social Development in Lithuania* (monthly)

Exchange Rates:

The talons replaced the ruble in October 1992 at the rate of RUB 1 = LTT 1. The litas replaced the talonas in June 1993 at the rate of LTT 100 = LTL 1.

Official Rate: (End of Period and Period Average):
The official exchange rate of the litas is set by resolution of the Bank of Lithuania's Board. Until February 1, 2002, the anchor currency of the litas was the U.S. dollar. Effective February 2, 2002, the litas are pegged to the euro.

International Liquidity:

Until November 1997 gold was valued at US$333 per fine troy ounce. Between December 1997 and November 1998, gold was valued at US$283 per fine troy ounce. Beginning in December 1998, gold is valued at US$273.4 per fine troy ounce in national sources. Since December 2001, the gold holdings have been revalued once per month on the last working day at the value of London gold price fixing. Previously, gold was revalued once per year on the last working day at the lowest gold price fixing during the year, if that value was lower than the book value.

Monetary Authorities:

Comprises the Bank of Lithuania, which undertakes all monetary authorities functions. † Beginning in March 2004, data are compiled in accordance with the European Central Bank's framework for monetary statistics using the national residency approach.

Banking Institutions:

Comprises commercial banks, branches of foreign banks, and since, January 1999, the credit unions. † Beginning in December 1994, overdrafts, all of which were previously included in *Claims on the Private Sector,* are properly classified by economic sector. † Beginning in March 2004, data are compiled in accordance with the European Central Bank's framework for monetary statistics using the national residency approach; data cover *credit institutions* only (namely, commercial banks, branches of foreign banks, and the credit unions).

Banking Survey:

† See notes on monetary authorities and banking institutions .

Money (National Definitions):

Base Money comprises currency in circulation and deposits of resident sectors at the Bank of Lithuania excluding deposits of central and other general government.

M1 comprises currency held by the public and demand deposits of the private sector, public nonfinancial enterprises, and nonbank financial institutions with the Bank of Lithuania and banking institutions. † Beginning in March 2004, M1 comprises currency in circulation and overnight deposits at monetary financial institutions (MFIs) held by the non-central government, non-MFI resident sectors.

M2 comprises M1 and time, savings, and foreign currency deposits of the private sector, public nonfinancial enterprises, and nonbank financial institutions with the Bank of Lithuania and banking institutions. † Beginning in March 2004, *M2* is equal to *M1* plus deposits with agreed maturity up to two years and de-

posits redeemable at notice up to three months held by the non-central government, non-MFI resident sectors at resident MFIs. *M3* is equal to *M2* plus marketable instruments issued by MFIs, namely repurchase agreements contracted by MFIs with non-central government non-MFI resident sectors, money market fund shares/units and debt securities with maturity up to two years issued by MFIs to non-central government, non-MFI resident sectors.

Interest Rates:

All interest rate data are from source B.

Bank Rate (End of Period):
Bank of Lithuania rate on overnight repurchase agreements.

Money Market Rate:
Average rate on interbank credit with maturities of up to one month. † Beginning in January 1998, average rate on one-day contracts between resident banks in national currency.

Money Market Rate (Foreign Currency):
Average rate on one-day contracts between resident banks in foreign currency.

Savings Rate:
Average rate offered by banks on savings deposits in national currency.

Savings Rate (Foreign Currency):
Average rate offered by banks on savings deposits in foreign currency.

Treasury Bill Rate:
Average auction rate on 91-day treasury bills. † Beginning in January 2000, average auction rate on one-year treasury bills.

Deposit Rate:
Average of rates offered by banks on time deposits of residents in national currency weighted by volume. † Beginning in January 2005, average of rates on new time deposits of households and non-financial corporations in national currency weighted by volume.

Deposit Rate (Foreign Currency):
Aaverage of rates offered by banks on time deposits of residents in foreign currency weighted by volume. † Beginning in January 2005, average of rates on new time deposits of households and non-financial corporations in euros weighted by volume.

Lending Rate:
Average of rates charged by banks on all loans and advances to residents in national currency weighted by volume. † Beginning in January 2005, average of rates on new loans to households and non-financial corporations in national currency weighted by volume.

Lending Rate (Foreign Currency):
Average of rates charged by banks on loans and advances to residents in foreign currency weighted by volume. † Beginning in January 2005, average of rates on new loans to households and non-financial corporations in euros weighted by volume.

Prices, Production, Labor:

Producer Prices:
Source S Laspeyres index. Reference period for prices is December of the year t–1 (t - the current year), and reference period for weights is the sales volumes of the year t–2. In December 2002 Statistics Lithuania adjusted the weightings' volumes of the reference period to the reference period of prices having applied

respective producer price indices. This adjustment also was applied to 1998–2002 years to produce a consistent time series. The index covers both domestic and exported industrial products. The reference period for the price indices has changed into 2000 (the year 2000=100). Since January 2003, 542 representative goods are selected for index compilation. Individual price data are collected for 1447 items from 415 enterprises, which in 1999, accounted for 75 percent of industrial output.

Consumer Prices:
Source S. Geographical Coverage: 19 regions; Number of Items in Basket: 796; Basis for Calculation: Weights are based on Household Budget Survey and are updated at approximately one-yearly intervals.

Wages: Average Earnings:
Annual data are derived from the annual survey on wages and salaries, which covers complete enumeration of enterprises, institutions, and organizations of all kinds of ownership. Quarterly data on average earnings are presented excluding individual enterprises. Since 2000, the quarterly data are derived from the quarterly survey; until this year, from the monthly survey. Due to this fact, data are not strictly comparable.

Industrial Production:
Source S. Weights Reference Period: 2000; Sectoral Coverage: mining, quarrying and manufacturing; Basis for Calculation: to calculate the indices, the aggregate value of sales for each industrial activity (or branch of industry) for each month is deflated by the corresponding producer price index.

Manufacturing Employment:
Data are from the same survey as the manufacturing production data. Data on total hours worked in the period are divided by the standard work hours for the period to obtain the equivalent numbers employed.

International Transactions:

Exports and Imports:
Source S data. The special system of recording trade transactions is used.

Government Finance:

Monthly and quarterly cash data are as reported by the Ministry of Finance. All data cover the consolidated central government. However, not all extrabudgetary operations financed by foreign grants and loans are covered. † In 1997, expenditure on health functions and their financing was shifted from local to central government. † Prior to 2004, to the extent possible, existing subannual *IFS* data were converted to the main aggregates that are presented in the *GFSM 2001* Statement of Sources and Uses of Cash (see the Introduction of the monthly *IFS* publication for details). Beginning in January 2004, monthly and quarterly data are reported in the *GFSM 2001* analytical framework The fiscal year ends December 31.

National Accounts:

As indicated by the country, data are compiled according to the *1993 SNA*. The coverage of the private sector activity is incomplete. Beginning in 1990, data are sourced from the Eurostat database. Eurostat introduced chain-linked GDP volume measures to both annual and quarterly data with the release of the third quarter 2005 on November 30, 2005. Chain-linked GDP volume measures are expressed in the prices of the previous year and re-referenced to 2000.

Luxembourg   137

Data are denominated in Luxembourg francs prior to January 1999 and in euros from January 1999 onward. An irrevocably fixed factor for converting Luxembourg francs to euros was established at 40.3399 Luxembourg francs per euro. In 2002, the Luxembourg franc was retired from circulation and replaced by euro banknotes and coins. Beginning in January 1999, with the implementation of Stage Three of the European Economic and Monetary Union (EMU), a euro area-wide definition of residency was introduced: All positions with residents of other euro area (EA) countries, including the European Central Bank (ECB), are classified as domestic positions, and foreign assets and foreign liabilities include only positions with non-euro area residents. Descriptions of the changes in the methodology and presentation of Luxembourg's accounts following the introduction of the euro are shown in the introduction to *IFS* and in the notes on the euro area page.

Date of Fund Membership:
December 27, 1945

Standard Sources:
B: Central Bank of Luxembourg, *Annual Report*
S: Statec, *Bulletin*
V: Eurostat

Exchange Rates:
Prior to March 5, 1990, there was a dual exchange rate system in which the primary rate, maintained within the cooperative exchange arrangement under the European Monetary System (EMS), was applicable to most current transactions, and the secondary or free market rate was applicable to most capital transactions. Between March 1990 and December 1998, the market rate maintained within the EMS was applicable to all transactions. Prior to January 1999, *Market Rate (End of Period and Period Average)* was the midpoint rate of the Luxembourg franc in the official market in Brussels. In January 1999, the Luxembourg franc became a participating currency within the Eurosystem, and the euro market rate became applicable to all transactions. In 2002, the Luxembourg franc was retired from circulation and replaced by euro banknotes and coins. For additional information, refer to the section on exchange rates in the introduction to *IFS* and the notes on the euro area page.

International Liquidity:
Beginning in January 1999, *Total Reserves minus Gold (line 1l.d)* is defined in accordance with the Eurosystem's statistical definition of international reserves. The international reserves of Luxembourg per the Eurosystem statistical definition at the start of the monetary union (January 1, 1999) in billions of U.S. dollars were as follows: *Total Reserves minus Gold,* $174; *Foreign Exchange,* $78; *SDRs,* $12; *Reserve Position in the Fund,* $84; *Other Reserve Assets,* $0; *Gold,* – $55; *Gold (million fine troy ounces),* – .191 ounces. *Foreign Exchange (line 1d.d):* Between March 1979 and December 1998, gold and foreign exchange holdings excluded deposits at the European Monetary Cooperation Fund (EMCF), and the holdings of European currency units (ECUs) issued against these deposits were included in *line 1d.d. Gold (Eurosystem Valuation) (line 1and):* Prior to June 1998, data pertained to gold holdings of the Institut Monétaire Luxembourgeois (IML). The government of Luxembourg held a claim on the IML, covered at all times by

the IML's gold holdings, which could include gold receivable from the European Monetary Institute (EMI). After June 1998, the gold retained by the Central Bank of Luxembourg (CBL)—the IML's successor—was sold (demonetized). Until December 1998, CBL's only gold account was for gold receivable from the ECB. The negative entries from January to May 1999 indicate a short position in the holdings of monetary gold, which was due to the delivery to the ECB of gold previously received under a gold loan from Belgium. Memorandum data are provided on *Non-Euro Claims on Euro Area Residents* and *Euro Claims on Non-Euro Area Residents,* which represent positions as of the last Friday in each month. For additional information, refer to the section on international liquidity in the introduction to *IFS* and the notes on the euro area page.

Monetary Authorities:

Comprises the CBL only, which beginning in January 1999 is part of the Eurosystem. The CBL was created on June 1, 1998 as a successor to the IML, which was largely a supervisory agency. Prior to June 1998, government interest rate policy was implemented through Banque et Caisse d'Epargne de l'Etat, a domestic commercial bank. Beginning in 2002, *Currency Issued (line 14a)* includes euro banknotes and coins and, until December 2002, any unretired Luxembourg francs. The recorded value of euro banknotes is based on a monthly allocation of total euro banknotes in circulation based on the Central Bank of Luxembourg's paid up share of the ECB's capital; it does not correspond to either the actual amount of euro banknotes placed in circulation by the CBL which is shown in memo line *Currency Put into Circulation (line 14m),* nor the actual circulation of banknotes within the domestic territory. See section *Euro banknotes and coins* in the introduction to *IFS.* Prior to January 1999, *Currency in Circulation (line 14a)* included Luxembourg notes and coins issued by the IML but did not include Belgian francs, which circulated as legal tender in Luxembourg. *Bonds and Money Market Instruments (line 16n.u)* include subordinated debt in the form of securities, other bonds, and money market paper. For a description of the accounts, refer to the section on monetary authorities in the introduction to *IFS.* Beginning with the data for end-November 2000, Monetary Authorities' *Foreign Assets (line 11), Foreign Liabilities (line 16c), Claims on Banking Institutions (line 12e.u),* and *Liabilities to Banking Institutions (line 14c.u)* are affected by a change from gross to net presentation of positions relating to the TARGET (Trans-European Automated Real-Time Gross Settlement Express Transfer) euro clearing system. (See *Recording of TARGET system positions* under *European Economic and Monetary Union (EMU)* in the introduction to *IFS.*) Beginning in 2002, *Claims on Banking Institutions (line 12e.u)* and *Liabilities to Banking Institutions (line 14c.u)* include "Intra-Eurosystem claims/liabilities related to banknote issue," which is a single net value representing the difference between the value of euro banknotes allocated to the CBL according to the accounting scheme of the Eurosystem for issuing euro banknotes, and the value of euro banknotes put into circulation by the CBL. See section *Euro banknotes and coins* in the introduction to *IFS.* Memo line *Net Claims on Eurosystem (line 12e.s)* equals gross claims on, less gross liabilities to, the ECB and other members of the Eurosystem. Comprises euro-denominated claims equivalent to the transfer of foreign currency reserves to the ECB, Intra-Eurosystem claims/liabilities related to banknote issue, net claims or liabilities within the TARGET clearing system, and other positions.

Banking Institutions:

Prior to January 1999, this section consolidated data on commercial banks operating in Luxembourg, including affiliates of foreign banks. The reports on the financial position of commercial banks forwarded to the IML were extensively revised at the end of 1992, leading to breaks in some series. *Money Market Fund Shares (line 26m.u)* include shares/units issued by money market funds. *Bonds and Money Market Instruments (line 26n.u)* include subordinated debt in the form of securities, other bonds, and money market paper. *Capital Accounts (line 27a):* Prior to January 1999, included subordinated debt securities and specific provisions. Beginning in January 1999, banking institutions comprise all resident units classified as other monetary financial institutions (other MFIs), as defined in *1995 ESA* standards, including money market funds. *Other Items (Net) (line 27r)* includes specific provisions, holdings of shares issued by other MFIs, and accruals on liabilities to third parties, such as for payment of taxes. For a description of the accounts, refer to the section on banking institutions in the introduction to *IFS. Central Government Monetary Liabilities (line 25.iu)* consist of post office deposit liabilities, which beginning in 1999 are a component of euro area monetary aggregates; data are unavailable prior to September 1997.

Banking Survey (Euro Area-wide Residency):

For a description of the methodology and accounts, refer to the section Banking Survey (Euro Area-wide Residency) in the introduction to *IFS.*

Money (National Definitions):

Prior to January 1999, *Money (line 39ma)* comprised currency outside banks, including an estimate for Belgian francs circulating as legal tender, and demand deposits (including demand deposits with the post office). *Quasi-Money (line 39mb)* comprised time and savings deposits of resident nonfinancial institutions. Beginning in January 1999, national monetary aggregates series are discontinued. Euro area aggregates are presented on the euro area page.

Interest Rates:

Deposit Rate (line 60l):
Rate on savings deposits with the Banque et Caisse d'Epargne de l'Etat.

Deposit Rate (lines 60lhs, 60lhn, 60lcs, and 60lcn):
See notes in the Introduction to *IFS.*

Lending Rate (line 60p):
Minimum rate on mortgage loans by the Banque et Caisse d'Epargne de l'Etat.

Lending Rate (lines 60phm, 60pcs, and 60pcn):
See notes in the Introduction to *IFS.*

Government Bond Yield (line 61):
† Weighted average yield to maturity on all government bonds quoted in the Luxembourg Stock Exchange. Prior to 1978, data referred to the average weighted yield to average maturity as then calculated by the Luxembourg Stock Exchange. For additional information, refer to the section on interest rates in the introduction to *IFS* and the notes on the euro area page.

Prices, Production, Labor:

Share Prices:
Source B, base 1967. It is calculated by the Luxembourg Stock Exchange and covers national companies.

Producer Prices:

Industrial products, source S index, weights reference period: 2000. Prices are ex-factory prices and cover the same industries as those under *Industrial Production,* except for electric power and gas. Value-added tax is excluded, but other taxes and subsidies are included.

Consumer Prices:

Source S. Weights Reference Period: annually re-weighted; Geographical Coverage: national territory (Grand Duchy of Luxembourg); Number of Items in Basket: 277; Basis for Calculation: the source for the weights at all levels of aggregation are National Accounts. Household Budget Survey results are integrated in the NA results.

Industrial Production:

Data are sourced from the OECD database, weights reference period: 2000. Data cover all industries, except construction and civil engineering. New enterprises are included as soon as they are created. Data have been adjusted by *IFS.*

Employment:

Source B, weights reference period: 2000. The index covers the whole economy.

International Transactions:

Luxembourg's trade with countries outside the Belgium-Luxembourg Economic Union (BLEU) is also part of the BLEU's foreign trade statistics which are shown on the page for Belgium. Beginning in 1997, trade data are for Luxembourg only, which includes trade between Belgium and Luxembourg.

Balance of Payments:

In the world tables, balance of payments data for Luxembourg are shown separately for 2002. For prior years, data are included under Belgium/Luxembourg. Historic current account data for Luxembourg are available in the detailed country pages.

Government Finance:

Annual data on general government are as reported for the *Government Finance Statistics Yearbook (GFSY).* The fiscal year ends December 31.

National Accounts:

GDP in the Luxembourg version used to be higher than GDP according to the *SNA,* to the extent that, depending on the special characteristics of the financial market, a very considerable proportion of imputed bank services is reported as exports. As indicated by the country, from 1995 onwards data have been revised following the implementation of the *ESA 95.* Beginning in 1999, euro data are sourced from the Eurostat database. Eurostat introduced chain-linked GDP volume measures to both annual and quarterly data with the release of the third quarter 2005 on November 30, 2005. Chain linked GDP volume measures are expressed in the prices of the previous year and re-referenced to 1995.

Macedonia, FYR   962

Date of Fund Membership:

December 14, 1992

Standard Sources:

A: National Bank of the Republic of Macedonia, *Monthly Bulletin*

S: Statistical Office of Macedonia, *Monthly Statistical Bulletin of the Republic of Macedonia and Macedonia Basic Economic Data*

Exchange Rates:

Market Rate (End of Period and Period Average):

Weighted average of daily transactions reported by commercial banks.

Monetary Authorities:

Comprises only accounts of the National Bank of the Republic of Macedonia (central bank). *Claims on Central Government (line 12a)* includes claims arising from the assumption by the government of certain liabilities of the former Socialist Federal Republic of Yugoslavia (SFRY) to the National Bank of the Republic of Macedonia. *Line 12a* and *Central Government Deposits (line 16d)* comprise accounts of the central government, social funds, and government agencies. † From November 1995, data reflect major changes in statistical reporting arrangements in the Former Yugoslav Republic of Macedonia, including improvements in the sectorization of accounts. Prior to November 1995, local governments were included in central government, and nonfinancial public enterprises and some government units were included in private sector.

Deposit Money Banks:

Comprises commercial banks and the Postal Savings House. *Claims on Central Government (line 22a)* and *Central Government Deposit (line 26d)* comprise accounts of central government, social funds, and government agencies. † See note on monetary authorities.

Monetary Survey:

† See note on monetary authorities.

Interest Rates:

All interest rate data are from source A.

Bank Rate (End of Period):

Reference rate for determining other rates charged by the central bank on discounting eligible commercial bills and loans.

Deposit Rate:

Lowest reported interest rate on household deposits with maturities of three to six months.

Lending Rate:

Midpoint rates for short-term lending to all sectors. † Prior to June 1995, lowest reported interest rate on short-term loans to the agricultural sector.

Prices, Production, Labor:

Producer Prices:

Source S. Weights reference period: previous year.

Consumer Prices:

Source S. Weights Reference Period: previous year. Laspeyres cost-of-living index for nonagricultural households.

Wages, Average Monthly:

Data are based on a regular monthly sample survey covering 70 percent of all employees. Annual data represent an average of monthly data.

Industrial Production:

Source S. Weights Reference Period: previous year; Sectoral Coverage: mining and quarrying, manufacturing industry, electricity, gas and water supply; Basis for Calculation: the weights of products are calculated as a share of value of gross output of each product into total gross output; the latest weights were calculated based on the data from the Annual Survey for Industry conducted in 2003.

International Transactions:

Source S. Special trade basis. Products intended for reprocessing or finishing are included.

International Investment Position:
Data are incomplete. Banking and official sector data are included. Private sector transactions are partially covered.

National Accounts:

Source S. Series are based on the *1993 SNA*, as indicated by the country. As the production-based GDP *(line 99bp)* is the official measure of GDP, the statistical discrepancy *(line 99bs)* represents the difference between the production-based GDP and the sum of the expenditure components shown.

Madagascar   674

Date of Fund Membership:
September 25, 1963

Standard Sources:
B: Central Bank, *Monthly Bulletin of Statistics*
S: National Institute of Statistics, *Monthly Bulletin*

Exchange Rates:
The ariary was introduced in January 2005 and replaced the malagasy franc at the rate of Ar1=FMG5.

Official Rate: (End of Period and Period Average):
Central bank midpoint rate. The official rate is managed flexibly and is adjusted according to a set of indicators.

Monetary Authorities:
Consolidates the Central Bank of Madagascar and monetary authority functions undertaken by the central government. † Beginning in 1979, claims on public enterprises are separately identified. The contra-entry to government foreign assets is included in *line 12a*. Foreign Liabilities *(line 16c)* comprises both short-term and long-term liabilities to nonresidents.

Deposit Money Banks:
Comprises commercial banks. † Beginning in 1979, data are based on an improved classification; as a result, bonds, central government lending funds, and credit from the central bank are separately identified.

Monetary Survey:
† See notes on monetary authorities and deposit money banks.

Interest Rates:

Base Rate:
Central Bank's reference rate representing a minimum rate on repurchase agreement operations and a minimum penalty rate on required reserve deficiencies, with the effective rates equal to the base rate plus the margins.

Money Market Rate:
Highest rate charged on overnight interbank loans.

Treasury Bill Rate:
Monthly average of interest rates on one-month, three-month, and six-month treasury bills sold at daily auctions.

Deposit Rate:
Highest rate offered on large three-month deposits at the commercial banks.

Lending Rate:
Highest rate charged on short-term loans.

Prices:

Consumer Prices:
Source B. Weights Reference Period: 2000; Geographical Coverage: four major urban centers of Madagascar (Antananarivo, Antsiranana, Fianarantsoa, and Toamasina); Number of Items in the Basket: 338–382 representative products; Basis for Calculation: the weights are derived from a national survey conducted in 1999 on health, education, and household expenditure.

International Transactions:
Source B.

Government Finance:
Annual data are as reported in the *Government Finance Statistics Yearbook (GFSY)* and cover the consolidated central government. The fiscal year ends December 31.

National Accounts:
Source B. As indicated by the country, the data are compiled in accordance with the *1968 SNA* and the *1993 SNA*.

Malawi   676

Date of Fund Membership:
July 19, 1965

Standard Sources:
B: Reserve Bank of Malawi, *Financial and Economic Review*
S: National Statistics Office, *Monthly Statistical Bulletin*

Exchange Rates:

Official Rate: (End of Period and Period Average):
Central bank midpoint rate. The official rate is pegged to a basket of currencies. From February 1994, the official rate is market-determined.

For the purpose of calculating the real effective exchange rate index *(line **rec**)*, the consumer price index used is a weighted average of six official price series for high-, medium-, and low-income groups in Lilongwe and Blantyre. The monthly data are derived by interpolating the weighted average of published quarterly data.

International Liquidity:
Data for *line 1d.d* include small foreign exchange holdings by the government.

Gold (National Valuation) (line 1and) is obtained by converting the value in national currency terms, as reported in the country's standard sources, using the prevailing exchange rate, as given in *line **de***, *line **ae***, or *line **we***.

Monetary Authorities:

Consolidates the Reserve Bank of Malawi (RBM) and monetary authority functions undertaken by the central government. The contra-entry to government foreign assets and Treasury IMF accounts is included in *line 16d,* while that for Trust Fund loans is included in *line 12a.*

Deposit Money Banks:

Comprises National Bank of Malawi and Stanbic Bank. Beginning in January 1998, includes First Merchant Bank and Finance Bank of Malawi.

Other Banking Institutions:

Comprises New Building Society, National Finance Company, Investment and Development Bank of Malawi, and Post Office Savings Bank. † Beginning in March 1988, comprises Inde Bank, New Building Society, National Finance Company, Leasing and Finance Company, Fincom Bank, Malawi Savings Bank, and CBM Financial Services.

Banking Survey:

† See note to other banking institutions.

Nonbank Financial Institutions:

Comprises life insurance companies and non-life insurance companies. Beginning in March 2004, includes the Old Mutual Insurance Company.

Money (National Definitions):

Reserve Money comprises currency in circulation and banker's correspondent and other accounts with the RBM. Currency in circulation refers to notes and coins issued by the RBM.
M1 comprises currency in circulation and transferable deposits. Currency in circulation refers to notes and coins issued by the RBM less the amount held by commercial banks. Transferable deposits refer to current account deposits in national currency of the private sector with commercial banks.
M2 comprises M1, fixed term and savings deposits in national currency and foreign currency deposits of the private sector with commercial banks.

Interest Rates:

Discount Rate (End of Period):
Rate charged by the RBM on loans to commercial banks.

Treasury Bill Rate:
Rate for 91-day treasury bills.

Deposit Rate:
Rate offered by commercial banks on three- to five-month time deposits.

Lending Rate:
Maximum rate charged by commercial banks on unsecured loans.

Government Bond Yield:
Yield on new issues of bonds.

Prices, Production, Labor:

Consumer Prices:
Source S. Weights Reference Period: October 1997-November 1998; Geographical Coverage: national territory; Basis for Calculation: Integrated Household Survey.

Industrial Production:
Source B index, weights reference period: 1984. Prior to 1988, manufacturing production, base 1970.

International Transactions:

Value data on *Exports* and total *Imports* are from source B. Revisions are made to annual data only; consequently, monthly and quarterly figures may not add up to annual data.

National Accounts:

Source S.

Malaysia   548

Data refer to Malaysia, i.e., to West Malaysia (the former State of Malaya) and East Malaysia (the former Sabah and Sarawak). Data do not include Singapore. Exceptions are noted.

Date of Fund Membership:

March 7, 1958

Standard Sources:

A: Bank Negara, *Annual Report*
B: Bank Negara, *Quarterly Economic Bulletin, Monthly Statistical Supplement*
S: Department of Statistics, *Monthly Statistical Bulletin*

Exchange Rates:

Official Rate: (End of Period and Period Average):
Closing interbank rate in Kuala Lumpur. Effective September 2, 1998, the official rate of the ringgit was pegged to the U.S. dollar at a rate of RM 3.80 per dollar. Effective July 21, 2005, the exchange rate operates as a managed float, with its value being determined by economic fundamentals and maintained against a trade-weighted index of Malaysia's major trading partners.

International Liquidity:

Gold (National Valuation) (line 1and) is equal to *Gold (Million Fine Troy Ounces) (line 1ad),* valued at SDR 35 per fine troy ounce and converted into U.S. dollars at the dollar/SDR rate **sa** on the country page for the United States. Source E: OECD

Monetary Authorities:

Comprises the Bank Negara Malaysia only. † Beginning in January 1992, data are based on an improved sectorization of the accounts. † Beginning in December 1996, data are based on a new reporting system which provides improved sectorization of the accounts. † Beginning in December 2001, data are based on an improved classification and sectorization of the accounts. † Beginning in December 2002, data are based on a new reporting system which provides improved classification and sectorization of the accounts.

Banking Institutions:

Comprises commercial banks and National Savings Bank. Beginning in December 1969, includes finance companies. † Beginning in December 1971 includes the Employees Provident Fund. † Beginning in January 1974, includes merchant banks. † Beginning in January 1992, includes discount houses and excludes the National Savings Bank and Employees Provident Fund. Data are based on an improved sectorization of the accounts. † Beginning in December 1996, data are based on a new reporting system which provides improved sectorization of the accounts. † Beginning in December 2001, data are based on an improved classification and sectorization of the accounts. † Beginning in December 2002, data are based on a new reporting system which provides improved classification and sectorization of the accounts.

Banking Survey:

† See notes on monetary authorities and banking institutions.

Money (National Definitions):

Reserve Money comprises currency in circulation, bankers' required reserves, bankers' excess reserves, and deposits of the private sector. Currency in circulation refers to notes and coins issued by Bank Negara Malaysia (BNM) less the amount of notes and coins held by banking institutions (commercial banks, finance companies, merchant banks, Islamic banks, and discount houses). Required reserves refer to the amount placed by banking institutions, except discount houses, with BNM in compliance with the Statutory Reserve Requirement. Excess reserves refer to cash in vault of the banking institutions and their demand deposits with BNM. Deposits of the private sector refer to the demand and time deposits placed by other financial institutions and public agencies with BNM.

Beginning in April 1997, *reserve money* excludes deposits of the private sector. As part of performing the role of banker to the government, BNM had been providing retail banking services to the other financial institutions and public agencies. In April 1997, BNM ceased to provide these services.

M1 comprises currency in circulation and demand deposits. Currency in circulation refers to the notes and coins issued by BNM less the amount held by commercial banks and Islamic banks. Demand deposits refer to the current accounts in national currency of the private sector with commercial banks and Islamic banks.

M2 comprises *M1* and narrow quasi-money. Narrow quasi-money refers to savings and time deposits, negotiable instruments of deposits, and repurchase agreements of the private sector with commercial banks and Islamic banks and foreign currency deposits of the private sector and foreign entities with commercial banks and Islamic banks.

M3 comprises *M2* and deposits placed with other banking institutions. Deposits with other banking institutions refer to savings and time deposits, negotiable instruments of deposits, and repurchase agreements of the private sector with finance companies, merchant banks, and discount houses and foreign currency deposits of the private sector and foreign entities with finance companies, merchant banks, and discount houses.

Nonbank Financial Institutions:

Comprises life insurance companies.

Interest Rates:

All interest rate data are from source B.

Discount Rate (End of Period):
Rate of discount on three-month treasury bills.

Money Market Rate:
Weighted average overnight interbank rate. Monthly rates refer to the average for the trading days of the month. Daily rates are calculated as the average of interbank deposit rates for the day, with individual rates weighted by the volume of transactions.

Treasury Bill Rate:
Average discount rate on three-month treasury bills.

Savings Rate:
Weighted average rate offered by commercial banks on savings deposits in national currency. The rate is weighted by deposit amounts in single rate savings accounts as well as multi-tiered savings accounts.

Deposit Rate:
Average rate offered by commercial banks on three-month time deposits to the private sector in national currency.

Lending Rate:
Weighted average rate offered by commercial banks on all loans in national currency. The rate is weighted by loan amounts.

Government Bond Yield:
Market yield to maturity on five-year government bonds.

Prices, Production, Labor:

All data on prices and production are from source S.

Share Prices:
Composite stock price index of the Kuala Lumpur Stock Exchange, weights reference period: 1977. The index is limited to 100 companies although the actual component companies can change from time to time and weighted by market capitalization. The monthly index is calculated from the average of the daily closing quotations.

Producer Prices:
Source S. Weights Reference Period: 2000; Coverage: agriculture, fishing, mining, manufacturing, and water, gas, and electricity sectors; Number of Items in Basket: 2009 commodities; Basis for Calculation: weights used in the index are derived from the Census of Economy 2000, Final National Accounts 2000 and other alternative sources of data for the value of production imports.

Consumer Prices:
Source S. Weights Reference Period: 2005; Geographical Coverage: whole national territory; Number of Items in Basket: 460; Basis for Calculation: weights are derived from the 2004–2005 Household Expenditure Survey.

Industrial Production:
Source S. Weights Reference Period: 2000; Sectoral Coverage: manufacturing, mining, and electricity sectors; Basis for Calculation: the weights are based on the group or industry's proportion of the total census of value added in the 2000 weights reference period.

International Transactions:

All trade data are from source B. Beginning 1965, imports of ships, aircraft, military weapons, bunkers, and ships' stores are excluded.

Government Finance:

Prior to 2000, quarterly and annual data on central government are derived from source A. † Beginning in 2000, annual data are as reported in the *Government Finance Statistics Yearbook (GFSY)* and cover the consolidated central government. The fiscal year ends December 31.

National Accounts:

Data are derived from source B.

Maldives   556

Date of Fund Membership:

January 13, 1978

Standard Sources:

A: Maldives Monetary Authority, *Annual Report*
B: Maldives Monetary Authority, *Quarterly Economic Bulletin*
S: Ministry of Planning and Development, *Statistical Yearbook of Maldives*

Exchange Rates:

Official Rate: (End of Period and Period Average):
Commercial bank midpoint rate. Effective October 19, 1994, the official rate of the rufiyaa was pegged to the U.S. dollar at a rate of Rf 11.77 per dollar. Effective July 25, 2001, the rufiyaa was devalued and fixed at Rf 12.80 per US$1.

International Liquidity:

Data for *Gold (National Valuation) (line 1and)* are calculated on the basis of cost of acquisition as given in the accounts of the monetary authority.

Monetary Authorities:

Prior to December 1981, data relate to the monetary authority functions of the Department of Finance (Treasury) and the State Trading Organization, which managed a large part of the official foreign exchange holdings. † Beginning in December 1981, comprises the Maldives Monetary Authority (MMA) only, which was established in that year. † Prior to January 1985, *Claims on Central Government (line 12a)* include claims on nonfinancial public enterprises and *Foreign Liabilities (line 16c)* include amounts of government foreign borrowing, with a contra-entry in *Claims on Central Government (line 12a)*.

Deposit Money Banks:

Comprises the Bank of Maldives Plc. and branches of foreign banks, namely the Bank of Ceylon, Bank of Credit and Commerce International, Habib Bank Ltd., Hong Kong and Shanghai Banking Corporation Ltd., and State Bank of India. † Beginning in December 1981, data are based on an improved sectorization of the accounts. † Prior to January 1985, *Foreign Liabilities (line 26c)* exclude nonresident deposits with domestic banks.

Monetary Survey:

† See notes on monetary authorities and deposit money banks.

Money (National Definitions):

Reserve Money comprises currency in circulation, commercial banks' deposits at the MMA, and demand deposits of public nonfinancial corporations at the MMA in national and foreign currency.
Narrow Money comprises currency outside the banking system, demand deposits of public nonfinancial corporations at the MMA in national currency, and demand deposits of public nonfinancial corporations, other financial corporations, and private sector at commercial banks in national currency.
Quasi Money comprises demand deposits of public nonfinancial corporations at the MMA in foreign currency, and savings and time deposits of public nonfinancial corporations, other financial corporations, and private sector at commercial banks in national and foreign currency.
Broad Money comprises narrow money and quasi money.

Interest Rates:

Discount Rate (End of Period):
Rate charged by the MMA on loans to commercial banks. Effective August 6, 2001, commercial banks have access to a Lombard window at the MMA with a maximum interest of five percentage points above the highest rate prevailing in the banking industry. † Beginning in November 2006, Repurchase Facility Rate offered by the MMA to commercial banks on short-term liquidity loans collateralized by treasury bills in national currency. The rate corresponds to the 28-day treasury bill rate plus seven percentage points.

Money Market Rate:
Average yield on overnight deposits in the interbank market.

Treasury Bill Rate:
Rate on 28-day treasury bills in national currency announced by the MMA.

Savings Rate:
Maximum rate offered by commercial banks on savings deposits in national and foreign currency. † Beginning in January 2004, maximum rate offered by commercial banks on savings deposits in national currency.

Savings Rate (Foreign Currency):
Maximum rate offered by commercial banks on savings deposits in foreign currency.

Deposit Rate:
Maximum rate offered by commercial banks on time deposits of six months to one year in national and foreign currency. † Beginning in January 2004, maximum rate offered by commercial banks on time deposits of six months to one year in national currency.

Deposit Rate (Foreign Currency):
Maximum rate offered by commercial banks on time deposits of six months to one year in foreign currency.

Lending Rate:
Maximum rate charged by commercial banks on loans of up to three months to the private sector in national and foreign currency. † Beginning in January 2004, maximum rate charged by commercial banks on loans of up to three months to the private sector in national currency.

Lending Rate (Foreign Currency):
Maximum rate charged by commercial banks on loans of up to three months to the private sector in foreign currency.

Prices, Production, Labor:

Consumer Prices:
Source B index, weights reference period: June 1995. Geographical coverage: whole country.

Fish Catch Index:
Source B data on live weight of total fish landings reported in metric tons.

Tourist Bed Night Index:
Source B data on monthly number of tourist bed nights based on receipt of tourist tax.

International Transactions:

Merchandise Exports f.o.b.:
The entries are derived from customs returns, supplemented by estimates of the purchases of consumer durables by travelers from India and Sri Lanka and other expenditures by all other tourists. Re-exports of ships not reported by customs are included.

Exports and Imports (f.o.b.):
Data are from "Customs, Male" as reported in sources B and S.

Government Finance:

Data for consolidated central government are as reported by the Maldives Monetary Authority. Beginning in 1990, annual data are as reported in the *Government Finance Statistics Yearbook (GFSY)* and cover the budgetary central government. The fiscal year ends December 31.

Mali   678

Date of Fund Membership:

September 27, 1963

Standard Sources:

B: Banque Centrale des Etats de l'Afrique de l'Ouest (Central Bank of West African States), *Notes d'information et Statistiques (Informative Notes and Statistics)*

N: Direction Nationale de la Statistique et de l'Informatique, Ministère du Plan, *Comptes Économique du Mali.*

Mali became the seventh member of the West African Economic and Monetary Union on June 1, 1984, joining Benin, Burkina Faso, Côte d'Ivoire, Niger, Senegal, and Togo. The Union, which was established in 1962, has a common central bank, the Central Bank of West African States (BCEAO), with headquarters in Dakar, and national branches in the member states. Guinea-Bissau joined the Union on May 2, 1997.

Exchange Rates:

Official Rate: (End of Period and Period Average):
Prior to January 1999, the official rate was pegged to the French franc. On January 12, 1994, the CFA franc was devalued to CFAF 100 per French franc from CFAF 50 at which it had been fixed since 1948. From January 1, 1999, the CFAF is pegged to the euro at a rate of CFA franc 655.957 per euro.

International Liquidity:

Gold is revalued on a quarterly basis at the rate communicated by the BCEAO, which corresponds to the lowest average fixing in the London market.

Monetary Authorities:

Comprises the national branch of the BCEAO only. The amount of currency outside banks is estimated by subtracting from the amount of CFA franc notes issued by Mali the estimated amounts of Mali's currency in the cash held by the banks of all member countries of the Union.

Deposit Money Banks:

Comprises commercial banks and development banks and includes certain banking operations of the Treasury and the Post Office. The Treasury accepts customs duty bills (reported separately in *line 22d.i*). Through its many branches, the Postal Checking System acts as the main depository for the private sector in the interior of Mali. *Claims on the Private Sector (line 22d)* include doubtful and litigious debts. † Beginning in 1979, *Central Government Deposits (line 26d)* include the deposits of the public establishments of an administrative or social nature (EPAS) and exclude those of the savings bank; *Demand and Time Deposits (lines 24 and 25)* include deposits of the savings bank and exclude deposits of EPAS; and *Claims on Private Sector (line 22d)* exclude claims on other financial institutions.

Monetary Survey:

The data reported agree with source B aggregates, as given in the table on the position of the monetary institutions, except for *line 31n,* for which source B treats long-term foreign liabilities and SDR allocations as a foreign liability, whereas *IFS* reports the former separately and includes the latter in *line 37r.* Moreover, valuation differences exist as a result of the *IFS* calculations of reserve position in the Fund and the SDR holdings, both components of *line 11,* based on Fund record. † Beginning in 1979, *Claims on Other Financial Institutions (line 32f)* includes claims of deposit money banks on other financial institutions; see deposit money bank notes for explanation of other break symbols.

Other Banking Institutions:

Liquid Liabilities (line 55l): † See notes on deposit money banks and monetary survey.

Interest Rates:

Bank Rate (End of Period):
Rate on repurchase agreements between the BCEAO and the banks. † Prior to October 1, 1993 data refer to basic discount rate offered by the BCEAO.

Money Market Rate:
Rate paid on overnight interbank advances.

Deposit Rate:
Rate offered by banks on time deposits of CFAF 500,000–2,000,000 for under six months.

Prices:

Consumer Prices:
Source B. Weights Reference Period: 1996; Geographical Coverage: Bamako metropolitan area; Number of Items in Basket: 321; Basis for Calculation: The weights are taken from a household expenditure survey conducted in 1996 in the Bamako metropolitan area.

International Transactions:

All trade data are from source S.

Government Finance:

Data are as reported by the Central Bank of West African States and cover budgetary central government as well as the budgets of special funds and annexed budgets. A statistical discrepancy results from the difference between the deficit and financing. † Beginning in 1980, data also cover extrabudgetary foreign grants and loans not recorded in the treasury accounts. † Data for 1980 and 1981 do not cover social security operations. † From 1989 to 1997, net lending and privatization receipts are included in revenue. The fiscal year ends December 31.

National Accounts:

Source N. Data are prepared in accordance with the *1968 SNA.*

Malta   181

Date of Fund Membership:

September 11, 1968

Standard Sources:

A: Central Bank, *Annual Report*

B: Central Bank, *Quarterly Review*
S: National Statistics Office, *Quarterly Digest of Statistics, Abstract*

Exchange Rates:

Official Rate: (End of Period and Period Average):
Closing central bank midpoint rate. The official rate is pegged to a weighted basket consisting of the pound sterling, the U.S. dollar, and the Euro. On May 1, 2005 the Maltese lira entered the Exchange Rate Mechanism II (ERM II) of the European Union at a central parity rate of MTL/EUR 0.4293. The average rates are calculated on the arithmetic mean of the daily opening and closing Central Bank of Malta middle rates.

International Liquidity:

Gold (National Valuation) (line 1and) is obtained by converting the value in national currency as reported in the country's standard sources using the national currency/dollar conversion rates utilized for balance sheet purposes. These conversion rates differ from the prevailing exchange rates reported in *IFS*.

Monetary Authorities:

Consolidates the Central Bank of Malta and monetary authority functions undertaken by the central government. The contra-entry to government foreign assets is included in *line 16d*. † Beginning in October 2003, the data are compiled from new, more detailed report forms.

Banking Institutions:

Comprises commercial banks and specialized financial institutions. † Beginning January 1995, data for offshore banks (international banking institutions) have been included in the consolidation. † Beginning in October 2003, the data are compiled from new, more detailed report forms, and include coverage of international banking institutions.

Banking Survey:

† See note on banking institutions.

Interest Rates:

Discount Rate:
The rate at which the central bank lends to credit institutions. † Beginning in February 2003, data refer to the central intervention rate used by the central bank to manage liquidity in the banking system, as discount rates were no longer in use.

Treasury Bill Rate:
Weighted average rate on 3-month Treasury bills sold through weekly auctions.

Deposit Rate:
Rate on six-month time deposits.

Lending Rate:
Weighted average rate on loans and advances extended by commercial banks.

Prices and Labor:

Consumer Prices:
Source B. Weights Reference Period: December 2002; Geographical Coverage: whole national territory; Number of Items in Basket: 355; Basis for Calculation: weights are derived from the 2000–2001 Household Budget Survey.

Industrial Production:
Source B. Base Year: 1997.

International Transactions:

Exports and Imports, c.i.f.: Source B.

Government Finance:

Beginning in 1998, monthly and quarterly data are as reported by the Central Bank of Malta and cover the consolidated central government, except for a relatively small amount of own revenues and the corresponding expenditures of extrabudgetary funds. Beginning in 1999, expenditure data exclude lending minus repayments, which have been reclassified as domestic financing. † Prior to 1999, to the extent possible, existing subannual IFS data were converted to the main aggregates that are presented in the *GFSM 2001* Statement of Sources and Uses of Cash (see the Introduction of the monthly *IFS* publication for details). Beginning in 1999, annual data are as reported in the *Government Finance Statistics Yearbook (GFSY)* and cover the consolidated central government. The fiscal year ends December 31.

National Accounts:

Source B.

Mauritania   682

Date of Fund Membership:
September 10, 1963

Standard Sources:
B: Central Bank, *Bulletin*
S: Department of Statistics and Economic Studies, *Monthly Statistical Bulletin*

Exchange Rates:

Official Rate: (End of Period and Period Average):
Central bank midpoint rate.

International Liquidity:

Gold (National Valuation) (line 1and) is obtained by converting the value in national currency terms, as reported in the country's standard sources, using the prevailing exchange rate, as given in *line de*, *line ae*, or *line we*.

Monetary Authorities:

Comprises the Central Bank of Mauritania. † The sectorization and classification of accounts have been revised from 1989 onwards. *Claims on Private Sector (line 12d)* includes loans to the Central Bank employees.

Deposit Money Banks:

Consolidates commercial banks and includes the accounts of the Islamic Bank. † The sectorization and classification of accounts have been revised from 1989 onwards. In addition, the following accounts are consolidated with the commercial banks' demand deposits, with a contra-entry in claims on central government demand deposits with the postal checking account and claims arising from the Treasury's function as a lender to the private sector in the form of custom bills accepted in payment of import and other indirect taxes.

Monetary Survey:

† See notes on monetary authorities.

Prices:

Consumer Prices:
Source S index for Mauritanian households, weights reference period: 2002. Geographical Coverage: Nouakchott; Number of Items in Basket: 361; Basis for Calculation: weights are derived from a survey conducted in 2002 from more than 1000 households.

Government Finance:

† Beginning in 1990, annual data are reported for publication by the Budget Directorate of the Ministry of Finance and cover the consolidated operations of the Treasury and operations financed with foreign resources not recorded in the treasury accounts. Revenue data are adjusted for uncashed checks. Expenditure data are reported on a payment order basis. Therefore, changes in domestic and foreign arrears are included in the financing. The fiscal year ends December 31.

National Accounts:

Data are from source S. National accounts are compiled according to the recommendations of the *1968 SNA*.

Mauritius   684

Date of Fund Membership:
September 23, 1968

Standard Sources:
B: Bank of Mauritius, *Quarterly Review*
S: Central Statistical Office, *Digest of Statistics*

Exchange Rates:

Market Rate (End of Period and Period Average):
Average of opening midpoint rates in the interbank foreign exchange market in Mauritius.

International Liquidity:

Gold is revalued on the basis of the monthly average quotations in London over the three preceding years, less a discount of 25 percent. *Gold (National Valuation) (line 1and)* is obtained by converting the value in national currency terms, as reported in the country's standard sources, using the prevailing exchange rate, as given in *line* **de**, *line* **ae**, or *line* **we**.

Monetary Authorities:

Comprises the Bank of Mauritius only. † Beginning in December 2001, data are based on an improved classification and sectorization of the accounts. † Beginning in June 2003, data are based on a new reporting system which provides improved classification and sectorization of the accounts.

Banking Institutions:

Comprises state and private commercial banks, branches of foreign banks, Post Office Savings Bank, and nonbank financial institutions authorized to transact deposit-taking business. † Beginning in December 2001, data are based on an improved classification and sectorization of the accounts. † Beginning in June 2003, includes offshore banks. Data are based on a new reporting system which provides improved classification and sectorization of the accounts.

Banking Survey:

† See notes on monetary authorities and banking institutions.

Money (National Definitions):

Reserve Money comprises currency in circulation, banker's correspondent and other accounts with the Bank of Mauritius (BoM), commercial banks' investment in BoM securities valued at cost, and transferable deposits of public nonfinancial corporations and private sector with the BoM in national currency. Currency in circulation refers to notes and coins issued by the BoM.
M1 comprises currency in circulation and transferable deposits. Currency in circulation refers to notes and coins issued by the BoM less the amount held by commercial banks. Transferable deposits refer to the current account deposits in national currency of state and local governments, public nonfinancial corporations, and private sector with the BoM and commercial banks.
M2 comprises M1 and time and foreign currency deposits. Time deposits refer to time, savings, and margin deposits in national currency of state and local governments, public nonfinancial corporations, and private sector with commercial banks. Foreign currency deposits refer to transferable, time, savings, and margin deposits of state and local governments, public nonfinancial corporations, and private sector with commercial banks. Beginning in September 2005, includes securities other than shares issued by commercial banks in national currency held by public nonfinancial corporations, private sector, and other financial corporations.
Broad Money comprises currency in circulation, transferable, savings, and time deposits, and securities other than shares issued by the BoM and banking institutions in national currency held by public nonfinancial corporations, private sector, and other financial corporations. Currency in circulation refers to notes and coins issued by the BoM less the amount held by banking institutions. Transferable deposits refer to the current account deposits in national and foreign currency of state and local governments, public nonfinancial corporations, private sector, and other financial corporations with the BoM and banking institutions. Savings and time deposits refer to term and margin deposits in national and foreign currency of state and local governments, public nonfinancial corporations, private sector, and other financial corporations with the BoM and banking institutions.

Interest Rates:

Discount Rate (End of Period):
Rate offered by the Bank of Mauritius on loans to commercial banks.

Money Market Rate:
Interbank deposits at call.

Savings Rate:
Minimum rate offered by commercial banks on savings deposits.

Deposit Rate:
Upper margin on three-month deposits.

Lending Rate:
Upper margin of rates on overdraft loans for prime customers.

Prices and Labor:

Share Prices:
Weights reference period: July 5, 1989. Prices are the arithmetic average of each session's share prices as quoted by the Stock

Exchange Commission of Mauritius, which publishes the series in, inter alia, its *Annual Reports.*

Consumer Prices:

Source B. Weights Reference Period: July 2001–June 2002; Geographical Coverage: whole national territory; Number of Items in Basket: 194; Basis for Calculation: weights are derived from the Household Budget Survey (HBS) conducted in 2001/02.

Employment:

Figures prior to 2004 refer to employment in large establishments, employing 10 or more persons and include foreign workers. After 2004 data refer to all establishments but exclude foreign workers and are based on the Continuous Multi-Purpose Household Survey which is used to estimate labor force, employment, and unemployment on a quarterly basis.

International Transactions:

Value data on total *Exports, Imports, cif,* and *Imports, fob* are from source B.

Trade indices are from source S data, weights reference period: 2003.

Government Finance:

Beginning in 1990, annual data are as reported for the *Government Finance Statistics Yearbook (GFSY)* and cover consolidated central government. † Changes in the coverage of the consolidated central government in 1992, 1993, 1994, and 1999 are as specified in *GFSY.* The fiscal year ends June 30.

National Accounts:

† Source S. As from 1998, the figures provided are based on information required for implementing the *1993 SNA.*

Mexico   273

Date of Fund Membership:

December 31, 1945

Standard Sources:

A: Bank of Mexico, *Annual Report*
B: Bank of Mexico, *Economic Indicators*
N: Instituto Nacional de Estadística Geográfia e Informática
S: Statistical Office, *Monthly Bulletin of Economic Information, Statistical Review*

Exchange Rates:

On January 1, 1993, the new peso, equal to 1,000 old pesos, was introduced. The denomination "new" was transitory and was used only on bills issued in January 1993 (series B) and in October 1994 (series C) but has been eliminated on bills issued beginning in 1996; therefore, the currency has been redenominated as pesos.

Market Rate (End of Period and Period Average):

On November 11, 1991, foreign exchange surrender requirements were eliminated, along with related exchange control measures that originated in the dual exchange system. Until October 31, 1991, the dual exchange market consisted of (1) a controlled market rate that applied to specific transactions amounting to about 70 percent of commercial and payments transactions and (2) a free market rate that applied to the remaining transactions. As of

November 1991, a more flexible exchange regime was introduced under which the peso fluctuated within an intervention band. As of August 1, 1996, the Bank of Mexico introduced a system for buying foreign exchange on the market, without abandoning its commitment to the floating exchange rate. Under this system, the Bank of Mexico organized monthly auctions of options that give financial institutions the right to sell U.S. dollars to the Bank of Mexico in exchange for Mexican pesos.

International Liquidity:

The data on *line 1d.d* include interest accrued but not collected on deposits, securities, and other obligations payable outside the national territory, loans granted to central banks, and SDR holdings, as well as the difference in favor of the central bank between the value of foreign exchange receivable and payable on forex futures in currencies other than the domestic currency. The central bank values gold holdings daily at the equivalent in U.S. dollars based on the dollar/ounce rate; the dollar/ounce rate is the arithmetical average of the rates quoted at opening on that day in London and at closing the previous day in New York.

Monetary Authorities:

Comprises the Bank of Mexico only. † Beginning in December 1977, data are based on an improved sectorization of the accounts. *Claims on Nonbank Financial Institutions* and *Liabilities to Nonbank Financial Institutions* include positions vis-à-vis the Fund for the Protection of Savings (FOBAPROA). † Beginning in January 1982, data reflect the introduction of a new reporting system, which provides an improved sectorization of domestic and foreign accounts. † Beginning in January 1997, data reflect methodological changes in compilation. The positions vis-à-vis the various sectors are shown gross, and accrued interest is classified with the corresponding financial instruments. *Capital Accounts* includes capital, capital reserves, and unallocated profits from the current year. † Beginning in December 2001, data are based on a new reporting system which provides improved classification and sectorization of the accounts.

Banking Institutions:

Comprises commercial banks, development banks, and national credit corporations. † Beginning in December 1977, data are based on an improved sectorization of the accounts. † Beginning in January 1982, data reflect the introduction of a new plan of accounts, which provides an improved sectorization of domestic and foreign accounts. *Claims on Nonbank Financial Institutions* and *Liabilities to Nonbank Financial Institutions* include positions vis-à-vis FOBAPROA. † Beginning in January 1997, comprises commercial banks, development banks, credit unions, savings and loan associations, investment funds, financial leasing companies, factoring companies, and specialized lending institutions.

Data reflect changes in the chart of accounts, accounting criteria, and the methodology for compiling the monetary accounts, which identify positions with nonresidents and with the various domestic sectors by financial instrument. Forwards and futures are recorded at nominal value, swaps at the gross amounts of the flows valued at market prices, and options at the market price of the option. *Capital Accounts* comprises paid-up capital (including subordinated debt with mandatory conversion issued under the PROCAPTE program), capital reserves, revaluation of assets, excess or insufficiency from the updating of the net worth, and profits/losses. *Claims on Central Government* includes holdings of CETES-UDIS, which are government securities received by commercial banks to document credit operations with the private sector. These private sector credit operations were transferred, for purposes of administration, to trust accounts recorded off the balance sheets of the banks. Commercial banks' holdings of CETES-UDIS as of December 31, 1998 were 199,314 million pesos and of the development banks were 17,820 million pesos. Beginning in December 1997, *Claims on the Private Sector* includes the portfolio previously associated with FOBAPROA. This portfolio amounted to 155,271 million pesos. † Beginning in December 2001, data are based on a new reporting system which provides improved classification and sectorization of the accounts.

Banking Survey:

† See notes on monetary authorities and banking institutions.

Nonbank Financial Institutions:

Comprises insurance companies, pension funds, guarantee corporations, general deposit warehouses, economic development funds, and stock exchange houses. † Beginning in December 2001, data are based on a new reporting system which provides improved classification and sectorization of the accounts.

Financial Survey:

† See notes on monetary authorities, deposit money banks, and nonbank financial institutions.

Money (National Definitions):

Base Money comprises bills and coins outside the Bank of Mexico.
M1 comprises bills and coins outside the banking system and deposits in checking and current accounts, which can be withdrawn through debit cards, in national and foreign currency of the private sector in banks.
M2 comprises M1 plus demand (other than deposits in checking and current accounts) and time deposits in national and foreign currency of the private sector in banks, federal government and private sector securities held by the private sector, and other instruments held by pension funds.
M3 comprises M2 plus demand and time deposits of nonresidents in banks and federal government securities held by nonresidents.
M4 comprises M3 and deposits of residents and nonresidents in branches abroad of domestic banks.
M4a comprises M4 and deposits and instruments of the public sector (federal, municipal, and state governments, nonfinancial public enterprises, and development trust funds).
M4 National Currency comprises all the instruments denominated in national currency that are included in M4.
M4 Foreign Currency comprises all the instruments denominated in foreign currency that are included in M4.

Interest Rates:

All interest rate data are from source B.

Money Market Rate:
Average of rates quoted by commercial banks on six-month bankers' acceptances.† Beginning in July 1988, average of rates quoted by commercial banks on three-month bankers' acceptances. † Beginning in March 1995, weighted average rate on

loans between financial institutions (TIIE). The rate is weighted by daily loan amounts.

Treasury Bill Rate:
Average yield on 90-day treasury bills. † Beginning in January 1988, average yield on 28-day treasury bills, calculated from the weighted average rate of discount on daily transactions among dealers on the Mexican Securities Exchange. For periods during which no auctions of treasury bills were held, no data are published.

Savings Rate:
Weighted average of gross rates agreed on operations during the month, payable to individuals. The rate is weighted by deposit amounts.

Deposit Rate:
Weighted average rate payable to individuals on 60-day time deposits. The rate is weighted by deposit amounts.

Average Cost of Funds:
Weighted average percentage cost of deposit-taking (CPP), including time bank deposits, promissory notes with yield payable at maturity, other deposits (except sight and savings), bankers' acceptances, and commercial paper with bank guarantees. † Beginning in February 1996, weighted cost of deposit-taking (CCP), including time bank deposits, promissory notes with yield payable at maturity, other deposits (except sight and savings), bankers' acceptances, and commercial paper with bank guarantees.

Lending Rate:
Lending rate indicator: Weighted average of amounts placed on the securities exchange at various terms with the yield curve calculated on commercial paper and stock certificates of qualified companies. The rate is weighted by the volume of amounts placed.

Government Bond Yield:
Weighted average yield on development bonds of 728 days. † Beginning in January 2000, weighted average yield on three-year fixed rate government bonds. † Beginning in December 2001, weighted average yield on ten-year fixed rate government bonds. The yield is weighted by issuance amounts.

Prices, Production, Labor:

Share Prices:
Source B, general share price index covering shares quoted on the Mexico City Stock Exchange, base October 1, 1978.

Producer Price Index:
Source B, weights reference period: 2003, based on a monthly survey covering 15,000 direct prices at 2,000 enterprises making up a representative sample of all economic activities throughout the national territory; the basket for the index is made up of 600 generic products.

Consumer Prices:
Source B. Weights Reference Period: 2000; Geographical Coverage: All cities with more than 20,000 inhabitants; Number of Items in Basket: 313; Basis for Calculation: 1989 National Income and Expenditure Household Survey (NIEHS) consisting of a sample of 12,800 households and the 1990 Population Census.

Wages, Monthly:
Source N index on average real remunerations in manufacturing, weights reference period: 1993.

Industrial Production:
Source N. Weights reference period: 1993; Sectoral Coverage: mining, manufacturing, construction, and electricity, gas and water; Basis for Calculation: the weights are based on the 1993 GDP of each activity subgroup in the Sistema de Cuentas Nacionales de México (SCNM) "Mexico's National Accounts System" classification.

International Transactions:
All trade data are from source S. Beginning in 1970, trade data exclude exports and imports of in-bond industries. Total exports are adjusted by the Bank of Mexico to reflect transaction values of certain commodities which are valued by Customs at administrative prices. Silver exports, which are not published in source S, are directly reported by the national authorities and included in total exports by *IFS*.

Government Finance:
Data are as reported in *Estadisticas Oportunas de Finanzas Publicas y Deuda Publica,* published by the *Direccion de Estadistica Hacendaria,* and cover consolidated central government, post office, and telecommunications. The fiscal year ends December 31.

National Accounts:
Source N. † As indicated by the country, beginning in 1988 data have been revised significantly following the implementation of the *1993 SNA.*

Micronesia, Federated States of   868

Date of Fund Membership:
June 24, 1993

Standard Source:
B: Federal States of Micronesia Banking Board

Exchange Rates:
Market Rate (End of Period):
There is no independent national currency in the Federated States of Micronesia (FSM). The U.S. dollar is legal tender that circulates freely.

International Liquidity:
Foreign Exchange (line 1d.d) comprises the government's (monetary authorities) holdings of foreign exchange.

Monetary Authorities:
Comprises the monetary authority functions of the government. The contra-entries to government foreign assets, Treasury IMF accounts, and SDR holdings are included in *line 16d.* There is no formal central bank in the FSM; the Bank of Hawaii (Pohnpei Branch) has been designated as the depository of the Fund's holdings of currency.

Banking Institutions:
Comprises commercial banks and the FSM Development Bank.

Interest Rates:
Savings Rate:
Average end-of-month rate on passbook savings deposits offered by banks.

Deposit Rate:
Average rate on six- to nine-month certificates of deposit offered by banks.
Lending Rate:
Average rate charged by banks on consumer loans.

Moldova   921

Date of Fund Membership:
August 12, 1992

Standard Sources:
A: National Bank of Moldova
S: Statistical Office

Exchange Rates:
Up to July 1993, the Russian ruble (supplemented by ruble denominated coupons) was the legal tender in Moldova. On August 9, 1993 the Moldovan ruble was introduced. On November 29, 1993 the Moldovan leu, equal to 1,000 Moldovan rubles, was introduced.
Official Rate: (End of Period and Period Average):
The official rate is the rate used by the National Bank of Moldova (NBM). Effective June 30, 2002, the exchange regime has been reclassified to the category managed floating with no pre-announced path for the exchange rate.

International Liquidity:
Total Reserves Minus Gold (line 1l.d) comprises NBM's holdings of SDRs, reserve position in the Fund, and convertible foreign exchange.

Monetary Authorities:
Comprises the National Bank of Moldova (NBM) only. *Foreign Assets (line 11)* includes claims on nonresidents in nonconvertible currencies and is broader than gross international reserves. † Beginning in January 1996, data are based on an improved sectorization of the accounts. † Beginning in December 2001, data are based on an improved classification and sectorization of the accounts. † Beginning in July 2005, data are based on a new reporting system which provides an improved classification and sectorization of the accounts.

Banking Institutions:
Comprises commercial banks. † Beginning in January 1998, data reflect the introduction of a new accounting system. † Beginning in December 2001, data are based on an improved classification and sectorization of the accounts. † Beginning in July 2005, data are based on a new reporting system which provides an improved classification and sectorization of the accounts.
Comprises commercial banks. † Beginning in January 1998, data reflect the introduction of a new accounting system.

Banking Survey:
† See notes on monetary authorities and banking institutions.

Money (National Definitions):
Reserve Money comprises currency in circulation, bankers' reserves, and transferable deposits of other financial institutions, nonfinancial public corporations, and private sector with the Na-

tional Bank of Moldova (NBM). Currency in circulation refers to notes and coins issued by the NBM less cash at the NBM's vaults. Bankers' reserves comprise required reserves and other deposits in national currency at the NBM and cash in the banks' vaults.

M1 comprises currency in circulation and transferable deposits. Currency in circulation refers to notes and coins issued by the NBM less cash at the NBM's vaults and currency held by banking institutions. Transferable deposits refer to current account deposits in national currency of other financial institutions, nonfinancial public corporations, and private sector with the NBM and banking institutions.

M2 comprises M1, time deposits, and money market instruments. Time deposits include time and savings deposits in national currency of other financial institutions, nonfinancial public enterprises, and private sector with the NBM and commercial banks. Money market instruments include securities other than shares issued by banking institutions in national currency held by other financial institutions, nonfinancial public enterprises, and private sector.

M3 comprises M2 plus foreign currency deposits of other financial institutions, nonfinancial public enterprises, and private sector with banking institutions.

Interest Rates:

Refinancing Rate:
Weighted average rate at which the NBM makes loans and advances to commercial banks. The rate is determined through credit auctions conducted by the NBM.

Money Market Rate:
Weighted average rate on funds obtained by commercial banks in the interbank market in national currency. The rate is weighted by loan amounts.

Money Market Rate (Foreign Currency):
Weighted average rate on funds obtained by commercial banks in the interbank market in foreign currency. The rate is weighted by loan amounts.

Treasury Bill Rate:
Weighted average rate on all treasury bills. The rate is determined through securities auctions conducted by the NBM.

Deposit Rate:
Weighted average rate offered by commercial banks on all newly accepted deposits in national currency. The rate is weighted by deposit amounts.

Deposit Rate (Foreign Currency):
Weighted average rate offered by commercial banks on all newly accepted deposits in foreign currency. The rate is weighted by deposit amounts.

Lending Rate:
Weighted average rate charged by commercial banks on new loans to customers in national currency. The rate is weighted by loan amounts.

Lending Rate (Foreign Currency):
Weighted average rate charged by commercial banks on new loans in foreign currency. The rate is weighted by loan amounts.

Prices and Labor:

Data are from source S.

Consumer Prices:
Weights Reference Period: 2002; Geographical Coverage: 11 cities of Moldova but excludes the Transnistrian region; Num-

ber of Items in Basket: 1200; Basis for Calculation: the weights are derived from the Household Income and Expenditure Survey of 2002.

International Transactions:
Source S.

Government Finance:
Annual data are as reported in the *Government Finance Statistics Yearbook (GFSY)* and cover the budgetary central government. The fiscal year ends December 31.

National Accounts:
Source S. As indicated by the country, data are compiled following the *1993 SNA*.

Mongolia   948

Date of Fund Membership:
February 14, 1991

Standard Sources:
A: Mongolbank, *Annual Report*
B: Mongolbank, *Monthly Statistical Bulletin*
S: State Statistical Office, *The Mongolian Economy (Statistical Yearbook), The Monthly Selected Statistics*

Exchange Rates:

Market Rate (End of Period and Period Average):
† From May 27, 1993 the midpoint of the average buying and selling rates that are freely determined on the basis of market transactions between commercial banks and the nonbank public. Also beginning on May 27, 1993 all exchange rates were unified in the context of the floating exchange rate system.

International Liquidity:

Gold (National Valuation) (line 1and) is valued at 4300 togrogs per gram since June 6, 1993; it was valued at 1600 Tog/gram from November 19, 1992; at 450 Tog/gram from September 12, 1991; at 60 Tog/gram from October 23, 1986; at 52 Tog/gram from March 27, 1985; at 40 Tog/gram from November 1, 1983; and at 32.03 Tog/gram from December 15, 1980.

Line 1d.d comprises balances held by the Mongolbank and small holdings by the Ministry of Finance since April 1993. Prior to April 1993, the State Bank (International) also held part of the official international reserves.

Monetary Authorities:
Consolidates the accounts of the Mongolbank, government SDR holdings, and the government's reserve position in the Fund and use of Fund credit.

Lines 12a and *16d* include local government budgetary units.

Deposit Money Banks:
Comprises commercial banks. Beginning in December 1996, data exclude nonperforming assets of commercial banks that were taken over by the government in exchange for government bonds.

Lines 22a and *26d* include local government budgetary units.

Interest Rates:

All interest rate data are from source B.

Bank Rate (End of Period):
Minimum rate charged by Mongolbank on automatic loans to banks to settle overdrafts in their clearing accounts.

Deposit Rate (End of Period):
Minimum rate for time deposits of three months and over.

Lending Rate (End of Period):
Average rate on commercial loans to prime borrowers.

Prices:

Data are from source S.

Consumer Prices:
Source S. Weights Reference Period: December 2000; Geographical Coverage: compiles for the capital city, Ulaanbaatar, and the 21 aimags (provinces); Number of Items in the Basket: 239 items in eight main item categories; Basis for Calculation: the basket was reweighed and the weight reference period was updated from 1999 to 2000. The new weights were being derived from the 2000 Household Income and Expenditure Survey (HIES).

International Transactions:

Source S data; trade in convertible currencies was valued at the commercial rate from 1990 to May 1993. Trade in nonconvertible currencies valued at official exchange rates.

Balance of Payments:
Data include transactions in nonconvertible currencies at the official cross rates.

Government Finance:

Monthly data are provided by the Ministry of Finance and cover the consolidated central and local government. The fiscal year ends December 31.

National Accounts:

Source S. As indicated by the country, data are compiled accouding to *1993 SNA*.

Montenegro, Rep. of   943

Date of Fund Membership:

January 18, 2007

Standard Sources:

B: Central Bank of Montenegro, *Statistical Bulletin* (monthly)
S: Statistical Office, *Statistical Yearbook*

Exchange Rates:

Market Rate (End of Period and Period Average):
Euro market rate. Since April 1, 2002, euro is the legal tender and the unit of account in the Republic of Montenegro. During the transition period January - March 2002, the deutsche mark and the euro were the parallel legal tender.

Monetary Authorities:

Comprises Central Bank of Montenegro. Central Bank of Montenegro does not issue currency. Euro is the legal tender and the unit of account in the Republic of Montenegro. See notes on Ex-

change Rates. *Other general government* comprises municipalities, social security funds, and the Development fund.

Banking Institutions:

Comprises commercial banks; banks in liquidation are excluded. *Other general government* comprises municipalities, social security funds, and the Development fund.

Banking Survey:

Deposit Money (line 34) and *Time, Savings, and Foreign Currency Deposits (line 35)* comprise depository liabilities only. Euro notes and coins are used as a domestic medium of exchange or for payments abroad; their amount in circulation, however, is not precisely known, and hence no attempt was made to calculate *Money* for the Republic of Montenegro. See notes for Monetary Authorities and Banking Institutions.

Interest Rates:

Treasury Bill Rate:
Yield on newly issued 182-day Treasury bills from the latest auction.

Deposit Rate:
Simple average of midpoints between maximum and minimum rates on euro deposits with maturity of 3–12 months offered by four largest banks.

Lending Rate:
Average rate on loans weighted by volume.

Prices:

Share Price Index:
NEX Montenegro Stock Exchange index of the basket of share prices of 20 largest companies weighted by capitalization, turnover, and the number of transactions (March 1, 2003 = 1000).

Population:

Source S.

Montserrat   351

Standard Sources:

A: Eastern Caribbean Central Bank, *Annual Report and Statement of Accounts*
B: Eastern Caribbean Central Bank, *Economic and Financial Review*
C: Eastern Caribbean Central Bank, *National Accounts Statistics*
N: Eastern Caribbean Central Bank, *Commercial Banking Statistics*

Exchange Rates:

Official Rate: (End of Period and Period Average):
The official rate is pegged to the U.S. dollar.

Monetary Authorities:

The accounts are compiled from data contained in the balance sheet of the Eastern Caribbean Central Bank (ECCB). The monetary authorities' accounts for Montserrat represent country attributable data for ECCB claims on and liabilities to the government of Montserrat and its resident deposit money banks, and estimates of Montserrat's notional share of the ECCB's foreign assets and liabilities and currency in circulation within the region. † Beginning in December 2001, data are based on a new reporting system which provides improved classification and sectorization of the accounts.

Banking Institutions:

Comprises commercial banks. † Beginning in December 2001, data are based on a new reporting system which provides improved classification and sectorization of the accounts.

Banking Survey:

† See notes on monetary authorities and banking institutions.

Money (National Definitions):

M1 comprises notes and coins held by the public and demand deposits in national currency of the private sector in commercial banks.

M2 comprises *M1* plus time, savings, and foreign currency deposits of the private sector in commercial banks.

Interest Rates:

Discount Rate (End of Period):
Rate charged by the ECCB on loans of last resort to commercial banks.

Money Market Rate:
Fixed rate on loans between commercial banks. The rate includes the commission charged by the ECCB as agent. † Beginning in October 2001, weighted average rate on loans between commercial banks. The rate is weighted by loan amounts.

Savings Rate:
Maximum rate offered by commercial banks on savings deposits in national currency. † Beginning in June 2003, weighted average rate offered by commercial banks on savings deposits in national currency. The rate is weighted by deposit amounts.

Deposit Rate:
Maximum rate offered by commercial banks on three-month deposits. † Beginning in March 1991, weighted average rate offered by commercial banks on deposits in national currency. The rate is weighted by deposit amounts.

Deposit Rate (Foreign Currency):
Weighted average rate offered by commercial banks on deposits in foreign currency. The rate is weighted by deposit amounts.

Lending Rate:
Maximum rate charged by commercial banks on prime loans. † Beginning in March 1991, weighted average rate charged by commercial banks on loans in national currency. The rate is weighted by loan amounts.

National Accounts:

Source C.

Morocco   686

Date of Fund Membership:

April 25, 1958

Standard Sources:

B: Bank Al-Maghrib, *Studies and Statistics*
C: Ministry of Finance
S: Division of Statistics, *Monthly Bulletin*

Exchange Rates:

Official Rate: (End of Period and Period Average):
Central bank midpoint rate. The official rate is fixed daily in terms of the French franc.
The weighting scheme used to calculate indices of nominal and real effective exchange rates (*lines* **nec** and **rec**) is based on data for tourism receipts as well as on data for merchandise trade.

International Liquidity:

Gold (National Valuation) (line 1and) is obtained by converting the value in national currency terms, as reported in the country's standard sources, using the prevailing exchange rate, as given in *line de, line ae,* or *line we*.

Monetary Authorities:

Consolidates the Bank Al-Maghrib and monetary authority functions undertaken by the central government. † Beginning in 1980, *Claims on Central Government (line 12a)* include the Fund drawings that have been transferred to the Treasury, and *Claims on Private Sector (line 12d)* exclude *Claims on Other Financial Institutions (line 12f)*. † Beginning in 1990, data are based on a more detailed classification of accounts. † For data beginning in 1997, see note on international liquidity.

Deposit Money Banks:

Comprises the commercial banks, the popular banks, and the Central Popular Bank. Private sector demand deposits with the postal checking system and the Treasury are shown separately. † Beginning in 1982, data are based on improved classification. † Beginning in December 1997, consolidates data on commercial banks, the popular banks, the Central Popular Bank, and five formerly specialized banking institutions. Of the five, three were previously classified as other banking institutions (the National Development Bank, the National Agriculture Bank, and the Crédit Immobilier et Hôtelier), and two were previously nonreporting (Fonds d'équipement and Bank Al-Amal). † See note on monetary authorities.

Monetary Survey:

† See notes on monetary authorities.

Other Banking Institutions:

Comprises the National Development Bank, the National Agriculture Bank, Crédit Immobilier et Hôtelier (hotel and building loans), Caisse de Dépôts et de Gestion (investment management), and Caisse des Marchés (guarantee and credit company). Almost all savings bank deposits are redeposited by the bank with the Caisse de Dépôts et de Gestion, and the remaining minor balance is made with the Treasury. † Beginning in December 1997, units previously classified as other banking institutions were reclassified as deposit money banks. †See note to section 20.

Interest Rates:

Discount Rate (End of Period):
Offer rate on seven-day credit auctions Source B.

Money Market Rate:
Data refer to the interbank lending rate.

Deposit Rate:
Rate on 12-month time deposits.

Lending Rate:
Maximum rate on short-term loans.

Government Bond Yield:
Medium-term series refers to rate on 5-year treasury bonds. Long-term series refers to rate on 15-year treasury bonds.

Prices, Production, Labor:

Wholesale Prices:
Source S, national index, weights reference period: 1977, covers 231 final products available in local markets (in nine important cities), including 77 items from the agricultural sector and 154 items from the industrial and energy sectors.

Producer Prices:
Source S. Weights Reference Period: 1997; Geographical Coverage: comprises 190 industrial units in Casablanca, three in Mohammedia, four in Rabat, one in Kenitra, one in Temara, and one in Skhirat; Number of items in Basket: 301; Basis for Calculation: weights are based on the value of production of the reference period.

Consumer Prices:
Source S. Weights Reference Period: 1989; Geographical Coverage: low income families in eight major cities. Prior to 1974 data refer to Casablanca only; Number of Items in Basket: 385; Basis for Calculation: weights are derived from a Household Expenditure Survey conducted in 1970–1971 among low-income families.

Manufacturing Production:
Source S index, weights reference period: 1992. It includes 3000 enterprises from among 14 branches of manufacturing.

Mining Production:
Source S index, weights reference period: 1992. It includes 10 branches of mining.

Employment:
Urban and rural population for ages 15 and older.

International Transactions:

All trade value data are from source S. Trade indices are compiled on weights reference period: 1976 and supplied directly by the Bank Al-Maghrib.

Government Finance:

Monthly data are from source B and cover the operations of the consolidated central government. The fiscal year ends December 31.

National Accounts:

Source B.

Mozambique   688

Date of Fund Membership:
September 24, 1984

Standard Source:
S: National Institute of Statistics

Exchange Rates:
On July 1, 2006, the new metical (MTn), equivalent to 1,000 of the old metical (MT) was introduced.

Market Rate (End of Period and Period Average):
Before April 1, 1992, the market rate referred to the official rate set by the Central Bank and covered most transactions. After that date, it refers to the rate at which commercial banks purchase from and sell to the public. Effective October 19, 2000, the exchange rate is determined as the weighted average of buying and selling exchange rates of all transactions of commercial banks and stock exchanges with the public.

Monetary Authorities:
Comprises the former Banco de Moçambique, which performed central and commercial banking functions. † Beginning in September 1989, data are based on an improved sectorization of the accounts. † Beginning in December 1991, comprises the Banco de Moçambique only. Data are based on an improved classification of the accounts. † Beginning in December 2001, data are based on an improved classification and sectorization of the accounts. † Beginning in December 2002, data are based on a new reporting system which provides an improved classification and sectorization of the accounts.

Banking Institutions:
Comprises commercial banks. † Beginning in December 1991, comprises the Banco Popular de Desenvolvimento, Banco Standard Totta de Moçambique, and Banco Comercial de Moçambique, which was the commercial department of the former Banco de Moçambique. Beginning in January 1994, includes the Banco Fomento Exterior and Banco Portugués do Atlântico. Data are based on an improved classification of the accounts. † Beginning in December 2001, data are based on an improved classification and sectorization of the accounts. † Beginning in December 2002, data are based on a new reporting system which provides an improved classification and sectorization of the accounts.

Banking Survey:
† See notes on monetary authorities and banking institutions.

Money (National Definitions):
Reserve Money comprises notes and coins in circulation and deposits in national and foreign currency of commercial banks in the Banco de Moçambique.

M1 comprises notes and coins in circulation outside the commercial banks and demand deposits in national and foreign currency of nonfinancial public enterprises, the private sector, and nonbank financial institutions in commercial banks.

M2 comprises *M1* plus advance notice and time deposits in national and foreign currency of nonfinancial public enterprises, the private sector, and nonbank financial institutions in commercial banks.

Interest Rates:
Discount Rate (End of Period):
Rate charged by the Banco de Moçambique on loans in national currency to commercial banks.

Money Market Rate:
Average rate on loans of up to seven days in national currency between commercial banks. † Beginning in January 2001, the Banco de Moçambique introduced a new method, which uses improved data from surveyed banks, for calculating interest rates.

Treasury Bill Rate:
Average rate on 91-day treasury bills denominated in national currency.

Deposit Rate:
Average rate offered by commercial banks on deposits of up to 180 days in national currency. † Beginning in January 2001, the

Banco de Moçambique introduced a new method, which uses improved data from surveyed banks, for calculating interest rates.

Lending Rate:
Average prime rate charged by commercial banks on loans in national currency. † Beginning in January 2001, the Banco de Moçambique introduced a new method, which uses improved data from surveyed banks, for calculating interest rates.

Prices:

Consumer Prices:
Source S. Data are reported by the Direcçao Nacional de Planificaçao and relate to a Laspeyres-type index for Maputo, weights reference period: December 2004.

International Transactions:
Source S.

National Accounts:
Source S. As indicated by the country, beginning in 1991, data are compiled according to the *1993 SNA.*

Myanmar 518

Date of Fund Membership:
January 3, 1952

Standard Source:
S: Central Statistical Organization, *Economic Indicators*

Exchange Rates:

Official Rate: (End of Period and Period Average):
Central bank midpoint rate. Beginning January 1975, the official rate is pegged to the SDR.

International Liquidity:
Gold (National Valuation) (line 1and) is equal to *Gold (Million Fine Troy Ounces) (line 1ad),* valued at SDR 35 per fine troy ounce and converted into U.S. dollars at the dollar/SDR rate **sa** on the country page for the United States. Source E: OECD

Monetary Authorities:
Consolidates accounts of the Central Bank of Myanmar and foreign assets of Myanma Foreign Trade Bank, Myanma Economic Bank, and Myanma Investment and Commercial Bank. The contra-entry to these foreign assets is included in *Other Liabilities to DMBs (line14n).* Compilation of *Reserve Money (line 14)* and *Claims on Deposit Money Banks (line 12e)* is based on accounts, some of which are maintained on a net basis.

Deposit Money Banks:
Comprises Myanma Economic Bank, Myanma Foreign Trade Bank, Myanma Agricultural Development Bank, Myanma Investment and Commercial Bank, and private commercial banks. Foreign assets of Myanma Foreign Trade Bank, Myanma Economic Bank, and Myanma Investment and Commercial Bank are reclassified in monetary authorities' foreign assets *(line 11)* with a contra-claim included in *Other Claims on Monetary Authorities (line 20n).* Also see note on monetary monetary authorities. Compilation of *Reserves (line 20)* and *Credit from Monetary Authorities (line 26g)* is based on accounts, some of which are maintained on a net basis.

Interest Rates:

Central Bank Rate (End of Period):
Rediscount rate of the Central Bank of Myanmar.

Deposit Rate:
Rate offered on six-month fixed deposits.

Lending Rate:
Rate charged on loans to private sector for financing working capital.

Government Bond Yield:
Interest rate on five-year government treasury bonds.

Prices:

Consumer Prices:
Source S. Weights Reference Period: 1997; Geographical Coverage: Yangon; Number of Items in Basket: 135; Basis for Calculation: the weights are derived from the 1997 household income and expenditure survey.

International Transactions:
All trade data are from source S.

Exports:
Data include re-exports.

Imports:
Current data are provisional, as they exclude government imports under special order and military goods.

Government Finance:
Annual data are as reported in the *Government Finance Statistics Yearbook (GFSY)* and cover the consolidated central government. The fiscal year ends March 31.

National Accounts:
† Data prior to 1974 refer to fiscal years ending September 30. Data from 1974 onward relate to the new fiscal year, ending March 31. For the year ending September 1974, that is, based on the old fiscal year, GDP at current market prices was estimated to be 14,852 million kyats. Data for *line 96f* comprise government and private consumption, when those data are not shown separately.

Namibia 728

Date of Fund Membership:
September 25, 1990

Standard Sources:
A: Ministry of Finance
B: Bank of Namibia, *Quarterly Bulletin*
C: Central Bureau of Statistics

Exchange Rates:

Market Rate (End of Period and Period Average):
The exchange rate of the Namibia dollar, which became legal tender on September 15, 1993, is the selling rate for the U.S. dollar. The Namibia dollar was established on par with the South African commercial rand. For an undetermined period after September 15, 1993, the South African commercial rand will also be legal tender in Namibia.

International Liquidity:

Gold (National Valuation) (line 1and) is obtained by converting the value in national currency terms, as reported in the country's standard sources and as given in *line* **ae**. Gold is revalued at the end of each month.

Monetary Authorities:

Comprises the Bank of Namibia (BON) only. † Beginning in December 2001, data are based on an improved classification and sectorization of the accounts. † Beginning in April 2002, data are based on a new reporting system which provides improved classification and sectorization of the accounts.

Banking Institutions:

Comprises commercial banks, Namibia Post Office Savings Bank, Agricultural Bank of Namibia, and National Housing Enterprise. † Beginning in December 2001, data are based on an improved classification and sectorization of the accounts. † Beginning in April 2002, data are based on a new reporting system which provides improved classification and sectorization of the accounts. Beginning in August 2003, data include the SWABOU Building Society which merged operations with a commercial bank.

Banking Survey:

† See notes on monetary authorities and banking institutions.

Money (National Definitions):

M1 comprises currency in circulation and transferable deposits. Currency in circulation refers to notes and coins issued by the Bank of Namibia (BON) less the amount held by banks. Transferable deposits refer to the current account deposits in national and foreign currency of other financial institutions, state and local governments, public nonfinancial corporations, and private sector with the BON and banks.

M2 comprises M1 and other deposits. Other deposits include time and savings deposits in national and foreign currency of other financial institutions, state and local governments, public nonfinancial corporations, and private sector with the BON and banks.

Interest Rates:

BON Overdraft Rate:
Rate is based on Bank of Namibia overdraft facility, which is available to commercial banks.

Money Market Rate:
Average rate on loans between banks. Prior to January 1996 data reflect rate charged in the South African interbank market.

Treasury Bill Rate:
Tender rate on three-month treasury bills.

Deposit Rate:
Rate offered by commercial banks on three-month time deposits.

Lending Rate:
Prime rate charged by major banks.

Government Bond Yield:
Yield on five-year government bonds. † Beginning in April 2002, yield on 15-year government bonds.

Prices:

Consumer Prices:
Source C. Weights Reference Period: 1993–1994; Geographical Coverage: Whole national territory; Basis for Calculation: The Namibia Income and Expenditure Survey was conducted by the National Planning Commission, covering the period of September 1993–August 1994.

International Transactions:

All trade data are from source C.

Balance of Payments:
The source of data is the Bank of Namibia. For explanatory information see *Balance of Payments, Namibia* published by the Bank of Namibia.

Government Finance:

Annual data are as reported in the *Government Finance Statistics Yearbook (GFSY)* and cover budgetary central government from 1990 onwards. The fiscal year ends March 31.

National Accounts:

Sources B and C.

Nepal   558

Unless otherwise indicated, monthly data refer to Nepalese months ending in the middle of the calendar months shown.

Date of Fund Membership:

September 6, 1961

Standard Sources:

B: Nepal Rastra Bank, *Quarterly Economic Bulletin*
S: Central Bureau of Statistics, *Statistical Bulletin*

Exchange Rates:

Market Rate (End of Period and Period Average):
Effective February 12, 1993, the dual exchange rate system was unified, and the exchange rate of the rupee is determined by linking it to the Indian rupee with cross rates against other currencies determined by commercial banks on the basis of demand and supply.

International Liquidity:

Central bank gold and foreign exchange holdings are as of the middle of the month while *lines 1b.d* and *1c.d* are at the end of the month.

Gold (National Valuation) (line 1and): Official gold is valued at US$42.22 per fine troy ounce.

Monetary Authorities:

Consolidates Nepal Rastra Bank and monetary authority functions undertaken by the central government. The contra-entry to Treasury IMF accounts and coin issues is included in *line 12a.*

Deposit Money Banks:

Consolidates the commercial banks, including the state-owned commercial bank, which engages in all commercial banking functions including those taken over from the central bank.

Interest Rates:

All interest rate data are from source B.

Discount Rate:
Rate charged by Rastra Bank to deposit money banks to refinance their working capital loans to other industries.

Deposit Rate:

Minimum rate offered by commercial banks on twelve-month time deposits.

Lending Rate:

Minimum rate charged by commercial banks on working capital loans to basic industries.

Government Bond Yield:

† Prior to 1984, *line 61* included government development bonds. Beginning in March 1984, annual coupon rate on national savings certificates with five years maturity issued by the government to mobilize funds from nonbank sources.

Prices:

Consumer Prices:

Source B. Weights Reference Period: fiscal year 1995–96 (starts in mid-July); Geographical Coverage: urban areas defined as government municipalities (about 13 percent of total population); Number of Items in the Basket: 301 items; Basis for Calculation: 1995–1996 Household Budget Survey in urban areas conducted over the 12-month period.

International Transactions:

All trade data are from source B and are based on customs data.

Government Finance:

Annual data are derived from source B and cover budgetary central government. Debt service payments and grants include foreign transaction in kind. The fiscal year ends July 15.

National Accounts:

Source B. As indicated by the country, the data are compiled in the framework of the *1968 SNA*.

Netherlands   138

Data are denominated in guilders prior to January 1999 and in euros from January 1999 onward. The guilder's irrevocable fixed conversion factor to the euro is 2.20371 guilders per euro. In 2002, the guilder was retired from circulation and replaced by euro banknotes and coins. Beginning in January 1999, with the implementation of Stage Three of the European Economic and Monetary Union (EMU), an alternative euro area-wide definition of residency was introduced: All positions with residents of other euro area (EA) countries, including the European Central Bank (ECB), are classified as domestic positions, and foreign assets and foreign liabilities include only positions with non-euro area residents. Descriptions of the changes in the methodology and presentation of the Netherlands' accounts following the introduction of the euro are shown in the Introduction to *IFS* and in the footnotes on the euro area page.

Date of Fund Membership:

December 27, 1945

Standard Sources:

B: Netherlands Bank
S: Statistics Netherlands
V: Eurostat

Exchange Rates:

Market Rate (End of Period and Period Average):

Prior to January 1999, the market rate refers to guilder midpoint rate in the Amsterdam market at 2:15 p.m. In January 1999, the guilder became a participating currency with the Eurosystem, and the euro market rate became applicable to all transactions. In 2002, the guilder was retired from circulation and replaced by euro banknotes and coins. For additional information, refer to the section on exchange rates in the Introduction to *IFS* and the footnotes on the euro area page.

International Liquidity:

Beginning in January 1999, *Total Reserves minus Gold (line 1l.d)* is defined in accordance with the Eurosystem's statistical definition of international reserves. The international reserves of the Netherlands per the Eurosystem statistical definition at the start of the monetary union (January 1, 1999) in billions of U.S. dollars were as follows: *Total Reserves minus Gold*, \$13,641; *Foreign Exchange*, \$9,766; *SDRs*, \$905; *Reserve Position in the Fund*, \$2,969; *Other Reserve Assets*, \$0; *Gold*, \$9,726; *Gold (million fine troy ounces)*, 33.835 ounces. *Foreign Exchange (line 1d.d)*: From March 1979 through December 1998, gold and foreign exchange holdings excluded deposits at the European Monetary Cooperation Fund (EMCF), and the holdings of European currency units (ECUs) issued against these deposits were included in *line 1d.d. Gold (Eurosystem Valuation) (line 1and)* is obtained by converting the value in national currency terms, as reported in the country's standard sources, using the prevailing exchange rate, as given in *line* **ae**. During August 1978-December 1998, gold was revalued every three years at 70 percent of the lowest annual average of the daily noon market prices in Amsterdam in the preceding three years. From January 1999 onward, gold is revalued at market rate at the end of each quarter. Memorandum data are provided on *Non-Euro Claims on Euro Area Residents* and *Euro Claims on Non-Euro Area Residents,* which represent positions as of the last working day of each month. For additional information, refer to the section on international liquidity in the Introduction to *IFS* and on the euro area page.

Monetary Authorities:

Comprises the Netherlands Bank, which is part of the Eurosystem beginning in January 1999, and coin issue of the general government. Before December 2001, the contra-entry to coin issue was included in *Claims on General Government (line 12a)*. As from January 2002, the contra-entry for government coin issue is recorded in *Other Items (Net) (line 17r)*. Beginning in 2002, *Currency Issued (line 14a)* includes euro banknotes and coins and, until December 2002, any unretired guilder. The recorded value of euro banknotes is based on a monthly allocation of total euro banknotes in circulation based on the Netherlands Bank's paid up share of the ECB's capital; it does not correspond to either the actual amount of euro banknotes placed in circulation by the Netherlands Bank which is shown in memo line *Currency Put into Circulation (line 14m)*, nor the actual circulation of banknotes within the domestic territory. See section *Euro banknotes and coins* in the introduction to *IFS*. *Bonds and Money Market Instruments (line 16n.u)* include subordinated debt in the form of securities, other bonds, and money market paper. For a description of the accounts, refer to the section on monetary authorities in the introduction to *IFS*. Beginning with the data for end-November 2000, Monetary Authorities' *Foreign Assets (line 11)*, *Foreign Liabilities (line 16c)*, *Claims on Banking Institutions (line 12e.u)*, and *Liabilities to Banking Institutions (line 14c.u)* are affected by a change from gross to net presentation of positions relating to the TARGET (Trans-European Automated Real-Time Gross Settlement Express Transfer) euro clearing system. (See *Recording of TARGET system positions* under *European Economic and Monetary Union (EMU)* in the introduction to *IFS*.) Beginning in 2002, *Claims on Banking Institutions (line 12e.u)* and *Liabilities to Banking Institutions (line 14c.u)* include "Intra-Eurosystem claims/liabilities related to banknote issue," which is a single net value representing the difference between the value of euro banknotes allocated to the Netherlands Bank according to the accounting scheme of the Eurosystem for issuing euro banknotes, and the value of euro banknotes put into circulation by the Netherlands Bank. See section *Euro banknotes and coins* in the Introduction to *IFS*. Memo line *Net Claims on Eurosystem (line 12e.s)* equals gross claims on, less gross liabilities to, the ECB and other members of the Eurosystem.

Banking Institutions:

This category comprises universal banks (including Postbank, the Bank for Netherlands Municipalities, and the Netherlands Polder Boards Bank), as well as securities credit institutions, savings banks, and mortgage banks that are subsidiaries of universal banks. *Claims on Monetary Authorities (line 20)* and *Credit from Monetary Authorities (line 26g)* refer to the Netherlands Bank and the holdings of coins issued by the general government. *Money Market Fund Shares (line 26m.u)* include shares/units issued by money market funds. *Bonds and Money Market Instruments (line 26n.u)* include subordinated debt in the form of securities, other bonds, and money market paper. For a description of the accounts, refer to the section on banking institutions in the Introduction to *IFS*.

Banking Survey (National Residency):

For a description of the methodology and accounts, refer to the section Banking Survey (National Residency) in the introduction to *IFS*.

Banking Survey (Euro Area-wide Residency):

For a description of the methodology and accounts, refer to the section Banking Survey (Euro Area-wide Residency) in the introduction to *IFS*.

Money (National Definitions):

The national concept of domestic liquidity (also called money supply or M3, *line 39m*) includes savings with an original maturity of less than two years but excludes liquid liabilities of the general and local governments. From 1995 onward, the seasonally adjusted series (*line 39m.c*) contains adjustments for items in transit. Beginning in January 1999, national monetary aggregate series are discontinued. Euro area aggregates are presented on the euro area page.

Nonbank Financial Institutions:

Comprises life insurance and pension funds. † Beginning in December 1985, data for insurance companies are based on a new and extended survey of the largest seven insurance companies, covering about 85 to 90 percent of the balance sheet total of all insurance companies. Data for pension funds cover the General Public Service Fund and other pension funds; data for the latter are based on returns from the largest such funds.

Interest Rates:

Rate on Advances (line 60a):
Interest rate charged by the Netherlands Bank on advances to credit institutions. Beginning in January 1999, central bank policy rates are discontinued. See Eurosystem policy rate series on the Euro Area page.

Money Market Rate (line 60b):
Average market rate paid on bankers' call loans.
Interest rate on savings deposits with minimum balance of f.10,000.

Deposit Rate (lines 60lhs, 60lhn, 60lcs, and 60lcn):
See notes in the Introduction to *IFS*.

Lending Rate (line 60p):
Prior to January 1999, referred to midpoint of the minimum and maximum interest charged on current account advances. Beginning in January 1999, represents base rate charged by commercial banks on loans.

Lending Rate (lines 60phs, 60pns, 60phm, 60phn, 60pcs, and 60pcn):
See notes in the Introduction to *IFS*.

Government Bond Yield (line 61):
The data refer to the most recent 10-year government bond. For additional information, refer to the section on interest rates in the Introduction to *IFS* and on the euro area page.

Prices, Production, Labor:

Share Prices:
Source B. The AEX Index, base 1983, covers 25 shares quoted on the Amsterdam Exchange and refers to the average of daily quotations.

Share Prices: Manufacturing:
Source S. The index, base 1985, comprised a sample of 127 shares; the index was discontinued at the end of 2002.

Producer Prices: Final Products:
Source S. Weights Reference Period: 2000; Coverage: three main industrial activities: mining and quarrying, industry, electricity and gas; Number of Items in the Basket: about 27,350 prices from about 3,695 commodities; Basis for Calculation: the weights are derived from yearly production statistics and "Make and Use" matrices of the national accounts. The weights are based on the 2000 production number.

Consumer Prices:
Source S. Weights Reference Period: 2000; Geographical Coverage: covering all private households in the country; Number of Items in Basket: the index covers some 80,000 prices of more than 1600 items; Basis for Calculation: the weights are derived primarily from National Accounts results on private consumption. Additional information at a more detailed level is taken from a 2000 Household Budget Survey.

Wages: Hourly Rates:
The index, weights reference period: 2000, covers wages in manufacturing only.

Industrial Production:
Source S. Weights Reference Period: 2000; Sectoral Coverage: mining, manufacturing, electricity and gas; Basis for Calculation:

the relative weight is derived from the value added from a monthly survey covering about 6600 establishments.

Industrial Employment:
Source S index. The data refer to the average number of employed at the beginning and the end of the quarter in manufacturing industries, mining, and public utilities.

International Transactions:

Data on exports and imports and trade indices are from source S.

Government Finance:

Cash data on central government are derived from unpublished sources of the "Rijkshoofdboekhouding" (Accounts Department of the Ministry of Finance) and cover the consolidated central government, excluding the social security funds. Data on general government are derived from source V. The fiscal year ends December 31.

National Accounts:

As indicated by the country, concepts and definitions are in accordance with the *1995 ESA*. Estimates include hidden activities but exclude illegal activities. Both annual and quarterly accounts are derived from a balanced framework of supply and use tables. Volume measures are annually re-weighted and chained Laspeyres series. Beginning in 1999, euro data are sourced from the Eurostat database. Chain linked GDP volume measures are expressed in the prices of the previous year and re-referenced to 2000.

Netherlands Antilles   353

See page for Netherlands

Standard Sources:

B: Bank of the Netherlands Antilles, *Quarterly Bulletin*
S: Bureau of Statistics, *Statistische Mededelingen*

Exchange Rates:

Official Rate: (End of Period and Period Average):
Central bank midpoint rate. The official rate is pegged to the U.S. dollar.
The weighting scheme used to calculate indices of nominal and real effective exchange rates (*lines* **nec** and **rec**) is based on data for aggregate bilateral non-oil trade flows for 1980.

International Liquidity:

Data include the offshore departments of commercial banks but exclude the transactions of banks operating in Aruba. Data for *line 1d.d* include small foreign exchange holdings by the government. *Gold (National Valuation) (line 1and)* is obtained by converting the value in national currency terms, as reported in the country's standard sources, using the prevailing exchange rate, as given in *line* **ae** or **we**.
Lines 7a.d and 7b.d refer to the U.S. dollar equivalents of *lines 21* and *26c,* respectively. They include accounts of the special offshore departments of commercial banks. The accounts of a number of other financial institutions dealing exclusively offshore are not included. *Line 7k.d* measures the balance sheet total for most of the offshore banking units (OBUs) licensed to offer a full range

of banking facilities to nonresidents. Data agree with source B and are directly reported to *IFS*.

Monetary Authorities:

Consolidates the Bank of the Netherlands Antilles and monetary authority functions undertaken by the central government. The contra-entry to government foreign assets and coin issues is included in *line 12a.* Data include the offshore departments of commercial banks but exclude the transactions of banks operating in Aruba.
Monetary authorities data agree with the source B table "Monetary Authorities Summary Account." Exceptions are as follows:
Claims on Private Sector in source B is net of long-term special foreign borrowing.
Reserve Money equals source B data on money base minus Island Government time deposits.

Deposit Money Banks:

Consolidates commercial banks. Data include the offshore departments of commercial banks, excluding banks in Aruba.

Monetary Survey:

Data include the offshore departments of commercial banks but exclude the transactions of banks operating in Aruba. Data agree with the source B table "Money-Creating Institutions Summary Account." The exception is as follows:
Claims on Private Sector in source B is net of long-term special foreign borrowing by the monetary authorities and commercial banks.
In the monetary survey (see introduction for the standard method of calculation), *line 32an* includes *Central Government Deposits* with Girosystem Curacao (*line 26d.i*), and *line 34* includes *Private Sector Deposits* with Girosystem Curacao (*line 24..i*). *Line 32b* includes the contra-entries for *lines 24..i* and *26d.i. Line 35* is equal to *Time and Savings* plus *Foreign Currency Deposits* (*lines 25a* and *25b,* respectively).

Interest Rates:

Discount Rate (End of Period):
Central bank official discount rate.

Treasury Bill Rate:
Interest rate on three-month treasury bills.

Deposit Rate:
Rate offered by commercial banks on passbook deposits.

Lending Rate:
Rate charged by commercial banks on prime loans.

Government Bond Yield:
Yield on medium- and long-term Government bonds.

Prices:

Consumer Prices:
Source S index covering Aruba, Curaçao, and from 1975 also Bonaire. † As of January 1986, data cover only Curaçao and Bonaire, base December 1984. Beginning in 1990, data cover only Curaçao, base February 1996.

International Transactions:

Exports and Imports:
Source S data; also published in source B. *Imports* are reported on a c.i.f. basis beginning 1971. † As of January 1986, data exclude

Aruba. Current data for total exports and imports are on a payments basis.

Government Finance:

Annual data are as reported for the *Government Finance Statistics Yearbook (GFSY)* and cover the budgetary central government. † Beginning in 1980, data also cover social security operations. † In 1986, the island government of Aruba became independent of the Netherlands Antilles. † Provisional data for 1995 do not include social security operations. The fiscal year ends December 31.

New Zealand 196

Date of Fund Membership:

August 31, 1961

Standard Sources:

B: Reserve Bank of New Zealand
S: Statistics New Zealand

Exchange Rates:

Market Rate (End of Period and Period Average):
Beginning in April 1991, figures are market midrates at 11 a.m., which the Reserve Bank republishes on its website. Prior to that date, figures were established at 3 p.m.

International Liquidity:

Gold (National Valuation) (line 1and) is equal to *Gold (Million Fine Troy Ounces) (line 1ad),* valued at SDR 35 per fine troy ounce and converted into U.S. dollars at the dollar/SDR rate **sa** on the country page for the United States. Source E: OECD

Monetary Authorities:

Consolidates the Reserve Bank of New Zealand and monetary functions undertaken by the central government. The contra-entry to government foreign assets is included in *line 16d;* the contra-entry to Treasury coin issues and the adjustment for Treasury IMF accounts are included in *line 12a.* † Beginning in September 1988, data are based on an improved sectorization of the accounts.

Banking Institutions:

Comprises trading banks. † From September 1988, comprised monetary financial institutions (MFI) whose deposits and private sector loans comprise more than 95 percent of the estimated total MFI market. Data are based on an improved sectorization of the accounts.

Banking Survey:

† See notes on monetary authorities and banking institutions.

Money (National Definitions):

M1 comprises currency outside M3 financial institutions plus check balances, less interinstitutional transaction balances and central government demand deposits. M3 financial institutions include the Reserve Bank of New Zealand, most registered banks, and other financial intermediaries of significant size.
M2 comprises M1 and all other call deposits not included in M1, less interinstitutional call balances.

M3R comprises currency outside M3 institutions and their total New Zealand dollar deposits, less interinstitutional deposits, central government deposits, and deposits from nonresidents. The national official measure of broad money M3 includes NZ dollar deposits from nonresidents.

Other Banking Institutions:

Comprises finance companies and savings banks. The data on finance companies relate to companies with outstanding loans and advances exceeding $NZ200,000 and with assets constituting about 90 percent of the total assets of all finance companies.

Nonbank Financial Institutions:

Comprises life insurance and reassurance companies.

Interest Rates:

All interest rate data are from source B.

Discount Rate (End of Period):
Until February 1999, rate at which the Reserve Bank discounted eligible 28-day Reserve Bank bills to the market. Beginning in March 1999, official cash rate (OCR) around which the Reserve Bank transacts with the market.

Money Market Rate:
Refers to the New Zealand Overnight Interbank Cash Average rate on secured and unsecured overnight transactions, direct or through brokers, between banks, which are price makers in the New Zealand cash market.

Treasury Bill Rate:
Tender rate on three-month treasury bills.

Deposit Rate:
Maximum rate offered by banks on 31- to 89-day small deposits. † Beginning in March 1988, quarterly weighted averages for registered banks' total deposits in national currency. † Beginning in January 1990, weighted average rate offered by New Zealand's six largest banks on six-month deposits of $NZ10,000 or more, each bank's rate being weighted according to its share of the group's total New Zealand dollar deposits.

Lending Rate:
Rate charged by banks on overdrafts. † Beginning in January 1987, weighted average base business rate charged by New Zealand's six largest banks, each bank's rate being weighted according to its share of the group's private sector claims.

Government Bond Yield:
Yield on government bonds. † Beginning in January 1987, rate on the five-year 'benchmark' bond, a specific bond selected by the Reserve Bank to provide a representative five-year government bond rate.

Prices, Production, Labor:

Share Prices:
General index on shares, base January 1968. † Beginning in June 1986, gross index calculated by the New Zealand Stock Exchange, which has a base of June 30, 1986 = 100. All shares of all public companies listed on the New Zealand Stock Exchange are contained within the index. Payments of a dividend, rights issues, cash issues, and the flotation of new companies each have a neutral effect on the index.

Producer Prices:
Source S. Weight Reference Period: fourth quarter 1997; Coverage: has two types of indexes: the *outputs indexes* which measure

changes in the prices received by producers and the *inputs indexes* which measure changes in the cost of production (excluding labor and capital costs); Number of Items in the Basket: approximately 13,000 individual commodity items are surveyed from about 3,000 respondents; Basis for Calculation: since March 1996, the PPI has been produced using industry groups defined by the Australian and New Zealand Standard Industrial Classification (ANZSIC).

Consumer Prices:

Source S. Weight Reference Period: second quarter 1999; Geographical Coverage: all resident households living in permanent dwellings; Number of Items in the Basket: expenditure weight index are derived from 2300 HES expenditure items group to about 360 items in the CPI regimen; Basis for Calculation: the annual Household Economic Survey (HES).

Labor Cost Index:

The index includes salaries and wage rates, overtime wage rates, and some nonwage labor-related costs like annual leave, medical insurance, and low-interest loans. It covers all employees aged 15 years and over in all occupations and all industries except domestic services.

Manufacturing Production:

Data are sourced from the OECD database. Index of manufacturing gross domestic product, base 1995–96, year beginning April 1.

Manufacturing Employment:

Source S data on persons employed in manufacturing.

International Transactions:

All data on trade are from source S. The index series are of the chain-linked Fisher Ideal type, base second quarter 2002. The merchandise export indexes are calculated using NZ dollar f.o.b.-values. The merchandise import indexes use NZ dollar v.f.d.-values (represent the value of goods excluding the cost of freight and insurance). Prior to the September 2003 quarter, the merchandise import indexes used c.i.f.-values.

Volume of Exports:

Source S Fisher index of volume of exports, base July 1988–June 1989. *Butter:* Source S data reported in thousand metric tons.

Volume of Imports:

Source S Fisher index of volume of imports, base July 1988–June 1989.

Balance of Payments:

Annual balance of payments data for years prior to 1980 are compiled on the basis of fiscal years ending March 31. From 1980 onwards, the data are on a calendar year basis.

International Investment Position:

Data are compiled as at March 31 each year until March 31, 1999. From March 31, 2000, data are available quarterly.

Government Finance:

Annual data are as reported for the *Government Finance Statistics Yearbook (GFSY)* and cover budgetary central government. Annual data refer to a fiscal year different from calendar year (fiscal year ends June 30 from 1990 onwards; fiscal year begins April 1 through 1988). Beginning in 1990, annual data are as reported in the *Government Finance Statistics Yearbook (GFSY)* and cover the budgetary central government. The fiscal year ends June 30.

National Accounts:

Source S. Lines *99a.c* and *99b.c* include a statistical discrepancy. As indicated by the country, from 1987 onwards data have been revised according to the *1993 SNA.*

Nicaragua 278

Date of Fund Membership:

March 14, 1946

Standard Sources:

A: Central Bank, *Annual Report*
B: Central Bank, *Quarterly Bulletin and Indicadores Economicos*

Exchange Rates:

On February 15, 1988 the new cordoba, equal to 1,000 old cordobas, was introduced. A new currency unit called córdoba oro, equivalent to one U.S. dollar, was introduced as a unit of account on May 1, 1990 and began to be circulated in August 1990. On March 4, 1991, the gold córdoba was devalued to US$0.2 per gold córdoba, equal to five million old córdobas. On April 30, 1991 the córdoba completely replaced the gold and the old córdoba as the sole legal tender. *IFS* money and banking accounts are now expressed in gold córdobas.

Principal Rate (End of Period and Period Average):

The córdoba is pegged to the U.S. dollar.

For the purpose of calculating effective exchange rates (*lines* **nec** and **rec**), a weighted average exchange rate index for U.S. dollars per cordoba is based on trade at the rates applicable for exports and imports.

Monetary Authorities:

Comprises the Central Bank of Nicaragua only. † Beginning in December 1983, data are based on a new reporting system. † Beginning in December 1996, data are based on an improved sectorization of the accounts. † Beginning in December 2001, data are based on a new reporting system, which provides an improved classification and sectorization of the accounts.

Banking Institutions:

Comprises commercial banks and finance companies. † Beginning in December 2001, data are based on a new reporting system which provides improved classification and sectorization of the accounts.

Banking Survey:

† See notes on monetary authorities and banking institutions.

Nonbank Financial Institutions:

Comprises the Financiera Nicaragüense de Inversiones. † Beginning in December 2001, data are based on a new reporting system which provides improved classification and sectorization of the accounts.

Money (National Definitions):

Base Money comprises currency in circulation, and banker's legal reserve and other accounts at the Central Bank of Nicaragua (CBN). Currency in circulation refers to notes and coins issued by the CBN.

M1 comprises currency in circulation and transferable deposits. Currency in circulation refers to notes and coins issued by the

CBN less the amount held by banking institutions. Transferable deposits refer to the current account deposits in national and foreign currency of the private sector with the CBN and banking institutions.

M1A comprises M1 and transferable deposits in national and foreign currency of the central government, state and local governments, and public nonfinancial corporations with banking institutions.

M2 comprises M1, other deposits, and securities other than shares issued by the CBN in foreign currency held by the private sector. Other deposits refer to time and savings deposits in national and foreign currency of the private sector with banking institutions.

M2A comprises M2 and other deposits in national and foreign currency of the central government, state and local governments, and public nonfinancial corporations with banking institutions.

M3 comprises M2 and transferable and other deposits of nonresidents in national and foreign currency with banking institutions.

M3A comprises M2A and transferable and other deposits of nonresidents in national and foreign currency with banking institutions.

Interest Rates:

Discount Rate (End of Period):
Rediscount rate charged by the Central Bank of Nicaragua on short-term loans to commercial banks.

Savings Rate:
Rate offered by commercial banks on savings deposits in national currency. † Beginning in January 1999, weighted average rate offered by commercial banks on savings deposits in national currency. The rate is weighted by deposit amounts.

Savings Rate (Foreign Currency):
Rate offered by commercial banks on savings deposits in foreign currency. † Beginning in January 1999, weighted average rate offered by commercial banks on savings deposits in foreign currency. The rate is weighted by deposit amounts.

Deposit Rate:
Average rate offered by commercial banks on one-month deposits in national currency. † Beginning in January 1999, weighted average rate offered by commercial banks on one-month deposits in national currency. The rate is weighted by deposit amounts.

Deposit Rate (Foreign Currency):
Average rate offered by commercial banks on one-month deposits in foreign currency. † Beginning in January 1999, weighted average rate offered by commercial banks on one-month deposits in foreign currency. The rate is weighted by deposit amounts.

Lending Rate:
Average rate charged by commercial banks on loans of up to 18 months in national currency. † Beginning in January 1999, weighted average rate charged by commercial banks on loans of up to 18 months in national currency. The rate is weighted by loan amounts.

Lending Rate (Foreign Currency):
Average rate charged by commercial banks on loans of up to 18 months in foreign currency. † Beginning in January 1999, weighted average rate charged by commercial banks on loans of up to 18 months in foreign currency. The rate is weighted by loan amounts.

Prices and Labor:

Consumer Prices:
Source B. Weights Reference Period: 1999; Geographical Coverage: covers 17 departmental capitals and two of the country's autonomous regions; Number of Items in Basket: 322; Basis for Calculation: the weights are derived from the Household Income and Expenditure Survey (EIGH) carried out in 1998–1999.

International Transactions:
Source B trade data in U.S. dollars.

Government Finance:
Monthly, quarterly, and annual data are derived from source B and information provided by the Central Bank of Nicaragua and cover budgetary central government. The fiscal year ends December 31.

National Accounts:
Source A.

Niger   692

Date of Fund Membership:
April 24, 1963

Standard Source:
B: Banque Centrale des Etats de l'Afrique de l'Ouest (Central Bank of West African States), *Notes d'information et Statistiques (Informative Notes and Statistics)*

Niger is a member of the West African Economic and Monetary Union, together with Benin, Burkina Faso, Côte d'Ivoire, Guinea-Bissau, Mali, Senegal, and Togo. The Union, which was established in 1962, has a common central bank, the Central Bank of West African States (BCEAO), with headquarters in Dakar, and national branches in the member states. Mali and Guinea-Bissau joined the Union on June 1, 1984 and May 2, 1997, respectively.

Exchange Rates:

Official Rate: (End of Period and Period Average):
Prior to January 1999, the official rate was pegged to the French franc. On January 12, 1994, the CFA franc was devalued to CFAF 100 per French franc from CFAF 50 at which it had been fixed since 1948. From January 1, 1999, the CFAF is pegged to the euro at a rate of CFA franc 655.957 per euro.

International Liquidity:
Gold is revalued on a quarterly basis at the rate communicated by the BCEAO, which corresponds to the lowest average fixing in the London market.

Monetary Authorities:
Comprises the national branch of the BCEAO only. The amount of currency outside banks is estimated by subtracting from the amount of CFA franc notes issued by Niger the estimated amounts of Niger's currency in the cash held by the banks of all member countries of the Union.

Deposit Money Banks:
Comprises commercial banks, the Development Bank, and the Credit du Niger, and includes certain banking operations of the

Treasury and the Post Office. The Treasury accepts customs duty bills (reported separately in *line 22d.i*). Through its many branches, the Postal Checking System acts as the main depository for the private sector in the interior of Niger. *Claims on the Private Sector (line 22d)* include doubtful and litigious debts.

† Beginning in 1979, *Central Government Deposits (line 26d)* include the deposits of the public establishments of an administrative or social nature (EPAS) and exclude those of the savings bank; *Demand and Time Deposits (lines 24 and 25)* include deposits of the savings bank and exclude deposits of EPAS; and *Claims on Private Sector (line 22d)* exclude claims on other financial institutions.

Monetary Survey:

The data reported agree with source B aggregates, as given in the table on the position of the monetary institutions, except for *line 31n,* for which source B treats long-term foreign liabilities and SDR allocations as a foreign liability, whereas *IFS* reports the former separately and includes the latter in *line 37r*. Moreover, valuation differences exist as a result of the *IFS* calculations of reserve position in the Fund and the SDR holdings, both components of *line 11,* based on Fund record. † Beginning in 1979, *Claims on Other Financial Institutions (line 32f)* includes claims of deposit money banks on other financial institutions; see deposit money bank notes for explanation of other break symbols.

Other Banking Institutions:

Liquid Liabilities (line 55l): † See notes on deposit money banks and monetary survey.

Interest Rates:

Bank Rate (End of Period):
Rate on repurchase agreements between the BCEAO and the banks. † Prior to October 1, 1993 data refer to basic discount rate offered by the BCEAO.

Money Market Rate:
Rate paid on overnight interbank advances.

Deposit Rate:
Rate offered by banks on time deposits of CFAF 500,000–2,000,000 for under six months.

Prices:

Consumer Prices:
Source B. Weights Reference Period: 1996; Geographical Coverage: City of Niamey; Number of Items in Basket: 346; Basis for Calculation: The weights are derived from the survey "WAEMU Prices" of 1996.

International Transactions:

All trade value data are from source B.

National Accounts:

Source N. According to the country, the framework is an adaptation of the *1993 SNA*.

Nigeria 694

Date of Fund Membership:
March 30, 1961

Standard Sources:
A: Central Bank, *Annual Report and Statement of Accounts*

B: Central Bank, *Monthly Report, Economic and Financial Review*
S: Federal Office of Statistics, *Digest of Statistics*

Exchange Rates:
Principal Rate (End of Period and Period Average):
Central bank midpoint rate. The official exchange rate is based on an allocation by the Central Bank of Nigeria of official foreign exchange receipts to the authorized dealers through a Dutch auction system. Between March 1992 and January 1993 the auction system was replaced by an interbank system under which the official exchange rate was freely determined in the interbank market.

International Liquidity:
Line 1d.d includes small holdings of foreign exchange by the Federal Government.
Gold (National Valuation) (line 1and) is obtained by converting the value in national currency terms, as reported in the country's standard sources, using the prevailing exchange rate, as given in *line* **ae** or **we**.

Monetary Authorities:
Consolidates the Central Bank of Nigeria and monetary authority functions undertaken by the central government. † Beginning in November 1992, data are based on an improved sectorization of the accounts.

Deposit Money Banks:
Comprises commercial banks. † Prior to December 1973, central government deposits with commercial banks were included in *Demand Deposits* and *Time, Savings, and Foreign Currency Deposits*. † Beginning in November 1992, comprised commercial banks and merchant banks. Data are based on an improved sectorization of the accounts.

Monetary Survey:
† See notes on monetary authorities and deposit money banks.

Other Banking Institutions:
Comprises merchant banks.

Interest Rates:
All interest rate data are from source B.

Discount Rate (End of Period):
Minimum rediscount rate offered by the Central Bank of Nigeria.

Treasury Bill Rate:
Rate on new issues of treasury bills.

Deposit Rate:
Weighted average rate offered by commercial banks on three-month deposits. Rate is weighted by deposit amounts.

Lending Rate:
Prime rate charged by commercial banks on first-class advances.

Prices and Production:
Consumer Prices:
Source B. Weights Reference Period: 1996–97; Geographical Coverage: urban and rural areas; Number of Items in Basket: 265 expenditure categories—several items are collected for same categories; Basis for Calculation: weights are determined based on the National Consumer Survey of 1996–97.

Industrial Production:
Source B index, weights reference period 1985 covering mining (mainly crude petroleum), manufacturing, and electricity.

Crude Petroleum Production:
Source B data.
Manufacturing Production in the eastern states was not included prior to the third quarter of 1971. The manufacturing production index is a component of the industrial production index.

International Transactions:
Data are from source B.

Government Finance:
Data are derived from source A and cover the operations of the budgetary central government. The fiscal year ends December 31.

National Accounts:
Lines 99a and *99b* include a statistical discrepancy. *Line 96f* includes increases and/or decreases in stocks. Prior to May 1981, national accounts data were reported in years beginning on April 1. The large fluctuations in 1995 were due to a movement away from a pegged exchange rate in 1994 to a market-determined exchange rate in 1995.

Norway   142

Date of Fund Membership:
December 27, 1945

Standard Sources:
A: Bank of Norway, *Annual Report*
B: Bank of Norway, *Economic Bulletin*
S: Statistics Norway, *Statistisk Manedshefte, Manedsstatistikk over Utenrikshandelen*

Exchange Rates:
Official Rate: (End of Period and Period Average):
The Norwegian krone was floated on December 10, 1992, with an aim of maintaining a stable krone exchange rate against European currencies.

International Liquidity:
Gold (National Valuation) (line 1and) is revalued monthly using the end-of-period London Gold Market Fixing price. In the period December 1999 to December 2001, gold was valued at 20 percent below market value as gold was traded in an illiquid market. Prior to this period, gold was valued according to historical cost. Data for *Foreign Exchange (line 1d.d)* do not include Government Petroleum Fund investments.

Monetary Authorities:
Beginning in 1976, data for the Bank of Norway are based on improved sectorization in national source data. From May 1996 to June 1999, the Government Petroleum Fund investments are included in *Foreign Assets (line 11)*, and the Government Petroleum Fund deposits are included in *Central Government Deposits (line 16d)*.

Deposit Money Banks:
Comprises the commercial and savings banks and the Postal Bank. † Beginning in 1976, data for state banks are based on improved sectorization in national source data.
Beginning in 1995, the P.O. Savings Bank and Postal Giro, the accounts of which were previously published under a sepa-

rate subsection of the deposit money banks, merged into the Postal Bank.

Monetary Survey:
See Introduction for the standard method of calculation.

Money (National Definitions):
Broad Money (line 39m) is defined as the money holding sector's possession of notes and coins, bank deposits (both in Norwegian kroner and foreign currencies), and certificates of deposits. Restricted deposits are not included in *Broad Money*. The money holding sector consists of local government, nonfinancial corporations, households, and other financial corporations (other than banks and state lending institutions).

Other Banking Institutions:
Comprises state lending institutions and mortgage institutions. Beginning in January 1984, data for *State Lending Institutions* include two additional banks. Beginning in 1988, data for *Mortgage Institutions* are based on a more detailed reporting of accounts.

Nonbank Financial Institutions:
Comprises life insurance companies.

Interest Rates:
Discount Rate (End of Period):
Marginal lending rate of the Bank of Norway.

Average Cost for Central Bank Funding:
Weighted average rate of interest on the Bank of Norway's overnight, fixed-rate, and subsidized loans to banks.

Deposit Rate:
Average rate on all time deposits with deposit money banks. Beginning in the second quarter of 2001, statistics for deposit rates have been revised in keeping with new specifications for banks' monthly balance sheets. As a result the deposit rate refers to deposits other than deposits on transaction accounts.

Lending Rate:
Average rate of interest on all loans extended by deposit money banks.
Three-Month Interbank Rate (Norwegian Interbank Offered Rate—NIBOR):
Norwegian kroner rate in the foreign exchange market, based on forward rates.

Government Bond Yield:
Yield to maturity on five-year government bonds.

Prices, Production, Labor:
Industrial Share Prices:
Source S index, weights reference period: January 1, 1983. The index refers to midmonth prices of manufacturing and mining shares quoted on the Oslo Exchange.

Producer Prices:
Source S. Weights reference period: 2000; Coverage: selling prices for the domestic market and for the exports of goods in the oil and gas extraction, mining, manufacturing (most activities), and electricity supply production sectors; Number of Items in Basket: data for the index are obtained from a sample of approximately 820 establishments; Basis for Calculation: weights based on output and export values from the year t–1 national accounts, and the data obtained from the sample survey are subsequently weighted by market share indices to arrive at the producer price index.

Consumer Prices:

Source S. Weights reference period: 1998; Geographical Coverage: whole national territory; Number of Items in Basket: 900; Basis for Calculation: the weights used in the index are derived from the annual Household Expenditure Surveys (using a moving average of the last three annual surveys available) and annual retail trade statistics at the branch level.

Wages: Monthly Earnings:

Source S index, weights reference period: 2000. Data refer to quarterly averages ending in March, June, September, and December. Annual figures are unweighted arithmetic averages of quarterly data.

Industrial Production:

Source S. Weights Reference Period: 1995; Sectoral Coverage: oil and gas extraction, mining and quarrying, manufacturing, and electricity supply industries; Basis for Calculation: the weights are based on the value added at factor cost of the different industries.

Crude Petroleum Production:

Source B data in thousand metric tons.

International Transactions:

All trade data are from the *Monthly Bulletin of External Trade.*

Trade indices are from source S, weights reference period: 2000. Volume data are Laspeyres indices, and unit value data are Paasche indices. The coverage of the trade data is slightly less comprehensive than in the national accounts and balance of payments. Items not included in the merchandise trade data are primarily certain goods shipped directly to and from oil fields, shipping and air companies' expenditures on fuel abroad, and direct export to foreign ships, oil rigs and air companies' expenditures abroad.

Balance of Payments:

Balance of payments data have been revised on an annual basis for 1992–93, but revised quarterly data for this period are not yet available.

International Investment Position: Data are incomplete for 1980–87.

Government Finance:

Annual consolidated central government cash data are as reported for the *Government Finance Statistics Yearbook (GFSY).* † Beginning in 1996, quarterly general government data are reported according to the *GFSM 2001* analytical framework. † Beginning in 2003, monthly budgetary central government data also are reported according to the *GFSM 2001* analytical framework. The fiscal year ends December 31.

National Accounts:

Source S. As indicated by the country, from 1978 onwards data have been revised following the implementation of improved compilation methods and the *1993 SNA.* GDP chain-linked volume measures are calculated based on the prices and weights of the previous year, using Laspeyres formula in general.

Oman   449

Date of Fund Membership:

December 23, 1971

Standard Sources:

A: Central Bank of Oman, *Annual Report*
B: Central Bank of Oman, *Bulletin*
S: Ministry of Development, *Monthly Statistical Bulletin*

Exchange Rates:

Official Rate: (End of Period and Period Average):
The official rate is pegged to the U.S. dollar.

International Liquidity:

Gold (National Valuation) (line 1and) is obtained by converting the value in national currency terms, as reported in the country's standard sources, using the prevailing exchange rate, as given in *line de, line ae,* or *line we.*

Line 3..d reports the foreign currency deposits of the State General Reserve Fund with the Central Bank.

Lines 7a.d and *7b.d* are based on balance sheet data which report gross claims on and liabilities to head offices, branches, and other banks abroad. Prior data included net figures.

Monetary Authorities:

Comprises the Central Bank of Oman only.

Deposit Money Banks:

Comprises commercial banks. † Prior to 1979, some components of foreign assets and foreign liabilities were reported on a net basis.

Monetary Survey:

† See note on deposit money banks.

Interest Rates:

Deposit Rate:
Source B. Weighted average interest rate on local currency time deposits.

Lending Rate:
Transactions-weighted average interest rate on all local currency loans.

Prices and Production:

Consumer Prices:
Source S. National CPI with weights reference period: 2000. The weights are derived from a household expenditure survey conducted between 1999–2000. The index includes 8101 items of goods and services from 1571 centers.

Crude Petroleum Production:
Index calculated from source B data.

International Transactions:

Exports:
Source S data, except for the value of *Crude Petroleum* exports. The value of crude petroleum exports is obtained by multiplying the volume by the export price. Volume exports and the export prices of crude petroleum are from source S. Data are based on monthly average government sales prices in U.S. dollars per barrel.

Imports, c.i.f.:
Source B data, excluding public sector imports and, prior to mid–1973, petroleum company imports and imports of contractors undertaking public development projects.

Government Finance:

Annual data are as reported in the *Government Finance Statistics Yearbook (GFSY)* and cover transactions or recurrent and capital budgets of central government (the operations of the State General Reserve Fund are not included). The fiscal year ends December 31.

Pakistan 564

Data on international liquidity and sections 10 through 40 prior to July 1977 refer to last Friday of the period.

Beginning in July 1974, the State Bank and scheduled banks' net positions vis-à-vis their offices and branches in former East Pakistan are reported in *lines 17r, 27r,* and *37r.* Prior data were on a gross basis and were included in the appropriate aggregates of sections 10, 20, and 30.

Date of Fund Membership:
July 11, 1950

Standard Sources:
A: State Bank, *Annual Report*
B: State Bank, *Bulletin*
S: Federal Bureau of Statistics
N: *Insurance Yearbook*

Exchange Rates:

Market Rate (End of Period and Period Average):
† Prior to July 22, 1998, the State Bank of Pakistan buying rate. From July 22, 1998 to May 18, 1999, the rate established by the State Bank of Pakistan. † Beginning on May 19, 1999, Free Interbank Exchange rate, as determined in the interbank foreign exchange market.

International Liquidity:

Gold (National Valuation) (line 1and) is obtained by converting the value in national currency terms, as reported in the country's standard sources, using the prevailing exchange rate, as given in *line* **de,** *line* **ae,** or *line* **we.** This line refers to gold revalued annually on the last working day of June on the basis of the closing market rates fixed in London.

Monetary Authorities:

Consolidates the State Bank of Pakistan and monetary authority functions undertaken by the central government. The contra-entry to Treasury IMF accounts and coin issues is included in *line 12a.*

Deposit Money Banks:

Comprises the scheduled banks. Monthly data for these banks, which include two development banks, are prepared by the State Bank for *IFS.* Beginning in January 2005, data are based on an improved classification and sectorization of accounts. *Central Government Lending Funds (line 26f)* pertain to resources provided by the government to finance lending by the industrial and agricultural development banks.

Foreign Assets (line 21) exclude and Claims on Private Sector (line 22d) include import bills discounted.

Monetary Survey:

IFS line 34 plus *line 35* differ from the source B measure on monetary assets, in that source B includes (1) deposits of international nonmonetary organizations at the State Bank and the deposits of nonresident nonbanks at scheduled banks, which *IFS* treats as foreign liabilities and nets in *line 31n,* (2) counterpart funds

which *IFS* reports separately, (3) government deposits at scheduled banks which are netted in *IFS line 32an,* and (4) postal savings deposits which *IFS* reports separately in the other banking institutions section. Beginning in January 2005, data are based on an improved classification and sectorization of accounts.

Other Banking Institutions:
Comprises Post Office Savings deposits.

Money (National Definitions):

Reserve Money comprises currency in circulation, bankers' required reserve deposits and clearing balances, and deposits of the private sector in national currency with the State Bank of Pakistan (SBP). Currency in circulation refers to notes and coins issued by the SBP and the Ministry of Finance.

M1 comprises currency in circulation and demand deposits of other financial corporations, public nonfinancial corporations, and private sector with commercial banks and the SBP in national currency. Currency in circulation refers to the notes and coins issued by the SBP and the Ministry of Finance less the amount held by commercial banks. † Beginning in June 2004 transferable deposits includes savings deposits of other financial corporations, public nonfinancial corporations, and private sector with commercial banks in national currency.

M2 comprises M1 and time and foreign currency deposits of other financial corporations, public nonfinancial corporations, and private sector with commercial banks.

Interest Rates:

Discount Rate (End of Period):
The State Bank of Pakistan rate on its repurchase facility. † Prior to January 1994, rate at which the State Bank of Pakistan made advances to scheduled banks against acceptable securities. Beginning in 1994, data refer to the State Bank of Pakistan discount rate for its three-day repo facility.

Money Market Rate:
Monthly average of daily minimum and maximum call-money rates.

Treasury Bill Rate:
Weighted average yield on six-month treasury securities. † Prior to July 1996, rate on six-month Federal Treasury Bill. Since July 1996, rate on six-month Federal Treasury Bond (STFB), which replaced the six-month Federal Treasury Bill.

Government Bond Yield:
Beginning in June 1989, data relate to monthly yields based on average prices quoted on the last Wednesday of the month for the 113/4 percent bond due for redemption in 2002.

Prices, Production, Labor:

Share Prices:
Index figures prior to 1982 have been reported with 1975–76 as weights reference period; those for 1982 and onwards, with 1980–81. The newer series have a wider coverage. The series shown are ratio-spliced. Source B. Data refer to midday quotes for the last Friday of the month for 242 common shares on the Karachi Exchange. The index is chained.

Wholesale Prices:
Source S. † Beginning in July 2002, weights reference period: 2000–01. Index numbers of wholesale prices including food, raw material, fuel, lighting, lubricants, and manufactures.

Consumer Prices:

Source S. Weights reference period: 2000–2001; Geographical Coverage: 35 urban centers of Pakistan; Number of Items in Basket: 374; Basis for Calculation: weights are derived from the Family Budget Survey conducted in 2000–2001.

Manufacturing Production:

Source S. Weights Reference Period: 1999–2000; Coverage: manufacturing; Number of Items in Basket: 100; Basis for Calculation: quantum index numbers of manufacturing.

International Transactions:

All trade data are from source S.

Value of Exports and Imports:

Export data include re-exports. Trade in military goods and silver bullions are excluded.

Volume and Unit Value of Exports and Imports:

Laspeyres indices, weights reference period: 1990–91. The export indices cover 96.5 percent of total exports, and the import indices cover 86.7 percent of total imports.

Government Finance:

Annual data are as reported for the *Government Finance Statistics Yearbook (GFSY)* and cover budgetary central government. The fiscal year ends June 30.

National Accounts:

Source S.

Panama   283

Date of Fund Membership:

March 14, 1946

Standard Sources:

S: Directorate of Statistics and Census, *Panamanian Statistics*, published in separate booklets as follows:
National Accounts (Series 342)
Government Finance (Series 343)
Prices (Series 351)
Foreign Trade (Series 331)
Social and Economic Indicators (Series 001)

Exchange Rates:

Official Rate: (End of Period and Period Average):
Rates are based on a fixed relationship to the U.S. dollar.

International Liquidity:

Lines 7a.d and *7b.d* relate to foreign accounts of deposit money banks operating under general licenses, as reported in section 20. In addition, there are international license banks (ILB) that deal freely with the foreign sector but are limited locally to interbank markets.

Monetary Authorities:

Consists of the National Bank of Panama (NBP) only. The NBP performs some central banking functions, i.e., fiscal agent for the Government, a clearing house for commercial banks, and holder of international reserves and positions vis-à-vis the IMF. † Beginning in October 1969, data are based on an improved sectoriza-

tion of the accounts. † Beginning in December 2001, data are based on an improved classification and sectorization of the accounts. † Beginning in December 2002, data are based on a new reporting system which provides improved classification and sectorization of the accounts.

Banking Institutions:

Consolidates private commercial and savings banks. Transactions between these banks and offshore banks, whose accounts are not shown here, are included in *Foreign Assets (line 21)* and *Liabilities (line 26c)*. † Beginning in December 2001, data are based on an improved classification and sectorization of the accounts. † Beginning in December 2002, data are based on a new reporting system which provides improved classification and sectorization of the accounts.

Banking Survey:

Money in Panama comprises U.S. notes and coin, Panamanian coin, and demand deposits. The banks' U.S. currency and their deposits in the U.S. are reported as part of *Foreign Assets (Net) (line 31n)*. The substantial private holdings of U.S. notes and coin in Panama are available either for use as money locally or for the financing of foreign payments; their amount is, however, not known, and hence no attempt has been made to calculate *Money* for Panama. The amount of Panamanian coin in circulation is small in comparison to U.S. currency. † See notes on monetary authorities and banking institutions.

Interest Rates:

Money Market Rate:
Rate on funds obtained by commercial banks on one-month deposits in the interbank market. † Beginning in February 2006, the rate is calculated as an average of the rates paid during the month.

Savings Rate:
Rate offered by commercial banks on savings deposits to nonfinancial corporations.

Deposit Rate:
Average rate offered by domestic banks on six-month time deposits. † Beginning in December 1992, weighted average rate offered by domestic banks on six-month time deposits. The rate is weighted by deposit amounts.

Lending Rate:
Average rate charged by banks on one- to five-year loans for trading activities.
† Beginning in June 1990, weighted average rate charged by banks on one- to five-year loans for trading activities. † Beginning in January 2000, weighted average rate charged by domestic banks on one- to five-year loans for trading activities. The rate is weighted by loan amounts.

Prices, Production, Labor:

Wholesale Prices:
Source S index of wholesale prices for the entire country, covering the agricultural, industrial, and import sectors, base 1987.

Consumer Prices:
Source S. Weights Reference Period: October 2002; Geographical Coverage: urban areas of the whole country; Number of Items in Basket: 211; Basis for Calculation: The data source is retail merchants.

Manufacturing Production:

Source S. General index of manufacturing production, base 1992, compiled by the Direction of Statistics and Census (D.E.C.). Laspeyres index; the weight for each product is derived as a percentage of its value in production in the reference year of the total value of the production within the class of activity. The weight for each industrial division is the percentage of its aggregated gross value of the total value of the manufacturing industry in 1992. The index includes 368 industrial units and 240 products.

International Transactions:

All trade data are from source S. Exports include re-exports and petroleum products.

Volume of Exports:

IFS average of commodities with a 1985 value of exports as weights.

Government Finance:

Monthly and quarterly data cover budgetary central government only. Data on outstanding debt are derived from the annual bulletin published by "Contraloría General de la República," entitled *Situacion Economica.* The fiscal year ends December 31.

National Accounts:

Source S. As indicated by the authorities, concepts and definitions are in accordance with the *1993 SNA.*

Papua New Guinea   853

Date of Fund Membership:

October 9, 1975

Standard Sources:

B: Bank of Papua New Guinea, *Quarterly Economic Bulletin*
S: National Statistics Office, *Economic Indicators, Abstract of Statistics*

Exchange Rates:

Market Rate (End of Period and Period Average):

Prior to 1994, central bank midpoint rate. Beginning in 1994, closing rate set at the foreign exchange auction in which commercial banks, the only authorized foreign exchange dealers, participate. The exchange rate floats independently with respect to the U.S. dollar and is determined freely in the interbank market.

International Liquidity:

Gold (National Valuation) (line 1and) was revalued at the end of December 2001 to reflect the market price of gold instead of the historical cost.

Monetary Authorities:

Comprises the Bank of Papua New Guinea only. † Beginning in December 2001, data are based on a new reporting system which provides improved classification and sectorization of the accounts.

Banking Institutions:

Consolidates the Government-owned Papua New Guinea Banking Corporation (PNGBC) and four private banks, of which one is a branch and three are subsidiaries of Australian banks. *Lines 22d* and *26c* exclude an external loan, administered by a commercial bank on behalf of a resident corporation, which was later refinanced without the intermediary of the monetary system. † Beginning in December 2001, comprises commercial banks, finance companies, merchant banks, savings and loans societies, and a microfinance company. Data are based on a new reporting system which provides improved classification and sectorization of the accounts. On April 9, 2002, the PNGBC merged operations with the Bank South Pacific, a private bank.

Banking Survey:

† See notes on monetary authorities and banking institutions.

Money (National Definitions):

Reserve Money comprises currency in circulation, deposits of banking institutions with the BPNG, and demand deposits of nonbank financial institutions and private sector with the BPNG.

M1* comprises of currency outside the banking system and demand deposits of nonbank financial institutions, provincial and local governments, nonfinancial public enterprises, and private sector with the BPNG and banking institutions.

M3* comprises M1* and quasi money. Quasi money comprises savings and term deposits of nonbank financial institutions, provincial and local government, nonfinancial public enterprises, and private sector with the BPNG and banking institutions.

Interest Rates:

All interest rate data are from source B.

Discount Rate (End of Period):

Rate charged by the Bank of Papua New Guinea (BPNG) on loans to banks. † Beginning in January 1993, maximum rate charged by the BPNG on loans to commercial banks against acceptable commercial paper. † Beginning in May 1995, rate refers to the Kina Auction Facility and is the weighted average of bids in national currency placed by commercial banks at the auction. On February 5, 2001, the Kina Auction Facility was replaced with the Kina Facility Rate (KFR) and an overnight REPO facility. The KFR is announced monthly and provides a signal to the market of the BPNG's monetary stance. Both the Kina Auction and the overnight REPO facilities were offered at fixed rates based on the KFR. The Kina Auction Facility was abolished on April 14, 2003. † Beginning in April 2003, term REPOs were introduced and is the rate on repurchase agreements in national currency between the BPNG and commercial banks. Margins on trading under the REPO facility are changed periodically by the BPNG. Trading under the REPO facility in unsecuritized.

Money Market Rate:

Average rate on loans between commercial banks.

Treasury Bill Rate:

Rate on 182-day treasury bills. Data refer to the second Thursday of the month. † Beginning in August 1994, weighted average rate on 182-day treasury bills in national currency at the last auction of the month.

Savings Rate:

Average rate offered by commercial banks on savings deposits in national currency.

Deposit Rate:

Weighted average rate offered by commercial banks on three- to six-month term deposits in national currency. † Beginning in January 1995, weighted average rate offered by commercial banks on deposits in national currency. Rate is weighted by deposit amounts.

Lending Rate:
Weighted average rate charged by commercial banks on loans in national currency. Rate is weighted by loan amounts.

Government Bond Yield:
Weighted average yield on all inscribed stock.

Prices and Labor:

Share Prices:
Kina Securities Share Index (KSi), base January 2, 2001. The index covers shares quoted on the Port Moresby Stock Exchange. Beginning in March 2006, the KSi includes debt securities.

Consumer Prices:
Source B index for six towns combined, weights reference period: 1977.

Total Employment:
Source B. Data refer to employment in trade, building and construction, transport, agriculture, forestry and fisheries, financial and business services, and manufacturing industries.

International Transactions:

All trade data are from source B.

Volume of Exports:
Source B, weights reference period: 1994.

Export Unit Value index is from source B, weights reference period: 1994.

Government Finance:

Monthly data are from unpublished sources, as provided by source B and cover the operations of the budgetary central government. The fiscal year ends December 31.

National Accounts:

Prior to 1977, data relate to fiscal years ending June 30. Since this date, data refer to calendar years.

Paraguay   288

Date of Fund Membership:

December 28, 1945

Standard Source:

B: Central Bank, *Monthly Statistical Bulletin*

Exchange Rates:

Market Rate (End of Period and Period Average):
From early 1998 onwards, the exchange rate is operated as a managed float. Prior to that, the exchange rate was determined freely in the market. The exchange rate is determined as the average of sales and purchases weighted by the volume of transactions of the main banks and exchange houses.
For the purpose of calculating effective exchange rates (*lines* **nec** and **rec**), a weighted average exchange rate index for U.S. dollars per guarani is based on trade for non-oil imports.

International Liquidity:

Gold (National Valuation) (line 1and) is valued on the basis of the international market price of the period in reference. *Monetary Authorities: Other Assets (line 3..d)* includes holdings of shares from the Latin American Export Bank.

Monetary Authorities:

Comprises the Central Bank of Paraguay (CBP) only. † Beginning in December 1988, data are based on an improved sectorization of the accounts. † Beginning in January 1995, data reflect the introduction of a new plan of accounts and are based on an improved sectorization and classification of the accounts. † Beginning in December 2001, data are based on a new reporting system which provides improved classification and sectorization of the accounts.

Banking Institutions:

Comprises commercial banks. † Beginning in January 1967, includes savings and loan associations. Data are based on an improved sectorization of the accounts. † Beginning in December 1988, includes the National Development Bank, savings and loans associations for housing, National Housing Bank, Cattle Fund, Credit Agency for Farm Equipment, Bank Employees Retirement and Pension Fund, finance companies, and Paraguayan Institute for Housing and Urbanization, which was abolished in March 1992. Data are based on an improved sectorization of the accounts. † Beginning in January 1995, comprises commercial banks, National Development Bank, and finance companies. Data reflect the introduction of a new plan of accounts and are based on an improved sectorization and classification of the accounts. † Beginning in December 2001, data are based on a new reporting system which provides improved classification and sectorization of the accounts.

Banking Survey:

† See notes on monetary authorities and banking institutions.

Money (National Definitions):

Base Money comprises notes and coins in circulation and bankers' reserves. Bankers' reserves include legal reserve requirements and demand deposits in national currency of commercial banks in the CBP.

M1 comprises notes and coins held by the public and demand deposits in national currency of the private sector in commercial banks.

M2 comprises M1 plus savings and time deposits and savings certificates in national currency of the private sector in commercial banks.

M3 comprises M2 and deposits in foreign currency of the private sector in commercial banks.

M4 comprises M3 and bonds and other securities in circulation issued by commercial banks.

M5 comprises M4 plus trust funds and mutual funds of the private sector in commercial banks.

Interest Rates:

Discount Rate (End of Period):
Rediscount rate charged by the CBP. † Beginning in September 1990, rate charged by the CBP on short-term liquidity loans to commercial banks.

Money Market Rate:
Average rate on loans between financial institutions in national currency.

Savings Rate:
Rate offered by commercial banks on savings deposits in national currency. † Beginning in January 1994, weighted average rate offered by commercial banks on savings deposits in national currency. The rate is weighted by deposit amounts.

Savings Rate (Foreign Currency):

Weighted average rate offered by commercial banks on savings deposits in foreign currency. The rate is weighted by deposit amounts.

Deposit Rate:

Rate offered by commercial banks on 180-day certificates of deposit in national currency. † Beginning in March 1998, weighted average rate offered by commercial banks on 90- to 180-day time deposits in national currency. The rate is weighted by deposit amounts.

Deposit Rate (Foreign Currency):

Weighted average rate offered by commercial banks on 90- to 180-day time deposits in foreign currency. The rate is weighted by deposit amounts.

Lending Rate:

Rate charged by commercial banks on loans in national currency. † Beginning in January 1994, weighted average rate charged by commercial banks on commercial, developmental, personal, and various loans in national currency. The rate is weighted by loan amounts.

Lending Rate (Foreign Currency):

Weighted average rate charged by commercial banks on commercial, developmental, personal, and various loans in foreign currency. The rate is weighted by loan amounts.

Prices:

Producer Prices:

Source B. Weights Reference Period: December 1995; Coverage: covers agricultural products, livestock, forestry, mining, and manufacturing; Number of Items in the Basket: 150 products; Basis for Calculation: two indices are calculated: one for local goods and another for imported goods. A general weighted index of local and imported goods is also compiled.

Consumer Prices:

Source B. Weights Reference Period: 1992; Geographical Coverage: urban households at the national level; Number of Items in the Basket: 293 products (goods and services); Basis for Calculation: June 1990–June 1991 Household Budget Survey (income and expenditure), fixed-weight Laspeyres index.

International Transactions:

All trade data are from source B.

Balance of Payments:

The entries shown in the columns for second quarters correspond to data for the first half of each year.

Government Finance:

Data are as reported in the *Government Finance Statistics Yearbook (GFSY)* and cover the budgetary central government. † The fiscal year ends December 31.

National Accounts:

Source B. As indicated by the country, concepts and definitions are in accordance with the *1953 SNA*.

Peru   293

Date of Fund Membership:

December 31, 1945

Standard Source:

B: Central Reserve Bank of Peru, *Weekly Bulletin*

Exchange Rates:

On February 1, 1985, the inti, equal to 1,000 soles, was introduced. On July 1, 1991, the nuevo sol, equal to one million intis, replaced the inti as the currency unit of Peru.

Market Rate (End of Period and Period Average):

Midpoint rate of interbank operations as published by the Superintendency of Banks and Insurance Corporations.

International Liquidity:

Line 1and is equal to *line 1ad,* converted into U.S. dollars at the dollar price of gold used by national sources, as reported to *IFS*. Gold acquired prior to June 1979 is valued at SDR 35 per ounce. Gold acquired from this date onwards is revalued once a month based on an accounting value equal to 85 percent of the international price shown in the London, New York, and Zurich markets.

Monetary Authorities:

Comprises the Central Reserve Bank of Peru only.

Deposit Money Banks:

Comprises the Bank of the Nation and private commercial banks. Beginning in May 1994, the new charter of the Bank of the Nation establishes its role as fiscal agent of the government.

Other Banking Institutions:

Comprises development banks, which are under liquidation. Beginning in May 2002, includes the Banco Agropecuario, which provides agricultural and livestock loans.

Money (National Definitions):

Liquidity comprises money and quasi-money in national and foreign currency.

Monetary Base comprises notes and coins issued and demand deposits in national currency of deposit money banks and other banking institutions at the Central Reserve Bank of Peru. Beginning in January 1994, excludes deposits of the Bank of the Nation and development banks.

Money comprises notes and coins held by the public and demand deposits in national currency of the private sector in deposit money banks and other banking institutions.

Quasi-Money in National Currency comprises time and savings deposits in national currency of the private sector in deposit money banks and other banking institutions and bonds and other securities in national currency issued by deposit money banks and other banking institutions which are held by the private sector.

Quasi-Money in Foreign Currency comprises time and savings deposits in foreign currency of the private sector in deposit money banks and other banking institutions and bonds and other securities in foreign currency issued by deposit money banks and other banking institutions which are held by the private sector.

Interest Rates:

Discount Rate (End of Period):

Central Reserve Bank of Peru's rediscount rate on short-term monetary regulation loans to commercial banks in national currency.

Discount Rate (Foreign Currency) (End of Period):

Central Reserve Bank of Peru's rediscount rate on short-term monetary regulation loans to commercial banks in foreign currency.

Money Market Rate:

Weighted average rate on noncollateralized loans between commercial banks in national currency. The rate is the arithmetic average of daily rates and is weighted by the individual banks' participation in total loans.

Money Market Rate (Foreign Currency):

Weighted average rate on noncollateralized loans between commercial banks in foreign currency. The rate is the arithmetic average of daily rates and is weighted by the individual banks' participation in total loans.

Savings Rate:

Average rate offered by commercial banks on savings deposits in national currency. The rate is converted to percent per annum by compounding monthly rates of interest.

Savings Rate (Foreign Currency):

Average rate offered by commercial banks on savings deposits in foreign currency.

Deposit Rate:

Weighted average rate offered by commercial banks on 31- to 179-day time deposits in national currency. † Beginning in February 1992, weighted average rate offered by commercial banks on all deposits in national currency. The rate is the arithmetic average of daily rates and is weighted by the individual banks' participation in total deposits.

Deposit Rate (Foreign Currency):

Weighted average rate offered by commercial banks on all deposits in foreign currency. The rate is the arithmetic average of daily rates and is weighted by the individual banks' participation in total deposits.

Lending Rate:

Weighted average rate charged by commercial banks on loans in national currency of 360 days or less. The rate is the arithmetic average of daily rates and is weighted by the individual banks' participation in total loans. † Beginning in February 1992, weighted average rate charged by the eight most important commercial banks on overdrafts and advances on current accounts, credit cards, discounts, and loans up to 360 days and mortgage loans in national currency. The rate is the geometric average of daily rates and is weighted by the individual banks' participation in total loans.

Lending Rate (Foreign Currency):

Weighted average rate charged by the eight most important commercial banks on overdrafts and advances on current accounts, credit cards, discounts, and loans up to 360 days and mortgage loans in foreign currency. The rate is the geometric average of daily rates and is weighted by the individual banks' participation in total loans.

Prices, Production, Labor:

Share Prices:

General share price index covering industrial and mining shares quoted in the Lima Stock Exchange, base December 1991.

Wholesale Prices:

Source B, weights reference period: 1994. A Laspeyres index that measures the evolution of prices of a representative group of goods traded in the wholesale markets in the Lima metropolitan area and 25 other cities. The index covers 394 products.

Consumer Prices:

Source B. Weights Reference Period: January 2002; Geographical Coverage: Metropolitan Lima; Number of Items in Basket:

515; Basis for Calculation: The weights used to calculate the CPI are derived from the multipurpose national survey conducted from October 1993 to September 1994 in Lima. These weights were changed in January 2002 as a result of a revision of the INEI methodology.

Industrial Production:

Source S. Weights Reference Period: 1994; Sectoral Coverage: agriculture and livestock, fishing, mining and fuel, manufacturing, construction, trade and other services sectors; Basis for Calculation: the weighting factor is the annual percentage structure of the 1994 base year value added.

Industrial Employment:

Source B. Monthly index of industrial employment in metropolitan Lima, weights reference period: October 1997. The index covers all registered enterprises employing at least 100 workers.

International Transactions:

All trade data are from source B. Prior to 1975, data on exports and imports in U.S. dollars were derived by conversion of national currency data into U.S. dollars. Annual figures include grants and other adjustments.

Volume of Exports:

IFS average of copper, crude petroleum, fishmeal, iron ore, silver, zinc, and lead with a 1995 value of exports as weights.

Unit Value of Exports:

IFS average of copper, crude petroleum, fishmeal, iron ore, silver, zinc, and lead with a 1995 value of exports as weights.

Government Finance:

Monthly and quarterly data are derived from source B and cover the budgetary central government. The fiscal year ends December 31.

National Accounts:

As indicated by the country, from 1990 onward data have been revised following the implementation of the *1993 SNA*.

Philippines   566

Date of Fund Membership:
December 27, 1945

Standard Source:
B: Central Bank: *Quarterly Bulletin, Statistical Bulletin*

Exchange Rates:

Market Rate (End of Period and Period Average):
Bankers' Association reference rate, which is the weighted average rate of all transactions conducted through the Philippines Dealing System during the previous day.

International Liquidity:

Gold (National Valuation) (line 1and) is the U.S. dollar value of official holdings of gold as reported in the country's standard sources. In early 1977 a number of offshore banking units (OBUs) and foreign currency deposit units (FCDUs) were established. OBUs deal freely with nonresidents but are permitted to undertake only limited domestic operations, essentially with the monetary system and Government. FCDUs are allowed to undertake longer-term foreign currency operations with residents. *Lines 7a.d* and *7b.d* are derived from the accounts of commercial banks (see section 20). They exclude OBU accounts but include most FCDU accounts as well as claims on and liabilities to OBUs. *Lines 7k.d* and *7m.d* relate to the foreign assets and foreign liabilities of OBUs. Their assets and liabilities with the monetary system are classified as part of the foreign sector accounts in sections monetary authorities, deposit money banks, and monetary survey.

Monetary Authorities:

Consolidates the Central Bank of the Philippines and monetary authority functions undertaken by the central government. The contra-entry to Treasury IMF accounts is included in *line 12a.* † Beginning December 1983, data are based on an improved sectorization of the accounts. † Beginning July 1993, data reflect the financial restructuring of the Central Bank of the Philippines. The Bangko Sentral ng Pilipinas (BSP) was created to take over the monetary authority functions of the former Central Bank of the Philippines. At the same time, the Central Bank-Board of Liquidators (CB-BOL), an agency of the central government, was created to liquidate the nonperforming assets of the former Central Bank of the Philippines. *Line 12a* includes claims on the CB-BOL. *Line 16c* includes foreign liabilities assumed by the BSP which, prior to July 1993, were included in *lines 16b* and *16d*.

Deposit Money Banks:

Comprises commercial banks and rural banks accepting demand deposits. † Prior to January 1976, *line 21* included and *line 22d* excluded certain claims on residents. Data are based on an improved classification of the accounts. † Beginning December 1983, data are based on an improved sectorization of the accounts.

Time, Savings, and Foreign Currency Deposits (line 25) includes prepayments required by the banks for letters of credit and small amounts of foreign currency deposits held by residents. Data for *line 26aa* refer to deposit substitutes. These relate to notes, certificates, and other instruments used by the banks to obtain term funds from the resident private sector other than through deposits.

Monetary Survey:

† See notes on monetary authorities and deposit money banks.

Other Banking Institutions:

Comprises development and savings banks.

Money (National Definitions):

Reserve Money comprises currency in circulation, bankers' reserves, and transferable deposits of the private sector with the Bangko Sentral ng Philipinas (BSP) less cash holdings of the Bureau of the Treasury (BTr). Currency in circulation refers to notes and coins issued by the BSP. Bankers' reserves include required reserves and clearing balances of commercial banks, thrift banks, rural banks and nonbanks with quasi-banking functions in national currency at the BSP.

Narrow Money comprises currency in circulation, transferable deposits, and managers' and cashiers' checks outstanding less commercial banks holdings of checks and other cash items. Currency in circulation refers to notes and coins issued by the BSP less cash at the BTr's vaults and currency held by commercial banks. Transferable deposits refer to current account deposits in national currency of other financial institutions, state and local gov-

ernments, nonfinancial public corporations, and private sector with the BSP and commercial banks.

Quasi-Money comprises other deposits in national currency. Other deposits refer to time and savings deposits in national currency of other financial institutions, state and local governments, nonfinancial public corporations, and private sector with commercial banks.

M3 comprises narrow money, quasi-money, and deposit substitutes. Deposit substitutes refer to money market borrowings by commercial banks such as promissory notes, repurchase agreements, commercial paper, and certificates of assignment with recourse.

M4 comprises M3 plus foreign currency deposits of other financial institutions, state and local governments, nonfinancial public corporations, and private sector with commercial banks.

Interest Rates:

Discount Rate (End of Period):
Rediscount rate for loans for traditional exports, which account for a large part of total rediscount credits. † Beginning in December 1985, the rediscount facility was unified and refers to the rediscount rate charged by the Central Bank of the Philippines on loans to banks in national currency.

Money Market Rate:
Weighted average rate on overnight loans between commercial banks, thrift banks, savings banks, and nonbank financial institutions with quasi-banking functions to cover reserve deficiencies. The rate is weighted by loan amounts.

Treasury Bill Rate:
Weighted average rate on 91-day treasury bills denominated in national currency. Rate is weighted by the volume of bills sold.

Savings Rate:
Rate offered by banks on savings deposits in national currency. Rate is calculated as the ratio of the amount of interest on the deposits of a sample of banks and the total outstanding amount of these deposits.

Savings Rate (Foreign Currency):
Rate offered by banks on savings deposits in foreign currency. Rate is calculated as the ratio of the amount of interest on the deposits of a sample of banks and the total outstanding amount of these deposits.

Deposit Rate:
Weighted average rate offered by commercial banks on 61- to 90-day time deposits in national currency. Rate is weighted by deposit amounts.

Deposit Rate (Foreign Currency):
Weighted average rate offered by commercial banks on 61- to 90-day time deposits in foreign currency. Rate is weighted by deposit amounts.

Lending Rate:
Weighted average rate charged by commercial banks on loans in national currency. Rate is weighted by loan amounts and is calculated as the ratio of the amount of interest on the loans of a sample of banks and the total outstanding amount of these loans.

Government Bond Yield:
Yield on two-year treasury notes. † Beginning in March 1998, average yield on two-year treasury bonds. The yield is that of the last issue of the month.

Prices and Production:

All data on prices are from source B.

Share Prices:

Index of the Manila Stock Exchange on commercial and industrial shares, base 1965. † Beginning in December 1972, stock price index of the Manila and Makati stock exchanges, base 1972.† Beginning in January 1978, stock price index of the Manila and Makati stock exchanges, base 1985. Beginning in April 1994, stock price index of the Philippine Stock Exchange, base 1985.

Mining and Sugar:

Average of daily quotations in the Manila and Makati stock exchanges, base 1972.

Producer Prices:

Source B. Weights Reference Period: 1994; Coverage: covers 276 sample manufacturing establishments ; Number of Items in the Basket: 548 manufactured goods; Basis for Calculation: the weights are revised every year based on the latest data available from the Annual Survey of Establishments/Census of Establishments (ASE/CE).

Consumer Prices:

Source B. Weights Reference Period: 2000; Geographical Coverage: covers about 9,500 outlets nationwide; Number of Items in the Basket: covers between 286 and 753 items, the number varying by province; Basis for Calculation: the weights are derived from the 2000 Family Income and Expenditures (FIES) data.

Manufacturing Production:

Source S. Weights Reference Period: 1994; Sectoral Coverage: manufacturing sector; Basis for Calculation: the weights used for the index are based on the 1994 Census of Establishments (CE).

International Transactions:

All trade data are from source B.

Government Finance:

Monthly, quarterly, and annual data are reported by source B and are derived from *Cash Operations Statements,* Bureau of Treasury. Data cover operations of the budgetary central government. The fiscal year ends December 31.

National Accounts:

Source B.

Poland   964

Date of Fund Membership:

June 12, 1986

Standard Sources:

A: National Bank, *Information Bulletin*
B: Central Statistical Office, *Statistical Bulletin*
S: Central Statistical Office, *Statistical Yearbook*

Exchange Rates:

The post-January 1, 1995 zloty is equal to 10,000 of the pre-January 1, 1995 zlotys.

Market Rate (End of Period and Period Average):
National Bank midpoint rate.

International Liquidity:

Gold (National Valuation) (line 1and): Gold is valued at US$400 per ounce.

An accurate bank/nonbank distinction of foreign accounts of deposit money banks is not available, in particular because on the liabilities side certain debts originally owed to foreign bank creditors have been taken over by foreign governments in the context of debt rescheduling. Deposit money banks' liabilities do not include interest payments in arrears, defined to cover also those rescheduled but not booked.

Monetary Authorities:

Comprises the National Bank of Poland (NBP) only. Accounts classified as general government include positions with central and local government. *Reserve Money (line 14)* includes foreign currency deposits. *Nonreserve Liabilities to Banks (line 16b)* includes NBP bills, reverse repurchase agreements, and NBP bonds. † Beginning in 1981, data are based on an improved reporting system. † Beginning in December 1991, data are based on a new system of accounts and an improved reporting system.

Deposit Money Banks:

Comprises commercial banks. Accounts classified as general government include positions with central and local government. *Nonreserve Claims on Monetary Authorities (line 20c)* includes NBP bills, reverse repurchase agreements, and NBP bonds. † See note to section 10.

Monetary Survey:

† See notes to sections 10 and 20.

Interest Rates:

All data are from source A.

Discount Rate (End of Period):
† Beginning in 1989, basic rate at which the National Bank of Poland rediscounts bills of exchange to commercial banks. All data are compiled following the recommendations of the *1993 SNA.* Beginning in 1990, data are sourced from the Eurostat database.

Money Market Rate:
Weighted average rate on outstanding one-month deposits in the interbank market. † Beginning January 1992, weighted average rate on outstanding deposits of one month or less in the interbank market.

Treasury Bill Rate:
Weighted average yield on 13-week Treasury bills sold at auctions.

Deposit Rate:
Rate offered on deposits of under one year by commercial banks in domestic currency. † Beginning in 1991, lowest rate offered by main commercial banks on 12-month deposits in domestic currency. † Beginning in March 1993, weighted average rate offered by commercial banks on households' deposits in domestic currency.

Lending Rate:
Lowest rate charged by commercial banks on credits with lowest risk rates. † Beginning January 1995, weighted average rate charged by commercial banks on minimum risk loans.

Prices, Production, Labor:

With the exception of share prices, data are derived from source B.

Share Prices:

Monthly average of the Warsaw Stock Exchange Price Index 20 (WIG 20), which is calculated on the basis of share prices of the twenty largest companies ranked by their capitalization.

Producer Prices:

Laspeyres index, weights reference period: 2000 covers sold production of the manufacturing, mining and quarrying, electricity, gas and water supply sectors represented by approximately 19000 items.

Consumer Prices:

The index covers 1800 goods and services from 307 districts. Since 1990, the weight system has been based on a household budget survey. The weights are revised every year.

Wages: Average Earnings:

The index, weights reference period: 1992, covers the socialized sector and excludes apprentices and outworkers (employees who contract for outside work).

Industrial Production:

Data are sourced from the OECD database, weights reference period: 1995. The indices cover the whole industry.

Industrial Employment:

Weights reference period: 1995. † Before 1991, the data covered only the socialized sector. Since 1991, covers both private and socialized units where the number of employed persons exceeds five.

International Transactions:

Exports and Imports:

Data in zlotys since 1982 are not comparable to previous yearly data which are in foreign exchange zlotys. Index numbers are on weights reference period: 1990. Since 1991, data include import and export invoices as well as customs declarations. Monthly and quarterly data on prices are derived as a ratio of turnover in zlotys to turnover volume. Annual data are obtained on the basis of direct surveys of price changes.

Balance of Payments:

The annual and quarterly data for the balance of payments are not fully compatible. Quarterly data are compiled, primarily, from records of cash settlement, with only restricted detail and limited adjustment to bring the statistics closer to the recommendations for coverage and timing contained in the IMF's *Balance of Payments Manual (Manual)*. The annual data, however, are compiled incorporating additional data, available only annually, to improve compliance with the recommendations contained in the *Manual* for the coverage, timing, and classification of transactions in the balance of payments.

Government Finance:

Monthly and quarterly data are as reported by the Ministry of Finance and cover, through July 1999, the consolidated central government, namely, the state budget, the Labor Fund, the Pension and Disability Fund, and the Social Insurance Fund. From August 1999, data on consolidated core operations of central government do not cover the Social Insurance Fund. The fiscal year ends December 31.

National Accounts:

All data are compiled following the recommendations of the *1993 SNA*. Beginning in 1990, data are sourced from the Eurostat database.

GDP Volume Measures:

Beginning in 1994, data at previous year prices are used to construct *line 99bvpzf*. Beginning in 1990, data are sourced from the Eurostat database. Eurostat introduced chain-linked GDP volume measures to both annual and quarterly data with the release of the third quarter 2005 on November 30, 2005. Chain-linked GDP volume measures are expressed in the prices of the previous year and re-referenced to 1995.

Portugal   182

Data are denominated in Portuguese escudos prior to January 1999 and in euros from January 1999 onward. An irrevocably fixed factor for converting escudos to euros was established at 200.482 escudos per euro. In 2002, the escudo was retired from circulation and replaced by euro banknotes and coins. Beginning in January 1999, with the implementation of Stage Three of the European Economic and Monetary Union (EMU), an alternative euro area-wide definition of residency was introduced: All positions with residents of other euro area (EA) countries, including the European Central Bank (ECB), are classified as domestic positions, and foreign assets and foreign liabilities include only positions with non-euro area residents. Descriptions of the changes in the methodology and presentation of Portugal's accounts following the introduction of the euro are shown in the introduction to *IFS* and in the notes on the euro area page.

Date of Fund Membership:

March 29, 1961

Standard Sources:

B: Banco de Portugal, *Boletim Estatístico*
S: National Institute of Statistics, *Monthly Bulletin of Statistics*; Portuguese Industrial Association, *Studies on Applied Economics*
V: Eurostat

Exchange Rates:

Market Rate (End of Period and Period Average):

Central bank midpoint rate. Central Bank indicative midpoint rate. Prior to January 1999, the official indicative rates for the U.S. dollar and other currencies were determined by the Banco de Portugal on the basis of market exchange rates data received by 12:00 p.m. from the main foreign exchange market-makers. These rates were a reference for bank bid-offer rates, which were freely determined. In January 1999, the escudo became a participating currency within the Eurosystem, and the euro market rate became applicable to all transactions. In 2002, the escudo was retired from circulation and replaced by euro banknotes and coins. For additional information, refer to the section on exchange rates in the introduction to *IFS* and the notes for the euro area page. *Real Effective Exchange Rates:* Prior to January 1998, calculations are based on a consumer price index that excludes rents.

International Liquidity:

Beginning in January 1999, *Total Reserves minus Gold (line 1l.d)* is defined in accordance with the Eurosystem's statistical definition of international reserves. The international reserves of Portugal per the Eurosystem statistical definition at the start of the monetary union (January 1, 1999) in billions of U.S. dollars were as follows: *Total Reserves minus Gold,* $9,087; *Foreign Exchange,* $8,273; *SDRs,* $135; *Reserve Position in the Fund,* $621; *Other Reserve Assets,* $60; *Gold,* $5,774 *Gold (million fine troy ounces),* 20.089 ounces. *Foreign Exchange (line 1d.d):* Foreign exchange holdings of the Treasury Department of the government of Portugal are included in reserves *(line 1dbd).* Beginning in January 1988, *line 1d.d* excludes deposits made with the European Monetary Cooperation Fund (EMCF); the holdings of European currency units (ECUs) issued by the EMCF against those deposits (and similar deposits of gold) are included in *line 1d.d. Gold (Eurosystem Valuation) (line 1and):* Prior to January 1980, *Gold (Million Fine Troy Ounces) (line 1ad)* was valued at SDR 35 per ounce and converted into U.S. dollars at the U.S. dollar/SDR exchange rate **sa** on the *IFS* page for the United States. From January 1980 to December 1987, *line 1and* was revalued at 70 percent of the average price of gold in the London market during the second half of 1979. From January 1988 to November 1998, *line 1and* excluded deposits of gold. From January 1999 onward, *line 1and* is revalued at market prices at the end of each month. Gold swaps within *line 1and* are treated as repurchase transactions that do not affect the volume of gold held. Memorandum data are provided on *Non-Euro Claims on Euro Area Residents* and *Euro Claims on Non-Euro Area Residents,* which represent positions as of the last Friday in each month. For additional information, see the section on international liquidity in the introduction to *IFS* and on the euro area page.

Monetary Authorities:

Prior to January 1999, this section consolidated the Banco de Portugal and monetary authority functions undertaken by the central government. The contra-entry to Treasury-IMF accounts and coin issue of the Treasury Department of the government of Portugal (Treasury) was included in *Claims on General Government (line 12a).* Beginning in January 1999, consists of the Banco de Portugal, which is part of the Eurosystem, and coin issue of the Treasury, with the contra-entry for Treasury coin issue recorded in *Other Items (Net) (line 17r).* Beginning in 2002, *Currency Issued (line 14a)* includes euro banknotes and coins and, until December 2002, any unretired escudos. The recorded value of euro banknotes is based on a monthly allocation of total euro banknotes in circulation based on the Banco de Portugal's paid up share of the ECB's capital; it does not correspond to either the actual amount of euro banknotes placed in circulation by the Banco de Portugal which is shown in memo line *Currency Put into Circulation (line 14m),* nor the actual circulation of banknotes within the domestic territory. See section *Euro banknotes and coins* in the introduction to *IFS. Bonds and Money Market Instruments (line 16n.u)* include subordinated debt in the form of securities, other bonds, and money market paper. For a description of the accounts, refer to the section on monetary authorities in the introduction to *IFS.* Beginning with the data for end-November 2000, Monetary Authorities' *Foreign Assets (line 11), Foreign Liabilities (line 16c), Claims on Banking Institutions (line 12c.u),* and *Liabilities to Banking Institutions (line 14c.u)* are affected by a change from gross to net presentation of positions relating to the TARGET (Trans-European Automated Real-Time Gross Settlement Express Transfer) euro clearing system. (See *Recording of TARGET system positions* under *European Economic and Monetary Union (EMU)* in the introduction to *IFS.*) Beginning in 2002, *Claims on Banking Institutions (line 12e.u)* and *Liabilities to Banking Institutions (line 14c.u)* include "Intra-Eurosystem claims/liabilities related to banknote issue," which is a single net value repre-

senting the difference between the value of euro banknotes allocated to the Banco de Portugal according to the accounting scheme of the Eurosystem for issuing euro banknotes, and the value of euro banknotes put into circulation by the Banco de Portugal. See section *Euro banknotes and coins* in the introduction to *IFS.* Memo line *Net Claims on Other Members of the Eurosystem (line 12e.s)* equals gross claims on, less gross liabilities to, the ECB and other members of the Eurosystem. Comprises euro-denominated claims equivalent to the transfer of foreign currency reserves to the ECB, Intra-Eurosystem claims/liabilities related to banknote issue, net claims or liabilities within the TARGET clearing system, and other positions.

Banking Institutions:

† Beginning in 1976, the statistical reporting of data was changed (the "residency" criterion was adopted to identify the "external sector," instead of the "foreign currency" or "domestic currency" criterion formerly used; also the split between the general government and the rest of the economy was implemented). Prior to January 1999, comprised all banks except saving banks and mutual agricultural credit banks, which were classified as nonbank financial institutions. Beginning in January 1999, consists of all resident units classified as other monetary financial institutions (other MFIs), defined in accordance with *1995 ESA* standards. Deposit accounts of emigrants that can be accessed by residents are classified as deposits of residents in *Demand Deposits (line 24)* or *Other Deposits (line 25). Money Market Fund Shares (line 26m.u)* include shares/units issued by money market funds. *Bonds and Money Market Instruments (line 26n.u)* include subordinated debt in the form of securities, other bonds, and money market paper. Beginning in January 1999, this line includes the market values of options and traded financial derivatives.

Banking Survey (National Residency):

For a description of the methodology and accounts, refer to the section Banking Survey (National Residency) in the introduction to *IFS.*

Banking Survey (Euro Area-wide Residency):

For a description of the methodology and accounts, refer to the section Banking Survey (Euro Area-wide Residency) in the introduction to *IFS.*

Money (National Definitions):

Prior to January 1999, *M1* comprised currency held by the public and sight deposits in national currency. *M2* equaled *M1* plus other liquid assets held by the nonfinancial sector, including time deposits, savings deposits, foreign-currency deposits of residents, certificates of deposit, repurchase agreements, and bonds redeemable up to two years issued by banks. *L* equaled *M2* plus short-term securities issued by the general government and held by the nonfinancial resident sector. Any of these aggregates did not include deposits of autonomous regions, local governments, and nonbanking financial institutions. Beginning in January 1999, national monetary aggregate series are discontinued. Euro area aggregates are presented on the euro area page.

Interest Rates:

Banco de Portugal Rate (End of Period) (line 60):
† Prior to 1987, the end-of-year rate on first tranche rate at which the Banco de Portugal rediscounted the financial claims held by the banking system. From 1987 until May 1991, first tranche rate

at which the Banco de Portugal rediscounted the financial claims held by the banking system. From May 1991 to January 1999, the rate on regular provision of liquidity announced by the Banco de Portugal. For months when no announcements were made, the rate corresponded to the weighted average of various auction rates for repurchase agreements used for provision of liquidity by the Banco de Portugal. Data were those from the last reserve maintenance period for the month on which an announcement or auction took place. Beginning in January 1999, the central bank rates are discontinued. Refer to Eurosystem policy rate series on the euro area page.

Money Market Rate (line 60b):
† Prior to 1986, weighted average rate for interbank deposits up to three days. From 1986 to 1991, weighted average rate for interbank deposits up to five days. † Beginning in 1992, weighted monthly average rate for interbank overnight transactions.

Treasury Bill Rate (line 60c):
Weighted monthly average rate on three-month treasury bills in the primary market, excluding underwriting by the Banco de Portugal (when it was allowed). † Prior to 1986, average rate of all treasury bills issued.

Deposit Rate (line 60l):
† Prior to 1990, administrative minimum rate offered by deposit money banks on time deposits with maturities of 180 days to one year. Beginning in January 1990, weighted monthly average rate offered by deposit money banks on time deposits with maturities of 181 days to one year.

Deposit Rate (lines 60lhs, 60lhn, 60lcs, and 60lcn):
See notes in the Introduction to *IFS*.

Lending Rate (line 60p):
† Prior to January 1990, administrative maximum rate on 91- to 180-day loans. Beginning in January 1990, weighted monthly average rate charged by deposit money banks on 91- to 180-day loans and advances to nonfinancial private enterprises.

Lending Rate (lines 60phs, 60pns, 60phm, 60phn, 60pcs, and 60pcn):
See notes in the Introduction to *IFS*.

Government Bond Yield (line 61):
† Prior to July 1993, weighted monthly average of daily yields on floating rate bonds. Beginning in July 1993, simple monthly average of daily yields on floating rate bonds. For additional information, refer to the section on interest rates in the introduction to *IFS* and on the euro area page.

Prices, Production, Labor:

Share Prices (line 62):
Beginning January 1988, data relate to the Lisbon Stock Exchange Share Prices Index including all shares listed on the official market. Prior to this date, data relate to the Bank of Portugal Share Prices Index calculated on the basis of shares having an average monthly trading value of over Esc 30 million and a trading frequency index greater than 90 percent.

Producer Prices:
Source S. Weights Reference Period: 2000; Coverage: mining and quarrying, manufacturing, and electricity, gas, and water sectors; Number of Items in Basket: 500 products, 2,498 enterprises, and 12,335 prices; Basis for Calculation: weights used for the index are based on sales to the domestic market in the year of 1995.

Consumer Prices:
Source S. Weights Reference Period: 2002; Geographical Coverage: whole national territory; Number of Items in Basket: 812;

Basis for Calculation: weights are derived from a Household Budget Survey conducted in 2000.

Industrial Production:
Source S. Weights Reference Period: 2000; Sectoral Coverage: mining and quarrying, manufacturing, electricity, gas and water industrial sectors; Basis for Calculation: weights are based on value added and the reference year for the weight structure is 1995.

International Transactions:

All trade data are from source S.

Balance of Payments:
As only a net figure is available for transactions in *Other Goods, Services, and Income* for the fourth quarter of 1978, this is entered in the line for gross debits. In line with this treatment the gross debit for the full year 1978 is calculated as the sum of the gross debits for the first three quarters and the net debit for the final quarter, while the gross credit shows the sum of the gross credits for the first three quarters. *Merchandise: Exports f.o.b. (line 77aad)* include exports of nonmonetary gold in the amount of (in millions of U.S. dollars) 531 for 1977, 370 for 1978, 197 for 1983 second quarter, 440 for 1983 third quarter, and 37 for 1983 fourth quarter.

Government Finance:

Data on general government are derived from source V. The fiscal year ends December 31.

National Accounts:

Source S. GDP chain-linked volume measures are calculated based on the prices and weights of the previous year, using Laspeyres formula in general.

Qatar 453

Date of Fund Membership:
September 8, 1972

Standard Sources:
A: Qatar Central Bank, *Annual Report, Quarterly Statistical Bulletin*
S: Customs Department, *Yearly Bulletin of Imports and Exports*

Exchange Rates:

Official Rate: (End of Period and Period Average):
The Qatar Central Bank midpoint rate. The official rate shows limited flexibility against the U.S. dollar.

International Liquidity:

Gold (National Valuation) (line 1and) is obtained by converting the value in national currency terms, as reported in the country's standard sources, using the prevailing exchange rate, as given in *line **ae** or **we***.

Monetary Authorities:

Consolidates the Qatar Central Bank and monetary authority functions undertaken by the central government. The contra-entry to Treasury IMF accounts is included in *line 16d* or *line 12a*. † Beginning December 1993, revised data are based on the availability of additional classification detail.

Deposit Money Banks:

Comprises locally owned commercial banks (including Islamic banks) and branches of foreign banks. Revisions to capital accounts are based on the availability of additional classification detail.

Interest Rates:

All interest rate data are from source A. Quarterly and annual interest rate data are averages of end-of-period monthly data.

Central Bank Rate:

The Qatar Central Bank Policy Lending Rate, the key rate used to signal the monetary policy stance, is the rate announced by the Qatar Central Bank on overnight loans between it and local banks through the Qatar Money Market Rate Standing Facility.

Deposit Facility Rate:

The Qatar Central Bank Policy Deposit Rate is the rate announced by the Qatar Central Bank of overnight deposits between it and local banks through the Qatar Money Market Rate Standing Facility.

Repo Rate:

Repurchase Rate for Qatar Central Bank repurchase operations conducted in domestic government securities of two-week or one-month maturity.

Money Market Rate:

Interbank interest rates in Qatari Riyal, weighted average of rates on overnight balances.

Savings Rate:

Weighted average of rates on one year time deposits.

Deposit Rate:

† Beginning mid-December 1993, statutory base rates on deposits of different maturities were unified, and data refer to the uniform base rate on local currency time deposits. Beginning July 2004, the deposit rate is the weighted average of rates on demand deposits.

Lending Rate:

Weighted average of rates on loans up to one year.

Prices and Production:

Consumer Prices:

Data are from source A, weight reference period: 2001. † Prior to 1986, the index is derived from a household expenditures survey held in DOHA between April 1982 and April 1983 among 500 households from various nationalities and income groups. The index includes 156 items and is computed by the Central Statistical Organization, weight reference period: 1981. † Prior to 1981, data refer to the consumer price index computed by the Ministry of Economy and Prices, base 1979.

Crude Petroleum Production:

Index is calculated from annual data through 1983 from source A, and monthly data through June 1984 supplied directly by the Monetary Agency (now the Central Bank). The data covered onshore and offshore production as well as production of the Al Bunduq field. Data for July 1984 onwards are based on production quantities as reported in the *Oil Market Intelligence.*

International Transactions:

Imports, c.i.f.:

Annual data are from source A, and monthly data are supplied directly by the Central Bank. Defense imports are excluded.

National Accounts:

Source A.

Romania   968

Date of Fund Membership:
December 15, 1972

Standard Sources:

S: *Anuarul Statistic al României* (Statistical Yearbook). Data are also supplied directly by the national authorities.

Exchange Rates:

On July 1, 2005, the new currency leu (RON), equal to 10,000 units of the old currency leu (ROL) was introduced.
Market Rate:
In February 1991 an interbank rate was implemented, which was applicable to an increasing number of commercial and individual transactions. Effective November 1991, the *principal rate* and *secondary rate* were eliminated, and all foreign exchange transactions are effected through the free market.

International Liquidity:

Gold (National Valuation): Gold is valued using the average cost method and is revalued monthly at market price. Prior to 2005, gold was valued using a fixed domestic price, revalued at the end of the year only. *Foreign Exchange:* Comprises gross balances held by the National Bank of Romania. For periods prior to November 1999, comprises gross balances held by the National Bank of Romania and the Romanian Foreign Trade Bank. The latter's holdings include a large part of Romania's foreign exchange reserves held for balance of payments purposes, but they also comprise working balances as well.

Monetary Authorities:

Claims on Government (line 12a) reflects the stock of treasury securities acquired by the National Bank of Romania (NBR) from the secondary market. *Government Deposits (line 16d)* include the current accounts of the general government (in RON and in foreign currency). *Transit Accounts (line 14x)* reflects collection items, clearing balances, and transit accounts payable to/receivable from clients. *Reserve money (line 14)* includes: vault cash, currency outside banks, required reserves (in RON and in foreign currencies) deposited with NBR, deposit-taking by the NBR, and certificates of deposit issued by the NBR. Reserve money, as compiled by the NBR, is defined as the sum of the following: vault cash, currency outside banks, and required reserves in RON deposited with the central bank. † Starting in 1990, data reflect significant classification changes resulting from the reform of the banking system, by which commercial operations of the NBR were transferred to the newly created Romanian Commercial Bank, and the former specialized banks were authorized to engage in any type of regular banking activity. † Beginning in 1993, substantial revisions were made to the classification of accounts and the compilation of data. † Beginning in December 2001, data are based on a new reporting system which provides an improved classification and sectorization of the accounts.

Banking Institutions:

The coverage of *Government Deposits (line 26d)* include medium- and long-term deposits intended to finance special and other extrabudgetary funds, and deposits representing state Treasury investments. *Transit Accounts (line 24x)* reflect collection items, clearing balances, and transit accounts payable to and receivable from depositors. *Demand Deposits (line 24)* include current accounts of households and demand deposits of nonfinancial enterprises (both public and private), insurance companies, and other nonbank nongovernment entities. *Time and Savings Deposits (line 25)* include households savings, time deposits of nonfinancial enterprises (both public and private), insurance companies, other nonbank nongovernment entities, as well as restricted deposits and certificates of deposit; all of the above instruments are denominated in national currency. *Claims on Nonbank Institutions (line 22g)* include credits to insurance companies, households, and other. † Beginning in December 1996, commercial banks' claims on the nonbank sector were reclassified into claims on nonfinancial public enterprises, private sector, and nonbank financial institutions. Since May 2003, credit cooperatives were reclassified as part of deposit money banks. † Beginning in December 2001, data are based on a new reporting system which provides an improved classification and sectorization of the accounts.

Banking Survey:

† See note on monetary authorities and deposit money banks.

Money (National Definitions):

*M1** comprises currency outside depository corporations and demand deposits in national currency of resident non-bank non-central government sectors.

*M2** comprises M1 and demand deposits in foreign currencies, and time and saving deposits in national and foreign currencies of resident non-bank non-central government sectors. Deposits at banks in liquidation are also included in *M2**.

Interest Rates:

Bank Rate (End of Period):
Structural Credit Rate, which is the predominant rate on central bank loans to commercial banks. Since February 2002, reference rate is calculated as a weighted average of the interest rates on NBR's deposit-taking and reverse-repo operations in the month prior to that of the announcement.

Treasury Bill Rate:
Rate on 91-day Treasury bills.

Prices, Production, Labor:

Producer Prices:
Source S. Weights Reference Period: 2000; Coverage: covers almost totally the mining, quarrying and manufacturing sectors as well as the energy sector; Number of Items in Basket: 16200; Basis for Calculation: the weights are valued by destinations for all aggregation levels have been determined from the Annual Statistical (structural) Survey in enterprises in 2000.

Consumer Prices:
Source S. Weights Reference Period: December 2004; Geographical Coverage: covering all private households; Number of Items in the Basket: about 1,500 locally collected items; Basis for Calculation: the weights are obtained from Household Budget Survey. Starting in 1999 the weights are updated annually using HBS data from year t–2. So, in 2005 the base year is 2003.

Wages, Average Earnings:
Source S. Geographical Coverage: entire country; Basis for Calculation: monthly sample survey enterprises and public authorities.

Industrial Production:
Source S. Weights Reference Period: 2000; Geographical Coverage: cover the manufacturing, mining, electricity, gas and water supply industries; Number of Items in the Basket: data are collected monthly from 7,000 enterprises.

International Transactions:

Source S. Based on the trade statistics compiled by the National Institute of Statistics (NIS) from customs documents and makes adjustments regarding timing coverage and valuation in respect of BOP purposes.

Balance of Payments:
Since April 2003, Romania's Balance of Payments has been expressed and disseminated in national publications in euro. While transactions denominated in other currencies are converted in euro at the rate prevailing at the time of the transactions, for data deriving from balance sheets of reporters, the exchange rate at the end of the reporting period is used. To the extent possible for those data derived from balance sheets, foreign exchange valuation changes are excluded from the Balance of Payments (Reserve Assets, Medium- and Long-Term Loans—Liabilities etc.). BOP and IIP data reported to the IMF to be published in the *IFSY* are converted from euro in U.S. dollars using the average quarterly EUR/USD rate.

Government Finance:

Quarterly data cover the general government. The fiscal year ends December 31.

National Accounts:

Source S. As indicated by the country, quarterly data were first produced and disseminated covering the quarters for 1997. The data are compiled in accordance with the methodology of the *1995 ESA* and the *1993 SNA*.

Russia   922

Date of Fund Membership:
June 1, 1992

Standard Sources:
B: Central Bank of Russia, *Monthly Bulletin*
S: State Statistical Office, *Monthly Bulletin*

Exchange Rates:

The post-January 1, 1998 ruble is equal to 1,000 of the pre-January 1, 1998 rubles.

Official Rate: (End of Period and Period Average):
Central Bank of Russia rate based on the Moscow Interbank Currency Exchange (MICEX) rate.

International Liquidity:

Gold (National Valuation) (line 1and) is valued at current quotations fixed by the Bank of Russia. † Prior to December 2005, gold was valued at US$300 per fine troy ounce.

Monetary Authorities:

Consolidates the accounts of the Central Bank of Russia and monetary authority functions conducted by the central government. All data include both ruble- and foreign-currency denominated accounts. Data before June 1995 were compiled by the IMF using basic accounting data and other information provided by the authorities prior to establishment of regular data reporting. The contra-entries to government holdings of foreign assets and the Treasury-IMF accounts are included in *lines 16d* and *12a*, respectively. Foreign assets and foreign liabilities comprise claims and liabilities in rubles and other currencies. General government comprises central and local government units and their extrabudgetary funds.

Deposit Money Banks:

Comprises commercial banks (including branches of foreign banks), the Savings Bank, and Vneshekonombank. All data include both ruble- and foreign-currency denominated accounts. Data before June 1995 were compiled by the IMF using basic accounting data and other information provided by the authorities prior to establishment of regular data reporting. General government comprises central and local government units and their extrabudgetary funds.

Money (National Definitions):

Base Money comprises currency in circulation, bankers' required reserves and correspondent accounts with the Central Bank of the Russian Federation (CBR), CBR bonds held by banking institutions, CBR obligations on reverse repurchase agreements with banking institutions, and reserve funds for foreign exchange operations deposited with the CBR. Currency in circulation refers to notes and coins issued by the CBR less the amount held in CBR vaults.

Reserve Money comprises currency in circulation, bankers' required reserves and correspondent accounts with the CBR, CBR bonds held by banking institutions, CBR obligations on reverse repurchase agreements with banking institutions, reserve funds for foreign exchange operations deposited with the CBR, and demand deposits of nonfinancial corporations in national currency with the CBR. Currency in circulation refers to notes and coins issued by the CBR less the amount held in CBR vaults.

Money comprises currency in circulation and demand deposits in national currency of nonmonetary financial institutions, public nonfinancial corporations, and private sector with the CBR and banking institutions. Currency in circulation refers to notes and coins issued by the CBR less the amount held in CBR vaults and by banking institutions.

M2 comprises currency in circulation and demand, time, and savings deposits in national currency public nonfinancial corporations and private sector. Currency in circulation refers to notes and coins in circulation outside the banking system.

Money supply comprises money plus quasi-money. Quasi-money refers to time and savings deposits in national currency and foreign currency deposits of nonmonetary financial institutions, public nonfinancial corporations, and private sector with the CBR and banking institutions.

Interest Rates:

All interest rate data are from source B.

Refinancing Rate (End of Period):
Rate at which the Central Bank of Russia lends to commercial banks.

Money Market Rate:
Weighted average rate on one-day loans in national currency of the Moscow interbank market. The rate is weighted by loan amounts.

Treasury Bill Rate:
Weighted average rate on government short-term obligations ("GKO") with maturities of up to 90 days. Beginning in April 1997, the rate is calculated on the basis of taxable "GKO" with remaining maturity of up to 90 days.

Deposit Rate:
Prevailing rate for one-month time deposits in denominations of more than Rub 300,000. † Beginning in January 1997, weighted average rate offered by commercial banks on time deposits of households in national currency with remaining maturity of up to one year. The rate is weighted by deposit amounts.

Lending Rate:
Weighted average rate on various regional commercial banks' loans of up to one year in national currency to legal entities (companies and organizations). † Beginning in January 1997, weighted average rate charged by commercial banks on loans of up to one year in national currency to legal entities (companies and organizations). The rate is weighted by loan amounts.

Prices, Production, Labor:

Source S.

Producer Prices:
Laspeyres index using weights of the penultimate year (e.g., for 2003 weights of 2001 are used) covering industrial enterprises sample.

Consumer Prices:
Laspeyres index using weights of the previous year, including 412 goods and services since 2003 in a sample circle of towns.

International Transactions:

Source S. *Exports (line 70..d)* and *Imports (line 71..d)* include adjustments for barter trade and for shuttle trade but exclude humanitarian aid and trade in fish and other marine products by Russian vessels operating overseas. † Data prior to 1994 exclude trade with the Baltic countries and the other countries of the former Soviet Union. Beginning in January 1994, data for imports c.i.f. are obtained by conversion from reported imports f.o.b. data using 10 percent c.i.f./f.o.b. factor.

International Investment Position:
Prior to 2000, data covered the banking sector, including credit institutions, Vnesheconombank (excluding assets and liabilities managed by Vnesheconombank as the agent of the government of Russia) and the Central Bank of Russia. Data on the government reserve assets are also included as part of reserve assets of Russia. Beginning in 2000, data include all sectors: general government, Central Bank of Russia and the banking sector, non-financial enterprises and households.

Government Finance:

Data are as reported by the Federal Treasury and cover operations of the budgetary central (federal) government. † From January 2002, budget accounts balances in foreign currency are included under net domestic financing. The fiscal year ends December 31.

National Accounts:

Source S. The expenditure components are compiled from data on 1) retail trade turnover and data on services that are adjusted for undercoverage, 2) budget documents, 3) annual surveys of capital formation of enterprises, and 4) balance of payments. The data on inventories are obtained from financial surveys and are adjusted to exclude holding gains at the total economy level. *Gross Domestic Product, Production Based (line 99bp)* is compiled from the production approach using data on gross output and intermediate consumption from production surveys, adjusted to exclude holding gains in inventories. The statistical discrepancy *(line 99bs)* represents the difference between the GDP from the production approach *(line 99bp)* and the sum of the expenditure components shown. As indicated by the country, data are in accordance with the *1993 SNA*.

Rwanda   714

Date of Fund Membership:
September 30, 1963

Standard Sources:
B: National Bank of Rwanda, *Quarterly Bulletin*
S: General Office of Statistics, *Bulletin of Statistics*

Exchange Rates:
Market Rate (End of Period and Period Average):
On March 6, 1995, Rwanda adopted a market-determined exchange rate system. Before then, the official rate was pegged to the SDR.

Monetary Authorities:
Comprises the National Bank of Rwanda only.

Deposit Money Banks:
Comprises the commercial banks. Excludes demand deposits with the Centre des Chèques Postaux (Postal System). Excludes the Caisse d'Epargne (Savings Bank), liquidated in 2000. † Beginning in 1981, the classification of external and government accounts has been improved.

Monetary Survey:
† See note on deposit money banks.

Other Banking Institutions:
Comprises the Development Bank and the Mortgage Loan Fund. Excludes the Union des Banques Populaires (Cooperative Bank) and Saving and Credit Cooperatives.

Interest Rates:
Discount Rate (End of Period):
Discount rate offered by the National Bank of Rwanda.

Deposit Rate:
Rate offered by deposit money banks on three-month deposits.

Prices:
Consumer Prices:
Source B. Weights Reference Period: 2003; Geographical Coverage: all urban areas; Number of Items in the Basket: 201and 457 items, respectively, for urban and rural areas; Basis for Calculation: their weights were based on national household budget-consumption surveys.

International Transactions:
Source B.

Government Finance:
From 1992 onwards, data are as reported by source B and cover consolidated central government. The fiscal year ends December 31.

National Accounts:
Source B. As indicated by the country, the data are compiled in the framework of the *1968 SNA*.

St. Kitts and Nevis   361

Date of Fund Membership:
August 15, 1984

Standard Sources:
A: Eastern Caribbean Central Bank, *Annual Report and Statement of Accounts*
B: Eastern Caribbean Central Bank, *Economic and Financial Review*
C: Eastern Caribbean Central Bank, *National Accounts Statistics*
N: Eastern Caribbean Central Bank, *Commercial Banking Statistics*
S: Statistical Office, *Annual Digest of Statistics*

Exchange Rates:
Official Rate: (End of Period and Period Average):
Rates are based on a fixed relationship to the U.S. dollar.

Monetary Authorities:
The accounts are compiled from data contained in the balance sheet of the Eastern Caribbean Central Bank (ECCB). The monetary authorities' accounts for St. Kitts and Nevis represent country attributable data for ECCB claims on and liabilities to the government of St. Kitts and Nevis and its resident deposit money banks, and estimates of St. Kitts and Nevis' notional share of the ECCB's foreign assets and liabilities and currency in circulation within the region. † Beginning in December 2001, data are based on a new reporting system which provides improved classification and sectorization of the accounts.

Banking Institutions:
Comprises commercial banks. † Beginning in December 2001, data are based on a new reporting system which provides improved classification and sectorization of the accounts.

Banking Survey:
† See notes on monetary authorities and banking institutions.

Money (National Definitions):
M1 comprises notes and coins held by the public and demand deposits in national currency of the private sector in commercial banks.
M2 comprises *M1* plus time, savings, and foreign currency deposits of the private sector in commercial banks.

Interest Rates:
Discount Rate (End of Period):
Rate charged by the ECCB on loans of last resort to commercial banks.

Money Market Rate:
Fixed rate on loans between commercial banks. The rate includes the commission charged by the ECCB as agent. † Beginning in October 2001, weighted average rate on loans between commercial banks. The rate is weighted by loan amounts.

Treasury Bill Rate:
Rate on three-month treasury bills.

Savings Rate:
Maximum rate offered by commercial banks on savings deposits in national currency. † Beginning in June 2003, weighted average rate offered by commercial banks on savings deposits in national currency. The rate is weighted by deposit amounts.

Savings Rate (Foreign Currency):
Weighted average rate offered by commercial banks on savings deposits in foreign currency. The rate is weighted by deposit amounts.

Deposit Rate:
Maximum rate offered by deposit money banks on three-month time deposits. † Beginning in March 1991, weighted average rate offered by commercial banks on deposits in national currency. The rate is weighted by deposit amounts.

Deposit Rate (Foreign Currency):
Weighted average rate offered by commercial banks on deposits in foreign currency. The rate is weighted by deposit amounts.

Lending Rate:
Maximum rate charged by commercial banks on prime loans. † Beginning in March 1991, weighted average rate charged by commercial banks on loans in national currency. The rate is weighted by loan amounts.

Lending Rate (Foreign Currency):
Weighted average rate charged by commercial banks on loans in foreign currency. The rate is weighted by loan amounts.

Prices:

Consumer Prices:
Source S. Weights Reference Period: 2001; Geographical Coverage: Basseterre and Sandy Point; Number of Items in Basket: 329; Basis for Calculation: weights are derived from the 1998 Household Income and Expenditure Survey.

International Transactions:
Source S.

Government Finance:
Data cover budgetary central government. The fiscal year ends December 31.

National Accounts:
Source C. There are no data for Increase/Decrease in Stocks. As indicated by the country, data have been revised following the implementation of the *1993 SNA*.

St. Lucia   362

Date of Fund Membership:
November 15, 1979

Standard Sources:
A: Eastern Caribbean Central Bank, *Annual Report and Statement of Accounts*

B: Eastern Caribbean Central Bank, *Economic and Financial Review*
C: Eastern Caribbean Central Bank, *National Accounts Statistics*
N: Eastern Caribbean Central Bank, *Commercial Banking Statistics*
S: Statistical Office, Government of St. Lucia, *Annual Statistical Digest*

Exchange Rates:

Official Rate: (End of Period and Period Average):
Rates are based on a fixed relationship to the U.S. dollar.
The weighting scheme used to calculate indices of nominal and real effective exchange rates (*lines* **nec** and **rec**) is based on data for tourism receipts and on data for aggregate bilateral non-oil trade flow for 1980–82.

Monetary Authorities:
The accounts are compiled from data contained in the balance sheet of the Eastern Caribbean Central Bank (ECCB). The monetary authorities' accounts for St. Lucia represent country attributable data for ECCB claims on and liabilities to the government of St. Lucia and its resident deposit money banks, and estimates of St. Lucia's notional share of the ECCB's foreign assets and liabilities and currency in circulation within the region. † Beginning in December 2001, data are based on a new reporting system which provides improved classification and sectorization of the accounts.

Banking Institutions:
Comprises commercial banks. † Beginning in December 2001, data are based on a new reporting system which provides improved classification and sectorization of the accounts.

Banking Survey:
† See notes on monetary authorities and banking institutions.

Money (National Definitions):
M1 comprises notes and coins held by the public and demand deposits in national currency of the private sector in commercial banks.
M2 comprises *M1* plus time, savings, and foreign currency deposits of the private sector in commercial banks.

Interest Rates:

Discount Rate (End of Period):
Rate charged by the ECCB on loans of last resort to commercial banks.

Money Market Rate:
Fixed rate on loans between commercial banks. The rate includes the commission charged by the ECCB as agent. † Beginning in October 2001, weighted average rate on loans between commercial banks. The rate is weighted by loan amounts.

Treasury Bill Rate:
Rate on three-month treasury bills. † Beginning in January 2004, rate on one-year treasury bills.

Savings Rate:
Maximum rate offered by commercial banks on savings deposits in national currency. † Beginning in June 2003, weighted average rate offered by commercial banks on savings deposits in national currency. The rate is weighted by deposit amounts.

Deposit Rate:
Maximum rate offered by deposit money banks on three-month time deposits. † Beginning in March 1991, weighted average rate

offered by commercial banks on deposits in national currency. The rate is weighted by deposit amounts.

Deposit Rate (Foreign Currency):
Weighted average rate offered by commercial banks on deposits in foreign currency. The rate is weighted by deposit amounts.

Lending Rate:
Maximum rate charged by commercial banks on prime loans. † Beginning in March 1991, weighted average rate charged by commercial banks on loans in national currency. The rate is weighted by loan amounts.

Lending Rate (Foreign Currency):
Weighted average rate charged by commercial banks on loans in foreign currency. The rate is weighted by loan amounts.

Prices:

Consumer Prices:
Source S. Weights Reference Period: April 1984; Geographical Coverage: Castries Administrative Area; Number of Items in Basket: 186; Basis for Calculation: weights are derived from the September–November 1982 Household Budget Survey for the Castries Administrative Area.

International Transactions:

All trade data are from source S. *Exports* include re-exports.

National Accounts:

Data are as reported by national authorities. Data differ from earlier estimates published in the *UN Monthly Bulletin of Statistics*.

St. Vincent & Grenadines   364

Date of Fund Membership:
December 28, 1979

Standard Sources:

A: Eastern Caribbean Central Bank, *Annual Report and Statement of Accounts*
B: Eastern Caribbean Central Bank, *Economic and Financial Review*
C: Eastern Caribbean Central Bank, *National Accounts Statistics*
N: Eastern Caribbean Central Bank, *Commercial Banking Statistics*
S: Statistical Unit, St. Vincent and the Grenadines, *Digest of Statistics*

Exchange Rates:

Official Rate: (End of Period and Period Average):
Rates are based on a fixed relationship to the U.S. dollar.
The weighting scheme used to calculate indices of nominal and real effective exchange rates (*lines* **nec** and **rec**) is based on data for tourism receipts and on data for aggregate bilateral non-oil trade flow for 1980–82.

Monetary Authorities:

The accounts are compiled from data contained in the balance sheet of the Eastern Caribbean Central Bank (ECCB). The monetary authorities' accounts for St. Vincent and the Grenadines represent country attributable data for ECCB claims on and liabilities to the government of St. Vincent and the Grenadines and its resident deposit money banks, and estimates of St. Vincent and the Grenadines' notional share of the ECCB's foreign assets and liabilities and currency in circulation within the region. † Beginning in December 2001, data are based on a new reporting system which provides improved classification and sectorization of the accounts.

Banking Institutions:

Comprises commercial banks. † Beginning in December 2001, data are based on a new reporting system which provides improved classification and sectorization of the accounts.

Banking Survey:

† See notes on monetary authorities and banking institutions.

Money (National Definitions):

M1 comprises notes and coins held by the public and demand deposits in national currency of the private sector in commercial banks.
M2 comprises *M1* plus time, savings, and foreign currency deposits of the private sector in commercial banks.

Interest Rates:

Discount Rate (End of Period):
Rate charged by the ECCB on loans of last resort to commercial banks.

Money Market Rate:
Fixed rate on loans between commercial banks. The rate includes the commission charged by the ECCB as agent. † Beginning in October 2001, weighted average rate on loans between commercial banks. The rate is weighted by loan amounts.

Treasury Bill Rate:
Rate on three-month treasury bills.

Savings Rate:
Maximum rate offered by commercial banks on savings deposits in national currency. † Beginning in June 2003, weighted average rate offered by commercial banks on savings deposits in national currency. The rate is weighted by deposit amounts.

Deposit Rate:
Maximum rate offered by deposit money banks on three-month time deposits. † Beginning in March 1991, weighted average rate offered by commercial banks on deposits in national currency. The rate is weighted by deposit amounts.

Deposit Rate (Foreign Currency):
Weighted average rate offered by commercial banks on deposits in foreign currency. The rate is weighted by deposit amounts.

Lending Rate:
Maximum rate charged by commercial banks on prime loans. † Beginning in March 1991, weighted average rate charged by commercial banks on loans in national currency. The rate is weighted by loan amounts.

Lending Rate (Foreign Currency):
Weighted average rate charged by commercial banks on loans in foreign currency. The rate is weighted by loan amounts.

Prices:

Consumer Prices:
Source S. Weights Reference Period: January 2001; Geographical Coverage: whole national territory; Number of Items in Basket: 256; Basis for Calculation: weights are based on the 1996–1997 Household Budget and Expenditure Survey.

International Transactions:

All trade data are from source S.

Government Finance:

Annual data are as reported for the *Government Finance Statistics Yearbook (GFSY)* and cover budgetary central government. The fiscal year ends December 31.

National Accounts:

Data are as reported by national authorities. Data differ from earlier estimates published in the *UN Monthly Bulletin of Statistics.* As indicated by the country, data have been revised following the implementation of the *1993 SNA.*

Samoa   862

Date of Fund Membership:
December 28, 1971

Standard Sources:
B: Central Bank of Samoa, *Bulletin*
S: Department of Statistics, *Quarterly Statistical Bulletin*

Exchange Rates:

Official Rate: (End of Period and Period Average):
The exchange rate is operated as a fixed peg arrangement against a composite of currencies. Central bank midpoint rate.

International Liquidity:
Foreign Exchange (line 1d.d) comprises holdings of the Bank of Samoa, the government, and the commercial banks.

Monetary Authorities:
Consolidates the Central Bank of Samoa and monetary authority functions undertaken by the central government. The contra-entry to government foreign assets and Treasury IMF accounts, SDR holdings, and coin issues is included in *line 16d.*

Deposit Money Banks:
Comprises commercial banks.

Other Banking Institutions:
Comprises Post Office Savings deposits.

Interest Rates:

Deposit Rate:
Rate offered by commercial banks on three- to six-month deposits.

Lending Rate:
Maximum rate charged by commercial banks.

Government Bond Yield:
Yield to maturity on seven-year government bonds.

Prices:

Consumer Prices:
Source S index, Weights reference period March 2004.

International Transactions:
† Prior to January 1977, data are based on customs clearances; diplomatic imports are included in total imports. After January 1977, data refer to actual imports landed in Samoa. All value data on trade are from source S. † October tala 1985 re-export value

data include the sale proceeds of an aircraft by the government for 2.54 million tala (equivalent to US $1.1 million). † Imports for August 1986 include the engine for a damaged aircraft valued at 3,676,019 tala. Effective May 2005, figures for imports, petroleum and petrol products have been revised since 2000 to exclude freight and insurance.

San Marino   135

Data are denominated in Italian lire prior to January 1999 as the currency of San Marino was the Italian lire under a monetary union agreement between Italy and San Marino. With the authority of the Council of the European Union (EU), Italy was empowered to negotiate agreements with San Marino to replace the monetary union agreement between itself and San Marino, making the euro the official currency of San Marino, providing access to payment systems and covering other monetary conditions. Pursuant to the new monetary agreement, San Marino adopted the euro and all data are denominated in euros from January 1999 onward. An irrevocably fixed factor for converting lire to euros was established at 1,936.27 lire per euro. In 2002, Italian lire banknotes and Sammarinese lire coins were retired from circulation and replaced by euro banknotes and coins. San Marino is obligated to apply EU rules regarding banknotes and coins.

Date of Fund Membership:
September 23, 1992

Standard Source:
B: Office of Economic Planning and Data Processing Center and Statistics, *Statistical Bulletin*

Exchange Rates:
Market Rate (End of Period and Period Average):
Refer to the section on exchange rates in the notes for the pages for Italy and for the euro area.

Monetary Authorities:
Comprises Banca Centrale della Repubblica di San Marino (Central Bank of the Republic of San Marino).

Deposit Money Banks:
Comprises private commercial and savings banks. Commercial banks are not subject to a legal reserve requirement, but instead to a liquidity requirement, under which banks must hold at least 10 percent of their deposits, less 10 times their capital, in the form of cash or bonds issued or guaranteed by the Sammarinese government, the Italian government, and/or international organizations. The reported data cover all of the asset management activities of banks but do not include custodial securities activities.

Monetary Survey:
Deposit Money (line 34) comprises Demand Deposits in Monetary Authorities (line 14d), and Demand Deposits in Deposit Money Banks (line 24).

Interest Rates:

Deposit Rate:
Data pertains to average rates weighted by the outstanding level of all time deposits.

Lending Rate:
Data pertains to average lending rates weighted by the outstanding level of all loans of more than 10,000 euros.

Prices and Production:

Consumer Prices:
Source S index, weights reference period: December 2002. Basket composed by 727 products.

Tourist Arrivals:
Source B.

National Accounts:

Source B. As indicated by the country, data are in accordance with the *ESA 95*.

São Tomé & Príncipe   716

Date of Fund Membership:
September 30, 1977

Standard Source:
B: Central Bank of São Tomé and Príncipe, *Monetary and Balance of Payments Statistics*

Exchange Rates:

Market Rate (End of Period and Period Average):
Between July 22, 1987 and December 2, 1994, São Tomé and Príncipe's currency, the dobra, was pegged to a basket of currencies of the country's seven major trading partners. Beginning in December 1994, the official exchange rate is determined daily as a weighted average of exchange rates in commercial banks, exchange bureaus, and the parallel market. The weights are based on the U.S. dollar value of the previous day's transactions reported by commercial banks and exchange bureaus and an estimate of the U.S. dollar value of transactions in the parallel market.

International Liquidity:
Foreign Exchange (line 1d.d) is the U.S. dollar value of deposits in foreign banks and holdings of foreign currency of the Central Bank of São Tomé and Príncipe.

Monetary Authorities:
Comprises the Central Bank of São Tomé and Príncipe only.

Banking Institutions:
Comprises commercial banks, namely, the International Bank of São Tomé and Príncipe, the Banco Comercial do Equador, and the Caixa Nacional de Poupança e Crédito.

Interest Rates:

Discount Rate (End of Period):
Rate charged by the Central Bank of São Tomé and Príncipe on loans to commercial banks.

Deposit Rate:
Rate offered by commercial banks on 91- to 180-day time deposits. † Beginning in August 2000, average rate offered by commercial banks on one-year time deposits.

Lending Rate:
Rate charged by commercial banks on 180-day loans. † Beginning in August 2000, average rate charged by commercial banks on one-year loans.

Saudi Arabia   456

Calendar:
The Islamic lunar year (Hijra year) is about eleven days shorter than the Gregorian year. The Gregorian calendar equivalent of the lunar year changes annually. Hence, after three years the difference amounts to one lunar month which must be skipped in the Gregorian calendar. The data in the monetary sections are compiled on the basis of the lunar calendar, and the end of lunar month data are allocated to the approximate equivalent of the Gregorian dates.

Date of Fund Membership:
August 26, 1957

Standard Sources:
A: Saudi Arabian Monetary Agency (SAMA), *Annual Report*
B: Saudi Arabian Monetary Agency, *Statistical Summary*

Exchange Rates:
Official Rate: (End of Period and Period Average):
The exchange rate of the Saudi Riyal is fixed at SR 3.75 per U.S. dollar.

International Liquidity:
† Beginning April 1978, *line 1d.d* excludes the foreign exchange cover against the note issue which together with *Monetary Authorities: Other Assets* are included in *line 11*. As of March 1978, this foreign exchange cover amounted to about US$5.3 billion. The authorities revised their methodology for classifying foreign assets to include the foreign exchange cover against the note issue, and provided revised data on *Foreign Exchange (line 1d.d)* for 1996 onward.
Beginning in March 1975, *Gold (National Valuation) (line 1and)* is equal to *line 1ad* valued at SDR 35 per fine troy ounce and converted into U.S. dollars at the dollar/SDR rate *line sa* on the *IFS* page for the United States.

Monetary Authorities:
Comprises the Saudi Arabian Monetary Agency (SAMA) only.

Deposit Money Banks:
† Beginning in 1983, data are based on improved classification. † Beginning December 1992, claims on public enterprises *(line 22c)* include claims on financial and nonfinancial public enterprises, and may include a small amount of loans and advances to central government. Demand deposits *(line 24)*, quasi-monetary deposits *(line 25a)*, and foreign currency deposits *(line 25b)* may include some central government deposits.

Monetary Survey:
In the monetary survey (see Introduction for the standard method of calculation), *line 35* equals *Quasi-Monetary* and *Foreign Currency Deposits (lines 25a and 25b)*, respectively. † See note on deposit money banks.

Other Banking Institutions:
† Prior to 1976, data refer to the Saudi Agricultural Bank. Thereafter, consolidates the Saudi Agricultural Bank, the Saudi Industrial Development Fund, the Public Investment Fund, the Real Estate Development Fund, and the Saudi Credit Bank. Foreign accounts relate solely to the Public Investment Fund.

Interest Rates:

Deposit Rate:
Simple average of daily interest rates on three-month deposits.

Prices, Production, Labor:

Share Prices:
End-of-period Domestic Share Index, base 1985, covering agriculture, cement, electricity, other industry, banking, and other services.

Wholesale Prices:
Laspeyres index, weights reference period 1988, covering 160 items, weighted by the import value of each item.

Consumer Prices:
Source A index covering all-income population of 16 cities, weights reference period 1999.

Crude Petroleum Production:
Calculated from production quantities reported in the *Oil Market Intelligence.*

International Transactions:

Exports:
Data are from source B. The volume index of petroleum exports is calculated as an average of crude and refined petroleum volumes with 1985 export values as weights. If actual data is uncurrent, the index is projected forward using total petroleum production. The crude petroleum price index *(line 76aad)* is calculated by *IFS* as the weighted average of official state sales prices of Light, Medium, and Heavy grade crudes. The weights are the average of estimated supply figures published in *Petroleum Intelligence Weekly (PIW)* from Dec. 6, 1982 through June 24, 1985.

Imports, c.i.f.:
Source B data. Defense imports are excluded.

National Accounts:

Data are published for Gregorian years.

Senegal   722

Date of Fund Membership:

August 31, 1962

Standard Source:

B: Banque Centrale des Etats de l'Afrique de l'Ouest (Central Bank of West African States), *Notes d'information et Statistiques (Informative Notes and Statistics).*
Senegal is a member of the West African Economic and Monetary Union, together with Benin, Burkina Faso, Côte d'Ivoire, Guinea-Bissau, Mali, Niger, and Togo. The Union, which was established in 1962, has a common central bank, the Central Bank of West African States (BCEAO), with headquarters in Dakar, and national branches in the member states. Mali and Guinea-Bissau joined the Union on June 1, 1984 and May 2, 1997, respectively.

Exchange Rates:

Official Rate: (End of Period and Period Average):
Prior to January 1999, the official rate was pegged to the French franc. On January 12, 1994, the CFA franc was devalued to CFAF 100 per French franc from CFAF 50 at which it had been fixed

since 1948. From January 1, 1999, the CFAF is pegged to the euro at a rate of CFA franc 655.957 per euro.

International Liquidity:

Gold is revalued on a quarterly basis at the rate communicated by the BCEAO, which corresponds to the lowest average fixing in the London market.

Monetary Authorities:

Comprises the national branch of the BCEAO only. The amount of currency outside banks is estimated by subtracting from the amount of CFA franc notes issued by Senegal the estimated amounts of Senegal's currency in the cash held by the banks of all member countries of the Union.

Deposit Money Banks:

Comprises commercial banks and development banks, and includes certain banking operations of the Treasury and the Post Office. The Treasury accepts customs duty bills (reported separately in *line 22d.i*). Through its many branches, the Postal Checking System acts as the main depository for the private sector in the interior of Senegal. *Claims on the Private Sector (line 22d)* include doubtful and litigious debts. † Beginning in 1979, *Central Government Deposits (line 26d)* include the deposits of the public establishments of an administrative or social nature (EPAS) and exclude those of the savings bank; *Demand and Time Deposits (lines 24 and 25)* include deposits of the savings bank and exclude deposits of EPAS; and *Claims on Private Sector (line 22d)* exclude claims on other financial institutions.

Monetary Survey:

The data reported agree with source B aggregates, as given in the table on the position of the monetary institutions, except for *line 31n,* for which source B treats long-term foreign liabilities and SDR allocations as a foreign liability, whereas *IFS* reports the former separately and includes the latter in *line 37r.* Moreover, valuation differences exist as a result of the *IFS* calculations of reserve position in the Fund and the SDR holdings, both components of *line 11,* based on Fund record. † Beginning in 1979, *Claims on Other Financial Institutions (line 32f)* includes claims of deposit money banks on other financial institutions; see deposit money bank notes for explanation of other break symbols.

Other Banking Institutions:

Liquid Liabilities (line 55l): † See notes on deposit money banks and monetary survey.

Interest Rates:

Bank Rate (End of Period):
Rate on repurchase agreements between the BCEAO and the banks. † Prior to October 1, 1993 data refer to basic discount rate offered by the BCEAO.

Money Market Rate:
Rate paid on overnight interbank advances.

Deposit Rate:
Rate offered by banks on time deposits of CFAF 500,000–2,000,000 for under six months.

Prices and Production:

Consumer Prices:
Source B. Weights Reference Period: 1996; Geographical Coverage: Dakar metropolitan area; Number of Items in Basket: 345;

Basis for Calculation: The weights are derived from a household expenditure survey of the Capital City (EDMC) in February–May 1996.

Industrial Production:
Source B index, weights reference period 1999, including food production, chemicals, mining, textiles, and energy.

International Transactions:

All trade data are from source B.

Balance of Payments:
The data for recent years are preliminary.

National Accounts:

Source S. As indicated by the country, the national accounts have been revised according to the *1993 SNA* beginning in 1996.

Serbia, Republic of   942

Date of Fund Membership:
December 14, 1992

Standard Sources:
B: National Bank of Serbia (NBS), *Statistical Bulletin* (monthly)
S: Statistical Office of the Republic of Serbia

Exchange Rates:
Official Rate: (End of Period and Period Average):
From October 2000, the dinar exchange rate is set within the managed float regime. The dinar exchange rate against the euro is formed at the fixing session organized every business day by the commercial banks in Serbia and the National Bank of Serbia. The mid-point between the buy and sell rate formed at the session is the official dinar/euro mid-point exchange rate. The official exchange rates for the dinar against other currencies are computed using the dinar/euro rate and the cross rates for the euro against other currencies as provided by the Reuters service. Prior to October 2000, data are based on the fixed exchange rate of the dinar against the deutsche mark.

International Liquidity:
Gold (National Valuation) (line *1and*) is valued at the average price in three international markets prevailing at the end of the previous year.

Monetary Authorities:
Consists of the National Bank of Serbia. Data for central government include positions of the federal government of the former State Union of Serbia and Montenegro. † From December 2003 data are based on an improved data collection, classification, and reporting system.

Banking Institutions:
Comprises commercial banks; banks in liquidation are excluded. Data for central government include positions of the federal government of the former State Union of Serbia and Montenegro. Claims on Central Government (line *22a*) include claims on government for frozen foreign-currency deposits. Restricted deposits include frozen foreign-currency deposits of the households; in July 2002 the liability for these deposits has been assumed by the central government. † From December 2003 data are based on an improved data collection, classification, and reporting system.

Money (National Definitions):
M1 comprises currency in circulation and dinar-denominated demand deposits.
M2 comprises M1 and dinar-denominated time deposits.
M3 comprises M2 and foreign currency deposits.

Interest Rates:
Bank Rate (End of Period):
Rate on the 14-day NBS repurchase agreement. † During the period November 2000-January 2005 data refer to the average rate on the NBS bills weighted by volume.

Money Market Rate:
Rate on the three-month interbank deposits (three-months Belgrade Interbank Offer Rate (BELIBOR)).

Treasury Bill Rate:
Average yield on three-month Treasury bills.

Deposit Rate:
Average rate on the dinar-denominated household and enterprise time and savings deposits weighted by outstanding amount.

Lending Rate:
Average rate on new dinar-denominated loans to households and enterprises weighted by volume.

Prices and Production:
Share Price Index:
BELEX–15 index of the Belgrade Stock Exchange.

Consumer Price Index:
Source S. Laspeyres retail price index; weights reference period: previous year.

Industrial Production:
Source S. Base Year: 1993, 1998, and 2003; Sectoral Coverage: mining and quarrying, manufacturing industry, electricity, gas and water supply. Weights are derived as value added shares.
International Transactions:
Source S. Data exclude transactions with Montenegro.

National Accounts:
Source S. Series are based on the *1993 SNA*, as indicated by the country. As the production-based GDP *(line 99bp)* is the official measure of GDP, the statistical discrepancy *(line 99bs)* represents the difference between the production-based GDP and the sum of the expenditure components shown.

Population:
Source S.

Seychelles   718

Date of Fund Membership:
June 30, 1977

Standard Sources:
B: Central Bank of Seychelles, *Quarterly Review*
S: Ministry of Administration and Manpower, Management and Information Systems Division, *Statistical Abstract*

Exchange Rates:

Official Rate: (End of Period and Period Average):
Prior to May 13, 1996, rates were based on a fixed relationship to the SDR. Beginning May 13, 1996, the Seychelles rupee is pegged to the Seychelles Trade and Tourism weighted basket. Beginning in September 2003, the Seychelles rupee is pegged to the U.S. dollar.

Monetary Authorities:

Comprises the Central Bank of Seychelles (CBS) only.

Banking Institutions:

Comprises commercial banks. † Beginning in December 2001, data are based on a new reporting system which provides improved classification and sectorization of the accounts.

Banking Survey:

† See notes on monetary authorities and banking institutions.

Nonbank Financial Institutions:

Comprises the Development Bank of Seychelles. † Beginning in December 2001, data are based on a new reporting system which provides improved classification and sectorization of the accounts.

Money (National Definitions):

M1 comprises currency held by the public and demand deposits of the private sector, public entities, and other financial institutions with commercial banks.
M2 comprises M1 and time, savings, and foreign currency deposits of the private sector, public entities, and other financial institutions with commercial banks.
M2(p) comprises M2 and pipeline deposits of the private sector, public entities, and other financial institutions with commercial banks. Pipeline deposits are the rupee equivalent of foreign exchange requests by clients.

Interest Rates:

Discount Rate (End of Period):
Bank rate on export finance loans. † Beginning in January 1989, rate charged by of the CBS on temporary advances to commercial banks for liquidity purposes using treasury bills as collateral. The rate for the advances against treasury bills is the simple average of the outstanding treasury bills plus five points whilst the rate on treasury bonds and government stocks is the same as that payable on the securities against which the advance is made.

Treasury Bill Rate:
Rate on 91-day treasury bills. † Beginning in January 1989, average rate on 91- and 365-day treasury bills.

Savings Rate:
Weighted average rate offered by commercial banks on savings deposits in national and foreign currency. The rate is weighted by deposit amounts.

Deposit Rate:
Weighted average rate offered by commercial banks on three-month time deposits in national and foreign currency. The rate is weighted by deposit amounts.

Lending Rate:
Weighted average rate charged by commercial banks on loans in national and foreign currency. The rate is weighted by loan amounts.

Government Bond Yield:
Average yield on one-, two-, three-, five-, seven-, and ten-year government bonds.

Prices and Labor:

Consumer Prices:
Source S index for households of all income levels, weights reference period 2001.

International Transactions:

All trade value and volume data are from source B.

Government Finance:

Data are as reported by source B and cover budgetary central government. The fiscal year ends December 31.

National Accounts:

Source S.

Sierra Leone 724

Date of Fund Membership:
September 10, 1962

Standard Source:
B: Bank of Sierra Leone, *Economic Review*

Exchange Rates:

Market Rate (End of Period and Period Average):
The central bank determines the exchange rate every Friday, based on the weighted-average rate of the commercial bank transactions in that week for customs valuations and official transactions.

Monetary Authorities:

Comprises the Bank of Sierra Leone (BSL) only. † Beginning in March 1996, data are based on an improved sectorization of the accounts.

Deposit Money Banks:

Comprises commercial banks. † See note on monetary authorities.

Monetary Survey:

† See note on monetary authorities.

Money (National Definitions):

Reserve Money comprises currency in circulation, commercial banks' correspondent and other accounts, and transferable deposits in national currency of rural banks, other financial corporations, public nonfinancial corporations, and private sector with the BSL. Currency in circulation refers to notes and coins issued by the BSL.
M1 comprises currency in circulation and transferable deposits. Currency in circulation refers to notes and coins issued by the BSL less the amount held by commercial banks. Transferable deposits refer to current account deposits in national currency of rural banks, other financial corporations, public nonfinancial corporations, and private sector with the BSL and commercial banks.

M2 comprises M1, fixed term and savings deposits in national currency and foreign currency deposits of other financial corporations, public nonfinancial corporations, and private sector with the BSL and commercial banks.

M2* comprises M1 and fixed term and savings deposits in national currency of other financial corporations, public nonfinancial corporations, and private sector with the BSL and commercial banks.

Interest Rates:

All interest rate data are from source B.

Treasury Bill Rate:
Coupon rate on new issues of treasury bills.

Deposit Rate:
Rate offered by commercial banks on one- to three-month time deposits.

Lending Rate:
Minimum rate charged by commercial banks on overdrafts.

Prices:

Consumer Prices:
Source B. Weights Reference Period: 1992; Geographical Coverage: 4 CPIs are produced in Sierra Leone, one each for four urban towns namely Freetown, Bo, Kenema and Makeni. The Freetown CPI is the one used officially; Number of Items in the Basket: 251 items, 150 of which are nonfood and 101 food items; Basis for Calculation: the CPI basket of goods for the four indices was derived from the 1989/90 Household Expenditure Survey Report.

International Transactions:

All trade data are from source B.

Government Finance:

Data cover the consolidated central government † Prior to 1998, the fiscal year ends June 30. The fiscal year ends December 31.

National Accounts:

Source B. As indicated by the country, concepts and definitions are in accordance with the *1993 SNA*.

Singapore   576

Date of Fund Membership:
August 3, 1966

Standard Sources:
B: Monetary Authority, *Quarterly Bulletin, Monthly Statistical Release, Monthly Statistical Bulletin*
N: Department of Statistics, *Yearbook of Statistics*
S: Department of Statistics, *Monthly Digest of Statistics*

Exchange Rates:

Market Rate (End of Period and Period Average):
Midpoint interbank rate at noon. Real effective exchange rates, based on consumer price indices for the Singapore dollar, reflect imperfect underlying movements in competitiveness.

International Liquidity:
Data for *line 1d.d* include gold holdings. *Line 1d.d* also includes government foreign exchange holdings.

Asian currency units (ACUs), which began operations in 1968, deal extensively with nonresidents but perform only limited domestic operations, primarily with deposit money banks. Their assets and liabilities with the monetary system are regarded as part of the foreign sector in data reported in sections 10, 20, and 30. Hence, *lines 7a.d* and *7b.d* include commercial bank accounts with ACUs. *Lines 7k.d.* and *7m.d* relate to the foreign assets and foreign liabilities, respectively, of ACUs and exclude both their accounts with the monetary system and inter-ACU accounts.

Monetary Authorities:
Consolidates the Monetary Authority of Singapore and monetary authority functions undertaken by the central government. The contra-entry to Treasury IMF accounts and government foreign assets is included in *line 16d*.

Currency Outside Deposit Money Banks (line 14a) excludes Singapore's estimated share of the currency issued by Malaya/British Borneo Currency Board and commemorative coins issued by the Board of Commissioners of Currency, Singapore.

Deposit Money Banks:
Comprises commercial banks and discount houses. † Beginning in April 1971, data are based on an improved sectorization of resident and nonresident accounts. Beginning in November 1998, includes Post Office savings deposits, previously classified within the other banking institutions.

Monetary Survey:
† See note on deposit money banks.

Other Banking Institutions:
Comprises finance companies and Post Office savings deposits. Beginning in November 1998, excludes Post Office savings deposits; they were reclassified within the deposit money banks.

Nonbank Financial Institutions:
Comprises life insurance offices.

Money (National Definitions):
M1 comprises currency in circulation (excludes commemorative, numismatic, and bullion coins issued by the Monetary Authority of Singapore and cash held by commercial banks and non-bank financial institutions) and demand deposits of the private sector in commercial banks in national and foreign currency.

M2 comprises M1 plus fixed, savings, and other deposits of the private sector in commercial banks in national and foreign currency and negotiable certificates of deposits in national currency.

M3 comprises M2 plus net deposits with non-bank financial institutions. Net deposits of non-bank financial institutions excludes these institutions' deposits with banks. Beginning in November 1998, with the acquisition of the Post Office Savings Bank by DBS Bank, Ltd., Post Office Savings Bank's data has been incorporated as part of the banking system in M1 and M2, and not as a non-bank financial institution in M3.

Interest Rates:
All interest rate data are from source B.

Money Market Rate:
The rates are the modes of the three-month interbank rates quoted by money brokers. Monthly data refer to the rates on the last Friday (or working day closest to the last Friday) of the month.

Treasury Bill Rate:
Rate refers to the closing offer prices quoted by the Singapore Government Securities (SGS) primary dealers. Beginning in January 2001, bid rate quoted by the SGS primary dealers. Monthly rates refer to the rates on the last Friday, or working day closest to the last Friday, of the month.

Savings Rate:
Average rate offered by the ten leading commercial banks on savings deposits.

Deposit Rate:
Average rate offered by the ten leading commercial banks on three-month time deposits.

Lending Rate:
Average minimum rate charged by the ten leading commercial banks.

Prices, Production, Labor:

All data on prices and production are from source S.

Share Prices:
Straits Times index, base August 28, 1998. The index covers common stocks, although not all components stocks are 100 percent represented and is weighted by market capitalization. The monthly index refers to the last closing quotation of the month.

Wholesale Prices:
Data refer to all items of the domestic supply price index (DSPI), which covers goods manufactured locally (excluding exports) and imported goods retained for domestic use, weights reference period 2000. The weight for each commodity item in the DSPI is proportional to the value of its total supply or availability in the domestic market in 2000.

Consumer Prices:
Source S. Weights Reference Period: October 2002–September 2003; Geographical Coverage: The central 90 percent of all households; Number of Items in Basket: 790; Basis for Calculation: The weights are derived from the results of the Household Expenditure Survey conducted between October 2002 and September 2003, and updated every five years.

Manufacturing Production:
Source S. Weights Reference Period: 2003; Sectoral Coverage: manufacturing sector; Basis for Calculation: the weights used in the index are based on the 2002 Census of Manufacturing Activities.

Employment:
Data refer to registered unemployment.

International Transactions:

All trade data are from source S.
Export and *Imports Volume* indices are calculated by *IFS* from export and import values and export and import price indices. The export volume index prior to 1978 and import volume index prior to 1975 were calculated by the Department of Statistics. *Exports* and *Imports (Direct Prices)* (source S) are based on sample surveys of exporters and importers; for exports, and imports, weights reference period 2000.

Government Finance:

Data are derived from unpublished reports and reported by Source B. Data cover the budgetary central government. The fiscal year ends March 31.

National Accounts:

Data are as reported in source N. *Lines 99a* and *99b* include a statistical discrepancy. As indicated by the country, data follow the implementation of the *1993 SNA*.

Slovak Republic 936

Date of Fund Membership:
January 1, 1993

Standard Sources:
B: National Bank of Slovakia (NBS), *Financial Statistics* (monthly)
S: Statistical Office of the Slovak Republic, *Monitor of the Economy of the Slovak Republic*

Exchange Rates:
Official Rate: (End of Period and Period Average):
National Bank of Slovakia's midpoint rate.

International Liquidity:
Gold (National Valuation) (line 1and) is valued at market prices. †
Prior to January 2002, *(line 1and)* is valued at US$42.22 per ounce.
Monetary Authorities: Other Liabilities (line 4..d) relate mainly to obligations to the Czech Republic in nonconvertible currencies.

Monetary Authorities:
Comprises the National Bank of Slovakia. † Beginning in August 2003, data are compiled in accordance with the European Central Bank's framework for monetary statistics using national residency approach.

Banking Institutions:
Beginning in January 2004, comprises all resident units classified as other monetary financial institutions (other MFIs) in accordance with *1995 ESA* standards. Prior to January 2004, comprises only the commercial banks including branches of foreign banks. General government comprises central government, local governments, and National Property Fund. † Beginning in January 1997, data on claims are based on improved sectorization of accounts. † Beginning in January 2003, data are based on an improved classification of accounts due to availability of more detailed information. † Prior to January 2003, data on *line 22a* refer to *Claims on General Government*, and data on *line 26d* refer to *General Government Deposits*. † Beginning in August 2003, data are compiled in accordance with the European Central Bank's framework for monetary statistics using national residency approach.

Banking Survey:
See notes on banking institutions. † Prior to January 2003, data on *line 32an* refer to *Claims on General Government (Net)*, comprising net claims on central government, inclusive of National Property Fund, and net claims on local governments. † Beginning in August 2003, data are compiled in accordance with the European Central Bank's framework for monetary statistics using national residency approach.

Interest Rates:
Bank Rate (End of Period):
National Bank of Slovakia's main policy rate. Starting in May 2001, the data refer to the rate on two-week repurchase agreements. Prior to May 2001, the data refer to the discount rate.

Money Market Rate:
Rate on one-month interbank deposits.

Deposit Rate:
Beginning in January 2005, weighted average interest rate offered on short-term (up to one year) deposits of non-financial corporations (S.11). From January 1996 to December 2004, weighted average interest rate offered on short-term (up to one year) deposits of the private sector during the reference period. During 1993–95, weighted average rate offered by commercial banks on all accepted deposits.

Lending Rate:
Beginning in January 2005, weighted average interest rate on short-term loans drawn by non-financial corporations (S.11). From January 1995 to December 2004, weighted average interest rate on short-term loans granted to the private corporate sector during the reference period. During 1993–94, weighted average rate charged by commercial banks on all outstanding credits.

Government Bond Yield:
Monthly average of yields on 10-year government bonds.

Prices, Production, Labor:
Data are from source S.

Producer Prices:
Laspeyres index, weights reference period: 2000, covers mining and quarrying, manufacturing, electricity, gas, steam, and water supply. Approximately 5800 prices are observed. The weights are based on the structure of industrial sales receipts in 2000.

Consumer Prices:
Source S. Weights Reference Period: 2003; Geographical Coverage: 90% of all households in the Slovak Republic; Number of Items in Basket: 707; Basis for Calculation: the weights are derived from a 2000 Household Budget Survey, adjusted for the results of the 2000 national accounts data.

Wages:
Data refer to average monthly wages in koruny for enterprises with 25 and more employees.

Industrial Production:
Source S. Weights Reference Period: 2000; Sectoral Coverage: mining and quarrying, manufacturing, electricity, gas and water supply sectors; Basis for Calculation: the weights are based on the annual data on value added.

Industrial Employment:
Index of number of workers employed in all enterprises, reported in thousands.

International Transactions:
Data are from source S.

Government Finance:
Data on general government are derived from source V. † Prior to 2004, to the extent possible, existing subannual *IFS* data were converted to the main aggregates that are presented in the *GFSM 2001* Statement of Sources and Uses of Cash (see the Introduction of the monthly *IFS* publication for details). Beginning in 2004, annual data are as reported in the *Government Finance Statistics Yearbook (GFSY)* and cover the consolidated central government. The fiscal year ends December 31.

National Accounts:
Concepts and definitions are in accordance with the *ESA 95*, as indicated by the country. Beginning in 1993, data are sourced from the Eurostat database.

Slovenia 961

Data are denominated in Slovenian tolars prior to January 2007 and in euros from January 2007 onward. An irrevocably fixed factor for converting tolars to euros was established at 239.640 tolars per euro. With Slovenia's entry into Stage Three of the European Economic and Monetary Union (EMU) in January 2007, a euro area-wide definition of residency was introduced: all positions with residents of other euro area (EA) countries, including the European Central Bank (ECB), are classified as domestic positions, and foreign assets and foreign liabilities include only positions with non-EA residents. In 2007, the tolar was retired from circulation and replaced by euro banknotes and coins. Descriptions of the methodology and presentation of Slovenia's accounts following the introduction of the euro are discussed under *European Economic and Monetary Union* in the Introduction to *IFS* and in the notes on the euro area page.

Date of Fund Membership:
December 14, 1992

Standard Sources:
A: Ministry of Finance, *Bulletin of Government Finance Statistics*
B: Bank of Slovenia, *Monthly Bulletin*
S: Statistical Office of the Republic of Slovenia, *Monthly Bulletin*

Exchange Rates:

Market Rate (End of Period and Period Average):
In January 2007, the Slovenian tolar became a participating currency within the Eurosystem, and the euro market rate became applicable to all transactions. In 2007, the tolar was retired from circulation and replaced by euro banknotes and coins. For additional information, refer to the section on exchange rates in the *Introduction* to *IFS* and the notes on the euro area page. Prior to January 2007, midpoint of the official tolar/U.S. dollar exchange rate, which was computed using the official tolar/Euro exchange rate and the market Euro/U.S. dollar exchange rate. The official tolar/Euro exchange rate was calculated daily by the Bank of Slovenia using a moving average of the daily market rates on the foreign exchange market over the preceding 60 days' interval.

International Liquidity:
Beginning in January 2007, *Total Reserves minus Gold (line 1l.d)* and *Foreign Exchange (line.1d.d)* are defined in accordance with the Eurosystem's statistical definition of international reserves. *Gold (Eurosystem Valuation) (line 1and)* is revalued monthly at market prices. In the period June 2001 to December 2006, gold was revalued monthly using end-of-month London gold market price; in the period 1999 to May 2001, gold was revalued quarterly; in the period 1995 through 1999, gold was revalued annually (at end-December); prior to 1995, gold was revalued semi-annually (at end-June and end-December). End-period London gold market price was used as the basis for revaluations. Memorandum data are provided on *Non-Euro Claims on Euro Area Residents* and *Euro Claims on Non-Euro Area Residents*. For additional information, refer to the section on international liquidity in the introduction to *IFS* and the notes on the euro area page.

Monetary Authorities:
Comprises the Bank of Slovenia, which beginning in January 2007 is part of the Eurosystem, and coin issue by the Treasury. Prior to January 2007, the contra-entry to Treasury coin issue was included in *Claims on General Government (line 12a)*. From

January 2007 onward, the contra-entry is included in *Other Items (Net) (line 17r)*. *Bonds and Money Market Instruments (line 16n.u)* include subordinated debt in the form of securities, other bonds, and money market paper. Beginning in January 2007, *Currency Issued (line 14a)* comprises euro banknotes and coins and unretired tolars. The recorded value of euro banknotes is based on a monthly allocation of total euro banknotes in circulation based on the Bank of Slovenia's paid up share of the ECB's capital; it does not correspond to either the actual amount of euro banknotes placed in circulation by the Bank of Slovenia which is shown in memo line *Currency Put into Circulation (line 14m)*, nor the actual circulation of banknotes within the domestic territory. See section *Euro banknotes and coins* in the introduction to *IFS*. Beginning in 2007, *Claims on Banking Institutions (line 12e.u)* and *Liabilities to Banking Institutions (line 14c.u)* include "Intra-Eurosystem claims/liabilities related to banknote issue," which is a single net value representing the difference between the value of euro banknotes allocated to the Bank of Slovenia according to the accounting scheme of the Eurosystem for issuing euro banknotes, and the value of euro banknotes put into circulation by the Bank of Slovenia (see section *Euro banknotes and coins* in the introduction to *IFS*. Memo line *Net Claims on Eurosystem (line 12e.s)* equals gross claims on, less gross liabilities to, the ECB and other members of the Eurosystem; it comprises euro-denominated claims equivalent to the transfer of foreign currency reserves to the ECB, Intra-Eurosystem claims/liabilities related to banknote issue, and net claims or liabilities within the TARGET(Trans-European Automated Real-Time Gross Settlement Express Transfer) clearing system, and other positions (see *Recording of TARGET system positions* under *European Economic and Monetary Union* in the introduction to *IFS*). † Beginning in January 2004, data are compiled in accordance with the European Central Bank's framework for monetary statistics; however, presentation of data during January 2004–December 2006 is based on the national residency approach only.

Banking Institutions:

Prior to January 2007 comprises commercial banks. Beginning in January 2007, comprises all resident units classified as other monetary financial institutions (other MFIs), in accordance with *1995 ESA* standards, including money market funds. † Beginning in January 2004, data are compiled in accordance with the European Central Bank's framework for monetary statistics; however, presentation of data during January 2004–December 2006 is based on the national residency approach only.

Banking Survey (National Residency):

See notes on monetary authorities and banking institutions. For a description of the methodology and accounts, refer to the section Banking Survey (Based on National Residency) – Euro Area under *European Economic and Monetary Union* in the Introduction to *IFS*.

Banking Survey (Euro Area-wide Residency):

For a description of the methodology and accounts, refer to the section Banking Survey (Based on Euro Area-wide Residency) under *European Economic and Monetary Union* in the Introduction to *IFS*.

Money (National Definitions):

Beginning in January 2007, national monetary aggregates series were discontinued. The euro area aggregates are presented on the euro area page.

M1 comprises currency in circulation and overnight deposits of non-central government, non-MFI resident sectors with resident MFIs. Currency in circulation is equal to currency issued by the central bank less currency in the central bank vault. † Prior to January 2005, *M1* comprises currency in circulation and demand deposits, including demand deposits of central government, enterprises and non-monetary financial institutions with the Bank of Slovenia.

M2 is equal to *M1* plus deposits with agreed maturity up to two years and deposits redeemable at notice up to three months of non-central government, non-MFI resident sectors with resident MFIs. † Prior to January 2005, *M2* is equal to *M1* plus securities in tolar, central government time deposit at Bank of Slovenia, and tolar time deposits of non-central government non-bank residents with the commercial banks and Bank of Slovenia.

M3 is equal to *M2* plus repurchase agreements contracted with other (non-MFI) resident sectors, money market fund shares/units, and debt securities with maturity up to two years issued to non-central government, non-MFI resident sectors. † Prior to January 2005, *M3* is equal to *M2* plus foreign currency deposits at commercial banks and foreign currency securities issued by commerical banks and held by non-banks.

Interest Rates:

Central Bank Rate (End of Period):
Prior to January 2007, rate on one-day lombard loans by Bank of Slovenia to banks, with the Bank of Slovenia bills or government securities used as collateral. In January 2007, the central bank rate was discontinued. See Eurosystem policy rate series on the euro area page.

Money Market Rate:
Prior to January 2007, annualized 30-day period average interest rate in the Slovenian interbank market on the unsecured Slovenian tolar deposits with the maturity up to 30 days, weighted by turnover. Beginning in January 2007, data refer to EURIBOR1M rate.

Treasury Bill Rate:
Rate on three-month treasury bills.

Deposit Rate (line 60l):
Prior to January 2007, period average rate on 31- to 90-day time deposits at commercial banks, weighted by stocks. Beginning in January 2007, rate on new deposits redeemable at notice with maturity up to three months calculated in accordance with the ECB's methodology.

Deposit Rate (lines 60lhs, 60lhn, 60lcs, and 60lcn):
See notes in the Introduction to *IFS*.

Lending Rate (line 60p):
Prior to January 2007, period average rate on short-term commercial bank loans weighted by stocks. Beginning in January 2007, rate on new loans of up to EUR 1 million to non-financial corporations with maturity up to one year calculated in accordance with the ECB's methodology.

Lending Rate (lines 60phs, 60pns, 60phm, 60phn, 60pcs, and 60pcn):
See notes in the Introduction to *IFS*.

Government Bond Yield:
Period average yield on government bonds with a 10-year residual maturity.

Prices, Production, Labor:

Data are from source S.

Share Prices:
Data refer to the Slovenian Stock Exchange Index (SBI 20) of the Ljubljana Stock Exchange.

Producer Prices:
Source S. Weights Reference Period: 2000; Coverage: manufacturing, mining and quarrying, electricity supply, and forestry sectors; Number of Items in Basket: 2000 price quotations; Basis for Calculation: weights are adjusted to the price reference period. Starting in 2001 the weights are revised annually.

Consumer Prices:
Source S. Weights Reference Period: 2005; Geographical Coverage: whole national territory; Number of Items in Basket: 648; Basis for Calculation: 2006 weights are based on the three-year average of expenditure from surveys in 2002, 2003, and 2004 recalculated (indexed) to the prices of December 2005, which is also the index base month.

Wages:
Data refer to average monthly gross wages in tolars. Data are obtained from a census conducted every month of all establishments in the public sector and of those in the private sector with three or more employees. As of January, 2005, establishments in the private sector with one or two employees are also taken into account.

Industrial Production:
Source B. Weights Reference Period: 2005; Sectoral Coverage: mining and quarrying, manufacturing and electrical energy, gas, steam and hot water sector of the Statistical Classification of Economic Activities (NACE Rev 1.1). Group 40.3 (Steam and hot water supply) and Division 41 (Collection, purification and distribution of water) are excluded; Basis for Calculation: weights are based on value added in the year 2000 and are corrected every year with the annual growth in the IPI.

Employment:
"Employed persons" are defined as persons aged 15 years and over who during the last week prior to the interview undertook any work for payment (in cash or kind), or family gain. The data on employment are obtained from the Labor Force Survey, a sample survey covering the whole territory of Slovenia, excluding inmates of institutions.

International Transactions:

All trade data are from source S. Prior to 1992, excludes exports and imports for processing and trade with former Yugoslav republics.

Government Finance:

Monthly data are derived from source A and cover budgetary central government. Prior to 2006, annual data are as reported for the *Government Finance Statistics Yearbook (GFSY)*. Beginning in 2006, data are reported in the *GFSM 2001* analytical framework. The fiscal year ends December 31.

National Accounts:

Estimates are derived by the Statistical Office. Data are compiled according to the *ESA 95*. Beginning in 1990, data are sourced from the Eurostat database. Eurostat introduced chain-linked GDP volume measures to both annual and quarterly data. Chain-linked GDP volume measures are expressed in the prices of the previous year and re-referenced to 1995.

Date of Fund Membership:
September 22, 1978

Standard Sources:
A: Central Bank of Solomon Islands, *Annual Report*
N: Ministry of Finance, *Annual Accounts*
S: Statistical Office, Ministry of Finance, *Statistical Bulletin*

Exchange Rates:

Official Rate: (End of Period and Period Average):
Central bank midpoint rate. The exchange rate of the Solomon Islands dollar is determined on the basis of a trade-weighted basket of the currencies of Solomon Islands' four major trading partners.

International Liquidity:

Foreign Exchange (line 1d.d) comprises holdings of the Central Bank and the central government.

Monetary Authorities:

Consolidates the Central Bank of the Solomon Islands (CBSI) and monetary functions undertaken by the central government. The contra-entries to Treasury IMF accounts and the central government's foreign assets are included in *line 12a* and *line 16d*, respectively. *Foreign Liabilities (line 16c)* includes the proceeds of Euro loans raised by the central government on behalf of the CBSI, pending passage of legislation to enable the CBSI to incur such liabilities on its own behalf.

Deposit Money Banks:

Comprises trading and savings banks.

Other Banking Institutions:

Comprises the Development Bank of Solomon Islands and Investment Corporation of Solomon Islands (formerly the Government Shareholding Agency). † Beginning in March 1987, included credit unions.

Banking Survey:

† See note on other banking institutions.

Nonbank Financial Institutions:

Comprises the National Provident Fund.

Interest Rates:

Treasury Bill Rate:
End-month yield on three-month treasury bills.

Deposit Rate:
Maximum rate offered by banks on 90-day deposits of up to SI$25,000.

Lending Rate:
Minimum rate charged by banks on advances and overdrafts.

Government Bond Yield:
Coupon rate offered on long-term development bonds issued by the Government.

Prices, Production, Labor:

Consumer Prices:
Source S retail price index, weights reference period: fourth quarter 1992, covering lower- and middle-income households in Ho-

niara. The index includes 166 items. † Prior to 1990, weights reference period: fourth quarter 1984.
Copra Production and *Fish Catch:*
Indices calculated from source S data, expressed in metric tons.

South Africa 199

Date of Fund Membership:
December 27, 1945

Standard Sources:
B: Reserve Bank, *Quarterly Bulletin*
C: Department of Customs and Excise, *Monthly Abstract of Trade Statistics*
S: Central Statistical Service, *Quarterly Bulletin of Statistics*

Exchange Rates:
Principal Rate (End of Period and Period Average):
A dual exchange rate system, consisting of a commercial rand rate and a financial rand rate, was in effect until February 7, 1983 and again between September 1985 and March 1995. The exchange rate of the commercial rand was determined in a managed floating system and applied to all current transactions. The financial rand applied to the local sale or redemption proceeds of South African securities and other investments in South Africa owned by nonresidents (other than former residents of South Africa), capital remittances by emigrants and immigrants, and approved outward capital transfers by residents. The exchange rate of the financial rand was determined freely by the supply and demand for financial rand balances. Beginning March 13, 1995, the government abolished the financial rand system and repealed all exchange control restrictions on the free convertibility and repatriation of the local sale proceeds on investments in South Africa owned by nonresidents. Thus, beginning March 13, 1995, a unitary exchange rate that applies to both current and capital transactions between residents and nonresidents is in effect. Data prior to that date refer to the commercial rand rate.

International Liquidity:
Data for *line 1d.d* include small foreign exchange holdings by the government.
Gold (National Valuation) (line 1and) is obtained by converting the value in national currency terms, as reported in the country's standard sources, using the prevailing exchange rate, as given in *line* **ag** or *line* **wg**. Data on gold in national sources revalue gold at the end of each month at the average of the last ten gold fixings during the relevant month on the London market, less 10 percent. *Line 3..d* comprises long-term loans to foreign countries, mainly for development purposes.

Monetary Authorities:
Comprises the South African Reserve Bank (SARB) only. † Beginning in January 1990, comprises the SARB and the Corporation for Public Deposits, a full subsidiary of the SARB. Data are based on improved sectorization and classification of the accounts. † Beginning in December 2001, data are based on improved sectorization and classification of the accounts. † Beginning in June 2002, data are based on a new reporting system which provides improved classification and sectorization of the accounts.

Banking Institutions:
Comprises private banking institutions (including the former commercial banks, discount houses, and equity building societies), mutual banks, Land Bank, and Post Bank. † Beginning in January 1992, data reflect the implementation of South Africa's Banks Act (Act No. 94 of 1990), which expanded the coverage of the banking sector and resulted in changes in the reporting and presentation of accounts. † Beginning in December 2001, data are based on improved sectorization and classification of the accounts. Prior to January 2002, *Claims on Central Government (line 22a)* and *Central Government Deposits (line 26d)* included the Public Investment Commissioners (PIC). Beginning in January 2002, the PIC were reclassified as nonbank financial institutions, following the incorporation of the PIC into the Public Investment Corporation. † Beginning in June 2002, data are based on a new reporting system which provides improved classification and sectorization of the accounts.

Banking Survey:
† See notes on monetary authorities and banking institutions.

Nonbank Financial Institutions:
Comprises insurance companies (short- and long-term insurers) and private pension and provident funds. Insurance Technical Reserves includes the contra-entry to the financial assets of the nonbank financial institutions. † Beginning in December 2001, data are based on improved sectorization and classification of the accounts. Beginning in January 2002, includes the Public Investment Corporation. † Beginning in June 2002, data are based on a new reporting system which provides improved classification and sectorization of the accounts.

Financial Survey:
† See notes on monetary authorities, banking institutions, and nonbank financial institutions.

Money (National Definitions):
M0 comprises notes and coins in circulation outside the South Africa Reserve Bank (SARB) and bankers' deposits with the SARB in national currency.
M1A comprises notes and coins in circulation outside the banking institutions and check and transferable deposits in national currency of households, local governments, public and private nonfinancial corporations, and nonbank financial institutions (including the Public Investment Commissioners (PIC) beginning in January 1996) with the banking institutions.
M1 comprises *M1A* and other demand deposits in national currency of households, local governments, public and private nonfinancial corporations, and nonbank financial institutions (including the PIC beginning in January 1996) with the banking institutions.
M2 comprises *M1* and other short- and medium-term deposits in national currency of households, local governments, public and private nonfinancial corporations, and nonbank financial institutions (including the PIC beginning in January 1996) with the banking institutions, and negotiable certificates of deposits and promissory notes issued by banking institutions in national currency held by households, local governments, public and private nonfinancial corporations, and nonbank financial institutions (including the PIC beginning in January 1996). Short- and medium-term (up to six month's unexpired maturity) deposits include time and savings deposits and savings bank certificates issued by the Postbank.

M3 comprises M2 and long-term deposits in national currency of households, local governments, public and private nonfinancial corporations, and nonbank financial institutions (including the PIC beginning in January 1996) with the banking institutions. Long-term deposits include national savings certificates issued by the Postbank.

Interest Rates:

Discount Rate (End of Period):
Lowest rate at which the South African Reserve Bank (SARB) discounts treasury bills to commercial banks. † Beginning in March 1998, rate determined by the SARB on repurchase agreements between the SARB and banks in national currency.

Money Market Rate:
Rate on loans between banks. † Beginning in March 1976, predominant quoted rate on interbank deposits at call. † Beginning in September 2001, refers to the South African overnight interbank average rate (SAONIA) which is the weighted average rate of unsecured interbank overnight transactions at market rates in national currency. The rate is weighted by loan amounts. † Beginning in March 2007, the SAONIA rate was discontinued and replaced by the South African Benchmark Overnight Rate (SABOR). SABOR is the volume-weighted average of interbank funding at a rate other than the current repo rate and the twenty highest rates paid by banks on their overnight and call deposits, plus a five percent weight for funding through foreign exchange swaps.

Treasury Bill Rate:
Tender rate on 91-day treasury bills in national currency. Monthly data are averages of each Friday of the month.

Savings Rate:
Weighted average rate offered by banks on savings deposits in national currency. The rate is weighted by deposit amounts.

Deposit Rate:
Predominant quoted rate on wholesale 88–91 day time deposits with clearing banks in national currency. † Beginning in January 2001, weighted average rate offered by banks on wholesale 88–91 day time deposits in national currency. The rate is weighted by deposit amounts.

Lending Rate:
Predominant prime overdraft rate charged by banks.

Government Bond Yield:
Yield on bonds with maturities of more than ten years traded on the bond exchange.

Prices, Production, Labor:

Share Prices:
Weighted index of monthly average prices of all ordinary shares listed on the JSE Securities Exchange South Africa (JSE), base 2000.

Producer Prices:
Source S. Weights Reference Period: 2000; Coverage: agriculture, forestry, fishing, mining and quarrying sector, manufacturing sector, and electricity, gas, and water sector; Number of Items in Basket: 4500; Basis for Calculation: weights are derived based on sales of products from 1995–1996.

Consumer Prices:
Source S. Weights Reference Period: 2000; Geographical Coverage: each of the nine provinces; Number of Items in Basket:

1500; Basis for Calculation: weights are derived from the Survey of Household Expenditure from 2000.

Manufacturing Production:
Source S. Weights Reference Period: 2000; Sectoral Coverage: manufacturing sector; Basis for Calculation: weights are based on the value added by each group in the 1996 Manufacturing Census.

Unemployment:
Until 1997, unemployment figures included all persons 15 and over, excluding Transkei, Bophuthatswana, Venda, Ciskei, and elsewhere persons enumerated at de facto dwelling place. From 1990 onward, the data include all persons aged 15–66 years.

International Transactions:

† Beginning in January 1998, foreign trade data refer to South Africa only, excluding intra-trade of the South African Common Customs Area. Prior to January 1998, trade data refer to the South African Common Customs Area, which includes Botswana, Lesotho, Namibia, South Africa, and Swaziland.

Exports:
Sources C and S, value of exports, f.o.b., including gold exports. From January 1973 to February 1980, export data excluded certain mineral oils.

Gold Output (Net):
Source B value of net gold output (balance of payments table).

† Imports c.i.f. and f.o.b.:
Data are from sources C and S. Prior to March 1980, petroleum products and defense equipment were excluded.

Volume of Exports:
Source S Laspeyres index of volume of domestic merchandise exports, weights reference period: 2000.

Volume of Imports:
Source S Laspeyres index of volume of imports, f.o.b., base 2000.

Unit Value of Exports:
Source S Paasche index of unit value of imports, f.o.b., base 2000.

Unit Value of Imports:
Source S Paasche index of unit value of imports, f.o.b., base 2000.

Government Finance:

Monthly, quarterly, and annual data are as reported by source B. Data cover the budgetary central government channeled through the consolidated Exchequer and Paymaster Accounts. † From January 1991 onward, data include the revenue, expenditure, and financing of the former Transkei, Bophuthatswana, Venda, and Ciskei (TBVC) and self-governing states. † From April 1994 onward, outstanding debt data include debt of the former TBVC countries and self-governing states. This debt was assumed by the national government in terms of Section 239 of the Second Amendment Bill of the Constitution of the Republic of South Africa. † From May 1997, outstanding debt data include part of Namibia's debt, guaranteed by South Africa before Namibia's independence and subsequently assumed by South Africa. † Prior to 2004, to the extent possible, existing subannual IFS data were converted to the main aggregates that are presented in the GFSM 2001 Statement of Sources and Uses of Cash (see the Introduction of the monthly IFS publication for details). Beginning in 2004, data are reported in the GFSM 2001 analytical framework. The fiscal year ends March 31.

National Accounts:

Source B. † Since 1985, national accounts data correspond to the new set of national accounts estimates first published in the first quarter of 1994 by the Reserve Bank. *Lines 99a* and *99b.c* include a statistical discrepancy. As indicated by the country, data from 1993 onward are compiled according to the *1993 SNA*.

Spain   184

Data are denominated in Spanish pesetas prior to January 1999 and in euros from January 1999 onward. An irrevocably fixed factor for converting pesetas to euros was established at 166.386 pesetas per euro. In 2002, the peseta was retired from circulation and replaced by the euro banknotes and coins. Beginning in January 1999, with the implementation of Stage Three of the European Economic and Monetary Union (EMU), an alternative euro area-wide definition of residency was introduced: All positions with residents of other euro area (EA) countries, including the European Central Bank (ECB), are classified as domestic positions, and foreign assets and foreign liabilities include only positions with non-euro area residents. Descriptions of the changes in the methodology and presentation of Spain's accounts following the introduction of the euro are shown in the introduction to *IFS* and in the notes on the euro area page.

Date of Fund Membership:
September 15, 1958

Standard Sources:
A: Bank of Spain, *Annual Report*
B: Bank of Spain, *Statistical Bulletin*
S: National Statistical Institute, *Monthly Bulletin of Statistics, National Accounts of Spain*
V: Eurostat

Exchange Rates:
Prior to 1999, the market rate was the midpoint rate established each business day in the Madrid exchange market by the Bank of Spain. In January 1999, the peseta became a participating currency within the Eurosystem, and the euro market rate became applicable to all transactions. In 2002, the peseta was retired from circulation and replaced by euro banknotes and coins. For additional information, see the section on exchange rates in the introduction to *IFS* and the notes for the euro area page.

International Liquidity:
Beginning in January 1999, *Total Reserves minus Gold (line 1l.d)* is defined in accordance with the Eurosystem's statistical definition of international reserves. The international reserves of Spain per the Eurosystem statistical definition at the start of the monetary union (January 1, 1999) in billions of U.S. dollars were as follows: *Total Reserves minus Gold,* $55,167; *Foreign Exchange,* $52,186; *SDRs,* $574; *Reserve Position in the Fund,* $2,189; *Other Reserve Assets,* $219; *Gold,* $5,617 *Gold (million fine troy ounces),* 19.539 ounces. *Foreign Exchange (line 1d.d):* Beginning in July 1988, excludes deposits made with the European Monetary Cooperation Fund (EMCF); the holdings of European currency units (ECUs) issued by the EMCF against those deposits (and similar deposits of gold) are included in *line 1d.d. Gold (Eurosystem Valuation) (line 1and):* In December 1981, gold was revalued from US $42.22 per ounce to US $298 per ounce. From March 1979 to December 1998, excludes deposits of gold at the EMCF. Prior to January 1999, *line 1and* was revalued based on the following formula: If

the average market price for the calendar year (or the fourth quarter, if lower) was greater than 150 percent of the current book price, the book price was increased by an amount equal to the difference between the average market price and 150 percent of the book price. Conversely, if the book price was more than 80 percent of the average market price during any number of months since the last price adjustment, then the book price was lowered to 80 percent of the average market price for that period. From January 1999 onward, gold is revalued at market prices at the end of each quarter. Gold swaps within *line 1and* are treated as repurchase transactions that do not affect the volume of gold held. Memorandum data are provided on *Non-Euro Claims on Euro Area Residents* and *Euro Claims on Non-Euro Area Residents,* which represent positions as of the last day in each month. For additional information, see the section on international liquidity in the introduction to *IFS* and the notes to the euro area page.

Monetary Authorities:
Prior to 1999, this section consolidated the Bank of Spain and monetary authorities functions undertaken by the central government. The contra-entry to Treasury coin issue was included in *Claims on General Government (line 12a).* Beginning in January 1999, consists of the Bank of Spain and coin issue of the government, with the contra-entry recorded for government coin issue in *Other Items (Net) (line 17r).* Beginning in 2002, *Currency Issued (line 14a)* includes euro banknotes and coins and, until December 2002, any unretired pesetas. The recorded value of euro banknotes is based on a monthly allocation of total euro banknotes in circulation based on the Bank of Spain's paid up share of the ECB's capital; it does not correspond to either the actual amount of euro banknotes placed in circulation by the Bank of Spain which is shown in memo line *Currency Put into Circulation (line 14m),* nor the actual circulation of banknotes within the domestic territory. See section *Euro banknotes and coins* in the introduction to *IFS. Bonds and Money Market Instruments (line 16n.u)* include subordinated debt in the form of securities, other bonds, and money market paper. This line also includes negotiable securities, held by other monetary financial institutions (other MFIs) only, issued by the Bank of Spain to absorb liquidity when reserves requirements were reduced in the early 1990s. *Capital Accounts (line 17a)* includes general provisions. Beginning in January 1999, excludes valuation adjustments associated with ECU claims on the EMI and claims representing advanced payments to the Treasury for the transfer of dividends. For a description of the accounts, refer to the monetary authorities section in the introduction to *IFS.* Beginning with the data for end-November 2000, Monetary Authorities' *Foreign Assets (line 11), Foreign Liabilities (line 16c), Claims on Banking Institutions (line 12e.u),* and *Liabilities to Banking Institutions (line 14c.u)* are affected by a change from gross to net presentation of positions relating to the TARGET (Trans-European Automated Real-Time Gross Settlement Express Transfer) euro clearing system. (See *Recording of TARGET system positions* under *European Economic and Monetary Union (EMU)* in the introduction to *IFS.*) Beginning in 2002, *Claims on Banking Institutions (line 12e.u)* and *Liabilities to Banking Institutions (line 14c.u)* include "Intra-Eurosystem claims/liabilities related to banknote issue," which is a single net value representing the difference between the value of euro banknotes allocated to the Bank of Spain according to the accounting scheme of the Eurosystem for issuing euro banknotes, and the value of euro

banknotes put into circulation by the Bank of Spain. See section *Euro banknotes and coins* in the introduction to *IFS*. Memo line *Net Claims on Eurosystem (line 12e.s)* equals gross claims on, less gross liabilities to, the ECB and other members of the Eurosystem. Comprises euro-denominated claims equivalent to the transfer of foreign currency reserves to the ECB, Intra-Eurosystem claims/liabilities related to banknote issue, net claims or liabilities within the TARGET clearing system, and other positions. † Beginning in 1983, data are based on a new system of accounts with a revised transactor breakdown. † From 1986, data reflect an introduction of a new reporting system. † In accordance with provisions of the Treaty of European Union, beginning in 1994 overdrafts or loans from the Banco de Espana to the government were prohibited. Accordingly, *Credit to Central Government (line 12a)* shows net Treasury indebtedness through 1993 and gross indebtedness (without deducting the Treasury's current account) from 1994 onward.

Banking Institutions:

Beginning in January 1999, consists of all resident units classified as other MFIs, defined in accordance with *1995 ESA* standards, including money market funds and the Instituto de Crédito Oficial (ICO). Prior to January 1999, excluded the ICO. *Claims on General Government (line 22a)* includes claims on general government in other euro area countries. Beginning in January 1999, data reflect changes in the recording of securities lending. *Bonds (Debt Securities) (line 26n.u)* includes bonds issued by the ICO and subordinated debt in the form of securities. Prior to January 1999, the latter were classified in *Other Items (Net) (line 27r)*. *Money Market Fund Shares (line 26m.u)* include shares/units issued by money market funds. *Bonds and Money Market Instruments (line 26n.u)* include subordinated debt in the form of securities, other bonds, and money market paper. *Central Government Deposits (line 26d.u)*: Prior to January 1999, included transitory accounts managed by other MFIs for collection of taxes prior to their transfer to the central government. *Capital Accounts (line 27a)* includes general provisions and specific provisions except those that imply liabilities to third parties, which are included in *Other Items (Net) (line 27r)*. *Other Items (Net)* includes holdings of shares issued by other MFIs, the value of options, and specific provisions for payments to third parties (i.e., pension funds and taxes). For a description of the accounts, refer to the section on banking institutions in the introduction to *IFS*. † Prior to 1983, the coverage of *line 24* is confined to the commercial and savings banks. Beginning in 1983, cooperative banks and money market intermediary companies are included. From 1983 onward, data are based on the new bank returns, which are aimed at a uniform reporting system for all financial institutions. † From 1986 onward, data reflect an introduction of a new reporting system.

Banking Survey (National Residency):

For a description of the methodology and accounts, refer to the section Banking Survey (National Residency) in the introduction to *IFS*.

Banking Survey (Euro Area-wide Residency):

For a description of the methodology and accounts, refer to the section Banking Survey (Euro Area-wide Residency) in the introduction to *IFS*.

Money (National Definitions):

Prior to January 1999, *M1* comprised currency held by the public and sight deposits in national currency. It did not include de-

posits of local governments and other banking institutions. *M2* comprised *M1* plus savings deposits. *M3* comprised *M2* plus other liquid assets including time deposits, foreign-currency deposits of residents, asset participations, liabilities under repurchase agreements, short-term securities issued by credit institutions, and long-term securities issued by deposit money banks excluding official credit banks. *ALP* comprised *M3* plus other liquid liabilities of financial institutions and short-term instruments issued by the general government and held by other resident sectors. Beginning in January 1999, national monetary aggregate series are discontinued. Euro area aggregates are presented on the euro area page.

Interest Rates:

Source B.

Bank of Spain Rate (End of Period) (line 60):
Prior to September 1977, rate at which the Bank of Spain discounted financial paper for commercial and saving banks. From September 1977 to January 1999, the weighted average of the interest rate on loans granted to the banking system, through auction, by the Bank of Spain. Data were for the last day of the month in which an auction took place. Beginning in January 1999, central bank policy rate series are discontinued. See Eurosystem policy rate series on the euro area page.

Money Market Rate (line 60b):
Daily average rate on interbank operations effected through the Bank of Spain's cable service.

Treasury Bill Rate (line 60c):
Prior to July 1987, the discount rate on three-month treasury bills. Beginning in July 1987, the discount rate on one-year treasury bills.

Deposit Rate (line 60l):
Rate offered by banks on six- to 12-month time deposits.

Deposit Rate (lines 60lhs, 60lhn, 60lcs, 60lcn, and 60lcr):
See notes in the Introduction to *IFS*.

Lending Rate (line 60p):
Rate charged by banks to discount three-month commercial bills.

Lending Rate (lines 60phs, 60pns, 60phm, 60phn, 60pcs, and 60pcn):
See notes in the Introduction to *IFS*.

Government Bond Yield (line 61):
Simple monthly average of daily yields on bonds with over two years maturity included in the government's Sistema de Anotaciones de Cuenta de Deuda del Estado (SACDE). For additional information, refer to the section on interest rates in the introduction to *IFS* and on the euro area page.

Prices, Production, Labor:

Share Prices:
Source B, index of Madrid Stock Exchange share prices, base December 1970. † Beginning January 1986, data refer to base December 1985.

Industrial Prices:
Source S Laspeyres index, weights reference period: 2000. The index covers the energy and manufacturing sectors of the industry. It is based on a monthly survey of 8000 industrial establishments with over 20 employees.

Consumer Prices:
Source S. Weights Reference Period: 2001; Geographical Coverage: The entire country; Number of Items in Basket: 484; Basis

for Calculation: The weights of the products are based on the Household Budget Continuous Survey (HBCS) and are revised every year.

Wages:

Source S index of hourly wages, weights reference period: weights are annually updated. The index covers establishments with 10 or more employees in the industrial sector, in part of the construction sector, and in the commerce, hotel and restaurant, road transportation, and banking and insurance sectors.

Industrial Production:

Source S. Weights Reference Period: 2000; Sectoral Coverage: energy, mining and manufacturing sectors, but excluding building; Basis for Calculation: the elementary indices are then weighted by 2000 gross output, and aggregated by value added to obtain the indices for branches and the general index for total industry.

Employment:

Source S. Data refer to the average number of employed persons for the quarter.

International Transactions:

All data on prices are from source B.

Volume of Exports and Imports:

Source S, Laspeyres type indices, weights reference period: 1995. *Export* and *Import Unit Values* are published by the country as export and import prices: Source S, Paasche type indices, weights reference period: 1995.

Balance of Payments:

Beginning in 1990, the annual and quarterly balance of payments data have been compiled by the Bank of Spain, on a transaction basis, in accordance with the methodology set forth in the *Balance of Payments Manual*, fifth edition. Balance of payments data for earlier periods were compiled by the Ministry of Economy and Finance in accordance with the methodology set forth in the *Balance of Payments Manual*, fourth edition, and have been converted to the presentation recommended in the fifth edition of the *Manual*.

Government Finance:

Data on general government are derived from source V. Monthly cash data are provided by source B and cover the budgetary central government. Privatization receipts are included in revenue. The fiscal year ends December 31.

National Accounts:

Data are from source S. As indicated by the country, from 1998 onwards data have been revised following the implementation of the *ESA 95*. Beginning in 1999, euro data are sourced from the Eurostat database. Eurostat introduced chain-linked GDP volume measures to both annual and quarterly data with the release of the third quarter 2005 on November 30, 2005. Chain linked GDP volume measures are expressed in the prices of the previous year and re-referenced to 1995.

Sri Lanka   524

Date of Fund Membership:

August 29, 1950

Standard Sources:

A: Central Bank, *Annual Report*
B: Central Bank, *Bulletin*

Exchange Rates:

Market Rate (End of Period and Period Average):
Commercial bank midpoint rate.

International Liquidity:

Data for *line 1d.d* include small foreign exchange holdings by the government.

Gold (National Valuation) (line 1and) is obtained by converting the value in national currency terms, as reported in the national sources, and is calculated on the basis of the cost of acquisition at the prevailing exchange rate, as given in *line* **ae**. † For 2000–2002, data on the volume of gold include the balances in the Gold Trading Account, the Gold Stock Account, and the Gold Fixed Deposit Account of the Central Bank of Sri Lanka. Beginning in 2003, the outstanding balance on the Gold Stock Account is excluded as this item is no longer classified as foreign reserves by the Central Bank of Sri Lank. Beginning in January 2000, gold valuation is based on market price.

Lines 7a.d and *7b.d* are the U.S. dollar equivalents of *lines 21* and *26c,* respectively. † Beginning in January 1999, they include the foreign accounts of the foreign currency banking units (FCBUs). Through their FCBUs, commercial banks may undertake foreign currency transactions with any nonresident and with designated residents, notably enterprises operating in the free trade zone of the Greater Colombo Economic Commission.

Monetary Authorities:

Consolidates the Central Bank of Sri Lanka and monetary authority functions of the central government through December 1985. The contra-entries to Treasury IMF accounts are included in *line 12a.* † Beginning in 1975, data are based on improved classification and sectorization. † Beginning in 1986 through 1995, data are based on partial coverage of IMF accounts. † Beginning in 1989, data are compiled from a new report form. † Beginning in January 1995, positions of the central bank with foreign currency banking units (FCBUs) are classified as positions with residents. † Beginning in 2002, data reported by the Central Bank of Sri Lanka are based on International Accounting Standards.

Deposit Money Banks:

Comprises the commercial banks. † Beginning in January 1995, FCBUs have been reclassified from nonresident entities to resident entities and have been included in the consolidation. In addition, fifty percent of the deposits of nonresidents previously classified in foreign liabilities *(line 26c)* have been reclassified as domestic deposits.

Monetary Survey:

† See note on monetary authorities.

Interest Rates:

Data are from source B. With the exception of *Bank Rate (End of Period),* quarterly and annual data are averages of end-of-period monthly data.

Bank Rate (End of Period):
Rate charged by the central bank on advances to commercial banks for their temporary liquidity needs.

Money Market Rate:
Maximum advance rate charged by commercial banks on inter-bank call loans.

Treasury Bill Rate:
Discount rate in the secondary market. † Beginning in August 1996, discount rate in the primary market.

Deposit Rate:
Weighted average rate on all commercial bank deposits excluding demand deposits; weights are the deposit amounts.

Lending Rate:
Weighted average prime lending rate of commercial banks; weights are the loan amounts.

Prices and Labor:

Share Prices:
Based on 1985 = 100. The All Share Price Index is an index of all equities traded on the Stock Exchange. The index is weighted by the market capitalization of each equity. Data are from Source B.

Wholesale Prices:
Wholesale price index, all items, weights reference period: 1974.

Consumer Prices:
Source B. Weights Reference Period: 1952; Geographical Coverage: Colombo; Number of Items in Basket: 219; Basis for Calculation: weights are derived from a Family Expenditure Survey among 455 manual workers' families in Colombo in 1949–1950.

International Transactions:

Trade data are from source B. *Export* and *Import* data are adjusted for timing and coverage differences.

Volume of Exports:
Source B. Weights Reference Period: 1997

Volume of Imports:
Source B. Weights Reference Period: 1997

Unit Value of Exports:
Source B. Weights Reference Period: 1997

Unit Value of Imports:
Source B. Weights Reference Period: 1990.

Government Finance:

Annual data are as reported for the *Government Finance Statistics Yearbook (GFSY)* and cover budgetary central government. The fiscal year ends December 31.

National Accounts:

Source B.

Sudan 732

Date of Fund Membership:
September 5, 1957

Standard Sources:
A: Bank of Sudan, *Annual Report*
B: Bank of Sudan, *Economic and Financial Bulletin, Foreign Trade Statistical Digest*
C: Ministry of Finance and Economy

Exchange Rates:
Since the country's independence in 1956 and end-July 1999, the pound had been in circulation. On July 31, 1999 the dinar, equal to 10 pounds, was introduced.

Market Rate (End of Period and Period Average):
Effective 1992, a unified exchange rate system was introduced. Under the new system, the exchange rate is determined by a committee of local bankers, without official intervention, and is quoted uniformly by all commercial banks. Since 1992, all restrictions on foreign currency have been lifted.

International Liquidity:
† Beginning in March 2000, data reflect an improved classification of accounts.

Monetary Authorities:
† Data reflect improvements in classification and sectorization beginning in 1983, 1992, 1997 and 2000. Prior to 1992, Claims on Central Government (line 12a) was net of central government deposits. *Claims on Central Government (line 12a)* includes accumulated interest arrears representing the counterpart to interest payable by the Bank of Sudan to foreign creditors on overdue government debt obligations. Beginning in March 2001, these accumulated interest arrears are separately identified in *line 12ag*.
† Beginning in March 2000, reserve money includes quasi-money deposit liabilities of the central bank.

Deposit Money Banks:
Comprises the accounts of the commercial banks and the consolidation of postal savings deposits. † See note on monetary authorities. † Beginning in 1985, data are based on a new bank reporting system. † Beginning in 1992, data reflect improvements in classification. † Beginning in 2006, data reflect improvements in classification.

Monetary Survey:
† See notes on monetary authorities and deposit money banks.

Prices and Labor:
Consumer Prices:
Source B index base January 1992=100 for middle income group. Data are compiled by the Department of Statistics and supplied by the Central Bank.

International Transactions:
All trade value data are from source B. Prior to 1995, annual trade value data refer to the fiscal year ending June 30, and from 1995 onward, trade value data are on a calendar year basis (year ending December 31). For the 1994–95 fiscal year, exports are 421.7 million U.S. dollars and imports are 1,023.4 million U.S. dollars.

Balance of Payments:
† Balance of payments data from 2002 incorporate changes introduced following an IMF balance of payments statistics technical assistance mission in June 2003. The main changes relate to the reclassification of capital account flows to direct investment in the reporting economy and improved data sources on loan repayments of general government.

Government Finance:
Annual data are as reported in the *Government Finance Staitstics Yearbook* and cover budgetary central government. The fiscal year ends December 31.

National Accounts:

GDP data are from source C. Prior to 1995, annual GDP refer to the fiscal year ending June 30, and from 1995 onward, annual GDP data are on a calendar-year basis (year ending December 31).

Suriname 366

Date of Fund Membership:
April 27, 1978

Standard Sources:
A: Bank of Suriname, *Annual Report*
S: General Bureau of Statistics, *Statistical News*

Exchange Rates:
On January 1, 2004, the Surinamese dollar, equal to 1,000 Surinamese guilders, replaced the guilder as the currency unit.

Market Rate (End of Period):
Central bank midpoint rate. Beginning July 1994, the Central Bank midpoint exchange rate was unified and became market determined. Beginning in March 2002, data reported correspond to the official rate.

International Liquidity:
Data for *line 1d.d* include small foreign exchange holdings by the government.
Gold (National Valuation) (line 1and) is obtained by converting for current periods the value in national currency terms, as reported in the country's standard sources, using the prevailing exchange rate, as given in *line* **ae**.

Monetary Authorities:
Comprises the Central Bank of Suriname only. † Beginning in December 1998, data are based on an improved classification and sectorization of the accounts. † Beginning in December 2001, data are based on an improved classification and sectorization of the accounts. † Beginning in January 2004, data are based on a new reporting system which provides an improved classification and sectorization of the accounts.

Banking Institutions:
Comprises commercial banks, one finance company, and two trust companies. Finance and trust companies are wholly owned by the commercial banks on whom they almost exclusively rely to finance their operations. † Beginning in May 2002, data are based on an improved classification and sectorization of the accounts. † Beginning in December 2001, data are based on an improved classification and sectorization of the accounts. † Beginning in January 2004, data are based on a new reporting system which provides an improved classification and sectorization of the accounts.

Banking Survey:
† See notes on monetary authorities and banking institutions.

Money (National Definitions):
M1 comprises banknotes and coins in circulation, treasury notes, and local currency demand deposits.
M2 comprises *M1* plus local currency time deposits of less than one year, 10 percent of local currency savings deposits, and gold certificates held by the public.

M3 comprises *M2* plus local currency time deposits with a maturity of more than one year and 90 percent of local currency savings deposits.

Interest Rates:

Money Market Rate:
Simple average of rates at which commercial banks borrow funds in the interbank market.

Deposit Rate:
Weighted average rate offered by commercial banks on all savings and time deposits. The rate is weighted by deposit amounts.

Deposit Rate in US Dollars:
Weighted average rate offered by commercial banks on all savings and time deposits in US dollars.

Lending Rate:
Weighted average rate charged by commercial banks on all loans. The rate is weighted by loan amounts.

Lending Rate in US Dollars:
Weighted average rate charged by commercial banks on all loans in US dollars.

Deposit Rate in Euros:
Weighted average rate offered by commercial banks on all savings and time deposits in euros.

Lending Rate in Euros:
Weighted average rate charged by commercial banks on all loans in euros.

Prices:

Consumer Prices:
Source S index of consumer prices, weights reference period October–December 2000. Number of Items in Basket: 240; Geographical Coverage: the index covers the city of Paramaribo and surrounding areas. Basis for Calculation: weights are based on the Household Budget Survey of June 1999–June 2000.

International Transactions:
Trade data, which are compiled by the Central Bureau of Statistics have been updated with the Bank of Suriname balance of payments data on a cash basis for current periods.

National Accounts:
Source B. According to the country, the national accounts of Suriname are based, as far as possible, on the *1993 SNA*.

Swaziland 734

Date of Fund Membership:
September 22, 1969

Standard Sources:
A: Central Bank, *Annual Report*
B: Central Bank, *Quarterly Review*
S: Central Statistical Office, *Annual Statistical Bulletin, Digest of Statistics*

Exchange Rates:

Official Rate: (End of Period and Period Average):
The lilangeni is at par with the South African rand (see note on the page for South Africa for a description of the exchange rates).

Monetary Authorities:

Comprises the Central Bank of Swaziland (CBS) only. † Beginning in December 2001, data are based on improved sectorization and classification of the accounts. † Beginning in August 2004, data are based on a new reporting system which provides improved classification and sectorization of the accounts.

Banking Institutions:

Comprises commercial banks and the Swaziland Development and Savings Bank. † Beginning in December 2001, data are based on improved sectorization and classification of the accounts. † Beginning in August 2004, data are based on a new reporting system which provides improved classification and sectorization of the accounts.

Banking Survey:

† See notes on monetary authorities and banking institutions.

Money (National Definitions):

M1 comprises currency in circulation outside the banking system and demand deposits of the private sector, local authorities and town councils, nonfinancial public enterprises, and nonbank financial institutions in national currency with the Central Bank of Swaziland and in national and foreign currency with commercial banks.

M2 comprises M1 plus time and savings deposits of the private sector, local authorities and town councils, nonfinancial public enterprises, and nonbank financial institutions in national and foreign currency with commercial banks.

Interest Rates:

All interest rate data are from source B.

Discount Rate (End of Period):
Rate at which the Central Bank of Swaziland discounts eligible domestic bills.

Money Market Rate:
Interbank call deposit rate.

Treasury Bill Rate:
Yield on treasury bills.

Savings Rate:
Midpoint rate offered by commercial banks on savings deposits.

Deposit Rate:
Midpoint rate offered by banks on three-month fixed term deposits.

Lending Rate (Prime Rate):
Rate charged by banks to their most creditworthy customers on short-term loans.

Prices and Labor:

Consumer Prices:
Source S. Weights Reference Period: January 1996; Geographical Coverage: Nine urban centers; Number of Items in Basket: 390; Basis for Calculation: The weights are derived from the Swaziland Household Income and Expenditure Survey (SHIES) conducted in 1995.

International Transactions:

All trade value data are from source B. *Imports, c.i.f.* include customs duties, excises, and sales taxes paid and are therefore not comparable to corresponding balance of payments data.

Government Finance:

Data are derived from source B and cover the budgetary central government. External debt data cover both budgetary central government and public guaranteed debt. The fiscal year ends March 31.

National Accounts:

Source B.

Sweden   144

Date of Fund Membership:

August 31, 1951

Standard Sources:

A: Sveriges Riksbank, *Yearbook*
B: Sveriges Riksbank, *Quarterly Review*
N: National Institute of Economic Research, *The Swedish Economy*
S: Central Bureau of Statistics, *Monthly Digest of Swedish Statistics, Statistical Reports*

Exchange Rates:

Official Rate: (End of Period and Period Average):
Since November 19, 1992, midpoint rate in the Stockholm foreign exchange market at the time of the fixing of exchange quotations each business day. During the period May 17, 1991–November 18, 1992, the official rate was pegged to the European currency unit (ECU). Prior to May 17, 1991, the official rate was pegged to an index of a basket comprising 15 currencies.

International Liquidity:

Gold (National Valuation) (line 1and) is valued according to market prices. † Prior to January 2004, *(line 1and)* is equal to *Gold (Million Fine Troy Ounces) (line 1ad),* valued at SDR 35 per fine troy ounce and converted into U.S. dollars at the dollar/SDR rate **sa** on the country page for the United States. Source E: OECD
Lines 7a.d and *7b.d* are obtained from detailed information with geographic breakdown and differ from *lines 21* and *26c.*
Lines 7a.d, 7b.d, 7e.d, and *7f.d:* † The banks' positions with their branches abroad are included.

Monetary Authorities:

Comprises Sveriges Riksbank. † Before 1986, the monetary authorities included Treasury coin issue.
† Beginning in September 1999, data are based on a revised reporting of accounts. † Beginning in December 2001, data are compiled in accordance with the European Central Bank's framework for monetary statistics using national residency approach.

Banking Institutions:

Beginning in December 2001, comprises all resident units classified as other monetary financial institutions (other MFIs) in accordance with *1995 ESA* standards. Prior to December 2001, consolidates the commercial banks, large savings banks, cooperative banks, and deposit liabilities to the private sector of the postal giro system.
Demand, Time, Savings, & Foreign Currency Deposits (line 25l):
From March 1990 to December 2000, data refer to the sum of liquid liabilities of commercial banks, large savings banks, cooperative banks, and the postal giro system. † Beginning in 1983, data reflect improved classification of accounts. † Beginning in Janu-

ary 1996, data on accounts of deposit money banks are not strictly comparable with earlier figures, owing to the adoption of the European Union accounting system. † Beginning in December 2001, data are compiled in accordance with the European Central Bank's framework for monetary statistics using national residence approach. Prior to December 2001, deposit money banks' positions with other banking institutions are classified in Other Items (net) (line 27r).

Banking Survey:

Money plus Quasi-Money (line 351):
See notes on monetary authorities and banking institutions.
From March 1990 to December 2000, data refer to the sum of liquid liabilities of the monetary authorities, commercial banks, large savings banks, cooperative banks, and postal giro system. Liquid liabilities comprise the public's holdings of notes and coins, deposits in Swedish kronor and foreign currencies with the deposit money banks, deposits in Swedish kronor with the Postal Giro, and certificates of deposit.

Money (National Definitions):

M0 comprises currency outside monetary financial institutions (MFIs), which is equal to currency in circulation minus currency held by MFIs.
M1 is equal to M0 plus Swedish crown and foreign currency demand deposits in MFIs from Swedish non-bank public.
M2 is equal to M1 plus other Swedish crown and foreign currency deposits in MFIs from Swedish non-bank public. Other deposits include time, savings, and other deposits with restrictions.
M3 is equal to M2 plus repurchase agreements, money market fund shares, and debt securities with maturity less than two years issued by MFIs held by Swedish non-bank public.

Other Banking Institutions:

Beginning in December 2001, institutions classified as other monetary financial institutions (other MFIs) in accordance with *1995 ESA* standards are included in Banking Institutions (section 20). Prior to December 2001, comprises mortgage institutions and finance companies. † Beginning in 1990 and in 1996, data are based on a revised reporting of accounts.

Nonbank Financial Institutions:

Comprises the nationwide life and casualty insurance companies. † Beginning first quarter 1996, data are based on an improved collection and classification system. Prior to the first quarter 1996, data on line *42d.l* refer to claims on the private sector.

Interest Rates:

Bank Rate (End of Period):
Source B. Beginning in July 2002, data refer to the reference rate set by the Riksbank at six-monthly intervals, and is based on the repurchase agreement rate applying at the end of the previous six-month period, rounded up to the nearest whole or half percentage point. Prior to July 2002, data refer to the official discount rate which was based on the average rate on six-month and five-year securities fixings during the previous quarter minus 2.5 percent. † Before March 1992, rate charged by the Riksbank to commercial banks on short-term loans.

Repurchase Rate:
† Prior to June 1994, data refer to the marginal rate charged by the Riksbank on the loans to banks. Beginning June 1994, the marginal rate has been replaced by the repurchase rate.

Money Market Rate:
Relates to the monthly average of daily rates for day-to-day interbank loans.

Treasury Bill Rate:
Rate on three-month treasury discount notes.

Deposit Rate:
From March 2000 onward, end-quarter average deposit rate of 11 largest commercial banks. † From December 1992 through February 2000, end-quarter average deposit rate at six largest banks. † Prior to December 1992, end-quarter average rate on savings deposits at deposit money banks.

Lending Rate:
From March 2000 onward, end-quarter average lending rate of 11 largest commercial banks. † From December 1992 through February 2000, rate on six largest banks' total lending, at end quarter. † Prior to December 1992, average rate on lending to households, at end-quarter.

Government Bond Yield:
Source B. Until December 1986, data refer to yields on government bonds maturing in 15 years; from January 1987 data refer to yields on bonds maturing in 10 years. Monthly data are mid-month yields; quarterly and yearly data are averages of monthly data.

Prices, Production, Labor:

Share Prices:
Source S data, base December 28, 1979. The general index refers to prices of all shares on the Stockholm Exchange as of the end of the month. The other series are components of the general index. Industrials share price index (base December 29, 1995) covers industrial conglomerates, vehicles and machinery, wholesalers, printing and office supplies, transportation, technical consultants, and miscellaneous industry subsectors. † Prior to December 1995, data refer to machinery/engineering industries share price index (base December 30, 1979), whose coverage differs from that of the industrials share price index.

Prices: Domestic Supply:
Source S data, weights reference period 1990. The index measures the price development in the producer and import stages for industrial goods consumed in the country. It is calculated by aggregating the Producer Price Index, home sales, and Import Price Index adjusted for customs and import charges.

Consumer Prices:
Source S. Weights Reference Period: 1980; Geographical Coverage: The whole country; Number of Items in Basket: 350; Basis for Calculation: The weights are derived from national accounts estimates of private consumption expenditures and revised every December.

Wages: Hourly Earnings:
Source S data, weights reference period 1994. The index refers to basic wages and supplements for overtime and shiftwork and covers workers in mining, quarrying, and manufacturing.

Industrial Production:
Source S. Weights Reference Period: 2000; Sectoral Coverage: whole industry; Basis for Calculation: the weights used for aggregation are the value added in the weights reference period.

Industrial Employment:
Source S series on employed labor force from January 1976, 16–64 years of age. Prior to 1976, the series related to ages 16–71.

The monthly survey covers 22,000 persons selected from all over the country.

International Transactions:

Beginning January 1977, data refer to actual imports and exports of the period. Prior to January 1977, data refer to exports and imports for which customs documents were processed by the Customs Office during the period. *Exports* and *Imports c.i.f.:* Source S data. *Export* and *Import Prices:* Reference year = 1990; annual chain-linked Laspeyres index with data comprising 1800 items for the Swedish market, about 850 for the export market, and about 1500 for the import market.

Government Finance:

Data on general government are derived from source V. † From 1970 through 1993, cash data are as reported in the *Government Finance Statistics Yearbook* and refer to a fiscal year ending June 30. † Beginning in 1994, cash data cover the operations of the budgetary central government and are derived from source S. Domestic financing data include operations of the National Debt Office for liquidity purposes. Debt data are derived from source B and cover the budgetary central government only. The fiscal year ends December 31.

National Accounts:

Data are from source S. *Line 93i* includes a statistical discrepancy. As indicated by the country, from 1994 onwards concepts and definitions are in accordance with the *1995 ESA*. Beginning in 1990, data are sourced from the Eurostat database. Eurostat introduced chain-linked GDP volume measures to both annual and quarterly data with the release of the third quarter 2005 on November 30, 2005. Chain linked GDP volume measures are expressed in the prices of the previous year and re-referenced to 2000.

Switzerland 146

Date of Fund Membership:
May 29, 1992

Standard Sources:

A: Swiss National Bank, *Annual Report, The Swiss Banking System*
B: Swiss National Bank, *Monthly Bulletin*
N: Message of the Federal Council to the Federal Assembly

Exchange Rates:

Market Rate (End of Period and Period Average):
Midpoint rate.

International Liquidity:

Data for *line 1c.d* refer to Switzerland's lendings to the Fund.
Gold (National Valuation) (line 1and) is obtained by converting the value in national currency terms, as reported in the country's standard sources, using the prevailing exchange rate, as given in *line de, line ae,* or *line we.*
Banks' foreign assets and foreign liabilities are equal to data reported in the text portion of source B, converted at the prevailing spot rate *(line ae).* The institutional coverage provided is broader than deposit money bank coverage mainly because the foreign accounts of most private banks and foreign banks operating in Switzerland are included. *Lines 7a.d and 7b.d* cover their own foreign assets and liabilities of resident banks (including those of

branches of foreign banks in Switzerland) that are subject to minimum reserve requirements on nonresident accounts. Nonresident branches of Swiss banks are treated as nonresident banks. Claims on and liabilities to Swiss citizens residing abroad, embassies, and international organizations residing in Switzerland are not included.
Lines 7k.d and 7m.d cover the trustee accounts of resident banks that are subject to minimum reserve requirements on nonresident accounts. A bank/nonbank distinction of these accounts is not available; however, it is known that *line 7k.d* consists mainly of claims on nonresident banks, whereas in *line 7m.d* the nonbank component is more dominant.

Monetary Authorities:

Consolidates the Swiss National Bank and monetary authority functions undertaken by the central government. The contra-entry to treasury coin issues is included in *line 12a.* Annual data are from source A, which provides a more detailed sectoral breakdown. † Beginning in March 1997, *Central Government Deposits* includes Deposits of the Confederation.

Deposit Money Banks:

† Before 1974, data relate to all banks in Switzerland, with data on nonresident branches of Swiss banks being consolidated into the accounts of the parent bank. Beginning in 1974, data relate to resident banks, which are subject to minimum reserves on external liabilities. † Beginning in 1982, data cover all banks, except for small Raiffeisen banks. † Beginning in 1984, consolidates banks that are subject to minimum reserves on foreign liabilities. † Beginning in 1996, data reflect a new reporting format. † Beginning in September 2006, data include all Raiffeisen banks, which means, that the total assets of all banks increased by approximately 0.7 percent, whereof the two most affected positions "mortgage claims" increased by 2.7 percent and "liabilities towards customers in the form of savings and deposits" increased by 3.9 percent. Annual data cover all banks and bank-like financial institutions as reported in *Das schweizerische Bankwesen.* Monthly data do not reflect the domestic monetary effect of the banking system's foreign transactions. *Demand Deposits (line 24)* includes *Post Office: Checking Deposits* previously published on a separate line; Counterpart adjustments are made to *Claims on Central Government (line22a).*

Monetary Survey:

† See notes on monetary authorities and deposit money banks.

Other Banking Institutions:

Comprises trustee accounts. † From 1996 onward, data reflect a new reporting format.

Interest Rates:

Bank Rate (End of Period):
Prior to January 2000, data refer to official discount rates. Beginning in January 2000, data refer to rates on short-term repurchase agreements at which the Swiss National Bank lends to commercial banks.

Money Market Rate:
Overnight Swiss franc deposit rates in international markets. Beginning in January 2000, data are end-of-period rates. Prior to that date, they are monthly averages.

Treasury Bill Rate:
Monthly average rate of interest on Federal Debt Register Claims.

Deposit Rate:

Rate of interest on three-month deposits with large banks. Beginning in January 2000, data are beginning-of-period rates. Prior to that date, they are end-of-period rates.

Lending Rate:

Rate of interest on first mortgages.

Government Bond Yield:

† Beginning in January 1998, data refer to spot interest rate on government bonds with 10-year maturity. Prior to that date, data cover government bonds with maturity of up to 20 years. Monthly data are based on prices of the last market day of the month. Quarterly and annual yields are end-of-period data.

Prices, Production, Labor:

Share Prices:

Source B index, base April 1, 1987; refers to the SBV–100 index, i.e., data on closing quotations at the end of the month for a composition of the 100 most regularly traded shares. The composition of the index is updated semiannually.

Producer Prices:

Laspeyres index, weights reference period: 2000, covers agriculture, forestry, industrial products, and energy sectors represented by 820 items. The weights are based on gross production value or turnover, if the gross production value is not available.

Prices: Home and Imported Goods:

Weights reference period: 2000; the weights are based on the turnover value of domestic producers and importers.

Consumer Prices:

Source B. Weights Reference Period: 2004; Geographical Coverage: the entire country; Number of Items in Basket: 1046; Basis for Calculation: the weights are based on the 2004 Income and Consumption Survey and are revised annually.

Wages: Hourly Earnings:

Source S index, weights reference period: 1993. Data covers all employees in the economy, except agriculture.

Industrial Production:

Source B. Weights reference period: 1993; Sectoral Coverage: mining and quarrying, manufacturing, and production and distribution of energy and water industrial sectors.

International Transactions:

Exports and Imports, c.i.f.:

Source B data. † Beginning in 1979, trade value data for the volume and unit value of imports included trade of gems, semi-precious stones, and antiques. Beginning in January 1, 1992, value data exclude diamonds, nonmonetary gold, works of art, collectors' pieces, antiques, and precious metals.

Petroleum:

Volume and Unit Value Indices:

Source B data, weights reference period: 1997. † From 1997 onward, new methodology is used to calculate the indices.

Import Prices:

Source B. For *line 76.x,* weights reference period: 2000, and the index is a component of the *Home & Imported Goods* index (*line 63s*).

Government Finance:

Quarterly and annual data are derived from source B. Data cover the operations of the budgetary central government. The fiscal year ends December 31.

National Accounts:

Source B. GDP chain-linked volume measures are calculated based on the prices and weights of the previous year, using Laspeyres formula in general.

Syrian Arab Republic 463

Date of Fund Membership:
April 10, 1947

Standard Sources:
B: Central Bank, *Quarterly Bulletin*
S: Central Bureau of Statistics, *Monthly Summary of Foreign Trade*

Exchange Rates:

Principal Rate (End of Period and Period Average):
The principal rate is an officially determined exchange rate. Beginning in January 2004, the multiple exchange rates for public and private sector transactions have been replaced by two rates: the state and public sector rate which is used for public sector transactions, and the private sector rate which is used for private sector transactions. Prior to January 2004, a number of different exchange rates were in use depending on the sector of the transactor and the purpose of the transaction.

International Liquidity:
Gold (National Valuation) (line 1and) is obtained by converting the value in national currency terms, as reported in the country's standard sources, using the prevailing exchange rate, as given in *line* **ae** or **we**.

Monetary Authorities:
Consolidates the Central Bank of Syria and monetary authority functions undertaken by the central government. The contra-entry to Treasury IMF accounts is included in *line 12a.*

Deposit Money Banks:
Comprises the six banks referred to as specialized banks in source B.

Interest Rates:

Discount Rate (End of Period):
Source B. Rate at which the Central Bank of Syria (CBS) discounts eligible commercial paper for banks not exceeding 120 days. CBS also quotes several other rates for loans and advances on commercial paper, for seasonal financing of agricultural and industrial operations, and for discounts to specialized credit institutions. Advances against government securities bear a rate of 1.0 percent per annum. CBS does not grant direct credit to business. The Council of Money and Credit, together with CBS, determine a ceiling for financing and rediscount operations of the Commercial Bank of Syria and other specialized banks. Banks are permitted to exceed this ceiling with the consent of CBS and the Minister of Economy and Trade. Borrowing from CBS within the quantitative limits may be considered a right of the banks, but CBS can finance banks more or less than the quantitative limits. CBS started regular operations on August 1, 1956, with a discount rate of 3.50 percent per annum. On July 11, 1962, the rate was changed to the present level of 5.00 percent.

Deposit Rate (Period Average):
Source B. Rate offered by specialized banks to current accounts and sight deposits of the private sector.

Lending Rate (Period Average):
Source B. Rate at which the Commercial Bank of Syria discounts private sector bonds.

Prices and Production:

Wholesale Prices:
Source B index, base 2000, covering all goods sold at wholesale markets in Damascus, except construction materials and highly fabricated goods.

Consumer Prices:
Source B. Weights Reference Period: 2000; Geographical Coverage: the whole country; Number of Items in Basket: 210; Basis for Calculation: the weights are derived from a household and expenditure survey conducted in 1996–97.

Industrial Production:
Source B index, weights reference period 2000. Covers mining, manufacturing, electricity, and gas. The basic indicators used are quantities produced in 78 main industries in Syria.

International Transactions:

Exports and Imports, c.i.f.:
All data are from source B. † Beginning in 2000, data have been calculated by authorities using a flexible exchange rate determined by the Ministry of Economy and Foreign Trade.

Trade indices:
Data are compiled on base 1990.

Government Finance:

Annual data are as reported for the *Government Finance Statistics Yearbook (GFSY)* and cover budgetary central government. The fiscal year ends December 31.

National Accounts:

Source B. *Line 99b* includes a statistical discrepancy.

Tajikistan   923

Date of Fund Membership:
April 27, 1993

Standard Sources:
B: National Bank of Tajikistan, *Monthly Statistical Bulletin*
S: State Statistical Agency, *Monthly Statistical Bulletin, Annual Economic Indicators*

Exchange Rates:
The Tajik ruble (TR) was introduced in May 1995. Beginning in November 2000, a new currency, the somoni (SM) replaced the Tajik ruble at the rate of SM 1 = TR 1000.

Official Rate: (End of Period and Period Average):
Prior to July 1, 2000, the official rate was established at the twice-weekly foreign exchange auctions in the Tajikistan Interbank Foreign Currency Exchange, which was eliminated in July 2000. Beginning in July 2000, the official rate is a weighted average of the established daily rates at the interbank foreign exchange market.

International Liquidity:
Gold (National Valuation) (line 1and) is equal to Gold (Thousands of Fine Troy Ounces) (line 1ad) valued at prevailing London market rates.

Monetary Authorities:
Comprises the National Bank of Tajikistan. Data are based on a new chart of accounts introduced at the end of 1998, broadly in line with international accounting standards. *Claims on Other Resident Sectors (line 12d)* include claims on other financial corporations, nonfinancial public and private enterprises, households, and nonprofit institutions serving households.

Deposit Money Banks:
Comprises all commercial banks in Tajikistan. Data are based on a new chart of accounts introduced in end–1998, which is broadly in line with International Accounting Standards. *Claims on Other Resident Sectors (line 22d)* include claims on other financial corporations, nonfinancial public and private enterprises, households, and nonprofit institutions serving households.

Interest Rates:
Source B.
Refinancing Rate (End of Period):
Rate charged by the National Bank of Tajikistan (NBT) on credits to commercial banks. Prior to January 2002, data refer to NBT's last credit auction rate plus a margin. † Beginning in January 2002, data refer to NBT Lombard rate calculated as last government securities auction rate plus a margin.

Deposit Rate:
Prior to January 2002, data (end-of-period) refer to weighted average rate offered by commercial banks on demand deposits and time deposits of all maturities in national currency. The rate is weighted by the outstanding amount of deposits. † Beginning in January 2002, data (period average) refer to weighted average rate offered by commercial banks on time and savings deposits of various maturities in national currency. The rate is weighted by the amount of new deposits accepted during the reference period.

Lending Rate:
Prior to January 2002, data (end-of-period) refer to weighted average rate charged by commercial banks on loans of all types and maturities in national currency to nonbank sectors. The rate is weighted by the outstanding amount of loans. † Beginning in January 2002, data (period average) refer to weighted average rate charged by commercial banks on loans of all types and maturities in national currency to nonbank sectors. The rate is weighted by the amount of new loans extended during the reference period.

Tanzania   738

Data refer to Tanzania, i.e., Tanzania Mainland, formerly Tanganyika, and Zanzibar, unless noted otherwise.

Date of Fund Membership:
September 10, 1962

Standard Sources:
A: Bank of Tanzania, *Economic and Operations Report*
B: Bank of Tanzania, *Economic Bulletin*
S: Bureau of Statistics, *Quarterly Statistical Bulletin*

Exchange Rates:

Official Rate: (End of Period and Period Average):
Central bank midpoint rate.

Monetary Authorities:

Comprises the Bank of Tanzania. Government foreign exchange is consolidated. † Beginning in December 1993, data are based on a new reporting system, which provides an improved classification of the accounts.

Deposit Money Banks:

Comprises commercial banks. † Beginning in June 1989, data are based on an improved sectorization of the accounts. † See note on monetary authorities.

Monetary Survey:

† See note on monetary authorities.

Other Banking Institutions:

Comprises Post Office Savings deposits. † See notes on monetary authorities and deposit money banks.

Money (National Definitions):

M0 comprises notes and coins issued and commercial banks' reserves. Banks' reserves include legal reserve requirements and clearing/settlement accounts.
M1 comprises currency held by the public and demand deposits of the private sector, nonfinancial public enterprises, and nonbank financial institutions with commercial banks.
M2 comprises M1 and time and savings deposits of the private sector, nonfinancial public enterprises, and nonbank financial institutions with commercial banks.
M3 comprises M2 and foreign currency deposits of the private sector, nonfinancial public enterprises, and nonbank financial institutions with commercial banks.

Interest Rates:

Discount Rate (End of Period):
Bank of Tanzania's rediscount rate on 35-day treasury bills. There is a spread of discount rates on commercial bills. An individual rate depends on the purpose for which the bill was drawn. For treasury bills of all maturities rediscounts are ½ of 1 percent and advances are 1 percent above the current rate for bills.

Treasury Bill Rate:
Rate on three-month treasury bills.

Savings Rate:
Average rate offered by commercial banks on savings deposits. † Beginning in July 2000, weighted average rate offered by commercial banks on savings deposits. The rate is weighted by deposit amounts.

Deposit Rate:
Rate offered by commercial banks on three- to six-month deposits. † Beginning in July 2000, weighted average rate offered by commercial banks on three-month deposits. The rate is weighted by deposit amounts.

Lending Rate:
Maximum rate charged by commercial banks on general purpose loans. † Beginning in January 1996, average rate charged by commercial banks on loans. † Beginning in July 2000, weighted average rate charged by commercial banks on loans. The rate is weighted by loan amounts.

Prices and Production:

Consumer Prices:
Source B. Weight Reference Period: 2001; Geographical Coverage: 20 urban towns of mainland; Number of Items in the Basket: 207 items; Basis of Calculation: 2000/2001 Household Budget Survey (HBS).

Manufacturing Production:
Source S. Weight Reference Period: 1995; Coverage: manufacturing establishments that on average have a labor force of 50 persons or more. The index covers more than 300 establishments that are surveyed, contributing more than 85% to total manufacturing gross output; Basis of Calculation: data are collected by means of the Quarterly Survey of Industrial Production and sent out by mail at the end of the reference period.

International Transactions:

Source B.

Government Finance:

Data are compiled by the Ministry of Finance and disseminated in the Bank of Tanzania's web page and in sources A and B. Revenue, grants, and expenditure data cover operations of the budgetary central government. The fiscal year ends June 30.

National Accounts:

Source B. As indicated by the country, the data are compiled in the framework of the *1968 SNA* but also includes certain elements of the *1993 SNA*.

Thailand   578

Date of Fund Membership:

May 3, 1949

Standard Sources:

B: Bank of Thailand, *Monthly Bulletin*
S: National Economic and Social Development Board, *National Income of Thailand*

Exchange Rates:

Official Rate: (End of Period and Period Average):
Average midpoint rate of all commercial banks. The official rate is determined on the basis of a weighted basket of currencies. † Effective July 2, 1997 the Bank of Thailand started operating a managed float for the baht exchange rate. In addition, the authorities introduced a two-tier currency market that creates separate exchange rates for investors who buy baht in domestic markets and those who buy it overseas.

International Liquidity:

Gold (National Valuation) (line 1and) is the U.S. dollar value of official holdings of gold as reported in the country's standard sources.
Gold is revalued annually at the end of the year.

Monetary Authorities:

Consolidates the Bank of Thailand, the Exchange Equalization Fund, and Financial Institutions Development Fund. For balance sheet purposes, gold is revalued annually at the afternoon quotation in London at the end of the year. Profits resulting from the revaluation of gold are set aside in a special reserve. † Beginning in January 1968 and December 1976, data are based on a new reporting system, which provides an improved classification and sectorization of the accounts. † Beginning in December 2001, data are based on an improved classification and sectorization of the accounts. † Beginning in January 2003, comprises the Bank of Thailand only. Data are based on a new reporting system which provides improved classification and sectorization of the accounts.

Banking Institutions:

Comprises commercial banks, Government Savings Bank, Bank for Agriculture and Agricultural Cooperatives, and Industrial Finance Corporation of Thailand. † Beginning in January 1968, data are based on a new reporting system, which provides an improved classification and sectorization of the accounts. Beginning in December 1974, includes the Government Housing Bank. † Beginning in December 1976, includes finance companies. A new system of bank returns was introduced that led to changes in the coverage of commercial bank data. Beginning in January 1996, includes the Export-Import Bank of Thailand. † Beginning in December 2001, data are based on an improved classification and sectorization of the accounts. † Beginning in January 2003, includes the Small and Medium Enterprises Bank of Thailand. Data are based on a new reporting system which provides improved classification and sectorization of the accounts. Beginning in September 2004, excludes the Industrial Finance Corporation of Thailand, which merged operations with a commercial bank, Thai Military Bank Public Company Ltd.

Banking Survey:

† See notes on monetary authorities and banking institutions.

Money (National Definitions):

M0 comprises currency in circulation and current account deposits of commercial banks, other financial institutions, local government, public nonfinancial corporations, and private sector with the Bank of Thailand (BOT). Currency in circulation refers to notes and coins issued by the BOT and central government less the amount held by the BOT and central government.

M1 comprises currency in circulation and transferable deposits. Currency in circulation refers to notes and coins issued by the BOT and central government less the amount held by the BOT, central government, and commercial banks. Transferable deposits refer to the current account deposits in national currency of other financial institutions, local government, public nonfinancial corporations, and private sector with the BOT and commercial banks.

Narrow Money comprises currency outside depository corporations and transferable deposits of other financial corporations, local governments, public nonfinancial corporations, and private sector with other depository corporations.

M2 comprises M1 and quasi-money. Quasi-money refers to time, savings, marginal, and foreign currency deposits of other financial institutions, local government, public nonfinancial corporations, and private sector with commercial banks.

M2a comprises M2 (less notes and coins held by finance companies and deposits of finance companies with commercial banks) and promissory notes issued by finance companies held by other financial institutions, local government, public nonfinancial corporations, and private sector.

M3 comprises currency in circulation; demand, time, savings, marginal, and foreign currency deposits of local government, public nonfinancial corporations, private sector, and other financial corporations with commercial banks and specialized financial institutions; and promissory notes issued by finance companies and finance and securities companies held by local government, public nonfinancial corporations, private sector, and other financial corporations.

Broad Money comprises currency outside depository corporations, including the currency issued by the government; transferable and other deposits of other financial corporations, local governments, public nonfinancial corporations, and private sector with other depository corporations; and securities issued by finance companies and held by other financial corporations, local governments, public nonfinancial corporations, and private sector.

Interest Rates:

All interest rate data are from source B.

Discount Rate (End of Period):
Discount rate offered by the Bank of Thailand.

Money Market Rate:
Rate on loans between commercial banks. † Beginning in January 1989, daily average of commercial banks' overnight rates for interbank lending.

Treasury Bill Rate:
Average rate on the total of accepted treasury bills sold at tender.

Deposit Rate:
Maximum rate offered by commercial banks on three- to six-month savings deposits.

Lending Rate:
Minimum rate charged by commercial banks on loans to prime customers.

Government Bond Yield:
Maximum coupon rate on bonds allotted to banks and other financial institutions in Thailand.

Prices:

Share Prices:
Composite stock price index of the Stock Exchange of Thailand, base April 30, 1975. The index covers common stocks and is weighted by market capitalization. The monthly index is calculated from the average of the daily closing quotations.

Producer Prices:
Source B. Weights Reference Period: 2000; Coverage: measures changes in the selling price received by domestic producers for their output; Number of Items in the Basket: 506 items; Basis for Calculation: the weights for major product groups are obtained from the 2000 input-output table. Disaggregated weights are based on turnover data obtained from surveys of major producers. The index is re-based and re-weighted each time the input-output table is revised.

Consumer Prices:
Source B. Weights Reference Period: 2002; Geographical Coverage: nationwide; Number of Items in the Basket: 373 items; Basis for Calculation: the weights are based on a Household Expenditure Survey conducted by the NSO in 2002 amd normally re-based every four years.

International Transactions:

All trade data are from source B, based on customs records. *Exports* include re-exports. *Imports* include gold and exclude military aid.

Unit Value of Exports and Imports:
Source B index numbers, national currency, base 1995. From January 1996 onward, unit value indices are calculated by using Fisher chained method. Volume indices are obtained by dividing value indices by Fisher chained unit value indices. *Export Volume* indices for individual commodities are based on source B data in metric tons.

Export Unit Value indices for individual commodities are calculated for *IFS* from reported value and volume data. The rice wholesale price index is the Thailand (Bangkok) index shown in the world table for commodity prices, and the rubber wholesale price index is the Malaysia (Singapore) index shown in the world table for commodity prices, both converted into baht at the period average exchange rate.

Government Finance:

Data are derived from source B and cover the operations of the consolidated central government. Expenditure exclude expenditure financed through foreign loans and grants. The fiscal year ends September 30.

National Accounts:

Data are from source S. *Line 99b* is derived from the production accounts; therefore, it differs from the sum of the expenditure components presented here.

Togo   742

Date of Fund Membership:
August 1, 1962

Standard Source:

B: Banque Centrale des Etats de l'Afrique de l'Ouest (Central Bank of West African States), *Notes d'information et Statistiques (Informative Notes and Statistics)*
Togo is a member of the West African Economic and Monetary Union, together with Benin, Burkina Faso, Côte d'Ivoire, Guinea-Bissau, Mali, Niger, and Senegal. The Union, which was established in 1962, has a common central bank, the Central Bank of West African States (BCEAO), with headquarters in Dakar, and national branches in the member states. Mali and Guinea-Bissau joined the Union on June 1, 1984 and May 2, 1997, respectively.

Exchange Rates:

Official Rate: (End of Period and Period Average):
Prior to January 1999, the official rate was pegged to the French franc. On January 12, 1994, the CFA franc was devalued to CFAF 100 per French franc from CFAF 50 at which it had been fixed since 1948. From January 1, 1999, the CFAF is pegged to the euro at a rate of CFA franc 655.957 per euro.

International Liquidity:

Gold is revalued on a quarterly basis at the rate communicated by the BCEAO, which corresponds to the lowest average fixing in the London market.

Monetary Authorities:

Comprises the national branch of the BCEAO only. The amount of currency outside banks is estimated by subtracting from the amount of CFA franc notes issued by Togo the estimated amounts of Togo's currency in the cash held by the banks of all member countries of the Union.

Deposit Money Banks:

Comprises commercial banks and development banks, and includes certain banking operations of the Treasury and the Post Office. The Treasury accepts customs duty bills (reported separately in *line 22d.i*). Through its many branches, the Postal Checking System acts as the main depository for the private sector in the interior of Togo. *Claims on the Private Sector (line 22d)* include doubtful and litigious debts. † Beginning in 1979, *Central Government Deposits (line 26d)* include the deposits of the public establishments of an administrative or social nature (EPAS) and exclude those of the savings bank; *Demand and Time Deposits (lines 24 and 25)* include deposits of the savings bank and exclude deposits of EPAS; and *Claims on Private Sector (line 22d)* exclude claims on other financial institutions.

Monetary Survey:

The data reported agree with source B aggregates, as given in the table on the position of the monetary institutions, except for *line 31n,* for which source B treats long-term foreign liabilities and SDR allocations as a foreign liability, whereas *IFS* reports the former separately and includes the latter in *line 37r.* Moreover, valuation differences exist as a result of the *IFS* calculations of reserve position in the Fund and the SDR holdings, both components of *line 11,* based on Fund record. † Beginning in 1979, *Claims on Other Financial Institutions (line 32f)* includes claims of deposit money banks on other financial institutions; see deposit money bank notes for explanation of other break symbols.

Other Banking Institutions:

Liquid Liabilities (line 55l): † See notes on deposit money banks and monetary survey.

Interest Rates:

Bank Rate (End of Period):
Rate on repurchase agreements between the BCEAO and the banks. † Prior to October 1, 1993 data refer to basic discount rate offered by the BCEAO.

Money Market Rate:
Rate paid on overnight interbank advances.

Deposit Rate:
Rate offered by banks on time deposits of CFAF 500,000–2,000,000 for under six months.

Prices and Labor:

Consumer Prices:
Source B. Weights Reference Period: 1996; Geographical Coverage: City of Lome; Number of Items in Basket: 362; Basis for Calculation: The weights are derived from the survey "WAEMU Prices" of 1996.

International Transactions:

All trade data are from source B.

Government Finance:

The data are provided by source B and cover the consolidated central government. The fiscal year ends December 31.

National Accounts:
Source B. The reference is the *1968 SNA*.

Tonga 866

Date of Fund Membership:
September 13, 1985

Standard Sources:
B: Data are provided by the National Reserve Bank of Tonga
S: Statistics Department, Ministry of Finance, *Statistical Abstract* and *Foreign Trade Report*

Exchange Rates:
Official Rate: (End of Period and Period Average):
The pa'anga has been pegged at par to the Australian dollar from November 1976 through February 8, 1991. Beginning February 11, 1991, the value of the pa'anga has been determined daily by reference to a weighted basket of currencies of Tonga's most important partners in trade and payments transactions. Beginning in November 1999, the official rate is the central bank midpoint rate.

International Liquidity:
Data for *Foreign Exchange (line 1d.d)* include small foreign exchange holdings by central government.

Monetary Authorities:
Comprises the National Reserve Bank of Tonga (NRBT) only.

Deposit Money Banks:
Comprises commercial banks.

Other Banking Institutions:
Comprises the Tonga Development Bank (TDB).

Money (National Definitions):
Reserve Money comprises currency in circulation and deposits of commercial banks at the NRBT.
M1 comprises currency outside commercial banks and the TDB and demand deposits of the private sector in national currency at commercial banks.
Quasi-Money comprises time, savings, and foreign currency deposits of the private sector at commercial banks and savings deposits of the private sector at the TDB.
M2 comprises M1 plus quasi-money.

Interest Rates:
All interest rate data are from source B.
Deposit Rate:
Rate offered by commerical banks on six-month time deposits.
Lending Rate:
Maximum rate charged by the Bank of Tonga on loans. † Beginning in September 1993, average rate, which is the total interest received and accrued on all performing loans and overdrafts, charged by the Bank of Tonga as of the last business day of the quarter, divided by the average size of the portfolio during the quarter. † Beginning in July 1994, weighted average rate charged by commercial banks on loans. The rate is weighted by loan amounts.

Prices and Labor:
Consumer Prices:
Source B. Weights Reference Period: 2000–2001; Geographical Coverage: Tongapatu division (main island of Tonga); Number of Items in Basket: 453; Basis for Calculation: the weights are derived from the urban household income and expenditure survey conducted in the period 2000–2001.

International Transactions:
All trade data are from source S.

National Accounts:
Data are as reported by the national authorities and are compiled on a fiscal year basis.

Trinidad and Tobago 369

Date of Fund Membership:
September 16, 1963

Standard Sources:
B: Central Bank, *Statistical Digest*
S: Central Statistical Office, *Quarterly Economic Report*

Exchange Rates:
Market Rate (End of Period and Period Average):
Effective April 13, 1993, the exchange rate of the TT dollar is market-determined. Prior to that date, the rates were based on a fixed relationship to the U.S. dollar.

International Liquidity:
Line 1d.d includes a share in small holdings of foreign exchange by the British Caribbean Currency Board.
Gold (National Valuation) (line 1and) is obtained by converting the value in national currency terms, as reported in the country's standard sources, using the prevailing exchange rate, as given in *line* **ae** or **we**.
External accounts of other financial institutions exclude nonbank financial institutions, namely, life insurance companies.

Monetary Authorities:
Consolidates the Central Bank of Trinidad and Tobago (CBTT) and monetary authority functions undertaken by the central government. † Beginning in December 1996, data are based on an improved sectorization of the accounts.

Deposit Money Banks:
Comprises commercial banks. † See note on monetary authorities.

Monetary Survey:
† See note on monetary authorities.

Other Banking Institutions:
Comprises post office savings deposits. † Beginning in December 1970, comprised other banklike institutions and development banks. Other banklike institutions comprise finance houses, merchant banks, trust and mortgage finance companies, and thrift institutions. † See note on monetary authorities.

Banking Survey:
† See note on monetary authorities.

Money (National Definitions):

Base Money comprises currency in circulation and commercial banks' deposits with the CBTT. Currency in circulation refers to notes and coins issued by the CBTT less the amount held by commercial banks and in the vaults of the CBTT.

M1A comprises currency in circulation, cashiers' cheques, and demand deposits in national currency of other financial corporations, state and local governments, public nonfinancial corporations, and private sector with commercial banks less cash items in the process of collection from other banks and net inter-branch clearings. Currency in circulation refers to notes and coins issued by the CBTT less the amount held by commercial banks and in the vaults of the CBTT.

M1C comprises M1A and savings deposits in national currency of other financial corporations, state and local governments, public nonfinancial corporations, and private sector with commercial banks.

M2 comprises M1C and time deposits in national currency of other financial corporations, state and local governments, public nonfinancial corporations, and private sector with commercial banks.

M2* comprises M2 and foreign currency deposits of other financial corporations, state and local governments, public nonfinancial corporations, and private sector with commercial banks.

M3 comprises M2 and time and savings deposits in national currency of other financial corporations, state and local governments, public nonfinancial corporations, and private sector with other banking institutions.

M3* comprises M2*, time and savings deposits in national currency and foreign currency deposits of other financial corporations, state and local governments, public nonfinancial corporations, and private sector with other banking institutions.

Nonbank Financial Institutions:

Comprises insurance companies.

Interest Rates:

All interest rate data are from source B.

Bank Rate (End of Period):
Rate at which the Central Bank of Trinidad and Tobago lends to commercial banks.

Treasury Bill Rate:
Average tender rate for three-month bills. The Central Bank also sells treasury bills of the latest issue to commercial banks and to the public, normally at a slightly lower rate.

Savings Rate:
Median of ordinary savings deposits rates offered by commercial banks.

Deposit Rate:
Weighted average rate offered by commercial banks on 6-month time deposits in national currency. The rate is weighted by deposit amounts.

Deposit Rate (Foreign Currency):
Weighted average rate offered by commercial banks on 6-month time deposits and 6-month certificates of deposit in foreign currency. The rate is weighted by deposit amounts.

Lending Rate:
Median of basic prime rates charged by commercial banks on loans.

Government Bond Yield:
Average of redemption yields on government bonds with remaining maturities exceeding 20 years.

Prices, Production, Labor:

Share Prices:
Composite price index covering commercial banking, conglomerates, manufacturing, property, trading, and nonbank finance shares quoted on the Trinidad and Tobago Stock Exchange, weights reference period: January 1983. The index is computed every trading day by the Trinidad and Tobago Stock Exchange Limited based on share closing prices and outstanding listed share capital.

Producer Prices:
Source B. Weights Reference Period: October 1978.

Consumer Prices:
Source B. Weights Reference Period: January 2003.

Industrial Production:
Source B. Weights Reference Period: 1995.

International Transactions:

Exports and Imports:
All trade value data are from source B, as compiled by the Central Statistical Office, and include merchandise under Processing Agreement.

Government Finance:

Annual data are as reported for the *Government Finance Statistics Yearbook (GFSY)* and cover consolidated central government. The fiscal year ends September 30.

National Accounts:

Source B.

Tunisia   744

Date of Fund Membership:
April 14, 1958

Standard Sources:
B: Central Bank, *Financial Statistics*
S: National Institute of Statistics, *Monthly Bulletin of Statistics*

Exchange Rates:

Market Rate (End of Period and Period Average):
Central bank midpoint rate.

International Liquidity:

Gold (National Valuation) (line 1and) is obtained by converting the value in national currency terms, as reported in the country's standard sources, using the prevailing exchange rate, as given in *line* **de**, *line* **ae**, or *line* **we**.

Lines 7a.d and 7b.d are derived from the accounts of commercial banks and exclude the foreign accounts of offshore banks operating in Tunisia.

Monetary Authorities:

Beginning in January 1998, items previously classified as *Claims on Deposit Money Banks (line 12e)* have been reclassified as *Claims on Private Sector (line 12d)*.

Deposit Money Banks:
Comprises commercial banks.

Monetary Survey:
Line 37r and *line 32d*: See note to section 10.

Other Banking Institutions:
Comprises the Economic Development Bank of Tunisia (BDET), previously known as the National Investment Corporation, the General Investment Bank (BGI), the Financial and Tourism Company (COFIT), the Tunisian National Savings Bank (CENT), the National Housing Savings Bank (CNEL), and the portfolio management companies (GEP, SIMPARI, SOFIGES, UF, and UTP). Data agree with those in source B.

Banking Survey:
Line 52d and *line 57r*: See note to section 10.

Interest Rates:
Discount Rate (End of Period):
Source B. The rate mainly applies to the rediscount of short-term commercial paper. Another rate exists that applies to the rediscount of financial paper and advances to banks in the form of guaranteed overdrafts. In November 1996 the Central Bank abolished its rediscount facility for preferential credit to certain sectors.
Money Market Rate:
Upper margin of interest on overnight interbank deposits.

Prices, Production, Labor:
Producer Prices:
Source B. Weights Reference Period: 1990; Coverage: all industrial goods manufactured and sold on the local market; Number of Items in Basket: 347 products in ten industries; Basis for Calculation: weights are based on the value of the 1990 sales.

Consumer Prices:
Source B. Weights Reference Period: 1990; Geographical Coverage: 18 communes representing the capital cities of governorates and communes having more than 50,000 inhabitants in 1994; Number of Items in Basket: 819; Basis for Calculation: weights are obtained from the 1990 Survey of Household Budgets and Consumption.

Industrial Production:
Source S. Weights Reference Period: 1990; Sectoral Coverage: manufacturing, mining, and energy sectors, excluding construction and public works; Basis for Calculation: the weights for the index are derived on the basis of the value added to factor costs, by sector.

Mining Production:
Source B. Weights Reference Period: 1990; no data were reported for 1984–1986.

Crude Petroleum Production:
The index is calculated from source B data in metric tons.

International Transactions:
All trade data are from source B.
Trade indices:
Data are compiled on weights reference period: 1990.

Government Finance:
Annual data are as reported for the *Government Finance Statistics Yearbook (GFSY)* and cover budgetary central government. The fiscal year ends December 31.

National Accounts:
Source B.

Turkey   186

Date of Fund Membership:
March 11, 1947

Standard Sources:
B: Central Bank, *Quarterly Bulletin*
S: State Institute of Statistics, *Monthly Bulletin of Statistics, Summary of Monthly Foreign Trade*

Exchange Rates:
On January 1, 2005, the New Turkish Lira (YTL), equal to 1,000,000 Turkish lira, was introduced.
Market Rate (End of Period and Period Average):
Official midpoint rate.

International Liquidity:
Gold (National Valuation) (line 1and) is equal to *Gold in Million Fine Troy Ounces (line 1ad)* valued at US$369.1 between 1988–97 and US$ 300 per ounce in 1998. Beginning in 1999, gold data are valued annually based on the price quoted on the London Stock Exchange on the last day of each year.

Monetary Authorities:
Source B, *Quarterly Bulletin.*
Comprises the Central Bank of the Republic of Turkey (CBRT), inclusive of transactions with the IMF undertaken by the Government of the Republic of Turkey. Contra-entries to the Government's transactions with the IMF are made to *Other Items Net (line 17r). Foreign Assets (line 11):* Convertible foreign assets are adjusted to include foreign exchange receivable from, and exclude foreign exchange payable to banking institutions under swap arrangements. Counterpart adjustments are made to the foreign assets of banking institutions *(line 21). Claims on Central Government (line 12a):* Data are adjusted to include securities sold, and exclude those purchased, under repurchase agreements with banking institutions. Counterpart adjustments are made in the accounts of banking institutions *(line 22a).* † Beginning in December 2002, data are based on improved sectoral and instrument classification of accounts.

Banking Institutions:
Source B, *Quarterly Bulletin.*
Comprises commercial banks and investment and development banks. *Foreign Assets (line 21):* See note for *line 11.* Beginning in October 1996, *Foreign Assets (line 21)* include foreign currency checks received, which were previously recorded among *Other Items (Net) (line 27r). Money Market Instruments (line 26aa):* Comprises banks' negotiable certificates of deposit; however, data for 1989–92 include some data for instruments with longer-dated maturities. † Beginning in December 2002, data are based on an improved sectoral and instrument classification of accounts.

Banking Survey:
See notes on monetary authorities and banking institutions.

Money (National Definitions):
M2 (broad money) comprises currency in circulation outside banking institutions and the demand, savings, and time deposits

in national and foreign currency held by resident, non-central government sectors at the central bank and banking institutions. Data are reported inclusive of accrued interest.

M3 comprises M2 plus some deposits of general government ("official deposits") at the central bank and banking institutions. Data for M3 are published excluding accrued interest.

Interest Rates:

Discount Rate (End of Period):
Source B. The rate at which the central bank lends to eligible banks and state economic enterprises.

Interbank Money Market Rate:
Weighted average annualized rate in the overnight interbank money market.

Treasury Bill Rate:
Weighted average auction rate on 3-month Treasury bills.

Deposit Rate:
Data refer to the rate on three-month time deposits denominated in Turkish lira.

Prices, Production, Labor:

Wholesale Prices:
Source S. Weights Reference Period: 2003; Coverage: agricultural, manufacturing, mining, and energy sectors nationwide; Number of Items in Basket: 762; Basis for Calculation: weights used for the index are based on the industrial production data and agricultural and mining and energy censuses of 2004.

Consumer Prices:
Source S. Weights Reference Period: 2003; Geographical Coverage: 26 regions and 81 cities throughout Turkey; Number of Items in Basket: 442; Basis for Calculation: weights and item basket are updated every year by means of continuous household budget surveys.

Industrial Production:
Source S. Weights Reference Period: 1997; Sectoral Coverage: manufacturing, mining and electricity, gas and water; Basis for Calculation: the weights for the index are derived from the weights reference period value added data of the activities covering all public sector establishments and those private sector establishments with 10 or more employees.

International Transactions:

Trade value and indices data in U.S. dollars are from source S. The volume indices are of the Laspeyres type with 2003 weights, and the unit value indices use the Fisher formula.

Government Finance:

Data are as reported for the *Government Finance Statistics Yearbook (GFSY)* and cover budgetary central government. The fiscal year ends December 31.

National Accounts:

Source S. Beginning in 1990, data are sourced from the Eurostat database.

Uganda 746

Date of Fund Membership:

September 27, 1963

Standard Sources:

B: Bank of Uganda, *Quarterly Economic Report*
G: Ministry of Finance and Economic Planning

Exchange Rates:

Principal Rate (End of Period and Period Average):
The principal rate is determined on the basis of a trade-weighted basket of currencies.

International Liquidity:

Foreign Exchange (line 1d.d) reflects the U.S. dollar value of foreign currency holdings, as reported by the Foreign Exchange Operations Department of the Bank of Uganda. † Prior to October 1984, data for *line 1d.d* are obtained by converting the shilling value of the Bank of Uganda's foreign exchange holdings, as maintained by the Accounts Department of the Bank of Uganda, using the prevailing exchange rate given in *line* **ae**.

Monetary Authorities:

Consolidates the Bank of Uganda and monetary authority functions undertaken by the central government. The Treasury IMF accounts are included in *line 12a*. † Prior to 1983, the main government accounts were shown on a net basis in *Claims on Central Government (line 12a)*. Beginning in June 1983, *line 12a* and *Central Government Deposits (line 16d)* are presented on a gross basis. † Beginning in June 1987, data are based on an improved sectorization and classification of the accounts.

Deposit Money Banks:

Comprises commercial banks.

Monetary Survey:

† See note on monetary authorities.

Money (National Definitions):

Base Money comprises currency in circulation, current accounts and other transaction balances of commercial banks, excluding banks in liquidation, and commercial bank investment in Bank of Uganda instruments. Currency in circulation refers to notes and coins issued by the Bank of Uganda.

M2 comprises currency in circulation and transferable and other deposits in national currency of nonbank financial corporations, state and local governments, public nonfinancial corporations, and private sector with commercial banks.

M2A comprises M2 plus certificates of deposit in national currency held by nonbank financial corporations, state and local governments, public nonfinancial corporations, and private sector with commercial banks.

M3 comprises M2A plus foreign currency deposits of nonbank financial corporations, state and local governments, public nonfinancial corporations, and private sector with commercial banks.

Interest Rates:

All interest rate data are from source B.

Bank Rate (End of Period):
Rate offered by the Bank of Uganda to commercial banks for general purposes.

Treasury Bill Rate:
Rate determined by the Bank of Uganda on 91-day treasury bills. † Beginning in May 1992, rate on 91-day treasury bills auctioned every two weeks.

Savings Rate:
Weighted average rate offered by commercial banks on savings deposits in national currency. Rate is weighted by deposit amounts.

Deposit Rate:
Rate offered by commercial banks on time deposits. † Beginning in June 1984, Rate offered by commercial banks on time deposits of less than 12 months.

Lending Rate:
Rate charged by commercial banks on credit to finance exports and manufacturing production.

Government Bond Yield:
Coupon rate on Government of Uganda stock with an original maturity of ten years.

Prices:

Consumer Prices:
Source S. Weight Reference Period: 1997–1998; Geographical Coverage: all households in Kampala; Number of Items in the Basket: 121 items; Basis of Calculation: based on the Uganda National Household Survey (UNHS) conducted between March-November 1997.

International Transactions:

Data are based on customs records from the Customs department of the Uganda Revenue Authority (URA), and are compiled by the Uganda Bureau of Statistics (UBOS), and the Bank of Uganda (BOU).

Imports, c.i.f.:
Data are for cash imports, imports without foreign exchange required, barter, and project imports valued at the official exchange rate.

Government Finance:

Data are reported by source B and cover budgetary central government. † Prior to 2002, to the extent possible, existing subannual *IFS* data were converted to the main aggregates that are presented in the *GFSM 2001* Statement of Sources and Uses of Cash (see the Introduction of the monthly *IFS* publication for details). The fiscal year ends June 30.

National Accounts:

Source S. As indicated by the country, the estimates are based primarily on the concepts and classifications of the *1968 SNA*.

Ukraine   926

Date of Fund Membership:

Weighted average rate on loans between commercial banks in foreign currency. The rate is weighted by daily loan amounts. September 3, 1992

Standard Sources:

B: National Bank of Ukraine
S: Ministry of Statistics of Ukraine

Exchange Rates:

On September 2, 1996, the Ukrainian hryvnia, equal to 100,000 karbovanets, was introduced.

Official Rate: (End of Period and Period Average):
The official rate is determined by the National Bank of Ukraine (NBU) and is set equal to the rate established at the Ukranian in-terbank exchange market one day before the last business day of the period. Effective January 1, 2002, the exchange arrangement of Ukraine has been reclassified to the category conventional pegged arrangement.

International Liquidity:

Data for *Foreign Exchange (line 1d.d)* comprise NBU's convertible currency and other liquid claims on nonresidents denominated in convertible currencies.

Monetary Authorities:

Comprises the National Bank of Ukraine (NBU) only. † Beginning in January 1998, data reflect the introduction of a new accounting system which provides an improved classification and sectorization of the accounts. † Beginning in December 2001, data are based on an improved classification and sectorization of the accounts. † Beginning in March 2004, data are based on a new reporting system which provides an improved classification and sectorization of the accounts.

Banking Institutions:

Comprises commercial banks and the Savings Bank. *Money Market Instruments (line 26aa)* comprise debt securities, tradable savings certificates, and fiduciary transactions. † Beginning in January 1998, data reflect the introduction of a new accounting system which provides an improved classification and sectorization of the accounts. † Beginning in December 2001, data are based on an improved classification and sectorization of the accounts. † Beginning in March 2004, data are based on a new reporting system which provides an improved classification and sectorization of the accounts.

Banking Survey:

See notes on monetary authorities and banking institutions.

Money (National Definitions):

Reserve Money comprises notes and coins issued by the National Bank of Ukraine (NBU) and demand deposits of banking institutions and the private sector at the NBU in national currency.

M0 comprises notes and coins issued by the NBU, excluding holdings of the NBU and other depository corporations.

M1 comprises M0 and transferable deposits in national currency. Transferable deposits comprise liabilities of depository corporations on demand deposits (current account deposits and settlement accounts) in national currency of other financial corporations, nonfinancial corporations, households and nonprofit institutions serving households.

M2 comprises M1, transferable deposits in foreign currency, and other deposits in both national and foreign currency with the NBU and other depository corporations. Other deposits comprise liabilities of depository corporations on other demand deposits (target deposits, deposits on clearing accounts, deposits on accounts of VAT taxpayers), time deposits and deposits on registered saving certificates which belong to other financial corporations, nonfinancial corporations, households and nonprofit institutions serving households.

M3 comprises M2 and securities other than shares in both national and foreign currency. Securities other than shares included in M3 comprise liabilities of deposit corporations on time debt securities and bearer saving (deposit) certificates, obtained by other financial corporations, nonfinancial corporations, households and nonprofit institutions serving households.

Interest Rates:

All interest rate data are from source B.
Refinancing Rate (End of Period):
Basic rate at which the NBU extends refinancing loans to banks for a specified period.

Money Market Rate:
Weighted average rate on loans in national currency at the interbank market. The rate is weighted by daily loan amounts.

Money Market Rate (Foreign Currency):
Weighted average rate on loans in foreign currency at the interbank market. The rate is weighted by daily loan amounts.

Deposit Rate:
Weighted average rate offered by commercial banks on deposits in national currency. The rate is weighted by deposit amounts.

Deposit Rate (Foreign Currency):
Weighted average rate offered by commercial banks on deposits in foreign currency. The rate is weighted by deposit amounts.

Lending Rate:
Weighted average rate charged by commercial banks on loans in national currency. The rate is weighted by loan amounts.

Lending Rate (Foreign Currency):
Weighted average rate charged by commercial banks on loans in foreign currency. The rate is weighted by loan amounts.

Prices and Labor:

Share Prices:
Capital weighted share price index covering shares quoted on the First Securities Trading System (PFTS), base October 1, 1997. The list of share of companies included in the index calculation includes the most liquid shares and is revised monthly.

Wholesale Prices:
Source S index. The index covers wholesale prices (before VAT and excise) of over 6,000 agricultural and industrial articles produced by about 2,000 resident enterprises, which account for a large proportion of agricultural and industrial production. Excludes services.

Consumer Prices:
Source S. Geographical Coverage: 27 regions; Number of Items in Basket: 270; Basis for Calculation: Weights are based on Household Budget Survey and are updated at approximately one-yearly intervals.

Wages:
Source S. Data show the average level of wages and salaries for employees in state and non-state sectors (including cooperatives, small enterprises, and industrial workshops/sections of collective farms and other nonindustrial organizations) per employee.

Industrial Employment:
Source S. The coverage is the same as for wages.

International Transactions:

Source S. *Exports (line 70..d)* and *Imports (line 71..d),* compiled from enterprise survey data, include oil and gas traded through pipelines.

Government Finance:

Annual data are as reported for the *Government Finance Statistics Yearbook (GFSY)* and cover budgetary central government. The fiscal year ends December 31.

National Accounts:

Source S. The expenditure components (*lines 96f–98c*) are compiled from data on (1) household budget survey, retail trade turnover (that includes adjustment for unofficial retail trade), and services, (2) fiscal reports, (3) surveys of capital formation and government documents, and (4) balance of payments. The data on inventories are obtained from a financial survey of enterprises and are adjusted to exclude holding gains. As indicated by the country, data are based on the *1993 SNA.*

United Arab Emirates   466

Date of Fund Membership:
September 22, 1972

Standard Sources:
A: Central Bank, *Annual Report*
B: Central Bank, *Bulletin*
S: Department of Planning, Abu Dhabi, *Statistical Abstract* and *Statistical Yearbook*

Exchange Rates:

Official Rate: (End of Period and Period Average):
Central bank midpoint rate.

International Liquidity:

Gold (National Valuation) (line 1and) is obtained by converting the value in national currency terms, as reported in the country's standard sources, using the prevailing exchange rate, as given in line **ae** or **we**.
Lines 7a.d and *7b.d* are the U.S. dollar equivalents of *lines 21* and *26c,* respectively. They exclude the foreign accounts of the restricted license banks (RLBs), first authorized in 1976. RLBs are not permitted to accept local currency deposits from nonbank residents but otherwise operate as commercial banks. RLB foreign assets and foreign liabilities, as reported in source B, are given in *lines 7k.d* and *7m.d,* respectively. The difference between these two lines essentially reflects the domestic credit extended by RLBs.

Monetary Authorities:

Consolidates the United Arab Emirates Central Bank and monetary authority functions undertaken by the central government. The contra-entry to Treasury IMF accounts, which are paid by the Government of Abu Dhabi, is included in *line 16d.*
The gold component of *line 11* is valued at the market-related cost of acquisition.
Beginning January 1990, data are provisional.

Deposit Money Banks:

Consolidates the accounts of the commercial banks operating in the seven United Arab Emirates.

Production:

Crude Petroleum Production:
Source B data covering production of the Abu Dhabi, Dubai, and Sharjah Fields. Data for current periods are based on production quantities as reported in the *Oil Market Intelligence.*

International Transactions:

Imports, c.i.f.:
Source B data covering imports into Dubai, Abu Dhabi, and Sharjah. Inter-emirate trade and transit trade are excluded, as are imports of gold and silver.

Government Finance:

Annual data are as reported for the *Government Finance Statistics Yearbook (GFSY)* and cover budgetary central government. The fiscal year ends December 31.

National Accounts:

Source S.

United Kingdom   112

Date of Fund Membership:
December 27, 1945

Standard Sources:
B: Bank of England, *Monetary and Financial Statistics*
S: Office for National Statistics, *Monthly Digest of Statistics, Economic Trends, Financial Statistics*

Exchange Rates:

Market Rate (End of Period and Period Average):
Midpoint rate at noon in the London market.

International Liquidity:

International Reserves (minus Gold) (line 1l.d) excludes the foreign assets of the central bank (Bank of England). This institutional separation reflects the fact that the ownership and purpose of the central government and Bank of England pools of foreign assets are different. The Exchange Equalization Account (EEA) holds the central government's foreign currency assets, owned by Her Majesty's Treasury but managed by the Bank of England acting as its agent. The EEA was established in 1932 to provide a fund that could be used for "checking undue fluctuations in the exchange value of sterling" (Section 24 of the Finance Act 1932). Any U.K. government intervention in the foreign exchange market would therefore be conducted through the EEA. The Bank of England manages its own holdings of foreign assets and gold which mainly arise from the Bank's routine banking business with its customers, from its operations in the U.K. money markets, and from U.K. participation in the euro payment system, TARGET. In accordance with the Chancellor of the Exchequer's letter of May 6, 1997 to the Governor of the Bank of England, the Bank may intervene in the foreign exchange market in support of its monetary policy objective. The Bank of England's holdings of foreign assets are, therefore, not considered by the U.K. authorities to be part of the U.K.'s international reserves. Data on the Bank of England's holdings of liquid foreign assets (including Gold) are shown for completeness under *Other Liquid Foreign Assets (line 1e.d)*. Net TARGET related balances are included in *Other Liquid Foreign Assets (line 1e.d)*.
From April 1979 to June 1999, international reserves were valued using parity exchange rates; non-dollar holdings were revalued each year at the average of their exchange rates against the U.S. dollar in the three months up to the end of March. This system

was amended in April 1980 in that the U.S. dollar valuation on the last working day of March was used—if that was lower than the three-month average. The only exception to this was Gold for which a discount was also applied. Hence, beginning in April 1980, gold was valued at the lower of either the average of the London fixing price for the three months up to the end of March, less 25 percent, or at 75 percent of its final fixing price on the last working day in March.
Banking Institutions: Foreign Assets (line 7a.d) includes banking institutions' claims on foreign central monetary institutions (CMIs) and other nonresidents in the form of loans and advances, overdrafts, commercial bills, sterling denominated acceptances, and from end–1985, bonds issued by nonresidents. *Foreign Liabilities (line 7b.d)* includes banking institutions' liabilities to foreign CMIs, and other nonresidents.
The data on external liabilities and claims are as reported in source B.

Monetary Authorities:

† Beginning in July 1999, consolidates the accounts of the Bank of England's Issue and Banking Departments, and central government functions relating to the issue of coin. Prior to July 1999, consolidates the accounts of the Bank of England's Issue Department, central government functions relating to the issue of coin, and the EEA.
Foreign Assets (line 11) comprises monetary authorities' claims on nonresidents and includes gross TARGET related claims on the European Central Bank (ECB) and other member countries of the TARGET payment system. Beginning with the data for end-November 2000, *Foreign Assets* are affected by a change from gross to net presentation of positions relating to the TARGET (Trans-European Automated Real-Time Gross Settlement Express Transfer) euro clearing system. (See *Recording of TARGET system positions* under *European Economic and Monetary Union (EMU)* in the introduction to *IFS*.) *Reserve Money (line 14)* comprises the monetary liabilities of the monetary authorities: Issue Department notes and Treasury coin in circulation, plus bankers' restricted and unrestricted deposits at the Bank of England. *Foreign Liabilities (line 16c)* comprises monetary authority liabilities to nonresidents, including gross TARGET related liabilities to the ECB and other members of the TARGET payment system. Beginning with the data for end-November 2000, *Foreign Liabilities* are affected by a change from gross to net presentation of positions relating to the TARGET euro clearing system. (See *Recording of TARGET system positions* under *European Economic and Monetary Union (EMU)* in the introduction to *IFS*.) *Other Items (Net) (line 17r)* includes Bank of England claims on U.K. banking institutions.

Banking Institutions:

† A new system of bank returns was introduced in 1975. As a result of this change, (1) money at call and money placed overnight are now reported in line 24 rather thatn in lin 25 – a shift of approximately 700 million pounds sterling – and (2) line 21 is estimated to have increased by about 1,3000 million pounds sterling. † Beginning in 1981, they comprise the U.K. monetary sector as described in the December 1981 issue of the Bank of England's Monetary and Financial Statistics, subject to the same exclusions as the banking sector. † Prior to 1987, building societies are treated as part of the private sector. Beginning in 1987, Comprises U.K. banks authorized under the Banking Act of 1987 and, beginning in January 1987, building societies as defined by the Building Societies Act of 1986. † In September 1992, a new

balance sheet report form was introduced for the building society sector in the U.K., resulting in a discontinuity for most of the building society data. † Prior to September 1997, the accounts of certain institutions in the Channel Islands and the Isle of Man were included as part of the U.K. banking institutions sector.

Banking Survey:

A break in series occurs in July 1999 as a result of the change in the definition of the monetary authorities' sector. A break in series occurs in January 1987 as a result of a change in the coverage of banking institutions. A break in series occurs in September 1992 as a result of new balance sheet report forms for the building society sector.

Money (National Definitions):

M0 comprises notes and coin in circulation outside the Bank of England, plus bankers' operational balances with the Bank of England. M4 comprises notes and coin in circulation outside the Bank of England and banking institutions in the U.K., plus non-bank private sector sterling deposits held with U.K. banking institutions. M4 differs from *Money plus Quasi-Money (line 35l)* because it excludes private sector foreign currency deposits, and sterling and foreign currency deposits of official entities (local authorities and public enterprises).

Interest Rates:

Money Market Rate:
Data refer to the interbank offer rate for overnight deposits.

Treasury Bill Rate:
Source B. This is the tender rate at which 91-day bills are allotted, calculated from source B data given in terms of the amount of the discount. Monthly data are averages of Friday data.

Treasury Bill Rate (Bond Equivalent):
Monthly data refer to the simple arithmetic average of the daily market yields on a bond equivalent basis for 91-day bills; this rate is used in calculating the SDR interest rate.
The *Eurodollar Rate in London* relates to three-month deposits. It is the average of daily quotations of broker bid rates at noon in London. Beginning December 1979, the data relate to the average of bid and offer rates at or near the end of the month.

Deposit Rate:
Source S (*Financial Statistics*). With effect from January 1984, monthly data are end-period observations of average rates, for the four main London clearing banks, on instant access savings accounts with a median balance currently of £10,000. Prior to that date, data refer to the rate on seven-day notice accounts of the London clearing banks.

Lending Rate:
Data refer to the minimum base rate of the London clearing banks as reported in source B.

Government Bond Yield:
Source B. These are theoretical gross redemption bond yields. Beginning June 1976, the calculations are based on a method described in source B, June 1976. *Short-Term:* Issue at par with five years to maturity. *Long-Term:* Issue at par with 20 years to maturity.

Prices, Production, Labor:

Industrial Share Prices:
Data refer to the average of daily quotations of 500 industrial ordinary shares, base 1985.

Prices: Manufacturing Output:
Source S. Weights Reference Period: 2000; Coverage: the country manufacturing industry; Number of Items in Basket: Approximately 9,000 price quotes are obtained covering 980 products; Basis for Calculation: data on sales in the base year as provided by the PRODCOM inquiry, the manufacturing products inquiry required by Eurostat.

Consumer Prices:
The general Retail Prices Index (RPI), Source S. Weights Reference Period: January 1987; Geographical Coverage: the whole country; Number of Items in Basket: containing some 650 individual goods and services from around 150 areas throughout the country; Basis for Calculation: the annual Expenditure and Food Survey and are updated each year.
The Consumer Price Index (CPI) in the UK National Statistics is the Harmonized Index of Consumer Prices (HICP).

Wages:
Data refer to average monthly earnings in the whole economy, base 2000.

Industrial Production:
Data are sourced from the OECD database. Weights Reference Period: 2002; Sectoral Coverage: covering the mining and quarrying (C), manufacturing (D) and electricity, gas and water supply (E) sectors of the Standard Industrial Classification 2003; Basis of Calculation: the monthly survey known as the Monthly Production Inquiry (MPI) is the main source of information for calculating the indices.

Employment, Seasonally Adjusted:
Data are taken from the *Employment Gazette* and refer to, for the entire U.K. economy, employees in employment, which covers salaried employees in all industries and services. Domestic servants, the self-employed, and military personnel are excluded.

International Transactions:

Value data on total *Exports* and *Imports* are from the Department of Trade and Industry. *Imports f.o.b.* are from source S. The figures are on a balance of payments basis and include various coverage adjustments to the customs returns, such as the value of ships purchased abroad.
Trade indices are from source S. Prior to 1970, trade indices refer to total unadjusted series. From January 1970. Volumes Indices refer to seasonally adjusted series.

Government Finance:

Data on general government are derived from source V. Monthly and quarterly cash data, which are not on a consolidated basis, are derived from sources B and S. Above-the-line transactions are compiled by the Office of National Statistics (ONS), while financing data are compiled by the Bank of England using different sources. Annual cash data, from 1999, are as reported in the *Government Finance Statistics Yearbook (GFSY)*. For the United Kingdom, *GFSY* data cover consolidated central government. The fiscal year ends December 31.

National Accounts:

Source S. *Line 99b.c* is "GDP-Average." By construction, the sum of the expenditure-based components is not equal to the "GDP-Average," leading to an official statistical discrepancy. As indicated by the country, data have been revised following the implementation of improved compilation methods and the *1993 SNA*. Beginning in 1990, euro data are sourced from the Eurostat database. Eurostat introduced chain-linked GDP volume measures to both annual and quarterly data with the release of the third quarter 2005 on November 30, 2005. Chain linked GDP volume measures are expressed in the prices of the previous year and re-referenced to 2000.

United States   111

Date of Fund Membership:
December 27, 1945

Standard Sources:
B: Board of Governors of the Federal Reserve System, *Federal Reserve Bulletin*
S: U.S. Department of Commerce, *Survey of Current Business Highlights of U.S. Export and Import Trade*
N: U.S. Treasury Department,
Treasury Bulletin and Monthly Treasury Statement

Exchange Rates:
Data relate to the par value through June 1974 and to the rate determined through a method known as the standard "basket" valuation thereafter.

International Liquidity:
Lines 7a.d and *.7b.d* are derived from the U.S. Treasury International Capital (TIC) reports. They differ from the commercial banks' *Foreign Assets (line 21)* and *Foreign Liabilities (line 26c)*, reported in section 20, mainly because they include the accounts of international banking facilities (IBFs). See notes on commercial banks in section on banking institutions. † Beginning in 1978, *Deposit Money Banks: Assets (line .7a.d)* and *Deposit Money Banks: Liabilities (line .7b.d)* reflect a broader coverage of international banking facilities (IBFs). Beginning in December 2001, data are based on a new reporting system for banking institutions.

Monetary Authorities:
Comprises the Federal Reserve Banks (FED) only. The data are derived from the FED monthly bulletin. *Currency Outside Banks (line 14a)* is currency outside the U.S. Treasury, Federal Reserve Banks, and commercial banks. † Beginning in December 2001, data are based on a new reporting system which provides improved classification and sectorization of the accounts.

Banking Institutions:
Comprises commercial banks, credit unions and savings institutions, and money market funds as defined in the FED Flow of Funds accounts. Commercial banks include U.S.-chartered commercial banks, foreign banking offices in the U.S., bank holding companies, and banks in U.S.-affiliated areas and exclude international banking facilities (IBFs). Savings institutions include savings and loan associations, mutual savings banks, and federal savings banks. The data are derived from the FED Flow of Funds quarterly publication.
Claims on Central Government (line 22a) exclude claims on government-sponsored credit agencies and government enterprises, which are included in *Claims on Nonbank Financial Institutions (line 22g)*. *Demand Deposits (line 24)* comprise checkable deposits as defined in the FED Flow of Funds accounts. † Beginning in December 2001, data are based on a new reporting

system which provides improved classification and sectorization of the accounts.

Banking Survey:
Money (line 34) comprises currency outside banks and checkable deposits in national currency of nonfinancial resident sectors other than the central government with banking institutions. *Money* differs from M1 of the FED monthly bulletin by the former's exclusion of travelers checks and by the fact that *IFS* money is an end-of-month stock while FED M1 is a monthly average of daily stocks. *Quasi-Money (line 35)* comprises all savings and time deposits in national currency of the nonfinancial resident sectors other than the central government with banking institutions. *Money plus Quasi-Money (line 35l)* differs from M2 of the FED monthly bulletin by the former's exclusion of travelers checks, overnight repurchase agreements, and overnight Eurodollar deposits and its inclusion of IRA/Keogh deposit accounts and institution-only money market funds. † See notes on monetary authorities and banking institutions.

Nonbank Financial Institutions:
Comprises other nondepository financial institutions as defined in the FED flow of funds accounts, including property-casualty insurance companies, life insurance companies, private pension funds, state and local government employee retirement funds, federal government retirement funds, mutual funds, closed-end and exchange-traded funds, government-sponsored enterprises (GSE), agency-and GSE-backed mortgage pools, issuers of asset-backed securities, finance companies, mortgage companies, real estate investment trust, security brokers and dealers, and funding corporations. The data are derived from the FED Flow of Funds quarterly publication. † Beginning in December 2001, data are based on a new reporting system which provides improved classification and sectorization of the accounts.

Insurance Companies & Pension Funds:
Comprises life and other insurance companies, private pension funds, and state and local government employee retirement funds that are included in the FED flow of funds accounts. The data are derived from the FED Flow of Funds quarterly publication.

Financial Survey:
† See notes on monetary authorities, banking institutions and nonbank financial institutions.

Money (National Definitions):
Monetary base comprises total reserves, required clearing balances and other adjustments to compensate for float at Federal Reserve Banks, the currency component of the money stock, and, for all quarterly reporters on the "Report of Transaction Accounts, Other Deposits and Vault Cash" and for all those weekly reporters whose vault cash exceeds their required reserves, the difference between current vault cash and the amount applied to satisfy current reserve requirements. Currency and vault cash figures are measured over computation periods ending on Mondays. *Seasonally adjusted monetary base* comprises seasonally adjusted, break-adjusted total reserves; the seasonally adjusted currency component of the money stock; and, for all quarterly reporters on the "Report of Transaction Accounts, Other Deposits and Vault Cash" and for all those weekly reporters whose vault cash exceeds their required reserves, the seasonally adjusted, break-adjusted difference between current vault cash and the amount applied to satisfy current reserve requirements.

M1: (1) currency outside the U.S. Treasury, Federal Reserve Banks, and the vaults of depository institutions, (2) travelers checks of nonbank issuers, (3) demand deposits at all commercial banks other than those owed to depository institutions, the U.S. government, and foreign banks and official institutions, less cash items in the process of collection and Federal Reserve float, and (4) other checkable deposits (OCDs), consisting of negotiable order of withdrawal (NOW) and automatic transfer service (ATS) accounts at depository institutions, credit union share draft accounts, and demand deposits at thrift institutions. *Seasonally Adjusted M1* is computed by summing currency, travelers checks, demand deposits, and OCDs, each seasonally adjusted separately.

M2: *M1* plus (1) overnight (and continuing-contract) repurchase agreements (RPs) issued by all depository institutions and overnight Eurodollars issued to U.S. residents by foreign branches of U.S. banks worldwide, (2) savings (including money market deposit accounts [MMDAs]) and small time deposits (time deposits—including retail RPs—in amounts of less than $100,000), and (3) balances in both taxable and tax-exempt general-purpose and broker-dealer money market funds. Excludes individual retirement accounts (IRAs) and Keogh balances at depository institutions and money market funds. Also excludes all balances held by U.S. commercial banks, money market funds (general purpose and broker-dealer), foreign governments and commercial banks, and U.S. government. *Seasonally Adjusted M2* is computed by adjusting its non-M1 component as a whole and then adding this result to seasonally adjusted M1.

M3: *M2* plus (1) large time deposits and term RP liabilities (in amounts of $100,000 or more) issued by all depository institutions, (2) term Eurodollars held by U.S. residents at foreign branches of U.S. banks worldwide and at all banking offices in the United Kingdom and Canada, and (3) balances in both taxable and tax-exempt institution-only money market funds. Excludes amounts held by depository institutions, the U.S. government, money market funds, and foreign banks and official institutions. Also excluded is the estimated amount of overnight RPs and Eurodollars held by institution-only money market funds. *Seasonally Adjusted M3* is computed by adjusting its non-M2 component as a whole and then adding this result to a seasonally adjusted M2.

L: *M3* plus the nonbank public holdings of U.S. savings bonds, short-term Treasury securities, commercial paper, and bankers acceptances, net of money market fund holdings of these assets. *Seasonally Adjusted L* is computed by summing U.S. savings bonds, short-term Treasury securities, commercial paper and bankers acceptances, each seasonally adjusted separately, and then adding this result to seasonally adjusted M3.

Debt: Debt of domestic nonfinancial sectors consists of outstanding credit market debt of the U.S. government, state and local governments, and private nonfinancial sectors. Private debt consists of corporate bonds, mortgages, consumer credit (including bank loans), other bank loans, commercial paper, banks acceptances, and other debt instruments. Data are derived from the Federal Reserve Board's flow of funds accounts. Debt data are based on monthly averages. This sum is seasonally adjusted as a whole.

Treasury Securities by Holders:

The data are taken from the FED Flow of Funds quarterly publication.

Interest Rates:

All interest rate data are from source B.

Discount Rate (End of Period):
Rate at which the Federal Reserve Bank of New York discounts eligible paper and makes advances to member banks. Establishment of the discount rate is at the discretion of each Federal Reserve bank but is subject to review and determination by the Board of Governors in Washington every fourteen days; these rates are publicly announced. Borrowing from a Federal Reserve bank is a privilege of being a member of the Federal Reserve system. Borrowing may take the form either of discounts of short-term commercial, industrial, and other financial paper or of advances against government securities and other eligible collateral; most transactions are in the form of advances. Federal Reserve advances to or discounts for member banks are usually of short maturity up to fifteen days. Federal Reserve banks do not discount eligible paper or make advances to member banks automatically. Ordinarily, the continuous use of Federal Reserve credit by a member bank over a considerable period of time is not regarded as appropriate. The volume of discounts is consequently very small. † Effective January 9, 2003 the rate charged for primary credit replaces that for adjustment credit. Primary credit, which is broadly similar to credit programs offered by many other central banks, is made available by the Federal Reserve Bank for short terms as a backup source of liquidity to depository institutions that are in sound financial condition.

Federal Funds Rate:
Weighted average rate at which banks borrow funds through New York brokers. Monthly rate is the average of rates of all calendar days, and the daily rate is the average of the rates on a given day weighted by the volume of transactions.

Commercial Paper Rate:
Rate on three-month commercial paper of nonfinancial firms. Rates are quoted on a discount basis and interpolated from data on certain commercial paper trades settled by the Depository Trust Company. The trades represent sales of commercial paper by dealers or direct issuers to investors.

Treasury Bill Rate:
Weighted average yield on multiple-price auctions of 13-week treasury bills. Monthly averages are computed on an issue-date basis. Beginning on October 28, 1998, data are stop yields from uniform-price auctions.

Treasury Bill Rate (Bond Equivalent):
Yield on actively traded three-month treasury bills adjusted to constant maturities. This rate is used in calculating the SDR interest rate.

Certificates of Deposit Rate:
Average of dealer offering rates on nationally traded certificates of deposit.

Lending Rate (Prime Rate):
Base rate charged by banks on short-term business loans. Monthly rate is the average of rates of all calendar days and is posted by a majority of the top 25 insured U.S. chartered commercial banks.

Mortgage Rate:
Contract rate on 30-year fixed-rate first mortgages.

Government Bond Yield:
Yield on actively traded treasury issues adjusted to constant maturities. Yields on treasury securities at constant maturity are

interpolated by the U.S. Treasury from the daily yield curve. This curve, which relates the yield on a security to its time to maturity, is based on the closing market bid yields on actively traded treasury securities in the over-the-counter market. These market yields are calculated from composites of quotations obtained by the Federal Reserve Bank of New York. *Medium-Term* rate refers to three-year constant maturities. *Long-Term* rate refers to ten-year constant maturities.

Prices, Production, Labor:

Share Prices:
Price-weighted monthly average covering 30 blue chip stocks quoted in the Dow Jones Industrial Average (DJIA). The NASDAQ Composite Index (base February 5, 1971) is a market capitalization-weighted index covering domestic and international-based common stocks, ordinary shares, American Depository Receipts (ADRs), shares of beneficial interest, REITs, Tracking Stocks and Limited Partnerships and excluding exchange traded funds, structured products, convertible debentures, rights, units, warrants and preferred issues. The S&P Industrials (base 41–43=10) is a Laspeyres-type index based on daily closing quotations for companies in the Industrials on the New York Exchange. The AMEX Average (base August 31, 1973) is a total-market-value-weighted index that covers all common shares, warrants, and (ADRs) listed.

Producer Prices:
Source: compiled by the Bureau of Labor Statistics (U.S. Department of Labor) and published in source S; Weights Reference Period: 1982; Coverage: the entire output of domestic goods-producing sectors; Number of Items in Basket: approximately 25,000 establishments providing close to 100,000 price quotations per month; Basis for Calculation: the weights are taken from the Economic Census conducted by the Census Bureau and are revised every five years.

Consumer Prices:
Source: compiled by the Bureau of Labor Statistics (U.S. Department of Labor) and published in source S. Weights reference period: 1982–1984; Geographical Coverage: covers all residents in urban areas; Number of Items in Basket: 305 entry level items representing all goods and services; Basis for Calculation: is computed using a modified Laspeyres methodology, the weights are derived from the Consumer Expenditure Surveys for 1993–95, and the average for those three years. Historically weights have been revised once every 10 years; however, starting in 2002, weights will be revised every other year.

Wages: Hourly Earnings (Mfg):
Source: compiled by the Bureau of Labor Statistics (U.S. Department of Labor). In June 2003, the Current Employment Statistics survey converted to the 2002 North American Industry Classification System (NAICS) from 1987 Standard Industrial Classification System (SIC). NAICS emphasis on new, emerging, service-providing, and high-tech industries. Both current and historical data are now based on NAICS.

Industrial Production:
Source B. Weights Reference Period: 1997; Sectoral Coverage: manufacturing, mining, and electric and gas utilities; Basis for Calculation: the weights are based on annual estimates of value added.

Crude Petroleum Production:
Data are from Energy Information Administration, U.S. Department of Energy.

Nonagricultural Employment, Seasonally Adjusted:
Data are from source B and represent an establishment survey that covers all full- and part-time employees who worked during or received pay for the pay period that includes the 12th of the month. The survey excludes proprietors, self-employed persons, domestic servants, unpaid family workers, and members of the Armed Forces.

Labor:
Data are compiled by the Bureau of Labor Statistics (U.S. Department of Labor). Beginning in January 2000, Employment data presents statistics from two major surveys, the Current Population Survey (household survey) which provides the information on the labor force, employment, and unemployment that marked Household Data and the Current Employment Statistics Survey (establishment survey) which provides the information on the employment, hours, and earnings of workers on non-farm payrolls that marked Establishment Data.

International Transactions:

All trade value data are from the U.S. Bureau of Census web site. Total trade data include trade of the U.S. Virgin Islands. Beginning January 1975, data include exports and imports, respectively, of nonmonetary gold, which prior to January 1975 are excluded. † Beginning in 1987, all trade data are reported on the revised statistical month based on import entry and export declaration transaction dates, whereas previous data reflect import entries and export declarations transmitted to the U.S. Bureau of the Census during a fixed monthly processing period. Export and import price data are Laspeyres-type indices with 1995 trade weights and are compiled by the Bureau of Labor Statistics, U.S. Department of Labor. Volume indices are Paasche-type indices derived for *IFS* from import and export value data divided by the respective Laspeyres price indices. The f.a.s. (free alongside ship) value is the value of exports at the U.S. seaport, airport, or border port of export, based on the transaction price, including inland freight, insurance, and other charged incurred in placing the merchandise alongside the carrier at the U.S. port of exportation. The value, as defined, excludes the cost of loading the merchandise aboard the exporting carrier and also excludes freight, insurance, and any charges or transportation costs beyond the port of exportation.

Government Finance:

Through September 1995, all monthly, quarterly, and annual data are derived from the quarterly *Treasury Bulletin,* which uses the *Monthly Treasury Statement of Receipts and Outlays of the United States Government (MTS)* as its source. Beginning in October 1995, revenue, expenditure, and financing data are derived directly from the *MTS,* while the *Treasury Bulletin* remains the source for debt data. The monthly, quarterly, and annual data cover the central government transactions of the unified budget and the off-budget agencies. Net borrowing includes changes in financial assets other than cash balances. The fiscal year ends September 30.

National Accounts:

Source: Bureau of Economic Analysis (BEA), U.S. Department of Commerce. The National Income and Product Accounts (NIPAs) are, in general, consistent with the *1993 SNA.* Volume and price data are calculated using the chained Fisher formula.

Uruguay 298

Date of Fund Membership:
March 11, 1946

Standard Sources:
B: Central Bank, *Statistical Bulletin, Indicators of Economic and Financial Activity*

Exchange Rates:
On March 1, 1993 the Uruguayan peso, equal to 1,000 new Uruguayan pesos, was introduced.

Market Rate (End of Period and Period Average):
Until June 19, 2002, the exchange rate was operated as a managed float. Effective June 20, 2002, the exchange rate regime was changed to a floating system.

International Liquidity:
Data for *Total Reserves minus Gold (line 1l.d)*, *Foreign Exchange (line 1d.d)*, and *Gold (lines 1ad and 1and)* include foreign exchange and gold holdings of the Central Bank of Uruguay (BCU) only. † Prior to March 1979, data include the holdings of the BCU and the Bank of the Republic of Uruguay. *Gold (National Valuation) (line 1and)* is the U.S. dollar value of official holdings of gold as reported in the country's standard sources.

Monetary Authorities:
Comprises the Central Bank of Uruguay (BCU) only. † Beginning in December 1975, data included only the central bank accounts that were generated from the end-of-month issue of provisional balance sheets produced every ten days by the BCU. Prior to January 1982, gold holdings are valued at the historical price of gold, and the gold component of *line 11* is not comparable with *line 1and* converted into national currency. Beginning in January 1982, however, the national currency value of gold holdings is based on the national valuation.† Beginning in December 1998, data are based on an improved sectorization and classification of the accounts.

Banking Institutions:
Comprises private banks. † Beginning in December 1975, includes the Bank of the Republic of Uruguay (BROU). † Beginning in December 1982, data are based on improved sectorization, which properly distinguishes between resident and nonresident transactions; in addition, data are based on actual, rather than preliminary, information. † Beginning in December 1998, includes the Mortgage Bank of Uruguay (BHU). Data are based on an improved sectorization and classification of the accounts.

Banking Survey:
† See notes on monetary authorities and banking institutions.

Nonbank Financial Institutions:
Comprises off-shore financial institutions.

Money (National Definitions):
Base Money comprises notes and coins in circulation and non-interest bearing demand and sight deposits in national currency of the private banks, BROU, Mortgage Bank of Uruguay (BHU), cooperatives of financial intermediation, local governments, nonfinancial public enterprises, and other financial institutions in the BCU.

M1 comprises notes and coins in circulation outside the banking system and demand deposits in national currency of the private sector, social security, nonfinancial public enterprises, and pension funds in private banks, BROU, and BHU.

M2 comprises M1 plus time and savings deposits in national currency of the private sector, social security, nonfinancial public enterprises, and pension funds in private banks, BROU, and BHU, and housing savings deposits in national currency of the private sector in the BHU.

Interest Rates:
All interest rate data are from source B.

Discount Rate (End of Period):
Effective rate established by the BCU for financial assistance in national currency to the private banks.

Discount Rate (Foreign Currency) (End of Period):
Effective rate established by the BCU for financial assistance in foreign currency to the private banks.

Money Market Rate:
Effective overnight rate on loans between private banks. The rate is an average of the last three days of the month.

Treasury Bill Rate (Foreign Currency):
Weighted average rate on 182-day treasury bills denominated in foreign currency auctioned by the BCU. Rate is weighted by the number of bills auctioned.

Savings Rate:
Average of the rates most frequently offered on savings deposits in national currency in the last three days of each month by the five most representative (determined as of July 1978) private banks. † Beginning in January 2002, average rate offered on savings deposits in national currency by private banks.

Savings Rate (Foreign Currency):
Average of the rates most frequently offered on savings deposits in foreign currency in the last three days of each month by the five most representative (determined as of July 1978) private banks. † Beginning in January 2002, average rate offered on savings deposits in foreign currency by private banks.

Deposit Rate:
Average of the rates most frequently offered on one- to six-month time deposits in national currency in the last three days of each month by the five most representative (determined as of July 1978) private banks. † Beginning in January 2002, average rate offered on one- to six-month deposits in national currency by private banks.

Deposit Rate (Foreign Currency):
Average of the rates most frequently offered on one- to six-month time deposits in foreign currency in the last three days of each month by the five most representative (determined as of July 1978) private banks. † Beginning in January 2002, average rate offered on one- to six-month deposits in foreign currency by private banks.

Lending Rate:
Average of the rates most frequently charged on ordinary loans in national currency not exceeding six months on the last day of each month by the five most representative (determined as of July 1978) private banks. † Beginning in January 2002, average rate charged on loans not exceeding six months in national currency by private banks.

Lending Rate (Foreign Currency):
Average of the rates most frequently charged on short-term commercial loans in foreign currency on the last day of each month by the five most representative (determined as of July 1978)

private banks. † Beginning in January 2002, average rate charged on loans not exceeding six months in foreign currency by private banks.

Prices, Production, Labor:

Wholesale Prices:
Source B index of wholesale prices, covering home and export goods in agriculture and manufacturing, base August 2001.

Consumer Prices:
Source S. Weights Reference Period: 1994–1995; Geographical Coverage: Montevideo; Number of Items in Basket: 310; Basis for Calculation: Household Expenditure and Income Survey.

Manufacturing Production:
Source B.

International Transactions:

All trade data are from source B.

Government Finance:

Monthly and quarterly data are derived from source B and cover budgetary central government. The fiscal year ends December 31.

National Accounts:

Source B.

Vanuatu   846

Date of Fund Membership:

September 28, 1981

Standard Sources:

A: Reserve Bank of Vanuatu, *Quarterly Economic Review* and *Annual Report*
S: National Planning & Statistics Office, *Statistical Bulletin*

Exchange Rates:

Official Rate: (End of Period and Period Average):
The official exchange rate is determined on the basis of an undisclosed transactions-weighted basket of currencies.

Monetary Authorities:

Consolidates the Reserve Bank of Vanuatu and monetary authority functions undertaken by the central government. The contra-entry to Treasury IMF accounts and government foreign exchange holdings is included in *line 16d*. † Prior to October 1994, separate data for claims on central government and claims on nonfinancial public enterprises were unavailable, and these data were indistinguishably included in *Other Items, Net (line 17r)*. In February 1997, the European Development Fund deposited ECU 3 million in the Reserve Bank of Vanuatu on account of a STABEX grant; these funds, which were withdrawn in March (ECU 1 million) and in April 1997 (ECU 2 million), are recorded as foreign liabilities and are matched by foreign assets.

Deposit Money Banks:

Comprises branches of foreign banks and the National Bank of Vanuatu. Foreign currency demand deposits, other than those of exempt nonreporting banks, trust companies, and other financial institutions, are included in *line 24*. The deposits of exempt non-reporting banks, trust companies, and other financial institutions, whose business is almost entirely offshore, are shown in *line 25e*. Line 26g includes, and *line 26d* excludes, the central government's foreign currency balances with domestic commercial banks, which are consolidated with the monetary authorities.

Monetary Survey:

† See note on monetary authorities.

Money (National Definitions):

Reserve Money comprises currency in circulation, banker's statutory reserve deposits (SRDs) and excess reserves, and transferable deposits in national currency of public entities excluding the central government at the Reserve Bank of Vanuatu (RBV). Currency in circulation refers to notes and coins issued by the RBV. The RBV uses SRDs as monetary policy instruments calculated as ten percent of all deposits in national currency and transferable deposits in foreign currency.

M1 comprises currency in circulation and transferable deposits. Currency in circulation refers to notes and coins issued by the RBV less the amount held by commercial banks. Transferable deposits refer to demand deposits in national currency of state and local governments, public nonfinancial corporations, private sector, and other banking institutions with commercial banks.

M2 comprises M1 plus transferable deposits in foreign currency of state and local governments, public nonfinancial corporations, private sector, and other banking institutions with commercial banks.

MV, Vatu Liquidity comprises M1 plus time, fixed, and savings deposits in national currency of state and local governments, public nonfinancial corporations, private sector, and other banking institutions with commercial banks.

M3 comprises M2 plus time, fixed, and savings deposits in national currency of state and local governments, public nonfinancial corporations, private sector, and other banking institutions with commercial banks.

MF, Foreign Currency Liquidity comprises M2 plus time, fixed, and savings deposits in foreign currency of state and local governments, public nonfinancial corporations, private sector, and other banking institutions with commercial banks.

M4 comprises M3 plus time, fixed, and savings deposits in foreign currency of state and local governments, public nonfinancial corporations, private sector, and other banking institutions with commercial banks.

Other Banking Institutions:

Comprises the Development Bank of Vanuatu, which ceased operations on September 30, 1998 and was liquidated.

Banking Survey:

† See note on monetary authorities.

Interest Rates:

All interest rate data are from source A.

Discount Rate (End of Period):
Rate offered by the Reserve Bank of Vanuatu on loans to commercial banks.

Money Market Rate:
Data refer to the overnight interbank lending rate.

Deposit Rate:
Representative rate quoted by commercial banks for three-month time deposits.

Lending Rate:
Representative rate for commercial banks' advances for commercial purposes.

Government Bond Yield:
Yield on three-year bonds. † Beginning in January 1989, yield on ten-year bonds.

Prices:

Consumer Prices:
Source S. Weights Reference Period: first quarter 2000; Geographical Coverage: two urban centers of Vanuatu: Port Vila and Luganville; Number of Items in the Basket: 760 goods/services items for Vila, and 680 for Luganville; Basis for Calculation: the weights are derived from urban dwellers expenditure patterns through the 1998 household surveys.

International Transactions:
All trade data are from source S.

Venezuela, Rep. Bol.   299

Date of Fund Membership:
December 30, 1946

Standard Sources:
A: Central Bank, *Economic Report*
B: Central Bank, Monthly Bulletin, *Quarterly Bulletin*

Exchange Rates:

Official Rate: (End of Period and Period Average):
Effective 1989, the multiple exchange rate system was replaced by a system of unified managed float that was maintained until June 1994. After a temporary closure, the exchange rate market was re-opened on July 11, 1994 under a system of exchange controls at a fixed rate of 170 bolivares per U.S. dollar. On December 11, 1995, the official rate of the bolivar was devalued from 170 bolivares per U.S. dollar to 290 bolivares per U.S. dollar. Effective April 22, 1996 the exchange rate regime was changed to a managed float with full convertibility. On July 8, 1996 an exchange rate band system was introduced with a width of 7.5 percent each way around the central parity which moves according to the annual inflation target. Effective January 1, 2001, the exchange rate band was moved by 7.5 percent to set the central parity rate of the band to the actual level of the exchange rate. Effective February 13, 2002, the exchange rate regime was changed to a floating system. On February 4, 2003, the bolivar was fixed at Bs 1,598 per US$1 and, therefore, the exchange regime was reclassified to the category of conventional pegged arrangement. Effective February 9, 2004, the bolivar was devalued and fixed at Bs 1,918 per US$1. Effective March 3, 2005, the bolivar was fixed at Bs 2,147 per US$1.
For the purpose of calculating effective exchange rates (*lines* **nec** and **rec**), a weighted average exchange rate index for U.S. dollars per bolivar is calculated as follows: Through November 1986, exchange rates were weighted by transactions in a basket of imports effected at various exchange rates; beginning December 1986, the rate is a weighted average of the market rate.

International Liquidity:
Gold (National Valuation) (line 1and) is the U.S. dollar value of official holdings of gold as reported in the country's standard sources.

Monetary Authorities:
Comprises the Central Bank of Venezuela only. † Beginning in December 1987, data are based on an improved reporting system. † Beginning in July 1996, data reflect the introduction of a new plan of accounts, which provides an improved sectorization and classification of the accounts.

Deposit Money Banks:
Comprises commercial and universal banks. Universal banks began operations on November 26, 1996. † See note on monetary authorities.

Monetary Survey:
† See note on monetary authorities.

Other Banking Institutions:
Comprises mortgage banks, National Savings and Loan System, and investment banks. † Beginning in July 1996, included financial leasing companies and investment funds. See note on monetary authorities. See note on monetary authorities.

Banking Survey:
† See note on monetary authorities.

Interest Rates:
All interest rate data are from source B.

Discount Rate (End of Period):
Rate charged by the Central Bank of Venezuela on credit to financial institutions through discounts, rediscounts, advances, and repurchase agreements.

Money Market Rate:
Weighted average rate on loans between financial institutions. The rate is weighted by loan amounts.

Savings Rate:
Weighted average rate offered by commercial and universal banks on savings deposits in national currency. The rate is weighted by deposit amounts.

Deposit Rate:
Weighted average rate offered by commercial and universal banks on 90-day time deposits in national currency. The rate is weighted by deposit amounts.

Lending Rate:
Average rate charged by commercial banks on loans. † Beginning in January 1990, weighted average rate charged by commercial and universal banks on industrial, agricultural, commercial, and car loans in national currency. The rate is weighted by loan amounts.

Government Bond Yield:
Effective weighted average yield on national public debt bonds traded in the Caracas Stock Exchange. † Beginning in January 1999, weighted average yield on national public debt bonds traded on the operations desk of the Central Bank of Venezuela. The yield is weighted by issuance amounts.

Prices, Production, Labor:

Industrial Share Prices:
The index, base 1968, refers to the average of daily quotations and covers ordinary and preference shares quoted on the Caracas and Miranda exchanges. † Beginning January 1990, the index, base January 1, 1971, refers to the average of daily quotations on the Caracas Stock Exchange. † Beginning December 1993, the index,

base December 1993, refers to the average of daily quotations on the Caracas Stock Exchange.

Wholesale Prices:
Source B indices, weights reference period 1997, covering home-produced and imported goods for domestic consumption.

Consumer Prices:
Source B. Weights Reference Period: 1997–98; Geographical Coverage: Caracas Metropolitan Area; Number of Items in Basket: 287; Basis for Calculation: weights are determined based on the Family Budget Survey of 1997–98.

Crude Petroleum Production:
Source B data.

International Transactions:

Exports:
All data are from source B, except volume of petroleum exports, which is the average of crude and refined petroleum with 1995 values of exports as weights, computed for *IFS*. Data for exports from 2003 exclude petroleum exports.

Imports, c.i.f.:
Source B data. Data for current periods are based on incomplete enumeration of customs documents and are subject to subsequent upward revision. † Value data for exports and imports in bolivares are U.S. dollar equivalents at the secondary rate until June 1987 and at the principal rate from July 1987 through June 1988. Thereafter, the relation between values expressed in bolivares and in U.S. dollars is no longer determined by a uniform rate.

Government Finance:

Monthly and quarterly data are derived from source B and cover budgetary central government only. † Prior to 2004, to the extent possible, existing subannual IFS data were converted to the main aggregates that are presented in the *GFSM 2001* Statement of Sources and Uses of Cash (see the Introduction of the monthly *IFS* publication for details). Beginning in 2004, annual data are as reported in the *Government Finance Statistics Yearbook (GFSY)* and cover the consolidated central government. The fiscal year ends December 31.

National Accounts:

Data are from source A. As indicated by the country, data are compiled according to the recommendations of the *1968 SNA*.

Vietnam 582

Date of Fund Membership:
September 21, 1956

Standard Source:
S: General Statistics Office, *Statistical Yearbook*

Exchange Rates:

Market Rate (End of Period and Period Average):
Data refer to the midpoint of the average buying and selling rates quoted by the commercial banks authorized to deal in the organized foreign exchange market.

International Liquidity:

Data for *Foreign Exchange (line 1d.d)* are the U.S. dollar equivalents of the sum of foreign currency, investments in foreign securities, and deposits with foreign banks, as reported by the State Bank of Vietnam. The reported value in national currency terms is converted to the U.S. dollar value using the prevailing end-of-period exchange rate, as given in *line* **ae**.

Gold (Market Valuation) (line 1and) is obtained by converting the value of official holdings of gold in national currency terms, as reported by the State Bank of Vietnam, using the prevailing end-of-period exchange rate, as given in *line* **ae**.

Monetary Authorities:

Comprises the accounts of the State Bank of Vietnam.

Banking Institutions:

Prior to December 1999, comprises 4 state-owned commercial banks (SOCBs) and 24 other credit institutions. Between December 1999 and November 2000, data cover 6 SOCBs and 81 other credit institutions (comprising 46 joint stock banks, 4 joint venture banks, 24 foreign bank branches, 6 finance companies, and the System of People's Credit Funds). Beginning in December 2000, the coverage was expanded to include 2 more foreign bank branches.

Finance companies are credit institutions that are permitted to engage in some banking activities but not permitted to accept demand deposits and to provide payment services (according to the Law on Credit Institutions). The System of People's Credit Funds is permitted to accept demand deposits.

Bonds and Money Market Instruments (line 26a) include bills and bonds that are issued by credit institutions.

Interest Rates:

Refinancing Rate (End of Period):
Rate charged by the State Bank of Vietnam on its lending facilities to all credit institutions.

Treasury Bill Rate:
Average monthly yield on 360-day treasury bills sold at auction.

Deposit Rate:
Average of rates at the end of period on 3-month deposits of four large state-owned commercial banks.

Lending Rate:
Average of rates at the end of period on short-term (less than 12 months) working capital loans of four large state-owned commercial banks.

Prices:

Consumer Prices:
Source S. Weight Reference Period: 2000; Geographical Coverage: 36 largest provinces representing the 8 economic regions; Number of Items in the Basket: 400 items; Basis of Calculation: the weights is derived from the 1998 Multipurpose Household Survey (MPHS) and relate to the expenditure pattern for households in each of the provinces.

International Transactions:
Source S.

National Accounts:

Source S. As indicated by the country, since 1996, concepts and definitions are in accordance with the *1993 SNA*.

The West African Economic Monetary Union (WAEMU) is a regional entity established by a treaty signed on January 10, 1994 and entered into force on August 1, 1994 after its ratification by all member countries. The aim of the treaty—built on the achievements of the West African Monetary Union (WAMU), established in 1962—was to create a new framework for fostering the achievement of the member countries' growth and development objectives. It was also to provide the credibility required to sustain the fixed exchange rate for the common currency.

The Union has a common central bank, the Central Bank of West African States (Banque Centrale des états de l'Afrique de l'Ouest (BCEAO)), with headquarters in Dakar and national branches in the member states. WAEMU comprises eight francophone countries: Benin, Burkina Faso, Côte d'Ivoire, Guinea-Bissau, Mali, Niger, Senegal, and Togo. Mali and Guinea-Bissau joined the Union on June 1, 1984 and May 2, 1997, respectively. The BCEAO issues the common currency of the WAEMU member countries, the CFA franc (CFA stands for "Communauté Financière Africaine" since 1958; from 1945 through 1958, CFA stood for "Colonies Françaises d'Afrique").

On December 17, 1993, the Council of Ministers of WAEMU decided to formally establish a regional financial market and mandated the BCEAO to carry out the project. The regional securities exchange (Bourse régionale des valeurs mobilières (BRVM)) was established as a private company in Abidjan and began operations in September 1998.

Compared to data published in the individual *IFS* pages for the WAEMU member countries, consolidated data published for the WAEMU as a whole embody two major methodological differences: (1) where relevant, a WAEMU-wide residency criterion is applied instead of a national residency criterion; (2) BCEAO headquarters' transactions are included in data presented in the sections "International liquidity" and "Monetary Authorities." BCEAO headquarters' transactions are not allocated to the member countries' national data.

Date of Fund Membership:

Benin (July 10, 1963), Burkina Faso (May 2, 1963), Côte d'Ivoire (March 11, 1963), Guinea-Bissau (March 24, 1977), Mali (September 27, 1963), Niger (April 24, 1963), Senegal (August 31, 1962), and Togo (August 1, 1962).

Standard Source:

B: Banque Centrale des Etats de l'Afrique de l'Ouest (Central Bank of West African States), *Notes d'information et Statistiques (Informative Notes and Statistics)*

Exchange Rates:

Official Rate: (End of Period and Period Average):
Prior to January 1999, the official rate was pegged to the French Franc. On January 12, 1994, the CFA franc (CFAF) was devalued to CFAF 100 per French franc from CFAF 50, which was the fixed rate adopted since 1948. From January 1, 1999 onward, the CFAF is pegged to the euro at the rate of CFAF 655.957 per euro.

Fund Position:

Data are the aggregation of positions of WAEMU countries.

International Liquidity:

Data include holdings by the BCEAO headquarters and the BCEAO agencies in member countries. *Gold (National Valuation) (line 1and)* is obtained by converting the value in national currency, as reported by the BCEAO source, using the prevailing exchange rate, as given in *line* **ae**. Gold in national currency is revalued by the BCEAO on a quarterly basis at the rate corresponding to the lowest average fixing in the London market.

Monetary Authorities:

Data, compiled from the BCEAO balance sheet, cover its headquarters and national agencies.

Deposit Money Banks:

This section consolidates national data by application of a WAEMU-wide residency criterion. For more details on national data, see country notes.

Interest Rates:

Bank Rate (End of Period):
Data refer to the rate on repurchase agreements between the BCEAO and banks. The repo rate was formally established on October 1, 1993.

Money Market Rate:
Rate paid on overnight interbank advances.

Deposit Rate:
Rate offered by banks on time deposits of CFAF 500,000–2,000,000 with a maturity of less than six months.

Prices and Production:

Share Prices (line 62):
Data relate to the Regional Stock Exchange (BRVM) Composite Index, base September 15, 1998=100, when the BRVM started operations. It covers all listed securities on the market.

Consumer Prices:
BCEAO harmonized index, weights reference period 1996. From January 2005, Guinea Bissau's CPI is taken into account in the calculation of the index.

National Accounts:
Source S.

West Bank and Gaza   487

Exchange Rates (End of Period):

The U.S. dollar is used for statistical reporting purposes. (See note on Exchange Rate for the United States).

Monetary Authorities:

Comprises the Palestinian Monetary Authority (PMA).

Deposit Money Banks:

Comprises commercial banks under the PMA's supervisory authority.

Interest Rates:

Deposit Rate:
Average rate on U.S. dollar denominated deposits of all clients weighted by volume.

Lending Rate:
Average rate on U.S. dollar denominated loans to all clients weighted by volume.

Yemen, Republic of   474

Date of Fund Membership:
May 22, 1970
The Republic of Yemen succeeded to the membership of the Yemen Arab Republic and of the People's Democratic Republic of Yemen on May 22, 1990.

Standard Sources:
B: Central Bank of Yemen
S: Central Statistical Organization

Exchange Rates:
Market Rate (End of Period and Period Average):
† Starting on July 1, 1996, data refer to the market rate. Prior to July 1, 1996, data refer to the official rate, which was pegged to the U.S. dollar. The official rate applied to most government transactions and was also referred to as the principal rate within the multiple exchange rate regime in effect prior to July 1, 1996. Effective January 1996, the official rate was changed from Yrls 50.04 to Yrls 100.08 per U.S. dollar. Effective March 29, 1995, the official rate was changed from Yrls 12.01 to Yrls 50.04 per U.S. dollar.

Monetary Authorities:
Comprises the Central Bank of Yemen. † Starting in December 1999, data are based on improved classification due to more detailed reporting.

Deposit Money Banks:
Comprises all commercial banks in Yemen. † Starting in December 1999, data are based on improved classification due to more detailed reporting.

Monetary Survey:
See notes on monetary authorities and deposit money banks.

Interest Rates:
Source B.

Discount Rate (End of Period):
The rate at which the Central Bank of Yemen rediscounts government securities.

Treasury Bill Rate:
Simple annualized rate on three-month treasury bills.

Deposit Rate:
Rate on savings deposits, which is a minimum rate on deposits at commercial banks set by the Central Bank of Yemen.

Lending Rate:
Simple arithmetic average of the maximum and minimum rates on short-term loans extended to the private sector by commercial banks.

Prices:
Consumer Prices:
Source S Laspeyres index, weights reference period: 1998, covering all major categories of personal consumption. Prices are col-
lected at varying frequencies from outlets in Sana's and Aden. Weights are derived from the household budget survey.

International Transactions:
Source S. Exports include re-exports.

Government Finance:
Annual data are as reported for the *Government Finance Statistics Yearbook (GFSY)* and cover budgetary central government. The fiscal year ends December 31.

National Accounts:
Source S.

Zambia   754

Date of Fund Membership:
September 23, 1965

Standard Sources:
A: Bank of Zambia, *Report and Statement of Accounts*
B: Bank of Zambia, *Quarterly Statistical Review*
S: Central Statistical Office, *Monthly Digest of Statistics*

Exchange Rates:
Official Rate: (End of Period and Period Average):
Bank of Zambia base rate. Prior to July 2003, the rate was determined in the auction market, with a 1.6 percent spread between buying and selling rates. Afterwards, it is calculated as the midpoint between the simple average of the primary dealers bid and offer rates.

International Liquidity:
Data for *line 1d.d* include small foreign exchange holdings by the government.
Gold (National Valuation) (line 1and) is obtained by converting the value in national currency terms, as reported in the country's standard sources, using the prevailing exchange rate, as given in *line* **dg** or *line* **ag**.

Monetary Authorities:
Comprises the Bank of Zambia (BoZ) only. † Beginning in December 1988, data reflect the introduction of a new accounting system which provides improved classification and sectorization of the accounts. † Beginning in January 1995, data are based on an improved sectorization of the accounts. † Beginning in December 2001, data are based on an improved classification and sectorization of the accounts. † Beginning in January 2003, data are based on a new reporting system which provides an improved classification and sectorization of the accounts.

Banking Institutions:
Comprises commercial banks. † Beginning in July 1971, data are based on a new reporting system, which provides an improved sectorization between resident and nonresident accounts and the government and private sectors. † Beginning in January 1998, data are based on an improved sectorization of the accounts. † Beginning in December 2001, data are based on an improved classification and sectorization of the accounts. † Beginning in January 2003, includes building societies and National Savings and Credit Bank. Data are based on a new reporting

system which provides improved classification and sectorization of the accounts.

Banking Survey:
† See notes on monetary authorities and banking institutions.

Money (National Definitions):
Monetary Base comprises currency in circulation, bankers' required reserves, bankers' excess reserves, and deposits of non-bank financial institutions, nonfinancial public enterprises, and private sector.

M1 comprises currency in circulation plus demand deposits in national currency, other than those of the central government, in the Bank of Zambia and commercial banks, and bills payable.

M2 comprises *M1* plus savings and time deposits in national currency and demand deposits in foreign currency, other than those of the central government, in commercial banks.

M3 comprises *M2* plus savings and time deposits in foreign currency, other than those of the central government, in commercial banks.

Interest Rates:

Discount Rate (End of Period):
Rate charged by the Bank of Zambia on loans to commercial banks.

Treasury Bill Rate:
Average rate on treasury bills.

Savings Rate:
Rate offered by commercial banks on savings deposits.

Deposit Rate:
Rate offered by commercial banks on three- to six-month deposits.

Lending Rate:
Rate charged by commercial banks on overdrafts.

Prices and Production:

Share Prices:
General index covering shares quoted in the Lusaka Stock Exchange, base January 1997.

Wholesale Prices:
Source B index, weights reference period: 1966.

Consumer Prices:
Source S. Weights Reference Period: 1993–1994; Geographical Coverage: whole national territory; Number of Items in Basket: 300; Basis for Calculation: Household Budget Survey, Laspeyres index.

Industrial Production and Mining Production:
Source B indices, † weights reference period: 1980.

International Transactions:
All trade value data are from source S.

Government Finance:
Annual data are as reported for the *Government Finance Statistics Yearbook (GFSY)* and cover budgetary central government. The fiscal year ends December 31.

National Accounts:
Source S.

Zimbabwe   698

Date of Fund Membership:
September 29, 1980

Standard Sources:
B: Reserve Bank of Zimbabwe, *Quarterly Economic and Statistical Review*
S: Central Statistical Office, *Monthly Digest of Statistics*

Exchange Rates:
On August 1, 2006, the new dollar (ZWN), equivalent to 1,000 of the old dollar (ZWD) was introduced.

Official Rate: (End of Period and Period Average):
Central bank midpoint rate. The official rate was pegged to a trade-weighted basket of currencies. As of June 30, 2001, the official rate is pegged to the U.S. dollar.

International Liquidity:
Gold holdings are valued on the first of each month at 50 percent of the daily average price of the Zurich closing quotation for the three-month period ended on the last day of the preceding month.

Monetary Authorities:
Comprises the Reserve Bank of Zimbabwe only.

Deposit Money Banks:
Consolidates the commercial banks, the discount houses, and the accepting houses. † Prior to December 1984, *line 22d* includes claims on state and local governments and claims on public financial enterprises. Subsequently, these claims have been identified and omitted from the series.

Monetary Survey:
Data for *Money (line 34)* agree with data for M1 as published in source B; however, data for *Quasi-Money (line 35)* differ from data for "near-money" as published in source B. "Near-money" is defined as fixed deposits (including savings deposits) with commercial banks with a maturity of less than 30 days, while quasi-money is equal to the sum of savings and fixed deposits at the deposit money banks and the quasi-monetary liabilities of the Reserve Bank. Therefore, M2 (total money and near-money), as published in source B, differs from the sum of *lines 34* and *35*. † See note on deposit money banks.

Other Banking Institutions:
Comprises the finance houses, the Post Office Savings Bank, and the building societies.

Banking Survey:
† See note on deposit money banks.

Interest Rates:
All interest rate data are from source B.

Bank Rate (End of Period):
Rate charged by the Reserve Bank of Zimbabwe on loans to banks. † Beginning in December 1998, rate charged on rediscounted loans and repurchase agreements.

Money Market Rate:
Rate charged by discount houses to buy three-month bankers' acceptances.

Treasury Bill Rate:
Yield on 91-day treasury bills.

Deposit Rate:
Rate offered by commercial banks on three-month deposits.

Lending Rate:
Rate charged by commercial banks on loans.

Prices, Production, Labor:

Share Prices:
Capital weighted share price index covering industrial shares quoted on the Zimbabwe Stock Exchange (ZSE), base 1967.

Consumer Prices:
Source S. Weights Reference Period: 1995; Geographical Coverage: Whole national territory; Number of Items in Basket: 337; Basis for Calculation: The weights are derived from the

Income, Consumption and Expenditure Survey conducted in 1995/96.

Manufacturing Production:
Source S index of volume of production of the manufacturing sector (all groups), 1980 = 100.

International Transactions:

All trade data are from source S. *Exports* include re-exports and are valued "Free On Rail" (F.O.R.) at point of dispatch.

Government Finance:

Annual data are as reported for the *Government Finance Statistics Yearbook (GFSY)* and cover consolidated central government. The fiscal year ends June 30.

National Accounts:

Lines 99a and *99b* include a statistical discrepancy.

Notes

Notes

Notes